Iran

Pat Yale
Anthony Ham
Paul Greenway

LONELY PLANET PUBLICATIONS
Melbourne • Oakland • London • Paris

IRAN

To Erzurum
To Tbilisi (Georgia)
YEREVAN
Mt Ararat (5137m)
Doğubayazıt
To Grozny (Russia)
◎ BAKU
Turkmenbashi
Gürbulak
Bāzārgān
Mākū
ARMENIA
AZERBAIJAN
AZERBAIJAN
Khoy
Jolfā
Julfā
Razi

MĀSULEH
Charming mountain village set in lush forest

CASPIAN SEA

TEHRĀN
Teeming metropolis with superb museums, palaces & restaurants

Lake Van
Yüksekova
Sero
Orūmīyeh
Tabrīz
Ardabīl
Astara
Āstārā
Bandar-é Anzalī
Gombad-é Kāvūs
Bandar-é Torkamān
Gorgān
A01

TURKEY
To Sanlıurfa
Mt Sahand (3707m)
Mt Sabalān (4811m)
Marāgheh
Māsuleh
Rasht
Rāmsar
Chālūs
Nōshahr
Bābol
Sārī
Shāhrūd
Dāmghān
A83

Mosul
Mahābād
Zanjān
Ismā'il Ābād
Qazvīn
Mt Damāvand (5671m)

TABRĪZ
Bustling modern city with fine historic monuments & 3km of bazaars

Soltānīyeh
Bījār
Karaj
Tajrīsh
TEHRĀN
Semnān

I R A Q
Sanandaj
Āli Sadr Caves
A02
A01
7

KĀSHĀN
Compact city with plenty of gardens, mosques & Islamic sites

Khosravi
A02
Bīsotūn
Kermānshāh
Hamadān
Qom
Lake Namak
Dasht-é

To Aleppo (Syria)
To Amman (Jordan)
BAGHDAD
Īlām
Borūjerd
Arāk
Kāshān
Khorram Ābād
Mt Oshtorān (4070m)
A02
7

ESFAHĀN
Old Persian capital with magnificent mosques, bazaars, teahouses & bridges

Karbalā
Najaf
Shūsh (Susa)
Dezfūl
Choqā Zanbil
Zardkouh Mountains
Shahr-é Kord
Esfahān
A02
Yazd

Zagros
Qomsheh
Ābādeh
A02

YAZD
Fascinating old desert city; centre of Zoroastrianism

To Amman (Jordan)
Ahvāz
Kārūn River
Abarqū
Yazd

Al-Basra
Khorramshāhr
Ābādān
Bandar-é Emām Khomeinī
Yāsūj
7

To Buraydah
KUWAIT
Pasargadae
Naqsh-é Rostam
Shīrāz
Persepolis
Kāzerūn
Lake Tashk
Sīrjān

KUWAIT CITY
Khārk Island
Būshehr
Mountains
Lake Bakhtīān
Fasā

S A U D I A R A B I A
PERSIAN
Firūz Ābād
Jahrom

GULF
Kangān

SHĪRĀZ
Ancient Persian centre with formal gardens, poets' tombs & mirrored shrines

Lāvān Island
Bandar-é Chārak
Bandar-é Langeh
Kīsh Island
Qeshm Island

To Mecca
Dhahran
◎ MANAMA
BAHRAIN

PERSEPOLIS
Awesome ruins of Achaemenid palaces with bas-reliefs; dramatic rock tombs nearby

Sharjah
Dubai
UNITED ARAB EMIRATES

To San'a
◎ RIYADH
◎ DOHA
QATAR
ABU DHABI

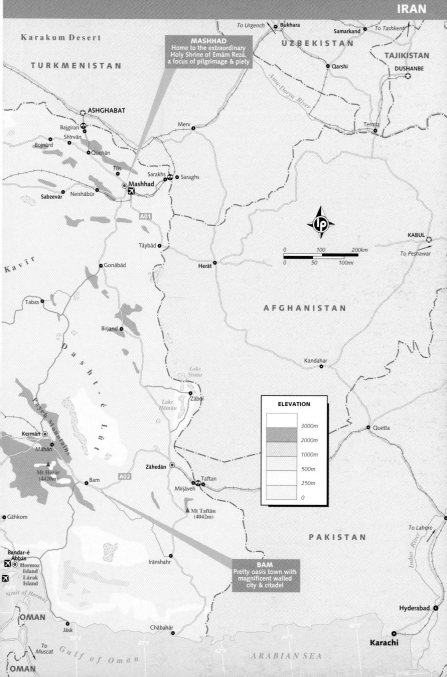

IRAN

Karakum Desert

TURKMENISTAN

UZBEKISTAN

TAJIKISTAN

To Urgench
Bukhara
Samarkand
To Tashkent

ASHGHABAT

Qarshi

DUSHANBE

Bajgiran
Shīrvān

Merv

Amu-Darya River

Termiz

Bojnūrd
Qūchān

Tūs

Sabzevār
Neishābūr

Sarakhs
Saraghs

Mashhad

MASHHAD
Home to the extraordinary
Holy Shrine of Emām Rezā,
a focus of pilgrimage & piety

A01

KABUL

To Peshawar

Tāybād

Kavīr

Gonābād

Herāt

AFGHANISTAN

0   100   200km
0   50   100mi

Tabas

Birjand

Lake
Sīstān

Dasht-e Lūt

Kandahar

Lake
Hāmūn

Zābol

Quetta

Kermān

Māhān

ELEVATION

Mt Hezār
(4420m)

A02

Bam

Zāhedān

Taftan

Mirjāveh

Mt Taftān
(4042m)

3000m

2000m

1000m

500m

250m

0

Gāhkom

PAKISTAN

Bandar-é
Abbās

Hormoz
Island

Lārak
Island

Irānshahr

To Lahore

Strait of Hormoz

BAM
Pretty oasis town with
magnificent walled
city & citadel

Indus River

Hyderabad

OMAN

Jāsk

Chābahār

Karachi

To
Muscat

Gulf of Oman

ARABIAN SEA

OMAN

Iran
3rd edition – July 2001
First published – August 1992

Published by
Lonely Planet Publications Pty Ltd ABN 36 005 607 983
90 Maribyrnong St, Footscray, Victoria 3011, Australia

Lonely Planet Offices
Australia Locked Bag 1, Footscray, Victoria 3011
USA 150 Linden St, Oakland, CA 94607
UK 10a Spring Place, London NW5 3BH
France 1 rue du Dahomey, 75011 Paris

Photographs
Many of the images in this guide are available for licensing from
Lonely Planet Images.
W www.lonelyplanetimages.com

Front cover photograph
Tiled arch in the Emām Mosque, Esfahān (Chris Mellor)

ISBN 0 86442 756 5

Contents – Text

FARSI (PERSIAN)   413

GLOSSARY   418

THANKS   421

INDEX   424

MAP LEGEND   back page

METRIC CONVERSION   inside back cover

Contents – Maps

The Authors

Pat Yale

Pat first travelled across Europe to Turkey in an old van that didn't look as if it would make it past Dover. After graduating, she spent several years selling holidays before throwing away sensible careerdom to head overland from Egypt to Zimbabwe. Returning home, she mixed teaching with extensive travel in Europe, Asia, Central America and South America. A full-time writer now, she has worked on many Lonely Planet titles, including *Turkey*, *Middle East, Britain, Ireland, London* and *Dublin*. She currently lives in Göreme in Turkey.

Anthony Ham

Anthony worked as a refugee lawyer for three years, during which time the people of the world came to visit him in his office. After tiring of daily battles with the Australian government, he set out to see the world for himself and restore his faith in humanity. He has been travelling throughout Asia and Africa ever since, discovering unimagined uses for his Masters degree in Middle Eastern politics. He is now based in Melbourne and works as a freelance writer and photographer, with his work appearing in a range of magazines and newspapers. For Lonely Planet, Anthony has worked on the *Africa*, *India, Middle East* and *North India* guides.

FROM THE AUTHORS

Pat Yale Among the many people who went out of their way to help me, I would particularly like to thank Zoreh Majdian at Magic Carpet Travel, Jacky Finstone of Imaginative Traveller and Lyn Hughes of Wanderlust magazine for persuading me that I could go it alone in Iran. Thanks, too, to Yavuz Salatacı in İstanbul for keeping his cool when I was losing mine in the anxious days before my visa was approved. In Iran, I was especially grateful to Ms Shahpar Roosta of Arg-é Jadid in Tehrān for all her help and encouragement, and to Ali Reza Mozaffari, without whose unstinting efforts I might still be standing in the Western Bus Terminal trying to find out the cost of a bus to Esfāhān. Pezhman Azizi was the perfect guide, endlessly patient with my many questions on every aspect of life in his country. I am also immensely indebted to Nazzer Khān for ensuring I didn't get lost in the Tabrīz bazaar; to Ahmad Shirmohammad for talking me through Iran's various trekking routes; to Babel Shaīmshiri for advice on mountaineering; to the two Farshīds for showing me around Rāmsar; and to Yavar Dehghani for accompanying me to Tōchāl. Thanks, too, to Golnaz Assadi, Lianne Bajalan, Nick Banks, Ian Hodges, Jaap and Abe Jawze, Mansur Johnson and Teresa Rumpf for all their travel tips, and to Craig Rosario and Martin Bjerke for being such great travel companions. Finally, I would like to thank

Anthony Ham for being such a great fellow author, Bethune Carmichael for his sterling support as editor and Hunor Csutoros for bringing order to my maps.

Anthony Ham Wherever I travelled in Iran, I found myself constantly overwhelmed by the many kindnesses shown by anything-but-ordinary people. Special thanks must go to my dear friend, Akbar, in Bam who personifies everything that is good about Iran, and Hajj Ali Khatib in Mashhad for his warmth, hospitality and friendship, not to mention his captivating performance on the road to Kalat. Particular thanks must also go to: Mohammed Ali and Behzad Poor for their generous hospitality in Bam, and Hadi for letting a complete stranger borrow his camera; Hossein and Ali in Yazd for their unfailing patience and hospitality; Hossein Vatany for his infectious love of Kermān; the Akhavan brothers in Kermān; the Ziaee brothers in Esfāhān for their help, and for letting me monopolise their phone on my birthday; Ehsan Nikravesh for helping me endure the heat in Bandar-é Abbas; Mansoor for his humour and enthusiasm in the humidity of Būshehr; Iraj Riahi, Ali and friends at the Nomad Carpet Shop in Esfāhān for sharing their love of their city and their carpets; Mina, Samira and Maryam in Emām Khomeinī Square in Esfāhān; Ali Kooroony for his gentle good humour in Shīrāz; Komeil Noofeili, also in Shīrāz, for his encyclopedic list of colloquialisms, Cockney accent and for sharing his considerable wisdom about Iran; Elham and Negar for their kindness in Yazd; and the students at the tourism college in Mashhad who shared with me a wonderfully memorable trip to Kalat. I hope that I will meet you all again one day.

Of the travellers I met, a big thank you to Agnes and Emmanuel for a lovely night in Yazd and to Pete and the Long Way Home crew for their invaluable information on driving in Iran. Thanks also to all those travellers who took the time to write with updates and suggestions.

Back home, I am especially grateful to my family and friends for their tolerance of my frequent absences, their understanding when a deadline approaches and the unfailing warmth of their welcome whenever I return home. At Lonely Planet, thanks to Michelle Glynn, Verity Campbell, Brett Moore, Bethune Carmichael, Hunor Csutoros and all the cartos. Finally, special thanks to Pat Yale, the coordinating author, who brought such wisdom to bear on this book.

This Book

David St Vincent researched and wrote the first edition of this book and Paul Greenway updated and revised the second edition. For this third edition, Pat Yale updated the introductory chapters, and the Tehrān, Caspian Sea and Western Iran chapters; Anthony Ham updated the Central Iran, Eastern Iran and Persian Gulf chapters.

FROM THE PUBLISHER

This edition of *Iran* was edited in Lonely Planet's Melbourne office by Bethune Carmichael, Isabelle Young, Kerryn Burgess, Evan Jones, Justin Flynn and Hilary Rogers. Hunor Csutoros coordinated the design and mapping, with assistance from Heath Comrie, Rod Zandbergs, Yvonne Bischofberger, Gus Balbontin, Csanád Csutoros, Sally Morgan, Corinne Waddell, Anna Judd and Lachlan Ross. Hunor also provided the climate charts and decorative borders. Special thanks to Kelli Hamblet and Martin Harris for the illustrations; Simon Bracken for the cover design; and Quentin Frayne and Emma Koch for the Language chapter.

Last but by no means least, thanks to authors Pat Yale and Anthony Ham for all their hard work.

THANKS
Many thanks to the travellers who used the last edition and wrote to us with helpful hints, advice and interesting anecdotes. Your names appear in the back of this book.

7

Foreword

ABOUT LONELY PLANET GUIDEBOOKS

The story begins with a classic travel adventure: Tony and Maureen Wheeler's 1972 journey across Europe and Asia to Australia. Useful information about the overland trail did not exist at that time, so Tony and Maureen published the first Lonely Planet guidebook to meet a growing need.

From a kitchen table, then from a tiny office in Melbourne (Australia), Lonely Planet has become the largest independent travel publisher in the world, an international company with offices in Melbourne, Oakland (USA), London (UK) and Paris (France).

Today Lonely Planet guidebooks cover the globe. There is an ever-growing list of books and there's information in a variety of forms and media. Some things haven't changed. The main aim is still to help make it possible for adventurous travellers to get out there – to explore and better understand the world.

At Lonely Planet we believe travellers can make a positive contribution to the countries they visit – if they respect their host communities and spend their money wisely. Since 1986 a percentage of the income from each book has been donated to aid projects and human rights campaigns.

Updates Lonely Planet thoroughly updates each guidebook as often as possible. This usually means there are around two years between editions, although for more unusual or more stable destinations the gap can be longer. Check the imprint page (following the colour map at the beginning of the book) for publication dates.

Between editions up-to-date information is available in two free newsletters – the paper *Planet Talk* and email *Comet* (to subscribe, contact any Lonely Planet office) – and on our Web site at www.lonelyplanet.com. The *Upgrades* section of the Web site covers a number of important and volatile destinations and is regularly updated by Lonely Planet authors. *Scoop* covers news and current affairs relevant to travellers. And, lastly, the *Thorn Tree* bulletin board and *Postcards* section of the site carry unverified, but fascinating, reports from travellers.

Correspondence The process of creating new editions begins with the letters, postcards and emails received from travellers. This correspondence often includes suggestions, criticisms and comments about the current editions. Interesting excerpts are immediately passed on via newsletters and the Web site, and everything goes to our authors to be verified when they're researching on the road. We're keen to get more feedback from organisations or individuals who represent communities visited by travellers.

Lonely Planet gathers information for everyone who's curious about the planet – and especially for those who explore it first-hand. Through guidebooks, phrasebooks, activity guides, maps, literature, newsletters, image library, TV series and Web site we act as an information exchange for a worldwide community of travellers.

Research Authors aim to gather sufficient practical information to enable travellers to make informed choices and to make the mechanics of a journey run smoothly. They also research historical and cultural background to help enrich the travel experience and allow travellers to understand and respond appropriately to cultural and environmental issues.

Authors don't stay in every hotel because that would mean spending a couple of months in each medium-sized city and, no, they don't eat at every restaurant because that would mean stretching belts beyond capacity. They do visit hotels and restaurants to check standards and prices, but feedback based on readers' direct experiences can be very helpful.

Many of our authors work undercover, others aren't so secretive. None of them accept freebies in exchange for positive write-ups. And none of our guidebooks contain any advertising.

Production Authors submit their raw manuscripts and maps to offices in Australia, USA, UK or France. Editors and cartographers – all experienced travellers themselves – then begin the process of assembling the pieces. When the book finally hits the shops, some things are already out of date, we start getting feedback from readers and the process begins again …

WARNING & REQUEST

Things change – prices go up, schedules change, good places go bad and bad places go bankrupt – nothing stays the same. So, if you find things better or worse, recently opened or long since closed, please tell us and help make the next edition even more accurate and useful. We genuinely value all the feedback we receive. A well travelled team reads and acknowledges every letter, postcard and email and ensures that every morsel of information finds its way to the appropriate authors, editors and cartographers for verification.

Everyone who writes to us will find their name in the next edition of the appropriate guidebook. They will also receive the latest issue of *Planet Talk*, our quarterly printed newsletter, or *Comet*, our monthly email newsletter. Subscriptions to both newsletters are free. The very best contributions will be rewarded with a free guidebook.

Excerpts from your correspondence may appear in new editions of Lonely Planet guidebooks, the Lonely Planet Web site, *Planet Talk* or *Comet*, so please let us know if you *don't* want your letter published or your name acknowledged.

Send all correspondence to the Lonely Planet office closest to you:

Australia: Locked Bag 1, Footscray, Victoria 3011
USA: 150 Linden St, Oakland, CA 94607
UK: 10A Spring Place, London NW5 3BH
France: 1 rue du Dahomey, 75011 Paris

Or email us at: talk2us@lonelyplanet.com.au

For news, views and updates see our Web site: www.lonelyplanet.com

HOW TO USE A LONELY PLANET GUIDEBOOK

The best way to use a Lonely Planet guidebook is any way you choose. At Lonely Planet we believe the most memorable travel experiences are often those that are unexpected, and the finest discoveries are those you make yourself. Guidebooks are not intended to be used as if they provide a detailed set of infallible instructions!

Contents All Lonely Planet guidebooks follow roughly the same format. The Facts about the Destination chapters or sections give background information ranging from history to weather. Facts for the Visitor gives practical information on issues like visas and health. Getting There & Away gives a brief starting point for researching travel to and from the destination. Getting Around gives an overview of the transport options when you arrive.

The peculiar demands of each destination determine how subsequent chapters are broken up, but some things remain constant. We always start with background, then proceed to sights, places to stay, places to eat, entertainment, getting there and away, and getting around information – in that order.

Heading Hierarchy Lonely Planet headings are used in a strict hierarchical structure that can be visualised as a set of Russian dolls. Each heading (and its following text) is encompassed by any preceding heading that is higher on the hierarchical ladder.

Entry Points We do not assume guidebooks will be read from beginning to end, but that people will dip into them. The traditional entry points are the list of contents and the index. In addition, however, some books have a complete list of maps and an index map illustrating map coverage.

There may also be a colour map that shows highlights. These highlights are dealt with in greater detail in the Facts for the Visitor chapter, along with planning questions and suggested itineraries. Each chapter covering a geographical region usually begins with a locator map and another list of highlights. Once you find something of interest in a list of highlights, turn to the index.

Maps Maps play a crucial role in Lonely Planet guidebooks and include a huge amount of information. A legend is printed on the back page. We seek to have complete consistency between maps and text, and to have every important place in the text captured on a map. Map key numbers usually start in the top left corner.

Although inclusion in a guidebook usually implies a recommendation we cannot list every good place. Exclusion does not necessarily imply criticism. In fact there are a number of reasons why we might exclude a place – sometimes it is simply inappropriate to encourage an influx of travellers.

Introduction

Whether under its ancient name of Persia or its modern name of Iran, the vast country that sprawls between Turkey and Iraq in the west and Pakistan and Afghanistan in the east has always held a great fascination for travellers. During the 1960s and '70s a steady stream of travellers made their way across the country, following the old hippy trail and bringing back tales of wonderful mosques with jewel-like tiles, of endless, rolling desert and of wonderfully hospitable people. All that came to an abrupt end, of course, in 1979 when those images were overlaid by images of the Islamic Revolution – black-veiled women with hands raised in protest and men screaming abuse against America and Israel. The Revolution was followed almost immediately by the horrors of the eight-year Iran-Iraq War, which claimed over a million lives. Not surprisingly tourism dwindled to a footnote in Iranian economic statistics.

In the last few years Iran has finally started to recover from the excesses of the Revolution and the aftermath of the war. The Iranian government is starting to promote tourism, but very cautiously and with a wary eye on the likely impact on its religious and cultural values of a sudden influx of rich non-Muslims. Western travel agencies have started to send tour groups back to Iran and the overland trail is back in business, with a steady trickle of visitors heading from Turkey to Pakistan or vice versa.

Iran has always had more than its fair share of sites to offer. For archaeology buffs, there are the famous ruins not just of ancient cities like Persepolis in central Iran, where you may find yourself wondering whether Iran doesn't have too many tourists already, but also of others like Takht-é Soleimān in western Iran where you may still have the place to yourself. For lovers of architecture there are hundreds of glorious mosques and mausoleums with domes that glitter like Fabergé eggs. Tehrān may be a traffic-choked urban nightmare but it also boasts a world-class array of museums where you can

11

examine some of the finest Persian carpets ever made and the treasures of dynasties from the Achaemenids to the Pahlavīs. For many people, highlights of their trip will be visits to the magnificent cities of Esfahān, Shīrāz, Kermān, Yazd and Bam, but lovers of the great outdoors can strike out into the Dasht-é Kavīr and Dasht-é Lūt deserts or the Zāgros and Alborz Mountains. It's even possible to ski down the slopes alongside Iran's nouveau riche. And shopaholics won't be able to tear themselves away from the ceramics, miniature paintings and world-renowned Persian carpets on sale in the bazaars.

However you choose to travel, Iran represents extremely good value for your hard-earned dollar, although you do have to be prepared to adapt to the very different social circumstances. The country is relatively easy to explore, with a cheap and extensive network of buses, trains and planes. There is also a reasonable range of accommodation in most places visitors will want to go, although solo travellers are in for thin pickings in their search for moderately priced single rooms.

These days Iran is also a remarkably safe country to travel around and Iranians, including the police and military, are very friendly. Although the strict dress code weighs particularly heavily on women (who may decide that summer is not the time to visit), the situation is slowly easing and there's no reason why even a lone woman can't travel around independently, provided she has deep reserves of self-confidence and self-sufficiency. Most women encounter less hassle than in Turkey or Pakistan, although it would be optimistic to assume that it never happens.

If you are the sort of traveller who is prepared to respect local people and their traditions, to be open-minded and to try to adapt to unfamiliar circumstances, post-revolutionary Iran is one of the most exciting, fascinating, welcoming, rewarding and, frankly, inexpensive countries yet to be 'discovered'. And *now* is the time to go.

Facts about Iran

HISTORY

Iran's ancient history is a catalogue of disasters and short-lived triumphs, of occasionally brilliant rulers succeeded by incompetents who failed to secure their inheritance. The last 20 years have seen it struggle to establish itself as the world's first Islamic theocracy.

The Original Iranians

Historians are still debating when the first inhabitants settled in what is now Iran, but ongoing excavations suggest that during Neolithic times small numbers of hunters probably lived in caves in the Zāgros and Alborz Mountains and in the south-east.

The first area where cities are known to have been established (in what is now Khūzestān province) was close enough to Mesopotamia and the great Sumerian civilisation to feel its influence. It was here that the Elamites established their capital at Shūsh. By the 12th century BC they are thought to have controlled all of western Persia, the Tigris Valley and the coast of the Persian Gulf. So powerful did the Elamites become that they even managed to defeat the Assyrians, carrying off in triumph the famous stone inscribed with the Code of Hammurabi, which is now in the Louvre in Paris.

About this time Indo-European Aryan tribes began to encroach on northern Persia. The Persians eventually settled in what is now Fārs province, while the Medes took up residence in western Persia, beating off the threat from invading Scythians and Cimmerians and even managing to hold their own against powerful neighbours to the west, the Assyrians and the Urartians (see the boxed text 'The Urartians' in the Western Iran chapter).

Very little is known about the Medes who left no written records of their own; instead we must depend on what is said about them by Assyrian and Greek historians and archivists. Although they first crop up in Assyrian records in 836 BC, there is nothing to

Persia or Iran?

Iran used to be called Persia, a name derived (like Farsi) from the name of Fārs province where the Aryan tribes had settled. In 1934 Rezā Shāh had the country's name changed to Iran – derived directly from Aryan (meaning 'of noble origin') – as part of his modernisation drive. But because the name 'Persia' had been so closely associated with art and culture, it's usual even today for people to talk of 'Persian' carpets and 'Persian' architecture.

indicate where they came from or how they managed to conquer an area that eventually extended from the Caspian Sea to the Zāgros Mountains. We do know that they took over most of the region during the reign of Sargon who died in 705 BC, that they were united under a chief called Dieoces in 673 BC and that they even managed to sack Nineveh, the Assyrian capital, in 612 BC. It is believed that they spoke a language similar to Old Persian. Their capital was at Ecbatana, more or less underneath what is now Hamadān.

The Achaemenids & the First Persian Empire

In the 7th century BC the king of one of the Persian tribes, Achemenes, managed to create a unified state in southern Iran, giving his name to what was to become the First Persian Empire, that of the Achaemenids, with its capital at Shūsh. It was during the reign of his great-grandson Cyrus II that the Persians became a real force to be reckoned with. Cyrus the Great (as he came to be known) expanded his territory until it stretched all the way from Pakistan to the Aegean coast of what is now Turkey. In 539 BC Cyrus the Great even captured Baghdad, omitting to have the population put to the sword and thus marking himself out as an unusually enlightened ruler for the time.

Cyrus colonised the old Median capital at Ecbatana, redeveloped Shūsh and built for

Iran's Timeline

BC

12th century Elamite Empire established with capital at Shūsh

c.750–550 Median Empire created in north and western Persia with capital at Ecbatana

550–330 Achaemenid Empire, First Persian Empire, set up with its capitals at Shūsh, Persepolis and Ecbatana; Zoroastrianism established as state religion

330 Alexander the Great invades Persia and sacks Persepolis

323 Death of Alexander the Great; Persian part of his empire falls to Seleucus I

312–162 Seleucid government; 'Hellenisation' of Persia

161 BC–AD 224 Parthian Empire

AD

224–637 Sassanian Empire, Second Persian Empire; Zoroastrianism the state religion

637–1050 Arab conquest of Persia followed by establishment of Islam as state religion; Umayyad caliphate governing from Damascus followed by Abbasid caliphate governing from Baghdad

1051–1220 Seljuk dynasty

1220–1335 Mongol dynasties govern from Tabrīz

1380–1502 Tamerlane and the Timurids govern from Qazvīn

1502–1722 Safavid dynasty governs from Esfahān, Third Persian Empire; Shiite Islam becomes state religion

1722–29 Brief period of Afghan rule

1736–47 Turbulent reign of Nāder Shāh

1747–79 More peaceful reign of Karīm Khān Zand from new capital at Shīrāz

1779–1925 Qajar dynasty

1906 Constitutional Revolution; first parliament established

1923 Rezā Khān comes to power as first Pahlavī shah

1941 Rezā Khān forced to abdicate in favour of his son Mohammed Rezā Pahlavī

1971 Lavish celebrations for 2500th anniversary of founding of Persian Empire

1974 Aftermath of oil crisis brings economic chaos to Iran

1979 Islamic Revolution brings Āyatollāh Khomeinī to power

1980 Creation of world's first Islamic Republic

1980–88 Iran-Iraq War

1989 Death of Āyatollāh Khomeinī

1997 Election of the reformist President Khatamī

---

himself a new home at Pasargadae, thereby establishing the pattern whereby Persian rulers circulated between three different capitals. He died in battle in 529 but his son, Cambyses II, headed west to capture most of Egypt.

Cambyses had only ascended the throne after arranging the murder of his brother, Smerdis, and while he was distracted in Egypt, a minor official called Magus Gaumata seized the throne, claiming to be Smerdis. Cambyses died mysteriously in 522 BC while still in Egypt, and Darius I (Darius the Great), a distant relative, moved quickly to be rid of Gaumata.

By then the empire was in disarray and Darius had to fight hard to re-establish it, dividing his sprawling inheritance into 23 satrapies to make it easier to govern. The magnificent complex at Persepolis was created to serve as the religious hub of an empire whose primary religion was Zoroastrianism (see the boxed text 'Zoroastrianism' in the Central Iran chapter for more details), while the Median capital at Shūsh became the administrative centre. Persepolis was liberally decorated with images of all the peoples now subject to the Achaemenids bringing tributes to the king. Darius eventually expanded the empire to India and pushed as far north as the Danube River.

After the Greek colonies of Asia Minor rebelled against their Persian overlord, Darius decided to invade mainland Greece in the hope of suppressing the city-states that supplied them. Thus commenced the long series of wars described by the Greek historian Thucydides in his book *The Persian*

Wars. In 490 BC Darius' armies were defeated at Marathon near Athens while he was busy putting down an uprising in Egypt. He died in 486 BC.

The subsequent defeat of Darius' son Xerxes at Salamis in Greece in 480 BC marked the effective end of the First Persian Empire. Artaxerxes made one last attempt to pull the splintering satrapies back together again but was powerless in face of the rising power of Macedonia to the west.

At the height of their power the Achaemenids ruled over one of the greatest of early civilisations. Paved roads suitable for horse-drawn carriages stretched from one end of their empire to the other, with caravanserais at regular intervals to provide food and shelter to travellers. The Achaemenids are also credited with having introduced the world's first courier service for transmitting mail around their territories.

Alexander the Great & the End of Persepolis

In the 4th century BC, fresh from conquering most of Greece, Egypt, Turkey and Iraq, Alexander the Great invaded Persia. After winning victories at Issus (333) and Gaugamela (331), Alexander routed Darius III who fled east to Bactria, only to be murdered by his cousin. Alexander spent several months at Persepolis, which was later burned down – the jury is still out on whether this was the accidental result of a drunken party or deliberate retaliation for the destruction of Athens by Xerxes.

Alexander's empire soon reached across Afghanistan, Pakistan and India, but after his death in 323 BC it was divided between three squabbling dynasties, with Persia controlled by the Macedonian Seleucids. Gradually the Greek language replaced Aramaic as the lingua franca, new towns were set up all over the region and Greek culture stamped itself on the older Persian one. But the Seleucids were soon in trouble with the ambitious satraps and the numerous feisty ethnic minorities nominally under their control, in particular with the nomadic Parthians. In 190 BC the Seleucids were further weakened by a great Roman victory over them at Magnesia.

The Parthian Takeover

The Parthians had settled the area of Persia between the Caspian and Aral Seas many centuries before. Under their great king Mithridates (171–138 BC), they started first to swallow most of Persia and then everywhere between the Euphrates in the west and Afghanistan in the east until they had more or less re-created the old Achaemenid Empire. They had two capitals, one at what is now Rey, the other at Ctesiphon in Iraq. Caught up in incessant ping-pong combat with the Romans over Syria, Mesopotamia and Armenia, they finally managed a great victory over an invading Roman army at Carrhae in 53 BC, but within a century the two were back to fighting each other for supremacy. Not nearly as despotic as later dynasties, the Parthians were responsible for the first flowering of Persian architecture.

The Sassanians & the Second Persian Empire

The Sassanians were a local dynasty from Fārs province who managed to resist the Hellenising tendencies of the Seleucids and Parthians. In AD 224 Ardeshir I (r. 224–41), leader of the Sassanians, rose up against the Parthians and started a 20-year push for power that soon saw him governing all the lands between Persia and the Indus. Ardeshir's son, Shāpūr I (r. 241–72), added Bactria to these gains and also fought with the Romans, culminating in a victory at Edessa in AD 260 when the Roman emperor Valerian was actually taken prisoner (a victory commemorated in the carvings at Naghsh-é Rostam, near Persepolis).

The Sassanians were followers of Zoroastrianism, which resulted in sporadic bursts of repression of other religions, especially Christianity, which was seen as too closely linked to Rome. They had their own language, Pahlavī, from which modern Farsi slowly developed. A few fire temples built during this period still remain, as do the ruins of Firūz Ābād, Tāq-é Bostān, and Neishābūr. The Sassanian capital was at Ctesiphon in modern Iraq.

The Sassanians also developed small industries, promoted urban development and encouraged trade across the Persian Gulf but soon they, too, were weakened by fighting. In the 6th century AD Khusro I (531–79) managed to fight off the invading Huns and started recovering lost ground. Khusro II (590–628) recaptured parts of Egypt, Syria, Palestine and Turkey. However, fighting among factions within the empire and wars against the Byzantine Empire slowly undermined the Second Persian Empire, which fell easy prey to the conquering Arabs in 637.

The Arabs & Islam

A crucial chapter in Persian history started when the Arabs defeated the Sassanians at Qadisirya in AD 637, following up with a victory at Nehāvand near Hamadān which marked the end of Sassanian power. The last Sassanian king, Yazdgard III (r. 632–51), was assassinated while still in power.

By the time of Mohammed's death in AD 632 the Arabs were firm adherents of Islam. The Persians found plenty to like in Islamic culture and religion, and happily forsook Zoroaster for the teachings of Mohammed without much need of persuasion from their conquerors. Only Yazd and Kermān (both of which clung to Zoroastrianism for a few centuries more) and a few isolated tribes in the mountains near the Caspian Sea held fast to their old religions.

At first the Umayyad caliphs held sway over Persia from their capital in Damascus, but in AD 750 a Shiite rebellion led to the elevation of the Abbasid dynasty who set up their capital near Baghdad. The Abbasid caliphs presided over a period of intellectual exuberance in which Persian culture played a major role. Persians also held many high offices at court, but the Arabic language and script became the norm for day-to-day business.

During the 9th century AD, Abbasid power started to crumble, and regional governors snatched the chance to set up their own local power-bases. In eastern Iran these new Iranian dynasties included the Safavids (868–903), the Tahirids (820–72) and the Samanids (874–1042) who set up their capital at Bukhara and revived the Per-

sian language, while in the west the Ziyarids (928–1042) and Buyids (942–1055) also resisted Arabisation and fought to hold on to Persian language and culture.

The Coming of the Seljuks

Inevitably, these local dynasties were no more able to hold onto their power. The Samanids became fatally dependent on Turkish soldiers, one of whom soon elbowed them aside to found his own Qaznavid dynasty (AD 998–1045); his son went on to grab what is now Sīstān ve Balūchestān province.

In turn they were ousted by the Seljuk Turks who pushed on through Persia, capturing Esfahān in 1051 and turning it into their capital. By the mid-11th century they had added eastern Turkey to their empire, and, despite numerous rebellions, they managed to maintain control with a large and well-paid army.

The Seljuk dynasty heralded a new era in Persian art, literature and science, distinguished by geniuses like the mathematician and poet Omar Khayyām. Theological schools were also set up throughout Seljuk territories to propagate their own Sunni branch of Islam.

The death of Malik Shāh in 1092 (possibly murdered by the Assassins – see the boxed text 'The Original Assassins', in the Western Iran chapter for more details) marked the end of real Seljuk supremacy, and once again a powerful empire splintered into weaker fragments.

Genghis Khan & After

In the early 13th century, the Seljuk Empire finally came to an end when the rampaging Mongols, under the leadership of Genghis Khan (Chinggis Khaan), came thundering across the Iranian plateau on their horses, leaving a trail of cold-blooded devastation in their wake.

Under the leadership first of Genghis Khan, and then of his grandson, Hulagu, the Mongol rulers managed to seize all of Persia, as well as an empire stretching from Beijing (China) to İstanbul (Turkey), leaving just tiny pockets of resistance in southern and northern Persia. Eventually they established a capital at Tabrīz (too close, as they later found out, to the Turks). It was Hulagu Khan who put an end to the stealthy power of the Assassins. After a flirtation with Christianity and Buddhism, Hulagu was forced by social pressures in Persia to adopt Islam. He called himself *il khān* (provincial khan or ruler), a name later given to the entire Ilkhanid dynasty (1259–1335) who followed him.

Tragically, the Mongols destroyed many of the Persian cities they conquered, obliterating much of Persia's documented history. Oddly enough, they later had a change of heart and matamorphosed into great patrons of the arts, leaving many fine monuments, including the wonderful Soltānīyeh Mausoleum, Gonbad-é Soltānīyeh, near Zanjān. It was during the ascendancy of the Mongols that Marco Polo travelled across Persia (see the boxed text 'Marco Polo in Persia'), and that Farsi replaced Arabic as the lingua franca. In 1335 the Mongol Empire came to an end when the death of Sultan Abu Said left it with no effective successor.

Tamerlane & the Timurids

The fragmented remnants of the Mongol Empire soon succumbed to invading forces from the east led by Tamerlane (Lame Timur) who swept on to defeat the Ottoman Turks in 1402. Tamerlane came from a Turkeyfied Mongol clan in what is now Uzbekistan. During his short reign, Tamerlane managed to stop the constant warring and moved the capital from Tabrīz to Qazvīn but he put down rebellions with brutal vigour; 70,000 people are said to have been executed in Esfahān alone.

When he died in 1405, Tamerlane's empire immediately started to fray at the edges. However, the Timurids in eastern Iran became great patrons of Persian art, encouraging in particular the miniaturists of Shīrāz; it was Gōhar Shād, the wife of one of the Timurid rulers, who was responsible for the beautiful mosque at the heart of the Mashhad shrine. Some parts of the Timurid domains eventually collapsed in the face of the Ottoman onslaught. Others came under the increasingly powerful and hostile influence of European colonialists (especially the Portuguese) who had established a foothold in the Persian Gulf.

The Black & White Sheep Turkmen

While the Mongols and Timurids were slogging it out in eastern Iran, assorted Turkman tribes were vying for power in the west. Eventually the Kara Koyunlu (Black Sheep) tribe, managed to set itself up in Tabrīz and to grab power in eastern Turkey. Having held strong for more than a century (1275–1468), they, in turn, gave way to the Ak Koyunlu (White Sheep) tribe who continued in power until 1514.

The Safavids & the Third Persian Empire

The Safavid dynasty started life quietly when it was founded by a Shiite Sufi called Sheikh Safī od-Dīn (d. 1334) whose power-base was around Ardabīl in north-west Iran. Shāh Ismāel (1502–24) soon went on to reconquer all the old Persian imperial heartlands, from Baghdad in the west to Herāt in the east, although he was forced out of western Iran by the Ottoman sultan, Selim the Grim.

Under Ismāel's son Tahmasp (1524–75), the capital was moved from Tabrīz to Qazvīn and Western monarchs started to take an interest in Persia.

The Safavids reached their peak under the brilliant Shāh Abbās I (Abbas the Great; r. 1587–1629) who finally crushed all the assorted Turkmen and Turkish factions to

Marco Polo in Persia

In the 13th century the famous Venetian world traveller Marco Polo crossed Iran en route from Italy to China with his father and uncle. On his way he passed through Tabrīz, Kashān, Yazd, Kermān, Hormoz, Tabas and Neishābūr. His *Book of Marco Polo*, originally written in French, has left us vivid accounts of these cities that make it clear the Mongols had by then settled down to peaceful enjoyment of their estates.

create what is thought of as the third great empire in Persian history (after the Achaemenid and Sassanian Empires).

The Safavid era saw a great flowering of Persian art and architecture; many of the finest monuments surviving today were erected in this period. It was also under the Safavids that Shiism was enshrined as Persia's state religion, bringing it into direct conflict with the Sunni Ottoman Empire.

The capital was moved once again, this time to Esfahān, which Abbās rebuilt with such splendour that it became the envy of other regional empires and of curious European visitors, one of whom, the French traveller Chardin, left a comprehensive record of what he saw. English companies were given business concessions, although the Portuguese, who controlled Hormoz Island in the Persian Gulf, were less welcome (see the boxed text 'The Portuguese on Hormoz Island' in the Persian Gulf chapter). The old caravan routes were revived and supplied with literally hundreds of new caravanserais.

The death of Abbās was the signal for a renewed period of bickering and fighting, which left the door wide open for Afghan invaders.

Afghan Interlude

The decline of the Safavids was hastened by an Afghan invasion of eastern Persia in 1722. The Afghans besieged the Persian capital Esfahān and eventually took control of the city, slaughtering thousands. The first Afghan ruler, Mahmud, eventually went mad and was murdered by a member of his own army.

During this brief interlude (1722–29), the Russians, under Peter the Great, attempted to intrude on Persian territory but didn't get far. The Turks once again invaded western and northern Persia.

Nāder Shāh & Karīm Khān Zand

The Safavids were briefly rescued from oblivion by a soldier of fortune, Nāder Shāh, who then decided he could do a better job as shah himself and proceeded to scatter the Afghans, Russians and Turks in all directions. For an encore he rushed off to

do a little conquering himself, returning from India laden with goodies, among them the Peacock Throne and the Kuh-é Nūr diamond. His constant warring rapidly wore out the country. It was a relief to all, both inside and outside Persia, when he was assassinated in 1747. He had governed for just 11 years.

After Nāder Shāh's murder, a Lor from western Iran, Karīm Khān Zand (1747–76), grabbed power. Almost uniquely, he had little interest in warfare. Instead he is remembered for moving the capital to Shīrāz and ruling less harshly than most of his predecessors. Karīm Khān Zand was called *vakīl* (regent) rather than shah.

The Qajars & the Constitutional Revolution

In 1779 a bitter and twisted eunuch Aga Muhammed Khān united the Āzārī Qajars and created a new capital in Tehrān. By 1795 he eventually wrested control of Persia from Karīm Khān Zand's ineffectual successors. Aga Muhammed Khān managed to hold onto the throne for only two years before he was murdered by his own servants, and his successors were not memorable; two even picked fights with Russia, which refused to be baited.

Soon, however, the Russians, as well as the British, had their eyes on Iran. The Russians were determined to use Iran to give them access to the Persian Gulf and thence to India, while the British were equally determined to keep the Russians well away from their sea routes to India. During the reign of big-bearded Fath Ali Shāh (1797–1834) Russia succeeded in capturing and keeping Azerbaijan, Armenia and Daghestan. Nasser al-Din Shāh was more interested in collecting art and building museums than in keeping control over Iran's considerable natural resources, and slowly but surely the Russians asserted control over northern Iran while the British dictated what happened in the south. In one particularly notorious incident, Nasser al-Din tried to sell exclusive rights to exploit all Iran's economic resources (including all the banks, mines and railways) for a one-off sum of UK£40,000 to be followed by payments of UK£10,000 for the next 25 years. He was forced to call off the deal once news of its absurdity leaked out.

Eventually, popular resistance to the sell-off of Persian resources to foreigners boiled over into revolt and the third-last Qajar shah, Muzaffar al-Din (1896–1907), was forced to introduce an embryo parliament, the first Majlis, in 1906, and a constitution, which would ensure that any laws passed would be in line with Shiite doctrine.

Worried that a shah who had been so helpful to them was being weakened, the Russians persuaded him to backtrack on his promises. In 1908 martial law and dictatorship were introduced by his ruthless son Shāh Mohammed Alī. This led to an uprising in Tabrīz in 1909 and Shāh Mohammed Alī was forced to abdicate in favour of his son who was still a child. The furore soon died down and in 1911 Shāh Ahmad quietly abolished the second Majlis.

During WWI both Britain and Russia occupied parts of Iran. Worried about the weakness of the Qajar shah, the growing influence of communist Russia and the German occupation of Iraq, Britain then threw in its lot with a charismatic and influential army officer, Rezā Khān, against Shāh Ahmad.

The Pahlavīs & the Lead-Up to Revolution

In 1921 Rezā Khān organised a coup d'etat and set up a puppet prime minister. By 1923 he felt confident enough to proclaim himself prime minister, naming his dynasty Pahlavī after the ancient language. The Qajar Empire was formally ended by the Majlis in December 1925.

During the first few years, Rezā Khān had to suppress several rebellions, and although he agreed to respect the authority of the Majlis, in fact he maintained almost complete control of Iran. The task facing him as he moved to modernise Iran along similar lines to his neighbour Mustafa Kemal Atatürk in Turkey was enormous. While the shahs had frolicked and fought, literacy in Iran remained very poor. The transport infrastructure was rudimentary,

the health system virtually nonexistent. Industry and agriculture were stagnant. Like Atatürk, Rezā Khān saw the need to improve the status of women and to that end he made the wearing of the traditional chador (black cloak) illegal. Like Atatürk, too, he insisted on the wearing of Western dress and moved to crush the power of the religious establishment, banning, for example, the traditional rituals to commemorate Hossein's martyrdom during Moharram.

Iran – as Persia was now to be called – was again neutral during WWII, but Britain and Russia established spheres of influence over vast areas of the country. In particular the Russians grabbed the Azerbaijan provinces and were only with difficulty winkled out again. In 1941, Rezā was forced into exile in South Africa when the Russians and British decided he was inclining towards the Axis powers. His 22-year-old son, Mohammed Rezā, succeeded him.

In 1943 at the Tehrān Conference, Britain, Russia and the USA signed the Tehrān Declaration, accepting the independence of Iran. However, the Russian forces were persuaded to depart only with great difficulty and American connivance. The young Mohammed Rezā regained absolute power but was completely in thrall to the West.

By now the Anglo-Iranian oil company was churning out petro-dollars by the million and there were calls for it to be nationalised. In 1951 the prime minister was assassinated and in his place came the 70-year-old nationalist Dr Mohammed Mossadeq, leader of the National Front Movement, swept into office on the back of promises to repatriate that money. Although he succeeded in getting Anglo-Iranian nationalised as the National Iranian Oil Company (a fact still celebrated with an annual public holiday), he had reckoned without the determination of the 'losers' – British Petroleum hit back by boycotting Iranian oil while more conservative factions in the government fomented economic turmoil. In 1953 the Shāh fled the country briefly but the CIA organised a coup to get Mossadeq out and he returned. Now the oil industry was denationalised but the

British monopoly was broken and the US gained a 40% stake in it.

The White Revolution & the Oil Crisis

Once Mossadeq was gone, the US government encouraged the Shāh to press ahead with a program of social and economic modernisation, dubbed the White Revolution because it was intended to take place without bloodshed. But although some headway was made with reducing illiteracy and emancipating women, it was all too fast for a conservative, and mainly rural, Muslim population. The religious establishment, the *ulema*, also took exception to land reforms that deprived them of some of their rights and to electoral reforms which gave votes to non-Muslims.

By 1962 Āyatollāh Khomeinī, then living in Qom, had started to emerge as a figurehead for opposition to the Shāh. In 1964 the Shāh approved a bill that gave US soldiers in Iran complete immunity from arrest. Khomeinī responded by claiming that he had 'reduced the Iranian people to a level lower than that of an American dog' since if anyone ran over a dog in America they would be prosecuted for doing so, while now if an American ran over an Iranian he could do so with impunity. The Shāh reacted by banishing Khomeinī who fled first to Turkey and then to Iraq.

In 1971 the Shāh organised lavish celebrations for the 2500th anniversary of the founding of the Persian Empire, hoping to make himself more popular by fanning the flames of nationalism. A vast pavilion built for the ceremonies still stands at Persepolis. At the same time a new 'Persian' calendar was introduced to replace the Arabic Islamic one.

The 1974 oil price revolution turned out to be the Shāh's undoing. In just one year the income from oil shot from US$4 billion to US$20 billion but the Shāh allowed US arms merchants to persuade him to squander this vast new wealth on huge arsenals of weapons that then stood rotting in the desert. Fortunes were wasted on inappropriate development schemes. The flood of petro-dollars ended up lining the pockets of a select few while galloping inflation made the vast majority of the country worse off than before. Then as the world slipped into recession, oil sales slumped, forcing the government to cut back on some of the planned social reforms.

The Islamic Revolution

Since the beginning of the Pahlavī dynasty there had been smouldering resistance that occasionally flared into violence. Students wanted faster reform, devout Muslims wanted reforms rolled back, and everyone attacked the Pahlavīs' conspicuous consumption. As the economy went from bad to worse under the Shāh's post oil-boom mismanagement, the growing opposition made its presence felt with sabotage and massive street demonstrations. The Shāh responded with all the force available to the absolute ruler of an oil-rich country backed by the major Western powers. His security force, Savak, earned a horrific reputation for torture and killing.

In the late 1970s the Shāh's efforts to save his tottering regime became increasingly desperate and brutal, and US support began to falter. In November 1978, he imposed martial law and hundreds of demonstrators were killed in street battles in Tehrān, Qom and Tabrīz. In December 1979 the Shāh made one last attempt to save the situation by appointing Shāpur Bakhtiāri as prime minister, However, Mohammed Rezā Pahlavī and his wife, Farah Diba, finally fled the country on 16 January 1979 (now a national holiday). In exile he was harried from country to country, eventually dying in Egypt in 1980.

Although in exile in Paris, Āyatollāh Khomeinī, the leading Shiite cleric, was acknowledged as the leader of the opposition, a ragbag group which covered everyone from fundamentalist Muslims to Soviet-backed leftists. Many saw him as a figurehead, who, once the Shāh was ousted, would retire to a position akin to that of a constitutional monarch. They were very wrong.

A charismatic figure commanding absolute loyalty among his followers, Āyatollāh Khomeinī returned to Iran on 1 February 1979 to be greeted by adoring millions. His fiery brand of nationalism and Islamic fundamentalism had been at the forefront of the revolt, but few westerners had realised how deep-rooted was his sup-

Āyatollāh Khomeinī

What can an outsider possibly say about Āyatollāh Khomeinī, a man regarded as a bogeyman in the West but revered as a saint by many – probably the majority – of Iranians? A family man whose wife hennaed her hair orange until his death; a religious leader who reduced the age at which 'women' could marry to nine; a war leader who sent wave upon wave of young men to their death on the Iraqi front by persuading them they would go straight to paradise as martyrs; the man who proclaimed the infamous fatwa against Salman Rushdie. Khomeinī will probably always remain a mystery to Western commentators.

The bare facts of his life are as follows. Born in the small village of Khomein in central Iran, Seyed Rūhollāh Mūsavī Khomeinī followed in the family tradition by studying theology, philosophy and law in the holy city of Qom. In the 1920s he earned the title of ayatollah (the highest rank of Shiite cleric) and settled down to teach and write.

He first came to public attention in 1962 when he opposed the Shāh's plans to reduce the clergy's property rights and emancipate women. In 1964 he was exiled to Turkey, before moving on to Iraq where he remained until 1978. Eventually he wound up in Paris where he plotted the Islamic Revolution with his friend Abol Hasan Bani-Sadr. After the Shāh fled in 1979, Āyatollāh Khomeinī returned to a tumultuous welcome and quickly took control of Iran. When he died in 1989, 10 million mourners turned out for his funeral in an unrivalled display of communal grief.

TAMSIN WILSON

port and how totally he reflected the beliefs and dreams of millions of Iranians.

The Aftermath of the Revolution

Once in control, Āyatollāh Khomeinī set about proving the adage that 'after the revolution comes the revolution'. His intention was to set up a clergy-dominated Islamic Republic, and he achieved this with brutal efficiency.

Much of the credit for undermining the Shāh's regime lay with groups like the People's Fedā'īyin and the Islamic People's Mojāhedīn, as well as the communists, but once the Shāh was safely out of the way they were swept aside. People disappeared from the streets, executions took place after brief and meaningless trials, and minor officials took the law into their own hands. It looked as if the country might topple into civil war.

Following a referendum in March 1979 in which an alleged 98.2% of the population voted in favour, the formation of the world's first Islamic Republic was announced on 1 April 1979. Āyatollāh Khomeinī became the Supreme Leader.

Almost immediately, the Islamic Republic found itself up against the rest of the world, accused of adopting confrontational policies designed to promote other Islamic revolutions. In November 1979, 400 Revolutionary Guards burst into the American embassy and took 52 of the staff hostage. Khomeinī's hand-picked prime minister Mehdi Bazargān proved unable to do anything about this and had to resign; in any case, Khomeinī quickly gave it his blessing. For the next 500 days the siege of the American embassy was to prove a thorn in the side of President Carter, who was helpless to get it lifted. Worse still, a *Boy's Own*-comic attempt to rescue the hostages ran aground quite literally when the helicopters supposed to carry them to safety collided in the desert. His failure to resolve the crisis almost certainly put paid to Carter's hopes for re-election.

In the middle of this crisis the first presidential elections were held and Abol Hasan Bani-Sadr, Khomeinī's friend since the days of his Paris exile, was selected, with Mohammed Ali Rajai as his prime minister. A new wave of executions followed the failed American rescue bid which renewed fears about espionage.

The Iran-Iraq War

All this pales into insignificance, however, compared with the Iran-Iraq War which raged from 1980 to 1988 and which is officially estimated to have killed 500,000 on each side. In 1980, hoping to take advantage of Iran's domestic chaos, Iraq's President Saddam Hussein made an opportunistic land grab on oil-rich Khūzestān province, claiming that it was a historic part of Iraq. He also had his eyes on capturing the Arvand River (Shatt al-Arab). It was a catastrophic miscalculation.

Saddam presented the shaky Islamic Revolution with an obvious enemy to rally against and with an opportunity to spread the revolution by force of arms. Although much smaller, Iraq was better equipped; however, Iran could draw on a larger population and a fanaticism fanned by its mullahs. For the first time since WWI the world witnessed the hideous reality of trench warfare and poison gas. (The Iranian government continues to claim that German companies sold the poison gas to Iraq.) Believing the Iraqi government to be the lesser of two evils, the Western powers and the USSR took Iraq's side, and weapons were only sold to Iran at vastly inflated black-market prices.

By July 1982 Iran had forced the Iraqis back to the border but by then Iran had developed its own agenda which included seeking to occupy Najaf and Karbala, two Iraqi towns of particular importance to Shiite Muslims (see the boxed text 'Karbala & Najaf' in the Western Iran chapter).

The war dragged on for another six years. During the war Iraq bombed nearly 3000 villages and 87 Iranian cities, virtually obliterating Ābādān and Khorramshāhr. About five million Iranians lost their homes and jobs,

'The Enemy'

Pick up any English-language Iranian newspaper and you can hardly hope to avoid references to 'the enemy' – as in 'Media should be pious, talented, reveal enemy plots'.

Who that enemy is never has to be spelt out since it is so well known to every single Iranian, but just in case you don't know, the twin bogeymen are Israel and the 'Great Satan' (aka the USA). Israel is blamed for taking land from the Palestinians and fermenting wars against Muslim states in the Middle East; the USA is seen as a pawn of the Israeli lobby. That aside, the US also supported the hated Pahlavīs and then threw in its lot with Iraq during the Iran-Iraq War. To top it off, the Americans shot down an unarmed Iran Air plane over the Persian Gulf in 1988.

Not quite up there in the premier division but trailing just behind comes Britain, seen as an American lackey, but also blamed for supporting the Shāh. Recently, relations between Iran and Germany (Iran's major trading partner) also took a nose-dive after a German businessman was sentenced to death for having sexual relations with an unmarried Muslim woman.

Most Iranians make a clear distinction between the governments of 'enemy' countries and the people who actually live in them. You're extremely unlikely to find people treating you as 'the enemy', even when you come from one of these pariah countries (unless, perhaps, you're an Israeli). On the other hand, you may find it affects how easily you can get a visa.

and some 1.2 million were forced to flee the area, many migrating to Mashhad, about as far as they could get from the war front without leaving Iran. The long-term damage to the soil (where many landmines are still hidden), environment, and flora and fauna is incalculable. The bill for war damage is estimated at a staggering US$1000 billion.

A cease-fire was finally negotiated in mid-1988, with neither side having achieved its objectives. Iranians refer to the war as the 'Iraq-imposed war' and its effects are still felt today, with newspapers continuing to report the deaths of injured war veterans on an almost weekly basis. The war only ended officially in August 1990, just before Iraq became embroiled in the Gulf War.

At the same time as the war was going on, the different factions within Iran continued to jostle for supremacy. In June 1981 a bomb blast at the headquarters of the Islamic Republican Party killed its founder Āyatollāh Beheshti and 71 others, including four cabinet ministers. A second bomb in August killed President Rajai and the new prime minister. Widely blamed for the chaos, ex-president Bani Sadr fled to France. By the end of 1982 all effective resistance to Khomeinī's ideas had been defeated.

Iran Today

When Āyatollāh Khomeinī died on 4 June 1989 he left an uncertain legacy. The Muslim clergy and the Revolutionary Guards immediately established their own, sometimes competing, bureaucracies and spheres of influence. The parliament was also factionalised.

Two months later, Hojjat-ol-Eslām Rafsanjānī was elected to the presidency, a post which had previously been largely ceremonial. Khomeinī's position as Supreme Leader passed to the former president, Āyatollāh Alī Khameneī. President Rafsanjānī was re-elected in 1993 and subsequently reconfirmed the fatwa (death sentence) that Khomeinī had issued against British author Salman Rushdie for blasphemy in his novel *The Satanic Veses*.

In 1995 the US slapped a trade embargo on Iran, alleging that Iran sponsors terrorist groups throughout the region and destabilises the peace process in the Middle East. Iran has also been blamed for the unsolved deaths by bombing of US Marines in Saudi Arabia, and the downing of the TWA airliner over Lockerbie in Scotland, now blamed on Libya. In spite of all the bad feeling, renegade factions in the USA were found to have sold arms to Iran in order to raise money to support the Contra rebels in Nicaragua. Relations between Iran and the US remain poor although at least the subject of improving them is back on the political agenda.

Much to the surprise of international monitors, in presidential elections in mid-1997, the moderate, and reform-minded Hojjat-ol-Eslām Seyed Mohammed Khatamī won 69% of the votes. It seems that many female voters, as well as young people who remember little about the Islamic Revolution and the excesses of the Shāh, are looking to Khatamī to modify the tone of the Islamic Revolution.

Unfortunately, whatever Khatamī may hope to do, his hands are tied by hard-line factions in the Majlis who make it impossible for him to speed the process of reform. The backlash against reform has taken many forms. During the winter of 1998 several intellectuals who were associated with the reform movement were assassinated; their deaths were still the subject of investigation at the time of writing.

President Khatamī

Hojjat-ol-Eslām Seyed Mohammed Khatamī was born in 1943, the son of an ayatollah from Yazd. Khatamī studied theology in Qom, and then took degrees in philosophy at Esfahān and Tehrān. In 1978, he was sent to Hamburg to establish an Islamic Centre, but returned after the Islamic Revolution to serve in the Majlis (Parliament).

Khatamī was appointed Minister of Culture & Islamic Guidance in 1982, but was forced to resign in 1992 because he was seen as caving in to the 'decadence' of the Western world. Later, Khatamī became a presidential adviser, then head of the National Library in Tehrān. To almost universal surprise he was elected president by a landslide in 1997, since when he has spearheaded a reform movement that is doing its best to roll back the excesses of the Islamic Revolution. How hard a task he faces was poignantly illustrated when a newspaper reported a speech by Khatamī in which he tried to explain that young people couldn't be expected to live their lives as if they were middle-aged. The paper followed the article up, a few paragraphs later, with a diatribe from a Qom cleric denouncing noisy car radios as un-Islamic!

In March 1999 local elections confirmed that the reformists were in the ascendancy. Shortly afterwards the popular reform-minded mayor of Tehrān Gholamhossein Karbashchi was jailed for corruption which led to student demonstrations. In July 1999 the police stormed into one of the dormitries of Tehrān University and attacked the students there. In the ensuing fracas at least one person was killed; perhaps 300 are still unaccounted for. (In the summer of 2000 the Majlis approved a bill barring the police from entering university campuses without permission from their principals in an attempt to prevent any repeat of this incident.)

During 2000, more than 30 reform-minded newspapers were closed down and their editors jailed. In August 2000 two reformist intellectuals arrived at Khorramābād airport, planning to address a student meeting in the town. They were prevented from leaving the airport and in the riot that broke out one policeman was killed and many people injured.

Still, there are signs of a slow thawing. Just how slow it is, though, can be judged by the fact that a law allowing primary school girls to wear colours other than black to school could be trumpeted as a reform.

GEOGRAPHY

The Islamic Republic of Iran (Jomhūrī-yé Eslāmī-yé Īrān) is bordered to the north by Armenia, Azerbaijan and Turkmenistan and the Caspian Sea; to the east by Afghanistan and Pakistan; to the south by the Gulf of Oman and the Persian Gulf; and to the west by Iraq and Turkey. With an area of 1,648,000 sq km, Iran is more than three times as large as France; nearly one-fifth the size of the entire USA; and nearly as big as Queensland, Australia. About 14% of Iran is arable land; 8% is forest; 47% is natural (ie, nonarable) pastures; and the remaining 31% is infertile land, including desert.

The central plain is mostly either sand or compacted silt and rock, and, except at its fringes where the tableland merges into the Zāgros and Alborz Mountains, most of its mountains are unconnected and low. The set-

Earthquake Zones

Iran is particularly susceptible to earthquakes, especially at the eastern and western ends of the Caspian Sea. There have been around 1000 registered earthquakes in the last 20 years, of which the most devastating killed more than 45,000 people in northern Iran in 1990. In 1997 another serious quake devastated the area around Ardabīl, killing over 550 people.

Experts believe that Iran should be ready for quakes measuring at least seven on the Richter scale every five years or so. A tragedy of epic proportions just waiting to happen is Tehrān, an uncontrolled urban mess of about 12 million people, mostly living in hastily built high-rise apartments.

tled areas are almost entirely confined to the foothills of mountains, though oasis towns, like Kermān, are growing very rapidly.

Mountains

Iran is dominated by three mountain ranges; the smaller, volcanic Sabalān and Tālesh ranges in the Azerbaijan provinces, which provide fertile pastures for nomads; the very long Zāgros range, stretching from Kordestān province to Bandar-é Abbās, which is so vast that it makes road construction and habitation very difficult (although it contains a lot of oil); and the majestic Alborz Mountains, which stretch from the border of the independent republic of Azerbaijan towards Turkmenistan, and is home to Iran's highest mountain, the permanently snow-capped Damāvand (5671m). About half the country is covered by mountains.

Deserts

The two great Iranian deserts, the Dasht-é Kavīr (more than 200,000 sq km) and the Dasht-é Lūt (more than 166,000 sq km), frame most of the north-east and east of the central plain.

Rivers & Lakes

Most Iranian rivers drain into the Persian Gulf, the Caspian Sea, or one of a number of salty and marshy lakes like Lake

Orūmīyeh and Lake Namak. The longest and sole navigable river is the Kārūn (890km) in the south-west. The Caspian Sea (Daryā-yé Khazar) is the world's largest lake, with an area of some 370,000 sq km. It is co-owned by Azerbaijan, Russia, Kazakhstan and Turkmenistan (see the boxed text 'The Mighty Caspian Sea' in the Caspian Sea chapter for more details). The largest lake wholly inside Iran is the 600-sq-km Lake Orūmīyeh in the north-west.

Persian Gulf

The Persian Gulf is 965km long, and becomes the Gulf of Oman east of the strategic Strait of Hormoz. The Gulf contains dozens of tiny islands, most of them uninhabited. Those that are, notably Qeshm and Kīsh, are being developed, attracting investors and tourists from the Gulf States. Other islands are used as bases for oil prospecting.

Hot Springs

Iran boasts an abundance of hot- and cold-water mineral springs, mostly in the Caspian provinces and around the volcanic areas of the north-western provinces. Water temperatures range from 19° to 49°C, so be very careful before jumping in. Hopeful tourist authorities claim a soak in these springs can cure all sorts of illnesses, from rheumatism and back pains to stomach ailments, but some contain chemicals that may do you more harm than good.

CLIMATE

Because of its size, topography and altitude, Iran experiences great climatic extremes. Winters (December to February) can be unpleasantly cold in most parts of the country, while in summer (June to August) temperatures as high as 50°C are nothing out of the ordinary. Regular rainfall is more or less restricted to the far north and west – generally also the coldest parts of Iran. Spring (March to May) and autumn (September to November) are the ideal times to visit.

In **western Iran** the climate is one of the coldest and wettest in the country. Temperatures well below zero are common between December and February; snow

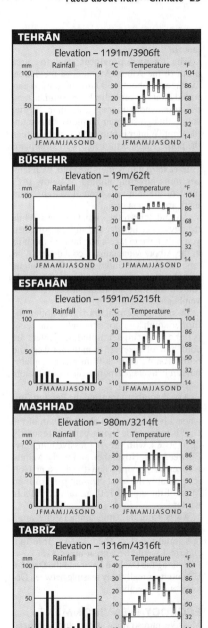

frequently remains until early spring, and later in the mountains.

The **Caspian provinces**, and the area north of the Alborz Mountains, receive an average of about 1300mm of rain. Year-round cloud cover helps keep summer temperatures more manageable than further south, though summer humidity can be unpleasant. Winter is milder than elsewhere in the north. Rainstorms can thwart your plans at any time.

In **eastern Iran** winters are cold, with temperatures hovering around or below 0°C; most of the rain falls around March. Summers are hot and dry.

Around **Tehrān** the climate varies. While the city can be hot, dry and stuffy in summer, you only have to take a bus into the foothills of the Alborz Mountains to cool down. Winters can be very chilly, especially at night, though any snow usually disappears by early March. Showers are frequent between November and mid-May.

In summer **central Iran** gets hotter the further south you go, although some relief is to be had at higher altitudes. Winters are cold, but not as severe as in the far west and north. Rainfall varies from place to place, but rarely averages more than about 250mm a year.

Avoid **southern Iran** and the **Persian Gulf coast** between early May and mid-October when anywhere within about 200km of the Gulf is going to be frying-pan hot (regularly up to 50°C), with very oppressive humidity. Between late November and early March, Khūzestān province and the Persian Gulf are probably the most pleasant parts of Iran. Most of the annual 150mm rainfall falls in winter.

Away from the Gulf, temperatures are a little lower. Summers are hot and dry, winters mild and dry. There's very little rain and frost would be a great novelty.

Visiting the **Dasht-é Kavīr** and the **Dasht-é Lūt** deserts is really only feasible between October and December.

ECOLOGY & ENVIRONMENT

Massive unrestrained urban and industrial development has caused irreparable envi-

Drought-Struck

In 2000, for the second year, running Iran's southern provinces suffered from severe drought, reckoned to have been the worst to hit for 30 years. More than half the population was left short of clean drinking water, and an estimated 800,000 sheep and cattle died of thirst or starvation. The waters of the Shāhīd Parsa Dam, which usually holds 11 million cubic metres of water, dried up, wildlife refuges were devastated, and lakes and lagoons shrivelled; thousands of baby flamingoes were reported to have died after Lake Bakhtegān in southern Iran contracted from 50,000 hectares to a few muddy puddles. Pakistan announced that desperate crocodiles and wild boars had been spotted rampaging across its borders in search of water.

ronmental damage to parts of Iran. The most depressing example of unplanned urban sprawl can be seen along the main road skirting the Caspian Sea. What could be described in guidebooks of only 20 years ago as a collection of quaint villages is now an unmitigated disaster with concrete homes and resorts stretching almost the entire way from Rasht to Sārī.

The air pollution of Tehrān is notorious, but an even greater tragedy is perhaps the contamination of the Persian Gulf by leaks from oil rigs and tankers, untreated sewage, and overly rapid development on the islands of Kīsh and Qeshm (see the boxed text 'The Persian Gulf' in the Persian Gulf chapter for more details). Since the demise of the USSR, pollution in the Caspian Sea has also increased and now threatens the internationally recognised wetlands of the Anzalī Lagoon at Bandar-é Anzalī. A joint Department of the Environment and UNDP plan to protect the Caspian was being tried out between Talesh and Kiashāhr ports at the time of writing.

Deforestation, erosion and overgrazing are also very evident on the southern slopes of the Alborz Mountains. To add to the problems there, walkers and tourists who should know better have left so much rubbish behind on Mt Damāvand that recently a 'Clean-up Damāvand Campaign' was initiated.

A recent report suggested that Iran was the world's third-biggest builder (after Turkey and China) of large dams more than 15m high. The drought of 2000 highlighted Iran's need to take measures to store water. However, large dam projects are increasingly controversial because of the impact on the environment. At the time of writing Iran was in the process of building 68 large dams.

In the last 30 years about 130,000 hectares of northern forest have been torn down and there is now a scheme to replant 4 million hectares of forest. There is also a so-called Environmental Protection Organisation, although this has been criticised for restricting itself to observing rather then to enforcing the laws that exist on paper. Although the government has set aside some areas to help preserve the native flora and fauna (see National Parks in the following Flora & Fauna section), you won't get the impression that protecting the environment is high on its list of priorities. It must be good news, though, that plans for nuclear power stations at Būshehr and Esfahān have been put on hold.

FLORA & FAUNA
Flora
Despite extensive deserts and unrestrained urban development, Iran still harbours more than 10,000 species of flora, many of them endemic. The northern slopes of the Alborz Mountains (up to about 2500m) are densely covered with broad-leaved deciduous forest, which forms the largest area of vegetation in Iran. Here you will find the same types of trees as in many European forests (oak, maple, pine and elm) as well as the less common Caucasian wing nut *(Ptero-carya fraxini-folia)*. Extracts from some of these trees are used to produce glue, and various resins and dyes. The loveliest pockets of forest are around Khalkhāl, south of Ardabīl; along the road between Ardabīl and Āstārā; and at Nahar Khorān, just south of Gorgān.

There are smaller, less dense forests of oak and juniper on the higher slopes of the central and north-west Zāgros Mountains, and in some southern parts of Khorāsān province. In contrast, southern and eastern Iran are almost bare, except for some scattered juniper trees. In the scrubland, you may spot prickly thrift *(Acantholimon)* and camel's thorn *(Alhagi camelorum)*. Palm trees grow on the southern coastal lowland, especially near the Strait of Hormoz, and around the luxuriant oases dotted about the bone-dry nothingness.

One of the few places dedicated to the protection of local flora is the Iranian National Flora Research Garden, Iran's largest horticultural research station. Near the village of Paykanshāhr, just off the highway between Tehrān and Karaj, the garden is open to the public from about 8 am to 3 pm daily, except Friday. Admission costs IR20,000.

Fauna
Mammals Of the 100 or so species of mammals found in Iran, about one-fifth are endemic. Most of the larger species (wolves, jackals, wild boars, hyenas, black bears and lynx) are more common in the unexplored forests of Māzandarān province. In the deserts and mountains, you're more likely to come across more sedate Persian squirrels and mongooses, galloping Persian gazelles, porcupines and badgers, the endemic Iranian wild ass, rabbits and hares, and the red, Jabir and Mesopotamian deer. Wild Bactrian camels still roam the provinces of Kermān, Sīstān va Balūchestān and Khorāsān, but most are domesticated and belong to nomadic or semi-nomadic communities.

Birds Look up and you'll be able to spot a wide variety of birds, both indigenous to Iran and migrants moving between Europe and Africa via the Middle East. Common species you're almost certain to see include black-and-white magpies, blue rollers, brown-and-green bee-eaters, and black-and-grey hooded crows. Among the less common birds are the golden eagle, found in the Caspian provinces; the tiny jiroft, found in Kermān province and along the Persian Gulf; the red-wattled lapwing; the yellow partridge; the delijeh and balaban falcon, found mainly in Hamadān province; and the black vulture and black kite, which live in the central plateau and deserts. Some migratory water birds include the greater flamingo, found in their thousands on Lake Orūmīyeh in spring, as well as the glossy ibis and the Smyrna kingfisher.

If you're staying in Tehrān you may also spot green parrots swooping from tree to tree in the grounds of the Sa'd Ābād Palace or flitting between the trees around the British embassy and the Hotel Naderi.

Fish The Persian Gulf is home to a wide range of tropical fish, as well as sharks, swordfish and porpoises. The Caspian Sea is home to salmon and other fish, as well as to the Caspian seal. It also has large shoals of sturgeon, which produce the world-famous caviar, although stocks are threatened by pollution (see boxed text 'Caviar Anyone?' in the Caspian Sea chapter). Some of the more common fish found in the streams around the Alborz Mountains include trout, chub and catfish.

Reptiles If you venture into the desert, you may stumble across a few snakes (rarely poisonous) and lizards, such as the metre-long waran, which abounds in the most desolate areas. In the mountains, Greek tortoises may amble across your path.

Endangered Species

As you travel round Iran, recoiling from tiles, carvings and paintings depicting one hunting scene after another, you might be forgiven for assuming there can't be a single large wild animal left in the country. One prize specimen that you're almost guaranteed not to see is the Persian lion, once the symbol of imperial Iran but generally believed to be extinct, bar one alleged sighting in a Māzandarān forest a few years ago.

However, although the lions and tigers are long gone, a few panthers and leopards do still manage to hang on in the depths of the forests. And despite the scenes of massed slaughter of wild boars on the walls at Taq-é Bostān in Kermānshāh there are,

---

Iran's National Parks

Central Iran
- Khabar va Rouchon, where Jabir deer roam, is about 200km south of Kermān city.
- Mehrouyeh, home to the black bear, is in the far south-east of Kermān province.
- Mooteh, established to protect antelope, is about 50km south-west of Kāshān.

Eastern Iran
- Tandoureh, home to the Oreal ram, ibex and even the odd leopard, is near Darregaz in Khorāsān province, on the border with Turkmenistan.

Persian Gulf
- Bakhtegān, established to protect migratory birds, is between Lakes Bakhtegān and Tashk, about 80km east of Shīrāz.
- Arjan, home to masked tits and waterfowl, is near Shīrāz.

Western Iran
- Assād Ābād, home to birds of prey such as delijeh and balaban falcons and to ibex, is just off the road between Hamadān and Kermānshāh.
- Bījār, home to hyenas, jackals and foxes, is about 15km north-west of Bījār town.

Caspian Sea
- Golestān, home to wild boar, goitred gazelles and assorted birdlife, is between Gorgān and the sea.
- Mian Kaleh, home to many waterfowl, is also on the Caspian.

mercifully, still a few boars left alive at the eastern end of the Caspian Sea.

Two of the more fascinating endangered species are the huge ibex-like Alborz red sheep, with its black beard and curvy horns, found in the Alborz Mountains; and the Oreal ram, with a white beard and enormous spiralling horns, found near the border with Turkmenistan.

Such has been the overfishing of the Caspian Sea recently that the prized sturgeon is rapidly heading for the endangered species list, along with the Caspian seal.

National Parks

Unesco has designated Lake Orūmīyeh as an 'area of special interest' to protect the multitude of migratory birds that rely on it for their habitat.

The Iranian government has also created a few national parks *(pārk-é-melli)* to protect its wildlife, although they're a far cry from the sort of national park you may be more used to: Iranian parks have no fenced areas or rangers, they are not mentioned on any maps and there are few laws to prevent hunting or development inside them. Still, if you have a hankering for wildlife and access to a vehicle, the following national parks are large and accessible. There's no public transport to get you to them, but some of the tour companies listed under Organised Tours in the Getting Around chapter will probably be able to help you reach them.

GOVERNMENT & POLITICS

After the Islamic Revolution, 98% of the population apparently voted to implement a unique form of Islamic government with three levels of political power. The Parliament, or Majlis, is made up of Islamic experts and revered Islamic leaders from around the country, as well as one representative each from the Jewish and Zoroastrian communities, and two from the Armenian Christians. The 270-seat Majlis has real power: It approves (but does not theoretically instigate) laws and economic decisions, but under the constitution it can 'investigate and examine all affairs of the country'.

The Majlis is dominated by the Velayat-é Faqih, or Supreme Leader. The first Supreme Leader was Āyatollāh Khomeinī, who created this position in accordance with his interpretation of the Quran. The Supreme Leader is chosen by the Assembly of Experts for life, and has the final say in the country's policies.

Among other things, he can select (and sack) the commander of the armed forces; declare war or peace; and veto the election of (or dismiss) the president. Having the knowledge to make decisions based on Islamic canon is a prime qualification. The current Supreme Leader is Āyatollāh Alī Khameneī.

The other powerful person in the Majlis is the Speaker, currently Mehdi Karroubi. The Iranian people vote to elect the Majlis every four years, but the candidates are carefully vetted before the elections.

According to the Iranian constitution, the second level of power, the Council of Guardians 'safeguards the Islamic ordinances and constitution'. It comprises 12 Islamic jurists and religious experts, all selected by the Supreme Leader. The Council's main purposes are to uphold Islamic values, ensure that the parliament remains free of corruption, and approve the handful of presidential candidates. Bills passed by the Majlis go to the Council of Guardians, which can halt a bill or send it back to the Majlis for amendment.

The president elects and manages the Cabinet, though final control rests with the Majlis. The president is elected every four years, but there are normally only four candidates to choose from. The current president is Hojjat-ol-Eslām Seyed Mohammed Khatamī who is responsible for the running of the country. He also appoints the ministers, who must be individually approved by the Majlis. Like the US president, the Iranian president can only serve for two terms.

Ex-president Rafsanjānī is now head of the Expediency Council, which he has revamped to give it more teeth. This body has the power to overturn the decisions of the Council of Guardians and approve bills

PROVINCES & PROVINCIAL CAPITALS

passed by the Majlis. The expediency council has 25 members, mostly elder statesmen.

There's little overt political opposition. Dissidents either live under harassment in Iran (like the members of the primary 'legal' opposition party, the Freedom Movement of Iran); or they operate political groups or terrorist organisations like the Mojāhedīn Khalq Organisation (MKO; see the boxed text 'The MKO' on the opposite page) in Iraq, Europe or North America.

Currently, Iran is divided into 28 provinces, each of them supervised by a governor general (ostāndār) based in the provincial capital. Places designated as towns are ruled by a *farmāndār*; those designated as villages by a *kadkodār*.

ECONOMY

Iran is still struggling to recover from the economic devastation caused by the Iran-Iraq War, which ended more than 10 years ago. Despite much talk of privatisation, more than 70% of industry remains government-owned, including the national airline (Iran Air); the majority share in the Indo-Iranian Joint Shipping Company, the country's largest shipping company; the major

The MKO

The Marxist Mojāhedīn Khalq Organisation started life as one of the groups responsible for overthrowing the Shāh. However, since it was not a religious-based grouping it soon found itself elbowed aside. It then turned to terrorism to oppose the regime it had been, at least in part, responsible for creating.

In 1981 the MKO planted a bomb that killed 72 government ministers and civil servants, including then President Mohammed-Ali Rajei and Prime Minister Javad Bahonar.

Although the MKO seemed to have disappeared from the headlines, in 2000 it was accused of several missile attacks launched in the direction of Ahvāz from Iraqi soil.

export earner, oil; and most media outlets. Private industry is beginning to make itself felt, but is heavily regulated by the state.

Official unemployment figures are pretty meaningless, but it's clear that the highest rates of unemployment (16% to 20%), and the lowest standards of living, are found among the Kurds and Lors of western Iran. Tehrān boasts the lowest level of unemployment (6%), below the national average of about 9%.

Iran's biggest export earners are, in order of importance, oil, carpets, chemicals, pistachios, tourism and caviar. Of these, oil is far and away the most important (see the boxed text 'Black Gold' for more details). Persian carpets are also vitally important; Iran produces nearly one-third of all traditional carpets and rugs made worldwide, currently earning more than US$2 billion per year from their export.

Industries such as steel and copper mining, cement and petrochemicals have in-creased production markedly in recent years. Iran has an estimated 20 trillion cubic metres of natural gas reserves (which should last more than 200 years). This has been an economic saviour, and pipelines are hurriedly being built to export this resource to gas-poor countries like Turkey. If you have already spent some time in Iran it will come as no surprise that one of the major manufacturing industries is the production of the Paykan, the family car seen all over the country. Nearly 80,000 are produced every year, overwhelmingly for domestic consumption.

One major hurdle to improving the economy is the trade embargo imposed by the US in 1995. At the time of writing, this is being ignored by European and Asian companies, keen to exploit Iran's vast gas and oil reserves, and by most governments in the region, but it still holds back recovery.

Iran is trying to lessen its dependence on Europe for imports and exports, and to

Black Gold

Oil was first drilled near Dezfūl in 1908, and at first it was mainly exploited by the Anglo-Iranian Oil Company. Ābādān quickly proved to be the most prolific site, and it wasn't long before it became a virtual colony of the international oil companies. However, in 1950 the Iranian government nationalised the oil companies to great popular acclaim, a fact still celebrated by an annual public holiday. These days oil is drilled in south-western Iran and in the Persian Gulf, and sent to refineries near Tehrān, Tabrīz, Arāk and Esfahān.

Iran is currently a member of the Organisation of Petroleum-Exporting Countries (OPEC), and is the organisation's third-largest oil exporter, just trailing Saudi Arabia and Norway. Oil is by far the biggest export earner, accounting for more than 40% of all government income. In accordance with quotas set by OPEC, Iran produces 3.7 million barrels per day, of which about 2.4 million is exported. At the time of writing the going rate per barrel had soared to more than US$30. Iran is estimated to own about 10% of the world's reserves, and new oilfields are still being discovered.

work with the nascent Central Asian republics, while attracting investment from the Gulf States and Asia. But because of the US embargo and a general distrust of the potentially volatile Iranian government, foreign investment continues to fall well below what Iran would hope.

Agriculture & Fisheries

Rice, grown mainly along the Caspian, used to be one of Iran's most important crops. However, these days its place as the most important staple foodstuff has been overtaken by bread, which is heavily subsidised and so cheaper: Wheat and barley are grown mainly in western Iran. Pomegranates, grapes, figs, dates and strawberries are grown in the less arid parts of the country; oranges, peaches, melons, apples and lemons in western Iran; and watermelons in Khūzestān province. Other important crops include sugar beet, potatoes, nuts, tea, tobacco, saffron and henna. Cotton is increasingly important, as is silk from the Caspian region. Pistachios from southern Iran make up 10% of non-oil exports.

The increasingly important Persian Gulf and Caspian fishing industry is mostly owned by the government. Caviar is a very lucrative export, with roughly half being collected from sturgeons near Bandar-é Torkamān.

Tourism

The present government is in two minds about developing the tourism industry. While it's clear that the lopsided economy could do with more strings to its bow, conservative factions in the Majlis are terrified of the 'cultural pollution' seen as an inevitable consequence of attracting more tourists. However, the year 2001 has been designated 'Visit Iran Year', with the unavoidable implication that the government is swaying towards encouraging tourism. As memories of the excesses of the Islamic Revolution and of the Iran-Iraq War recede, the number of Western visitors to the country will undoubtedly rise.

At the time of writing, most foreign visitors were Russians, Pakistanis, Azerbaijanis, Turks and Gulf State Arabs. Of Western tourists, by far the biggest contingent come from Germany. The conservatives want to encourage more visitors from Islamic countries who they hope will be more sympathetic to their cultural idiosyncrasies.

POPULATION & PEOPLE

In 1956, Iran's population was just 19 million, but by 2000 it had soared to around 73 million; by 2015, the authorities fear that it will reach 110 million. Since WWII there has been a steady move from the countryside to urban areas, worsened by the upheavals caused by the Iran-Iraq War, when millions of internal refugees moved to the large towns. Many Iranian towns have doubled in population since the Revolution, without any corresponding increase in housing. About 60% of the population now live in cities, and about 15% are shoe-horned into Tehrān. Only about 300,000 nomads continue to roam the plains and mountain pastures.

Iran's location at the crossroads of Arabia, Turkey and Central Asia and the ever-shifting frontiers of the old Persian Empire have ensured that the modern population is a very mixed bag ethnically. Many of the minority groups are adherents of the Sunni branch of Islam rather than the Shiite branch espoused by the majority of Iranians.

Despite this, ethnic strife isn't much of a problem in Iran, although there have been problems between the Iranian government and Kurdish separatists, as in neighbouring Turkey and Iraq. What racial animosity the Persians have is largely reserved for Afghan refugees, who tend to get blamed for almost every unresolved murder case or suspicious going-on from Khorāsān to Khūzestān.

Persians

Persians, or Farsis, make up perhaps 50% of the population of Iran. They are the descendants of the original Elamite and Aryan races who first set up camp in the central plateau back in the 2nd millennium BC and gave Persia its original name.

Āzārīs

Āzārīs make up perhaps 20% of the population and mainly live in small villages in the

Azerbaijan provinces. The Āzārīs are related to the Turks, although they are almost entirely Shiite whereas the Turks are predominantly Sunni. But all Āzārīs, whether in Iran, Turkey or the independent republic of Azerbaijan to the north, are united by Āzārī, a language descended many centuries ago from Anatolian Turkish, but now accepted as a language in its own right.

Older Āzārī men traditionally wear soft goat's wool hats, and Tabrīz, the main town of the region, is one of the few places in Iran where you may still see men wearing ties, branded un-Islamic by the central authorities.

Following a period of tension after the Islamic Revolution, there is now more contact between the Iranian Āzārīs and the people of the republic of Azerbaijan, although private visits in either direction are still limited and have been restricted by border closures in the past.

Kurds

Although they have been around longer than any other people in the region (at least since the 2nd millennium BC), the Kurds have never been able to establish their own nation. There are perhaps 12 million Kurds living in eastern Turkey, with more in north-eastern Iraq and small pockets of Syria. Perhaps five million Kurds live in Iran, mainly in the western provinces of Kordestān, Zanjān and Kermānshāh. Once strongly nomadic, they have mostly settled in the cities now.

The Kurds are divided into various tribes, including the Sanjābī and Kalhor, and speak different dialects of Kurdish, a language quite different from Farsi. Most Kurds are Sunni Muslims, although sometimes with local twists. A minority are Yezīdīs, a sect that combines elements of Islam with paganism.

The men often wear boiler suits with baggy pants and a cummerbund, while Kurdish women wear layer upon layer of colourful dresses, not always covered up with a chador.

Lors

Making up perhaps 2% of the population, Lors are thought to be part Persian and part Arab in origin, although they are probably a mix of the Kassites, who settled in western Iran some 2000 years ago, and the Medes.

The Lors mainly inhabit villages in the western province of Lorestān, while Lor nomads live in several other mountainous regions of western Iran. Under the Pahlavīs, some dissidents were exiled and sent to Zanjān and Khorāsān provinces, where they still live. The most famous Lor was the benevolent Karīm Khān Zand, who ruled Persia for a few years in the 18th century.

The Lors either speak a dialect of Arabic known as Avesta, or their own language known as Lorī. They are renowned for their horsemanship, sheep farming, metalwork and production of carpets and rugs. The Lors are reluctant to toe the government line, so they're not especially popular with Tehrān. Nor is this region the subject of much development.

Arabs

About 2% of the population are Arabs and most of them live in Khūzestān province, on some of the smaller Iranian islands in the Persian Gulf, and along the southern coast, where they have become partly Persianised and are known as Bandarīs, from the Persian word for 'port'. Descended from Arab, black African and mixed stock, the Bandarīs have darker skins than the Persians. Many Bandarīs are Sunni Muslims.

Bandarī women have their own style of dress, consisting of colourful embroidered or printed layers of wraps over loose trousers, leg bracelets and sandals or flip-flops (thongs), and, sometimes, owlish masks (see the boxed text 'The Masked Women of Mīnāb' in the Persian Gulf chapter). The men usually wear an *abba*, a long, sleeveless robe, usually white, with sandals and sometimes a turban. The traditional Bandarī dress is most commonly seen in Hormozgān province, especially on the islands.

Elsewhere Arab men usually wear a traditional floor-length shirt-dress called a *thobe* or *dishdasha*, as well as a loose headscarf called a *gutra*. Most Iranian Arabs still speak a dialect of Arabic.

Turkmen

The Turkmen who make up about 2% of Iran's total population mostly live in the Torkaman Sahrā, the plain occupying much of the east of Māzandarān province and the north of Khorāsān province, close to the Central Asian republic of Turkmenistan.

Of Turkic origin, Turkmen tend to be tall, and their faces show a mixture of Mongolian and Caucasian features. A few of the men still wear huge sheepskin hats (*telpek*), either white and fleecy or black with thick ringlets like dreadlocks, with baggy trousers tucked into knee-length boots and white shirts under knee-length cotton jackets, traditionally cherry-red. Women wear heavy ankle-length silk dresses over colourful trousers and huge scarf-shawls decorated with floral designs.

Turkmen speak their own Turkic language and have a typically nomadic liking for Sufism.

Nomads

Even though most of Iran's 20th-century governments have encouraged them to settle, there are still many different nomadic groups. The **Bākhtiarīs** (Bactrians) live in the more remote parts of the provinces of Chahārmahāl va Bakhteyārī and Khūzestān provinces, though many have also settled in towns.

Most of the **Baluchīs** (whose name means 'Wanderers') are still at least semi-nomadic, perhaps because the extremely arid region where they roam is hardly suited to a settled life. They occupy the thinly populated desert region covering the far south-east of Iran and the far west of Pakistan. Able riders, they are famous for their camel races.

The **Qashqā'īs** mainly live in Fārs province and many are still nomadic. Like so many of Iran's minority peoples, the Qashqā'īs are of Turkic stock and have always been hard to subjugate. Their women wear strikingly colourful dresses, which they rarely bother to hide beneath chadors.

EDUCATION

Schooling is compulsory for children aged from six to 11, and an impressive 95% of Iranian children currently receive primary or secondary schooling. Government-run schools are free of charge, though an increasing number of expensive private schools are being established.

At the level of higher education, demand far outstrips supply and only the cleverest and most favoured students can get a place at one of the state universities. Though the Iranian government claims that more than one million Iranians currently attend university, about half of them study at private universities. Many affluent Iranians still send their children to study in Europe if they possibly can. It may come as a quite a surprise to learn that there are more women than men studying in Iranian universities.

One of the successes of the Shāh's White Revolution was the Literacy Movement, which aimed to teach everyone to read and write. Literacy rates in Iran are impressively high: About 77% of the population can read and write, compared with just 25% in neighbouring Pakistan. The literacy rate is inevitably higher in the cities (about 85%) than in the countryside (70%).

SOCIETY & CONDUCT
Traditional Culture

No-one could possibly visit Iran and come away without realising how profoundly different its culture is even from that of neighbouring Islamic countries like Turkey and Pakistan. The most obvious ways in which the differences manifest themselves are in the absolute sexual segregation of society (right down to separate bread queues for men and women) and in the way that women are expected to dress. There's no doubt that the black chador is very much a part of Iranian tradition (you only need to look at the paintings on display in the Golestān Palace in Tehrān to understand that women didn't suddenly start wearing them in 1979) but what is interesting is how women have been expected to continue wearing this traditional dress while men have quietly been allowed to drop the multiple layers of garments they too used to wear in the past.

[Continued on page 51]

ARTS OF IRAN

Many Iranian art forms predate the Arab conquest, but since nearly all of them reached their peak within the Islamic era, religious influences are rarely completely absent.

In Iran, as in all Islamic societies, art favours the nonrepresentational, the derivative and the stylised over the figurative, the innovative and the true-to-life. Geometrical shapes and complex floral patterns are especially popular in Iranian art. Traditionally, Islam has forbidden the representation of living beings, but if you're more used to travelling in countries that follow the Sunni branch of Islam where such images almost never appear, it may come as a surprise to arrive in Iran and see examples of portraiture and images of animals in most of the museums and palaces.

Architecture

Persian architecture has had a very long and complex history, and is often regarded as the field in which Persia made its greatest contribution to world culture. Although Persian styles differ sharply from those of other Islamic architectural traditions, they have strongly influenced building throughout much of the Islamic world, especially in Central Asia, Afghanistan, Pakistan and India.

The two important religious influences on Persian architecture have been Zoroastrianism (dominant before the Arab conquest of AD 637) and Islam. Most of the greatest buildings were built for a religious purpose, and even in secular buildings religious influences are rarely entirely absent – even Persian churches often incorporate Islamic features.

What Makes Persian Architecture Unique? If there is one defining aspect of Persian architecture, it is its monumental simplicity combined with its lavish use of surface ornamentation and colour. The ground plans of ordinary Persian buildings are usually very simple, mixing only a few standard elements: a courtyard and arcades, lofty entrance porticoes and four *iwans* (barrel-vaulted halls opening onto the courtyard).

SIMON RICHMOND

The typical Persian mosque design evolved from the plan of the Prophet Mohammed's house in Medina. It consists of an entrance iwan which leads into a large courtyard surrounded by arched cloisters. Behind these are four inner iwans, one of them featuring a decorated niche indicating the direction of Mecca, the focal point of the interior of the mosque. In the Islamic world in general this is usually called a mihrab although in Iran this term is also used to refer to

Inset: Fabulous tiles decorate the dome of the Emāmzādeh-yé Alī Ebn-é Hamzeh in Shīrāz (photo by Phil Weymouth)

Right: The great blue dome, with black and white spider's web tracery, on top of the tomb of Shāh Ne'matol-lāh Valī in Māhān. The dome was built by Shāh Abbās I.

the cut-out space in the ground in front of it. According to many commentators, the four-iwan design can be traced back to old Zoroastrian ideas about the four elements and the circulation of life.

These basic features are often so densely covered with rich decoration that observers are led to imagine that the architecture is far more complex than it actually is. Since the depiction of religious figures is not part of the Islamic artistic tradition, the decorations are normally geometric, floral or calligraphic, although this is not as absolute in Shiite Iran as in Sunni states. A wall's decoration sometimes consists of nothing but mosaics forming the names of Allah, Mohammed and Ali, repeated perhaps hundreds of times in highly stylised script (masonry calligraphy). Often they are so closely moulded into the design that they appear to be an intrinsic part of the structure. The colours need to be bright and bold because the sunlight can be so harsh.

Earliest Days The only substantial remains left from before the 7th century BC are those of the remarkable Elamite ziggurat (tiered temple) at Choqā Zanbīl in south-western Iran. The ancient inhabitants of Persia imbued their mountains with great religious symbolism and built the characteristic pyramidal ziggurats to imitate them. The earliest builders used sun-dried mud bricks; baked brick was already being used for outer surfaces by the 12th century BC.

Pre-Islamic Architecture The surviving sites from the Achaemenid era (559–330 BC) include the magnificent ceremonial palace complexes and royal tombs at Pasargadae, Naqsh-é Rostam, Persepolis and Shūsh. These are decorated with bas-reliefs of kings, soldiers, suppliants, animals and the winged figure of the Zoroastrian deity Ahura Mazda.

Remains from the Achaemenid era show links with the old ziggurats both in their shape and decoration. The Achaemenid style also incorporated features taken from Egyptian and Greek architecture. They

PAT YALE

Left: The Towers of Silence in Yazd are the last earthly stop for Zoroastrians before their ascent to heaven, courtesy of the local vulture population.

built colossal halls supported by stone and wooden columns with typically Persian bull's-head capitals. Materials were imported from throughout Persia and beyond but the most usual building materials were sun-dried brick and stone.

Alexander the Great's arrival in 331 BC effectively ended the Achaemenid style of architecture in Persia. Instead the influence of Greece and Macedonia grew even stronger. No great examples remain today, although the Temple of Artemis at Kangāvar near Kermānshāh was built with Greek capitals to honour a Greek goddess. Under the Parthians (190 BC–AD 224), a few characteristically Persian features, including the iwan, began to put in an appearance.

In the Sassanian period, buildings became larger, heavier and more complex. The four-iwan plan with domed, square chambers became increasingly common. Decoration became more adventurous and more use was made of colour, especially in frescoes and mosaics. The Sassanians built fire temples throughout their empire, and the simple plan of the earliest examples was retained throughout the pre-Islamic era, even in the design of churches.

The Arab Period The Arab conquest didn't immediately supplant the well-developed Sassanian style but it did introduce the Islamic element that was to have such a pervasive impact on the Persian arts. Not only did the Arab period (AD 637–1050) shape the nature and basic architectural plan of religious buildings, but it also defined the type of decoration – no human representation, however stylised, was to be permitted, and ceremonial tombs or monuments also fell from favour. In place of grand palace complexes built as symbols of royal majesty came mosques designed as focal points for the social life of ordinary people.

The 9th–11th Centuries As Sassanian and Arab ingredients merged, a distinctly Persian style of Islamic architecture evolved. From about the mid-9th century, under the patronage of a succession of enlightened rulers, there was a resurgence of Persian nationalism and Persian values. Architectural innovations included the high, pointed arch, stalactites (elaborate stepped mouldings used to decorate recesses) and an emphasis on balance and scale. Calligraphy became the principal form of architectural decoration, which sometimes consisted wholly of inscriptions. Little remains of the architecture of these early centuries, although one good example is the Jāmeh Mosque at Nā'īn.

The period also marks the emergence of a series of remarkable tower tombs, usually more secular than religious in purpose. Built of brick and

Right: Stone carving in the Emām Mosque, Esfāhān

MARTIN MOOS

The Best of Persian Architecture

- **Choqā Zanbīl** This Elamite ziggurat is perhaps the most impressive single structure surviving from before the 7th century BC (see the Central Iran chapter for more details).
- **Persepolis** The finest surviving monument from the Achaemenid period (see the Central Iran chapter for more details).
- **Gonbad-é Kāvūs** A tower tomb near the town of Gonbad, this is the most extraordinary survival from the 11th century (see the Caspian Sea chapter for more details).
- **Jāmeh Mosque** The finest building left from the Seljuk period, located in Esfahān (see the Central Iran chapter for more details).
- **Soltānīyeh** This mausoleum near Zanjān is the most magnificent surviving Mongol structure (see the Western Iran chapter for more details).
- **Azīm-é Gōhar Shād Mosque, Kabūd Mosque** The best surviving examples of Timurid architecture inside Iran in Mashhad (see the Eastern Iran chapter for more details), and Tabrīz (see the Western Iran chapter for more details) respectively.
- **Golestān Palace, Takieh Mo'aven ol-Molk** Two of the finest examples of overblown Qajar style in Tehrān (see the Tehrān chapter for more details), and Kermānshāh (see the Western Iran chapter for more details) respectively.

usually round, they show a development of ornamentation starting with little more than a single garter of calligraphy and graduating to elaborate basket-weave brickwork designed to deflect the harsh sunlight.

The Seljuks Many of the Seljuk rulers (1051–1220) took a great personal interest in patronage of the arts. Architectural developments included the double dome, designed to achieve the best visual impact from both interior and exterior, a widening of vaults, improvement of the squinch and refinement of glazed tilework. A meticulous unity of structure and decoration was attempted for the first time, based on rigorous mathematical principles. Stucco, incorporating arabesques and Persian styles of calligraphy, was increasingly used to enhance brick surfaces.

The Mongols Although often seen as a dark age in Iranian history, the Mongol period (1220–1335) actually added quite a lot to the development of Persian architecture. The conquest of Persia by Genghis Khan and his rampaging hordes was at first purely destructive, and many Persian architects fled the country, but later the Mongols, too, became patrons of the arts. The Mongol style, designed to overawe the viewer, was marked by towering entrance portals, colossal domes and vaults reaching into the skies. It also saw a refinement of tiling, often based on geometric and floral lines, and calligraphy, often in the formal angular Kufic script imported from Arabia. Increasing attention was paid to the interior decoration of domes, which were more closely moulded into the whole design.

The Timurids

The Timurids (1380–1502) went on to refine the Seljuk and Mongol styles. Their architecture featured an exuberance of colour and a greater harmony of structure and decoration. Even in buildings of colossal scale, they avoided the monotony of large empty surfaces by judicious use of translucent tiling. Arcaded cloisters around inner courtyards, open galleries, and arches within arches were notable developments.

PHIL WEYMOUTH

The Safavids

Under a succession of enlightened and cultivated rulers, most notably Shāh Abbās I, came the final refinement of styles that marked the culmination of the Persian Islamic style of architecture. Its greatest expression was Shāh Abbās I's royal capital of Esfahān, a supreme example of town planning, with one of the most magnificent collections of buildings from one period anywhere in the Islamic world. At its centre is the vast Emām Khomeinī Square, still one of the world's largest squares, with the superb Emām Mosque as its focal point. There are other fine examples of Safavid architecture at Qazvīn, while the Holy Shrine of Emām Rezā at Mashhad gained much of its present magnificence in Safavid times.

The death of Shāh Abbās I in 1629 marked the beginning of the end for the golden age of Persian architecture. The Madraseh-yé Chāhār Bāgh, in Esfahān, is an outstanding architectural work for its period, but it and other buildings of the late Safavid period are really little more than a swan song.

PAT YALE

Top Right: The Madraseh-yé Khān in Shīrāz dates from the 17th century.

Bottom Right: Qajar-era tiles from the Golestān Palace, Tehrān

The Qajars The Qajar period marks the rather unhappy transition between the golden age of Persian architecture under the Safavids and the creeping introduction of Western-inspired uniformity from the mid-19th century onwards. Now widely regarded as tasteless, flimsy and uninspired, the Qajar style did nevertheless produce a few fine buildings, including the Emām Khomeinī mosque in Semnān, the Eram Palace in Shīrāz and the Golestān Palace in Tehrān.

Quirks of Persian Architecture All along the great trade routes from east to west **caravanserais** (hostels with stabling for animals) were set up to facilitate trade. Although the earliest caravanserais date back to Seljuk times, many of those surviving in Iran date from the reign of the great Shāh Abbās I who was credited with establishing a network of 999 such structures. In cities they were often built right beside the bazaar to facilitate the transfer of goods from beast to shelf and back again. It's easy to see this arrangement in Esfahān.

In the hot southern deserts you will see the remains of mud-brick ice houses which were built to store ice through the summer. Most have a long wall against which water was thrown. As soon as it froze it was scraped off and stored in an adjoining building, often a stepped dome. The one at Aabargu near Yazd resembles a circular ziggurat with the wall peeling off to one side.

In the countryside near Esfahān you may see curious circular towers standing alongside village houses. These were pigeon houses where pigeons were reared for meat and manure.

For details about wind towers, see the boxed text 'The Bādgīrs of Yazd' in the Central Iran chapter.

ANTHONY HAM

Tiles

Everywhere you go in Iran you will see glistening, multi-coloured tiles, coating the walls, domes and minarets of mosques, and decorating the edges of every kind of building from schools to government offices. The tiled domes of Iranian mosques, reminiscent of Fabergé eggs in the vividness of their colouring, are likely to remain one of your abiding memories of Iran.

The art of Persian tile production dates back to the Elamite period. However, the real glory period for the tile-makers came during the Safavid period, and especially in the 16th century. Tiles from that period come in two main

Left: The pinnacle of tile art: Seven-colour tile mosaics decorate the Emām Mosque in Esfahān.

forms. The very best are really mosaics – look closely at the walls and you'll see that the patterns have been picked out in tiny pieces of tile rather than created in one piece. Less fine are the *haft rengi* (seven-coloured) tiles, which are normal square tiles with a painted surface. Since these were not as hard-wearing as mosaic tiles, haft rengi tiles normally appear only on the inside of buildings.

By the time of the Qajars, Persian tile-making had passed its prime. On the other hand Qajar buildings often make up in quantity of tiles for what they lack in quality. Examples that illustrate this point are the courtyard walls of the Golestān Palace in Tehrān and the walls of the wonderful Takieh Mo'aven ol-Molk in Kermānshāh. In neither case do the individual tiles match up to anything you'll see in the Emām Mosque in Esfahān. On the other hand the sheer number and variety of tiles means you'll be hard-pressed to turn up your nose at them.

Painting

The earliest known distinctively Persian style of painting dates back to the Seljuk period (1051–1220) and is often referred to as the Baghdad School. Early painting was mainly used to decorate manuscripts and Qurans, though some fine 13th-century pottery found near Tehrān also reveals a unique early Persian style of art. During the Mongol period (1220–1335), paintings were used to decorate all sorts of books, especially poetry books.

In the 16th century an important school of Persian art developed in Tabrīz, under the guidance of Sultan Mohammed. Designs and patterns produced by this school also influenced the design of contemporary carpets. Persian art later flourished under the auspices of the great Shāh Abbās, who turned Esfahān into a flourishing centre for the arts. By the 18th century, all the distinctive features of Persian art started to fade as artists fell under the influence of India and Europe.

Since early Persian artists rarely signed their names to their work, not much is known about most of these artists.

Right: Painted hunting scene in the Golestān Palace in Tehrān

PAT YALE

PATRICK SYDER

Calligraphy

Not only was the Quran faithfully reproduced as a whole, but verses from it, and the holy names of Allah and Mohammed, were used as decorations on religious buildings and elsewhere, as they are to this day. The formal, upright Kufic style of calligraphy was imported from the Arabian Peninsula, but several distinctly Persian calligraphic styles also emerged, some of them so elaborate that they are almost illegible, eg, *nashki*, which later developed into another renowned style known as *thulth*.

By about the 16th century, Shīrāz and Esfahān were producing some of the finest calligraphy in the Islamic world. Some of the very best examples of ancient and modern calligraphy can be seen at the Rezā Abbāsī Museum in Tehrān. Rezā Abbāsī was himself a renowned 16th-century calligrapher.

Miniatures

The Persian miniature-painting tradition started in the 15th century, and had a second flowering during the period when the Safavid capital was at Qazvīn. Later, artists from eastern Iran, who had studied under the great Muhammedī in Herāt (now in Afghanistan), also started to influence this form of art.

Persian miniature paintings are now deservedly famous throughout the world, and the best examples show great intricacy and attention to detail. Favourite subjects include courting couples in traditional dress, polo matches and hunting scenes. Some of the best modern miniatures come from Esfahān. Although a few fine examples can be seen in Iranian museums, most of the early works are housed in museums and private collections in Britain.

Illustrated Manuscripts

Neatly combining Persia's two traditions of fine penmanship and miniature painting are the illustrated manuscripts you can see on display at the Rezā Abbāsī Museum in Tehrān. Most of the manuscripts are books of poetry with the themes beautifully illustrated alongside the text. However, some manuscripts are decorated Qurans that, while still nonfigurative, go beyond just beautiful handwriting.

Modern Art

One of the best-known and loved modern Iranian artists and sculptors is Sayyed Alī Akhbar Sanati, whose work is on display in the Kermān

Left: A calligraphy expert at work

Contemporary Arts Museum and the Sizdah-é Aban Museum in Tehrān. See those sections for more details.

Textile Printing

Everywhere you go in Iran you will see hand-printed tablecloths and wall hangings, most of them made in Esfahān. Wooden blocks are used to apply patterns in black, red, blue, yellow and green to what are basically beige cloths. These are then washed in the river to fasten the colours. It is thought that textile printing has been practised in Iran since Sassanian times.

PHIL WEYMOUTH

Music

Fortunately, things have moved on from the dismal situation fours years ago when the Tehrān prayer leader could denounce *all* forms of music as evil. Although you won't hear much Western music in Iran (except the elevator Muzak versions of pop songs and Richard Clayderman), these days most Iranians are familiar with the big names of Western pop thanks to satellite TV and the Internet. Almost every taxi driver, especially in Tehrān, seems to keep a cache of Turkish pop classics stashed under the dashboard.

Increasingly, shops selling cassettes and CDs are taking their place on high streets, although very often they only stock one master version of each album, which must then be re-taped for would-be buyers. Most of the musicians featured are Iranians and all of them are men since women singers are still taboo.

Right: Wooden blocks are used to print the designs onto cloth.

There are occasional music festivals, such as the annual Iranian Epic Music Festival (usually held in Tehrān in about April). However, it's hard to track down exact details, because although foreigners are welcome, these festivals are really intended for Iranians. If you're particularly interested in attending a festival it might be worth asking one of the tour companies listed under Organised Tours in the Getting There & Away chapter for advice.

Classical Traditional Persian music is simply poetry set to a musical accompaniment. Like epic poems, some 'epic songs' are very long and masters can spend most of their lives memorising the words. The instruments used as backing include the *tar*, a stringed instrument rather like the Indian sitar; the *dahol* and *zarb*, large and small drums respectively; the *nay* and *sorna*, a flute and oboe; and the *daryereh*, an outsized tambourine. Most of these instruments can be seen in the Ethnographical Museum in the Golestān Palace in Tehrān.

One singer particularly worth listening out for is Shāhram Nazerī, who has managed to combine traditional Iranian lyrics and poetry (often Hāfez or Sa'dī) with traditional Iranian music livened up to make it more inviting for a new young audience.

Folk The most appealing and melodious forms of traditional music are heard among the ethnic minorities, such as the Turkmen in the remote regions of Khorāsān province. The Āzārīs favour a unique style of music, often based around a love song, whereas the Kurds have a distinctive music based mainly around the lute and their own versions of epic songs, called *bards*.

The Lors often use an oboe-like instrument, while along the Persian Gulf a type of bagpipe called the *demam* is popular. The music of Sīstān va Balūchestān is understandably similar to that of Pakistan and played on instruments like the *tamboorak* (similar to the Pakistani *tambura*, a type of harmonium).

Perhaps not surprisingly, the lyrics of most traditional music revolve around Islam although some songs are based on love and others celebrate victories over invading armies centuries before.

Pop Although almost all modern music continues to be religious, slowly but surely Iranian pop music is starting to re-emerge, albeit under the watchful eye of the Iranian authorities. Many of the songs borrow rhythms and melodies from slightly out-of-date Western dance music tunes. Many of the best Iranian musicians (including the much-admired 'Ebi') fled Iran after the Islamic Revolution. They still perform abroad (the female singer Googosh's recent comeback concert in Toronto attracted an audience of 12,000) and tapes of their concerts circulate illicitly within Iran.

At the time of writing, perhaps the most popular young pop singer was Shadmehr Aghili who plays the violin and sings mainly love songs. Holding his own against younger newcomers was Mohammed Noori, who was popular before the Revolution and still sings songs about nationalism. Clarinet-playing Farhad, who has performed with Eric Clapton, was banned in the past as a dangerous left-winger, but has now been rehabilitated.

Literature

Overwhelmingly the most important form of writing in Iran is poetry, and the big-name writers, who everyone has heard of, are all primarily poets – Omar Khayyām, Hāfez, Sa'dī and, above all, Ferdōsī (see the boxed text 'The Great Iranian Poets' over the page).

Poetry While no-one knows the exact date of origin of the *Avesta*, the first known example of Persian literature, it is known that Persian poetry first blossomed in the 9th century AD. With influences drawn from other nearby empires, various forms of Persian poetry developed. Typical were the *mathnavi*, with its unique rhyming couplets, and the *ruba'i*, similar to the quatrain (a poem of four lines).

These styles later developed into the long and detailed 'epic poems', the first of which was Ferdōsī's *Shāh-namah*, finished in 1010 with 50,000 couplets! Many epic poems celebrated the glories of the old Persia before whichever foreigners had most recently invaded and occupied the country. The last truly great 'epic poem', *Zafar-nam*, covered the history of Islam from the birth of Mohammed to the early 14th century.

Poems of more than 100 nonrhyming couplets, known as *qasidas*, were the next major form of Persian poetry. Famous exponents were Anvarī and Sanjar. Moral and religious poetry became enormously popular following the success of Sa'dī's most famous poems, the *Būstan* and *Golestān*. By the 14th century, smaller *qazal* poems, which ran to about 10 nonrhyming couplets, were being used for love stories. Qazal poetry was made famous by Hāfez and is still practised today. Persian poets rarely produced anything exceptional after the 14th century.

Less well known, and one of the few noted female poets, is Parvin E'tesami, renowned for her religious poems, *Mecca of the Heart* and *Eye and Heart*. She died at 35 and is buried in Qom without any memorial.

Novels Sadly, not many Iranian novels have been translated into English. One that has is *The Blind Owl* by the 20th-century writer Sadeq Heydat, perhaps the best-known Iranian novelist outside Iran. The most popular of Iran's female writers is probably Simin Daneshvar, whose novel *Shaveshun* deals with life in Iran between the two world wars. Her husband Jalal Al-é Ahmad's novels *The School Principal* and *The Pen* have also been translated into English.

Iranians themselves tend to prefer short stories to novels. A selection of these are included in Minou Southgate's compendium *Modern Persian Short Stories*.

Story-Telling In a preliterate society, formal story-telling was often an extremely popular art form and Iran was no exception, with story-tellers taking their seat in teahouses every evening to entertain the assembled men. Unfortunately, the coming of television has more or less seen off the story-tellers; these days if you ask Iranians about story-tellers, they tend to pull a face and say 'boring'. Tracking down a genuine teahouse with traditional story-tellers is extremely difficult, but the Sofre Khane Sonnati Sangalag teahouse in Tehrān's Shāhr Park occasionally stages 'tourist' versions, which can be quite fun.

The Great Iranian Poets

Iranians venerate their great poets, often because they promoted Islam and protected the Persian language and culture during times of occupation. Many poets have large mausoleums, and streets and squares named after them: Ferdōsī and Omar Khayyām are buried in huge (separate) gardens near Mashhad; and Sa'dī and Hāfez have whole mausoleum complexes devoted to them in Shīraz.

For more information about Hāfez and Sa'dī, contact the Hāfez and Sa'dī Study Centre (☎/fax 0711 21071), PO Box 71455-414, Shīrāz, Fārs.

Ferdōsī

Haim Abulqasim Ferdōsī, first and foremost of all Iranian poets, was born in about AD 940 near Tūs. He was famous for developing the *ruba'i* (or quatrain) style of 'epic' historic poems. His most famous work is undoubtedly the *Shāh-nama* (Book of Kings), which he started when he was 40, and finished some 30 years later. When completed, this truly epic poem included close to 50,000 couplets. However, the Turkish king to whom he presented it was incensed that it contained no references to Turks and so rejected it. Ferdōsī died old, poor and grief-stricken.

These days Ferdōsi is seen as the saviour of Fārsī, which he chose to use at a time when the culture was being steadily Arabised. Without his writings many details of Persian history and culture might also have been lost. All in all Ferdōsī is credited with having done much to help shape the Iranian self-image.

Omar Khayyām

Omar Khayyām (Omar the Tentmaker) was born in Neishābūr in about 1047. He is probably the best-known Iranian poet in the West because many of his poems, including the famous *Rubaïyat*, were translated into English by Edward Fitzgerald; in Iran he is more famous as a mathematician, historian and astronomer, in particular for his studies of the Gregorian calendar and algebra. Although there is some speculation about what he actually wrote, Omar Khayyām is famous for his *ruba'a* (quatrain) poems, which many Iranians find far too gloomy. He died in 1123.

Hāfez

Khājé Shams-ed-Dīn Mohammed, or Hāfez (meaning 'One Who Can Recite the Quran from Memory') as he became known, was

Pottery

Pottery is one of the oldest Persian art forms and examples have been unearthed from burial mounds dating from the 5th millennium BC. Early pieces were probably for ornamental rather than domestic use, with elaborately detailed animals such as boars and ibex dominating

The Great Iranian Poets

born in Shīrāz in about 1324. His father died while he was still young, so the boy was educated by some of the city's leading scholars. Apart from memorising the Quran at an early age, he also became very interested in literature and wrote many verses that are still used in everyday speech today. Much of his poetry, known as the *Dīvān-é Hāfez*, has a strong mystical and virtually untranslatable quality; much of it was also about wine, nightingales and courtship.

Although he lived in turbulent times, Hāfez refused many generous invitations to some of the great courts of the day, both inside and outside Iran, because of his love for his birthplace. He died in 1389.

The Ārāmgāh-é Hāfez (Hāfez' Tomb) in Shīrāz

Sa'dī

The other great Shīrāzi poet, Sheikh Mohammed Shams-ed-Dīn (known by his pen name of Sa'dī), lived from about 1207 to 1291. Like Hāfez, he lost his father at a tender age, his education was entrusted to some of the leading teachers of Shīrāz and many of his elegantly phrased verses are still commonly used in conversation. His most famous works, the *Golestān* (Rose Garden) and *Būstān* (Garden of Trees), have been translated into many languages and his tomb has become something of a pilgrimage site.

the design. Persian pottery was initially unglazed, but glazed pottery dating back to the Elamite period has been unearthed from Choqā Zanbīl. In the 1st millennium AD, pottery was painted with the simple geometric, floral and animal motifs that developed into the characteristic Persian style. The lotus flower (called a *niloofar* in Farsi) has always been recognised as a symbol of life and of women; it features on a lot of Persian pottery, although the importance of the lotus predates the Arab conquest.

From the 9th century onwards, Persia's detailed and colourful (mainly blue and green) glazed pottery became world famous. The nomads of Khorāsān province had by then created their own style of glazing, adding early Islamic lettering styles like kufic to the design. Persian pottery reached its zenith in the 13th century, when a new type of clay was used to make the pottery more durable and several dazzling new colours were introduced. Chinese influences became very strong during the Mongol period, when figurative designs became quite commonplace, and remained so until the mid-18th century when the quality of Persian pottery started to decline.

The best examples of ancient Persian pottery have been unearthed at Neishābūr, near Mashhad; Rey, near Tehrān; and near Gorgān. Many of these early finds can be seen in the Glass & Ceramics, Rezā Abbāsī and National Museums in Tehrān, though some of the best examples are in the Louvre (Paris) and other museums outside Iran.

Marquetry

One of the most intricate styles of woodwork is *moarraq*, or marquetry. Initially influenced by artisans from India, a particular Persian style of marquetry slowly developed through the centuries. Several different woods including betel, walnut, cypress and pine are used, with the inlaid pieces made from animal bones, shells, bronze, silver and gold. Genuine Persian moarraq contains no paint; the colours come from the inlaid pieces.

Designs are often religious, but some simply show animals or birds. The designs are traced on paper and then pasted onto plywood. The design is then filled out with the required wood, the inlaid pieces are inserted, and the final product is coated with varnish. Moarraq is often used for furniture but visitors usually buy it in the form of ornamental boxes.

PATRICK SYDER

Cinema

Iran's film-making history dates back to *The Lor Girl* made in 1933. These days, dozens of Iranian films are churned out every year, most of them violent action flicks with names like *Play with Death* and *Escape from Hell*. However, recently a new school of Iranian realist cinema, fixated on the nitty-gritty detail of life and often focusing on children, has been proving hugely successful overseas.

Since films made in Iran must comply with the usual restrictive Islamic and political directions, some frustrated directors have

Left: A cinema in Shīrāz.

ANTHONY HAM

Top: The jewel-like dome of the Bogheh-yé Seyed Roknaddīn, in Yazd, is one of the earliest examples of the use of extensive tile mosaics.

PHIL WEYMOUTH

Middle Left: The Chehel Sotūn Palace (Palace of Forty Columns) was originally a royal pavillion used for receiving foreign dignitaries. Much of the building incorporates features exquisitely carved from wood, such as the intricate windows beneath its porch.

PATRICK SYDER

Middle Right: The dazzling minarets of the Jāmeh Mosque in Yazd date from the Muzaffarid period, during which the idea of an overall tile-mosaic pattern appeared for the first time.

SIMON RICHMOND

Bottom: Emām Khomeinī Square is Esfahān's masterpiece. At the southern end stands the Emām Mosque, the glory of Safavid architecture. Its great portal leads to a towering *iwan* and then to the mosque itself. The complex is not aligned with the elegant arcades surrounding the square because it must point in the direction of Mecca.

PATRICK SYDER

PHIL WEYMOUTH

PATRICK SYDER

PHIL WEYMOUTH

PAT YALE

PHIL WEYMOUTH

Top Left: Each of Iran's ethnic minorities takes pride in a unique musical heritage. The *sorna*, a woodwind instrument, is played by Baluchīs.

Top Right: Many cloth dyers in Esfahān's bazaar still use natural pigments.

Middle Left: Esfahān's bazaar provides a great opportunity to see artisans at work: a cloth printer (top) uses carved wooden blocks to create black, red, blue, yellow and green patterns on calico; the work of the coppersmith (bottom) can take on astonishing proportions.

Middle Right: While Iran is becoming internationally renowned for its art-house films, you are more likely to come across the blood-and-guts type in local cinemas.

Bottom: Persian miniature painting is delicate and beautifully refined. The tradition, which dates as far back as the 15th century, is still alive in Esfahān's bazaar.

decided to move elsewhere. But although Iranian films invariably revolve around the theme of good transcending bad, they rarely have an overt Islamic message.

If you happen to be in Tehrān during the annual Fajr International Film Festival (usually in late February), try to see a couple of new Iranian masterpieces, bearing in mind that they will be in Farsi, without English subtitles. Recent films especially well worth looking out for when you get back home include:

Blackboards Directed by the gifted Samira Makhmalbaf (daughter of Mohsen Makhmalbaf), this film won the Special Jury Prize at Cannes in 2000. It tells the story of a group of teachers who wander the mountains of western Iran looking for students, with blackboards strapped to their backs. (See the boxed text 'The Makhmalbafs – Father and Daughter' for more information about this director and her father.)

Gabbeh Directed by Mohsen Makhmalbaf, this film centres on a *gabbeh*, a type of Persian carpet made by Qashqā'ī nomads, and on a nomad girl with the same name.

Leila Last in a trilogy, directed by Dariush Mehrjoui, this film tells the story of a childless woman and her struggles with her husband and her family.

Taste of Cherry Directed by Abbas Kiarostami, this film was co-winner of the prestigious Palme d'Or at the 1997 Cannes Film Festival, despite being very controversial inside Iran because it deals with suicide, a taboo subject in Islam.

The Makhmalbafs – Father and Daughter

Born in 1957 in Tehrān, Mohsen Makhmalbaf first gained infamy when he was imprisoned for four years after fighting with a policeman. He was released during the Islamic Revolution in 1979 and started to write books before turning to film-making in 1982. Since then he has produced more than a dozen films, including *Boycott, Time for Love,* and, more recently and provocatively, *Salaam Cinema* and *Gabbeh*. Many of these films are based on taboo subjects: *Time for Love* was filmed in Turkey because it broached the topic of adultery; and *Marriage of the Blessed* was a brutal film about the casualties of the Iran-Iraq War.

Although Makhmalbaf refuses to follow the strict Islamic guidelines for local film-making, he enjoys comparative artistic freedom because he is so well known. The support provided to Makhmalbaf in the early 1990s by the then Minister of Culture, Seyed Mohammed Khatamī was one of the reasons why Khatamī had to resign. Ironically, he is now President of Iran, elected in a landslide partly because he was seen as a defender of artistic expression.

In 1997 Makhmalbaf's daughter Samira produced her first film *The Apple* – about children who had been locked inside a house in Tehrān for years – to critical acclaim. In 2000 her second film *Blackboards* was a smash hit at the Cannes Film Festival; she was the youngest director ever to have shown a film there. Samira has said that she intends to devote some of the prize money from *Blackboards* to building a school in Kordestān province.

The White Balloon Scripted by Abbas Kiarostami and directed by Jafar Panahi, this film, which tells the story of a young girl who loses her money while on the way to buy a goldfish, won several international awards.

Zinat Directed by Ebrahim Mohktari, this simple story of a nurse at a health centre, also won plaudits at international film festivals.

Other critically acclaimed films include Bahman Farmanara's *Smell of Camphor, Smell of Jasmine*; Majid Majidi's *Children of Heaven* and *The Color of God*; and Maryam Shariar's *Daughters of the Sun*.

Theatre

Almost all forms of Iranian theatre are based on Islam, and the most important is the *ta'ziyeh*, or passion play, which means 'mourning for the dead', and actually predates the introduction of Islam into Iran. These plays are staged in every Iranian city, town and village during the anniversary of Karbala, the battle in AD 680 in which Emām Hossein, the grandson of the Prophet, was murdered (see Public Holidays & Special Events in the Facts for the Visitor chapter for more details).

During the two days of mourning, groups of boys and men dressed in black shirts walk through the city streets, hitting their chests and backs with a chain called a *shallāgh*. Others play drums and brass instruments, lead the chanting, and carry flags and weapons symbolising the struggle against the infidels. The highlight for the participants and the hundreds of spectators comes when mounted warriors dressed in traditional fighting outfits re-enact the martyrdom of Hossein.

The groups then move to a public place, sometimes a bazaar or town square, where a temporary platform or stage has been erected. Here actors carrying dangerous-looking weapons continue to re-enact the martyrdom, often with rather too much passion. The followers of Hossein are usually dressed in green, while the followers of his enemy Yezid are dressed in red. One actor has to play Shemr, the man believed to have killed Hossein. It's a dangerous role since in the past some audiences have become so caught up in the play that they have actually killed 'Shemr'. Traditional poems are recited and dramatic songs sung to an accompaniment of Iranian flutes and drums. Many spectators openly weep. Others pray for health, wealth or a future family.

Note that this is a time when passions can run particularly high. It may not be especially wise to attend a passion play unless specifically invited and accompanied by Iranians.

[Continued from page 34]

The Iranian Way of Life These days the overwhelming majority of Iranians live in towns, most of them in fairly simple homes with basic sanitation and cooking facilities. Not surprisingly the most extreme differences in lifestyle can be found in Tehrān where people living in the northern suburbs lead a life not much different from that in the West, listening to the same music, eating the same food, watching the same television programs and films courtesy of satellite TV and the Internet. You'll see women in northern Tehrān whose headscarves could hardly slide much further back on their heads and who are clearly wearing very little beneath their trench coats. On the other hand, those same women probably roll up for work every day (13% of the workforce is female) cloaked from head to toe in black. Interestingly, a recent report found that 90 Iranian publications were being run by women.

In southern Tehrān, in contrast, it's a rare women who ventures onto the streets without a chador clenched tightly between her teeth. In these parts of town satellite TV is a luxury few people can afford. It's a rare husband, too, who would as much as carry a dirty dish to the sink, let alone do any housework.

Because of the absolute sexual segregation of society, marriage is crucially important. With almost no social situations in which they can meet unchaperoned, most Iranians get married very young, to partners chosen by their parents. In desperation some people resort to driving up and down the main streets of northern Tehrān handing out business cards with their telephone numbers on to likely-looking members of the opposite sex. Not surprisingly, the divorce rate, especially in cities, has started to rise, a situation probably exacerbated by the fact that more and more women are gaining a good education, enabling them to work for a living and making them less ready to put up with bad behaviour on the part of a spouse.

These days it's a rare man who can afford to take up his Islamic right to have four wives.

Hospitality to Strangers Hospitality to strangers and travellers is still very much a part of Iranian culture and Iranians are, generally, very welcoming towards foreigners (sometimes almost embarrassingly so). Traditionally, anyone for whom you do a favour has a duty to do another for you at some later date. Of course in practical terms there is no way that foreigners can repay in kind all the Iranians who give them a meal, hospitality or accommodation, but you might like to consider bringing small gifts from home to give to people who are especially kind to you (tape recordings of the *Gypsy Kings* go down especially well...).

Dos & Don'ts

Provided you observe the same simple courtesies as you would at home and keep within Iranian law and customs, most Iranians will forgive the occasional social gaffe. However, it's worth bearing in mind the

---

Marriage, Although Not Until Death Do Us Part

One of the most surprising features of prudish Iran is so-called temporary marriage, or *sigheh*, an institution unique to Shiite Islam.

Sigheh permits a man and woman (who can't be a virgin) to 'marry' for anything from a few hours to a few months with the blessing of a mullah. Although this is sometimes defended as a way for women widowed in the Iran-Iraq War to continue to have a sex life, or as a way for young people to do the same, most commentators see it as little more than legalised prostitution.

Not surprisingly, it's a subject many Iranians prefer not to talk about. However, during the early part of 2000 an English-language newspaper reported that 125 temporary marriages had been registered in the preceding three-month period, a 60% increase on the number recorded during the same period in 1999. The number of permanent marriages recorded in the same period has dropped by 3%.

following guidelines to avoid inadvertently giving offence.

In general, it's wise to be punctual for appointments, while understanding that Iranians themselves don't always turn up on time. Try to adjust yourself to the Iranian sense of time and build the occasional delay into your itinerary. Most people working in tourism are used to Western ideas about punctuality and will rarely keep you waiting.

Don't expect to be able to get straight to the point when dealing with Iranians. Preliminary conversation is likely to be confined to inquiries after each other's health over at least three cups of tea.

Iranians usually exchange presents when visiting friends. Bringing a few souvenirs from home is a great idea. If you have no suitable gift to offer, a dinner invitation will mean a lot to your hosts.

Never accept a present or service of any kind without first refusing three times, and expect an Iranian to behave in the same way if you offer anything to them. This tradition, known as *ta'arof*, is absolutely fundamental to Iranian social intercourse (see the boxed text 'Ta'arof' for more details).

Be wary about making comments to strangers that may incriminate yourself or another person, even if intended innocently or as a joke. Don't be the first person to open a discussion about politics or religion with a stranger. Remember that your views may appear just as extremist to some Iranians as theirs do to you.

Never sit down next to a member of the opposite sex who is not your spouse or a close relative unless specifically invited to do so, even if there is no other spare seat.

Holding hands in public seems to be making a quiet comeback, especially in Tabrīz, but in general you shouldn't shake hands or make physical contact with a member of the opposite sex in public.

Respect the dress code at all times and treat all copies of the Quran with the utmost respect. If looking at one in a bookshop, for example, try not to let your fingers stray onto the actual text.

Always remove your shoes when walking in the carpeted part of a mosque or other Islamic religious building, and when entering a private house, unless you're specifically invited to keep them on.

Most houses and hotels have a pair of sandals by the entrance to the lavatory. These should be exchanged for indoor slippers on entering and leaving and shouldn't be taken into the rest of the house.

Never turn your back on anyone, point the sole of your foot at anyone, or walk in front of someone who is praying. If you do

Ta'arof

Negotiating the intricacies of Iranian rules of etiquette can be a minefield. Much of it centres around *ta'arof* which essentially means that a person says something merely out of politeness. Although most offers of hospitality are genuine, ta'arof can result in Iranians getting stuck with unwanted guests who have taken the offer of a meal at face value – always refuse three times but, if they continue to insist, feel no hesitation in accepting. Shopkeepers have also got themselves into trouble by 'refusing' payment, only to find a Western traveller taking them seriously and heading straight for the door.

There is a less serious side to ta'arof. Like the Iranian practice of insisting that whoever they're with goes through the door first. It can make entering a room a drawn-out process as each invites the other with *'befamayīd'*, 'please'. Frustrated by this practice, the British who were in Iran used to tell the following joke, which is still repeated by Iranians today:

A woman who became pregnant never seemed to be able to give birth. The pregnancy had lasted over 30 years when finally two thirty-something twins were born with beards and walking sticks. Their furious father (the mother was clearly too exhausted to speak) demanded an explanation, to which the sons replied that they had spent the whole time arguing over who would be born first.

so inadvertently, excuse yourself by saying *'bebakhshid'*.

Rather than say 'no' outright and risk causing offence, Iranians will use any number of circumlocutions and diplomatic half-promises which are easily misunderstood by foreigners. Frankness and conciseness are not highly regarded by most Iranians.

When complimenting someone (eg, when telling a mother how beautiful her child is), always add *māshallāh* (God has willed it) for fear of invoking divine nemesis. People often believe that beauty and goodness are the gifts of God and can be taken away again at any time.

In Iran you need to be more careful than usual about what you say and in whose company you say it and there are some subjects (feminism, atheism, Zionism, free love and Salman Rushdie) best steered clear of unless you know somebody very well. It's also an offence to criticise any of the ayatollahs or to defame any of the prophets of Islam. On the other hand, you're going to feel a bit of a fool raving about the headscarf as this year's must-have fashion item when the women you are with are just itching to throw theirs away. Let the Iranian take the conversational lead and you probably won't go far wrong.

It may come as a surprise to discover just how many Iranian jokes revolve around money, religion and sexual infidelity. People also think it perfectly normal to launch into inquiries about your salary, standard of living and marital status on the briefest of acquaintances. Indeed, 'Are you married?' and 'How many children do you have?' are standard ice-breakers.

For advice on when and when not to take photographs, see the Photography & Video section in the Facts for the Visitor chapter.

The Dress Code The Iranian dress code is not only inspired by Quranic commands and reinforced by social custom but also rigidly reinforced by law. The dreaded religious police, the Komīteh, may be pretty much confined to barracks these days, but flouting the rules here remains much more than just bad manners. Although the dress code impacts most heavily on women (see

the Women Travellers section in the Facts for the Visitor chapter for vital information about what women must wear in Iran), it would be a grave error for a man to wear shorts, unless swimming at a segregated beach or playing official sports. On the other hand, it's perfectly acceptable these days for men to wear loose short-sleeved shirts or T-shirts.

Laws on dress are more strictly enforced during Ramazān and during Moharram, the month of mourning (see Public Holidays & Special Events in the Facts for the Visitor chapter for more details). Be particularly careful what you wear when entering a mosque or dealing with officialdom and when visiting somebody's home.

In a country where moustaches were once worn so long they had to be held up to eat, facial hair seems to be falling from favour; most of the really bushy beards you'll see these days are on mullahs or TV celebrities. Long hair on men remains a no-no; if yours is long, you'd be well-advised to cut it or at least tie it back.

For some reason, ties are seen as a symbol of Western cultural imperialism. You rarely see anybody wearing one except, perhaps, at a wedding. While we were researching this book the authorities on Kīsh Island actually announced that no-one wearing a tie would be admitted to local shops and hotels, but this may turn out to be a short-lived aberration.

Visiting Mosques Non-Muslims are completely forbidden to enter the Hazrat-é Masumeh (the shrine of Fātimeh) at Qom, and the Āstān-é Ghods-é Razavī (Holy Shrine of Emām Rezā) at Mashhad. Otherwise, most mosques will allow non-Muslims to visit except during Friday services and on mourning days. Some mosques won't allow photography anywhere near the mosque; and you should *never* take photos inside a functioning mosque.

Always take your shoes off when approaching the carpeted areas of a mosque (and make sure your feet and/or socks are clean). At larger mosques, there is usually an attendant who looks after the shoes of visitors and will make it clear to you if you shouldn't enter. Some historic mosques and other Islamic buildings have been turned into museums or simply abandoned. At some there is a nominal charge for admission, but others are major tourist attractions where you should expect to pay a normal entrance fee.

RELIGION

The Islamic Republic of Iran is, of course, overwhelmingly Muslim, and Islam is the state religion. Iran follows the Shiite sect of Islam rather than the more common Sunni sect followed in other Islamic countries. According to official statistics, 98.8% of the population follow Islam, of whom 95% are Shiites. The figures for the minorities – Christians (0.7%), Jews (0.3%), Zoroastrians (0.1%) with another 0.1% recorded as Sikhs and Buddhists – are probably an underestimate as many people play safe and call themselves Muslims on official documents. In general, it's not wise to say you're an atheist, or agnostic, concepts barely understood in Iran. Most Iranians will happily accept that you are a Christian, but it's probably best to avoid telling anyone if you are Jewish.

The recognised non-Muslim minorities pose little threat to the Iranian government and in return for their acquiescence they are granted certain concessions; for example, in matters of moral law they are allowed to be tried by their own religious leaders. Religions that seek to convert Muslims are not tolerated. Although Baha'ism was developed in 19th-century Iran, the 250,000-odd Baha'is are not allowed to practise their faith openly because it claims to be a purified form of Islam. Many Baha'is have emigrated since the Revolution.

Islam

Muslims believe the religion preached by the Prophet Mohammed to be God's final revelation to humanity. For them, the Quran, the Word of God revealed through the Prophet, supplements and completes the earlier revelations around which the Christian and Jewish faiths were built, and corrects human misinterpretations of those earlier revelations. For example, Muslims believe that Jesus was a prophet second only to Mohammed in importance, but that his followers later introduced into Christianity the heretical idea that Jesus was the son of God. They also regard Abraham, Moses and several other Christian and Jewish holy men as prophets. Mohammed, however, was the 'Seal of the Prophets', the last to have come.

Sunnis & Shiites The main division in the Islamic world is between Sunnis and Shiites. The schism that divided the Muslim world into these two broad camps took place after the death of the Prophet. When Mohammed died in AD 632, he left no clear instructions as to who should succeed him as leader. Some felt that leadership of the community should remain with the Prophet's family and supported Ali bin Abi Taleb, Mohammed's cousin and son-in-law and one of the first converts to Islam, but the majority of the community chose Abu Bakr, the Prophet's closest companion, as caliph, or leader. Ali was also passed over in two subsequent leadership contests.

Ali eventually became the fourth caliph in 656, but was assassinated five years later by troops loyal to the Governor of Syria, Mu'awiyah bin Abu Sufyan, a distant relative of the Prophet who subsequently set himself up as caliph.

The Muslim community then split into two competing factions. The Sunnis favoured the Umayyads, the dynasty established by Mu'awiyah, while the Shiites continued to believe that descendants of the Prophet through Ali's line should lead the Muslim community. The split widened and became permanent when Ali's son Hossein was killed in brutal circumstances at Karbala in 680 (see the boxed text 'Karbala & Najaf' in the Western Iran chapter for more details).

Over the centuries, Sunnism has developed into the 'orthodox' strain of Islam. Most Muslims are Sunnis, except in Iran, where the overwhelming majority are Shiite, a term derived from 'Shi'at' Alī', meaning 'Partisans of Ali'.

The Five Pillars of the Faith

All Muslims are expected to observe the five pillars of the faith:

Profession of Faith (Shāhadah) To become a Muslim you need only state the Islamic creed: 'There is no God but God, and Mohammed is the messenger of God'. To the end of this, Shiite Muslims add, 'and Ali is the representative of God'.

Prayer (Salat) Muslims are required to pray five times every day, although in practice Shiites only do so three times a day by performing all the necessary rituals for two sets of prayers immediately after each other on two occasions. Before praying Muslims are required to perform ritual ablutions. In Sunni mosques they usually do this using a fountain; in Shiite mosques they may well do so using a pool of water. During prayers, a Muslim must perform a series of prostrations while facing the direction of the Kaaba, the ancient shrine at the centre of the Grand Mosque in Mecca. Most Iranian hotel rooms contain an arrow or sign indicating the direction of Mecca, as well as a prayer rug and a mohr, a special tablet of clay which Shiites use when prostrating themselves to stop their foreheads touching what could be unclean ground. Shiite Muslims adopt a different posture to Sunnis when they commence praying. Their prayer leader, or imam, stands in a space cut out in front of the niche facing towards Mecca. The idea behind this is that, as the man in the congregation closest to Allah, he should make himself physically lower than everyone else as a sign of humility. Shiites call this hole in the ground the mihrab while for Sunnis the mihrab is the niche facing towards Mecca.

Alms-Giving (Zakat) Muslims are required to give a portion of their annual income to help the poor. Most Iranian streets are lined with alms-boxes to make such giving easy.

Fasting (Sawm) Mohammed received his first revelation during the month of Ramazān in AD 610. Muslims mark this event by fasting from sunrise until sunset through Ramazān each year. (See Public Holidays & Special Events in the Facts for the Visitor chapter for more details.)

Pilgrimage (Haj) All Muslims who are able to do so are required to make the pilgrimage to Mecca at least once in their lifetime. This pilgrimage should be performed during a specific few days in the first and second weeks of the Muslim month of Zū-l-Hejjeh. Visiting Mecca at any other time of the year is regarded as an umrah, or 'little pilgrimage', rather than a full-blown haj.

Because Shiites have rarely held temporal power their doctrine came to emphasise the spiritual position of their leaders, the imams *(emāms)*, over that of secular rulers.

The Muslim Faith For all Muslims, whether Sunni or Shiite, the essence of Islam is the belief that there is only one God and that it is their duty to believe in, and serve, Him according to the rules written in the Quran. In Arabic, *islam* means submission; a *muslim* is one who submits to God's will.

Among many other duties incumbent on Muslims, the best known, and least understood in the West, is 'jihad'. This word is usually translated into English as 'holy war' but literally means 'striving in the way of the faith'. Exactly what this means has been the subject of fierce debate among Muslim scholars for the last 1400 years. Some have tended to see jihad in spiritual, as opposed to martial, terms. These days in Iran, for example, you'll hear more about the 'construction jihad', the post-Revolution push to build more roads and install electricity and water pumps in rural areas, than about the fiery kind.

Muslims are forbidden to eat or drink anything containing pork, alcohol, blood or the meat of any animal that died of natural causes instead of being slaughtered in the

The 12 Imams

Iranian Shiite Islam recognises 12 imams as the direct successors to the Prophet Mohammed. Of these imams, by far the most important are the first imam, Ali; the third imam, Hossein; the eighth imam, Rezā; and the 12th imam, Mohammed al-Muntazar, better known as the Mehdi, or Mahdi (The One Led By God). However, every Iranian has their own favourite imam and you'll see appeals for their protection written on the backs of buses, as in 'Ya Emām Rezā' (Watch over me, Emām Rezā).

While all the other imams died normal deaths or were murdered, the 12th imam is said to have simply disappeared into a cave under the mosque at Smarra in Iraq in 878. Shiites believe that the 12 imams were the only men entrusted to interpret the Quran. In the absence of the Hidden Imam, the Awaited One, the present government makes its decisions in his name. It is believed that the return of the Mahdi, accompanied by the Prophet Jesus, will signal the end of tyranny and injustice and a return to peace on earth.

prescribed manner. Consequently, you will find no pork products on sale in Iran and although people will tell you that a lot of illicit drinking goes on behind doors, the only 'liquor' on sale is nonalcoholic beer. Muslim women may not marry non-Muslim men, although Muslim men are permitted to marry other 'peoples of the book' (ie, Christians or Jews but not Hindus or Buddhists).

Sharia'a Law Since the Islamic Revolution, Iran has been governed according to Sharia'a law. Like jihad, the term Sharia'a (usually translated as 'Islamic Law') sends shivers down Western spines. The Sharia'a is the general body of Islamic legal thought derived from the Quran and the *Sunnah* (a body of works recording the sayings and doings of the Prophet) rather than a legal code in the Western sense of the term. Sometimes it is quite specific – as in the case of inheritance law and the punishments laid down for certain offences – but often it simply offers a set of guidelines.

With enough research and the help of analogy, a learned scholar or judge should be able to determine the proper Islamic position on any situation from the Quran and the Sunnah.

It is partly because Sharia'a law permits capital and corporal punishment that the West condemns Iran for its poor human rights record. While it's certainly true that in the aftermath of the Revolution many people were executed after summary trials, the number of executions is steadily coming down

again; most of those executed today are murderers or drug smugglers; executions take place in public only for the most heinous offences. Flogging remains the prescribed penalty for drinking or failing to wear hejab, but women are rarely whipped these days. Persistent thieves can be sentenced to have two fingers (but not apparently whole hands) cut off.

Christianity

Christianity thrived in Iran long before the introduction of Islam, and some of its first saints were martyred in Persia. The majority of Iranian Christians are Armenians, who settled at Jolfā on Iran's northern border and were then moved to 'New Jolfā' in Esfahān by Shāh Abbās I.

There are smaller communities of Protestants, Roman Catholics, Catholics (Chaldean Rite), Orthodox Christians, Adventists, Nestorians and others. The Episcopal Church of Iran (part of the Anglican Communion) has churches in Tehrān, Esfahān, Shīrāz and Kermān, all of which welcome fellow Christians. The largest communities are in Orūmīyeh, Tabrīz, Tehrān (in particular around Nejātollāhī Ave), Esfahān (especially in the suburb of Jolfā), Shīrāz and the Azerbaijan provinces.

There are churches in almost every large Iranian town, but they are often hard to find. Many are not marked on maps even in Farsi, and most are hidden behind high walls, making them almost unidentifiable from the street.

Zoroastrianism

Zoroastrianism was the state creed of the early Persian Empires and at one stage it was practised all the way to the Mediterranean. Slowly but surely it was pushed back by Christianity in the west and Buddhism in the east, before Islam eventually overcame all three. These days there are very few Zoroastrians left in Iran (perhaps 30,000), most of them living in Yazd (their traditional centre), Shīrāz, Kermān, Tehrān and Esfahān.

Zoroastrian symbolism played an important part in Iranian art and you'll see Zoroastrian symbols on many of Iran's most famous pre-Islamic monuments. Some aspects of their faith still appeal to Iranian Muslims. See the boxed text 'Zoroastrianism' in the Central Iran chapter for more details.

Judaism

The Jewish population has fallen sharply since the Islamic Revolution. Perhaps 25,000 Jews remain in Iran, mainly in small communities in Hamadān, Tehrān, Shīrāz and Esfahān, where they are active in the bazaar and the jewellery trade. There is a synagogue in Hamadān and a mosque dedicated to a Jewish prophet in Shūsh.

In 2000 a group of Shīrāzi Jews were arrested and convicted of spying for Israel after a trial the West regarded as unfair. It seems likely that more of the remaining Jews will take that as a signal that the time has come to move on.

LANGUAGE

Iran's official language is Farsi (Persian), an Indo-European language. The other main regional languages spoken in Iran are Āzārī, Kurdish, Arabic and Lorī (spoken by the Lors), but you may also hear Gīlākī (spoken in Gīlān province), Balūchī (in Sīstān va Balūchestān province) and Turkmen (in Khorāsān province). Turkmen and Āzārī are both Turkic languages, related to but different from 'İstanbullu' Turkish as spoken in Turkey. Many Āzārīs and Turkmen have no problems understanding İstanbullu Turkish from watching Turkish television, so if you've managed to pick up a few phrases (even just the numbers) on your way across Turkey it could stand you in good stead – especially as there are quite a lot of Āzārī taxi drivers and hoteliers in Tehrān.

See the Language chapter at the back of this guidebook for some important Farsi

Transliterating Farsi

The Arabic script was adapted to Persian after the introduction of Islam, but there is no standard method of transliterating Farsi into English to make it easy for English speakers to pronounce it. There are also big differences between colloquial Farsi, the language of everyday speech, and classical Farsi, which an Iranian would use for reading a speech or writing a book.

In this book we have tried to use the spellings you will see on signs and maps in Iran to avoid possible confusion. Where there are alternative spellings of place names we have placed the most common alternatives in brackets after the first mention of the place.

Transliteration of the 'gh' sound is particularly problematic. You may see Qom written as Ghom, Qazvīn written as Ghazvīn and Qajar written as Ghajar, but the 'q' transliteration seems to be the most generally favoured, so that's the one we've gone with unless you're more likely to see the alternative spelling (eg, if it's a hotel that uses the 'gh' transliteration in its name). Hope that's all clear!

Throughout this book the following accented letters have been used in many Farsi words, especially in proper names:

ā	as the 'a' in 'far'	ō	as the 'o' in 'mole'
é	as the 'e' in 'bet'	ū	as the 'u' in 'rule'
ī	as the 'i' in 'marine'		

words and phrases, transliterated into English and written in the Persian script. The Lonely Planet *Farsi phrasebook* has all you need for a longer stay.

Almost every Iranian with whom you will do business will know the 'English' numerals, so a pocket calculator is very handy for 'discussing' prices.

PERSIAN CARPETS

The best known Iranian cultural export, the Persian carpet, is far more than just a floor covering to an Iranian. A Persian carpet is a display of wealth, an investment, an integral part of religious and cultural festivals, and used in everyday life, eg, as a prayer mat.

History

The earliest known Persian carpet, which probably dates back to the 5th century BC, was discovered in a remote part of Siberia, suggesting that carpets were made in Persia more than 2500 years ago.

Historians know that by the 7th century AD, Persian carpets made of wool or silk had become famous in court circles throughout the region. Their quality and subtlety of design were renowned, and carpets were exported to places as far away as China, although for many centuries they must have remained a great luxury in their country of production, with the finest pieces reserved for royalty.

The early patterns were usually symmetrical, with geometric and floral motifs designed to evoke the beauty of the classical Persian garden. Towards the end of the pre-Islamic period, stylised animal and human figures (especially royalty) became more popular.

After the Arab conquest, Quranic verses were incorporated into some carpet designs, and prayer mats began to be produced on a grand scale; secular carpets also became a major industry and were highly prized in European courts. Very few examples remain from before the 16th century, however, and little is known of early methods of weaving and knotting, or of differences in regional styles. The classification of existing pieces is often arbitrary.

During the 16th and 17th centuries, carpet making was given a high level of royal patronage, and a favoured designer or weaver could expect great privileges. Sheep were bred specifically to produce the finest possible wool for weaving, and vegetable plantations were tended with scientific precision to provide permanent dyes of just the right shade. The reign of Shāh Abbās I marks the peak of Persian carpet production, when

Inset: A tribal *gabbeh*, incorporating dogs to ward off evil spirits (photo by Glenn Beanland)

Right: Persian carpets derive much of their prestige from the elegance and sophistication of their designs.

GLENN BEANLAND

the quality of the raw materials and all aspects of the design and weaving were raised to a level never seen before or since.

Towards the end of the 17th century, as demand for Persian carpets grew, standards of production began to fall and designs became less inspired. Although a long period of relative stagnation followed, this has to be seen in perspective, for the finest Persian carpets of the 18th century and later still often led the world in quality and design. The reputation of modern Persian carpets has not entirely recovered from the introduction of artificial fibres and dyes earlier this century.

Persian Carpets Today

Persian carpets are a huge export earner for Iran but there are problems: The hand-weaving, which made Persian carpets so special, is being supplanted by modern factories; young Iranians are not interested in learning traditional weaving methods; and cheaper, often blatantly copied, versions of 'Persian' carpets are being produced in India and Pakistan (where child labour is sometimes used). The US embargo on the import of Persian carpets (now lifted) didn't help.

Iran relies on the prestige still evoked by the the term 'Persian carpet' and recently recaptured a large slice of the world's trade in carpets and rugs. While some authorities hope that the export of Persian carpets will top US$17 billion a year by 2020, pragmatists concede that the cost of making genuine handmade Persian carpets and rugs will increase until consumers are happier admiring them in museums than forking out to buy them.

Types of Carpets & Rugs

Persian carpets come in three main sizes: The *mian farsh* carpet is up to 3m long and up to 2.5m wide; the *kellegi* carpet is about 3.5m long and nearly 2m wide; and the *kenareh* carpet is up to 3m long and 1m wide. The best are made from wool (from sheep and goats, and occasionally camels), although its quality varies from region to region. Cotton is cheaper and easier to use than wool, and silk is used mainly for decorative rugs as it is not practical for everyday use.

Modern designs are symbolic or religious (eg, a lamp indicates the sacred lamp in Mecca); or reflect the everyday life of the weaver; or are inspired by whatever surrounds the weaver, eg, trees, animals and flowers, particularly the lotus, rose and chrysanthemum. Common designs include *miri-bota*, the leaf pattern also found in northern Indian rugs and probably a forerunner to the paisley patterns of the West.

One different type of rug you may come across is the *kilim*, a double-sided flat-woven mat without knots. These rugs are thinner and softer than knotted carpets and rarely used as floor coverings. They are popular as prayer mats (*kilim* is Turkish for 'prayer mat') and wall hangings.

Weaving

Most handmade carpets are woven from wool. The wool is spun, usually by hand, and then rinsed, washed and dried. It is then dyed to ensure

PHIL WEYMOUTH

an even colour throughout the rug. In the past, dyes were extracted from natural sources like herbs, skins of fruit and vegetables, and plants (eg, indigo for blue, madder for red and reseda for yellow). These days, however, chemical dyes are used, mainly aniline (which sometimes fades) and chrome. Later the rug is washed again to enhance the natural colours. Chemicals are sometimes used in this washing process.

Traditionally, nomad carpet-weavers (usually women) used horizontal looms, which are lightweight and transportable. Their carpets and rugs were less detailed and refined because their equipment was not so sophisticated, but the quality of wool was often high. Designs were either conjured up from memory, or made up as the weaver worked. These carpets and rugs were woven mainly for domestic use or occasional trade, and were necessarily small because they had to be portable.

In the villages, small workshops have simple upright looms, where men and women can create better designs, more variety. Designs are usually standard or copied from existing carpets or designs. Recently, city factories and village workshops mass-producing carpets of monotonous design and variable quality for, the sake of a quick buck, have more or less pushed nomad weavers out of the picture.

Knots You may come across the terms 'Persian (or *senneh*) knot' (known in Farsi as a *farsi-baf*) and 'Turkish (or *ghiordes*) knot' *(turki-baf)*. Despite the names, both are used in Iran: The Turkish knot is common in the Azerbaijan provinces and in western Iran. Without getting too technical, the Turkish knot is looped around two horizontal threads, with the yarn lifted between them, while the Persian knot loops around one horizontal thread and under the next. The difference is not obvious to the layperson.

As a rough guide, an everyday carpet or rug will have up to 30 knots per sq cm, a medium-grade piece 30 to 50 knots per sq cm, and a fine one 50 knots or more per sq cm. A prize piece might have 500 or more knots per sq cm, but nowadays museums are the only places where you will find such attempts at perfection. The higher the number of knots per sq cm, the better the quality and, of course, the higher the price.

Right: Carpet designs decorate the wall of a bazaar workshop

A nomad weaver can tie around 8000 knots a day; a weaver in a factory, about 12,000 knots a day.

Finding the Best

Experts argue over their favourite regions. Some claim that the carpets from Kermān province are the most colourful and soft; that those from Tabrīz offer the greatest variety; that those from Nā'īn boast the highest number of knots; that those from Qom are often most traditional; and that those from Kāshān are stronger and more dependable. The widest range – but not the cheapest prices – can be found in the bazaars in Tehrān, Esfahān and Shīrāz. In many cases the name of a carpet indicates where it was made or where the design originated.

If you have the time, you could try and hunt out something special in the following places:

- **Āzarbāyjān Provinces** The *heriz* and *mehriban* carpets found near the Azerbaijan border have bold designs, often featuring hunting scenes and tales from Ferdōsī's poem *Shāh-namah* on a mud-coloured background with bizarre fringes. Weavers invariably use Turkish knots.

- **Kermān Province** Kermān province is renowned for its soft and often very large carpets. They are very colourful, containing shades of green (although not too much, as green is sacred to Islam) and usually made from locally grown cotton. Designs feature flowers, nuts and fruit, as well as portraits of famous Iranians and foreigners.

- **Khorāsān Province** Carpets from this area are influenced by the nomadic Turkmen and the Arabs. They are often made from cotton and feature designs in red.

- **Kordestān Province** Popular, but perhaps less varied than those found in the villages of Lorestān, are the carpets and rugs made by the Kurds of western Iran. The two main centres for their production are Sanandaj and Bījār where particularly hard-wearing rugs are made.

PHIL WEYMOUTH

Left: Ironing the finished product

- **Lorestān Province** To help push-start the local economy, the Iranian government is promoting the traditional *gabbeh* carpets and rugs made by the Lors. Originally gabbehs featured plain patterns, but influences from India and wars over the centuries have introduced harsh black and white to symbolise bravery and victory. Lori carpets are normally made from local wool; the dyes are made from the skin of fruit such as pomegranates, and from herbs that are now hard to find. Designs may contain sporting and hunting scenes, local monuments or mosques.

- **Qom** In Qom, you are more likely to find *gul-i-bulbul* carpets, made from goat's wool and featuring designs with birds and flowers. The best are gorgeous, but these days many carpets sold in Qom are mass-produced for pilgrims.

Buying Carpets & Rugs

Iranians have had more than 2000 years to perfect the art of carpet-making – and just as long to master the art of carpet-selling. With hundreds of different types of carpets, it's going to take a Western novice several years of study to be on equal terms with a shrewd Iranian carpet dealer. If you don't know your warp from your weft, or your Turkish knot from your Persian knot, it might be worth reading up a little before visiting Iran, or taking an Iranian friend with you when you go shopping (bearing in mind that professional 'friends' who make a living from commission are as much a fact of life in Iran as in Turkey).

If you know what you're doing, you might be able to pick up a bargain, but it's worth remembering that dealers in Western countries often sell Persian carpets for little more than you'd pay in Iran (plus postage) – and carpet sellers in your home country know the market, bargain better, buy in bulk and save on transport costs. You are much less likely to be ripped off by your local warehouse dealer than by a Persian bazaar merchant. Unless you're an expert, never buy a carpet or rug as an investment – buy it because you like it, and even then only if you have some idea what sort of price you'd pay for a similar piece back home.

Before buying, lie the carpet flat on the floor and check for bumps or other imperfections. Small bumps will usually flatten out with wear but big ones are probably there to stay; if you're still sold on the carpet, look disappointed and expect a price cut. To check if a carpet is handmade, turn it over; on most handmade pieces the pattern will be distinct on the underside (the more distinct, the better the quality), although this is not an absolute rule. The most common pile material is wool, which is tough and practical,

PHIL WEYMOUTH

Right: Carpets for sale in the Shīrāz bazaar

and the best wool used is Iranian. Silk carpets are magnificent but they're largely decorative.

Taking Them Home

The whole business of clearing a carpet through customs and getting it to your doorstep usually takes one month (but allow two) and adds roughly one-third to the cost. Some of the larger, older and more valuable carpets cannot be exported without special permission, so always check that yours doesn't fall into this category before paying for it. Also make absolutely sure whether you'll have to pay transport costs or duties on delivery, and get everything down on paper. If in doubt, it's better to arrange to pay on delivery so you don't risk being charged twice. The service is generally reliable, but it's up to you to work out a fail-safe agreement with the agent.

Regulations for exporting Persian carpets can be confusing, so check the current situation with a reputable carpet dealer. Currently, each foreigner can take out of Iran one Persian carpet, or two small Persian rugs, totalling 12 sq metres in size. If you want to buy anything larger, or buy more than two rugs, and take them out of Iran, the authorities might regard you as a carpet trader although these days they don't necessarily check too closely.

More Information

For more information about Persian carpets and rugs visit the annual Grand Persian Carpet Exhibition & Conference in Tehrān, usually held in August, or visit the exquisite collection in the Carpet Museum in Tehrān. You could also contact the Export Promotion Center of Iran (☎ 021-212 896, fax 204 2858) at PO Box 1148, Tajrīsh, Tehrān, which organises the carpet fair. The *Iran Carpet* map produced by Ramezani Oriental Carpets, available at the Gita Shenasi map shop in Tehrān, indicates the location of carpet-weaving centres.

Any of the following books could also prove useful:

Oriental Carpets: A Buyer's Guide by Essie Sakhai. Useful for anyone contemplating buying a carpet who doesn't know their *ghiordes* knot from their *senneh*.

Oriental Rugs in Colour by Preben Liebetrau. Probably the most useful guide to carry around, this pocket-sized book includes an explanation of the carpets and rugs of Iran and Turkey.

Persian Kilims by A Hull & N Barnard. This lavishly illustrated volume covers most of what you'll need to know about Persian carpets and rugs.

Persian & Other Oriental Carpets for Today by N Fokker. This concise history of carpets includes an explanation of carpet-making in Iran and Turkey.

Some of the oldest and finest Persian carpets and rugs are housed in museums outside Iran: For example, in the national museums in Munich and Berlin, the royal palaces in Denmark, and the Victoria & Albert Museum in London, which houses the Ardabīl Carpet, one of the best known of all Persian carpets (see the boxed text 'The Ardabīl Carpet' in the Western Iran chapter for more details).

Top: Urban carpet production begins with meticulous planning and the creation of a design 'cartoon' or template. The importance of new and innovative designs arose during the Safavid period when carpets began to be mass produced for export.

Middle: With a design 'cartoon' completed, weaving can begin. As work on the carpet progresses, the carpet-maker regularly checks the emerging pattern against the template. In urban workshops, hand-made carpets are woven on large, upright looms. The work requires great dexterity and concentration: Fine carpets can contain over 100 knots per square centimetre!

Bottom: The finished product is displayed and sold in local bazaars, and the ensuing bargaining process is a time honoured tradition. Merchants will draw the buyer's attention to the prestige and quality of the carpet, and to its potential to actually improve with age.

The styles of Persian carpets are seemingly endless.

Top: This carpet from Qom depicts hunters pursuing deer. The design dates from the Safavid period.

Middle Left: A Toyserkan design from western Iran; tribal carpets usually feature simple designs and exceptionally high-quality wool.

Middle Right: A finely woven Habibian carpet from Nā'īn that depicts mosaics on the inside of a dome.

Bottom: A Tabrīzī carpet with a design that dates from the 17th century.

Facts for the Visitor

SUGGESTED ITINERARIES

As long as the problems in obtaining an Iranian visa persist, your itinerary may be dictated to a very large extent by how long you can persuade officialdom to let you stay.

One Week

People on transit visas may only be able to stay in Iran for a week to 10 days. If that's all you can get, it's probably best to restrict yourself to seeing two or three main towns. If you fly into Tehrān consider staying there to see the museums and palaces for two days, before flying to Esfahān, Iran's most

architecturally stunning city, for another two days and then spending another three days in and around Shīrāz and Persepolis.

There's a clear overland travellers' route from Turkey to Pakistan via Mākū, Tabrīz, Tehrān, Kāshān, Esfahān, Shīrāz, Yazd, Kermān and Bam, and although it's just about possible to do this in 10 days, you would spend almost all of your time travelling and see little of the country.

Two Weeks

Most travellers manage a visa and extension totalling at least two weeks. With two

---

Highlights

Iran's three Unesco World Heritage Sites should not be missed. They are the spectacular ruins of the Achaemenid religious capital at **Persepolis**; the dramatic Elamite ziggurat at **Choqā Zanbīl**; and the entire **Emām Khomeinī Square** complex in Esfahān.

Many people come to Iran just to see the wonderful mosques. For sheer architectural splendour you can hardly beat the **Emām Mosque** and **Sheikh Lotfollāh Mosque** in Esfahān and the **Jāmeh Mosque** in Yazd, although if it's the spectacle of religious fervour that you're after, the **Holy Shrine of Emām Rezā** in Mashhad is a must.

The huge 14th-century mausoleum, the **Gonbad-é Soltānīyeh**, near Zanjān, is also well worth a visit for its architecture, as is the beautiful **Sheikh Safī-od-Dīn Mausoleum** in Ardabīl.

In Shīrāz, the **Ārāmgāh-é Hāfez**, the tomb of the renowned poet Hāfez, is worth visiting primarily for its garden. Other splendid gardens worth visiting especially in spring include the **Bāgh-é Eram** in Shīrāz, and the famous **Bāgh-é Tārīkhī-yé Fīn**, near Kāshān.

The **Chehel Sotūn Palace** in Esfahān has spectacular wall paintings, which miraculously survived the Islamic Revolution. Bigger and absolutely intriguing is the newly restored **Golestān Palace** in Tehrān.

Particularly exciting **bazaars** can be found in Tabrīz, Esfahān and Shīrāz.

Of Iran's less well-known archaeological sites two of the more spectacular are **Takht-é Soleimān**, near Takab in western Iran, and **Tāq-é Bostān** in Kermānshāh.

No-one interested in carpets will want to miss the **Carpet Museum** in Tehrān. The collections in the **National Jewels** and **Rezā Abbasī Museums** in Tehrān are also spectacular and much better displayed than those in the **National Museum of Iran**, also in Tehrān.

In a class of its own is the ancient mud-brick city of **Arg-é Bam** in Bam. Still inhabited, the **old quarter of Yazd** repays many hours of wandering, as do the streets of Kāshān with their fine **old houses**. The **bridges of Esfahān**, with their wonderful teahouses, are other must-see attractions.

For lovers of natural attractions, the **Alī Sadr Caves**, near Hamadān, may also prove a highlight. The mountain village of **Māsuleh**, near Rasht, makes a great place to hang out for a few days, while the scenery en route to the **Castles of the Assassins**, near Qazvīn, is some of the most beautiful and unspoilt in Iran.

---

weeks at your disposal, you can follow the same route as people passing straight through on a one-week visa but you should have more time to stop and look at the places along the way. If you come into Iran from Turkey you could visit Tabrīz (one day) and Takht-é Soleimān (one day), then travel to Tehrān (two days), Kāshān (one day), Esfahān (two days), Shīrāz and Persepolis (two days), Yazd (two days), Kermān (two days) and Bam (one day), before leaving for Pakistan. Don't forget, though, that much of your time will be spent in transit between these towns; you might want to consider flying straight to Tehrān from Tabrīz and then heading south to Kāshān to allow more time in Esfahān and Shīrāz.

One Month

Given the size of Iran, this is probably the optimum length of time to stay. With more time at your disposal, you could visit Tabrīz and use it as a base to visit Jolfā, Kandovan and Marāqeh (four days). Then head on to Takht-é Soleimān (one day), Hamadān (one day) and Kermānshāh (one day).

Next, head for Tehrān (three days). From Tehrān you could head up to Māsuleh near Rasht (one day), stopping at Qazvīn (one day) to visit Alamut (one day) and Zanjān to visit Soltānīyeh (one day). Then you could continue east along the Caspian Sea (three days) or fly to Mashhad and back (two days).

Alternatively, backtrack to Tehrān and head south for Kāshān (two days), Esfahān (three days), Shīrāz and Persepolis (three days), Yazd (two days), Kermān (two days) and Bam (one day), before leaving for Pakistan.

This itinerary leaves plenty of time for travelling between towns, although if you want to squeeze in as much as possible you might be able to manage an excursion from Shīrāz to the Persian Gulf for two or three days, basing yourself in Bandar-é Abbās or Būshehr.

Two Months

If you are among the very few who manage to wangle a visa and a couple of extensions for two months, you could spend longer in all the places mentioned in the one-month itinerary, or consider flying to more remote regions such as Mashhad, Bandar-é Abbās, Būshehr or Ahvāz for a few days. If you have time left over and feel a bit adventurous, try and do some skiing, hiking or some other activity, depending on the season.

PLANNING
When to Go

The most agreeable time to visit the south coast is during winter, but the north-west and north-east are at their best between mid-April and early June, and late September and early November. High summer is unpleasantly hot in most of the country, but especially along the Persian Gulf coast. For more specific information about the weather in different parts of the country, see the Climate section in the Facts about Iran chapter.

You should aim to avoid visiting Iran during the long, cold, northern winter, and over the Iranian New Year or Nō Rūz (about 21 March). School holidays run for about two weeks after the Iranian New Year and from about 20 May in the south (elsewhere, from about 5 June), finishing on about 6 September. However, even in the popular Caspian region, they are unlikely to disrupt your travel plans too much.

Many people prefer not to visit Iran during Ramazān, the Muslim month of fasting, when most restaurants close between dawn and dusk, and tempers can be strained (see Public Holidays & Special Events later in this chapter for more details).

What Kind of Trip

What kind of trip you make in Iran may be dictated by your nationality and what kind of visa you can get. Although most people are able to get a transit or tourist visa for independent travel, some nationalities (especially Americans and to a lesser extent the British) may well only be able to get a visa if they book an organised tour.

These days, travelling around Iran independently is perfectly feasible, even on your own. However, you do need to bear in mind that the evenings can drag for lack of entertainment, and that communication with locals can be limited because of the language barrier. Taking an organised tour will certainly alleviate these frustrations, but will be far more expensive and much less flexible (see the boxed text 'To Tour or Not to Tour?' for more details). One disadvantage of travelling alone is that single rooms are rare and you will often have to fork out for a twin, which bumps up costs considerably. For some time to come, women will probably feel more comfortable travelling in a group or with a male or female companion.

Most people will be lucky to get more than a two-week visa, in which case even hardened overland travellers should consider taking advantage of Iran's extensive network of cheap flights to avoid wasting precious daylight hours staring out of the window of a bus at seemingly never-ending desert.

Maps

The maps in this guidebook should satisfy most travellers, although people driving through the country may need more detailed city maps to help them get in and out of the suburbs.

The undisputed king of Iranian map-making is Gita Shenasi, which publishes an impressive array of maps covering all the major cities and some of the mountain ranges. Most of the older maps list the names of the streets, suburbs and squares in English, although everything else, including the text and indexes, is in Farsi.

You can sometimes buy Gita Shenasi maps outside Tehrān, but if you're going to be staying for some time and don't think the maps in this guidebook will be sufficient, visit the Gita Shenasi office (☎ 021-670 9335, fax 670 5782) in Tehrān at 15 Ostad

---

To Tour Or Not To Tour?

In general, Lonely Planet advocates the do-it-yourself option as the best way to get to grips with a new country. However, in the case of Iran this may not always be realistic because of the difficulties with getting a visa for independent travel.

An increasing number of overseas tour operators are organising tours to Iran (see Organised Tours in the Getting There & Away chapter for contact details). Usually these last for two or three weeks and take in the main highlights, including the Tehrān museums, Esfahān, Shīrāz, Yazd, Kermān and Bam, with, perhaps, a detour to the Caspian coast, Hamadān and Mashhad. Given how cheap travelling in Iran is, most of these tours are extremely expensive, especially if you want to book a single room. You may also feel that they stop you trying cheaper restaurants and hotels, as well as excluding you from contact with local people other than the tour guide.

On the plus side, having a guide can be particularly useful when travelling in a country with such a different culture, when you are unlikely to be able to read many of the signs, and when you may arrive with preconceived ideas that don't necessarily mesh with reality. A guide will, for example, ensure that you don't run aground over the dress code, which is particularly reassuring for women travellers. Some tour companies also use buses with blacked-out windows so their female clients can travel the long distances between one town and another without having to wear their scarves. If you have to travel in high summer, you will also be very grateful for the air-conditioning on tour buses.

When deciding which tour to take it's often worth looking at how many 'free days' they offer. While free days sound great in theory, in practice if yours are in Shīrāz, Esfahān or Tehrān it could mean you end up having to pay a lot of quite hefty admission fees yourself instead of having them included in the tour price.

A word of warning about 'extra nights' at the start and end of your tour. Many flights to Iran arrive in the early hours of the morning, before you can check into your hotel. Unfortunately tour companies often charge extortionate prices for booking 'extra nights'. You'd do well either to book directly with the hotel via fax or to wait until you arrive and hope you can book a room for the normal price on the spot.

Shahrīvar St, Razī St, Valiasr Crossroads, Enqelāb-é Eslāmī Ave (PO Box 14155/3441).

Gita Shenasi's *Map of the Islamic Republic of Iran* (1:2,000,000) will satisfy most visitors. Train buffs may like to buy their *General Map of Railways: Islamic Republic of Iran & Its Corridors*, which shows the rail system, and includes history, as well as a table of distances, in English and Farsi.

The best dual-language map is the *Tourist Map of the Islamic Republic of Iran* (1:2,500,000), published by the Ministry of Culture & Islamic Guidance and available in some tourist offices. It marks all the main roads, railway lines, and petrol stations.

Bartholomew's *Iran* (1:2,500,000) is still occasionally available, but the best English-language map available outside the country is GeoCentre's *Iran* (1:2,000,000), which is clearer and more readable than most locally produced maps.

Trekkers and mountain climbers may want to pick up the relevant TPC or ONC topographical maps published by the Defence Mapping Agency in the USA. Gita Shenasi publishes climbing maps such as *Central Alborz*, *The Peaks of the Sabalan* and *Damāvand and its Ridges,* but their usefulness is limited because many places are marked only in Farsi. Kassa Mountaineering & Tourism (☎ 021-751 0463, fax 751 0464, ℮ KASSA@intelimet.net), 9 Maghdi Alley, Sharīatī St, Tehrān, also produces a useful climbing map called *Takht-é Soleimān and the Alankosh Region.*

What to Bring

There's no longer any need to arrive in Iran weighed down with toiletries and foodstuffs. Most day-to-day essentials can be bought in Tehrān or the big cities at very reasonable prices.

You may want to consider bringing a universal sink plug – since Muslims always wash in running water, hotels rarely provide plugs. Although toothpaste and soap are cheap and readily available, toilet paper is less easy to track down and can be pricey; on the other hand, boxes of tissues are cheap and ubiquitous so you can always improvise. Women should also bring tampons since these are almost impossible to find in Iran. Men needn't bother taking shaving gear along; even if they don't fancy growing a beard it's easy to find a barber.

Since Iranians suck sugar through their teeth, you'll rarely be given a teaspoon to stir yours. Most restaurants also only supply spoons and forks as eating utensils, so you may want to bring your own knife, fork and spoon. Even when they're out on short shopping trips, Iranians carry their own cups to take advantage of the endless free water supplies without having to share the communal cups provided; you may want to do likewise.

Given that Iran can still be politically volatile, it's not a bad idea to pack a short-wave radio to keep abreast of world news. A torch (flashlight) could come in handy for occasional power cuts, and it's surprising how often Swiss Army knives and compasses manage to justify the space they take up in your baggage.

Packing your own medical kit (see the Health section) is sensible, especially if you will be travelling off the beaten track or have specific medical requirements. You may also want to bring small presents from home for Iranian friends.

Unless you fancy early night after early night, don't forget to bring several large and interesting books. Pack earplugs for when you've decided it really *is* time to sleep.

Hotels are sometimes happy to hold luggage for guests, and some train stations have luggage lockers. Surplus gear and souvenirs can be posted out of Iran safely and cheaply.

Clothing For essential advice on what is considered acceptable clothing in Iran, see the Society & Conduct section in the Facts about Iran chapter, and the Women Travellers section later in this chapter.

In summer, take lightweight, easily washable clothes of natural fabrics, a cardigan or pullover for the cooler evenings, a pair of sunglasses and a hat which will protect your face from the sun. (Iranian women sometimes wear a hat over their headscarf. It may look silly but it beats the hell out of being burnt to a crisp.)

In winter, take mostly warm clothing, including a coat, scarf and hat, and two or three thin sweaters rather than one thick one. You may also want to take boots or shoes equipped to cope with heavy snow and slippery pavements. An umbrella is useful at any time unless you're travelling in the deep south.

RESPONSIBLE TOURISM

When travelling in a country like Iran, which has had somewhat fraught relations with the outside world, it's more than usually important that travellers do their bit as diplomats, respecting local customs as much as possible even when these seem very alien to them (as with the female dress code). Locals are usually thrilled if you take an interest in their way of life and try to master a few words of Farsi.

As elsewhere, travellers should aim to minimise their impact on the environment. Littering is a big problem in Iran. Always be sure to clear up after yourself properly; you might even feel you could clear up some of the mess left behind by other people.

While in Iran it's especially important to be sensitive to people's religious beliefs. Always make sure you're properly dressed and welcome before rushing into particularly holy shrines.

The best way to ensure as much of the money you spend as possible goes into the local economy is to choose hotels and tours run by Iranians, rather than foreigners. Until tourism picks up a bit more, this is pretty theoretical since few foreign companies have invested in Iranian tourism as yet. If you book a tour from abroad, much of your money will inevitably go to the foreign tour company, but if you travel independently most of your money will probably stay in Iran.

To find out more about the human rights situation in Iran, consult the *Amnesty International Handbook*.

TOURIST OFFICES
Local Tourist Offices

The ominous-sounding Ministry of Culture & Islamic Guidance is responsible for 'cultural affairs, propaganda, literature and arts, audiovisual production, archaeology, preservation of the cultural heritage, tourism, press and libraries'. You may have noticed how far down the list the word 'tourism' was squeezed in, giving you a fair indication of how unimportant tourism is to the Iranian government. However, things are slowly changing and it's possible that a separate tourism department will be created eventually.

The ministry has a tourist office in every provincial capital, but only a handful can provide any useful information for foreigners. A few local government authorities also run tourist offices; most have (or can find) someone who speaks English, but they rarely stock maps or brochures. With the exceptions of Tabrīz and Esfahān, it's rarely worth going out of your way to visit Iranian tourist offices but the addresses and phone numbers of some of them are listed in the relevant sections just in case the situation improves.

Tourist offices are generally open from 8 am to 2 pm, Saturday to Wednesday, and from 8 am to noon on Thursday.

There are also small information booths at the main bus terminals, train stations and international airports, but these are of limited usefulness because staff don't always speak any English.

Tourist Offices Abroad

Sorry, but there are none. You could try to prise some information from your nearest Iranian embassy or consulate, but don't hold your breath. The best source of information about anything to do with Iran (besides this guidebook, of course) is the Internet. See Internet Resources later in this chapter for more details.

VISAS & DOCUMENTS

How ready the Iranians are to give you a visa depends on the state of relations with your government when you apply. Citizens of small inoffensive countries like Ireland, New Zealand and San Marino tend to come out of this lottery best. Israelis are not allowed in under any circumstances; nor are women who refuse to wear appropriate clothing. US citizens are increasingly welcome, but may still have to join an organised tour to get a visa.

Passport

Make sure your passport has several spare pages for visa extensions and stamp-happy immigration officials. Your passport must be valid for more than six months after your intended departure.

Most hotels want to hold onto your passport during your stay because the police will almost certainly visit and want to take down your details. If you don't leave your passport at reception, you risk being asked to supply it to the police in person, even in the middle of the night. The best compromise is to leave your passport at reception overnight then ask for it back during the day in case you need to show it to the police when you are out (unlikely), or need to change money at the bank. If you don't want to leave your passport at reception, providing the receptionist with a photocopy of the most important pages (ie, the ones with your photo, personal details and visa) will sometimes be allowed.

If you *do* leave your passport at reception, be sure to pick it up again before departing. It can be a long way back again if you forget!

Visas

Visitors from the Gulf States (Bahrain, Kuwait, Oman, Qatar, Saudi Arabia and the UAE) don't need a visa to enter Iran. Everyone else does. People from the Former Yugoslav Republic of Macedonia and Turkey can get a three-month tourist visa on arrival, or at a diplomatic mission beforehand. Japanese travellers can also get a three-month tourist visa at an Iranian embassy without difficulty. For the rest of us, however, landing that visa tends to be something of a headache, especially if you are from the United States, Canada, Britain or Croatia.

Deciding how to set about getting a visa can be confusing, but the best *general* advice if you're planning to fly into Iran is to apply for a tourist visa (valid for two weeks or one month) in your home country as early as possible before setting out. Alternatively, if you plan to travel overland to Iran, apply for a transit visa (usually valid for five to 10 days) along the way, allowing plenty of time for the paperwork to be sorted out.

It doesn't help that visa regulations vary from one Iranian embassy to another; some only issue transit visas, a few are happy to supply one-month tourist visas, while others try hard to put you off the idea of applying in the first place. At the time of writing, for example, the Iranian embassy in İstanbul (Turkey) was turning away visa applications from anyone applying outside their country of residence unless they had a sponsor in Iran. However, the embassy in Ankara and the consulate in Erzurum were still continuing to process applications from non-Turks.

Sometimes it's next to impossible to get a visa in your home country, whereas the embassy in another country will issue you with a tourist visa in 48 hours. In general, consulates in countries that attract few applicants (Beijing, Budapest, Warsaw, Dubai and New Delhi have been reported as particularly helpful) are the most likely to oblige with visas, but that's not a hard and fast rule. At the time of writing, Erzurum, in Turkey, was one of the easiest places in the world to get an Iranian visa.

If you can't get a visa in your home country, that doesn't mean you must give up altogether. Either telephone the Iranian consulate in a neighbouring country (see Embassies & Consulates later in this section) or drop in at every consulate on your way to Iran. If you can only get a short transit visa, don't worry – getting an extension inside Iran is often far easier than getting any sort of visa in the first place (see Visa Extensions later in this section).

Nor should you be put off if you're refused a visa the first time you apply; just try again.

> We telephoned one of the most expensive hotels in Tehrān and reserved a suite for two, posing as well-off businessmen. We explained to the Āzādī that we needed a confirmation of the reservation to arrange the red tape and they immediately faxed that. With this reservation I approached the Iranian embassy in Budapest and they issued the visa within a week. We then cancelled the hotel reservation some weeks before departure.
>
> **Eirik Softeland**

Visa costs are as difficult to predict as the application process, but in general the price for most travellers seems to work out as the equivalent of about US$50; for example, for Brits in London the visa cost is UK£30, Canadians in Canada pay C$65 and Germans in Germany are slugged DM80. However, sometimes you can be landed for much more than this – and if you have to use an agency to help you the price can become quite astronomical.

When applying for a visa, you will need to complete two or three application forms, supply up to four passport-size photos and pay the visa fee into a nearby bank. You may also be asked to provide a photocopy of your air tickets in and out of Iran; a letter from your employer (rare); a letter of recommendation from your embassy if you're applying for the visa outside your home country; proof of funds (rare); and any student or press cards. Your visa may also be marked with your intended points of entry and exit, car registration number and the names of any travelling companions. Foreign women don't need to be wearing a headscarf in their passport photos, but they *must* be wearing a headscarf in the photos used for the visa application.

If you are arranging your visa through a relative, travel agency or business contact in Iran, they will need your full personal details and passport information, an outline itinerary, your flight details, and any other information likely to help your cause. Your sponsor will then forward an authorisation number from the Ministry of Foreign Affairs in Tehrān, which you use to collect your visa from the relevant embassy. You can ask for the authorisation number to be faxed from Iran to the relevant Iranian embassy, and for your passport to be returned to you by mail (preferably certified), but this is bound to be less reliable than calling to pick it up in person.

While it may take several weeks for authorisation to come through even for a transit visa, you don't normally have to leave your passport at the embassy while you

Dodgy Passports

If you hold an American, Canadian, British or Croatian passport you are in for a particularly difficult time when it comes to getting a visa. As one traveller writes...

My original plan was to go by boat from Dubai to Iran, then through Turkmenistan on a transit visa to Uzbekistan. Unfortunately I am now going to have to fly direct from Dubai via Kyrgyzstan to Uzbekistan as I have found it impossible to get an Iranian visa, probably because I have a British passport and refuse to go on a group tour. I have tried the embassies in Oman, Australia and UAE, and although I have been listened to sympathetically I have got nowhere. I tried one travel agent who wanted US$150 to provide a visa reference number and never bothered to reply when I suggested that this was rather high. In addition I was pissed off to lose the US$100 fee I'd sent to the embassy in Canberra, Australia. They advised me *after* they'd returned my passport that they were unable to return the fee as I was British! On further inquiry this policy appears to apply also to Americans, Canadians and Croatians. So the message seems to be if you are one of these four and don't want to go on a package, forget it.

Len Hobbs

The simple, but costly, way round the problem is to book on a tour in which case the tour operator will sort out the paperwork for you. Otherwise, you may have more luck getting a transit visa.

But things are easing up and we have received many letters from Americans who *did* manage to get visas. One couple wrote to say that they booked everything ahead so that they were 'almost on a tour except no tour operator was involved'; they then sent all the confirmations in with their application along with a letter expressing a great interest in Islamic art. The message must be, if at first you don't succeed, try, try again!

wait. So if, for example, you are applying in Delhi, India, you can apply for the visa (but keep your passport), travel around India for a few weeks and then come back to pick up your Iranian visa later on. One traveller reported how he used the Internet in Gilgit (Pakistan) to apply for a visa through a Tehrān travel agency who had it ready and waiting for him to pick up in Islamabad when he got there a few weeks later.

While we don't advocate lying on your application form, don't complicate matters unnecessarily by claiming you're something unloved like a journalist; it's better just to say that you're a teacher, student or nurse.

If you have access to the Internet, check out the excellent Web site created by the Iranian embassy in Ottawa, Canada (www .salamiran.org). This lists the telephone and fax numbers of major Iranian embassies, provides advice on visas and even supplies a visa application form, which you can download or print.

Remember that every part of every day counts towards the expiry of your visa, so if you cross the border at five minutes before midnight, one day of your precious visa has already been used up. And whatever you do, don't overstay your visa. While this may not cost a lot to rectify, it can take up to a week to sort out the paperwork.

Visa Agencies If you're short of time and/or having trouble getting a visa you may want to approach Magic Carpet Travel in the UK who can help you get a visa (see Organised Tours in the Getting There & Away chapter for contact details) but charges UK£70 for doing so.

In France you have to apply for a visa through AITO (ITTO; ☎ 01 56 59 91 86, fax 01 45 61 16 20, ⓔ aito.france@wana doof.fr), 9 Avenue de Friedland, 75008 Paris.

Transit Visas Transit visas are usually issued for a stay of five or 10 days. They are mainly given to foreigners who are travelling overland to Iran (eg, to anyone travelling through Iran to Turkey or Pakistan). Travellers often pick them up along the way, in İstanbul or Ankara (Turkey), New Delhi

(India) or Karachi (Pakistan). The main advantage of a transit visa is that you don't normally need a sponsor in Iran to get one.

In theory, transit visas should be issued within a few days, but it often takes two or three weeks and you may still need a letter of recommendation from your embassy if you apply from outside your home country. Transit visas are normally valid for three months (ie, you must enter Iran within three months of the date of issue), but double-check this when you apply.

A transit visa can be extended once you get inside Iran, but usually just for the same number of days as the original visa.

Tourist Visas Tourist visas are mainly issued to people flying into Iran on business, to visit family or as part of an organised tour group. These visas are usually issued for stays of two weeks or one month, but they may also be given for a set number of days, especially if you're going on a tour. You may be asked to provide an itinerary of your trip. Tourist visas are generally valid for three months (ie, you must enter Iran within three months of the date of issue).

The rules about whether you need an Iranian sponsor to get a tourist visa differ from one embassy to another. If you don't have a sponsor, ask another embassy in a neighbouring country about their rules for a tourist visa, or apply for a transit visa instead and get it extended inside Iran.

If you still need to provide a sponsor and don't have one, get in touch with a travel agency in Iran (see the Organised Tours section in the Getting There & Away chapter for contact details). These agencies will probably charge up to US$100 for their services (on top of the visa fee). Obviously, if the only service you want them to provide is help with a visa it will cost more than if you're signing up for one of their tours or booking accommodation with them.

Business Visas To get a two-week or one-month (extendable) business visa you must have a business contact in Iran who can sponsor your visit through the Ministry of Foreign Affairs in Tehrān. Business visas are generally valid for three months (ie, you must enter Iran within three months of the date of issue).

Visa Extensions The general rule with any Iranian visa is that you can get one, and sometimes two, extensions of up to two weeks each without too much hassle. If you're lucky, one extension of one month is possible, although there's not much chance of getting a second extension.

Normally you can only apply for an extension two or three days before the original visa is due to expire. If you have a five- or seven-day transit visa, get it extended as soon as you can in a city where you are more likely to be successful and bear in mind that on Thursday afternoon, Friday and public holidays nothing will get done. Visa extensions are normally handled at the provincial police headquarters *(shahrbānī)* or a provincial government office *(shahrdārī)*, though sometimes you must go to a special Foreign Affairs office, or some place with an unpleasant name like the Aliens Bureau (the addresses are listed under Information in the relevant sections). However, while the relevant offices in every provincial capital can, in theory, extend your visa, those in cities that receive relatively few tourists (eg, Semnān, Rasht) will probably refuse to help. It's

better not to waste precious time applying except at the few places known to extend visas happily.

Most people find the visa-extension office in Tehrān more trouble than it's worth because there are so many other non-Iranians hoping for extensions on their paperwork (although we have had a couple of letters from readers reporting success there). However, the best places to try are Tabrīz, Esfahān, Shīrāz, Kermān, Mashhad and Zāhedān, which is just as well because, with the exception of Zāhedān, these are also pleasant places to hang around and wait.

Onward Tickets
These days it's an unlucky traveller who gets asked to show their onward ticket out of Iran either when applying for a visa or when arriving in the country.

Travel Insurance
A travel insurance policy to cover theft, loss and medical problems is a good idea. Some policies offer lower and higher medical-expense options; medical costs in Iran may not be the highest in the world, but you need to check whether a lower-priced policy would allow you to be flown home for treatment if necessary.

How to Extend Your Visa
Here's how to go about getting a visa extension:

- Find the visa extension office and go there when it's open.
- Present yourself neatly and be polite. Women must be wearing a headscarf as they should in the photos they submit with their application form. It's probably best for foreign women travelling on their own to visit the office with a male friend.
- Fill out the visa application form in duplicate. If the visa officer does not speak English, and you need to do it in Farsi, find someone else who can help. It's okay to take the application form away and to return it when it's complete.
- Deposit IR10,000 in whichever branch of Bank Melli you're told and bring back a stamped receipt.
- Provide two photocopies of the front or back pages of your passport (ie, the ones with photos and personal details) and of your original Iranian visa, together with two passport-sized colour photos.
- You may have to supply a cardboard folder. In Tehrān, you may even have to provide two paperclips.
- You may get your visa extension on the spot, a few hours later or even the next day. If you explain that you're in a hurry to see his lovely country, the visa officer may hurry things up. Forget it in Tehrān though.

Make sure you check the small print carefully since some policies exclude 'dangerous activities', which can include scuba diving, motorcycling and even trekking.

You may prefer a policy that pays doctors or hospitals directly rather than expecting you to pay on the spot and claim later. If you know you will have to make a claim, make sure you keep all the necessary documentation. Some policies ask you to make a reverse charges call to a centre in your home country where an immediate assessment of your problem can be made. However, this may not be very easy to organise in Iran.

Make sure that the policy covers Iran *and* adjacent countries if you're travelling on. Some insurers, particularly in the US, still consider the region a 'danger zone' and either exclude it altogether or insist on exorbitant premiums.

Driving Licence & Permits
See Car & Motorcycle in the Land section of the Getting There & Away chapter for information about the paperwork needed if you are bringing a car into Iran.

Student & Youth Cards
The cost of visiting Iran's many tourist attractions can quickly mount up. With a current International Student Identity Card (ISIC) and a smattering of relevant words in Farsi, you can get a 50% discount at many major sites, including the National Museum of Iran, Carpet Museum and Glass & Ceramics Museum (all in Tehrān), the Emām Mosque (in Esfahān) and the old city of Bam. It's worth showing your card wherever you go. However, there are no longer any student discounts at Persepolis.

Vaccination Certificates
In theory if you're travelling to Iran from an area infected with yellow fever you could be asked to show an up-to-date vaccination certificate. In reality, we have never heard of anyone being asked to do so.

Copies
It's wise to photocopy all important documents (passport data page and visa page, credit cards, travel insurance policy, air/bus/train tickets, driving licence etc) before you leave home. Leave one copy with someone at home and keep another with you, separate from the originals. Although travellers cheques are next to worthless in Iran, you may be carrying them if you intend to travel on to Turkey, Pakistan or anywhere else – in which case make sure you've copied their numbers, too.

EMBASSIES & CONSULATES
Iranian Embassies & Consulates
Iranian embassies and consulates abroad include:

Australia (☎ 02-6290 2421, fax 6290 2431) 25 Culgoa Crt, O'Malley, ACT 2606
Azerbaijan (☎ 12-92 64 53, fax 98 07 95) 4 Bouniat Sardaroff St, Baku
Canada (☎ 613-235 4726, fax 232 5712, @ iranemb@salamiran.org) 245 Metcalfe St, Ottawa, Ontario K2P 2K2
France (☎ 01 47 20 30 95, fax 01 40 70 01 57) 4 Ave d'Iena, 75016, Paris
Germany (☎ 030-841 9180) Podbielskiallee 67, D-14195, Berlin
  Consulate General in Frankurt: (☎ 069-560 0070, fax 560 0713) Eichendorffstrasse 54
  Consulate General in Hamburg: (☎ 040-514 4060, fax 511 3511) Bebelalle 18
Ireland (☎ 01-885 881, fax 834 246) 72 Mount Merrion Ave, Blackrock, Dublin
Japan (☎ 3-3446 8011, fax 3446 2383)10-32-3 Chome Minami Aazabu, Minato-ku, Tokyo
Netherlands (☎ 070-354 8483, fax 392 4921) Duinweg 24, 2585 JX, The Hague
New Zealand (☎ 04-862 976, fax 863 065)151 Te Anau Rd, Roseheath, Wellington
Pakistan (☎ 051-822 694, fax 824 839) House 222-238, St 2, G-5/1, Islamabad
  Consulate General in Karachi: (☎ 021-530 638, fax 530 594) 81 Shahrah-i-Iran, Clifton Beach, Karachi
  Consulate General in Lahore: (☎ 042-870 274, fax 870 661) 82-E-1, Gulberg III
  Consulate in Peshawar: (☎ 0521-412 59) corner Park & University Rds
  Consulate in Quetta: (☎ 081-737 25, fax 752 55) 2/33 Hali Rd
Syria (☎ 011-222 6459, fax 222 0997) Al-Mezzeh, Damascus
Turkey (☎ 312-438 2195, fax 440 3429) Tahran Caddesi 10, Kavaklīdere, Ankara

Your Own Embassy

It's important to realise what your own embassy – the embassy of the country of which you are a citizen – can and can't do to help you if you get into trouble. Generally speaking, it won't be much help in emergencies if the trouble you're in is remotely your own fault. Remember that you are bound by the laws of the country you are in. Your embassy will not be sympathetic if you end up in jail after committing a crime locally, even if such actions are legal in your own country.

In genuine emergencies, you might get some assistance, but only if other channels have been exhausted. For example, if you need to get home urgently, a free ticket home is exceedingly unlikely – the embassy would expect you to have insurance. If you have all your money and documents stolen, it might assist with getting a new passport, but a loan for onward travel is out of the question.

Some embassies used to keep letters for travellers or have a small reading room with home newspapers, but these days the mail-holding service has usually been stopped and even newspapers tend to be out of date.

It's a good idea to register with your embassy if you plan to be in Iran for any length of time, especially if you're travelling independently or will be heading off the beaten track.

Consulate General in İstanbul: (☎ 212-513 8230, fax 511 5219) Ankara Caddesi 1/2, Cağaloğlu
Consulate in Erzurum: (☎ 442-218 3876, fax 316 1182) just off Atatürk Bulvarı
UK (☎ 020-7584 8101, fax 7589 4440) 27 Princes Gate, London SW7 IPX
USA (☎ 202-965 4990) The Iranian Interests Section is in the Pakistan embassy, 2209 Wisconsin Ave, NW, Washington, 20007

Embassies & Consulates in Iran

Most countries have embassies in Tehrān. They are generally open from 9 am to noon for visa applications and from 2 to 4 pm for collecting visas, Saturday to Wednesday, although much shorter working hours are also possible. Most embassies of Islamic countries close on Thursday afternoon and all day on Friday, although Western (and

Turkish) embassies may close on Friday and Saturday instead. The following embassies are in Tehrān (area code ☎ 021) unless otherwise stated:

Armenia (☎ 670 4833, fax 670 4657) 1 Ostad Shahriar St, Razī St, Jomhūrī-yé Eslāmī Ave
Australia (☎ 872 4456, fax 872 0484) 13 Eslāmbōlī St, 23rd St
Azerbaijan (☎ 221 5191, fax 228 4929) 10 Mālak St, Sharī'atī Ave
Bahrain (☎ 877 9112) 248 Zoubin St, Āfriqā Hwy
Canada (☎ 873 2623, fax 873 3202) 57 Shahīd Sarafraz St, Motahharī Ave
France (☎ 228 0372) 85 Nofl Lōshātō St
Germany (☎ 391 3329, fax 390 1144) 324 Ferdōsī St
India (☎ 875 5103, fax 875 5973) 46 Mir-emad Ave, corner Ninth St & Dr Beheshtī St
Consulate in Shīrāz: (☎ 071-337 612) Lane No 21, 233 Bāgh-é Eram St
Consulate in Zāhedān: (☎ 0541-222 337) Off Emām Khomeinī St
Japan (☎ 871 3396, fax 886 2515) corner Bucharest & Fifth Sts
Netherlands (☎ 890 6011, fax 875 7052) 36 Jahansouz Alley, Sarbedaran St, Motahharī Ave
New Zealand (☎ 8757052, fax 875 7056) 57 Javad Sarafraz St, Motahharī Ave
Pakistan (☎ 934 332, fax 935 154) Block No 1, Etemādzādeh Ave, Jamshidābād Shomalī St, Dr Hossein Fātemī Ave
Consulate in Mashhad: (☎ 051-29 845) Opposite Melli Park
Consulate in Zāhedān: (☎ 0541-223 389)
Syria (☎ 205 9031, fax 205 9409) Āfriqā Hwy, 19 Iraq St
Turkey (☎ 311 5299, fax 311 7928) 314 Ferdōsī St
Consulate in Orumīyeh: (☎ 0441-228 970) Beheshtī St
Consulate in Tabrīz: (☎ 041-554 3134, fax 553 3190) 156 Khiyabani Sharīatī Cenubi
Turkmenistan (☎ 254 2178, fax 258 0432) 39 Fifth Golestān St, Pāsdārān Ave
UAE (United Arab Emirates) (☎ 878 1333, fax 878 9084) 355 Vahid Dastjerdi Ave
Consulate in Bandar-é Abbās: (☎ 0761-38 262) Nasr Blvd
UK (☎ 675 5011, fax 670 0720) 143 Ferdōsī St
USA The Swiss embassy, 59 West Farzan St, Āfriqā Hwy, has a US Interests Section (☎ 878 2964, fax 877 3265), but while the Swiss embassy may be able to help in an emergency it is not allowed to offer the full range of consular services.

CUSTOMS

These days Iranian officialdom is fairly relaxed about what foreigners take into and out of the country; chances are your bags won't be searched at all.

You are allowed to import, duty-free, 200 cigarettes, 50 cigars or 250g of tobacco and a 'reasonable quantity' of perfume but absolutely no alcohol.

On arrival you will be asked to fill out a fairly standard customs declaration, which you show to the customs officer, who stamps it. You must keep this form until you leave, when another customs officer will probably give it a cursory glance. At international airports your luggage may be inspected, but foreigners are often whisked through customs quickly. At the Iranian borders, you will probably be shown through customs without your bags being inspected. The only things that are likely to attract interest are foreign magazines, audio cassettes, and video cassettes, whether blank or not. Be careful about the books you bring in – anything, however harmless, with a picture of a women showing flesh or hair is liable to be confiscated.

On departure, if you have the customs form that you filled out on arrival you'll be very unlucky if anyone shows much interest in your bags.

Export Restrictions

You may take out anything you legally imported into Iran, and anything you have purchased, including handicrafts other than carpets or rugs up to the value of IR150,000 (hang on to your receipts), as long as they are not for 'the purpose of trade'. Many traders, aware of the restriction of IR150,000, are willing to undervalue goods on receipts issued to foreigners.

You can also take out one or two Persian carpets or rugs (see the Persian Carpets special section at the end of the Facts about Iran chapter), 150g of gold, and 3kg of silver, without gemstones. If you want to exceed these limits, you will need an export permit from the local customs office (in Tehrān, visit the Edareh-yé Koll-é Gomrokāt, or General Office of Customs, near

the Golestān Palace in the southern part of the city).

Officially you need permission to export anything 'antique' (ie, more than 50 years old), including handicrafts, gemstones, coins and manuscripts. (The authorities are particularly sensitive about the export of old or valuable Qurans.) Unfortunately the staff are not trained in antique identification, so there is always a slight risk that anything vaguely 'antique' looking could be confiscated.

Until recently you were supposed to get a permit from the Ministry of Culture & Islamic Guidance before exporting a musical instrument. Although this regulation has now been relaxed, a question mark still hovers over the export of old *tars* (stringed instruments). If you are worried that an expensive item might be confiscated, have a word with the customs office before buying. Hand baggage is rarely searched on departure.

In 2000 the US embargo on the import of Iranian goods was lifted for carpets, caviar and pistachios. It remains in force for other items and you should consult US customs authorities before leaving home to check what can and cannot be imported.

Currency Declaration

Despite a notice at all the international borders asking you to declare your money to the Bank Melli, the officials will only be interested if you are importing more than US$1000. Marginally over that amount, and they'll probably wave you away.

Duty-Free Zones

The islands of Kīsh and Qeshm, and the port of Chābahār, are duty-free zones. Before buying any souvenirs or electronic goods at these places, make inquiries about customs regulations for bringing them back to mainland Iran. The customs rules are complicated and the procedures an absolute nightmare. It's probably best to avoid buying anything duty-free at these places.

MONEY
Currency

Although the official unit of currency in Iran is the Iranian rial, Iranians usually talk in terms of *tōmāns*, a unit equal to 10 rials. (In writing, prices are usually expressed in rials.) Since people usually omit to say what unit of currency they're talking about, you need to make absolutely sure whether you're both talking rials or tōmāns before agreeing to a price. After a while you will get to know the approximate price of everyday items and will be able to assess whether prices are being given in rials or tōmāns. The exceptions are the few goods such as handicrafts and souvenirs where prices can vary enormously. When hailing an empty taxi, a '200' fare in rials means it's a shared taxi, while a '200' fare in tōmāns means it's private. (See the boxed text 'Rials or Tōmāns?' for more details.) Throughout this book we use the abbreviation 'IR' to indicate Iranian rials.

Although there are coins for IR1, IR2, IR5, IR10, IR20, IR50, IR100 and IR250, only the latter three denominations are at all common. Indeed, so rare are IR1 coins (no longer minted) that they are considered lucky despite being utterly worthless. There are notes for IR100, IR200, IR500, IR1000, IR2000, IR5000 and IR10,000. Hang onto filthy IR100, IR200 and IR500 notes to pay shared-taxi fares. Most of the time no-one seems to care what state rial notes are in, then out of the blue someone will reject one on the grounds that it has a tiny tear or is too grubby.

Banknotes are easy to read, as the numbers and names are printed in Farsi and English. However, coins are only marked in Farsi and Arabic numerals.

Some mid-range and top-end hotels continue to quote their prices in US dollars, but these days they're usually happy to accept the equivalent amount in rials.

Exchange Rates

Although the Central Bank continues to publish 'official exchange rates', since the demise of the black market (see the Black Market entry later) these are only used by importers/exporters. The rates listed in the table are the 'free market' (unofficial) rates, offered by everyone from banks to street moneychangers. There is no point in bringing any currencies other than US dollars, UK pounds or deutschmarks with you. In-

Rials or Tōmāns?

No sooner have you crossed the Iranian border than you will come up against the idiosyncratic local practice of talking about prices in *tōmāns* even though the currency is denominated in rials. While most travellers eventually get used to this, at first it is completely bamboozling. One tōmān is worth 10 rials, so it's a bit like shopkeepers in Australia or the US asking for 10 cents whenever they wanted $1, or as if their British equivalents were to ask for 10 pence whenever they wanted UK£1.

To make matters worse, the *bazaaris*, the shopkeepers in the bazaar, sometimes say one tōmān as shorthand for IR100 or even IR1000. Forget it! You'll never understand them unless you get them to show you the rial price on a calculator.

deed, you are strongly advised to bring only US dollars. Unofficial exchange rates are published every day in the English-language press.

country	unit		rial
Germany	DM1	=	IR3490
UK	UK£1	=	IR11,200
USA	US$1	=	IR7980

Surplus rials can be changed back into foreign currency at a major bank, but only if you can show the original exchange receipt and have the time to be very persistent. Officially, you are not allowed to take more than IR200,000 out of the country.

Exchanging Money

For some time to come it will be best to think of Iran as a purely cash economy. It cannot be emphasised strongly enough that if you want to make life easy for yourself you will only use US dollars cash in Iran. Travellers cheques can only be exchanged in big cities and then with difficulty, delay and considerable cost; American Express cheques can *never* be cashed. MasterCard cannot be used, nor can Visa, American Express or Diners Club (with the rare exception of a few well-connected carpet dealers).

Because changing money is such an iffy business, you're advised to do all your financial transactions in the big towns most accustomed to travellers (Tehrān, Esfahān, Shīrāz and Tabrīz) even though it means carrying big wads of rials round with you most of the time.

Most of the top hotels have money-changing facilities, but usually just for their guests.

Cash Given the government's distaste for all things American, it is ironic that the major currency for all foreign trade is the mighty US greenback. Ideally, you should bring nothing with you but US dollars in cash; a few banks and moneychangers will accept UK pounds and deutschmarks, but you'll probably end up wasting a lot of time trying to persuade them to do so.

Your US dollar bills should be unmarked and undamaged in any way and should be the new-style notes printed since 1995 with the president's head very large in the centre. Ideally you should bring only denominations of US$100; you'll get a slightly less favourable exchange rate for smaller notes. If you bring deutschmarks, make sure they're DM100 bills.

There is a thriving business in UAE dirhams along the Persian Gulf coast, and in the north there is a small trade in Russian roubles. Turkish lira are treated with the utmost scorn everywhere except close to the Turkish border; ditto for the Afghan and Pakistani currencies. There is a small trade in Iranian currency in most neighbouring countries, especially in the Laleli district of Istanbul.

Travellers Cheques Don't bother bringing travellers cheques of any denomination or currency to Iran. The only bank that regularly claims to welcome travellers cheques is Bank Melli, but it sometimes wants 10% or even US$10 *per cheque* as commission. You will also face a long wait while the paperwork is completed. When asked how long he would take to change a travellers cheque, the cashier at Bank Melli in Ferdōsī St, Tehrān said 'two or three months'! Even

allowing for faulty English that implies a very long wait...

The US trade embargo against Iran means that you can't cash American Express travellers cheques or any other cheques issued by an American bank.

ATMs Although Iran has a functioning network of ATMs (cashpoint machines), they can only be used with locally issued bank cards. Theoretically this means that Iran could soon be linked up electronically to the banks of the rest of the world. Don't hold your breath though.

Credit Cards Up until 2002, an increasing number of mid-range hotels (and all top-end places) were accepting MasterCard but *not* Visa and certainly not American Express. Even if your MasterCard was issued in the US, it may still have been useless because of the US trade embargo.

However, the government has banned the use of MasterCard so you must now carry your spending money in cash.

This may not be a bad thing; getting authority from the relevant credit-card office used to take up to 30 minutes. Waiting for a cash advance to be authorised also involved a delay or up to one or two hours. A commission of 5% was also sometimes charged, both for cash advances and for purchases.

International Transfers It is possible to have money transferred from overseas to a bank in Iran. However, this is likely to take anything from three days to two weeks. If possible, have the money sent through a branch of an Iranian bank. Otherwise see what can be worked out through a bank in Tehrān, with a moneychanger or with your tour operator.

Most major Iranian banks have branches in Europe (mainly in the UK, France and Germany), but they are not represented in the USA or Australasia.

Banks Although it sometimes seems as if every fourth building in Iran is a bank, only a very few are interested in changing money and then usually only US dollars cash. In every provincial capital, you can change money at the central branch of the Bank Melli. In larger cities you may also be able to change money at the central branches of the other major banks: Bank Mellat, Bank Tejarat, Bank Sepah and Bank Saderat. Banks that offer foreign-exchange facilities nearly always have the sign 'Exchange' or 'Foreign Exchange' displayed in English near the entrance. At these banks there should be someone who speaks English. You will need to take your passport with you when changing money in a bank.

Most banks are open between 8 am and 4 pm Saturday to Wednesday, and between 8 am and noon on Thursday, although banks along the Persian Gulf coast usually close for the afternoon and reopen in the early evening year-round. Bank branches inside hotels keep their own peculiar hours, and airport banks open whenever international flights arrive or depart. Banks at the Iranian borders are usually open for the same hours as the border.

To add to all their other delaying tactics, banks are sometimes reluctant to change money before 10.30 am when the new exchange rate arrives from their head office.

Black Market Until 2000, Iran had a flourishing black market. However, since the government permitted banks to offer the free-market exchange rates, this has effectively died. These days you will get the same exchange rate (give or take the odd 10 rials) whether you change your money in a bank, at a hotel, in an exchange office or with a street moneychanger.

Moneychangers Easily the quickest way to change cash is with an official money exchange office. These can be found in several major cities, including Tehrān – look for small shops with the words 'Currency' or 'Exchange' in English. These offices mainly want US dollars, but may accept British pounds or deutschmarks as well.

However much of a hurry you're in, changing money in an exchange shop is much more sensible than doing so with a street moneychanger. You're much less likely to get ripped off because you know where to find the office again and they won't want a visit from the police if you complain.

Even though it means carrying around a fair wad of rials, try and change enough money at one exchange office to last a week or so because it may be a while until you come across another one. If you can't find an official money-exchange office, ask at a souvenir or carpet shop in the local bazaar; someone there may be able to help you, or find someone who can. Otherwise, try your hotel reception.

Security

In general, Iran is a very safe country to travel in, with a very low level of theft and robbery. However, the number of instances of bag-snatching etc is starting to rise and you would be wise to take the same sort of security precautions that you would elsewhere. Carry most of your money in a moneybelt under your clothes, and consider keeping perhaps one US$100 bill hidden in a secret pocket sewn into your clothes. Never leave money or valuables in your hotel room; give them to the reception for safe keeping.

For more information on possible problems, see Dangers & Annoyances later in this chapter.

Costs

At the budget end of the market, Iran is a very cheap country to travel in, especially as regards food and transport. You might get by on IR80,000 a day if you're prepared to stay in *mosāferkhūnehs* (cheap lodging houses), live on sandwiches and use only overland transport. However, unless you thrive on discomfort, it would be better to work on a budget of around IR120,000 a day. This is enough for decent budget accommodation (and the occasional splurge on a decent middle-range place), one good cooked meal every day, first-class transport by bus and shared taxi, chartered taxis around town (and sometimes in the countryside) and visits to all the important tourist attractions. On IR150,000 a day you could add in the cost of internal flights and a few more decent meals and mid-range hotels. If you want to stay in top-end hotels you'll be looking at more like IR400,000 a day.

On a tight budget your biggest single cost is likely to be the admission fees for tourist attractions; unless you can get a student card (see Visas & Documents earlier in this chapter), you may be forced to rationalise these visits. Solo travellers may also find accommodation eats into their budget because single rooms are few and far between. Finding someone to share with would certainly save you money, but unfortunately until tourism picks up, the only places you're likely to bump into other solo travellers are along the main travellers' route from Turkey to Pakistan.

Staying in cheap accommodation is a good way to save money, but paying an extra IR10,000/15,000 for a single/double will often add considerably to your comfort level. Sleeping on buses is not recommended as a way of economising, but taking a sleeper on an overnight train is certainly worth considering.

Costs for most things are higher in Tehrān, but easily the most expensive place in Iran is Kīsh Island, the luxury, duty-free port and holiday centre in the Persian Gulf. Iranian transport costs are wonderfully low. Indeed, two of the biggest bargains are internal air fares and taxi fares. Take advantage of them while you can.

Dual Pricing One controversial aspect of travelling in Iran is the dual-pricing system for foreigners and locals. Foreigners are charged 10 times as much as locals to enter tourist attractions, which can mean they are not much cheaper to visit than attractions at home. The only way to get around this is to produce a student card (see Visas & Documents earlier in this chapter).

All mid-range and top-end hotels, plus those at the top of the budget range, are also allowed to charge foreigners much higher prices than locals and to ask for US dollars. Unlike entrance fees, you can sometimes negotiate a discount on room rates, although it's very rare that you'll end up paying the same as an Iranian. As long as you're happy to stay in mosāferkhūnehs this isn't much of a problem, but if you want to stay in reasonable hotels and are travelling alone it can mean you end up paying more for indifferent accommodation than you would in Turkey and much, much more than you would pay in Pakistan.

Some travellers get very upset about dual pricing, but before launching into a diatribe about how unfair it is, it's worth remembering that foreigners often earn 10 times as much as Iranians as well.

All international air and ferry tickets bought by foreigners in Iran must be paid for in US dollars. However, at the time of writing you could still pay the same price as Iranians for internal flights, and in rials, too. But, since a new fuel tax was recently introduced to try and make foreign drivers pay more than locals for petrol, it doesn't look as if dual pricing of internal flights can be far away.

Tipping & Bargaining

Tipping is not a big deal in Iran, although you will be expected to leave a gratuity of about 10% if you eat in decent restaurants. This is the case even when 'service' is already included in the bill. It is also normal to offer a small tip or present to anyone who guides you or opens a building that is normally closed. If your offer is initially refused, you should persist in making it three times before giving up (see the boxed text 'Ta'arof' in the Facts About Iran chapter for more information on this important Iranian custom).

As elsewhere in the Middle East, bargaining is a way of life in Iran. However, for a first-time visitor it can be hard to know when it's appropriate to bargain and when it isn't. As a rough guide, you can tell whether the price of an item is negotiable by whether or not it has a price label. In the bazaar, virtually all prices are negotiable, whereas in shops people may think you very strange if you start bargaining. Even if there is no listed price, you may find that everywhere in town charges almost exactly the same price anyway.

Fares in private taxis are always negotiable, although the prices for other forms of transport (including shared taxis) are set by the government. Rates in mid-range hotels and mosāferkhūnehs are open to negotiation, although top-end hotels won't normally budge. Restaurant prices are fixed, but food in bazaars (but not shops) is sometimes negotiable. Everything else is negotiable, particularly handicrafts. It's impossible to lay down hard-and-fast rules about bargaining – in one place the first price asked may be 50% above the going rate, in another 500%, while in a third it may be exactly the same as the locals pay. If you always assume that you are being cheated, you will probably end up offending people, but if you always accept the first price you are offered you will surely be taken for a ride more than once.

Once you have agreed on a price, you can't change it; if, for example, you don't fix a price at the outset when chartering a taxi, it is too late to complain about it later. The only sure way to avoid getting done is to know what the price should be, and unfortunately to acquire this knowledge you probably have to spend longer in Iran than your visa will allow. In any case, the 'correct' price can vary from place to place.

Don't get too worried about all the constant bargaining – it usually turns out that you've been arguing frantically over the rial equivalent of US$0.20.

POST & COMMUNICATIONS

Post and telephone offices are often combined in smaller towns, while in larger cities they're separated. These offices are rarely marked in English, but are fairly obvious from the post boxes or telephone booths nearby.

Postal Rates

Postage is very cheap. The cost of sending an airmail postcard to Europe, North America and Australasia is IR500. The cost for a normal-sized letter by airmail to anywhere outside Iran should be IR1500, but be careful if you buy the pretty letter-cards you see on sale at tourist attractions as they cost IR4250 to mail.

Sending Mail

The international postal service is reliable and reasonably swift. Postcards sent by air usually reach Europe in four or five days, or in four weeks if they're sent by sea. In contrast, the domestic postal service is reliable but slow, and sending a letter from Iran to the other side of the world often takes no longer than getting it from one part of Iran to another.

It is not safe to send cash through the post. If you're sending mail to a complicated address or to somewhere remote, try to get someone to write the address in Farsi on the envelope. Post boxes are few and far between, except outside post offices.

Some Iranian stamps are very colourful so you may want to leave plenty of space on your envelope or postcard for them. Post office clerks are usually happy to let foreigners rummage through the latest issues, or you can buy some of the collectors' items at upwards of twice the face value.

Parcel Post Although the parcel post is also pretty reliable, sending a parcel out of Iran is an exercise in form shuffling, guaranteed to take twice as long as you expect. Take your unwrapped package to the parcel post counter *(daftar-é amānāt-é postī)* at the head post office *(postkhūneh-yé markazī)* in the provincial capital. There it will be checked, packaged and signed for in triplicate. The sections on Customs (earlier in this chapter) and Shopping (later) list the current customs regulations for some handicrafts and carpets, although the customs officer on duty at the head post office generally has discretion over what can be posted abroad. You may be asked to show your passport so don't forget to take it with you.

Receiving Mail

You can have mail, including parcels, sent to you care of the local head post office anywhere in Iran, although the service is very little used, even in Tehrān. Ask friends to write your name very clearly and to underline your surname. Since most people fronting up at the poste restante counter *(daftar-é post restānt)* are foreigners, mail is filed according to the English alphabet. Always ask the clerk to check under the initials of your first name, surname and title; bearers of multi-barrelled surnames are in for a lot of fun. Poste restante mail appears to be held almost indefinitely, even if you ask to have it forwarded. Take your passport with you when you go to check your mail. If a letter has arrived, you may be asked to pay a nominal collection fee.

Telephone

Except in very remote parts of the country, making telephone calls is easy: You should be able to get a line through to your home country in less than 30 minutes (and often within a few seconds), from most hotels and private homes, as well as from telephone or post offices. However, international calls are not cheap and you should, perhaps, be a little careful what you say.

Increasingly you can use a *kard telefon* (telephone card) to make calls from public phone boxes in big cities. This is much easier than trying to find the right number of appropriately sized coins for local calls. The cards are usually on sale wherever there are lines of phone boxes for IR10,000 each. You may be able to find the right coins for the phone in shops near the phones, too.

Calls within Iran Most public telephone boxes are only good for local calls. They were built aeons ago and still use IR50 coins (for one or three minutes, depending on the sort of phone) even though these are almost

Telephone Turmoil

For the last couple of years Iran has been updating its telephone system in line with other countries. In Tehrān in particular this means that many numbers now have seven digits. However, it's no good hoping for consistency; even in Tehrān a company may still have a seven-digit phone number and a six-digit fax number; elsewhere the number of digits in any given number remains pretty random.

This is an ongoing process. In an ideal world it would be possible to say 'as of such-and-such a date, all numbers in city X will change to Y'. Unfortunately, even the locals are lucky if they get more than a few weeks notice of a change.

impossible to find. Local calls are so cheap, however, that your hotel will probably let you make a few calls free of charge. Airports and major bus stations usually have at least one public telephone permitting free local calls.

Otherwise, you can use private payphones, available at most hotels and at some shops. These cost IR50 for three minutes and only accept the copper variety of the IR50 coin. Place the coin in the slot and, when the call is answered, push the button and your coin will disappear.

Calls within Iran can be made from private homes, hotels (for an extra charge), some telephones at airports and bus stations, or outside most post or telephone offices. Although charges are low, you'll need a large pocketful of IR50 or IR100 coins, or a telephone card, to talk for more than a minute or two. You can also book internal calls at telephone offices; you give the number to the receptionist and wait to be directed to a booth, hopefully after just a few minutes. From smaller villages, it's often difficult to make a call at busy times.

In this book, telephone area codes are listed under the place name, or included as a prefix to the telephone numbers elsewhere in the text.

International Calls from Iran You can make international calls at a telephone office (*markaz-é telefon* or *edāre-yé koll-yé mokhābarāt*) in any city or town, though it is easiest from places like Tehrān, Tabrīz, Esfahān or Shīrāz. Long-distance calls can also be made from most hotels and some mosāferkhūnehs. Always check how much commission will be charged, but it's often easier to use a hotel phone rather than have to wait at the telephone office.

For international calls, you will be charged for a minimum period of three minutes plus each subsequent minute or part thereof. The cost per minute (with a minimum of three minutes) is IR9600 to Europe or Australia, and IR13,500 to the USA.

If there is no connection, there should be no charge, although one irritated reader wrote to complain of being made to pay even though their call had not gone through.

You can't make a reverse-charge call to or from Iran.

International Calls to Iran The international dialling code for Iran is ☎ 098.

Telegraph

You can send telegrams out of Iran in English or within Iran in Farsi from almost all main telephone offices and the occasional special telegraph office *(telegrāfkhūneh)*. This is far cheaper than sending a fax if you don't need to fill a full A4 page. Charges to most Western countries are around IR150 a word with a minimum of seven words. International telegrams out of Iran rarely take more than a couple of working days to get through, and staff seem to try hard. One traveller reported that the telegraph office at Emām Khomeinī Square in Tehrān 'even called my hotel because they were not sure of the French spelling'!

Fax

You can usually send faxes from the main post and telephone office in the provincial capital, from many mid-range and top-end hotels, and from some budget hotels.

It's normally cheapest to use the post or telephone office, but easier to use your hotel. From the post office in Emām Khomeinī Square in Tehrān, it costs IR15,000 rials per A4 page to the UK, Europe and Australia, and IR18,000 to North America.

Email & Internet Access

Internet cafes have started to put in an appearance in Iran, and most big towns with a tourist trade now have either at least one dedicated Internet cafe or shops/hotels that will let travellers use their computers to send emails. We have included the addresses of Internet cafes that were open at the time of research, but by the time you read this it is likely that more will have opened. Check out www.netcafes.com for a complete list of Iranian Internet cafes.

If you plan to carry a portable computer, remember that the power supply can be erratic, which could damage your equipment. It's worth investing in a universal AC adaptor, which will enable you to plug it in anywhere without frying the innards.

Also, your PC-card modem may or may not work once you leave your home country – you won't know for sure until you try. The safest option is to buy a reputable 'global' modem before you leave home, or buy a local PC-card modem if you're spending an extended time in Iran. You may also find that the telephone sockets are different from the ones you're used to, so ensure that you have at least a US RJ-11 telephone adaptor that works with your modem. You can almost always find an adaptor that will convert from RJ-11 to the local variety. Check www .teleadapt.com or www.warrior.com for more information on travelling with a portable computer.

INTERNET RESOURCES

The World Wide Web is a rich resource for travellers. You can research your trip, hunt down bargain air fares, book hotels, check on weather conditions or chat with locals and other travellers about the best places to visit (or avoid!). At the Lonely Planet Web site (www.lonelyplanet.com) you'll find succinct summaries on travelling to most places on earth, postcards from other travellers and the Thorn Tree bulletin board, where you can ask questions before you go or dispense advice when you get back. You can also find travel news, while the subWWWay section links you to the most useful travel resources elsewhere on the Web.

Of Iran's many Internet providers, Neda (www.neda.net) is one of the most popular. Listed here are some Iran-specific Web sites:

Ankaboot Excellent search engine for topics ranging from Iranian history to arts and architecture. www.ankaboot.com

Cultural Heritage Foundation Provides news on archaeological excavations, restoration of monuments etc. www.chf-iran.com

Iran Export All the business advice you may need. www.iran-export.com

Iran Mania Excellent search engine for topics ranging from Iranian history to arts and architecture. www.iranmania.com

Iran Touring & Tourism Organisation Gives lots of background information on Iran together with a listing of ITTO hotels.
www.itto.org

Net Iran Colourful and informative Iranian Government site lists embassy contact details, customs rules etc.
www.netiran.com

Payvand Excellent links to permanent sites on Iran and a helpful travel section.
www.payvand.com

Salam Iran A site created by the Iranian embassy in Ottawa. Useful for visa information (there's even a visa application form on the site).
www.salamiran.org

Tehrān Times Online edition of this English-language daily paper together with an archive.
www.tehrantimes.com

BOOKS

Most books are published in different editions by different publishers in different countries. As a result, a book might be a hardcover rarity in one country while it's readily available in paperback in another. Fortunately, bookshops and libraries search by title or author, so your local bookshop or library should be able to advise you on the availability of any of the books listed in this section.

You should be particularly careful about what books you take into Iran, as anything with a hint of immorality on the cover or in the title, anything disrespectful to the government or, of course, anything written by Salman Rushdie is likely to be confiscated. You can pick up old novels in French, English and German from a couple of Tehrān bookstalls, but generally you should bring all your own reading material and lots of it – the social scene in Iran is not exactly riveting.

Lonely Planet

Lonely Planet covers the region extensively. We have guides to *Turkey*; *Pakistan*; *Central Asia*; *Georgia, Armenia & Azerbaijan*; *Bahrain, Kuwait & Qatar*; and *Oman & the UAE*. For broader coverage, pick up *Middle East* (which covers the Gulf States, plus Egypt, Iran, Iraq, Israel and the Palestinian Territories, Jordan, Lebanon, Libya, Syria, Turkey and Yemen) or *İstan-*

bul to Kathmandu which covers this classic travel route via Iran.

Lonely Planet also publishes a *Farsi phrasebook*, and *Black on Black: Iran Revisited* by AM Briongos, a travel story about a Spanish woman's return to visit friends in the country where she had studied before the Revolution.

Guidebooks

Other than this one, there are very few modern guidebooks about Iran. If you browse in Iranian bookshops, you may be able to pick up a few very outdated but fascinating guidebooks written before the Islamic Revolution.

A Travel Guide to Iran by MT Faramarzi. Widely available in Iran, this locally produced guidebook shamelessly lifts whole chunks of Lonely Planet word for word, but the 'Millennium Edition' also contains some interesting background information and mildly useful maps.

Travel

Given the problems faced by women travelling in Iran, it's interesting how many travel books about the country have been written by women.

Out of Iran by Sousan Azadi. This is the revealing, and very frightening, autobiography of a member of the Westernised Iranian elite who stayed on after 1979, resolutely refusing to give up the pleasures of life proscribed under the Islamic Republic. The story closes with her escape from Iran in 1982, in the untrustworthy hands of Kurdish smugglers.

Journeys in Persia and Kurdistan by Isabella Bird. Written in 1889 and hard to get hold of, this is a vivid account, taken from her letters, of the adventures of one of those crazy English female travellers of the turn of last century.

The Road to Oxiana by Robert Byron. Widely acknowledged as one of the greatest travel books ever, this is a vividly observed and often hilarious diary of a slow passage from England to the River Oxus (the Amu Darya) in north-west Afghanistan via Iran. Although Byron has a scholarly preoccupation with Islamic architecture, the book remains a classic travel book for its lively descriptive prose and for its often biting sketches of contacts with local people and encounters with disobliging officials.

Travels in Persia 1673-1677 by Sir John Chardin. Extremely interesting for the historical period it describes, this book is available at the bookshop in the Lāleh Hotel in Tehrān.

Persia and the Persian Question by GN Curzon. This two-volume opus is characteristically scathing about all things Persian. (Curzon is probably most famous for saying: 'My name is George Nathaniel Curzon. I am a most superior person.') A historical work as well as a travel book, the original is hard to come by, but an abridged reprint, *Curzon's Persia*, skips the heavier historical chapters.

Danziger's Travels: Beyond Forbidden Frontiers by Nick Danziger. A true modern adventurer, Danziger travelled through Turkey, Iran, Afghanistan, Pakistan and China to Hong Kong, without much regard for tiresome formalities like visas or entry and exit stamps. It is loaded with enough hair-raising adventures to make all but the most seasoned traveller feel inadequate.

Daughter of Persia by Sattareh Farman Farmaian. This is the life story of the daughter of one of the last scions of the Qajar dynasty; an interesting contrast to Sousan Azadi's account of the same period.

Through Persia in Disguise by Sarah Hobson. Published in 1973, this intriguing book describes the author's journey through Iran disguised, for protection, as a boy. It's a sobering reminder that Iranian religious zeal didn't suddenly kick-in in 1979.

A Short Walk in the Hindu Kush by Eric Newby. One of those gloriously eccentric travel books that could only have been written by an Englishman, it follows the author and friend's haphazard 1950s jaunt from England to the Hindu Kush by way of Turkey and Iran.

Blind White Fish in Persia by Anthony Smith. Story of four Oxford University students who travelled to Iran in 1950 to study the *qanats* around Kermān.

Honeymoon in Purdah by Alison Wearing. Excellent account of a recent journey through Iran, written by a young women with a great ear for dialogue and the witty story.

History, Archaeology & Politics

Persia: History and Heritage by J Boyle. This is the best book to buy for an overview of Iranian history, carpets, literature, painting, architecture, pottery and so on.

Persia, *A Heritage of Persia* and *The Golden Age of Persia* by Richard Frye. These were three of the best books on the history and culture of Iran published before the Revolution.

Iran: From the Earliest Times to the Islamic Conquest by R Ghirshman. Although written in 1954, this history is still the easiest to read and includes plenty of pictures to help you make sense of the various archaeological sites. You can buy it at the book kiosk on Enqelāb Ave, near the junction with Valiasr Ave, Tehrān.

The Longest War – The Iran-Iraq Military Conflict by Dilip Hiro. A harrowing, comprehensive, if a little dense, chronology of the conflict that cost more than a million lives.

Shah of Shahs by Ryszard Kapuscinski. This is one of the best books on modern Iran, covering the period from the fall of Mossadeq through to the early days of the Islamic Revolution. It is a highly readable account of the excesses of the Shāh and the fear felt by ordinary Iranians in face of the SAVAK secret police.

Persia: An Archaeological Guide by Sylvia Matheson. Most of the information in this scholarly but readable companion to every significant ancient ruin in Iran is still valid, though some of the travel details are inevitably outdated and it only covers sites up to the Seljuk era.

A List of the Historical Sites and Ancient Monuments of Iran by Nosratollah Meshkati. Although as dry as it sounds, this exhaustive work summarises every place worth visiting. It is for the archaeological enthusiast, rather than the average tourist.

Iran After the Revolution: Crisis of an Islamic State by Saeed Rahnema & Sohrab Behdad. Through a number of essays by prominent Muslims and Islamists, this book outlines the achievements (or lack of them) of Iranian governments since the Islamic Revolution.

Behind Iranian Lines and *Lifting the Veil* by John Simpson. Although hard to get hold of, these books by a veteran BBC journalist offer two of the best accounts of life after the Islamic Revolution. Simpson shared Khomeinī's flight from Paris to Tehrān in 1979 and took full advantage of an invitation to return in 1987.

Religion

Among the Believers by VS Naipaul. Naipaul's religious travel book contains some very funny anecdotes about Iran.

Islam: Ideology and the Way of Life Afzalur Rahman. Easy to read and well set out, this is a useful guide for any non-Muslim wanting to learn more about Islam.

Society & Culture

Culture Shock by Maria O'Shea. This book offers a thorough look at how life is lived in modern Iran and is particularly useful if you will be travelling alone or for an extended period.

Censored!

Two books written since the Revolution have resulted in uproar. Best known is *The Satanic Verses*, Salman Rushdie's sprawling novel, which was supposed to have had a club of readers who hadn't managed to get past page 15 before furious Islamic fundamentalists seized upon it and turned it into one of the most notorious books every written. Famously, Āyatollāh Khomeinī slapped a *fatwa* (legally binding edict) for blasphemy on Rushdie in 1989. The author was forced to go into hiding, while publishers and translators worldwide faced death threats which were sometimes acted on; in just one incident in Turkey, 37 people were burned to death in a hotel where the man responsible for the Turkish translation of the book was staying. Although President Khatamī said in 1998 that the Iranian government would not send anyone to kill Rushdie, the incident soured relations between Britain and Iran for more than a decade. You'd be well advised to avoid all reference to it.

The second most hated book in Iran is Betty Mahmoody's *Not Without My Daughter*, the supposedly true story of how an American mother journeyed to Tehrān with her Westernised husband and child, only to have him metamorphose into a wife-beating monster who locked her up and refused to let her return home. The problem with this book is the unrelentingly grim picture it presents of Iran and the Iranians ('Have *you* ever seen Iranians eating cockroaches?' I was asked, to which the answer was of course no). Interestingly, the book was co-authored with William Hoffer, whose previous efforts had included the equally Middle East-hating *Midnight Express*. No matter – the book was a runaway bestseller, being reprinted four times in just one year.

Cookbooks

A Taste of Persia by Najmieh K Batmanglij. A hundred-odd Iranian recipes adapted for modern kitchens.

The Art of Persian Cooking Forough Hekmat. The definitive book about Iranian cuisine (including how to make your own kebabs when you get home), this is available at the Gulestan Bookshop in Tehrān.

Poetry

All three of these books are available at the bookshop at Hāfez's tomb in Shīrāz.

Fifty Poems of Chemsed Din Mohammed Hafiz by Hāfez. This definitive work of the renowned Shīrāzī poet includes Farsi poems translated into English, German and French.

Rubaïyat of Omar Khayyam by Omar Khayyām. This volume includes poems translated into English, French and Arabic.

Sadi's Gulistan or Flower Garden by James Ross. This is the most renowned collection of poems by the famous Shīrāzī poet Sa'dī translated into English.

Art, Architecture & Handicrafts

Persian Glass by Shinji Fukai. Everything you need to know about Iranian glassware.

Introducing Persian Architecture by Arthur Upham Pope. This short illustrated book is a concise introduction to Iranian architecture up to the end of the Safavid period. It is widely available in Iranian museum bookshops.

Novels

Whirlwind by James Clavell. This novel includes some historical information, but although it makes a gripping read, the mood is often gloomy.

The Last Migration by Vincent Cronin. This novel looks at the life of some of Iran's nomads as they struggle to resist the pressure to settle.

For novels written by Iranian authors, see Literature, in the Arts of Iran special section in the Facts About Iran chapter.

FILMS

Probably the most famous film about Iran that has been made since the Revolution is *Not Without My Daughter*, the dramatised version of the book of the same name. If the book didn't go down well in Iran, you can imagine how this Hollywoodisation of it was viewed (see the boxed text 'Censored!' for more information).

CD-ROMS

One widely available CD-Rom is *Irania – Glory of the Past: 3rd Millennium BC to 7th*

Century AD, which has fantastic graphics and informative commentary on places like Choqā Zanbīl. It is produced by Vista Ara, Multimedia Cultural Institute in Tehrān (e vistaara@dpi.nit.ir) and would make an excellent souvenir.

NEWSPAPERS & MAGAZINES

Of the 70 newspapers published every day in Iran, four are in English: the *Tehrān Times*, *Iran Daily*, *Iran News* and *Kayhan International*. If you can ignore their extreme bias against the US and Israel, all contain some interesting news articles from around the world culled from reputable journalism agencies, as well as some dry-as-dust stuff about Iranian politics. The *Iran Daily* includes a Farsi Press Watch section, which lets you find out what the Iranian papers are saying. The classified ads are also very useful, especially if you'll be staying a while.

All four newspapers are readily available in Tehrān, although you can usually pick up copies (perhaps a few days old) at bookstalls in big towns around the country, too.

Several good English-language magazines have been produced over the years, but at the time of writing they all seemed to have folded. It's well worth looking out for back issues of *Silk Road* in particular, a glossy magazine about tourism with good and detailed articles about the main tourist sites.

In Tehrān and occasionally elsewhere, you can pick up copies of *Time* (IR23,000) and *Newsweek* (IR20,000). They're worth buying just for the pictures of the American president's wife with her neckline blacked out and Wimbledon tennis stars with their legs blacked out!

RADIO & TV

All official Iranian radio and television stations are controlled by the state and will be for a long time to come. However, many wealthier Iranians have access to satellite television, making the censorship rather pointless.

Radio

Most radio stations are based in Tehrān and relayed to each province, although many provinces also have their own stations broadcasting in minority languages such as Kurdish, Lors, Arabic and Āzārī. In 1997, former president Rafsanjānī inaugurated a Youth Radio Network to 'help strengthen the educational infrastructure of Iran's youth', so you can be sure that heavy metal and rap music won't feature too much.

The BBC World Service, most European international radio services and Voice of America can be picked up in most parts of the country. Many Iranians listen to the BBC, rightly distrustful of the state media. Short-wave radios have been found in the most unlikely places, from the lowliest Afghan refugee's hovel to the bedside of the late Āyatollāh Khomeinī, who was reportedly an avid follower of the BBC Persian Service.

TV

There are five television channels in Iran – imaginatively known as Channels 1, 2, 3, 4 and 5. They are all based in Tehrān, though a few programs emanate from some of the provinces. The few foreign programs screened are wholesome fare, like the adventures of *Skippy The Bush Kangaroo*, or *The Little House on the Prairie*, all badly dubbed into Farsi; *Mr Bean* has a very big following in Iran. Over religious holidays, all the channels show nothing but religious programs.

At around 11 pm, on Channel 4, there is a 15-minute news bulletin in English, but it's of limited interest as it concentrates mainly on the minutiae of presidential tours etc.

In a very few upmarket hotels you will be able to see satellite TV (even occasionally CNN). Iranians who want to buy a satellite dish are supposed to make a special application to the relevant ministry, and permits are usually only granted to foreigners or Iranians who have already lived in the West and experienced its 'decadence', rendering them unlikely to be corrupted further. Confiscating illegal satellite dishes in Tehrān is big business – but then so is installing them!

PHOTOGRAPHY & VIDEO
Film & Equipment

Most towns in Iran have at least one photographic shop for film and/or development, although the range of film and camera equipment available is limited (except in Tehrān and Mashhad). Kodak, Agfa and Fuji are the most commonly available film brands, with the average price for a roll of 24 exposures (print film) IR12,500; Kodak slide film, including processing, costs around IR30,000. Always check the 'best before' date on the side of the box in case it has been stored for ages in less than ideal conditions. Ideally you should try and bring as much equipment and film as you are likely to need. Normal camera batteries are widely available, but lithium batteries will be much harder to track down.

All over Iran there are small backroom photographers, recognisable by the faded samples displayed at their entrances, specialising in portraits. Many of them do passport photos, ready for collection the next day, for about IR8000 for four colour shots. Few will take pictures of women without their headscarves on.

Technical Tips

For most of the year lighting conditions during the day are good, so you can usually afford to use very slow speed film. In fact one of the main problems is that the strong sunlight throws reflections on the lens (preventable with a lens hood), casting very noticeable shadows, which can spoil an otherwise good photograph. For this reason, buildings are often best photographed with the light directly overhead. For panoramic shots, however, the very bright light around noon can make photos look washed out and lacking in depth; often you'll find better light conditions just after sunrise or just before dusk.

Many mosques and other buildings are poorly lit inside, so you'll need long exposures (several seconds), a powerful flash or faster film to take decent pictures of them. A portable tripod can be very useful.

These days video cameras have amazingly sensitive microphones, and you might be surprised by how much sound will be picked up. This can be a problem if there is a lot of ambient noise; filming by the side of a road might seem OK when you do it, but back home you might find you're stuck with a cacophony of traffic noise. One good rule for beginners is to try and film in long takes without moving the camera around too much.

If you have a digital or video camera, make sure you keep the batteries charged and bring the necessary charger, plugs and transformer. Bring your own video cassettes, but remember that customs officials may confiscate blank or used cassettes if they think there's anything 'immoral' on them.

Restrictions

You shouldn't have any problems photographing most of the things that tourists are expected to photograph, but elsewhere be prepared for a lot of stares if you stroll around with a camera slung over your shoulder.

You are not generally allowed to take photos inside a mosque (the shrine of Emām Khomeinī near Tehrān is one exception to this rule) but it's usually fine outside or in the grounds of the mosque, provided you're respectful towards worshippers. Some mosques and museums don't allow cameras at all (or charge you for using them), but there is always a sign indicating any restrictions.

At government buildings, look out for 'No Photography' signs or pictures of cameras with a cross through them. Don't take photos near any airport, naval dockyard, roadblock, military installation, embassy/consulate, prison, train station, telephone office or police station, or within several kilometres of any border. If in doubt, ask first – although during the research for this book one of the authors nearly got into trouble for taking pictures of tiles on a building she believed to be a mosque from the far side of the road. It turned out to be a police station!

Photographing People

Most Iranians are happy to have their picture taken provided you ask first, and quite often it's hard to get children away from the front of your lens. However, sometimes even if you ask nicely, the answer will still be no – the shopkeepers in the Shīrāz bazaar seem to be a particularly coy bunch. Never point a lens at women without permission and anticipate refusal. Think carefully before photographing anyone in a mosque.

Airport Security

Almost all airports have X-ray machines for checking luggage, but the customs guards are usually happy to inspect camera bags separately. One reader reported having film damaged by the machine at Kermān airport.

TIME

Compared with westerners, Iranians place little value on time. Promises like 'I'll see you at seven' should never be taken literally, especially when the meeting is at your place. However, Iranians generally expect foreigners to be punctual.

Time throughout Iran is 3½ hours ahead of Greenwich Mean Time (GMT). Clocks go forward one hour between mid-March and mid-September. When it's noon in Tehrān (outside summer time), the time elsewhere is:

location	time
New York	3.30 am
UK	8.30 am
Turkey	11.00 am
Azerbaijan	11.30 am
Pakistan	1.30 pm
Turkmenistan	1.30 pm
Sydney	6.30 pm

ELECTRICITY

The electricity system is on 220V, 50 cycles AC, and sockets have two circular holes. Since few hotels have a backup generator, keep a torch or some candles in an easily accessible part of your luggage ready for the occasional power cut.

WEIGHTS & MEASURES

Various parts of the Persian Empire used to have their own system of weights and measures, but nowadays the metric system has permeated to almost every corner of Iran. There is a standard conversion table at the back of this book.

You may still come across the *sīr* (about 75g) and the *chārak* (10 sīr) in some remote places. Gold and other precious metals are still often measured by the *mesghāl*, equal to 4.7g. Feet and nautical miles continue to be used in aeronautical and naval circles.

LAUNDRY

There are reliable laundries and dry cleaning services in most Iranian cities although they're not always easy to find. At the time of writing there were no laundrettes. The better hotels will have a laundry service for guests. If you want the hotel to do your laundry you may have to give it to the housekeeper, or leave it on your bed. Your clothes will be scrubbed thoroughly, lovingly ironed, and usually returned the next day. Expect to pay about IR500 per item.

Few laundries will accept underclothes, and laundry workers (who are mostly male) will certainly not accept female underwear. You can wash your 'smalls' in the hotel sink; hot water is plentiful and washing detergent and soaps widely available. If you're doing your own washing, a universal bath plug is indispensable.

TOILETS

Iranian toilets are sometimes the squat kind; even if you pay US$40 for a hotel room, you may still get a squat toilet. Public toilets are few and far between and may not be that clean; mosques always have toilets; a main park in the centre of town is another good place to look, as is a petrol station. There are always toilets at bus and train stations and airport terminals. Museums usually have clean Western-style toilets. There's rarely a charge for using the toilet and if there is it's usually just IR100.

Toilet paper is usually only provided in top-end hotels since most Iranians use their left hand and an urn of water. Some grocery shops sell toilet paper, but it may take some time to hunt down, so stick with the ubiquitous boxes of tissues. Many toilets are not designed for paper and there should be a bucket next to the toilet where you place used toilet paper. Most toilets have flushes, although sometimes you have to pour water down the hole.

HEALTH

In general, Iran is a very healthy country to travel in. Standards of hygiene are quite high (you'll see plastic gloves used to handle food) and most people will experience nothing worse than the occasional bout of travellers' tummy, or exhaustion from overdoing it in the sun. You're highly unlikely to catch any tropical diseases. The information in this section is mainly here in case you're the unlucky one person in a thousand who goes down with something worse.

Predeparture Planning

Immunisations Plan ahead for getting vaccinations as some of them require more than one injection, while some should not be given together. It's a good idea to get medical advice at least six weeks before you travel. Some vaccinations should not be given during pregnancy nor to people with allergies – discuss this with your doctor. Be aware that children are more likely to get ill while travelling, as are pregnant women.

Discuss your requirements with your doctor, but vaccinations you should consider for Iran include the following:

Diphtheria & Tetanus Vaccinations for these two diseases are usually combined and are recommended for everyone. After an initial course of three injections, boosters are necessary every 10 years.

Polio Everyone should keep up to date with this vaccination, which is normally given in childhood. A booster every 10 years maintains immunity.

Hepatitis A This vaccine provides long-term immunity (possibly more than 10 years) after an initial injection and a booster at six to 12 months. Alternatively, an injection of gamma globulin can provide short-term protection against hepatitis A – two to six months, depending on the dose given. It is not a vaccine, but a ready-made antibody collected from blood donations. It is reasonably effective and, unlike the vaccine, is protective immediately, but because it is a blood product, there are current concerns about its long-term safety. Hepatitis A vaccine is also available in a combined form with hepatitis B vaccine. Three injections over a period are required, the first two providing substantial protection against hepatitis A.

Typhoid Vaccination against typhoid may be required if you are travelling for more than a couple of weeks in Iran. It is now available either as an injection or as capsules to be taken orally.

Hepatitis B This vaccine may be recommended for long-term travellers to Iran or travellers at

Medical Kit Check List

Following is a list of items you should consider including in your medical kit – consult your pharmacist for brands available in your country.

☐ **Aspirin or paracetamol (acetaminophen in the USA)** – for pain or fever
☐ **Antihistamine** – for allergies, eg, hay fever; to ease the itch from insect bites or stings; and to prevent motion sickness
☐ **Cold and flu tablets, throat lozenges and nasal decongestant**
☐ **Multivitamins** – consider for long trips, when dietary vitamin intake may be inadequate
☐ **Antibiotics** – consider including these if you're travelling well off the beaten track; see your doctor, as they must be prescribed, and carry the prescription with you
☐ **Loperamide or diphenoxylate** –'blockers' for diarrhoea
☐ **Prochlorperazine or metaclopramide** – for nausea and vomiting
☐ **Rehydration mixture** – to prevent dehydration, which may occur, for example, during bouts of diarrhoea; particularly important when travelling with children
☐ **Insect repellent, sunscreen, lip balm and eye drops**
☐ **Calamine lotion, sting relief spray or aloe vera** – to ease irritation from sunburn and insect bites or stings
☐ **Antifungal cream or powder** – for fungal skin infections and thrush
☐ **Antiseptic (such as povidone-iodine)** – for cuts and grazes
☐ **Bandages, Band-Aids (plasters) and other wound dressings**
☐ **Water purification tablets or iodine**
☐ **Scissors, tweezers and a thermometer** – note that mercury thermometers are prohibited by airlines
☐ **Sterile kit** – in case you need injections in a country with medical hygiene problems; discuss with your doctor

special risk, for example those working as medics or nurses. Vaccination involves three injections, with a booster at 12 months. More rapid courses are available if necessary.

Rabies Vaccination should be considered by those who will spend a month or longer in Iran, especially if they are cycling or travelling to remote areas, and for children (who may not report a bite). Pretravel rabies vaccination involves having three injections over 21 to 28 days. If someone who has been vaccinated is bitten or scratched by an animal, they will require two booster injections of vaccine; those not vaccinated require more.

Tuberculosis The risk of TB to travellers to Iran is very low, unless they will be living with or closely associated with local people in high risk areas, like refugee camps. Vaccination against TB (BCG) is recommended for children and young adults living in these areas for three months or more.

Note that if you are arriving in Iran from a yellow-fever-infected country (mainly sub-Saharan Africa and parts of South America), you will, in theory need a vaccination certificate for yellow fever before you'll be allowed in the country.

Malaria Medication Malaria is one of the world's great killer diseases. In Iran, an estimated 22,000 people had malaria at the time of writing. The risk to travellers not great, but is highest between March and October, especially in the Persian Gulf region. Discuss with your doctor whether you need to take antimalarial drugs. These do not prevent you from being infected, but kill the malaria parasites during their development and significantly reduce the risk of becoming seriously ill or dying. You need to get expert advice on antimalarials, as there are many factors to consider, including the area to be visited, the risk of exposure to malaria-carrying mosquitoes, the side effects of medication, your medical history, your age and whether you're pregnant. Travellers to isolated areas could consider carrying a treatment dose of medication for use if symptoms occur.

Health Insurance Make sure that you have adequate health insurance. See Travel Insurance under Visas & Documents earlier in this chapter for details.

Travel Health Information Lonely Planet's *Travel with Children* includes advice on travel health for younger children.

Everyday Health

Normal body temperature is up to 37°C (98.6°F); more than 2°C (4°F) higher indicates a high fever. The normal adult pulse rate is 60 to 100 per minute (children 80 to 100, babies 100 to 140). As a general rule the pulse increases about 20 beats per minute for each 1°C (2°F) rise in fever.

Respiration (breathing) rate is also an indicator of illness. Count the number of breaths per minute: Between 12 and 20 is normal for adults and older children (up to 30 for younger children, 40 for babies). People with a high fever or serious respiratory illness breathe more quickly than normal. More than 40 shallow breaths a minute may indicate pneumonia.

There are a number of excellent travel health sites on the Internet. From the Lonely Planet home page there are links at www.lonelyplanet.com/weblinks/wlheal.htm to the World Health Organization and the US Centers for Disease Control & Prevention.

Before setting out, British travellers might like to contact MASTA, the Medical Advisory Service for Travellers Abroad (☎ 0906-822 4100), Keppel St, London WC1E 7HT, which produces up-to-date fact sheets on health precautions for individual countries tailored to the sort of travelling you will be doing. Calls are charged at 60p per minute.

Other Preparations Make sure you're healthy before you start travelling. If you are going on a long trip make sure your teeth are OK. If you wear glasses take a spare pair and your prescription.

Basic Rules
Food On the whole, food hygiene in Iran is pretty good, although the occasional kebab is left too long before reheating. If you have a particularly sensitive stomach you might want to peel vegetables and fruit or wash them with purified water. Avoid ice cream if there's any risk it might have been melted and refrozen (eg, where there's been a power cut in the last day or two). Some locals will

advise you to steer clear of *dūgh*, the Iranian yogurt drink, if it is being sold from uncovered urns on the pavement where dirt can easily get in.

If a place looks clean and well run and the vendor also looks clean and healthy, then the food is probably safe. In general, places that are packed with travellers or locals will be fine, while empty restaurants are questionable. The food in busy restaurants is cooked and eaten quickly with little standing around and is probably not reheated.

Water In general, Iranian tap water is safe to drink; where it isn't we have said so in the text. Bottled water is available in the big towns, but you may have to look pretty hard for it elsewhere. On the other hand, bottled soft drinks are available everywhere. Tea or coffee should be fine as the water should have been boiled.

Medical Problems & Treatment

Self-diagnosis and treatment can be risky, so you should always seek medical help where necessary. An embassy, consulate or five-star hotel can usually recommend a local doctor or clinic. Although we give drug dosages in this section, they are for emergency use only; correct diagnosis is vital. In this section we have used the generic names for medications – check with a pharmacist for brands available locally.

Ideally, antibiotics should only be administered under medical supervision. Take

Fluids

While in Iran, especially in summer, always make sure you drink enough – don't rely on feeling thirsty to indicate when you should drink. Not needing to urinate or voiding small amounts of very dark-yellow urine is a danger sign. Always carry a water bottle with you on long trips. Excessive sweating can lead to loss of salt and therefore muscle cramping. Salt tablets are not a good idea as a preventative, but in places where salt is not used much, adding salt to food can help.

only the recommended dose at the prescribed intervals and use the whole course, even if the illness seems to be cured earlier. Stop immediately if there are any serious reactions and don't use the antibiotic at all if you are unsure that you have the correct one. If you are allergic to commonly prescribed antibiotics like penicillin, keep this information with you (eg, on a bracelet) when travelling.

Medical Services Medications If you require a particular medication take an adequate supply, as it may not be available locally. There is usually a minimal charge for medicines on prescription, more than 90% of which are made in Iran, but few are labelled in English. Be careful when buying drugs as the expiry date may have passed or correct storage conditions may not have been available.

If you're looking for a particular medicine over the counter, try to find out its generic name rather than its Western brand name, which may not be recognised in Iran. Take the prescription with you wherever you travel, to show that you are legally using the medication – it's surprising how often over-the-counter drugs from one place are illegal without a prescription or even banned in another. Pharmacies are easy to spot in Iran, and often have the word 'drug' in English on the shop window. Pharmacists are well-trained, and usually speak enough English to make sure you get the right medication.

Medical Facilities If you are mildly sick, seek advice from someone at your hotel or an Iranian friend. They should be able to find a reputable doctor who speaks English and will come to your hotel. If your situation is more serious, contact your embassy, which should be able to recommend a reputable doctor and/or hospital. They may even arrange everything for you if you're lucky.

If the illness or injury is life-threatening, contact your embassy immediately and consider flying home (assuming you have medical insurance to cover the costs).

The standard of medical facilities varies greatly throughout Iran. The best place to fall ill is Tehrān since a disproportionate number of doctors and medical establishments are in the capital. Many of the doctors in Tehrān and the major provincial cities received their training in the West and you shouldn't have much problem finding one who speaks English (there are also lots of female doctors). In less developed areas, medical facilities are often far from adequate. Treatment is never free, which means you absolutely must have travel insurance with health cover.

Doctors' surgeries are often concentrated around the major hospitals, and along main roads in the centre of town. Standard consultations are very cheap (about IR10,000), but if you want a good doctor who has been trained in a foreign country and speaks English, expect to pay more (perhaps IR50,000).

There are also plenty of pharmacies (and homeopathic treatment centres) in the big towns, although the range of drugs available is relatively limited. In the bazaars you may see men selling unpackaged drugs, including antibiotics, which would be issued on prescription only at home. It's unwise to buy these as there are no instructions for use and they may be past their use-by date.

Although we list all sorts of emergency telephone numbers in this book, you should be aware that the chances of finding someone speaking English on the other end of the line are small. In an emergency you might be better off summoning a taxi to get you to a hospital unless there is an Iranian with you to call an ambulance.

Environmental Hazards

Pollution Air pollution is a major problem in Tehrān, most of all in summer. Tehrānīs tell visitors, almost with pride, that they live in one of the world's most polluted cities. If you start spluttering and coughing, and develop headaches and stomach pains, after a day or two in the capital, you're probably just reacting to the unhealthy air. Head for the hills of northern Tehrān and you'll probably stage a miraculous recovery. Asthmatics won't want to hang around Tehrān too long either.

Esfahān and Kermān also suffer badly from air pollution, especially in winter when fuel burned for heating compounds the normal problems created by traffic and industrial waste.

Sunburn It would be very easy to get sunburnt in Iran, especially in summer. Always use a sunscreen, a hat, and a barrier cream for your nose and lips. Calamine lotion or a commercial after-sun preparation are good for mild sunburn. Protect your eyes with good quality sunglasses.

Heat Exhaustion There's a real risk of heat exhaustion if you're travelling in Iran, especially in the summer and in the south. Dehydration and salt deficiency can cause heat exhaustion. Take time to acclimatise to high temperatures, drink sufficient liquids and do not do anything too physically demanding.

Salt deficiency is characterised by fatigue, lethargy, headaches, giddiness and muscle cramps; salt tablets may help but adding extra salt to your food is better.

Heatstroke This serious, occasionally fatal, condition can occur if the body's heat-regulating mechanism breaks down and the body temperature rises to dangerous levels. Long, continuous periods of exposure to high temperatures and insufficient fluids can leave you vulnerable to heatstroke.

The symptoms are feeling unwell, not sweating very much (or at all) and a high body temperature (39° to 41°C or 102° to 106°F). Where sweating has ceased, the skin becomes flushed and red. Severe, throbbing headaches and lack of coordination will also occur, and the sufferer may be confused or aggressive. Eventually the victim will become delirious or convulse. Hospitalisation is essential, but in the interim get victims out of the sun, remove their clothing, cover them with a wet sheet or towel and then fan continually. Give fluids if they are conscious.

Prickly Heat Prickly heat is an itchy rash caused by excessive perspiration trapped under the skin. It usually strikes people who have just arrived in a hot climate. Keeping cool, bathing often, drying the skin and using a mild talcum or prickly heat powder may help, as may renting an air-conditioned room.

Hypothermia People travelling in northwest Iran in winter, or mountaineers and trekkers, could theoretically fall victim to hypothermia. Hypothermia occurs when the body loses heat faster than it can produce it and the core temperature of the body falls. It is surprisingly easy to progress from very cold to dangerously cold due to a combination of wind, wet clothing, fatigue and hunger, even if the air temperature is above freezing. It is best to dress in layers; silk, wool and some of the new artificial fibres are all good insulating materials. A hat is important, as a lot of heat is lost through the head. A strong, waterproof outer layer is essential. Carry basic supplies, including food containing simple sugars and fluid to drink to generate heat quickly.

Symptoms of hypothermia are exhaustion, numb skin (particularly toes and fingers), shivering, slurred speech, irrational or violent behaviour, lethargy, stumbling, dizzy spells, muscle cramps and violent bursts of energy. Irrationality may cause sufferers to claim they are warm and try to take off their clothes.

To treat mild hypothermia, first get the person out of the wind and/or rain, remove their clothing if it's wet and replace it with dry, warm clothing. Give them hot liquids – not alcohol – and some high-energy, easily digestible food. Do not rub victims: Instead, allow them to warm themselves slowly. This should be enough to treat the early stages of hypothermia. Early recognition and treatment of mild hypothermia is the only way to prevent severe hypothermia, which is a critical condition.

Altitude Sickness Mountaineers could also suffer from the lack of oxygen at high altitudes (over 2500m), which affects most people to some extent. The effect may be mild or severe and occurs because less oxygen reaches the muscles and the brain, requiring the heart and lungs to compensate by working harder. Symptoms of Acute Mountain Sickness (AMS) usually develop during the first 24 hours at altitude, but may be delayed up to three weeks. Mild symptoms include headache, lethargy, dizziness, difficulty sleeping and loss of appetite. AMS may worsen without warning and can be fatal. Severe symptoms include breathlessness, a dry, irritative cough (which may progress to the production of pink, frothy sputum), severe headache, lack of coordination and balance, confusion, irrational behaviour, vomiting, drowsiness and unconsciousness. There is no hard-and-fast rule as to what is too high: AMS has proved fatal at 3000m, although it's more usually dangerous at 3500m to 4500m.

Treat mild symptoms by resting at the same altitude until recovery, usually in a day or two. Paracetamol or aspirin can be taken for headaches. If symptoms persist or become worse, however, *immediate descent is necessary*; even 500m can help. Drug treatments should never be used to avoid descent or to enable further ascent.

Some doctors recommend acetazolamide and dexamethasone for the prevention of AMS; however, their use is controversial. They can reduce the symptoms but they may also mask warning signs; severe and fatal AMS has occurred in people taking these drugs. In general we do not recommend them for travellers.

To prevent acute mountain sickness:

- Ascend slowly – have frequent rest days, spending two to three nights at each rise of 1000m. If you trek to a high altitude, acclimatisation takes place gradually and you are less likely to be affected than if you fly there directly. If possible you should sleep at a lower altitude than the greatest height reached during the day. Also, once above 3000m, care should be taken not to increase the sleeping altitude by more than 300m per day.
- Drink extra fluids – mountain air is dry and cold, and moisture is lost as you breathe. Evaporation of sweat may occur unnoticed and result in dehydration.
- Eat light – high-carbohydrate meals have more energy.
- Avoid alcohol – it may increase the risk of dehydration.
- Avoid sedatives.

Jet Lag Jet lag is experienced when a person travels by air across more than three time zones (each time zone usually represents a one-hour time difference). It occurs because many of the functions of the human body (such as temperature, pulse rate and emptying of the bladder and bowels) are regulated by internal 24-hour cycles. When we travel long distances rapidly, our bodies take time to adjust to the 'new time' of our destination, and we may experience fatigue, disorientation, insomnia, anxiety, impaired concentration and loss of appetite. These effects will usually be gone within three days of arrival, but to minimise the impact of jet lag:

- Rest for a couple of days prior to departure.
- Try to select flight schedules that minimise sleep deprivation; arriving late in the day means you can go to sleep soon after you arrive. For very long flights, try to organise a stopover.
- Avoid excessive eating (which bloats the stomach) and alcohol (which causes dehydration) during the flight. Instead, drink plenty of non-carbonated, nonalcoholic drinks such as fruit juice or water.
- Avoid smoking.
- Make yourself comfortable by wearing loose-fitting clothes and bringing an eye mask and ear plugs to help you sleep.
- Try to sleep at the appropriate time for the time zone you are travelling to.

Motion Sickness Eating lightly before and during a trip will reduce the chances of motion sickness. If you are prone to motion sickness try to find a place that minimises movement, such as near the wing on aircraft, close to midships on boats or near the centre on buses. Fresh air usually helps; reading and cigarette smoke don't. Commercial motion-sickness preparations, which can cause drowsiness, have to be taken before the trip commences. Ginger (available in capsule form) and peppermint (including mint-flavoured sweets) are natural preventatives.

Infectious Diseases

Diarrhoea Simple things like a change of water, food or climate can all cause a mild bout of diarrhoea, but a few rushed toilet trips with no other symptoms are not indicative of a major problem.

Dehydration is the main danger with any diarrhoea, particularly in children or the elderly as dehydration can occur quite quickly. Under all circumstances *fluid replacement* (at least equal to the volume being lost) is the most important thing to remember. Weak black tea with a little sugar, soda water, or soft drinks allowed to go flat and diluted 50% with clean water are all good. With severe diarrhoea a rehydrating solution is preferable to replace minerals and salts lost. Commercially available oral rehydration salts (ORS) are very useful; add them to boiled or bottled water. In an emergency you can make up a solution of six teaspoons of sugar and a half-teaspoon of salt to a litre of boiled or bottled water. Urine is the best guide to the adequacy of replacement – small amounts of concentrated urine suggest that you need to drink more. Keep drinking small amounts often and stick to a bland diet as you recover.

Gut-paralysing drugs such as loperamide or diphenoxylate can be used to bring relief from the symptoms, although they do not actually cure the problem. Only use these drugs if you do not have access to toilets, eg, if you *must* travel. Note that they are not recommended for children under 12 years.

Medical Treatment Antibiotics may be required if you have diarrhoea with blood or mucus (dysentery), any diarrhoea with fever, profuse watery diarrhoea, persistent diarrhoea which doesn't improve after 48 hours or severe diarrhoea. These suggest a more serious cause so avoid gut-paralysing drugs.

In these situations, a stool test may be necessary to diagnose what bug is causing your diarrhoea, so you should seek medical help urgently. Where this is not possible the recommended drugs for bacterial diarrhoea (the most likely cause of severe diarrhoea in travellers) are norfloxacin 400mg twice daily for three days or ciprofloxacin 500mg twice daily for five days. These are not recommended for children or pregnant women. The drug of choice for children would be co-trimoxazole with dosage dependent on weight. A five-day course is given. Ampicillin or amoxycillin may be given in pregnancy, but medical care is necessary.

Persistent Diarrhoea Two other causes of persistent diarrhoea in travellers are giardiasis and amoebic dysentery.

Caused by a common parasite, symptoms of giardiasis include stomach cramps, nausea, a bloated stomach, watery, foul-smelling diarrhoea and frequent gas. Giardiasis can appear several weeks after you have been exposed to the parasite. The symptoms may disappear for a few days and then return; this can go on for several weeks.

Symptoms of amoebic dysentery are a gradual onset of low-grade diarrhoea, often with blood and mucus. Cramping abdominal pain and vomiting are less likely than in other types of diarrhoea, and fever may not be present. It will persist until treated and can recur and cause other health problems.

You should seek medical advice if you think you have giardiasis or amoebic dysentery, but where this is not possible, tinidazole or metronidazole are the recommended drugs. Treatment is a 2g single dose of tinidazole or 250mg of metronidazole three times daily for five to 10 days.

Fungal Infections Fungal infections occur more commonly in hot weather and are usually found on the scalp, between the toes (athlete's foot) or fingers, in the groin and on the body (ringworm). You get ringworm (which is a fungal infection, not a worm) from infected animals or other people. Moisture encourages these infections.

To prevent fungal infections wear loose, comfortable clothes, avoid artificial fibres, wash frequently and dry yourself carefully. If you do get an infection, wash the infected area at least daily with a disinfectant or medicated soap and water, and rinse and dry well. Apply an antifungal cream or powder. Try to expose the infected area to air or sunlight as much as possible and wash all towels and underwear in hot water, change them often and let them dry in the sun.

Hepatitis Hepatitis is a general term for inflammation of the liver. It is a common disease worldwide. There are several different viruses that cause hepatitis, and they differ in the way that they are transmitted. The symptoms are similar in all forms of the illness, and include fever, chills, headache, fatigue, feelings of weakness and aches and pains, followed by loss of appetite, nausea, vomiting, abdominal pain, dark urine, light-coloured faeces, jaundiced (yellow) skin and yellowing of the whites of the eyes. People who have had hepatitis should avoid alcohol for some time after the illness, as the liver needs time to recover.

Hepatitis A is transmitted by contaminated food and drinking water. You should seek medical advice, but there is not much you can do apart from resting, drinking lots of fluids, eating lightly and avoiding fatty foods. **Hepatitis E** is transmitted in the same way as hepatitis A; it can be particularly serious in pregnant women.

There are almost 300 million chronic carriers of **hepatitis B** in the world. It is spread through contact with infected blood, blood products or body fluids, for example through sexual contact, unsterilised needles and blood transfusions, or contact with blood via small breaks in the skin. Other risk situations include having a shave with contaminated equipment. The symptoms of hepatitis B may be more severe than type A and the disease can lead to long-term problems such as chronic liver damage, liver cancer or a long-term carrier state. **Hepatitis C** and **D** are spread in the same way as hepatitis B and can also lead to long-term complications.

There are vaccines against hepatitis A and B but none currently against the other types of hepatitis. Following the basic rules for food and water (hepatitis A and E) and avoiding risk situations (hepatitis B, C and D) are important preventative measures.

HIV & AIDS Infection with the human immunodeficiency virus (HIV) may lead to acquired immune deficiency syndrome (AIDS), which is a fatal disease; the WHO estimates that about 1000 people in Iran may be HIV positive. Any exposure to blood, blood products or body fluids may put the individual at risk. The disease is often transmitted through sexual contact or dirty needles – vaccinations, acupuncture, tattooing and body piercing are potentially as dangerous as intravenous drug use. HIV/AIDS can also be spread through infected blood transfusions; some countries do not screen blood used for transfusions. If you do need an injection, ask to see the syringe unwrapped in front of you, or take a needle and syringe pack with you.

Malaria This serious and potentially fatal disease is spread by mosquito bites. While the risk of catching malaria in Iran is small, antimalarials may be recommended for travel to some parts of the country, including Lorestān, Boyerahmad va Kohgīlūyeh, Khūzestān and Chahārmahāl va Bakhteyārī provinces and the southern part of Fārs, southern part of Kermān and Sīstān va Balūchestān provinces. Get expert advice on malaria prevention from your doctor or a travel health clinic before you go.

Symptoms of malaria range from fever, chills and sweating, headache, diarrhoea and abdominal pains to a vague feeling of ill-health. Seek medical help immediately if malaria is suspected. Without treatment malaria can rapidly become more serious and can be fatal.

If medical care is not available, malaria tablets can be used for treatment. You need to use a *different* malaria tablet from the one you were taking when you contracted malaria. The standard treatment dose of mefloquine is two 250mg tablets and a further two six hours later. For Fansidar, it's a single dose of three tablets. If you were previously taking mefloquine and cannot obtain Fansidar, then other alternatives are Malarone (atovaquone-proguanil; four tablets once daily for three days), halofantrine (three doses of two 250mg tablets every six hours) or quinine sulphate (600mg every six hours). There is a greater risk of side effects with these dosages than in normal use, so medical advice is desirable. Be aware also that halofantrine is no longer recommended by the WHO as emergency stand by treatment, because of side effects; it should only be used if no other drugs are available.

You're advised to try and prevent mosquito bites at all times. The main messages are:

- Wear light-coloured clothing.
- Wear long trousers and long-sleeved shirts.
- Use mosquito repellents containing the compound DEET on exposed areas (prolonged overuse of DEET may be harmful, especially to children, but its use is considered preferable to being bitten by disease-transmitting mosquitoes).
- Avoid perfumes or aftershave.
- Use a mosquito net impregnated with mosquito repellent (permethrin).
- Impregnating clothes with permethrin effectively deters mosquitoes and other insects.

Cuts, Bites & Stings
See Less Common Diseases for details on rabies, which is passed through animal bites.

Cuts & Scratches Wash any cut well and treat with an antiseptic such as povidone-iodine. Where possible avoid bandages and Band-Aids, which can keep wounds wet.

Bedbugs & Lice Bedbugs live in various places, but particularly in dirty mattresses and bedding, evidenced by spots of blood on bedclothes or on the wall. Bedbugs leave itchy bites in neat rows. Calamine lotion or a sting-relief spray may help.

All lice cause itching and discomfort. They make themselves at home in your hair (head lice), your clothing (body lice) or in your pubic hair (crabs). You catch lice through direct contact with infected people or by sharing combs, clothing and the like. Powder or shampoo treatment will kill the lice. Infected clothing should then be washed in very hot, soapy water and left in the sun to dry.

Bites & Stings Bee and wasp stings are usually painful rather than dangerous. However, in people who are allergic to them, severe breathing difficulties may occur and require urgent medical care. Calamine lotion or a sting-relief spray will give relief and ice packs will reduce the pain and swelling. There are some spiders with dangerous bites but antivenins are usually available. Scorpion stings are notoriously painful. Scorpions often shelter in shoes or clothing.

Ticks You should always check all over your body if you have been walking through a potentially tick-infested area as ticks can cause skin infections and other more serious diseases. If a tick is found attached, press down around the tick's head with tweezers, grab the head and gently pull upwards.

Avoid pulling the rear of the body as this may squeeze the tick's gut contents through the attached mouth parts into the skin, increasing the risk of infection and disease. Smearing chemicals on the tick will not make it let go and is not recommended.

Snakes To minimise your chances of being bitten always wear boots, socks and long trousers when walking through undergrowth where snakes may be present. Don't put your hands into holes and crevices, and be careful when collecting firewood.

Snake bites do not cause instantaneous death and antivenins are usually available. Immediately wrap the bitten limb tightly, as you would for a sprained ankle and attach a splint to immobilise it. Keep the victim still and seek medical help, if possible bringing the dead snake for identification (don't attempt to catch the snake if there is a possibility of being bitten again). Tourniquets and sucking out the poison are now comprehensively discredited.

Women's Health
Gynaecological Problems Antibiotic use, synthetic underwear, sweating and contraceptive pills can lead to fungal vaginal infections, especially when travelling in hot climates. Fungal infections are characterised by a rash, itch and discharge and the usual treatment is an antifungal such as nystatin, miconazole or clotrimazole pessaries or vaginal cream. If these are unavailable, alternative treatments are a vinegar or lemon-juice douche, or yogurt. Maintaining good personal hygiene and wearing loose-fitting clothes and cotton underwear help prevent these infections.

Sexually transmitted infections are a major cause of vaginal problems. Symptoms include a smelly discharge, painful intercourse and sometimes a burning sensation when urinating. Medical attention should be sought and male sexual partners must also be treated. Besides abstinence, the best thing is to practise safer sex using condoms.

Pregnancy Pregnant women should think carefully before travelling to Iran in high summer, especially if heading for areas where there is some risk of malaria (see above).

Most miscarriages occur during the first three months of pregnancy. Miscarriage is not uncommon and can occasionally lead to severe bleeding. The last three months should also be spent within reasonable distance of good medical care. A baby born as early as 24 weeks stands a chance of survival but only in a good modern hospital. Pregnant women should avoid all unnecessary medication, although vaccinations and malarial prophylactics should still be taken where needed. Additional care should be taken to prevent illness and particular attention should be paid to diet and nutrition. Alcohol and nicotine, for example, should be avoided.

Less Common Diseases
The following diseases pose a small risk to travellers in Iran, and so are only mentioned in passing. Seek medical advice if you think you may have any of these diseases.

Cholera Outbreaks of cholera often follow natural disasters like earthquakes and are generally widely reported, so you can avoid the problem areas; a few cases were reported in southern Iran in 2000 following the drought.

This is the worst of the watery diarrhoeas and medical help should be sought. *Fluid replacement is the most vital treatment* – the risk of dehydration is severe as you may lose up to 20L a day. If there is a delay in getting to hospital, start taking tetracycline; the adult dose is 250mg four times daily, but it is not recommended for children under nine years or for pregnant women. Tetracycline may help shorten the illness but adequate fluids are required to save lives.

Leishmaniasis This is a group of parasitic diseases transmitted by sandflies, which are found in many parts of the Middle East. Cutaneous leishmaniasis affects the skin tissue causing ulceration and disfigurement, and visceral leishmaniasis affects the internal organs. Seek medical advice as laboratory testing is required for diagnosis and correct treatment. Avoiding sandfly bites is the best precaution. Bites are usually itchy and yet another reason to cover up and apply repellent.

Rabies This fatal viral infection is found in Iran. Many animals can be infected (eg, dogs, cats and bats) and it is their saliva which is infectious. Any bite, scratch or even lick should be cleaned immediately and thoroughly. Scrub with soap and running water, and then apply alcohol or iodine solution. Medical help should be sought promptly to receive a course of injections to prevent the onset of symptoms and death.

Tetanus This disease is caused by a germ which lives in soil and in the faeces of horses and other animals. It enters the body via breaks in the skin. The first symptom may be discomfort in swallowing, or stiffening of the jaw and neck; this is followed by painful convulsions of the jaw and whole body. The disease can be fatal. It can be prevented by vaccination.

Tuberculosis (TB) TB is a bacterial infection usually transmitted from person to person by coughing but which may be transmitted through consumption of unpasteurised milk. Milk that has been boiled is safe to drink, and the souring of milk to make yogurt or cheese also kills the bacilli. Travellers are not usually at great risk as close household contact with the infected person is usually required to catch the disease.

Typhus This disease is spread by ticks, mites or lice. It begins with fever, chills, headache and muscle pains followed a few days later by a body rash. There is often a large painful sore at the site of the bite and nearby lymph nodes are swollen and painful. Typhus can be treated under medical supervision. Seek local advice on areas where ticks pose a danger and always check your skin carefully after walking in a danger area (see Ticks earlier). An insect repellent can help, and walkers in tick-infested areas should consider having their boots and trousers impregnated with benzyl benzoate and dibutylphthalate.

WOMEN TRAVELLERS
Attitudes Towards Women

Islam, and in particular the Iranian interpretation of Islam, imposes many constraints on women, and no foreign woman should visit Iran unless she is prepared to adapt to the social code. You may not agree with it, but if you are not prepared to observe the rules you will simply be refused entry, or have an extremely unpleasant time; even under President Khatamī, Iran is not the place to make a feminist statement.

In general, the main hassle for foreign women is having to wear unusual clothing and lots of it. How you feel about this will probably depend on lots of things (not least the weather), including your own views on personal freedom. But some foreign women who have travelled through Pakistan and/or Turkey say they feel more comfortable in Iran where the level of harassment is lower.

Unfortunately, you can feel very isolated because of difficulties in making contact with local people. Even when you're travelling with a man, you will find that Iranian men and Iranian women in the company of an Iranian man will talk almost exclusively to the foreign man. This can be unsettling, especially if the conversation lasts for several hours over dinner, and you, as a woman, are rarely even acknowledged.

These days people are less wary of approaching foreigners, but if you want to make friends it's going to take a bit of self-confidence. You may find it easier to stick to befriending Iranian women, but as not many of them speak English (except some middle- or upper-class Tehrānīs) you may need to try to learn some Farsi. Unless you're prepared to make an extra effort, you may find yourself marginalised and so miss out on the best that Iran has to offer.

On the plus side, a foreign woman will sometimes be considered an honorary male and be accepted into all-male preserves, like teahouses, in a way that no Iranian woman would ever be. Of course, you can also enter female society far more than any man (Iranian or foreign). Unaccompanied foreign women are often treated with extra courtesy and indulgence because of their perceived vulnerability. When it comes to finding scarce hotel accommodation or plane tickets, or lining up at places like the visa-extension office, an unaccompanied woman is almost certainly at an advantage over a man.

Safety Precautions

Many Iranian men have very distorted ideas about Western women. Even if you're wearing all the necessary excess clothing, you may *still* have men leering and making sidelong comments (especially in southern Tehrān); nor is groping entirely unknown,

especially in shared taxis. However, not every male who speaks to you has ulterior motives. If you keep to the dress and social codes, most local people will respect you. Never lead men on. In Iran, the man does the wooing.

Although the risk of serious assault is almost nonexistent, you should still take normal safety precautions. Always lock the door of your hotel room, for example, since you may get the odd person who will try to open it using the 'I've got the wrong room' excuse. Normally, they're just curious to see what you look like without a scarf and coat.

Women can stay in cheap hotels (although the most basic mosāferkhūnehs may not be the best environments for them), and can often share rooms with a foreign male companion, even if he is not their husband (see Unmarried Foreign Couples in Dangers & Annoyances later in this chapter for more details on sharing rooms with men).

If you are harassed, tell your persecutor firmly, but politely, to desist (English will do), and try to enlist the sympathy of other Iranians. If they think that someone is behaving badly towards you, they are very likely to stop him out of shame. If you scream blue murder the situation could get out of hand. If the problem persists, a mere mention of the police should have a sobering affect. Thanks to social constraints, you will rarely be alone with an Iranian male unless you want to be, but if it looks as if that might happen when you don't want it, it's wise to be very cautious.

Holidaying in Hejab

It probably didn't help that I was travelling in Iran in August when temperatures were often in the 40s. Had it been winter I might have found wearing a headscarf more tolerable. As it was, there was never a day when my heart didn't sink as I pinned that wretched piece of cloth into place.

'Why?' I asked various people along the way. 'I'm not a Muslim so why must I dress as if I were?'

'It's to show respect for our culture', a museum curator ventured. He had been to the Punjab. 'Did you wear a turban then?' I asked him. He recoiled, horrified.

'It's to protect you', someone else tried. 'It's like the feminists of the 1970s who chose to wear dungarees.' Hmmm, well, forgive me but I'd like to decide for myself whether I need protection. Besides, did it stop the men in the back row of the taxi running their hands across my thigh? Did it hell!

Finally in desperation they would try 'Well, it's only for a few weeks.' Yes, and there's the rub. I could at least take my headscarf off when I reached the border but there are many women in Iran who would give their eye teeth for that privilege but who are obliged to wear hejab day in, day out from the year they turn nine. Every time I put on my scarf I was reminded of the way their right to dress as they chose had been stolen from them. It was no way to feel relaxed on holiday.

Pat Yale

My bum got pinched, touched a few times and in untouristy areas I was constantly followed by men. I couldn't even stop on a bench for a few minutes without them surrounding me. I tried all methods, including ignoring them, telling them to go, insulting them, then threatening to call the police, but nothing seemed to deter them, although I must say I never felt unsafe. I was wearing proper hejab at all times and some people mistook me for a local. I was much more comfortable when I was with foreign men.

Aisling Halleman

Khatamī & Women's Rights

While Minister for Culture under President Rafsanjānī, Khatamī allowed a female pop singer to hold a concert in Tehrān (for a female audience). He lost his cabinet post for doing so.

Since unexpectedly becoming president in 1997, Khatamī has put new emphasis on the status of women, stating that discrimination between men and women oppresses both men *and* women. He has appointed a woman as one of his vice-presidents, and two women serve as deputy cabinet ministers. All the women in the current Masjid (Parliament) are from reformist groups supporting President Khatamī.

In 1996 the first female prosecutor was appointed and in 1997 four women were named as family court judges. Crimes against women are occasionally reported in the media now, when not so long ago they were kept secret.

One woman, Farah Khosravi, has even announced her intention to stand for election as president in 2001, even though Article 115 of the constitution stipulates that only a man can hold the office.

Some foreign women may feel happier travelling in Iran in a group or with a male companion, but neither is essential. It might be a good idea to wear a wedding ring even if you're not married, to ward off unwelcome attention, and at times it may be sensible to say that your husband is travelling with you or about to join you, but in general, Iranians understand that foreigners have different rules. Iranian women do travel unaccompanied, although less often than Western women.

Some restaurants and teahouses have separate areas set aside for women and families. Where that's the case, you will be directed straight to them.

What to Wear

By law, all females over the age of nine must wear the *hejab*, the general term to describe the type of Islamic dress required for females in Iran. Signs in public places show two possible variants on correct hejab: The chador, an all-encompassing, head-to-toe black 'tent' (which is what 'chador' means in Farsi); or a *magnae* (a wimple-like scarf-shawl), *rouposh* (baggy trench coat) and trousers.

These days foreign women can get away with wearing their normal clothes, provided their head, shoulders, arms, legs and body are completely covered up and the shape of their body is concealed. Even socks are no longer absolutely essential. If you're coming to Iran from Pakistan or India a *shalwar-kameez* makes the perfect garment, provided the top is long enough to completely cover your bottom.

The only times when foreign women *must* wear a chador are when visiting the city of Qom or the shrines at Shīrāz and Mashhad. If you do choose to wear a chador more generally, it will earn you respect, but chadors are utterly unmanageable garments with no zips or buttons so that they must be held closed with the hands or teeth. Unless you've grown up wearing one, you'll find it almost impossibly unwieldy to travel in.

Locals will tell you that you no longer need to dress in black (indeed, the *in* colour for 2000 was a pale blue) but since perhaps 90% of Iranian women still do wear black, choosing to wear a lighter colour will make you stand out even more. Whatever you do, don't wear red, the colour associated with Yezid, the enemy of Emām Hossein. Women travelling with tour groups seem to wear whatever colours they like without any problem.

If you will be travelling in summer, light fabrics are strongly recommended. You can easily buy suitable clothes inside Iran, bearing in mind that you will have to be wearing something all-concealing enough to please the immigration officials when you arrive. In particular, the bazaars are full of scarves in all sorts of shapes, colours and sizes. These days few people bat an eyelid if you have your fringe or the front of your hair showing. On the other hand, were you to venture onto the streets without a scarf there would almost certainly be trouble.

Here are the thoughts of some other women travellers on the dress dilemma:

I bought a long, black garment together with a scarf in Dubai. I wore my normal make-up and open Birkenstock sandals. There were no hassles when I arrived (at Tehrān airport). The headscarf was a damned nuisance for a photographer, so I went to the nearest market and got a piece of square material sewn into a triangle for US$1. You insert your head into the narrow end, inside out; then when it's in about the right position you turn the rest of it over your head and bingo! – you have the same head-dress that 90% of Iranian women wear.

Venise Alstergen

Plain colours need not be worn, neither on the headscarf nor the coat; and a chador is only required when it is handed over at the entrance to a shrine. If you arrive wearing one, or looking more of a devout Muslim than the local women, you will probably be derided, as my friend and I were when we invested in long robes, black headscarves with not a hair visible and scraped our faces clean of all make-up. We purchased some lighter, patterned clothes, let our fringes out and felt instantly less gauche. It transpires that looking smart and well-presented will earn the tourist more respect than wearing a chador.

Barunka O'Shaughnessy

I was only once criticised for my dress. I was sitting by the river in Esfahān with my legs crossed. My ankle-length dress had ridden up and exposed a few centimetres of flesh above the less-than-attractive black socks and shoes. A middle-aged woman wrapped in a black chador came up and signed that I should adjust my dress. It reminded me of my school days when the nuns would tell me to pull my socks up!

Cheryl Rivers

What to Bring

For most women the main difficulty when packing is to find garments in their wardrobe 'suitable' for Iran. However, tampon-users may want to pack enough to get them through their trip. Tampons are very hard to find and, if you do manage to track them down, ridiculously expensive.

GAY & LESBIAN TRAVELLERS

Homosexuality is illegal in Iran and theoretically punishable by hundreds of lashes or worse (although foreigners would probably be deported instead). This should not deter gay and lesbian travellers from visiting Iran (questions about sexuality are not asked on visa applications or at immigration) although they should refrain from all overt signs of affection in public. It has been suggested that there are cruising areas around the harbour in Bandar-é Anzali, and in parts of Esfahān and Tehrān. However, you'd be ill-advised to run needless risks while in Iran.

DISABLED TRAVELLERS

As long as you are healthy and come with the right frame of mind, there is no reason why disabled travellers shouldn't enjoy much of what Iran has to offer. Depending on the nature of your disability, you may wish to fly rather than take long-distance buses or trains.

Although special facilities for the disabled are rare, Iran is having to come to terms with more than 300,000 people left disabled by the Iran-Iraq War. As a result wheelchair ramps are starting to appear (although it will be a long time before you can depend on their presence). Only the more upmarket hotels are likely to have elevators big enough for wheelchairs and European-style sit-down toilets.

You should bring your own medications, and prescriptions, although medical facilities in the major cities are quite good.

SENIOR TRAVELLERS

There's no reason why fit, healthy senior travellers shouldn't enjoy Iran just as much as younger people (indeed, older women may arguably find the dress code less intrusive than their younger counterparts). Iranian culture has it that a man doesn't become 'complete' until he's 40, so this is not a society likely to discriminate against older visitors.

TRAVEL WITH CHILDREN

In Iran, foreign children will be the source of much amusement and curiosity, which may drive them (and you) to despair after a while. Nappies (diapers), powders, most simple medications and so on are available in the big cities, although you may want to bring your own to save having to hunt about. The hardest thing will be trying to keep children entertained in a country where journeys are often long and the attractions often extremely 'adult'. It is debatable how many mothers would want to bring their young daughters here as long as the rule obliging them to wear hejab once they reach the age of nine is in force. Anyone contemplating taking children to Iran should read *Travel with Children* by Lonely Planet's Maureen Wheeler. She has travelled all around the world with her kids and lived to tell the tale.

DANGERS & ANNOYANCES
Security

Iran is starting to live down its past reputation as a dangerous country for westerners to visit. Open hostility towards Western visitors (even Americans) is very rare and rapidly diminishing. We continue to receive letters from foreigners who have been overwhelmed by the kindness and generosity shown to them during their visit, regardless of their own nationality. If you do your best to fit in with local customs, you are unlikely to be treated with anything but courtesy and friendliness.

Western embassies advise their nationals to register with them on arrival, especially if you will be in Iran for 10 or more days, or plan to visit remote places.

At the time of writing, the British Foreign and Commonwealth Office was advising travellers not to travel to Sistān va Balūchestān and Kermān provinces or to travel overland to Pakistan. Although they are probably being overly cautious, you might want to check the latest Foreign and Commonwealth Office Travel Advice on www.fco.gov.uk/travel/; the USA's State Department Travel Warnings on travel.state.gov/travel_warnings.html; or Australia's Department of Foreign Affairs and Trade Consular Travel Advice on www.dfat.gov.au/consular/advice/advices_mnu.html.

Police & Security Forces The Iranian Law Enforcement Forces (LEF) have a far better reputation for probity and efficiency than their counterparts in adjacent countries. There are several different police forces (their exact names and uniforms even confuse locals), but as long as you behave yourself and dress appropriately you shouldn't have problems with any of them.

The police force that used to be most worrying to travellers was the dreaded Komīteh (Komīteh-yé Enqelāb-é Eslāmī; the Islamic Revolutionary Committee, or 'religious police'). Their members are recognisable by short stubbly beards, black collarless shirts and green fatigues, their symbol being an arm with a bandaged hand clutching a rifle. Their primary roles are the monitoring of internal security and the enforcement of Islamic law, which used to mean tackling even foreign women over the slightest infringement of the dress code. Although you should still be particularly obsequious if any of them crosses your path, these days they seem to be pretty much confined to barracks. In two months in Iran our female author was never once bothered by the Komīteh.

Partly in response to a couple of recent instances in which drug smugglers held tourists to ransom (all were released unharmed), in 2000 it was announced that a wholly new police force would be set up specifically to protect tourists. By the time you read this, it may actually have happened.

Bogus Police More worrying are the growing number of reports of bogus police stopping tourists on the street, demanding to see passports and money and then making off with them. Most of these reports come from Tehrān, Shīrāz and Esfahān. The following story is typical:

> Four men in a white Paykan tried to stop us at Beheshtī St (Esfahān), near Emām Khomeinī Square. One of them yelled 'Police!' He flashed some identity card that for all we knew may have been his membership card for the local carpet-makers' council...The fact that they didn't come out of the car and wore civilian clothes puzzled us. They motioned us to come to the car, but we disobeyed (and) kept walking to the square. When they realised we wouldn't listen, the driver put the car into reverse and dashed into Āyatollāh Dastgheib St.
>
> **Martine van de Kreeke**

Genuine police officers would never pull a stunt like this. Should something like this happen to you, demand to go to your hotel or to a police station.

Security Checks Although soldiers and policemen roam the streets and patrol the highways checking on the movements of pedestrians and road users, they rarely trouble foreigners. Sexually segregated passport and baggage inspections and body frisks are routine for everyone on entry to some train stations and ports, at all airports, at some public gatherings and sometimes outside post and telephone offices, museums and other public buildings. After a fatal bomb blast a few years ago, security at public places in Mashhad and at the shrine of Emām Khomeinī in Tehrān is tighter than anywhere else in the country.

Foreigners are expected to carry their passports with them at all times, although this can be tricky when hotels also like to hang onto them throughout your stay. In fact, you may be best off leaving your passport at the hotel so that if you're stopped by bogus police you can say you haven't got it with you. In the unlikely event of your being stopped by genuine police officers, there's no need to worry provided your visa is in order.

Cameras can easily arouse suspicion; for more advice, see the Photography & Video section earlier.

Checkpoints See the Getting Around chapter for information about the frequent roadblocks-cum-checkpoints around the countryside.

Crime

In general, Iran is one of the safest countries for foreign visitors, but of course crime does still exist (and seems to be rising), so it pays to take the usual precautions. When travelling long distances by public transport, especially on international services, keep your passport, money and camera with you at all times as there is a slight possibility of theft by other passengers or at the frequent checkpoints en route. The occasional pickpocket operates in some crowded bazaars, and we have heard the odd story of bag snatching from Esfahān.

Theft from a hotel room is very unlikely, since the staff keep careful watch over visitors and residents. Nonresidents often have to leave their identity cards at reception if they want to go upstairs; in most places they're barred from any part of the hotel except the ground floor and restaurant. Hotels are locked or guarded at night. Most places also have a safe for guests' valuables. The theft of motorcycles is increasingly common, particularly in Tehrān. Even locals worry about parking their cars in the streets of Zāhedān, and anywhere near the Afghan and Pakistani borders (see Car & Motorcycle in the Getting Around chapter for more discussion on this).

The most valuable possession westerners usually bring to Iran – and the hardest to replace – is a foreign passport. Largely because of the difficulty Iranians face in travelling to Western countries, but also partly because of underworld operations, there is a booming black market in forged and stolen foreign passports. Take the usual precautions and keep your passport strapped to your body.

Traffic

Iran has one of the world's worst road accident rates. More than 200,000 road accidents are *reported* every year; no-one knows how many more go unreported. That works out at a rate of one accident per year for every 15 vehicles on the road. Every year more than 15,000 people die on Iranian roads.

If you have travelled elsewhere in the region, Iran's traffic chaos may come as little surprise, but if you have arrived from the West, you will be horrified. No-one pays a blind bit of notice to road rules. The willingness of a car to stop at a red light at a busy intersection is directly proportional to the number of armed traffic police the driver can see within rifle range. Some cars and all motorbikes use the designated bus lanes that usually go in the *opposite* direction to the rest of the traffic. Motorbikes speed through red lights, drive on footpaths and careen through crowded bazaars, all of which might be funny if it wasn't so damn dangerous.

The Jubs

In almost every Iranian city the main streets are lined with canals or *jubs*, which originally served to distribute drinking water through the city, but now serve as rain-water channels-cum-rubbish-collecting repositories. At the best of times they're a hazard for anyone crossing a road without looking carefully (especially women encumbered in tightish long skirts). After rain they can quickly turn into raging torrents.

While traffic in major cities rarely goes fast enough to cause a serious accident, never underestimate the possibility of dying a horrible death while crossing the road. Vehicles never stop at pedestrian crossings and there are far too few footbridges or underpasses. You will quickly realise that there's little alternative to stepping out in front of the traffic, as the Iranians do, and hoping that the drivers will slow down. It may not be much consolation, but the law says that if a driver hits a pedestrian the driver is always the one at fault and the one liable to pay blood money to the family of the victim.

Unmarried Foreign Couples

Unmarried foreign couples used to find it very difficult to share a room while travelling around Iran. Recently, however, hotel staff are starting to understand the weird wishes of foreigners and don't usually ask too many questions. One way to avoid problems is to wear a wedding ring; hotel receptionists usually accept that foreign females don't take their husbands' family name on marriage, since Iranian women don't either.

> I had planned to go to Iran by myself, but eventually a (male) friend of mine joined me. In the visa application we wrote we were married (he is Dutch, I am Italian, and we applied in Switzerland). Nobody ever doubted it, apart from a hotel owner who did not believe that people of different nationalities can be married. We just said it is possible, and that was it.
>
> **Anonymous**

Overcharging

Several readers have written to complain of overcharging, especially, by taxi drivers in Esfahān. Tabrīz has been identified as a town whose inhabitants are more than usually keen to fleece foreigners, so always ask about the price even of food and drink to be on the safe side. If you hand over a large note, don't be surprised if the recipient expects to keep the change.

Political Crises

Iran is no stranger to political crises and although the situation seemed fairly stable at the time of writing, it can always change. Regardless of your nationality, it's wise to stay clear of all political gatherings – don't take photos, don't discuss what's going on with anyone you don't know well and keep a low profile. It's a good idea to bring a short-wave radio with you, so you can keep in touch with what's happening in Iran and elsewhere in the region.

EMERGENCIES

The following emergency telephone numbers are available throughout Iran, although you'll be lucky if you find anyone on the other end of the line who speaks English:

Accidents	☎ 197
Ambulance	☎ 115
Emergency Assistance	☎ 198
Fire Brigade	☎ 125
Police	☎ 129

If you're having no luck dialling these numbers, get straight onto your embassy who should be able to help if it's a real emergency.

Throughout this book we have listed local telephone numbers for emergency assistance in the relevant Information sections.

LEGAL MATTERS

Like most things in Iran, the legal system is based on Islamic principles although the system is not as extreme as in countries such as Sudan or Iraq where various parts of one's anatomy can be lopped off for infringing the law. See the Religion section in the Facts about Iran chapter for a rundown on the meaning of Sharia'a law.

Generally, the same activities that are illegal in your home country are illegal in Iran, the difference being that the penalties laid down are much harsher. For most minor crimes, foreigners will probably get deported although it is possible to fall foul of the law big time, as one German businessman found out when he was sentenced to death for having sex with an unmarried Muslim woman.

It would be a very silly person who considered using drugs (or alcohol) in Iran. The penalties for drug use and smuggling are extremely harsh. Carrying the smallest amount of hashish can result in a minimum six-month jail sentence, and don't expect any assistance from your embassy, a fair trial or a comfortable cell. We strongly urge you to avoid using, carrying or selling any type of drugs or alcohol.

There are two 'crimes' which foreigners may not be aware of. Homosexual activity is highly illegal and has resulted in the death penalty for some Iranians. Deliberate refusal to comply with the hejab (the Islamic law on women's dress) can also result in a public flogging (although a foreigner is much more likely to be deported).

Getting Arrested
In the very unlikely event that you get arrested, it's best not to reply to, or appear to understand, any questions in Farsi. If you do choose to answer questions, do so politely, openly and diplomatically. Since the primary motives for arresting a foreigner are usually curiosity, mild suspicion and the desire to appear powerful, answer your interrogators so that their curiosity is satisfied, their suspicion allayed and their sense of their own self-importance flattered. Take special care not to incriminate yourself or anyone else, especially anyone Iranian, with a careless statement. Get in contact with your embassy in Tehrān as soon as possible.

BUSINESS HOURS
Opening and closing times are more erratic in Iran than you may be used to, but you can rely on most businesses closing all day on Friday and perhaps on Thursday afternoon (the Iranian weekend). Many businesses close during the afternoon for a siesta (from about 1 pm to 3 or 4 pm); along the hot Persian Gulf, this siesta understandably stretches until about 5 pm. The only thing that rarely stops during this time is public transport.

The most likely time to find anything open is between 9 am and noon, daily except Friday. In general, banks open from 8 am to 4 pm daily except Friday (8 am to noon on Thursday), and government offices open from 8 am to 2 pm daily except Friday (8 am to noon on Thursday). Iran Air offices are usually open from 7.30 am to 6 pm daily (7.30 am to noon on Friday). Museums usually open from 8.30 am to 6 pm in summer (5 pm in winter), with one day off, usually Monday or Tuesday. Post and telephone offices usually open every day from 8 am to 7 pm, except in smaller towns where they may close at 5 pm. Private businesses keep more or less Western hours – from 8 or 9 am to 5 pm daily except Friday and Thursday afternoon. Shops may stay open until 8 or 9 pm.

CALENDARS
Three calendars are in common use in Iran: The Persian solar calendar is the one in official and everyday use; the Muslim lunar calendar is used for Islamic religious matters; and the Western (Gregorian) calendar is used in dealing with foreigners and in some history books. As a result, Iranian newspapers have three dates along their mastheads. For example, 30 August 2000 also appeared as Shahrivar 9 1379 (Persian) and Jamadi-ul-Awai 29 1421 (Muslim). The Zoroastrians also have their own calendar (see the boxed text 'The Iranian Calendars' opposite), but this is less likely to have any effect on foreigners.

There is no easy way of converting a date from one system to another except by referring to an Iranian diary or calendar. This is particularly important when booking public transport or extending your visa, when you will be thinking in terms of the Gregorian calendar while the clerk at the other end

The Iranian Calendars

Persian Calendar

The modern Persian solar calendar, a direct descendant of the ancient Zoroastrian calendar, is calculated from the first day of spring in the year of the Hejira, the flight of the Prophet Mohammed from Mecca to Medina in AD 622. It has 365 days (366 every leap year), with its New Year (Nō Rūz) usually falling on 21 March according to the Western calendar. Dates given in the Persian calendar sometimes have AHS added after the year when written in English. The names of the Persian months are as follows:

season	Persian month	approximate equivalent	season	Persian month	approximate equivalent
Spring (Bahār)	Farvardīn	21 Mar–20 Apr	Autumn (Pā'īz)	Mehr	23 Sep–22 Oct
	Ordībehesht	21 Apr–21 May		Ābān	23 Oct–21 Nov
	Khordād	22 May–21 Jun		Āzar	22 Nov–21 Dec
Summer (Tābestān)	Tīr	22 Jun–22 Jul	Winter (Zāmestān)	Dei	22 Dec–20 Jan
	Mordād	23 Jul–22 Aug		Bahman	21 Jan–19 Feb
	Shahrīvar	23 Aug–22 Sep		Esfand	20 Feb–20 Mar

Muslim Calendar

The Muslim calendar, which is used to some extent in all Islamic countries, starts from the month before the Hejira, but is based on the lunar year of 354 or 355 days, so that it is currently out of step with the Persian solar calendar by some 40 years. The names of the 12 months of the Muslim calendar in Farsi are: Moharram, Safar, Rabī'-ol-Avval, Rabī'-ol-Osānī (or Rabī'-ol-Ākhar), Jamādī-l-Ūlā (or Jamādī-ul-Awai), Jamādī-l-Okhrā (or Jamādī-ul-Sami), Rajab, Sha'bān, Ramazān, Shavvāl, Zū-l-Gha'deh and Zū-l-Hejjeh.

The Zoroastrian Calendar

The Zoroastrian calendar works to a solar year of 12 months of 30 days each, with five additional days. The week has no place in this system, and each of the 30 days of the month is named after and presided over by its own angel or archangel. The 1st, 8th, 15th and 23rd of each month are holy days. As in the Persian calendar, the Zoroastrian year begins in March at the vernal equinox. The months of the Zoroastrian calendar (most of which have the same names as the Persian calendar) run as follows:

season	Zoroastrian month	season	Zoroastrian month
Spring (Bahār)	Farvardīn	Autumn (Pā'īz)	Mehr
	Ordībehesht		Ābān
	Khordād		Āzar
Summer (Tābestān)	Tīr	Winter (Zāmestān)	Dei
	Amordād		Bahman
	Shahrīvar		Andarmaz

is thinking in terms of the Persian calendar. If your visa extension is written only in Farsi be sure to get an Iranian to check the date on it for you and to cross-check with a calendar.

Traditionally, both Persian and Muslim days were reckoned as starting at sunset, but nowadays midnight is usually regarded as the start of the Persian day.

PUBLIC HOLIDAYS & SPECIAL EVENTS

It is vital to note the dates of the public holidays, especially if you are travelling on a short visa that you hope to extend at a government office. Just about everything closes on a religious holiday, although not necessarily on a national holiday. Over public holidays, transport will still function normally, and hotels will remain open, but only restaurants in a few upmarket hotels will stay open.

Religious Holidays

The religious holidays listed here follow the Muslim lunar calendar, which means that the corresponding dates in the Western calendar vary considerably every year. They are normally celebrated with a public holiday, extended for a day or more if it falls near the Iranian weekend, but you probably won't know this unless you read Farsi. The dates of religious holidays can change suddenly; for example, in 1997 the Supreme Leader moved the anniversary of the death of the Prophet's daughter Fatima forward by three weeks. Check the newspapers for upcoming holidays.

Eid-é Fetr (1 to 3 Shavvāl) – the Festival of the Breaking of the Fast that marks the end of Ramazān (see later in this section). After sunset on the last day of Ramazān, Muslims spill out onto the streets, drivers honk their horns in celebration, and virtually everyone joins in an orgy of overeating.

Qadir-é Khom (18 Zū-l-Hejjeh) – commemorates the day that the Prophet Mohammed appointed Emām Alī as his successor while returning to Mecca.

Ashūra (9 & 10 Moharram) – the anniversary of the martyrdom of Hossein, the third Shiite imam, in battle at Karbala in October AD 680. This is celebrated with religious dramas and sombre parades of devout Shiite men in black shirts, some of whom whip themselves with chains until they draw blood (see Theatre in the 'Arts of Iran' special section, in the Facts about Iran chapter).

Arbaeen (20 & 21 Safar) – the 40th day after 9 & 10 Moharram

Birthday of the Prophet Mohammed (17 Rabī'-ol-Avval)

Anniversary of the death of Fatima (3 Jamādī-ul-Sami) – Fatima was the daughter of the Prophet Mohammed.

Ramazān For many Muslims, the month of dawn-to-dusk fasting, known in Iran as Ramazān, is not an unpleasant ordeal but a chance to perform a ritual cleansing of body and mind. Some people, especially in towns, don't fully observe the fast, but most do for at least part of the month. Ramazān is imposed on everyone in Iran, but foreigners

Mourning Days

Mourning is a very big deal in Iran. Whole sections of the bazaar are devoted to the production of black flags which are hung out on public mourning days (eg, on the anniversary of the death of Fatima, the daughter of the Prophet). When I asked why the flags had not come down after this anniversary I was told: 'We have 12 imams, not to mention the Prophet, and they all had families, so we're always mourning somebody'.

On mourning days, museums will close and non-Muslims will be less welcome in mosques. Such entertainment as there is in the big cities will be suspended until the mourning period is over. Traditionally, mourning lasts for 40 days; it's just as well that this period isn't observed on all these occasions or nothing in the country would ever be open.

The most intense period of mourning occurs in Moharram to commemorate the death of Emām Hossein at Karbala (see the boxed text 'Karbala & Najaf' in the Western Iran chapter for more details).

Pat Yale

and non-Muslims can still eat, drink and smoke behind closed doors. Some Muslims are exempted from the fast (eg, pregnant and menstruating women, travellers, the elderly and the sick), but they mustn't eat or drink in front of others who are fasting.

Ramazān can be a trying period, particularly when it coincides with a spell of hot weather. It is considered a great sin to drink alcohol during Ramazān, and the penalties are stiffer even than at other times of year. The Komīteh is at its most active at this time, often on the lookout for anyone not dressed respectfully.

Domestic airlines still serve food to passengers in the daytime, and roadside cafes still cater for travellers. Many hotels keep their restaurants open in the daytime, or at least allow foreigners to order food in their rooms (guests can consider themselves travellers and so free from the obligation to fast). Other restaurants either close altogether or open only after dark. Many shops selling food remain open throughout Ramazān, so you can buy food to eat in your room.

Although you shouldn't have many problems in the larger cities, you may not be able to find any food at all during the daytime in rural areas and small towns. For this reason, Ramazān is probably not the best time to travel adventurously. Also, businesses and shops keep odd hours, tempers can flare and very little serious business gets done. Public transport continues to function, but often to reduced schedules. Not surprisingly, Eid-é Fetr, the day after Ramazān ends, is celebrated in grand style.

National Holidays

Just to confuse matters, national holidays follow the Persian solar calendar, and usually fall on the same day each year according to the Western calendar. If they fall near the Iranian weekend, an extra holiday is sometimes declared. As over religious holidays, most government offices are closed, which can disrupt your travel plans.

Dahe-yé Fajr or **The 10 Days of Dawn** (1–10 February; 11–21 Bahman) – the lead up to Āyatollāh Khomeinī's coming to power. They are often celebrated in Tehrān with concerts and other cultural events.

Magnificent Victory of the Islamic Revolution of Iran (11 February; 22 Bahman) – the anniversary of Khomeinī's coming to power in 1979.

Oil Nationalisation Day (20 March; 29 Esfand) – commemorates the day in 1951 when the Anglo-Iranian Oil Company was taken into Iranian hands.

Eid-é Nō Rūz (21–24 March; 1–4 Farvardīn) – Iranian New Year

Islamic Republic Day (1 April; 12 Farvardīn) – the anniversary of the establishment of the Islamic Republic of Iran in 1979.

Sīzdah Bedar (2 April; 13 Farvardīn) – the 13th day of the Iranian New Year, when Iranians traditionally leave their houses for the day.

Heart-Rending Departure of the Great Leader of the Islamic Republic of Iran (4 June; 14 Khordād) – commemorates the death of Āyatollāh Khomeinī in 1989. About 500,000 Iranians flock to Tehrān, Qom (where he trained and lived) and the village of Khomein (where he was born). Try not to be in Tehrān around this event; if you are, don't expect to find anything open or to be able to get on any transport.

Anniversary of the Arrest of Āyatollāh Khomeinī (5 June; 15 Khordād) – in 1963, Khomeinī was arrested after urging the Muslims of the world to rise up against the superpowers.

Anniversary of the Death of Dr Seyed Beheshtī (28 June; 7 Tīr) – the anniversary of the 1980 bomb blast at a meeting of the Islamic Republic Party which killed Dr Seyed Beheshtī and several others.

Day of the Martyrs of the Revolution (8 September; 17 Shahrīvar)

Nō Rūz Even before the Achaemenid period, the coming of spring was celebrated on a large scale throughout Persia, and today the Iranian New Year, or Nō Rūz, is a huge family celebration. Starting on the spring equinox (around 21 March), Iranians traditionally return to their home villages and towns to celebrate the New Year with friends and relatives.

On Sīzdah Bedar, the 13th day of the Persian New Year, Iranians avoid the bad luck associated with the number 13 and go to the countryside for a picnic. At this time, some unmarried women pray to find a husband during the coming year, plates are sometimes smashed, traditional food is cooked and children play games.

It is very difficult to find hotel accommodation over the Iranian New Year (for about 10 days before and after 21 March), and all forms of public transport are very heavily booked. Most businesses, including many restaurants (except those in good hotels), will close for about five days after the start of New Year (ie, from about 21 to 25 March inclusive). Although Nō Rūz is great fun if you are visiting Iranian friends, it is not a very sensible time to travel to Iran otherwise, as one expatriate Iranian returning home confirmed:

As I was visiting family, I specifically visited during the Iranian New Year. This is a great time to get everyone together, but definitely the wrong time to visit Iran and its many attractions. This is the only time Iranians have off and whilst this time of year is very festive (very much like Christmas) most, if not all, Iranians are on vacation at this time, and everyone will be visiting the sites you want to visit!

Azar Marashian

The Seven 'S's

The lead-up to the Iranian New Year is traditionally a time for spring-cleaning. Closer to the big day, tables are specially laid according to a tradition called *haft seen*, or Seven 'S's: Seven articles must be placed on the table, the Farsi names of which all start with the letter 's'. These include seeds (*sabzī*), apples (*sīb*), garlic (*sīr*), vinegar (*serkeh*), a gold coin and a bowl with goldfish in it. Mothers are also expected to eat symbolic hard-boiled eggs, one for every child. During the day bonfires are also lit for people to jump over.

At the stroke of midnight, the family recites a special prayer seeking happiness, good health and prosperity, and then the serious eating and partying begins. A special Nō Rūz rice dish is passed around, and the older folk give presents (*eidi*) to the young. For the next two weeks, most families visit relatives and friends all over the country, placing the *sabzī* on the roof of their car as they drive off so they will blow away and so dispel bad luck.

Festivals

Two festivals worth watching out for if you're in Tehrān are the Iranian Epic Music Festival, usually held in April, and the Fajr International Film Festival, usually held in February. You will need to watch the English-language papers or ask a travel agent for exact dates.

ACTIVITIES

If you love the great outdoors and can get a visa long enough to allow it, Iran has plenty of space and scenery where you can trek, climb and even ski to your heart's content.

Trekking

Short Treks The vast distances, difficulties with getting more than short visas and jittery security forces are hardly conducive to long-distance trekking, but Iran still offers many excellent one-day walks. Possibilities exist in northern Tehrān, around Darband and Tōchāl; on Hormoz Island; at Kalardasht, Māsuleh and Nahar Khorān in the Caspian region; and around Kermān, Orūmiyeh and Takht-é Soleimān (for more details see those sections in the main text). Wherever you go, take food and water, a jumper and wet weather gear, and a compass and a map. If possible, let someone know where you are going and when you expect to be back.

Longer Treks If you can stay long enough to appreciate them, Iran also offers several five- to seven-day hikes across mountains and through forests, a few challenging mountain climbs and a couple of full-scale expeditions for the more adventurous.

In remote regions, especially near borders, you may stumble across military/police/security areas; an Iranian guide or a few phrases of Farsi should smooth over any misunderstandings. Drinking water is often scarce, so take your own supplies in the desert regions, and purification tablets or water filters in other places.

For treks of more than a couple of days in remote areas, you should take camping equipment, including a good sleeping bag. Though some mountains have huts for climbers, these may be closed, full or inadequate, so carrying a tent is a good idea. Although you can often buy a limited range of foods at villages along the way, you may prefer to bring food and cooking equipment from town.

One of the best trekking routes is across the Alborz Mountains from Karaj, near Tehrān, to Chālūs on the Caspian Sea. This route has several advantages as it's easily accessible by public transport, including private taxi; the area is densely populated, with many villages along the way where you can find food, water, shelter and directions; and it's a relatively easy trek.

Other popular trekking routes in the Caspian region include from Ābyek to Abbās Ābād, via Mt Alam; from Garmabdar to Nōshahr; and from Shāhrūd to Gorgān. Most of these routes will take about five to seven days, depending on how much mountain climbing you do and whether you use public transport some of the way.

Desert Treks The two most difficult areas to explore are probably the Dasht-é Kavīr and Dasht-é Lūt deserts, but with the right preparation and an experienced guide, there is no reason why you cannot trek across at least some of the Dasht-é Kavīr. Only the very toughest travellers would undertake this alone; most will prefer to go on an organised trek with one of the agencies listed later in this section.

One main trekking route taking at least eight days (about 300km) heads from Vārāmīn to Kāshān, via the eastern side of Lake Namak (you can save three days' trek by renting a car as far as Mobarakiyeh). If you have a 4WD, and get permission from the relevant authorities (ask the Mountaineering Federation people how to go about it), it's possible to drive the whole way in two to three days.

Another awesome 20- to 30-day trek, possible with a lot of preparation and an experienced guide, travels the roughly 700km from Vārāmīn to Tabas in the middle of the desert. An experienced guide will find water along the way and steer well clear of the drug smugglers who cross the Lūt between Afghanistan (or Pakistan) and Turkey (and the police following hard on their footsteps). Talk to the people at the Mountaineering Federation if you are interested in undertaking such an awe-inspiring journey.

Crossing the barren wastes of the Dasht-é Kavīr desert nearly put paid to Alexander the Great so no-one should contemplate venturing here alone.

Rock Climbing

If clambering about on rocks is more your thing, there are several excellent and accessible places to try. Closest to Tehrān is Band-Yakh-Chal, one hour's drive north of Tajrish Square. The rocks here soar to 15m and can be climbed if you have suitable bolts. They're very busy on Friday. Alternatively, 40km north of Karaj and west of the Amīr Kābir Reservoir, you can go rock climbing at Pol-Khab (The Place of Good Sleeping).

Further afield, the rocks around Bījār in Kordestān province are begging to be explored; the rocky hills which line the main road through Khorram Ābād are easy to reach and extensive; the road between Ker-

mānshāh and Bīsotūn is lined with awesome rocks and cliffs, some with ancient statues and inscriptions carved into them; and the rocky hills around Mākū are especially accessible, although you should probably stay within eyesight of town or take a guide because of the proximity of the Turkish border.

Mountaineering

It may come as a surprise to learn that Iran boasts several high mountains, some of them permanently snowcapped. Most can be climbed by anyone fit without special equipment, experience or a guide, although you should always check the situation before embarking on a mountain trek. The best time to climb most Iranian mountains is between early June and the end of August.

The magnificent Alborz Mountains north of Tehrān contain about 70 peaks more than 4000m high. The best known is Iran's highest mountain, Damāvand (5671m) – for more details, see Mt Damāvand in the Around Tehrān section of the Tehrān chapter.

Other mountains you might want to climb include Mt Alam (see the Around Nōshahr & Chālūs section in the Caspian Sea chapter); Mt Sabalān (see the Around Tabrīz and Around Ardabīl sections of the Western Iran chapter); Mt Sahand (see the Around Tabrīz section of the Western Iran chapter); and Mt Oshturān (see the Around Khorram Ābād section of the Western Iran chapter).

In addition, you could try the snowcapped Mt Taftān (4042m) volcano, near the Pakistani border; and Mt Hezār (4420m) and Mt Lālezār (4374m) in the Pāyeh Mountains, south of Kermān. The Zardkouh Mountains west of Esfahān can also be climbed using Shahr-é Kord as a base; the highest point is Mt Zardkouh (4337m). Or there is the Dena Range, north-west of Shīrāz, with 37 peaks over 4000m, the highest of them Mt Gash Mastan (4460m).

Guides & Porters The best time to climb in Iran is between June and the end of August (or until the end of September if the weather holds). The cost of a guide depends on your bargaining skills, the number of climbers in the group, the equipment needed, the length of the trip and the difficulty of the route you want to undertake. You should probably assume you will need to pay about US$40 a day for an English-speaking guide and US$25 for a donkey to carry your equipment.

Equipment Purchase & Rental There are three camping shops about 200m along the walking trail that starts at the end of the ski lift at Darband, in northern Tehrān (see the Around Tehrān section of the Tehrān chapter for details) that rent out mountaineering gear. Staff speak little English, so can offer only limited advice.

There's an expectedly good and accessible mountaineering shop in Tehrān. Varzesh Kooh is on the fourth floor of a building in the south-eastern corner of Ferdōsī Square, beside a travel agency. It sells sleeping bags, backpacks, crampons, ice axes and Koflach boots.

Otherwise, try Kassa Mountaineering & Tourism, which has plenty of equipment for hire; it's near the Mountaineering Federation office in central Tehrān.

Maps There are very few specialised trekking or mountain-climbing maps on Iran available in English. If you want to climb any of the mountains described in this book, either take a guide or try and get hold of the relevant TPC or ONC series of topographical maps published by the Defence Mapping Agency in the USA before you leave home. Once in Iran, contact Kassa Mountaineering & Tourism or try the Gita Shenasi map shop in Tehrān, which should at least have a map of the Alborz Mountains in stock.

Trekking & Mountaineering Agencies Some of the travel agencies listed under Organised Tours in the Getting Around chapter will be able to help you organise walking and climbing holidays. For specialised advice on trekking and mountaineering trips in Iran, try contacting the following agencies:

Kassa Mountaineering & Tourism (☎ 021-751 0463, fax 751 0464, e KASSA@intelimet.net) 9 Maghdi Alley, Sharīatī St, Tehrān. This private trekking agency offers a full range of trekking and climbing tours, desert expeditions etc. It is run by Ahmad Shirmohammad, an experienced climber who speaks English.

Mountaineering Federation of Iran (☎ 021-883 9928, fax 836 641) 15 Varzandeh St, Mofatteh Ave, Tehrān; PO Box 15815/1881. About 200m up from the former US embassy is a side alley which accommodates most of Iran's sporting organisations. The undisputed experts in anything relating to mountain climbing, and trekking, the Mountaineering Federation people are a mine of information and advice. Staff speak English, or can find someone who does.

Skiing

Immediately after the Revolution, skiing in Iran was banned. The ban was lifted in 1988 and the restrictions on behaviour on the ski slopes considerably eased in 1997.

Iran is now one of the least expensive skiing destinations in the world. The season is long and the snow is often powdery. Of the dozen or more downhill skiing areas near Tehrān, only three – Darbansar, Shemsak and Dīzin – are easily accessible, and have reliable facilities and equipment for hire (see the Around Tehrān section in the Tehrān chapter for more details). There is also good downhill skiing available near Tabrīz (see the Around Tabrīz section in the Western Iran chapter for more details). For cross-country skiing, try the Kalardasht region near the Caspian Sea, or anywhere around Mt Damāvand.

Men and women have to ski on different slopes (the women's slopes are apparently easier), and there are separate ski lifts for both sexes. Women must still wear hejab on the lower slopes, and recent reports suggest a new mountain police force has been set up to discourage mingling of the sexes even on the higher slopes.

The season in the Alborz Mountains (where most of the slopes are located) gets going about mid-January and lasts until just after the Iranian New Year (about 21 March), although around Tabrīz, it can last as late as mid-May. The resorts are particularly busy around Iranian New Year. The slopes are packed with Iranians on Thursday and Friday, and with diplomats and expats on Saturday, but on other days you may have some parts to yourself. Lifts normally operate between 9 am and 4 pm daily.

All the resorts have upmarket hotels, which normally charge from about US$30 to US $100 for a room. Their restaurants normally serve Western and Iranian food at reasonable prices. Use of the ski lifts costs as little as IR40,000 a day. You can hire full equipment (ie, skis, poles and boots, but not clothes) at the resorts for about IR40,000 a day, or from a couple of camping shops along the walking trail at Darband in northern Tehrān.

For more information, contact the Skiing Federation (☎/fax 881 1785), 4th Floor, 14 Varzandeh St, Tehrān.

Cycling

There is only one cycle track in the whole country and it's on Kīsh Island. Although Iran's flat, well-surfaced country roads are well-suited to leisurely cycling, there is no tradition of cycling and 30 seconds in city traffic will be enough to put you right off the idea. See Bicycle in the Getting Around chapter for more details.

Diving

The only place in Iran with a recognised site for scuba diving and snorkelling is Kīsh Island, which is horribly expensive. See the Kīsh Island section in the Southern Iran chapter for more information.

Fishing

If you can persuade someone to let you on their boat, the best place to head for is the Caspian Sea where salmon, bream, mullet and sturgeon are found in large quantities. You can also catch trout in the Sefīd River, in the Caspian region, and fish in the Karaj River and Karaj Lake, several streams around Mt Damāvand, the Zāyandeh River, near Esfahān, and the Kārūn River in the south-west. The only places to buy or rent fishing equipment are a couple of shops at the southern end of Ferdōsī St in Tehrān.

Hang-Gliding

The cliff near the village of Lārijān, midway between Tehrān and Āmol, is where intrepid, mainly expat hang-gliders practise their stuff on weekends, much to the amazement of hundreds of awe-struck Iranian picnickers.

Water Sports

Water-skiing and other water sports are possible on many rivers and lakes, but the main place for rich Tehrānīs and expats to go is Karaj Lake, north of Karaj. Water-skiing is also possible, if you have the equipment, on Vahdat Dam, near Sanandaj, and Anzalī Lagoon, near Bandar-é Anzalī (although the latter is a waterfowl sanctuary so it's debatable how environmentally sound an idea this is). Women must still wear full hejab, which may not help the aerodynamics of water-skiing.

Beaches

A few sandy beaches along the Persian Gulf and the Caspian Sea are open to the public, but Iranians are not really sun-worshippers and even if they were, the dress code (women must swim in full hejab) and sexual segregation of the beaches takes much of the potential fun out of lying on them. The coast along the Caspian has a few expensive hotels with private beaches, but don't expect the Costa del Sol or French Riviera.

Don't swim anywhere in the Persian Gulf unless you see locals paddling about; one reason for the recent decline in pearl fishing is the increase in the local shark population.

COURSES

Even if there were more courses to sign up for, you probably wouldn't get a visa long enough to learn much. The English-language newspapers sometimes advertise courses in Farsi, but these are mainly for diplomats who don't have to fret about visa extensions. One place recommended by a reader is the International Farsi Centre (☎ 021-271 7120) on Valiasr St which has summer courses. Alternatively, your embassy may be able to put you in touch with a private Farsi tutor.

Traditional Iranian music classes are sometimes organised by the Arghanoun Cultural & Musical Association in Tehrān (☎ 021-826 2584). These classes aim to show foreigners and Iranians how to play traditional instruments and explain some of Iran's musical history at the same time. Look in the classifieds in the English-language press for details of these and any other courses that may occasionally pop up.

WORK

Unless you have a skill that is in particular demand (like engineering or medicine), are married to an Iranian or are a Shiite Muslim, your chances of finding legal, paid work in Iran range from negligible to nil. Some Iranian companies (mostly government enterprises) take foreigners on short-term contracts, but they don't recruit inside Iran. Even if you did get a job offer, the work permit is no mere formality – westerners are only likely to get one if a government department or semi-government organisation is prepared to lobby the Ministry of Labour very hard on their behalf.

The many English-language schools don't want casual labour, and even if you found one that did, you wouldn't get a work permit without family ties to Iran. In any case, wages are lamentable by Western standards and only a limited amount can be repatriated easily. For foreigners living in Iran (eg, spouses of diplomats), some jobs are advertised in the English-language newspapers.

ACCOMMODATION

Generally, Iran has a reasonable choice of accommodation, from the cheap and cheerful to the opulent and luxurious. If you turn up late at night in certain places at certain times of the year you will have trouble, but even if you front up in Mashhad at midnight at the peak of the pilgrimage season, someone will probably take pity on you before you have to start looking for a park bench.

All hotels, and some mosāferkhūnehs (lodging houses), are categorised and inspected by the Ministry of Culture & Islamic Guidance. Hotels are classified according to a star system, with five stars for a luxury establishment with private bathrooms, and one star for a place offering only simple accommodation with at least some bathroom or shower facilities. There is also a grading system for mosāferkhūnehs, which classes them as 'superior', '1st class' or '2nd class'. In the last of these categories you should expect almost unimaginable deprivations – there may not even be a shared shower. Nor is the star system much indication of the service you can expect; a mosāferkhūneh may

be able to rustle up tea at all hours whereas a four-star hotel's teahouse closes at 9 pm.

In general, our budget category covers mosāferkhūnehs, a few backpacker lodges, and one- and two-star places that offer a reasonable price for foreigners; mid-range covers two- and three-star hotels, and top end covers four- and five-star hotels. In a few places along the Caspian, there are also homestays (a room in someone's home) and suites or villas (fully equipped apartments). Prices are generally lowest in the east and south-east of the country, and highest in Tehrān and along the Caspian coast. In small towns or villages with no hotels, some mosāferkhūnehs charge everyone more because of the lack of competition.

Most mid-range and all top-end places can charge foreigners in US dollars, but now that the black market has died even if they quote the price in dollars they will almost certainly accept rials. Even on a tight budget it's still worth asking about rooms in the middle range, because almost all hotels in this price bracket will be prepared to drop their prices if it's quiet (although forget it if the place is run by the government agency, ITTO). Always try to talk to the hotel manager who is more likely to be ready to negotiate than other hotel staff.

If you are offered the 'foreigners price' of around US$25/40 for a single/double in a mid-range hotel, you could try asking for the 'Iranian' price, although this rarely works unless you are particularly assertive and speak Farsi. If that fails, ask for a reduction to, say, US$15/25, using the reasonable argument that the foreigners' price is way too high, or that you may stay more than one night.

You are unlikely to have problems finding a room in your price range except over the Iranian New Year and in Mashhad during the pilgrimage season. If you can't find anywhere, you can ask at the tourist office for help, or at the local police station (although you won't have much say over what sort of accommodation they get you).

Single hotel rooms are a rarity, so lone travellers will often have to fork out for a double.

Guests must fill out a registration form on arrival. Usually, the hotel will also want to keep your passport in case the police want to inspect it.

As in other parts of the Middle East, checkout time at hotels is often 2 pm – great if you want a lie-in, not so great if you arrive in the early hours exhausted after an overnight journey since it almost certainly forces you to pay for another night's accommodation.

There are no set rules about whether breakfast is included in the price, but the further away from Tehrān you go, the less likely it is to be included. In any case, many places will supply a cooked breakfast with plenty of tea for about IR3000. Almost every place to stay can supply a business card with their name, address and telephone number in Farsi and English, useful for asking directions if you get lost.

You rarely need to bring your own soap or towel when staying in an Iranian hotel. On the other hand there's rarely any toilet paper.

Camping

Camping on a regular basis is not really a viable option. Because of fears about security, the authorities don't like anyone other than nomads pitching tents at unofficial sites. Almost everywhere in Iran except the few government camp sites and private land where the owner has given someone permission to camp can be classified as an unofficial camp site.

Since many parts of the country are military or restricted zones and it's not always immediately obvious when you are near one, there is a risk of unknowingly camping in an area where your presence would attract a great deal of suspicion. Naturally, camping anywhere within binocular (or machine-gun) range of a border is inadvisable; be especially careful to avoid camping anywhere near the Afghanistan or Pakistan borders, or near the Kurdish parts of northern Iraq and south-eastern Turkey.

Long-distance trekkers and mountaineers who obviously need to camp should still discuss plans with the provincial tourist office first. The office may be able to write a letter of introduction, arrange a guide or help in other ways. It can also alert you to dangers such as wild animals or security problems. Bring camping and cooking equipment with you, although a few shops in Tehrān rent out gear (see the Trekking section in Activities earlier).

Mosāferkhūnehs

At the bottom end of the market you will probably end up staying in mosāferkhūnehs (literally 'travellers' houses'). Many of them don't have signs in English, so try to learn to recognise the Arabic script for the word 'mosāferkhūneh'. A mosāferkhūneh can offer anything from a bed in a noisy, grotty, male-only dormitory (for about IR12,000 per person per night) to a small, simple, private room, usually with just a sink, for perhaps IR20,000. Sometimes there is not even a shared shower on the premises.

Sadly, the police refuse to let all mosāferkhūnehs accept foreigners. However, even if you get turned away in one place, if you try a virtually identical place across the road, the manager may turn out to have the necessary documents. If you're stuck for somewhere to stay, go to the police station and see if you can persuade them to give you a permit allowing you to stay at a local mosāferkhūneh. Finding one that will accept foreigners is particularly hard in Būshehr, Bandar-é Abbās, Hamadān, Kermānshāh, Esfahān, Mashhad and Kāshān.

It has to be said that we receive a lot of complaints about the cleanliness and/or noisiness of many of the mosāferkhūnehs 'recommended' in this book, but until the Iranian tourism industry picks up enough for more cheapies to be built, there's little alternative but to include the ones that will take foreigners for the benefit of people travelling on the tightest budgets. Lone women, in particular, may not find many of them suitable places to stay.

Hotels

The Farsi words for hotel are *mehmūnkhūneh* or *mehmūnpazīr* but these days the word 'hotel' is commonly used in signs and understood by locals.

Some rooms in one-star hotels are similar in standard to private rooms in mosāfer-khūnehs, although others are surprisingly good value. A room in a decent one-star place should have a bathroom with shower (usually hot) and a toilet. There is often an added extra such as a telephone, television or fridge (useful for keeping food and drinks cold). In some one-star hotels, at least one member of staff can make a stab at conversation in English. Prices in this range start at about IR30,000/40,000 and go up to about IR50,000/70,000, depending on your negotiating skills.

In a two- or three-star hotel you may be able to have a conversation in English with the manager. You should also get a private bathroom with hot shower and toilet, and almost certainly with a TV and fridge. There may well be a reasonable hotel restaurant.

Prices for foreigners will often be quoted in US dollars although you will probably be able to pay the equivalent amount in rials. Prices for hotels in this range start at about US$20/30 for a single/double and go up to as much as US$50/70. If you normally stay at budget places, don't be afraid to check out a few places in the mid-range as well. If you bargain hard, you can sometimes get mid-range comfort at budget prices.

Most four- and five-star hotels will have all sorts of extras such as shops in the lobby, restaurants serving Western food, traditional teahouses, 24-hour room service and an overnight laundry service. A few also have bookshops, private taxi services, hairdressers, swimming pools and, of course, shops selling Persian carpets. Rooms are fairly luxurious, but prices are very high, starting from US$50/70 for a single/double and finishing at something like US$100/150. Prices are almost never negotiable.

Especially at the more expensive hotels, you should beware of taxes of 17% to 25% slapped on top of already high prices. Before agreeing to a price, ensure it includes everything.

Homestays

The other budget alternative, which is only available in a few towns along the Caspian Sea, is a homestay (the word is widely understood in the relevant towns). These are simply spare rooms, with or without private facilities, in the homes of locals, and cost from IR25,000 to IR50,000 for a double room (singles are rarely available). At a homestay, the rooms are invariably clean and the prices usually negotiable. This is also a good way to meet a local family.

Suites/Villas

At Rāmsar and a few other places on the Caspian Sea, Qom and Mashhad, you can rent a fully equipped self-catering apartment. These suites or villas (the words are understood by locals) usually consist of two bedrooms, a sitting room, a bathroom and a kitchen. Depending on your negotiating skills, and the seasonal demand, this luxury can cost as little as IR50,000 per suite – an absolute bargain and well worth a splurge.

FOOD

At its best, Iranian cuisine is excellent. With its emphasis on the freshest of ingredients and its relatively low levels of red meat and fat, it is also remarkably healthy. The problem is that to enjoy the best of Iranian cooking you need to be invited into Iranian houses. Unfortunately, budget travellers tend to get stuck with two or three standard dishes of kebabs or chicken, with rice, vegetables and bread.

Except in the more Westernised households, Iranians often prefer to eat at low tables on the floor in their homes. Cutlery normally consists of a fork and spoon. Eating with your hands is less common than in Arab countries or Pakistan, but where it seems to be expected, never put your left hand into a communal food dish; the left hand is used for something else altogether. That mainstay of restaurant meals, the kebab, is less commonly eaten at home where soups and stews are more usual.

For a list of basic food words, see the Language chapter at the back of this guidebook.

Local Food

Main Dishes Generally, the Iranian diet is based on rice, bread, fresh vegetables, herbs and fruit. Meat, usually minced or cut into small chunks, is used to add flavour but is rarely the dominant ingredient (except in kebabs, of course). The standard meats are lamb or mutton, though beef and veal also turn up from time to time; for religious reasons, pork never does. The most expensive meat is chicken, which is often spit-roasted and served whole or by the half. Goat, camel and buffalo meat are eaten in rural areas. Sadly, fish can be hard to find even on the Persian or Caspian coasts.

Lots of fresh herbs and spices, particularly turmeric, saffron, nutmeg and cardamom, are used in Iranian cooking. Nuts, and fresh or dried fruit, are commonly added to meat and poultry dishes to create a peculiarly Iranian blend of the sweet and the savoury.

The main dish served in restaurants throughout Iran is the *kabāb*. The standard *chelō kabāb* is a long thin strip of meat or mince served with a mound of rice or with bread and grilled tomatoes. *Kabāb-é makhsūs* (special kebab) is a larger strip of meat made of better quality lamb; *kabāb-é barg* (literally, 'leaf kebab') is thinner and more variable in quality. The cheapest and most common version is the *kabāb-é kūbīdé* (literally, 'ground kebab'), made out of minced meat. If you watch this being made, you may never eat one again (the 'meat' is kneaded hurriedly, and placed on the skewers by hand, the fingers forming the corrugations). Kebabs are usually sprinkled with *somāq* (sumac) and accompanied by a raw onion, a pat of butter and a bowl of yogurt to stir into the rice.

Another Iranian favourite is *jūjé kabāb*, marinated chicken kebab served in the same way as a normal kebab. Chicken kebab is more expensive than normal kebab and of variable quality. *Fīllé kabāb* is made with lamb fillet and is invariably delicious.

Kebabs are grilled for a few minutes over either charcoal or a gas-heated flame (the gas-cooked version is better avoided). If you are travelling as a twosome and are not particularly big eaters, you should be able to share a plate of kebabs topped up with tomatoes, bread, rice, soup and salad.

As a change from kebabs you may get served either soup or stew as a main course.

Iranian *sūp* (soup) is usually made from lentils and tomato paste and is thick and filling. A particularly popular variety is *āsh*, often made from yogurt and barley.

One gem of a main course that even budget travellers will be able to afford to eat is *ābgūsht*, a soup-stew combination, commonly served in teahouses and roadside cafes, where it is also known as *dīzī*; eaten with *sangak* bread, it makes a filling and inexpensive meal. The best ābgūsht is served in Tabrīz and along the walking trails of northern Tehrān (see the boxed text 'Eating Ābgūsht' in the Western Iran chapter for advice on how to eat this dish).

Khōresht is a blanket term for any kind of thick meaty stew made with vegetables and chopped nuts and served with rice. One of the prizes of Iranian cooking is *fesenjān*, a meat stew made with pomegranate juice, walnuts, aubergine and cardamom. It's quite an honour to be served this in an Iranian home; a few restaurants catering to tourists also serve it. *Qormeh-yé sabzī* is a rather bitter stew made from lamb, spinach and dried lime.

Like Turkish *dolmas*, Iranian *dolmehs* are vegetables, fruit or vine leaves stuffed with a mixture of vegetables or meat (or both), and rice. *Kofta* are meatballs, similar to Turkish *köfte*.

Yogurt, called *māst* and similar to Greek or Turkish yogurt, is a staple of Iranian cuisine. It's sometimes served on its own with *lavāsh* bread, or is mixed into rice, diced cucumber or other vegetables, fresh herbs and spices. It is also served as a side dish in many restaurants.

Tables in restaurants are usually set with lavāsh bread, cubes of cheese, rings of onion and a green salad.

Rice Rice is often served in vast helpings, although a government policy of subsidising wheat instead of rice means that rice is slowly being supplanted by bread as the major 'filling' element of meals. Rice from the rainy plains of Māzandarān province is thought of as some of the world's best. However, the best rice is often sold to Russia; what you eat in Iran may well have been imported from Thailand or elsewhere.

In general, rice is called *berenj*. *Chelō*, boiled or steamed rice, forms the basis of meals such as *chelō morgh* (chicken and rice). Rice cooked with other ingredients like nuts and spices is called *polō*.

Iranian rice is always fluffy and tender, never sticky or soggy. Often the cook will steam rice with yogurt or an egg yolk to make a crunchy golden crust at the bottom of the pan, which is broken up and served on top of the rice. Saffron is also frequently used to add flavour and colour. If rice is served with a knob of butter on top, blend this in as the Iranians do; it really livens it up if it's bland or dry.

Bread Iranian bread, known generally as *nūn*, is readily available for a few hundred rials. There are four main varieties, which are either baked in a cavernous clay furnace or briefly plunged into the flames of a pit-oven.

For breakfast in hotels you usually get lavāsh, the least appetising of Iranian breads. It's flat, thin and cardboard-like, and keeps for months. Crisp, salty *barbarī* has a glazed and finely latticed crust and is best eaten hot from the oven. The elite of Iranian breads is *sangak*, a thicker, oval-shaped bread, baked on a bed of stones to give it its characteristic dimpled appearance; make sure all the stones are removed before putting your teeth into it. (This bread is so popular there's actually a black market in it, with people prepared to pay more than the normal price to get their hands on it.) In Tehrān you may also come across *taftūn*, a crisp bread about 1cm thick and oval-shaped, with a characteristic ribbed surface. Along the Caspian Sea, French-style baguettes are also available.

Bakeries are not always terribly obvious and groceries usually sell only lavāsh. Look for little knots of people peering in at an open window and you'll probably find one eventually.

Nuts & Fruit These are passed around Iranian houses all day long and eaten in copious quantities. Most Iranian fruit is good, some of it among the best in the world. There are very few fruits that will not grow in Iran; even bananas can be found in south-ern Balūchestān although they're much more expensive than, say, apples and pears. Particularly recommended are pomegranates, peaches, watermelons, and rosy-fleshed grapefruits, which are fine to eat without sugar. You may also want to try a fig-peach which looks exactly like what is it – a cross between a fig and a peach.

Iranian almonds, hazelnuts and pistachios are all excellent.

Ice Cream, Cakes & Sweets After dinner, try to find somewhere that serves ice cream, especially the soft-serve variety in a crunchy cone costing just a few hundred rials. In most hot or touristy places there are prominently positioned ice-cream stalls; if the shop and the vendor look clean there's a fair chance the ice cream is safe.

Everywhere you go in Iran you'll find cake shops selling a wide range of sweet titbits (the macaroons are especially delicious). Cakes are sold by weight (usually IR1000 per 100g) so it's easy to try out all sorts of different types during your stay. Some shops have chairs and tables where you can sit down and eat your cakes with a cold drink, although rarely with a tea or coffee.

Iranian confectionery can be too sweet for some tastes, but if you have a sweet tooth, try some delicious and refreshing *pālūdeh* from Shīrāz, chewy *gaz* from Esfahān or the many delicious products made from honey, particularly in north-western Iran.

Western Food

Western-style dishes, particularly steaks and schnitzels but occasionally spaghetti bolognaise and other such delicacies, are available at some of the better restaurants, particularly in upmarket hotels. These may not be perfect or cheap (IR10,000 to IR15,000 a dish) compared to Iranian food, but they are worth an occasional splurge to boost morale and satisfy whingeing taste buds.

Fast Food

Along the main streets in town, you will see dozens of clean, modern hamburger joints where you can buy reheated sausage or hamburger meat ('sausage' and 'hamburger' are always understood by the men behind the counter), placed between a fresh roll and topped with tomato and pickles. These are Iranian-style hamburgers, as distinct from the more expensive Western-style hamburgers served in more upmarket places. Iranian-style hamburgers are always cheap: about IR4000 with a soft drink.

Everywhere you go you will find simple *kabābīs* (kebab shops) selling kebabs and cold drinks. Look for one that seems clean (most kabābīs are fairly hygienic). The price of a plate of kebabs with accompaniments depends on what you choose (see Main Dishes earlier for the options).

In the larger towns, brightly decorated restaurants selling 'fast' food like pizzas, and hamburgers are popular with locals of both sexes. They're often surprisingly good even if the service is not particularly 'fast'.

Vegetarian Food

Unless you are cooking for yourself, it would be hard to maintain a healthy diet in Iran without eating some animal products. As one traveller wrote: 'Three of the four vegetarians in my group succumbed, and the fourth looked pretty ropey.' The Farsi for 'I am a vegetarian' is *geyāh khār hastam*.

Most restaurants offer at least one vegetable dish, but sometimes small pieces of meat will have been used for flavouring. The main alternative is a salad, a standard component of meals in decent restaurants anyway. One dish to look out for is *kūkū*, a thick Iranian omelette cut into wedges and served hot or cold; spinach kūkū is a delicious staple of Iranian cooking.

Some snack bars sell Lebanese-style felafels, Indian-style samosas or meat-free khōreshts; look in the freezer but bear in mind that even a seemingly meat-free stew could have been made with meat stock. A few stalls sell boiled eggs or roasted potatoes in their jackets; otherwise they have kebab-style skewered tomatoes or onions to eat with bread, rice and salad.

It's probably better to buy your own food and supplement it with vitamin tablets if you think you may not be getting a balanced diet. Nuts, fruits, and vegetables such as cucumbers, tomatoes and pickles are excellent, readily available and very cheap. There's also plenty of fresh bread, as well as cheese and eggs for nonvegans.

> We're both vegetarians and didn't have too much trouble finding tasty food everywhere we went. We liked Shīrāz in particular because of the abundance of felafel sandwiches and samosas.
>
> **Jonathan Ruel**

Restaurants

The standard of restaurants varies considerably. You can eat at a kabābī, a hamburger joint or a restaurant (the best are often in hotels), or enjoy a drink or snack in a cake shop or teahouse. There are even a few excellent pizza places. However, if you want, for example, a cup of tea, a cola and a cake, you may have to go to three different places.

Most restaurants, except those in hotels, close by 7 pm on Friday; after this you may struggle to find somewhere to eat. On religious holidays, almost everywhere selling food will shut, markets and bazaars included.

Many restaurants are invisible from the main road in basements or upper storeys with only a Farsi sign at street level. The fact that a restaurant has a sign in English doesn't necessarily mean that there will be a menu in English, or that anyone working there will understand English. The easiest eating places to spot are the hamburger joints and kabābīs which tend to be gathered around the main squares in the towns.

Many restaurants don't have even a menu in Farsi, let alone English. To order, try to learn a few important words, point at the appropriate phrases in the Language chapter at the back of this book, or indicate something in the display window. Try to learn the Arabic numerals so you know the prices.

Hotel restaurants are often the best places to enjoy good meals, and they are open to anyone, including nonguests. The standard of the hotel is usually reflected in the range of meals, type of food and prices, but it's always worth at least checking the menu in more expensive hotels; some upmarket hotel restaurants offer excellent meals for about IR30,000 (about US$2.5).

Most hotel restaurants serve breakfast at least to guests. This normally consists of lavāsh bread with goat's milk cheese, yogurt, jam and honey, often accompanied by a fried or boiled egg, and always washed down with gallons of tea. They usually open for lunch between noon and 2 pm but often don't open again for dinner until about 8 pm. For lunch or dinner, kebabs, chicken and rice are bound to feature on the menu. If you're lucky there may also be fish, fesenjān and other stews too.

Although hotel restaurants rarely bother to segregate their guests, you will occasionally find a restaurant or cafe where women and families are expected to sit apart from lone men. Where this is the case, you will be directed to the right place to sit.

Self-Catering

If you are staying in mosāferkhūnehs self-catering may help you vary your diet. Most mosāferkhūnehs have little kitchens for making tea, and the owners may be prepared to let you use them to cook proper meals as well. Almost everywhere you're likely to stay has shops selling a limited range of tinned goods plus cheese, butter, yogurt and lavāsh bread. In the big towns you'll also find sections of the bazaar where you can shop for meat, fish and vegetables.

DRINKS
Nonalcoholic Drinks

Tea Iran's national drink is undoubtedly *chāy* (tea), served scalding hot and black in a small glass cup without a handle. According to the rules of Iranian hospitality, a host is honour-bound to offer a guest at least one cup of tea before considering any sort of business, and the guest is expected to drink it. Only in the most upmarket hotel restaurants will you be offered milk with your tea.

The tea tray is always set with a bowl of *ghand* (sugar cubes), often crudely hacked from huge rocks of sugar. It is customary to dip the sugar cube into the glass of tea to 'clean' it, then to place the cube between the front teeth before sucking the brew through it. In the mouth of a novice the ghand lasts a matter of seconds; an Iranian

can keep it going for a whole cup or more. If you want to stir the sugar into your tea, you'll probably have to bring your own teaspoon; these are rarely supplied in Iran.

If the tea is too hot and you're in a hurry, pour your tea into the saucer provided and slurp it loudly. Sometimes a bowl of mints is placed on the table. These are for sucking, rather than for putting into your glass. Also on the table may be lumps of yellow *nabot*, a sweet made from the sugar that crystallises on a piece of string dipped in a cauldron of sugar solution.

Coffee Iranian *qahveh* (coffee) is the same as Turkish coffee. Coffee is served strong, black and sweet, with a spoon to stir the sugar. Remember to let the brew settle and then drink only three-quarters of it, unless you enjoy coffee grains. Nescafé is making inroads into Iran, but it's still very expensive so you'd better look jolly pleased if anyone offers you a cup. Instant coffee is often served with milk, and sometimes made into an excellent milk shake.

Coffee is rare outside the upmarket restaurants. If you can't live without your caffeine fix, bring your own jar from home and learn how to ask for a glass of hot water in Farsi.

Other Drinks All sorts of delicious fresh fruit juices and milkshakes are served at ice-cream parlours, cafes and street stalls throughout Iran. Milk shakes are often semi-prepared in electric milk-shake makers, and then pepped up with some ice cream or milk, and ice.

As a general rule, if fruit juice is orange in colour, it's made from rock melon (cantaloupe) or carrot; light yellow is banana or honeydew melon; and if it's any other colour, you'd better ask! While these fruit drinks are considerably more expensive (IR2000 to IR2500) than soft drinks, the reduction in damage to your teeth often outweighs the damage to your wallet. Some cafes will not serve drinks to people who are not eating.

Tehrān boasts some of the purest tap water in the world; it comes straight from springs in the Alborz Mountains and is clean and tasty. Outside Tehrān, tap water varies in quality,

Time for Tea

Iran is famous for its teahouses, whether the traditional male-only versions, all bare walls and lines of men engaged in silent enjoyment of their *qalyans* (water pipes) or the new-look versions that welcome tourists of either sex. Listed here is a selection of our favourites, although you're bound to find your own.

- **Chāykhāneh-yé Sardār, Kermān** This teahouse is more of a local hangout, with tables indoors and out, where you can smoke a qalyan and get to know the locals.
- **Chāykhūneh-yé Vakīl, Kermān** Hugely popular, if unashamedly tourist-oriented, teahouse in a vaulted basement with small pools inside the bazaar. Come here to sip tea and perhaps buy some Kermān embroidery.
- **Citadel Gatehouse, Bam** Above the gatehouse of Bam citadel is a cosy teahouse with little alcoves pleasantly decorated with pictures of old Bam. Make sure you try one of their delicious date cookies.
- **Grounds of Hāfez's Tomb, Shīrāz** After visiting the tomb you'll want to sip tea in the walled tea garden at the back of the garden, a perfect place to try out smoking a qalyan.
- **Grounds of Qazvīn Museum** Behind the museum building is a small, simple teahouse frequented mostly by locals but where you'll be welcome to puff on a qalyan.
- **Hamūm-é Khān, Yazd** Also known as the Chāykhūneh-yé San'ati, this teahouse is in a restored underground hammam (bathhouse) and serves food as well as tea round its several restful pools of water.
- **Hezardestān Traditional Teahouse, Mashhad** This beautiful un121derground teahouse is festooned with carpets, samovars and antique water pipes. There's live music nightly.
- **Khājū Bridge, Esfahān** For many people a visit to the teahouse beneath the arches of the Khājū Bridge, with its idiosyncratic collections of teapots, glasses etc festooning walls and ceiling, will be a highlight of their visit to Esfahān.
- **Sa'd Ābād Museum Complex, Tehrān** This teahouse is in the grounds of the complex, just past the entrance. Recline outdoors on *takhts* (thrones) and enjoy the sounds of parrots screeching in the plane trees above you.
- **Sofre Khane Sonnati Sangalag, Tehrān** This pleasant, airy teahouse in Tehrān's Pārk-é Shahr sometimes offers lunch-time musical entertainment.

---

although it's generally safe to drink in most places. Outside the big towns, bottled water isn't always easy to come by, but you will usually find urns of water provided on street corners, in the grounds of museums etc.

Dūgh is a popular Iranian cold drink made from churned sour milk or yogurt, mixed with either sparkling or still water and sometimes flavoured with mint and other herbs.

Although Pepsi, Coca-Cola and Fanta are only occasionally available there are all sorts of locally bottled soft drinks. Avoid buying canned drinks as they cost about 10 times more because the container is expensive and not reusable. A bottle of cola or orange fizzy stuff costs about IR1000 and it doesn't much matter which type you ask for; you get what is available.

One of the better local brands of 'Iranian beer' *(mā'-osh-sha'īr)* is Delster, but international brands of nonalcoholic beer alternatives such as Oranjeboom and Bavaria are also available. Prices range from about IR2500 for a bottle of locally brewed stuff to a comparatively pricey IR4000 for an imported brand in a decent restaurant.

Alcoholic Drinks

Alcohol is strictly forbidden to Iranian Muslims, although it is still permitted for religious purposes (communion wine in churches) and to non-Muslims with special permission. There is a black market in alcohol, and staff of an unnamed airline are rumoured to sell duty-free Western-made liquor in shops in northern Tehrān, but we strongly advise you to steer well clear of alcohol during your stay.

The Komīteh keeps an eye out for parties and sometimes acts on tip-offs. The best-organised parties have a relay of lookouts; whenever the red alert is raised, the music is turned off, all the women make sure they are dressed properly, and the men head off for another room or a neighbour's flat. The host makes sure that anything incriminating is either extremely well hidden or flushed down the lavatory. This frequently rehearsed routine can be performed in less than two minutes.

ENTERTAINMENT

Iran offers very little in the way of organised entertainment or nightlife. Bring a book. Bring lots of them. Most Iranians keep themselves amused by visiting family and friends, playing with their children, watching satellite TV or seeing the latest Hollywood movies courtesy of the Internet (if they can afford it, of course).

Other favourite activities for young Iranians at a loose end include eating out, drifting between the homes of friends and relatives, window-shopping, playing street-football, and walking, motorcycling or driving in no particular direction for no particular reason. On Friday, many Iranians visit friends and relatives, or go to the country for picnics. Many Tehrānīs flock to the lower slopes of the Alborz Mountains for a spot of hiking.

Teahouses

The chāykhūneh, or teahouse, is a great Iranian institution. It's normally an all-male retreat, although foreign women are often allowed as temporary honorary males. In the teahouse, regulars sit all day drinking pot after pot of chāy, chatting, and smoking the qalyan (see the boxed text). The chāykhūneh used to be, and still sometimes is, a centre for social life and for the exchange of news, information and gossip; a bit like a bar or pub in Western countries. Until the Revolution, many chāykhūnehs served up poetry recitals, storytelling, animal shows and other cultural performances

---

Watch That Cup

Given the importance of the teahouse to Iranian male social life, it's not surprising that a whole etiquette has grown up around the cups and pipes. Turn your cup sideways on your saucer and people might conclude that you are gay. Turn it upside down on the saucer and you will insult a specific person nearby; place the saucer on top of the cup and you insult the entire teahouse.

The qalyan (water pipe) is seen as an entity complete in itself and it's an absolute no-no to light your cigarette from its coals. In rougher parts of towns like Tabrīz, such disrespect for the way things are done could actually lead to a fight – although of course most Iranians will make allowances for you as an ignorant foreigner.

---

alongside the tea, but nowadays very few still practise the old traditions.

It is fascinating to watch the manager of the teahouse do his stuff. Strong tea is usually brewed in a kettle and placed on top of an urn called a samovar, full of piping hot water. The tea served is a combination of the concentrate in the kettle and hot water from the samovar, and is served in tiny glasses for about IR500 a glass (IR1000 or more in tourist-oriented places).

A range of new-look teahouses aimed at men and women are appearing in the bigger towns. Usually in basements or upstairs or in the grounds of museums and palaces, these teahouses are attractively decorated and have qalyans or nārgīlehā (water pipes) for men and women, who stretch out on takhts (benchlike 'thrones') to enjoy them. They usually serve simple meals such as ābgūsht or have cakes and biscuits. Look for sketches of tea glasses or water pipes to find these places.

Cinemas

Each city has a few cinemas along the main street, but unfortunately few of them show the Iranian films that have been such big hits in the West. Instead they tend to concentrate on violence, with the dialogue in Farsi of course. Still, going to the cinema

Smoking the Qalyan

One of the most evocative smells in Iran is that of a *qalyan* or *nārgīleh* (water pipe) bubbling away in an Iranian teahouse. Sitting and puffing on a pipe, oblivious to the outside world, will help you acclimatise to the Iranian state of mind. It's a very sociable traditional custom that all foreigners, including women, can enjoy, and perhaps the greatest act of cultural integration that you can make, short of converting to Shiite Islam. You'll also get a mild buzz as you draw up the tobacco smoke and make that satisfying bubbling noise.

offers a chance to witness a different slice of Iranian social life.

Only as recently as 1997 were a few foreign films officially allowed into Iran. They're shown at selected (and often remote) cinemas in northern Tehrān, heavily censored to delete all 'immoral' scenes or sexual references and badly dubbed into Farsi. While some films, eg *Malcolm X* and *Dances With Wolves*, are American, they are chosen because they denigrate the American way of life and the politics of Uncle Sam.

Discos & Nightclubs
Dream on.

Chess & Cards
Though played in Iran for at least 1500 years, chess became illegal shortly after the Revolution on the grounds that it encourages the practice of betting, which is *haram* (forbidden by Muslim law). Chess sets were traded on the black market until early 1989, when the game became legal again by a final goodwill edict of Āyatollāh Khomeinī. Possession of playing cards, banned for the same reason, is still a criminal offence.

Quran Recital Contests
About the only cultural activity to have flourished since the Islamic Revolution, Quran recital contests can be quite interesting for the sheer range of contestants (haggard old men and mullahs to boys of about seven) and for the incredible powers of

memory they demonstrate. However, you will have to be invited, and you must dress and act appropriately.

SPECTATOR SPORTS
Football (soccer) is the major sport in Iran. The national championship lasts from about October to June, and games are played throughout the country on Thursday and Friday. Iran has a fine international side that qualified for the 1998 World Cup, and several Iranians play in major European football leagues, particularly in Germany.

Second in popularity is wrestling, which you can sometimes see if you ask around at a *zūrkhāneh* – see the boxed text later for more details. Iranian wrestlers often do well in international competitions. Other popular sports are volleyball, basketball, swimming, karate, fencing and horse riding.

One of the more unlikely sports you might see in Iran is cricket, which is played at Chābahār as well as Tehrān. If cricket is a little too sedate for you, go to the auto drag races held at the Āzādī Stadium in Tehrān. If you've spent a long time travelling around Iran, you will appreciate the irony of paying money to witness hundreds of racing cars scream around in a circle. In Sīstān va Balūchestān province, you may be able to see a traditional camel race.

Polo is probably a Persian invention, and was certainly played here during the reign of Darius the Great. Some 2000 years later, Shāh Abbās I used to enjoy watching his courtiers play the odd chukka in the main square in Esfahān. However, the game seems to have died out since the Revolution.

Iran, particularly Tehrān, has excellent sports facilities and there is always some international sporting carnival going on somewhere. Foreigners are normally welcome to attend; check out the sports sections in the English-language newspapers.

The requirement to wear hejab at all times severely restricts what women can do in the field of sport. The shooter Lida Fariman is the only Iranian woman to have excelled in the international sporting arena in recent times.

The Zūrkhāneh

SIMON RICHMOND

Unique to Iran, the *zūrkhāneh* (literally, the 'house of power' or 'strength') dates back hundreds of years. Its appeal lies somewhere between sport, theatre and a religious experience, at least for the participants. A group of 10 to 15 men, standing around the perimeter of a lowered pit, perform a series of highly ritualised dances, feats of strength and demonstrations of male virility, all to the accompaniment of a leader who sits on an elevated platform, pounding out a frenetic drumbeat. To further blur the lines between the sacred and the profane, the leader sings epic songs and recites poetry by Hāfez, which speak of mythical heroes and Golden Ages, while the performers whirl dervish-like in the centre of the floor. The performance, which takes place in a small, traditional gymnasium decorated like a shrine, is open to the public and usually free (a small donation is sometimes expected). Strangely enough, you won't see too many local women in attendance – Western women are welcomed as honorary men. Then again, if you've had your fill of being surrounded by testosterone, there are perhaps more relaxing ways to spend an evening.

SHOPPING

Iran is a great place to buy souvenirs, and you'll find it hard not to indulge yourself. Thanks to the shortage of tourists, mass production is not common, prices are low and the quality is generally high, even at the budget end of the market. Naturally, the bazaar is the best place to start looking, although much of what is on sale in places like Kermān, Kāshān and Hamadān is more likely to suit local tastes. Conversely, in places like Esfahān and Shīrāz where foreign tourists are more common, the goods may be more inviting but it is much harder to get a good price. If you're not keen on haggling and don't have much time to look around, the government-run Iran Handicrafts Organisation has fixed-price shops in most provincial capitals.

Various places in Iran specialise in specific products. Often, knowing the best place to buy something is as important as getting a good price.

Export restrictions apply to some goods (for more information, see Customs earlier in this chapter).

Art

In theory the best place to buy *mīnyātūrhā* (miniatures) is Esfahān, although perhaps 95% of what you'll find there has been made purely for the tourist market.

The better miniatures are likely to cost at least US$40. Real miniatures should be painted on paper rather than camel bone, which is what most people will try and sell you. Have a look in Manūchehrī St in Tehrān, which has some of the best examples. Tehrān Bazār, Khorramābād and Orūmīyeh are also good for miniatures, and *qābhā-yé aks* (picture frames) are good in Orūmīyeh.

Books

Most cities (except Tabrīz and Orūmiyeh) have bookshops that sell a range of English-language books about Iran with glossy photographs. Although expensive by Iranian standards, they are usually a bargain compared with what they would cost at home. Look out in particular for any books with photos by N Kasraian, a renowned Iranian photographer.

Carpets

See the Persian Carpets special section at the end of the Facts about Iran chapter.

Ceramics & Pottery

There are dozens of shops and factories selling *sefālgarī* (ceramics) and *mōzā'ī-hā* (mosaic tiles) at Lālejīn, near Hamadān; Marāqeh, near Tabrīz; Mīnāb, near Bandar-é Abbās; and around Rasht and Māsuleh.

Clothes

Givehs (lightweight shoes) and *abas* (traditional coats without sleeves) are available in Kermānshāh and Khūzestān provinces. Uniquely embroidered abas from villages near Bandar-é Abbās and Būshehr make great souvenirs.

All sorts of beautiful garments made from a silk called *tirma* are found in Yazd province. Traditional woollen Kurdish coats and hats from Kordestān and Īlām provinces are popular. The women of Māsuleh knit fine woollen socks which make good souvenirs.

Electronic Goods

Iran hasn't signed any international copyright agreements, so computer software is very cheap. Compare the prices in the shops around Jomhūrī-yé Eslāmī Ave in Tehrān.

Glassware

Intricate *shīsheh ālāt* (glassware) can be bought in Yazd, Tehrān and Meimand, near Kermān.

Jewellery

Be wary unless you know what you're doing when buying *javāher ālāt* (jewellery), although there is plenty of gorgeous stuff to choose from: traditional jewellery from Kordestān; turquoise from Mashhad; and silver filigree necklaces and earrings from villages in Zanjān province.

Leather & Silk

Bags made from *charmīneh* (leather) from Hamadān and Yazd are popular, and Tabrīz is renowned for its *abrīshom* (silk).

Metalwork

Some souvenirs to pick up include knives from Zanjān; anything made of silver or gold from Khūzestān province, Kermān or Shīrāz; and *servīs-hā-yé chāy* (tea sets) and qalyans made from *mes* (copper) and *beronz* (bronze).

Spices & Henna

Za'farān (saffron) from Mashhad, and *hannā* (henna), particularly from Tabrīz, are readily available.

Stamps

The handful of traders near the post office at Emām Khomeinī Square in Tehrān are the best people to see about buying *tambrhā* (postage stamps) as souvenirs. Some old commemorative issues can also be bought at the main post office in Yazd.

Woodwork

For carvings and *ja'behā* (inlaid boxes), it's hard to go past those available in Orūmīyeh and Esfahān. For baskets and knick-knacks made from bamboo, look around Rassht and nearby villages. For *moarraq* (marquetry) try Esfahān.

Getting There & Away

You can enter or leave Iran by air, road or sea, but the only train route currently open to passengers is from Pakistan. Most business travellers and foreigners on package tours come and go by air, while most independent travellers do so by road. Foreigners rarely use the sea routes across the Persian Gulf, although these make an interesting way of arriving or departing. At the time of writing, entering or leaving Iran via the Caspian Sea was not a realistic option as the boats were sporadic and schedules almost impossible to come by.

AIR
Airports & Airlines
Despite its political isolation, Iran has an impressive array of international flights. Most land at Mehrābād international airport in Tehrān, but some regional airlines use the other international airports, at Esfahān, Shīrāz, Mashhad, Bandar-é Abbās and Ahvāz. The HUGE Emām Khomeinī international airport, currently under construction to the south of Tehrān, will replace Mehrābād airport, but not during the lifetime of this book.

Iran Air is officially called the Airline of the Islamic Republic of Iran, and has the Homa, a mythical bird, as its symbol. The government-owned national carrier, it offers service with an Islamic flavour (ie, no pork and absolutely no alcohol). Women flying on Iran Air used to have to wear hejab from the time they arrived at the departure airport, but this rule seems to have been relaxed. These days, as on other international carriers, it seems to be all right to hold off on wearing the headscarf until the descent to Iran is announced (you may want to double-check before arriving at the airport though). Iran Air flights of less than 4½ hours are nonsmoking.

Iran Air offers a vast network of flights to Asia, the Middle East and Europe, with fewer direct flights to North America and Australia. Before you board your flight,

your Iranian visa is likely to be scrutinised thoroughly several times.

The prices listed in this book for Iran Air flights are for summer (April to October); in winter, there are sometimes discounts (as well as fewer flights).

Iran Asseman, Mahan Air and Caspian Air operate a handful of international flights, but standards of service and comfort are unlikely to be high.

Buying Tickets
An air ticket alone can gouge a great slice out of anyone's budget, but you can reduce the cost by finding discounted fares. Stiff competition has resulted in widespread discounting and passengers flying in economy can usually manage some sort of discount.

For long-term travel there are plenty of discount tickets, valid for 12 months and allowing multiple stopovers with open dates. For shorter-term travel to Iran you may be able to find short-lived promotional offers.

When looking for a bargain air fare, go to a travel agency rather than directly to the airline. From time to time, airlines do have promotional fares and special offers, but generally they only sell fares at the official listed price.

Another alternative is to book on the Internet. Many airlines offer some excellent fares to Web surfers. They may sell seats by auction or simply cut prices to reflect the reduced cost of electronic selling. Many travel agencies around the world have Web sites, which can make the Internet a quick and easy way to compare prices, a good start for negotiating with your favourite travel agency. Online ticket sales work well if you're doing a simple one-way or return trip on specified dates. However, online fare generators are no substitute for a travel agent who knows all about special deals, has strategies for avoiding stopovers and can offer advice on things like which airline offers the best vegetarian food.

The days when some travel agents would fleece travellers by running off with their money are, happily, almost over. Paying by credit card generally offers protection as most card issuers provide refunds if you can prove you didn't get what you paid for. Similar protection can be obtained by buying a ticket from a bonded agent, such as one covered by the Air Transport Operators License (ATOL) scheme in the UK. Agents who only accept cash should hand over the tickets straight away and not tell you to 'come back tomorrow'. After you've made a booking or paid your deposit, call the airline and confirm that the booking was made. It's generally not advisable to send money (even cheques) through the post unless the agent is very well established – some travellers have reported being ripped off by fly-by-night mail-order ticket agents.

You may decide to pay more than the rock-bottom fare by opting for the safety of a better-known travel agency. Firms like STA Travel, which has offices worldwide, Council Travel in the USA and Usit Campus (formerly Campus Travel) in the UK are not going to disappear overnight and offer good prices to most destinations.

If you purchase a ticket and later want to make changes or get a refund, you need to contact the original travel agency. Airlines only issue refunds to the ticket purchaser – usually the agent who bought the ticket on your behalf. Many travellers change their routes halfway through their trips, so think carefully before you buy a ticket that is not easily refundable.

Student & Youth Fares Full-time students and people under 26 have access to better deals than other travellers. 'Better deal' doesn't always mean a cheaper fare, but can include more flexibility to change flights and/or routes. You have to show a document proving your date of birth or a valid International Student Identity Card (ISIC) when buying your ticket and boarding the plane. There are plenty of places around the world where nonstudents can get fake student cards, but if you get caught using one you could have your ticket confiscated.

Frequent Flyers Most airlines offer frequent-flyer deals that can earn you a free air ticket or other goodies. To qualify, you have to accumulate sufficient mileage with the same airline or airline alliance. Many airlines have 'blackout periods' when you can't fly for free on your frequent-flyer points. The worst thing about frequent-flyer programs is that they tend to lock you into one airline, and that airline may not always have the cheapest fares or most convenient schedule.

Buying International Tickets in Iran
Foreigners can use rials to buy tickets on internal flights within Iran, but all tickets on international flights out of Iran must be bought with US dollars cash (or with MasterCard, but not American Express or Visa). Since the airlines operating out of Iran have little problem filling seats, there are very few discounted fares.

It is often hard to confirm, change or buy an Iran Air ticket for an international flight at Iran Air offices in Iran, which normally only handle tickets for domestic flights; you will have to go to an office in a city served by Iran Air international flights. Iran Air

Air Travel Glossary

Alliances Many of the world's leading airlines are now intimately involved with each other, sharing everything from reservations systems and check-in to aircraft and frequent-flyer schemes. Opponents say that alliances restrict competition. Whatever the arguments, there is no doubt that big alliances are the way of the future.

Courier Fares Businesses often need to send urgent documents or freight securely and quickly. Courier companies hire people to accompany the package through customs and, in return, offer a discount ticket which is sometimes a bargain. However, you may have to surrender all your baggage allowance and take only carry-on luggage.

Fares Airlines traditionally offer 1st class (coded F), business class (coded J) and economy class (coded Y) tickets. These days there are so many promotional and discounted fares available that few passengers pay full fare.

Lost Tickets If you lose your airline ticket, an airline will usually treat it like a travellers cheque and, after inquiries, issue you with another one. Legally, however, an airline is entitled to treat it like cash and if you lose it then it's gone forever. Take very good care of your tickets.

Onward Tickets An entry requirement for many countries is that you have a ticket out of the country. If you're unsure of your next move, the easiest solution is to buy the cheapest onward ticket to a neighbouring country or a ticket from a reliable airline which can later be refunded if you do not use it.

Open-Jaw Tickets These are return tickets where you fly out to one place but return from another. If available, this can save you backtracking to your arrival point.

Overbooking Since every flight has some passengers who fail to show up, airlines often book more passengers than they have seats. Usually excess passengers make up for the no-shows, but occasionally somebody gets 'bumped' onto the next available flight. Guess who it is most likely to be? The passengers who check in late. If you do get 'bumped', you are normally offered some form of compensation.

Reconfirmation Some airlines require you to reconfirm your flight at least 72 hours prior to departure. Check your travel documents to see if this is the case

Restrictions Discounted tickets often have various restrictions on them – such as needing to be paid for in advance and incurring a penalty to be altered or cancelled. Others are restrictions on the minimum and maximum period you must be away.

Round-the-World Tickets RTW tickets give you a limited period (usually a year) in which to circumnavigate the globe. You can go anywhere the carrying airlines go, as long as you don't backtrack. The number of stopovers or total number of separate flights is decided before you set off and they usually cost a bit more than a basic return flight.

Ticketless Travel Airlines are gradually waking up to the realisation that paper tickets are unnecessary encumbrances. On simple one-way or return trips, reservations details can be held on computer and the passenger merely shows ID to claim their seat.

Transferred Tickets Airline tickets cannot be transferred from one person to another. Travellers sometimes try to sell the return half of their ticket, but officials can ask you to prove that you are the person named on the ticket. On an international flight, tickets are compared with passports.

often throws in two internal flights with an international ticket, but this is not as generous as it sounds since internal Iranian flights rarely cost more than US$10.

For a list of the head offices of the major airlines that fly to and from Tehrān, see the Getting There & Away section in the Tehrān chapter.

Second-Hand Tickets Occasionally you'll see advertisements on youth-hostel bulletin boards or in newspapers for 'second-hand tickets' where somebody has purchased a return ticket or a ticket with multiple stopovers and now wants to sell the unused portion.

The prices offered may look very attractive but, unfortunately, these tickets are usually worthless for international travel as the name on the ticket must match the name on the passport of the person checking in. Some people reason that the ticket seller can check you in with his or her passport, and then give you the boarding pass. Wrong again! Usually the immigration people want to see your boarding pass, and if it doesn't match the name in your passport, then you won't be able to board your flight.

What happens if you purchase a ticket and then change your name, for example because of marriage or divorce? If the name on the ticket doesn't match the name in your passport, you could have problems, especially with a country like Iran, which tends to be hyper-suspicious of foreigners. Be sure to have something like your old passport to prove that the old you and the new you are the same person.

Precautions Once you have your ticket, write the number down, together with the flight number and other details, and keep the information somewhere separate. If the ticket is lost or stolen, this will help you to obtain a replacement.

It's sensible to buy travel insurance as early as possible. If you buy it the week before you fly, you may find, for example, that you're not covered for delays to your flight caused by industrial action, or for cancellation costs should you unexpectedly become sick. See Travel Insurance in the

Visas & Documents section of the Facts for the Visitor chapter for further information.

Travellers with Special Needs

Given adequate notice, most international airlines can cater for people with special needs; travellers with disabilities, perhaps, or people with young children, even children travelling alone.

Travellers with special dietary preferences (vegetarian, kosher etc) can request appropriate meals. If you're travelling in a wheelchair, most international airports can provide an escort from check-in desk to plane, but although you may be able to depend on ramps, lifts, toilets and phones in Western airports, it's not wise to depend on these at the Iranian end.

Airlines usually allow babies up to two years of age to fly for 10% of the adult fare; a few let them fly free of charge. Many international airlines provide nappies (diapers), tissues, talcum and all the other paraphernalia needed to keep babies clean, dry and half happy, but don't rely on Iran Air to come up trumps. For children between the ages of two and 12, the fare on international flights is usually 50% of the regular fare or 67% of a discounted fare.

Departure Tax

At the time of writing almost all international airlines included the Iranian international departure tax of IR70,000 in their fares or collected it at the time of the ticket sale; you should not have to pay anything as you are leaving the country, although it might be wise to hold on to IR70,000 just in case.

The USA & Canada

Despite the limited tourism between the USA and Iran, it's not too hard or expensive to find a flight from the USA to Tehrān either directly or via Europe or the Middle East. Iran Air currently has flights to Boston, Chicago, Detroit, Houston, Los Angeles, Miami, Minneapolis, New York, San Francisco, Seattle and Washington. Return fares from New York to Tehrān on Lufthansa start from US$1600; from Los Angeles they start from US$2100.

Of the many indirect possibilities, the cheapest fares seem to be via Europe on British Airways or KLM, or via the Middle East on Emirates Airlines (from the United Arab Emirates), Pakistan International Airlines (PIA) or Kuwait Airways. One good place to look for bargains is the classifieds section of the *Iran Times*, published in Washington. Otherwise, try Explorer Travel Consultants in New York (☎ 212-239 1012) or Travelure in California (☎ 818-247 6960, fax 244 3882).

Council Travel, the USA's largest student travel organisation, has around 60 offices in the USA; its head office (☎ 800-226 8624) is at 205 E 42nd St, New York, NY 10017. Call it for the office nearest you or visit its Web site (www.ciee.org). STA Travel (☎ 800-777 0112) has offices in Boston, Chicago, Miami, New York, Philadelphia, San Francisco and other major cities. Call the toll-free 800 number for office locations or visit its Web site (www.statravel.com).

If you check with a few travel agencies, or surf the Net, you could pick up a return ticket to Tehrān from Los Angeles, via Europe, for as little as US$1150. From New York, return flights to Tehrān, via Europe, are comparatively better value at about US$850. Most travel agencies recommend the better airlines, such as Lufthansa (via Frankfurt), but with them you may be looking at US$2200 return from the west coast, or US$1800 return from the east coast, to Tehrān.

Iran Air also has indirect flights from Tehrān to Montreal, Toronto and Vancouver. Flights from Toronto or Montreal to Tehrān with Air Canada and Lufthansa via Frankfurt start from US$1200 return; flights from Vancouver from US$2200.

Australia & New Zealand

The only direct flights between Australia and Iran are between Sydney and Tehrān a couple of times a week, but there are several good indirect options: Malaysia's MAS airline flies from most Australian cities to Kuala Lumpur, with connections to Tehrān on Iran Air, for A$1220/1996 one way/

return in low season; and Kuwait Airlines works with various Asian and Australian carriers to fly via Asia and Kuwait to Tehrān for A$1005/1774 one way/return in low season.

Two agencies well known for cheap fares are STA Travel and Flight Centre. STA Travel (☎ 03-9349 2411) has its main office at 224 Faraday St, Carlton, Victoria 3053, and offices in all major cities and on many university campuses. Call (☎ 1300 360 960 Australia-wide for the location of your nearest branch or visit STA's Web site (www.statravel.com.au). Flight Centre (☎ 131 600 Australia-wide) has a central office at 82 Elizabeth St, Sydney, and there are dozens of offices throughout Australia. It also has a Web site (www.flightcentre .com.au).

Otherwise, one of the best places to check out flights to Iran is Homa Travel, Chatswood Central, 1-5 Railway St, Chatswood, NSW 2067 (☎ 02-9413 3655, fax 9413 3677). The company is run by an expatriate Iranian who knows what it's all about.

There are no direct flights to New Zealand so Kiwis will have to take a connecting flight via Sydney or Asia, which will inevitably cost a bit more than Australians have to pay. Flight Centre (☎ 09-309 6171) has a large central office in Auckland at National Bank Towers (corner Queen and Darby Sts) and many branches throughout the country. STA Travel (☎ 09-309 0458) has its main office at 10 High St, Auckland, and has other offices in Auckland as well as in Hamilton, Palmerston North, Wellington, Christchurch and Dunedin.

The UK

One of the cheapest flights from London to Tehrān, via Rome, is with Alitalia or KLM for UK£350 return. Other relatively cheap flights between London and Tehrān are on Lufthansa and Swissair.

Discount air travel is big business in London. Advertisements for many travel agencies appear in the travel pages of the weekend broadsheets, such as the *Independent* on

Saturday and the *Sunday Times*. Look out for the free magazines, such as *TNT*, which are widely available in London – start by looking outside the main railway and underground stations.

For travellers under 26 and students, a popular travel agency is STA Travel (☎ 020-7361 6144), which has an office at 86 Old Brompton Rd, London SW7 3LQ, and other offices in London and Manchester. Visit its Web site (www.statravel.co.uk). This agency sells tickets to anyone, but caters especially to young people and students.

Other recommended travel agencies include Trailfinders (☎ 020-7938 3939), 194 Kensington High St, London W8 7RG; Bridge the World (☎ 020-7734 7447), 4 Regent Place, London W1R 5FB; and Flightbookers (☎ 020-7757 2000), 177-178 Tottenham Court Rd, London W1P 9LF.

Continental Europe

Iran Air and several major European carriers fly directly between most western European cities and Tehrān. Cheaper tickets are often offered by the following European airlines: Lufthansa, Air France, Aeroflot, Alitalia, Austrian Airlines, KLM, SAS and Swissair.

For something a little different, you could try the twice-weekly flight between Tehrān and Varna in Bulgaria on Balkan Airlines.

Across Europe many travel agencies have ties with STA Travel, where cheap tickets can be purchased. Outlets in major cities include: Voyages Wasteels (☎ 08 03 88 70 04, this number can only be dialled from within France; fax 01 43 25 46 25), 11 rue Dupuytren, 756006 Paris; STA Travel (☎ 030-311 0950, fax 313 0948), Goethestrasse 73, 10625 Berlin; Passaggi (☎ 06-474 0923, fax 482 7436), Stazione Termini FS, Galleria Di Tesla, Rome; and ISYTS (☎ 01-322 1267, fax 323 3767), 11 Nikis St, Upper Floor, Syntagma Square, Athens.

France has a network of student travel agencies that supply discount tickets to travellers of all ages. OTU Voyages (☎ 01 44 41 38 50) has a central Paris office at 39

Ave Georges Bernanos (5e) and 42 offices around the country. Check their Web site at www.otu.fr.

Acceuil des Jeunes en France (☎ 01 42 77 87 80), 119 rue Saint Martin (4e), is another popular discount travel agency.

General travel agencies in Paris that offer some of the best service and deals include Nouvelles Frontières (☎ 08 03 33 33 33), 5 Ave de l'Opéra (1er), or check their Web site at www.nouvelles-frontieres.com; and du Monde (☎ 01 42 86 16 00) at 55 rue Sainte Anne (2e). Return fares to Tehrān start at around US$400 (FFR3200) on Austrian Airlines.

Germany, Belgium, Switzerland, the Netherlands and Greece are also good places for buying discount air tickets.

In Belgium, Acotra Student Travel Agency (☎ 02-512 86 07) at rue de la Madeline, Brussels, and WATS Reizen (☎ 03-226 16 26) at de Keyserlei 44, Antwerp, are both well-known agencies.

In Switzerland, SSR Voyages (☎ 01-297 11 11) specialises in student, youth and budget fares. In Zurich, there is a branch at Leonhardstrasse 10 and there are others in most major Swiss cities, as well as a Web site (www.ssr.ch).

One recommended Amsterdam travel agency is Malibu Travel (☎ 020-626 32 30) at Prinsengracht 230.

In Athens, check the many travel agencies in the backstreets between Syntagma and Omonia Squares. For student and non-concession fares, try Magic Bus (☎ 01-323 7471, fax 322 0219).

Middle East & Africa

Not surprisingly, most countries in the Middle East and the Persian Gulf region offer regular flights to Iran. These flights are used almost exclusively by local businessmen, local tourists and pilgrims, and there are few discounted fares, although you can save money by carefully choosing which airport you fly into.

At the time of writing, Iran Air, Iran Asseman or partner national carriers offered the following flights from Tehrān to Middle East destinations: Abu Dhabi (UAE; once weekly,

US$121), Manama (Bahrain; three times weekly, from US$92), Damascus (Syria; twice weekly, US$134), Doha (Qatar; twice weekly, from US$101), Dubai (UAE; 14 times weekly, from US$90), Kuwait (nine times weekly, US$117) and Sharjah (UAE; twice weekly, US$60). The fares listed are for one-way journeys. Generally speaking, return fares cost exactly double the one-way fare. It's also worth checking whether there are flights to your destination from Shīrāz, Būshehr, Bandar-é Abbās, or Qeshm or Kīsh Islands. If the distance is shorter, you may find the fare is also cheaper!

The new international airports on Qeshm and Kīsh Islands also have flights with Iran Air and other regional airlines.

Surprisingly, Iran Air doesn't have any services to Africa, not even to Cairo.

Turkey Because the two countries are neighbours, and road transport is regular and cheap, there are few flights between Iran and Turkey and no discounted fares. Iran Air flies between Tehrān and İstanbul for US$237/465 (one way/return) on Monday and Friday. Turkish Airlines flies the same route daily but for US$368 each way. Flight times are very inconvenient, bringing you into Tehrān in the early hours of the morning.

Central Asia

The option of flying via one of the former Soviet states in Central Asia is a fascinating way to enter or leave Iran, though flights are not frequent and are prone to change and cancellation.

At the time of writing, Iran Air, Iran Asseman or partner national carriers offered the following flights from Tehrān to Central Asian destinations: Almaty (Kazakhstan; once weekly, US$272), Ashghabat (Turkmenistan; departing three times weekly, US$100), Baku (Azerbaijan; once weekly, US$137), Bishkek (Kyrgyzstan; departing twice weekly, US$210), Dushanbe (Tajikistan; twice weekly, US$165) and Tashkent (Uzbekistan; once weekly, US$220). The fares listed are for one-way journeys. Generally speaking, return fares cost exactly double the one-way fare.

The Rest of Asia

To avoid a long overland trip from the subcontinent you may want to consider flying, although you may have to backtrack if you wish to visit eastern Iran, because flights go straight to/from Tehrān.

Between Iran and India, Iran Air and Air India fly from Tehrān to Mumbai (Bombay) once weekly for US$307/614 one way/return. Between Iran and Pakistan, Iran Air and PIA fly from Tehrān to Karachi for US$159/239 once weekly.

Elsewhere in Asia, JAL and Iran Air fly between Tehrān and Tokyo (US$860/1720, twice weekly); and Iran Air goes to Kuala Lumpur for US$693/1386. Mahan Air recently started flying to Bangkok (US$480), Hanoi (US$690), Hong Kong (US$660), Jakarta (US$730), Manila (US$730), Seoul (US$754) and Singapore (US$611). All these prices are for return tickets.

LAND

For decades, the traditional overland passage, the 'Hippy Trail', between Europe and Kathmandu or anywhere in India was fraught with difficulty. While the situation in Afghanistan still deters all but the truly fearless (for which read, foolish), the 1990s saw the opening of several new overland routes through this part of the world.

Border Crossings

Currently, it is safe and easy to travel overland into Iran from Turkey and Pakistan, and the more adventurous are successfully crossing into Iran from the borders with the former Soviet states of Armenia, Azerbaijan and Turkmenistan. However, the border with Afghanistan is currently closed; nor can independent travellers cross into Iraq from Iran.

Car & Motorcycle

Driving across Iran is a relatively easy and surprisingly popular way to get around.

To bring your own vehicle into Iran, you must be more than 18 years old and have a current international driving permit. For the vehicle, you'll need a *carnet de passage* (temporary importation document), which can be obtained from the relevant international automobile organisation in your country. For further information about driving to and around Iran, contact the Touring & Automobile Club of the Islamic Republic of Iran (☎ 21-874 0411, fax 874 0410), PO Box 15875/5617, 12 Nobakht St, Khorramshahr Ave, Tehrān.

> Travellers with car but without carnet have to direct themselves to the so-called 'company', a small firm on the [Bāzārgān] border that helps you with all the necessary documents... Of course this takes more time [without a carnet] – we spent three days in the 'hell of Bāzārgān'. For all the services and documents we paid US$80.'
>
> **Rob van den Berg**

Recently we have been hearing from travellers who were charged a fuel tax when they tried to bring a car into Iran without a carnet. The idea behind it seems to be to bring the price of cheap Iranian petrol up to nearly what it would have cost the foreigner at home. We have heard of one reader who wrote to the government to complain about this tax and received a full refund. Don't hold your breath...

> Coming overland from Pakistan into Iran by [diesel engine] car...we drove to the last gate [and were told] to go back to the Boundary Terminal Management. The person in charge told us we had to go to the bank and pay US$174! It took a long time to find out we had to pay this amount because the oil price is so low in Iran. So it's a kind of fuel tax. If you have a tourist visa you don't have to pay – only if you have a transit visa. But [the embassies in India and Pakistan] issue transit visas only...Other tourists came by car and agreed very quickly. They went to the bank and paid with two notes of US$100. First they didn't want to give any change. Meeting people coming from the opposite direction they told us they didn't have to pay but their car had a petrol engine.
>
> **Johanna de Bresser**

In theory if you have a carnet de passage no such tax should be levied. It may be as well to calculate it into your likely costs anyway.

Customs officials seem to assume that all foreigners driving foreign vehicles are poten-tial drug smugglers, so while it may take just an hour to walk through the Iranian border, taking a vehicle across can take five hours or more (the reader quoted above who wrote of a three-day delay was surely exceptional). Plan ahead and bring loads of patience. It doesn't help that there are lots of different offices to visit at the Bāzārgān border and that none of them are signposted in English.

The officials will probably note your vehicle's details in your passport to make sure you don't leave the country without it. Third-party insurance is compulsory for foreign drivers but may be very difficult to obtain outside Iran (if you do get it, make sure the policy is valid for Iran and accredited with Iran Bimeh, the Iranian Green Card Bureau). If you buy it at the Bāzārgān border you may get charged US$22 when it costs only US$8 just down the road in Mākū.

Drivers report that Iranian oil is of poor quality. If coming from Turkey, you might want to change your oil in Doğubayazıt before approaching the border.

There are no motorbikes over 700cc in Iran so if you bring one in you must expect to attract a great deal of attention.

For information about driving around Iran, see the Car & Motorcycle section in the Getting Around chapter.

Turkey

There are two main crossings along the 1270km border with Turkey. The busy main one is at Gürbulak (Turkey) and Bāzārgān (Iran), where there are hotels, moneychanging facilities and regular transport on either side of the border. This border is one of the most congested bottlenecks in West Asia and the delays can be wearisome. For further details, see Bāzārgān in the Western Iran chapter. Foreigners can also cross the border at Yüksekova (Turkey) and Serō (Iran), although you need to plan the timing of this crossing more carefully since there is nowhere to stay on either side of the border. For further details, see Serō in the Western Iran chapter.

Bus Travelling by bus you have two options. The easier is to take a direct long-distance

The Silk Road

No one knows for sure when the miraculously fine, soft, strong, shimmering and sensuous fabric spun from the cocoon of the *Bombyx* caterpillar first reached Europe from China. The Parthians were the most voracious foreign consumers of Chinese silk by the close of the 2nd century BC. By about 100 BC, the Parthians and the Chinese had exchanged embassies and inaugurated official bilateral trade along the caravan route that lay between them. Thus the Silk Road was born, in fact if not in name.

It took up to 200 days to traverse the 8000km route, though geographically the Silk Road was a complex and shifting proposition. It was no single road, but rather a web of caravan tracks that threaded through some of the highest mountains and bleakest deserts on earth. Though the road map expanded over the centuries, the network had its main eastern terminus at the Chinese capital Ch'ang-an (now Xian); west of there, the route divided at Dunhuang, one branch skirting the dreaded Taklamakan desert to the north, while the other headed south. The two forks met again in Kashgar, where the trail headed up to any of a series of mountain passes.

The Silk Road entered Iran anywhere between Merv (now in Turkmenistan) and Herāt (now in Afghanistan), and passed through Mashhad, Neishābūr, Dāmghān, Semnān, Rey, Qazvīn, Tabrīz and Mākū, before finishing at Constantinople (now İstanbul). In the winter, the trail often diverted in a more westerly direction from Rey, and passed through Hamadān to Baghdad.

Goods heading west and those heading east didn't fall into discrete bundles. In fact, there was no 'through traffic'; caravanners were mostly short and medium-distance hauliers who marketed and took on freight along a given beat according to their needs and inclinations. At any given time any portion of the network might be beset by war, robbers or natural disaster. In general, the eastern end was enriched by the importation of gold, silver, ivory, jade and other precious stones, wool, Mediterranean coloured glass, grapes, wine, spices and – early Parthian crazes – acrobats and ostriches. Goods enriching the western end were silk, porcelain, spices, gems and perfumes. In the middle lay Central Asia and Iran, great clearing houses that provided the horses and Bactrian camels that kept the goods flowing in both directions.

The Silk Road gave rise to unprecedented trade, but its true glory and unique status in human history were the result of the interchange of ideas, technologies and religions that occurred among the very different cultures trading along it. Religion alone presents an astounding picture of diversity and

---

bus to, say, Tehrān or Tabrīz from İstanbul, Ankara or Erzurum, although this involves lengthy delays while you wait for everyone on the bus to be cleared through customs and immigration (as a lone foreigner, you might be done and on your way in less than an hour).

Every week, several long-distance buses travel between İstanbul and Ankara to Tehrān (see Getting There & Away under each destination in the regional chapters for details). From İstanbul, the buses leave from outside Tehran Tur (☎ 0212-512 5497, fax 511 8076), 268 Ordu Caddesi, Laleli, at 1 pm; from Ankara they leave from the big ASCİ bus terminal (tickets are on sale at 36 Paris Ave, opposite the American embassy). Whether from İstanbul or Ankara, tickets to Tehrān cost around US$35. Those in the know swear that it's better to take the Ankara bus, which is full of students and embassy workers, rather than the İstanbul bus, which is full of traders and so more likely to be taken apart at customs.

However, it is far better to break up the journey between Turkey and Iran, and enjoy some of eastern Turkey and western Iran along the way. Taking a bus to – but not across – either border will also do away with waiting for up to 50 fellow passengers to clear customs. You can cross the border between Doğubayazıt (Turkey) and Mākū (Iran) in one day by bus. It's even possible

The Silk Road

tolerance that would be the envy of any modern democratic state. Manichaeism, Zoroastrianism, Buddhism, Nestorian Christianity, Judaism, Confucianism, Taoism and the shamanism of the grassland nomads coexisted, and in some cases mingled, until the coming of Islam.

Eventually the Silk Road was abandoned when sailors from the new European colonial powers discovered alternative sea routes in the 15th century. But in the past few years the Silk Road has once again attracted interest, this time for trade between Iran and the newly opened Central Asian republics, and as a tourist attraction.

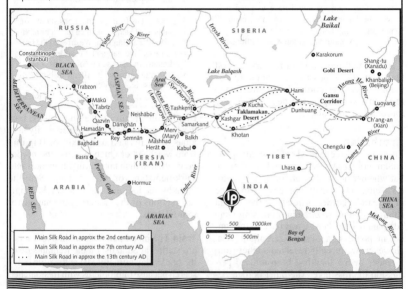

- – – Main Silk Road in approx the 2nd century AD
- ——— Main Silk Road in approx the 7th century AD
- · · · Main Silk Road in approx the 13th century AD

to cross in one day from Erzurum (Turkey) to Tabrīz (Iran) if you start early and get through the border with minimum fuss.

Expect longer than usual delays in winter as the high mountain passes near both borders are frequently snowbound.

For about 10 days either side of the Iranian New Year (Nō Rūz; 21 March), Iranian buses are not allowed to operate international services, although Turkish buses just keep on going.

Car & Motorcycle Most motorists will arrive in Iran via Turkey, crossing the border between Gürbulak and Bāzārgān or between Yüksekova and Serō. Be prepared for a long wait and a thorough vehicle search at

either border, especially at Bāzārgān where the line of waiting vehicles can stretch to the horizon.

Armenia

The border between Iran and Armenia is only 35km long, with one crossing point in Iran at Noghdooz. Before attempting this crossing by any mode of transport be sure to double-check with an Armenian embassy that it is still open. If crossing from Iran, bear in mind that the border between Turkey and Armenia is closed; to reach Turkey overland you will have to travel on via Georgia. For more information on the crossing at Noghdooz, see Jolfā in the Western Iran chapter.

Because of the car it took us 23 hours to have all our papers done (four hours on the Armenian side refusing to pay a bribe, 19 hours on the more polite and hospitable Iranian side). At the border we had to pay US$47 for using Iranian roads and oil. The following day at the administration border in Jolfā...we had to pay US$80 out of the US$100 asked for car insurance, even though we had our own. They said we could have avoided it with the carnet de passage – which we could not get, having bought the car in Georgia.

Arnaud Moreillon & Ben Pillonel

Unconfirmed reports from readers suggest that it might be possible to obtain an Armenian visa at the border. Before trusting to this, and wasting a journey, ask at the tourist office in Tabrīz.

Azerbaijan

There are two recognised crossings along the 768km border between Iran and Azerbaijan, but whether or not they are open to foreigners seems to be a matter of luck. At the time of research, border officials at the Āstārā (Iran) to Astara (Azerbaijan) crossing were adamant that the border was open to foreigners in possession of an Azerbaijani visa. However, we recently received a letter from a reader saying they had been refused permission to cross here. The other border, between Jolfā (Iran) and Julfā (Azerbaijan), was also said to be open but leads only to the exclave of Nakhichevan; to proceed to Baku you need to fly across Armenia, making this crossing of dubious usefulness. It's absolutely essential to double-check the situation with the Azerbaijani embassy in Baku or Tehrān before trying to cross either of these borders.

See the Āstārā section in the Caspian Sea chapter and the Jolfā section in the Western Iran chapter for more details.

Bus Every day a bus travels from Tehrān to Baku, via Āstārā. Taking the bus is certainly cheaper than flying, but means you must cope with the inordinate delays entailed in crossing the Āstārā border in any sort of vehicle – it may end up being quicker to cross the border yourself and then hitch a ride on any public transport heading north or south.

Turkmenistan

Although this border is very long (1206km), the only recognised crossing points are at Sarakhs (Iran) and Bajgiran (Iran). See the Sarakhs section in the Eastern Iran chapter for full details.

We took a bus from the main bus station (in Mashhad) to Quchan and then took a minibus to the border at Bajgiran. We crossed the border on foot. We had some troubles entering Turkmenistan because one of our visas had a slight writing error on it. After a 16-hour 'sit-and-sleep strike', they finally let us in.

Ad Ragas

Bus No direct buses travel through the border from either side, but you can easily take a bus or shared taxi to Sarakhs or Bajgiran from Mashhad or Quchan, cross the border yourself, and then take further transport into Turkmenistan (or vice versa). See the Sarakhs section, and the Quchan & Bajgiran sections of the Eastern Iran chapter for more details.

Train The brand new railway line and modern station at Sarakhs, on the Iranian side of the border, lay virtually idle at the time of research because of problems with mismatched railway gauges. It's worth double-checking with a travel agency in case trains start running during the lifetime of this book.

Afghanistan

At the time of research, it was foolish for anyone to consider trying to cross into war-torn Afghanistan.

Pakistan

Along the 830km border with Pakistan, the only recognised crossing for foreigners (and the only one you should use unless you have permission from immigration officials from both countries) is between Mīrjāveh (Iran) and Taftan (Pakistan). See the Zāhedān and Taftan sections in the Eastern Iran chapter for details on using public transport and driving across this border.

Bus There is no direct bus across the Mīrjāveh-Taftan border from either side, but this is not a problem because using a combination of any conceivable types of road transport, or the train, is very easy.

Train Once a week, a Pakistani train putters along the track between Quetta and Zāhedān. Though the train saves you changing transport midstream and is quaint (well, for the first few hours at least), taking a combination of bus, minibus and shared taxi to either side of the border and crossing it on foot is far quicker.

There are plans to lay a track between Kermān and Zāhedān, but for many years to come travellers will have to take a bus west from Zāhedān.

Iraq

The only crossing into Iraq, at Khosravī in Kermānshāh province, is used by Kurdish refugees coming from Iraq, by Iranian pilgrims and by the very occasional organised tour group. It is not open to independent travellers.

Syria

Iran and Syria have no common border, but each week several buses make the three-day journey between Tehrān or Tabrīz and Damascus. While we were researching this book the Iranian and Syrian rail authorities agreed on a project to connect their two countries by train via Turkey. This is unlikely to happen any day soon, but it's worth asking on arrival just in case.

SEA

Iran has 2410km of coastal boundaries along the Persian Gulf, Gulf of Oman and Caspian Sea, but there are very few ways to enter or leave Iran by sea.

Persian Gulf

The main shipping agency for trips across the Persian Gulf is Valfajre-8, which operates car ferries from Bandar-é Abbās to the United Arab Emirates. There are services to Sharjah (twice weekly, IR320,000, one class only); and to Dubai (once weekly, IR400,000/450,000 1st/2nd class). Schedules change regularly, so always make local inquiries or check with the Valfajre-8 office (☎ 889 2933, fax 892 409) at the end of Abyar Alley, on the corner of Shahīd Azodi St and Karīm Khān-é Zand St, in Tehrān.

A few ships also connect Būshehr with Bahrain, Qatar and Kuwait. By the time you read this a new ferry service from Būshehr to Bahrain may also have started operating; see Būshehr in the Persian Gulf chapter for more details.

Caspian Sea

At the time of research there didn't seem to be any regular passenger boat services on the Caspian Sea.

However, the occasional boat probably does operate to Baku (Azerbaijan) from Bandar-é Anzalī or Nōshahr. Your best hope of finding out anything more definite probably lies with one of the travel agencies listed under Organised Tours in the Getting Around chapter.

ORGANISED TOURS

Many travellers visit Iran on an organised tour, a situation that is likely to continue as long as reasonable-length visas for independent travellers are so difficult to obtain. You too may want to consider an organised tour, bearing in mind that so few Iranians outside the tourist industry speak much English; a good tour guide should be able to provide you with all sorts of insights into the places and culture you've come to see.

Because Iran is not yet a significant tourist destination, not many foreign travel agencies bother organising regular tours. You can ask your travel agent about tours, but by far the best thing to do is to contact one of the following agencies directly, or to use the Internet; these days some companies deal exclusively over the Net and don't even have a recognised office.

Costs of organised tours naturally depend on the length of the tour, the mode of transport, the type of accommodation and the current exchange rate, but tend to be expensive, and you often sacrifice a lot of flexibility and independence.

The following are some experienced and reputable agencies that offer organised tours to Iran from outside the country. (For a list of travel agencies that offer tours from within Iran, see Organised Tours in the Getting Around chapter.)

The USA & Canada

Americans may feel more comfortable going on an organised tour, and may not be able to get a visa otherwise. The Internet resources listed in the Facts for the Visitor chapter have good links to Web sites in the US and Canada that provide information about organised tours to Iran.

Bestway Tours & Safaris (☎ 604-264 7378, fax 264 7774, e bestway@bestway.com) 3526 West 41st Ave, Vancouver, BC, V6N 3E6. This company runs several more-adventurous trips. Web site www.bestway.com

Distant Horizons (☎ 800-333 1240, fax 562-983 8833, e disthoriz@aol.com) 350 Elm Ave, Long Beach, CA 90802. This impressive outfit focuses on senior travellers.

Geographic Expeditions (☎ 415-922 0448, fax 346 5535, e info@geoex.com) 2627 Lombard St, San Francisco, CA 94123. This company describes its tours as 'strenuous', which is probably another term for 'busy'.

Iran Tours Corporation (☎ 816-436 7791, fax 436 2875, e pardis@irantours.com) Pardis Travel Agency, 1006 Quince Orchard Rd, Gaithersburg MD 20878. This company offers an excellent range of tours and has an office in Tehrān.

Silk Road Tours (☎ 604-925 3831, fax 925 6269, e travel@silkroadtours.com) This agency offers package and tailor-made tours and can help with visa arrangements.

Voyage Afrolympic (☎ 514-274 0000, fax 270 5457) This company is based in Montreal.

Australia & New Zealand

Classic Oriental Tours (☎ 02-9657 2020, fax 9261 3320, e travel@classicoriental.com.au) 3/35 Grafton St, Woollahra, NSW 2025 Web site: www.classicoriental.com.au/Iran.htm

Diamond Persian Rug Gallery (☎ 03-9882 7451, fax 9836 4849) 201 Camberwell Rd, East Hawthorn, Victoria 3132. Though primarily a Persian carpet importer, the Iranian owner also runs three-week tours to Iran.

Equitrek (☎ 02-9913 9408, fax 9970 6303, e nelly@equitrek.com.au) This company offers riding tours of Iran from May to October. Web site: www.equitrek.com.au

Russian Passport/Red Bear Tours (☎ 03-9867 3888, fax 9867 1055, e passport@travelcentre.com.au) Suite 11a, 401 St. Kilda Rd, Melbourne, Victoria 3004 Web site: www.travelcentre.com.au

Sundowner Adventure Travel (☎ 03-9600 1934, fax 9642 5838) 600 Lonsdale St, Melbourne, Victoria 3004. Sundowner runs trips through Iran, often combined with Pakistan and/or Turkey.

The UK

Ace Study Tours (☎ 01223-835 055, fax 837 394) Church Farm Offices, Sawstan Rd, Babraham, Cambridge CB2 4AP. This is the best place to ask about study tours and Farsi language tours. Web site: www.study-tours.com

Exodus (☎ 020-8675 5550) 9 Weir Rd, London SW12 OLT. One of the many tours this company runs all over the world is to Iran. Web site: www.exodus.co.uk

Hinterland Travel (☎ 01883-743584) 2 Ivy Mill Lane, Godstone, Surrey RH9 8NH. Hinterland claims to be able to show you the 'real Iran', tied in with trips to Turkmenistan and Uzbekistan.

Imaginative Traveller (☎ 020-8742 8612, fax 8742 3045, e info@imaginative-traveller.com) 14 Barley Mow Passage, Chiswick W4 4PH. This company offers highly professional two- and three-week tours of all the main highlights of Iran, including those of the Caspian region.

Magic Carpet Travel (☎ 01344-622832) 1 Fieldhouse Close, Ascot, Berkshire SL5 9LT. Run by an Iranian woman, this company tailor-makes tours to specific needs and arranges visas for independent travellers. Web site: www.magic-carpet-travel.com

McCabe Travel (☎ 020-8675 8886, fax 673 1204) 53/55 Balham Hill, London, SW12 9DR

Silk Road Travellers Club (☎ 0800-093 8008, fax 01491-637617, e info@silkroadtravel.co.uk) St Mary's Court, Henley-on-Thames, Oxon RG9 2AA. This company offers occasional two-week tours of the highlights of Iran.

Continental Europe

Association Culturel de Voyages (☎ 01 40 43 20 21, fax 01 40 43 20 29) 39 rue des Favorites, 75738, Paris Cedex, France

Catai Tours (e catai@catai.es) Based in Spain, this company is ideal for Spanish-speaking travellers. Web site: www.catai.es/eafrica.html

Clio
France: (☎ 01 53 68 82 82, fax 01 53 68 82 60)

34 rue du Hameau, 75015, Paris. This company also has offices in Lyon and Marseille.
Switzerland: (☎ 22-731 70 26) 11 rue du Mont-Blanc CH1201, Geneva

Malibu Travel Inc (☎ 20-623 4912, fax 638 2271, ⓔ malibu@euronet.nl) Damrak 30, NL-102 LJ, Amsterdam, The Netherlands
Web site (in Dutch): www.etn.nl/malibu

Orients (☎ 01 46 34 29 00, fax 01 40 46 84 48) 29 rue des Boulangers, 75005, Paris, France

VS Studienreisen GmbH (☎ 030-213 8832, fax 213 8842) Augsburgerstrasse 31, D-10789, Berlin, Germany

Middle East

Iran Discovery Tours (☎ 0097-14 527 678, fax 591 459, ⓔ irdidar@safineh.net) This Dubai-based company, which has been recommended by readers, can organise tailor-made tours and help with visa arrangements.

Getting Around

Although transport in Iran isn't as developed as it is in the West, it's considerably better than that of most other countries in the region. Iran has 39 airports, more than 155,000km of roads, and 7740km of railways, so finding something going your way is easy. Public transport is frequent, reliable and relatively safe. What's more it's unbelievably cheap. Two of the best bargains in the country are taxi fares and domestic plane fares. There can't be many other places in the world where you can fly right across the country for less than US$20.

Whichever form of transport you favour, try to book tickets as early as you can; even if you change your plans and have to forfeit your bus or train ticket, or pay a small surcharge for changing a plane ticket, there's security in knowing you have confirmed tickets at times that suit you. However, it's only over the Nō Rūz, Ramazān and Eid al-Fitr public holidays that you are likely to have serious trouble finding transport. At these times bus fares can also double or triple. For more information about these holidays, see Public Holidays & Special Events in the Facts for the Visitor chapter.

Roadblocks are a fact of life on Iranian roads. They're usually located at major road junctions and a few kilometres either side of big towns, and are most frequent near the borders, particularly near Pakistan and Afghanistan, and on roads heading north from the major Persian Gulf ports.

AIR

For the time, being domestic air fares in Iran must be some of the world's cheapest. Even if you normally prefer to experience a country by travelling overland, you should still consider taking a few flights here because: a) your time is probably limited, b) your visa will probably not be long enough for you to get to remote cities by public transport, c) the country is vast and the scenery often monotonous, and d) flights (particularly on Iran Air) are reliable, frequent and safe. One

of these days someone is going to think of introducing dual pricing (ie, different prices for locals and foreigners) on air fares, so enjoy the chance to flit about the country by air for less than what you'd pay at home for bus tickets while you can.

Domestic Air Services

Iran's two major internal airlines are Iran Air and Iran Asseman. Both are well set up, with computerised offices, so you can book and/or confirm any domestic flight from anywhere in the country. Iran Air boasts an extensive network of flights to most provincial capitals, as well as places of interest to travellers, and is worth using almost exclusively because it's far more reliable than the other airlines. Flight details are included in the relevant Getting There & Away sections throughout this book.

Iran Asseman is the most viable alternative to Iran Air. However, its schedules are often a complete mystery even to Iran Asseman staff and timetables change regularly, so be wary. Asseman doesn't always have an office in a town to which it flies, in which case book with a reputable travel agent.

There are five other quirky domestic airlines to choose from – Caspian Airlines, Kīsh Air, Mahan Air, Qeshm Air and Saha Air – but their schedules are virtually impossible to track down, and flights are infrequent and unreliable. The offices of these airlines don't exist, or are hard to find, or are closed when you do find them, but if you still want their contact details, see Getting There & Away in the Tehrān chapter. It's better to book with an authorised travel agent or at the relevant airport.

If you try to book a flight and it's full, don't give up hope immediately. It may appear that way a week before the flight, but four days before departure additional seats often mysteriously appear. If there's still no luck, try again the day before departure. As a last resort, you can always try to get a ticket at the airport on the day of departure.

If you give the airlines plenty of notice, they rarely charge an extra fee if you change departure dates. There may be an IR2000 charge if you change the point of origin or destination within a few days of the departure date, and there can be a cancellation fee of up to 40% of the ticket price if you cancel within 24 hours of departure. There's little chance of getting a full refund for cancelled tickets. The departure tax is included in the fares on domestic flights.

It's a good idea to get to the airport a good hour ahead of domestic departures. This allows you enough time to sort yourself out at the terminal, check in your luggage, and struggle through the two or three x-ray machines, personal checks of hand baggage and frisks. Seats are allocated on the more popular flights, but on some less popular ones, you find your own seat once you are on the plane.

BUS

In Iran, if you can't get somewhere by bus (or minibus), the chances are that *no-one* wants to go there. More than 20 bus companies offer hundreds of services all over the country, so business is highly competitive, the fares are very cheap and, generally, there are regular departures. Most buses are comfortable, with your own cushioned seat, and standing is not normally allowed.

Don't be confused by the names of the destinations on a bus – it is quite common for a bus travelling between, for example, Khorram Ābād and Ahvāz, to have 'Tehrān-İstanbul' written on the front or side in English. Other English phrases written on the bus don't always translate well; our favourite is 'We Go To Trip Goodby'.

Bus Companies

Most bus companies are cooperatives, referred to simply as Cooperative Bus Company No X *(Sherkat-é Ta'āvonī Shomāré X)*, or whatever number it is. The best cooperatives, with the most extensive network of services, are TBT (Cooperative Bus Company No 15) and Cooperative Bus Company No 1 (often with the word 'Taavoni' or 'Bus No One' written on it).

There are also a few private bus companies, like Sayro Safar (or Seir o Safar), which offer more luxury, for a slightly higher price. In most cases, the differences between bus companies are small. It's not worth seeking out a specific company. Just take whichever bus is going your way when you want it.

Bus Stations

With a few notable exceptions, bus stations *(termīnāls)* are way out in the suburbs of every major town, easy enough to reach by shared taxi, less so by local bus. In some cities, there's more than one bus station; if in doubt, ask someone at your hotel or charter a taxi to the relevant station.

Bus stations are usually well set up and easy to use once you get the hang of it, although there are rarely any signs in English or anyone speaking English at the information desk. The different bus companies have individual offices inside a building or huddled around the bus departure area. Just ask 'Shīrāz?', 'Esfahān?' and someone will direct you to the right desk.

Often it's easy enough to find a tout shouting out the destination of a bus about to leave. In larger stations, they will probably approach you and (often annoyingly) guide you to the office of the company they work for. Claims that their bus is 'leaving now' should be treated with a grain of salt.

Bus stations always have somewhere to buy food and drink. Bigger stations may also have an information booth, post office, police station and somewhere to leave your bags, but there's rarely a hotel nearby.

If you're leaving a junction town such as Zanjān, you may need to flag down a passing bus on the road instead of going to the station. Position yourself near enough to the window to shout out your destination, but close enough to the kerb to avoid getting run over – a combination that is not as simple as it sounds. Roadblocks, roundabouts, service stations and junctions are the best places to hail passing buses.

Classes

Long-distance bus often have two classes, which are given a variety of different names.

'Lux' means regular (2nd) class, while 'super' is 1st class, but there may also be 'super lux' which is not much more super or luxurious than the other two. Super may also be called 'Volvo' where that is the type of vehicle being used. Lux buses have a few more seats than super or Volvo, so they're slightly less comfortable, if cheaper. For long trips, especially in summer, it's worth paying for super or Volvo class. If it's a short trip or seats are at a premium, just take whatever comes. Unless specified otherwise, the bus fares included in this book are for lux buses.

If you are travelling alone, you will often be given a single seat along one side of the bus. Try and avoid the seats at the back of the bus as they're on top of the back wheels and the engine; passengers picked up along the way also tend to congregate at the back. In summer it's vital to try and avoid being seated on the side that will be facing into the sun.

Tickets

You can buy tickets up to a week in advance at the bus station or at ticket offices in some larger cities (travel agencies never handle bus tickets). If time is tight, it's a good idea to buy a ticket one or two days before you want to travel. Booking an onward ticket as soon as you arrive also saves you making a special trip to the station (if there's no ticket office in town).

However, most people don't bother prebooking seats. Between major cities such as Shīrāz and Esfahān one bus company or another is bound to be departing at least every half-hour, while in medium-sized towns such as Hamadān and Kermān, you're unlikely to have to wait more than an hour for something going your way. Only in smaller places, where there may only be one or two buses a day to your destination, is it essential to book ahead.

Even if the bus you want to travel on seems to be full it's still worth going to the bus station at the time of departure and letting the driver, ticket collector and man at the bus-company office know that you're after a seat. There's a fair chance that someone with a prebooked ticket won't turn up, or that they can find you a seat at the back. Looking desperate, helpless and lost always helps.

The tickets themselves are incomprehensible. If you don't read Farsi, you won't know if the scrawled (Arabic) numbers indicate the day of departure, time of departure, bus number, seat number, platform number, bus company number or fare. Before handing over your money, always triple-check these details; then check again with the driver, his assistant or other passengers to make sure you get on the right bus. Waiting in the bus company office is a good idea – the staff will invariably look after you and show you to your seat.

Unfortunately a lot of buses leave in mid-afternoon and drop you at your destination in the early hours of the morning, a particular drag in winter.

Costs

Bus tickets are extremely cheap, averaging about IR25 per kilometre on longer routes (slightly more on shorter trips). Throughout this book we have provided fare tables that show the cheapest bus fares on the main routes. These should be taken as guidelines only since on many routes there are competing companies offering different fares. Prices will inevitably rise in line with inflation during the lifetime of this book. The highest fares are on 'Volvo' buses. Many locals will assure you that it's worth paying a little extra for the greater comfort and safety record of these vehicles.

The Journey

Don't count on averaging more than 60km/h on most bus journeys. Although many of them continue overnight, the buses are rarely comfortable enough to allow a good night's sleep and they're not recommended as a way of cutting down on accommodation costs. Some of the longer journeys (eg, Mashhad to Ahvāz) take more than 24 hours. It can get very cold at night, even in spring and autumn, so make sure you bring warm clothes. Try to get a seat at the front in winter, because the heater is usually only powerful enough to keep the driver and the front couple of rows of passengers cosy.

Is This Seat Free?

Choosing where to sit on Iranian transport is fraught with difficulty. On city buses, even men and women who are married to each other are not allowed to sit together; men sit at the front of the bus, women at the back.

In contrast, on intercity buses and minibuses, seating is generally arranged so that women sit next to women and men next to men unless they're couples or family. A man is not expected to sit next to an unrelated woman even if there's only one spare seat left on the bus, and people will move around until the gender mix is right.

If you decide to take a shared taxi you will find people hopping in and out of the front and back like yo-yos in an attempt to ensure that unrelated men and women don't end up side by side. Decide to take the Tehrān Metro, however, and you'll find that anything goes. The biggest surprise comes on sleeper trains when unless you specify that you want a single-sex compartment you may find yourself assigned to a mixed one.

On any trip of more than six hours you'll almost certainly stop every now and then at a roadside cafe serving kebabs, tea and cold drinks. Ice-cold water is normally available on the bus, but bring your own cup as the locals do to avoid having to share the communal one. Smoking is not permitted on Iranian buses.

The bus driver will stop on the outskirts of every major town so that his tachograph can be checked by the police as a precaution against speeding. Occasionally at these checkpoints (or at roadblocks along the way) a customs official or policeman may get in the bus and walk up and down, presumably looking for obvious smugglers or dissidents. They may ask to see your passport, more out of curiosity than anything else. Just do what they say, and answer questions politely and briefly. We have never heard of any traveller having any trouble at the roadblocks; the officials seem to be under instructions to be nice to foreigners, which is very reassuring.

In places near the borders or the Persian Gulf, customs searches are more thorough. The official will often look more closely at the passengers and search hand luggage. Often, everyone has to get out of the bus, identify their luggage, carry it up the road, and wait while the vehicle is searched. Very rarely will your main luggage be searched individually. Again, foreigners are often given special consideration and rarely have to suffer the indignation of intrusive baggage searches.

Several readers have complained that bus schedules often mean you arrive in a town in the early hours of the morning; it's worth checking the time of arrival when you book. Punctuality is not always guaranteed though.

MINIBUS

Minibuses are often used for shorter distances to and from minor towns and villages. Sometimes they're an alternative to the bus but sometimes there's no choice between a minibus or bus; just take whichever is going your way. Minibuses are particularly popular along the Caspian coast, and between the Caspian towns and Tehrān.

Minibuses are marginally more expensive than buses, but not enough to worry about. They often travel faster than the larger buses and inevitably carry fewer passengers so they spend less time dropping off and picking up. On the downside, they're not as comfortable as bigger buses and usually leave only when they're full which can mean a long wait on less popular routes. You pay for tickets before you get on, during the trip or when you get off.

Minibuses sometimes leave from a special station and sometimes from the main bus station. If in doubt, just charter a taxi and tell the driver you want to go to the *termīnāl-é Rasht, Tehrān* or wherever. Arriving in a town, they have a nasty habit of depositing you in the middle of nowhere. Luckily, hopeful taxi drivers are likely to be waiting.

TRAIN

Iran's rail network is especially impressive if you consider the mountainous terrain that the tracks must often pass through: The great trans-Iranian railway built in the 1930s to connect the Caspian Sea at Bandar-é Torkamān with the Persian Gulf at Bandar-é Emām Khomeinī is one of the great engineering achievements of the 20th century.

All trains start out from Tehrān, so to get from Tabrīz to Kermān, for example, you would have to travel to Tehrān and change. Travellers heading to Pakistan by train can only get as far as Kermān and must then continue by bus to the border, although for years there have been plans to extend this line.

Unfortunately, there are only a few services a week to popular places such as Esfahān and Kermān and none at all to Shīrāz. Stations are often remote and buying a ticket can be difficult. Departure and arrival times for anywhere other than the start and finish points of the journey are usually lousy, and, generally, you must prebook at the station, then wait hours for the train to arrive.

However, there are also some advantages to using the railway. Trains are usually comfortable (at least in 1st class), fairly efficient, reasonably fast and always cheap. For overnight trips a 1st-class sleeper makes a much more comfortable way to go than the bus. Also, some trains pass through pleasant scenery while buses speed through one dreary town after another (the best scenery and service is probably on the Tehrān-Tabrīz route). And trains have a better safety record than the buses.

A guard usually comes round to take orders for tea to be served in your compartment. Long-distance trains also have a restaurant car although the choice of food is very limited; passengers in the know tend to bring their own food. Iced water is available. Security is better than in India or Russia, but chain your luggage to something solid if you leave your compartment, or ask someone to look after it. You can ask to be seated in a nonsmoking or single-sex compartment.

Classes

All trains have at least two classes and some have three. You can buy tickets for any class at the place the train is leaving from, but if you want to buy a ticket from anywhere along the route, you may only be able to buy

For Train Buffs

Most travellers end up using buses, minibuses and shared taxis to travel around Iran, but for anyone who is interested in trains, there is much to like about Islamic Republic of Iran Railways. Here are a few facts and figures:

Track length: 7740km
Gauge: 1.435m
Locomotives: 566
Passenger coaches: 1066
Annual passengers: 9.7 million
Train stations: 299
Longest train line: Tehrān to Bandar-é Abbās (1483km)

2nd-class tickets. If 2nd class is too crowded for you, you can often upgrade to 1st class along the way, provided there's space.

On overnight trains (usually to or from Tehrān) the 1st-class carriages have sleepers with four or six bunks as in India, Pakistan and Turkey. Oddly enough, they are not all sexually segregated and one reader wrote to complain of having a man in another bunk stroking her arm in the night. Women travelling alone should make a point of asking for a single-sex sleeper.

'Express' train services are a little faster than the 'regular' ones because they stop at fewer stations.

Tickets

Buying tickets is a hassle. In most cases, you can only buy tickets at the train station itself, though Esfahān does have a booking office in the city, and in Yazd, a travel agency sells tickets. Travel agents in Tehrān can organise tickets for you, and it's well worth paying their small service charge to avoid having to face the scrum at the Tehrān station booking office. Buying a ticket at any station along a route is a matter of pot luck and waiting. You're probably better off taking a bus.

In Tehrān and major towns such as Esfahān, Tabrīz and Mashhad where trains originate, you can buy tickets up to one month in advance. Advance bookings cost an extra 20%, but it's worth paying considering how cheap tickets are anyway. It's never possible to book a return ticket; you will have to do that when you arrive at your destination.

If you're having no luck buying a ticket on your own, see if there's someone at the station who's willing to do the queuing, arguing and negotiating for you for a small consideration.

Costs

As a rough guide, a seat in 2nd class costs about the same as 'lux' class on the bus, and a 1st-class train seat about twice as much as 'super' class on the bus.

For the prices of specific train tickets, see the relevant destination in this book.

TAXI

Unlike taxis elsewhere in the world, Iranian taxis – whether shared or privately chartered – are remarkably cheap and worth considering even if you're on a tight budget.

Shared Taxi

Between major towns less than three hours apart by car, you can almost always find a shared taxi to travel in. Speed is the main advantage because shared taxis are generally more uncomfortable than buses. Two people are expected to squeeze into the front passenger seat, so never sit there unless you have no choice. Three people will share the back of the taxi, which is not too uncomfortable unless you're built like an NBA basketballer or a sumo wrestler.

Shared taxis need fewer people to fill them, so they usually depart fairly quickly. Though some buses leave half-empty, knowing they will pick up passengers along the way, shared taxis *never* leave with an empty seat unless a passenger agrees to pay for it. Drivers sometimes stop for toilet breaks, but beware of ordering something to eat and then finding the driver ready to go before you've eaten the first mouthful.

To distinguish a shared taxi from a private one you need to know the word *savari* (shared taxi), although in places that tend to be a hassle, like the Tabrīz bus station, the drivers will assure you their vehicle is a savarī but still try to demand the private

taxi fare. Most of the time, savarīs are the ubiquitous Iranian-made Paykans, but taxi drivers around the Caspian provinces use huge, battered (but sometimes lovingly restored) Mercedes Benzes.

As a general rule, shared taxis cost three times more than the 'lux' buses. This may seem a lot more in rials, but if you work it out in your own currency shared taxis are still cheap and worth using for quick trips, especially through dull stretches of countryside. If you want to hurry up a departure, you can always pay for an empty seat; if your Farsi is good enough, you can even arrange to pay the difference between the full fare and any fare the driver may pick up along the way.

Taxi drivers are generally honest and considerate, with the notable exception of a few operating out of Esfahān. For the etiquette of who to sit next to in a shared taxi see the boxed text 'Is This Seat Free?' earlier in this chapter.

Shared taxis usually leave from inside or just outside the relevant bus terminal, though occasionally there are special terminals for shared taxis heading in particular directions. If in doubt, charter a private taxi and ask the driver to take you to the relevant pick-up point for a shared taxi going your way. You can't prebook a seat in a shared taxi; they leave when they're full.

Private Taxi

Almost every single taxi in the country is available for private hire. If you have heaps of cash or are travelling in a group, chartering a taxi is worth considering: it allows you to stop for photos; you can arrange to stop off at places along the way; you can leave when you want to; and there is more space in the vehicle.

Needless to say, the price of a private taxi is open to negotiation. One excellent way to avoid getting ripped off is to ask the driver of a shared taxi for the price per person for a certain trip. For example, the price per person in a shared taxi from Tabrīz to Orūmīyeh is IR12,500. Multiply this figure by five (the number of passengers in a shared taxi); therefore IR62,500 is what you should expect to pay for this trip in a private

The Popular Paykan

Even though the situation is starting to change, nine out of 10 cars on Iranian roads are white Paykans. The Paykan is an exact replica of the Hillman Hunter, which Britain stopped producing decades ago. Daewoo and Peugeot now have factories in Iran, and cars manufactured overseas are also imported via Kīsh Island so the days of the Paykan monopoly must surely be numbered.

taxi, unless you want to make a detour or stop to examine the lake. In general, the cost of hiring a taxi should be about IR400 per kilometre on a one-way journey and IR600 on a return journey.

PIK-UP

Occasionally, especially in southern Iran around Bandar-é Abbās, you may come across a utility with a canvas cover called a *pik-up* (pick-up). If you're tall, try to get to the pik-up early and negotiate a price for the front seat, which will be far more comfortable than the back. Prices are very cheap, but the comfort level is also very low.

CAR & MOTORCYCLE

A growing number of travellers are taking a vehicle across Iran as part of a trip between Europe and the Indian subcontinent. This naturally gives you a lot of flexibility, although you need to bear in mind that the distances are great, the scenery often monotonous and the traffic (at least in the towns) truly horrendous.

Road surfaces are generally excellent, as are the dirt tracks if you're bringing a motorbike. On the other hand it's not wise to drive at night because of occasional potholes and the risk of bumping into tractors and other vehicles crawling along the road with no lights. Strong crosswinds can be a problem for bikers keen to overtake slow-moving trucks.

Just about every road sign is in English, including directions to almost every city, town and village, the names of main roads and squares in most towns, and general safety instructions. If there are no signs in English

along the road, you are probably somewhere you shouldn't be (ie, near the border or in a military area), or somewhere you don't want to be (ie, on a boring stretch of nothingness).

Heaven forbid that you should have any sort of accident, but if you do and you're in Tehrān, ring the Road Accident Department (☎ 197). Elsewhere ring the local police headquarters; most have individual traffic accident departments. You should never move the vehicle from the road until the police have come to make their report. In general, the bad news is that, as a foreigner, you are likely to be held responsible for the accident.

If you are driving your own vehicle, you should always slow down and get ready to stop at roadblocks. Usually if you wind down your window, smile nicely, and give the officials your best 'I don't know what to do and I don't speak Farsi' look, you will be waved straight through. The worst that can happen is that you have to show your passport, licence and vehicle documents. You're unlikely to have any hassles as long your documentation is in order.

You should never drive off the main road near the Pakistan, Iraq or Afghanistan borders; if you don't come across suspicious drug smugglers, you will probably come across suspicious customs and police officials instead.

There are large towns at least every 100km throughout the country except in the remote deserts of eastern Iran (where you should carry extra food and water), but petrol stations can be few and far between – it's as well to keep your tank topped up. Be particularly careful when filling up as there is nothing on the fuel pumps to indicate which is diesel and which petrol.

When arriving in big cities, look for a hotel with secure off-street parking, not always easy to find because hotels are often in the town centre, where every square centimetre is used for something more important. However, some cities have parking lots, identifiable by a big letter 'P' in blue, or a picture of a car and an arrow; you'll often find them just off a busy main road. Unless you have exceptional driving skills, and an excellent insurance policy, try to leave your

Road Distances (km)

	Ahvāz	Ardabīl	Bandar-é Abbās	Būshehr	Esfahān	Gorgān	Hamadān	Kermān	Kermānshāh	Khorram Ābād	Mashhad	Orūmīyeh	Qazvīn	Rasht	Shīrāz	Tabrīz	Tehrān	Yazd	Zāhedān
Ahvāz	---																		
Ardabīl	1310	---																	
Bandar-é Abbās	1280	1930	---																
Būshehr	490	1610	930	---															
Esfahān	750	1030	960	580	---														
Gorgān	1270	770	1730	1630	840	---													
Hamadān	640	670	1420	1050	470	730	---												
Kermān	1230	1630	490	880	660	1440	1130	---											
Kermānshāh	490	790	1770	970	650	920	190	1290	---										
Khorram Ābād	380	930	1330	860	370	900	260	1030	320	---									
Mashhad	1770	1330	1380	1650	1220	570	1230	890	1420	1390	---								
Orūmīyeh	1060	530	2030	1550	1070	1300	610	1740	580	870	1800	---							
Qazvīn	880	480	1650	1360	560	530	230	1220	420	490	1080	770	---						
Rasht	1040	270	1660	1520	760	500	400	1360	590	670	1070	800	170	---					
Shīrāz	660	1520	620	300	490	1320	950	570	1110	860	1380	1320	1050	1250	---				
Tabrīz	1080	220	1930	1560	1040	1000	610	1640	590	880	1500	310	480	490	1530	---			
Tehrān	870	590	1330	1230	440	400	340	1040	530	500	890	910	150	330	930	600	---		
Yazd	1080	1270	660	730	300	1080	730	360	950	670	920	1380	830	1000	450	1280	680	---	
Zāhedān	1760	2160	740	1400	1190	1520	1660	530	1820	1560	950	2270	1760	1900	1100	2170	1570	890	---
Zanjān	970	380	1650	1340	760	720	330	1360	420	590	1210	590	180	350	1240	280	320	1000	1890

car near your hotel, and use public transport to get around the city. Be especially careful about leaving your car unattended anywhere in eastern Iran – it may be stolen, stripped, driven across the border of Afghanistan or Pakistan, and bought by a drug smuggler before you've finished your plate of kebabs.

The maps in this guidebook are mainly designed for people using their feet and/or public transport. If you will be driving into large towns like Shīrāz, Esfahān, Mashhad or Tehrān (try not to!), you'd be well advised to try and get hold of the relevant Gita Shenasi map to help you find your way in and out. For more details, see Maps in the Facts for the Visitor chapter.

The best source of information on driving around Iran is the Touring & Automobile Club (☎ 021-874 0411, fax 874 0410) at 12 Nobakht St, Khorramshāhr Ave, Tehrān.

The following is a description of the reaction to that rare sight in Iran, a female motorcyclist:

One of the bikers I met there was a woman travelling alone. As you might expect, she attracted a huge amount of interest, but had no problems other than sometimes finding a place to stay. One place in particular she was refused, so she sat outside the hotel until they changed their minds. She said she brought the traffic to a standstill at a nearby roundabout. Eventually she went to the police who wrote something for the hotelier and she was reluctantly allowed to stay. She didn't even have to pay and was just told to clear out ASAP in the morning (without breakfast – charming!).

Nick Banks

Road Rules

Driving your own vehicle across Iran is not a task to be taken lightly. The major concern for anyone who hasn't driven in this part of the world before will be the appalling traffic, especially worrying for anyone on a motorbike.

In theory at least, the rule of the road is that everyone drives on the right, but even this can't be depended upon; faced with a one-way street going the wrong way, the average Iranian driver sees nothing wrong with reversing down it. The theory is that you give way to the traffic coming onto a roundabout, which seems a tad unimportant when some drivers simply drive the wrong way round it. Take 10 Iranian car drivers and an otherwise deserted open road and you can be sure that all 10 will form a convoy so tightly packed that each of the rear nine can read the speedometer of the car in front. The phrase 'optimum braking distance' might as well not exist. Any vehicle going less than 100km/h on the open road is probably driven by a petrified foreigner, and only foreigners wear motorcycle helmets or use seat belts.

The worst offenders of all are the motorcyclists who treat pavements as if they were main roads with complete disregard for pedestrians. Vehicle insurance is a must, and not just for legal reasons.

Petrol & Repairs

As you would expect, petrol is ridiculously cheap – IR400 per litre for petrol and IR100 for diesel – and Iranians will stare in disbelief if you tell them how much you pay for petrol at home. There are petrol stations (open every day) in or just outside every major town, but these are often choked with impatient shared taxis, trucks, buses, minibuses and private vehicles, so fill up completely whenever you can and always carry extra supplies, just in case.

So many Iranians drive their own vehicle that even the tiniest settlement has a shop where you can arrange repairs, usually somewhere on the outskirts or along the main arterial roads. The price for repair work is open to negotiation, and you should always be careful of inferior spare parts, or unscrupulous mechanics (or anyone else) taking an undue interest in your car.

In the height of summer, tyre blow-outs are common because of the scalding heat. The average Iranian driver needs less than five minutes to swap over a tyre.

Drivers have suggested that if you have a problem with your vehicle, your best bet is to talk to a truckie; many of them have been outside the country and speak a foreign language.

Rental

The concept of car rental barely exists in Iran, not least because without a functioning system for accepting credit cards it's hard for anyone leasing a car to be sure they can make good any damage. Instead, 'car rental' here means chartering a taxi, either privately or through a travel agency – any of those listed under Organised Tours later in this chapter will be able to help you with this.

BICYCLE

A fair smattering of travellers have also started cycling across Iran, spurred on by the excellent quality of the roads and the friendliness of most of the people met along the way. However, before deciding to cycle you need to consider the vast distances involved, the dodgy traffic, and the hot, tedious stretches of desert road with few villages along them. You will need to carry lots of water; enough food to last the long stretches between villages (where there is always something to eat); camping equipment if you are not sticking to major towns; a decent map of Iran; and a phrasebook.

Bear in mind that you may arrive in a village or small town and find either nowhere to stay at all or only a hotel that charges more than you can afford. In that case you may have to load your bike on a bus or truck and head for the next big town. This is also the thing to do if you get tired or your visa is about to expire.

The biggest drawback with cycling, as with most other activities in Iran, is the need to stay covered up. We have received varying reports from travellers: some say that it's fine to wear cycling gear when actually on the road as long as you have clothes at hand to cover up as soon as you stop; others say that women in particular must be covered at all times.

> Cycling in cycling shorts was NO problem... When we asked the customs officer at the border how people think about half-nude Western cyclists, he laughed and answered that the Iranian soccer team never plays in ski dresses...and as long as you are doing 'official' sports, you can follow its 'official' dress code. But take care – if you

stop to buy something or have a short rest, you are suddenly out of this rule and need to be dressed correctly.

Chrisian Wagner

In Chalūs we had a really bad experience with the police. When we're cycling my 'wife' doesn't wear a long coat. This is never a problem because people understand that it is impossible to cycle in a chador. But in Chalūs she left her bike for a moment to look for a bakery and forgot to put on her coat...the policeman that saw her took her to the police station...[where] they wouldn't let her go and show them her coat and bicycle... When they (finally) saw the coat (in combination with the bicycles) we could go.

Geieje van der Berg & Tony Verschoor

One reader sent us a newspaper clipping about a ban on female cyclists in the Caspian resort of Ramsār but this seems to have been a short-lived aberration.

The trouble is that Iranians themselves rarely use bikes. In an interview about her film *The Day I Became a Woman*, which was filmed on the Kīsh Island cycle track and in which women cyclists feature prominently, director Marziye Meshkini explained:

[The government] does not tolerate even the simplest form of modern exercise such as cycling. This is not a haphazard example...you can't ride a bicycle even in Tehrān... There is no written law in the country that forbids women to ride bicycles, but the unwritten law (that is, tradition) does not allow women to do a simple exercise like that. In other words, it is a taboo.

Iran News, Sept 2000

The other snag is that finding repairers and spare parts can be tricky. One good cycle shop is Saba Docharkh (☎ 021-878 0651), 16 Anahita St, Āfriqā Expressway, Tehrān. Otherwise, bring whatever you may need.

There is nowhere to rent bicycles for long distances, so bring your own.

HITCHING

Hitching is never entirely safe in any country, and we don't recommend it. Travellers who decide to hitch should understand that they are taking a small but potentially seri-

ous risk. However, many people do choose to hitch, and the advice that follows should help to make their journeys as fast and safe as possible.

Hitching, as understood in the West, is a novel concept in Iran. Although you will often see people standing by the roadside waiting for a lift, they are actually waiting for space in a bus, minibus or shared taxi, for which they expect to pay. Occasionally drivers will offer foreigners a free ride in return for English practice or out of simple hospitality, but you won't get very far if you hang around waiting for these chance encounters. Except when visiting remote archaeological sites, you should always depend on cheap, reliable public transport.

It goes without saying that women should *never* hitch in Iran.

BOAT

Despite the lengthy stretches of coast along the Caspian Sea and the Persian Gulf, there are very few domestic passenger boat services. Ferries travel between the mainland and some islands in the Persian Gulf. For example, regular boats for Kīsh Island leave from Bandar-é Langeh, Bandar-é Abbās and Bandar-é Chārak. They depart less often for more remote and less interesting islands in the Persian Gulf. Numerous speedboats travel between Bandar-é Abbās and Hormoz and Qeshm Islands.

There are currently no passenger services between towns along the Persian Gulf, or along the Iranian coast of the Caspian Sea. Occasional passenger boats putter along the Kārūn River, Iran's only navigable river, and ferries across Iran's largest lake, Orūmīyeh, supplement the unfinished causeway. Otherwise, that's about it.

LOCAL TRANSPORT
To/From the Airport

Only a few international and domestic airports have special bus services or even public buses, so in most cases you'll have to get to and from domestic flights by private or shared taxi. Sometimes a combination of public buses and shared taxis is possible, but this is generally more trouble then it's worth, especially if you're arriving in a strange town for the first time and have luggage with you.

At most airports, you will be met by a gaggle of taxi drivers foaming at the mouth in anticipation of overcharging a naive foreigner. If you're worried about the price of a private taxi, ask a local, or look for fellow passengers to share the cost. Some cities have official airport taxis, marked as such in English. These are invariably more expensive than normal private taxis, so avoid them if you can.

See the Getting Around section in the Tehrān chapter for information about how to get to and from the airport in Tehrān by taxi.

Bus

Most Iranian towns and cities have local bus services. The buses are often new and Iranian-made, though in the outer suburbs of Tehrān you may be astounded to see a converted double-decker bus imported from England a few decades ago. Because local buses are often crowded, and shared and private taxis are ubiquitous and cheap, only the most adventurous or frugal bother using them.

Local buses are difficult to use unless you know exactly where they're going, or you can speak and read Farsi. Bus numbers and destinations are marked only in Farsi (sometimes in English in Tehrān and Shīrāz). If in doubt, ask a local – most will be more than happy to help (even if you don't entirely understand their reply).

Bus stops are clearly marked, often with a circle in red and blue. Buses do not always set out and return by the same route, and services change frequently without notice. You buy your tickets in little booths along the main streets of the cities or at the bus stations. Tickets normally cost IR100, though depending on the distance and the city, a trip can cost IR200 to IR300 (ie, two or three tickets).

On local buses, small children of both genders and all women have to sit at the back of the bus. Because so few women travel by bus, women often get a seat while men have to stand, squashed like sardines, at the front. This segregation can be complicated if you are travelling as a mixed couple and need to discuss when to get off. Bus travellers give their tickets to the driver either before they get on, or after they get off, depending on the local system – but women must pass their tickets to the driver while leaning through the front door of the bus, without using the steps into the front of the bus.

Minibus

If you think using local buses is a hassle, don't even bother trying to use the infrequent and desperately crowded minibuses. Quite often they are so crammed with passengers that you can hardly see out of the window to tell where you are going. You normally pay in cash when you get on – about IR200 a ticket. Men and women get a seat anywhere they can; there is no room for segregation. Minibuses stop at normal bus stops.

Trolleybus

Tehrān boasts one environmentally friendly electric trolleybus line – even if its dedicated lane is more often used by carbon-monoxide-belching buses and recalcitrant motorcyclists. The same system of paying and segregation applies as for local buses.

Metro

Iran's first underground railway system has finally opened. For details of the first line of the Tehrān Metro, see Getting Around in the Tehrān chapter.

Taxi

For many Iranians and just about every foreign traveller, a shared or private taxi is the quickest and most hassle-free way of getting around a town or city.

Shared Taxi In most towns and cities, shared taxis duplicate or even replace local bus services. They usually take up to five passengers: two in the front passenger seat, three in the back, rarely more. A shared taxi will nearly always be a Paykan sedan, usually coloured orange, or with a dash of orange somewhere. After a while you will get used to them, especially if you try them out somewhere other than Tehrān first.

Shared taxis usually travel between major squares and along major roads in every town and city. They often make slight detours for passengers at no extra charge; for a longer detour, you may be charged IR300 or so extra. Shared taxis hang around places where they are most likely to get fares (bus stations, train stations, airports, major town squares) or you can hail one on the road.

Normally, getting a shared taxi goes something like this. Lean out a few metres from the kerb, far enough for the driver to hear you shout your destination but close enough to the kerb to dash back again if you have to. If the driver has a spare seat, he will slow down for a nanosecond while you shout your destination.

When you want the driver to stop you simply say *kheilī mamnūn* (thank you very much) or make any other obvious noise. Drivers appreciate exact change, so try and keep plenty of coins and those filthy IR200 and IR500 notes handy; you normally pay after the car has stopped.

Fares, which are fixed by the government, range from about IR200 to IR2000, depending on the distance and the city (Tehrān's fares are naturally the most expensive while Yazd's are some of the cheapest). Always try and see what other passengers are paying before you hand over your money.

If you get into an empty shared taxi, particularly in Esfahān and Tehrān, it's often assumed that you want to charter it privately.

Likewise, if everyone else gets out the driver may decide that you are now a private fare. Whenever possible try to take only taxis with other people in them.

Private Taxi Any taxi without passengers, whether obviously a shared taxi, or a more expensive private taxi, can be chartered to go anywhere in town. Unless it's a complicated deal including waiting time, simply hail the vehicle, tell the driver where you want to go, and ask the price, including waiting time. Immediately offer about half what he suggests but expect to end up paying about 70% of the originally quoted price. It's hardly worth haggling over the odd IR1000.

Agency Taxi Agency taxis, or 'telephone' taxis, don't normally stop to pick up passengers; you have to order them by telephone or at an agency office. There are taxi agency offices in even the smallest towns and hundreds of them in Tehrān. Some of the top hotels run their own taxi services, and any hotel or *mosāferkhūneh* (lodging house) can order a taxi for a guest. Naturally, this is the most expensive way of using taxis, but you get a better car, the comfort of knowing there will be someone to complain to if anything goes wrong, and, possibly, a driver who speaks English.

ORGANISED TOURS

Few Iranian travel agencies organise trips for foreigners within Iran: They mainly sell airline tickets or act as local operators for foreign travel companies. Furthermore, English is not usually spoken, attractions are Islamic in nature and the standard of food and accommodation may not be quite what you were expecting. Most organised tours around Iran start and finish in Tehrān, with a quick look around the capital before concentrating on the must-sees: Shīrāz and Esfahān, with either Tabrīz or Kermān and possibly Bam thrown in.

The handful of Iranian travel companies listed here offer something different. All are well established and used to catering for foreigners. Most can organise tailor-made tours to suit particular interests and can help you get your visa. It's better not to just ring up or turn up at their office and expect to be off on a tour within the day; most need prior notice to organise a tour. Most can provide guides who speak English, French, German or Japanese, and sometimes Spanish or Italian. Costs depend on the length of the tour, the mode of transport, the type of accommodation and the current exchange rate. Foreigners will be expected to pay in foreign currency, usually US dollars.

The following companies are all based in Tehrān (area code ☎ 021), although most have offices in the other major cities:

Arg-e-Jadid (☎ 881 1072, fax 882 6112, atc@neda.net) 296 Motahharī Ave, Tehrān 15886

Azadi International Tourism Organisation (AITO; ☎ 873 2191, fax 873 2195, aito@www.dci.co.ir) 37 AITO Bldg, 8th St, Ahmād Ghasir Ave (PO Box 15875/1765). There are branches in Paris and Frankfurt.

Caravan Sahra (☎ 750 2229, fax 882 6036, caravan@caravansahra.com) Caravan Sahra Bldg, 29 Qaem Maqam-e Farahani Ave, Tehrān 15899. There is another branch on the ground floor of Lāleh International Hotel (☎/fax 895 5253).

Gardesh Travel Agency (☎ 817 7239, fax 817 2729) 56 Ind Bldg, Sepahbod Qaranī Ave

Iran Air Tours (☎ 875 8390, fax 875 5884) 191 Motahharī Ave, at Mofatteh St crossroads

Iran Touring & Tourism Organisation (ITTO; ☎ 655 687, fax 656 800) 154 Keshāvarz Blvd. This is a quasi-government tourist bureau operated by the Ministry of Culture & Islamic Guidance, which runs many of Iran's two- and three-star hotels while acting as a travel agency as well.

Pasargad Tour (☎ 205 8833, fax 205 8866, info@pasargad-tour.com) 146 Āfriqā Hwy, Tehrān 19156

Persepolis Tour & Travel Agency (☎ 880 5266, fax 880 8534) 100 Nejātollahī St

Sogol Tour & Travel Co (☎ 884 9083, fax 884 9085, sogol@neda.net.ir) 65 Zohreh St, Modarres Hwy (PO Box 16315/439)

Tavakoli International Travel & Tour (☎ 880 4700, fax 657 262, tavakoli@sama.dpi.net.ir) 25 Falahpoor St, Nejātollahī St

Tehrān

☎ 021 • pop 12 million

Sadly, there's no longer so much as the slightest whiff of the Orient about the Iranian capital. Pollution, chronic overcrowding and a lack of responsible planning have conspired to turn Tehrān into a metropolis you're best off getting into and out of as quickly as possible, although most travellers end up spending several days in this grim city whether they want to or not.

One obvious drawback is the heavy smog, which hovers ominously over the city, blocking out views of the mountains for much of the time. At certain times of the year, especially in summer, it descends with unbearable effect and drives people out of Tehrān in coughing, wheezing droves, while the radio warns those with heart conditions not to leave their houses.

Even worse than the smog is the traffic that gives rise to it. It might not matter quite so much about the distances between one sight and another were it not for the appalling, out-of-control traffic, which turns even the shortest journey into a frightening obstacle course.

You can see the main sights in three days or so, hopefully long enough to transact any important business that may detain you in the capital. However, if you do need to stay longer, Tehrān's pluses include a decent choice of hotels and some of the best restaurants in the country. In general, facilities are far ahead of those in the provinces, and most Tehrānīs are friendly and welcoming. With time to explore in greater depth you'll find plenty of museums to keep you busy and at weekends it's fun to get out and about with the picnickers in northern Tehrān.

Wherever you go in Tehrān you will be confronted with the poignant images of men who died in the Iran-Iraq War, gazing down at you from murals on the sides of buildings or from billboards along the roads.

HISTORY

Human settlement of the region dates from Neolithic times, but Tehrān, which started

Highlights

Tehrān Province p187

● Tehrān p154
South Tehrān &
Tehrān Bazaar p161
Central Tehrān p168

• Gawping at the Achaemenid gold in the Rezā Abbāsī Museum and at the diamond-studded globe in the National Jewels Museum

• Admiring carpets you could never afford to buy in the Carpet Museum

•• Drinking tea in the grounds of the Sa'd Ābād Museum complex or along the paths at Darakeh and Darband

• Exploring the wonderful Golestān Palace

• Visiting the shrine of Emām Khomeinī and the war graves at Behesht-é Zahrā

as a small village in the foothills of the Alborz Mountains, developed very slowly and its rise to prominence was largely accidental. A succession of visitors to Tehrān from the 10th to 13th centuries AD described it as a village of half-savages who lived in underground dwellings and practised highway robbery. In AD 1197, after the Mongols sacked the nearby town of Rey (at that time the major urban centre in central Persia), Tehrān began to develop in its place as a small, moderately prosperous trading centre.

TEHRĀN

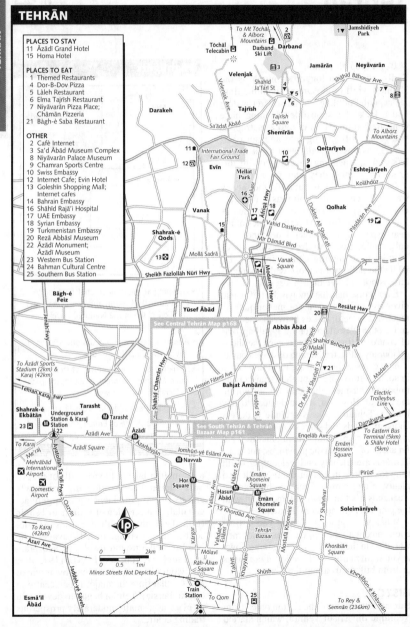

PLACES TO STAY
11 Āzādī Grand Hotel
15 Homa Hotel

PLACES TO EAT
1 Themed Restaurants
4 Dor-B-Dov Pizza
5 Lāleh Restaurant
6 Elma Tajrīsh Restaurant
7 Niyāvarān Pizza Place;
    Chāmān Pizzeria
21 Bāgh-è Saba Restaurant

OTHER
2 Cafè Internet
3 Sa'd Ābād Museum Complex
8 Niyāvarān Palace Museum
9 Chamran Sports Centre
10 Swiss Embassy
12 Internet Cafe; Evin Hotel
13 Goleshīn Shopping Mall;
    Internet cafes
14 Bahrain Embassy
16 Shāhīd Rajā'ī Hospital
17 UAE Embassy
18 Syrian Embassy
19 Turkmenistan Embassy
20 Rezā Abbāsī Museum
22 Āzādī Monument;
    Āzādī Museum
23 Western Bus Station
24 Bahman Cultural Centre
25 Southern Bus Station

In the mid-16th century AD, Tehrān's attractive natural setting, many trees, clear rivers and good hunting brought it to the attention of the early Safavid king, Tahmāsb I. Under his patronage, gardens were laid out, brick houses and caravanserais were built, and heavily fortified walls were erected to protect the town and its steadily increasing merchant population. As it continued to grow under the later Safavid kings, European visitors wrote of its many enchanting vineyards and gardens.

Threatened by the encroaching Qajars, Karīm Khān Zand transferred his army here from his capital at Shīrāz in 1758, intending to move in on his enemy. At the same time he refortified Tehrān and began the construction of a royal residence. Perhaps he had intended to move his capital here eventually, but when his army killed the Qajar chieftain Mohammed Hasan Khān and took his young son Agha Mohammed Khān hostage, Karīm Khān abandoned the unfinished palace and returned to Shīrāz.

In 1789, Agha Mohammed Khān declared Tehrān his capital, and six years later he had himself crowned as shah of all Persia. He destroyed the city walls of Shīrāz, disinterred the corpse of Karīm Khān and carried it back to Tehrān in a final act of revenge. Tehrān then was little more than a dusty town of around 15,000 souls but it continued to grow slowly under later Qajar rulers.

From the early 1920s, the city was extensively modernised on a grid system, and this period marked the start of the phenomenal population growth and uncontrolled urban development that continues to this day. In 1887, the population was 250,000; by 1930 it had only increased to 300,000. By 1939, it had rocketed to half a million, with the city's rapid expansion slowing only during WWII. By 1956, however, the population was 1.8 million; by 1976, it had risen to 4.5 million; and by the time of the 1986 census, Tehrān's population had soared to more than 8.7 million. Exact figures for the current population are unavailable; news reports usually say that it's still eight million but in reality it may well be as high as 12 million.

ORIENTATION

Tehrān is so vast that getting lost at least once is inevitable, no matter what form of transport you take. Thankfully, most of the streets that you are likely to visit have signs in English, but there are areas without street signs in any language, for example, around the Tehrān Bāzār, south of Pārk-é Shāhr, around the Iranshāhr Hotel, and in the ugly and appallingly crowded suburbs of southern Tehrān.

Tehrān is sharply divided between north and south. The south is cheaper, more congested and generally less appealing, but does have lots of cheap hotels, especially around Emām Khomeinī Square, which also hosts a big bus terminal, an underground station, and the main post and telephone offices. The north is more inviting, with slightly less chaotic traffic and cleaner air, but since there are few cheap hotels in the north most travellers are forced to base themselves south of Enqelāb Ave.

Tehrān is bisected north-south by Valiasr Ave, which runs for more than 20km from Tajrīsh to the train station. One of the main streets running from east to west is Āzādī Ave, which starts at the Āzādī Monument, near the airports, and becomes Enqelāb Ave east of Enqelāb Square.

If you need landmarks, the Alborz Mountains, known as the North Star of Tehrān, are to the north, and the huge telephone office at Emām Khomeinī Square dominates inner southern Tehrān. If you want to use public transport, it helps to try to get to know the names and locations of the main squares as soon as you can. It's worth noting that many north-south roads slope downwards as they head south.

Maps

If you're only stopping in Tehrān for a few days and seeing the major sights, the maps in this chapter should be adequate. If you want to explore the city in depth, walk a lot or visit friends or places in remote suburbs, you may need a more detailed map, in which case head straight for the Gita Shenasi map shop (☎ 670 9335, fax 670 5782), 15 Ostad Shahrīvar St, Razī St, Valiasr Crossroads,

Confusing Addresses

The good news is that street names are signposted in English in most big Iranian cities. To find your way about by taxi it's often enough just to say the names of the two biggest streets close to your destination, or to ask for the nearest main square, and then work it out from there.

The bad news is that written addresses can be horribly confusing. One address may contain as many as three street names, starting from the most important highway or square nearby, then progressing to a smaller avenue which runs off it, and finally to the street where (hopefully) you'll find the building you're looking for. The word *kheyābūn* (street or avenue) is often omitted from addresses and, despite their appearance on many maps, the names of suburbs rarely feature in an address.

In Tehrān there are a few particular catches. Āfriqā Ave, for example, is also called Jordan Ave after a barely remembered American philanthropist; Nejātollāhī St is often called Villa St; and Emām Khomeinī Square is sometimes called Tup Khuneh after the cannons that are fired there to announce Nō Rūz (the Iranian New Year) and the end of each day's fasting during Ramazān.

Enqelāb-é Eslāmī Ave, 11337, Tehrān, and take a look at its various offerings.

INFORMATION
Visa Extensions

Unfortunately, Tehrān is the worst place in the country to apply for a visa extension, primarily because so many people, especially Afghans and Pakistanis, apply here. To make matters worse, the office is hopelessly understaffed, so you may have to spend up to five days of your precious time waiting for an extension. For suggestions on better places to try to extend your visa, and how to go about it, see Visas & Documents in the Facts for the Visitor chapter.

If you have to apply for your extension in Tehrān, the place to do so is the Department of Aliens' Affairs (☎ 890 4560; *not* the Ministry of Foreign Affairs near Emām Khome-inī Square) on Khalantarī St, just off Nejā-tollāhī St. A branch of the Tejarat Bank on the corner makes a handy landmark, as does the long line (or huddle) of bearded Afghans.

The office is open daily except Friday and public holidays. You can drop your paperwork off between 7.45 am and 1 pm (11 am on Thursday) and call back for your extension between noon and 1.30 pm (between 10.30 and 11.15 am on Thursday). Get there as early as you can to stand any chance of beating the queues. Foreigners with a bit of cheek can usually get away with looking helpless and jumping the queue. There is usually a separate line for women, so foreign females may be able to spend less time lining up. They won't get their visas any more quickly though.

Tourist Offices

The fact that there is no tourist office in Tehrān says everything about the relative unimportance of tourism to the city. It's possible the situation may change now that the need to attract visitors is rising on the political agenda so it's worth double-checking with your hotel when you arrive. Although it is part of the Ministry of Culture & Islamic Guidance, the Iran Touring & Tourism Organisation (ITTO; ☎ 655 687, fax 656 800) at 154 Keshāvarz Blvd, is a travel agency rather than a tourist office. It is excellent for booking tickets and local tours, but not really set up for advice or recommendations.

There's a tourist information booth with English-speaking staff at the airport but they may not even be able to supply a map of the city. The train station also has English-speaking staff at its information desk but they are only able to provide information on train times and prices. The main bus stations have information counters, but you'll be lucky to find anyone who speaks English.

Money

If you arrive by air, you will probably have to change some money at the airport to pay for a taxi at least. The Bank Melli branch, just after the immigration counter at the international airport, will change most major currencies in cash and travellers cheques, and provide cash advances (in rials) on MasterCard but not Visa.

Although every second building in Tehrān seems to be a bank, only a handful of the larger branches will change your money; your best bet is to try the ones along Ferdōsī St and around Ferdōsī Square. The best place to go is Bank Melli (central branch), on Ferdōsī St, which changes travellers cheques (but not American Express), albeit reluctantly; counter 12 provides cash advances in rials (and sometimes, surprisingly, in US dollars) on MasterCard. None of the banks in northern Tehrān will change money. You can try the upmarket hotels, but check that the rate is as good as you'd get elsewhere first.

Even when you've found a bank ready to change your money, it's unlikely to be a speedy process so you may prefer to frequent one of the semi-official exchange offices along northern Ferdōsī St (on the eastern side) and around Ferdōsī Square, or along Jomhūrī-yé Eslāmī Ave. These are also the places to go to find street money-changers; just take the shortest of strolls and you will be approached by men blatantly waving wads of rials. It's obviously much wiser to change money at a shop or at your hotel than with anyone who guides you into a laneway where it may be hard to check exactly how much money you're getting.

Post

Most travellers use the post office to the west of Emām Khomeinī Square, on Emām Khomeinī Ave. Although not marked in English, it's easily recognisable by the line of post boxes outside. It is open from 8 am to 7 pm every day, but on Friday stamps are available only until 5 pm. You can also send a fax from here. If you want to have mail sent to you via poste restante, ask to have your letters clearly labelled Poste Restante, Post Office, Emām Khomeinī Square, South Tehrān, to avoid any chance of them being directed to any other post office in the city.

Telephone & Fax

The main telephone office, for telegrams, faxes and telephone calls, is on the south side of Emām Khomeinī Square. The telephone booking office inside is quite well organised and staff, some of whom speak English, can usually connect your call in a few minutes. The office is open 24 hours every day. Despite the massive size of the building the public entrance is tucked away rather inconspicuously to the side, off Nāser Khosrō St.

There are lots more telephone offices and phone boxes all over town, especially in the main squares. Most of the bigger and better hotels can also arrange international calls, although you obviously pay more – sometimes much more – for this service.

Email & Internet Access

Tehrān has several Internet cafes, usually charging around IR20,000 an hour. Most of them, however, are not in the most convenient of locations for short-term visitors. There are two Internet cafes on the second floor of the Golestān Shopping Mall. Other possibilities include:

Café Internet (☎ 270 1751, fax 270 1359) Bagh Shater Sports Centre, Sh Asadollahi St, Darband St
Future Way (☎ 895 4863, fax 895 7562, e cybercafe@neda.net) 84 Keshāvarz Blvd, in central Tehrān
Internet Café (☎ 878 8778) 31 Ayeneh Vanak Building, Vanak St (corner of Kordestan Hwy), Kharshad
Internet Café (☎ 207 8606) Business Centre, Evin Hotel, Evin Rd, Shahīd Chamrān Hwy

Of these, Future Way is probably the most conveniently located.

Internet Resources

As yet there are not many dedicated Tehrān sites. You might want to look at www .farsinet.com/tehran, which gives the dates and venues of events, as well as some images of the city and news on recent developments such as the metro. To find out what the weather will be like try the USA Today site (www.usatoday.com/weather). For other Iranian sites that may have useful Tehrān links, see Internet Resources in the Facts for the Visitor chapter.

Travel Agencies

Tehrān is dotted with travel agencies, many of the better ones along, or near, Nejātollāhī St in central Tehrān. Most do little more than sell airline tickets; a few work as local operators for overseas tour companies. For a list of reliable agencies based in Tehrān that run local tours, have English-speaking staff and are useful for buying train and plane tickets, see Organised Tours in the Getting Around chapter.

Bookshops

Finding books to read in English (or any European language) is hard. Your best bets are two pavement kiosks, one on Ferdosī St called Ferdōsī Bookshop, the other on Enqelāb Ave, just west of the junction with Valiasr Ave. Both sell pre-Revolutionary titles only, including a surprising number of raunchy novels by Henry Miller. They also sell a pretty random selection of old and new English-language magazines. The Gulestan Bookshop in Manūchehrī St sells Arthur Upham Pope's *Introducing Persian Architecture* and Forough-es Saltaneh Hekmat's *The Art of Persian Cooking*.

Enqelāb Ave, south of Tehrān University, boasts one of the longest stretches of bookshops in the world; mainly wall-to-wall shops selling texts in Farsi about medicine, architecture and other scholastic pursuits. Kaleme International Bookshop sells books for English-language students; it's a good place to pick up classics such as *Moby Dick* or *The Pickwick Papers*. Just east of Enqelāb Square there are a couple of book-lined passages; in Zaban Kedi you can pick up Longman titles, again aimed at English language students, along with copies of *The Times of India* and some German novels.

There are bookshops inside most top-end hotels. Prices for books are high by Iranian standards but well below what you'd pay in Western countries. The best is the Evin Bookshop in the Lāleh International Hotel, which stocks things like the *Cambridge History of Iran* and Sylvia Matheson's *Persia – An Archaeological Guide*. Unfortunately it seems to open only when the owners feel like it.

The National Museum of Iran has a good bookshop, with souvenir books in English at tourist prices. The bookshop at the Sa'd Ābād Museum complex in north Tehrān also boasts one of the best range of tourist-oriented books in English about Iran.

Laundry

Tehrān is not overrun with laundries and dry-cleaning services, although your hotel should be able to arrange something.

Toilets

Almost all the museums, palaces and other buildings open to the public have clean toilets, as do all but the smallest restaurants. In an emergency duck into the grounds of the nearest mosque or into a park, where the state of cleanliness or otherwise will depend on the local caretaker.

Medical Services

Tehrān has by far the largest concentration of doctors and hospitals in Iran, and the quality of medical care is reasonably high by international standards. Most doctors in Tehrān received training in the West, and you should have few problems finding one who speaks English (or French or German).

The best place to find the surgery of a reputable doctor is along the more upmarket streets, such as Valiasr Ave, Keshāvarz Blvd or Tāleqānī St, and near major hospitals. One private ambulance service is Iran Emdad (☎ 6436 662); otherwise ring the public ambulance number (☎ 115).

It's best to ask your embassy to recommend a doctor or hospital but if you have no luck getting their advice, the following hospitals are accessible, clean and reputable:

Arad Hospital	(☎ 761 001)
Dey Hospital	(☎ 887 0031)
Emām Khomeinī Hospital	(☎ 938 081)
Mehr Hospital	(☎ 656 130)
Mehrād Hospital	(☎ 859 0004)
Pārs Hospital	(☎ 650 051)
Shāhīd Rajā'i Hospital	(☎ 291 001)
Tehrān Clinic	(☎ 872 8113)

Dentists regularly advertise in the *Tehrān Times*, although you might want to check with your embassy for a recommendation first.

Tehrān is reasonably well stocked with pharmacies although whether they will have a full range of medications is another matter. If you need to find a 24-hour pharmacy you're best off asking your hotel receptionist for assistance; if they don't know of somewhere, ask them to phone the pharmacy line (☎ 191) to find out where the nearest branch is.

Emergency
If an emergency takes place during normal business hours and is not immediately life-threatening, it's worth contacting your embassy. It should be able to provide the current emergency numbers, and possibly some translation assistance. There are police stations all over the city. If you need to find one, contact your embassy first, or talk to someone at your hotel about getting some help with translating. (For more information on what your embassy can and can't do

for you, see the boxed text 'Your Own Embassy' in the Facts for the Visitor chapter.)

Otherwise, you could try ringing one of the telephone numbers listed under Emergencies in the Facts for the Visitor chapter.

Dangers & Annoyances
Traffic Of all Iran's many, many cars, almost half are registered in Tehrān, and at times it can seem as if all of them are on the road (or footpath) at the same time. It would be hard to overestimate the risk of an accident in this nightmarish traffic. Even if you're on foot, danger still lurks whenever you try to cross the road – cars, and worse still motorbikes, come at you from every direction.

Traffic lights remain something of a novelty, contraflow bus lanes are an omnipresent hazard, and you'll search in vain for bridges or underpasses in most parts of town. For advice and more information on surviving Tehrān's traffic, see the boxed text 'Crossing the Road'.

Crossing the Road

Day one and I'm opening the door to get out of a taxi when a motorcyclist cuts between the car and pavement. I knock him off his bike and the windscreen smashes. 'I'm so sorry. It's my fault,' I stammer, mortified, but a crowd gathers and to my surprise they take my side. 'This happens every day, every minute. It's *not* your fault,' one man tells me firmly. The motorcyclist picks up his bike and slinks away.

Day two and I'm trying to cross a road when someone decides to try and park behind me. The space isn't big enough so they thump me in the back hard enough to bruise me with their wing-mirror.

Day three and my driver takes one look at the traffic choking the roundabout and decides to drive round it in the opposite direction. We escape death by inches.

Even for habitual city dwellers, the Tehrān traffic is likely to come as a nasty shock. The city's unplanned growth means that traffic lights and pedestrian crossings are luxuries no-one has planned for, with the result that every junction is a knot of cars and motorbikes, all beeping their horns and trying to force their way through. Buses hurtle down contraflow traffic lanes and motorcyclists use pavements as short cuts round the traffic jams. Indeed, the simplest way to make life more tolerable for everyone would be to ban motorbikes from the city centre. However scary it seems, you will have to learn to cross the road as the Iranians do unless you want to find yourself still standing by the roadside when your visa expires.

Forget 'look right, look left, look right again' (or vice versa). In Tehrān you should never cross *any* road without looking left, right, back, front and then doing it all over again. Preferably cross with a group of other people. This means waiting until a group of people have gathered and then stepping boldly out in front of the cars, looking straight ahead and never faltering. That way you're less likely to be mown down.

Pat Yale

Pollution Closely linked to the general problem of the traffic is that of pollution. In summer one breath is all it takes to absorb the full horror of Tehrān's toxin-laden air. Nearly 40% of all transport is in small cars, mainly Paykans, which pump more than 50 million tonnes of carbonated gases, including 1.3 million tonnes of carbon monoxide, into the air every year. In Tehrān alone vehicles use up 10 million tonnes of fossil fuels each year and it's getting worse. If the pollution starts to hurt your throat, or you have asthma, it may be best to head for the hills – Darband or Mt Damāvand, for example.

Crime Until recently, crime was pretty negligible even in Tehrān. However, more thefts are starting to be reported and it's wise not to walk around with flashy jewellery, money belts outside your clothes, or bags and cameras hanging off your shoulder. At the time of writing, mobile phones were the most popular target for thieves. The odd carjacking has also been reported, although you'd have to be very unlucky to get caught up in anything so serious.

SOUTH TEHRĀN

South of Jomhūrī-yé Eslāmī Ave you can visit several of Tehrān's best museums, including the National Museum of Iran, together with the Golestān Palace complex and the Tehrān Bāzār. On a short visit of a day or so this may be all you have time for.

National Museum of Iran

A visit to the National Museum of Iran (☎ 670 2061), also known as the Archaeological Museum of Iran, may well prove one of the highlights of your trip to Tehrān. The contents will probably mean more to you if you come here after you've seen the main archaeological sites – particularly Persepolis – around the country, so you may want to save your visit until the end of your trip.

The museum's grand recessed entrance, designed by the French architect André Godard, is modelled on a Sassanian palace. Inside you'll find a marvellous collection, including ceramics, pottery, stone figures and carvings, mostly taken from excavations at Persepolis, Ismā'īl Ābād (near Qazvīn), Shūsh, Rey and Tūrang Tappeh. Although there's some English labelling, one reader wrote to point out that the museum's layout hasn't changed in 30 years.

Among the finds from **Shūsh**, there's a stone capital of a winged lion, some delightful pitchers and vessels in animal shapes, and colourful glazed bricks decorated with double-winged mythical creatures. A copy of the stone detailing the Code of Hammurabi found at Shūsh is also displayed (the original is in the Louvre in Paris).

Among the finds from **Persepolis**, you can see a 6th-century BC relief from the audience hall of the Treasury of Darius I; a frieze of glazed tiles from the central hall of the Apadana Palace; a famous trilingual inscription from the time of Darius I; a bull-headed capital and carved staircase; a statue of a sitting dog that looks as if it was carved just weeks ago; and four foundation tablets inscribed in cuneiform.

One of the more startling exhibits is the **Salt Man** from Zanjān, thought to have been a miner who died in the 3rd or 4th century, whose body, white hair, beard, leather boots and tools were also preserved by the salt in which he was buried. Rather more comical is a **bronze statue of a prince**, a huge moustache bristling on a head obviously made separately from the body and better suited to a smaller monument. Look out also for a selection of **Lorestān bronzes** dating back to the 8th century BC (for more information about these bronzes see the boxed text 'Lorestān Bronzes' in the Khorram Ābād section of the Western Iran chapter).

The museum has a sign in English, just north-west of the post office on Emām Khomeinī Ave, directly opposite a small park. It is open from 9 am to 6 pm daily except Monday. Admission costs IR60,000 which includes entry to the Museum of the Islamic Period next door.

Museum of the Islamic Period

Next door to the National Museum (and included in the same entrance ticket) is the Museum of the Islamic Period, which contains two floors of exhibits from a selection

SOUTH TEHRĀN & TEHRĀN BAZAAR

PLACES TO STAY
2 Mashhad Hotel
4 Āzādī (Liberty) Hotel
6 Iranshāhr Hotel
7 Marmar Hotel
13 Parsa Hotel
19 Tehrān Apartment Hotel
25 Shirāz Hotel
26 Hotel Markazi; Hotel Sa'di
32 Sadaf Hotel
37 Hotel Shams
42 Hotel Piroz; Misaq Hotel
44 Hotel Naderi; Cafe Naderi
51 Hāfez Hotel
52 Hotel Gilanow
53 Ferdōsī Grand Hotel
60 Farvardin Guest House
61 Hotel Arman
62 Asia Hotel

63 Hotel Khayyam
64 Hotel Khazar Sea; Mosāferkhūneh Tabrīz
65 Hotel Mashhad
67 Hotel Tehrān Gol
68 Aria Hotel

PLACES TO EAT
3 Sahra Restaurant
5 Koswar Restaurant
24 Gulestan Bookshop
27 Ultimate Fried Chicken Joint
45 Bābā Tāher Restaurant
58 Ferdōsī Kabābī
70 Sofre Khane Sonnati Sangalag

OTHER
1 Skiing Federation; Mountaineering Federation

8 Syrian Arab Airlines
9 Aeroflot
10 Iran Air; Kuwait Airways
11 Iran Asseman Booking Office
12 Iranian Photographers' Centre
14 Kaleme International Bookshop
15 Book Kiosk
16 Tezātre Shāhr (City Theatre)
17 Armenian Embassy
18 Gita Shenasi Map Shop
20 Air France
21 Bank Sepah
22 Emām Khomeinī Souvenir Shop
23 Ferdōsī Bookstand

28 UK Embassy
29 French Embassy
30 Pā Manār Mosque
31 Mosque
33 Customs Office (Edareh-yé Koll-é Gomrokāt)
34 Ark Mosque
35 Golestān Palace
36 Bank Melli
38 Great Bazaar Entrance
39 Emām Khomeinī Mosque
40 Jāmeh Mosque
41 Armenian Church of St Thaddeus
43 Glass & Ceramics Museum
46 Turkish Embassy
47 National Museum of Art

48 Madraseh va Sepahsālār Mosque
49 German Embassy
50 Bank Melli; Central Bank; National Jewels Museum
54 National Museum of Iran; Museum of the Islamic Period
55 Ministry of Foreign Affairs; Telephone, Post & Telegraph Ministry Museum; Malek National Museum & Library
56 Post Office
57 Coin Museum
59 13 Aban Museum
66 Public Bathhouse
69 Telephone Office

of Islamic arts including calligraphy, carpets, ceramics, woodcarving, stone carving, miniatures, brickwork and textiles. Look out particularly for the silks and stuccowork from Rey, portraits from the Mongol period, an impressive collection of Sassanian coins and gorgeous 14th-century wooden doors and windows. In the middle of the 1st floor is a shrine surrounded by Qurans, written in assorted scripts from different centuries. Look out also for the beautiful Paradise Door, a 14th-century lustre-painted mihrab (niche in a mosque indicating the direction of Mecca) from Qom, and a 19th-century inlaid door from Esfahān.

Captions are in English, and English-speaking guides are in theory available at the reception desk. The opening hours are the same as for the National Museum next door.

There's an excellent **bookshop** on the 1st floor, with many titles in English. Postcards,

videos, maps and dictionaries are also on sale.

To see both museums you should probably allow a good three hours. Bring something to eat and drink as there's no cafe in either place.

Glass & Ceramics Museum

North of the National Museum of Iran on Sī Tīr St is the impressive Glass & Ceramics Museum (☎ 670 8153), housed in a beautiful building dating back to Qajar times. Built as a private residence for a prominent Persian family, it later housed the Egyptian embassy and was converted into a museum in 1976.

The building marks a move away from purely Persian traditions, successfully blending features of both Eastern and Western styles. The graceful wooden staircase and the classical stucco mouldings on the walls and ceilings are particularly delight-

---

Who's That Man?

Wherever you go in Iran you will find streets named after the same group of men. Everyone knows who Āyatollāh Khomeinī was, but what of some of the others?

Āyatollāh Beheshtī

Āyatollāh Beheshtī founded the Islamic Republic Party (IRP) in 1979. He took part in the negotiations over the US embassy hostages but was killed a year later by a bomb planted in IRP headquarters by the Mojāhedīn Khalq Organisation (MKO).

Āyatollāh Tāleqānī

Āyatollāh Tāleqānī was a much-admired cleric who was horrifically tortured by the last shah in the 1970s and died soon afterwards.

Amīr Kabīr

Amīr Kabīr was the nickname of Mirza Taghī Khān, a reformist prime minister who served from 1848 to 1851 and who was executed at the command of Naser al-Din Shāh in the Bāgh-é Tārīkhī-yé Fīn near Kāshān.

Valiasr

Valī-yé Asr means 'Prince of This Time', a nickname for Mehdi, the 12th imam (for more details, see the boxed text 'The 12 Emams' under Religion in the Facts about Iran chapter).

Dr Alī Sharīatī

Dr Alī Sharīatī, who died in 1977, combined radical political thought with socially conscious traditionalism. He was a particular inspiration to many women, and although he was killed by the last shah he continues to inspire many Muslims.

ful, and there are many delicate carvings and other decorations.

The museum has hundreds of exhibits, mainly from Neishābūr, Kāshān, Rey and Gorgān, dating from the 2nd millennium BC. They're organised chronologically into galleries, with each piece labelled in English and lovingly displayed as if individual thought had been given to it; there are even explanations in English about, for example, the Persian glass-blowing tradition. The ground-floor shop sells an English guide-book, as well as lots of books on Persian art, and some replicas of items on display.

The museum is open from 9 am to 5 pm daily except Monday and public holidays. Admission costs IR25,000.

Malek National Museum & Library

Heading back from the National Museum of Iran towards Emām Khomeinī Square you'll see on your left the **Bāgh-é Melli** (National Garden Arch), a huge tiled arch, which leads through to a pedestrian street. On your left you'll see the Malek National Museum and Library, which contains a small but interesting and varied collection of 19th-century furnishings, decorative arts, miniatures, and paintings by Kamal ol-Molk. One vast painting shows Nasīr al-Din Shāh reviewing the troops with his son and Commander-in-Chief Mirza Mohammed Khan – they're huge and the troops tiny, to reflect their relative importance. For lovers of coins, there's an excellent, well-labelled collection dating back to the 6th century BC.

The basement contains a collection of stamps and several fine carpets, some of them made to order for the private collector Haji Hussein Agha Malek.

The museum is open from 8.30 am to 1.30 pm daily except Friday. Admission costs IR10,000.

13 Aban Museum

Right on the north-west corner of Emām Khomeinī Square is a small building that was once used as a stable by the shah. Now the 13 (Sizdah-é) Aban Museum, it's crammed solid with life-size bronze statues by the fa-mous modern Iranian sculptor Seyed Alī Akbar-e San'atī. Most striking is a group sculpture representing the political prisoners taken by the Pahlavīs, a human sea of prisoners in chains. Unsurprising statues include those of the poets Ferdōsī and Sa'dī, and Shāh Abbas I and Nader Shāh. What the crucified Christ is doing here is more of a mystery. A few San'atī watercolours, especially of cats, are also on display.

The museum is open from 8 am to 7 pm daily except on public holidays. Entry costs just IR1000. There's no sign but if you peep round the various doors on the north-west corner of Emām Khomeinī Square you'll soon find it.

National Jewels Museum

If you walk north from Emām Khomeinī Square along Ferdōsī St, you'll come to the National Jewels Museum (☎ 311 2369), owned by the Central Bank but actually housed behind the central branch of the Bank Melli. If you've already visited the art gallery at the Golestān Palace you will have seen the incredible jewellery with which the Safavid monarchs adorned themselves. Come here to gawp at the real things.

Believe it or not, at least one war has been fought over these jewels. Most of the collection dates back to Safavid times when the shahs scoured Europe, India and the lands of the Ottoman Empire for booty with which to decorate the then capital, Esfahān. However, when Mahmud Afghan invaded Iran in 1722, he plundered the treasury and sent its contents to India. On ascending the throne in 1736, Nader Shāh Afshar despatched courtiers to ask for the return of the jewels. When their powers of persuasion proved unequal to the task, he sent an army to prove that he was serious. To get the soldiers off his back Mohammed Shāh of India was forced to hand over the Daryā-yé Nūr and Kuh-é Nūr diamonds, the Peacock Throne and other assorted treasures. After Nader Shāh's murder in 1747, Ahmed Beg again plundered the treasury and dispersed the jewels. The Kuh-é Nūr diamond found its way to England where it remains to this day.

The Peacock Throne

In 1798 Fath Ali Shāh ordered a new throne encrusted with 26,733 gems to be made for himself. Set into its top was a carved sun, set with precious stones, so the throne became known as the Sun Throne. Later Fath Ali married a woman called Tavous Tajodoleh, nicknamed Tavous Khanoum or Lady Peacock, and the throne became known as the Peacock Throne in her honour. Somehow the story became muddled and later commentators believed the throne had been brought to Iran from India.

On your way into the museum pick up a guidebook at the shop for IR6,000; nothing inside is labelled so without it you won't be able to make much sense of the exhibits. Make sure you don't miss the **Daryā-yé Nūr** (Sea of Light), a pink diamond weighing 182 carats and said to be the largest uncut diamond in the world; the **Peacock (or Naderī) Throne** (see the boxed text); the tall **Kiani Crown** made for Fath Ali Shāh in 1797; the crowns worn by the last shah and his wife Farah; and the 34kg **Globe of Jewels**, made in 1869 using 51,366 precious stones – the seas are made from emeralds, the land from rubies (Iran, England and France are set in diamonds).

The museum is in a basement vault behind the central branch of Bank Melli; look for the huge iron gates, and a couple of machine-gun toting guards. Not surprisingly, cameras and bags must be left at reception. Be careful not to touch anything or you'll set off ear-piercing alarms.

This museum is open from 2 to 4 pm on Saturday, Sunday, Monday and Tuesday. Entry costs IR30,000.

Golestān Palace

Striking south from Emām Khomeinī Square along Khayyām St you will come to the Golestān Palace complex (☎ 311 8335), where seven buildings open to the public are set around a lovely garden. Although there was a Safavid citadel on this site, it only became a palace in the reign of Karīm Khān Zand. It was the Qajar ruler Nasser al-Din

Shāh (1848–96), impressed by what he'd seen on visits to Europe, who built it up into the fine complex you see today. Originally it would have been much bigger, with inner and outer sections to encompass offices, ministries and private living quarters, but much of it was pulled down under the Pahlavīs.

The following description assumes you start your visit at the Marble Throne Verandah then continue in a clockwise direction round the tiled courtyard.

Immediately opposite the entrance is the **Ivān-e Takht-é Marmar** (Marble Throne Verandah), a mirrored, open-fronted audience hall dominated by a magnificent throne supported by human figures and constructed from 65 pieces of alabaster. It was made in 1801 for Fath Ali Shāh, a monarch who managed a staggering 200-odd wives and 170 offspring. This hall was used on ceremonial occasions, including coronations like that of Rezā Shāh in 1925.

A narrow corridor leads off to a side room covered with murals of the fictional kings described in Ferdōsī's *Shāh-namah* – look for Zahhak, the king with two snakes on his shoulders that had to be fed with human brains. Other pictures depict royal births and musicians performing in the royal gardens. Don't miss the painting of Fath Ali Shāh – he's the one with the beard so thick you'd swear it was a falsie!

If you leave the Marble Throne Verandah and turn left you'll come to the **Negâr Khane** (Art Gallery), which displays a fine collection of Qajar works of art. It was the brainchild of Nasser al-Din Shāh, who'd been particularly captivated by European museums. Especially interesting are the portraits of the shahs wearing the jewels and crowns you can see in the National Jewels Museum, and pictures of everyday life in 19th-century Iran by Kamal ol-Molk and Mehdi. Women were certainly wearing chadors back then too. The difference is that the men were also swaddled in three layers of clothing.

Continue in a clockwise direction around the courtyard and you'll come to the **Haze Khâne** (Pool Room), used to house a collection of mediocre works of art given to the shahs by European monarchs. It's a pretty room with the eponymous pool in the middle but if you're pushed for time this would be one of the more missable parts of the complex.

The next museum you come to is the **Shams-Al Emarāt**, the tallest palace of its day and designed to mix European and Persian architectural traditions. A sequence of mirrored and tiled rooms display a collection of calligraphy, together with furniture and vases given to the shahs by European monarchs, especially the French.

The two soaring buildings nearby that look like minarets are, in fact, **wind towers**, first erected in the reign of Fath Ali Shāh (see the boxed text 'The Bādgīrs of Yazd' in the Central Iran chapter for more information on wind towers).

Next up is a basement room containing a fountain and the **Historic Photograph Gallery**, with pictures of Nasser al-Din's wives in curious tutu-like skirts. Most interesting of all is a photograph showing the inside of one of the Zoroastrian Towers of Silence, with bodies in varying states of decay, some still sitting upright (see Yazd in the Central Iran chapter).

The tiny **Tālār-e Almās** (Diamond Hall) displays 19th-century decorative arts in a room with red frescoed walls and tiled floor. This is another section that would be expendable if you're pushed for time.

Finally you come to the **Ethnographical Museum** (☎ 311 0653), which contains some fascinating tableaus, including one of a Qajar wedding and another of a traditional teahouse complete with storyteller. Particularly interesting is the model of a dervish, his clothes completely covered with Quranic texts, carrying a *kashkool* (a sort of handbag on a chain) and an axe. Upstairs you can inspect models wearing the traditional dress of the various different regions of Iran.

Restoration work was still in progress at the time of writing, and by the time you read this, other parts of the palace complex may also be open to the public. The gardens, too, should be much prettier once the work of repairing the pools is complete.

The palace complex is open from 9 am to 3 pm daily except Thursday. Admission to each of the museums costs IR10,000. There's a pricey but pretty teahouse and a decent book-cum-souvenir shop in the grounds.

Other Museums

The **Telephone, Post & Telegraph Ministry Museum** (☎ 670 0503) is on your right after you enter the Bāgh-é Melli arch leading to the Ministry of Foreign Affairs complex. It's open from 8.30 am to 4.30 pm daily except Friday.

The **Coin Museum** (☎ 311 1091) is right behind the Bank Sepah branch, just s of Emām Khomeinī Square.

The **National Museum of Art** (☎ 311 6329), north of Bahārestān Square, contains a collection of fine ceramics and handicrafts. It is open from 8 am to 4 pm Saturday to Wednesday (closed on public holidays). Entry costs IR10,000.

Tehrān Bazaar

Far more than just a market place, Tehrān Bazaar is traditionally the Wall St of Tehrān and hence Iran, where the prices of staple commodities are fixed. Sadly, it's gradually declining in size, importance and the quality of its shops, and many merchants have moved their businesses out to more salubrious surroundings. Never much of an architectural jewel, the bazaar has grown haphazardly and can be rather sleazy, but with time on your hands you might want to spend the odd hour or so here.

The main entrance to the bazaar is along 15 Khordād Ave. The bazaar is a city within a city, encompassing more than a dozen mosques, several guesthouses, a handful of banks (not for changing money), one church and even a fire station. Each corridor specialises in a particular commodity: copper, paper, gold, spices and carpets, among others. In the carpet area expect to be pounced on and whisked off on a tour that inevitably ends with a highly professional demonstration of the hard sell. You'll also find tobacconists, shoemakers, tailors, broadcloth sellers, bookbinders, flag sellers, haberdashers, saddlers, tinsmiths, knife makers and carpenters. The best way to explore the bazaar is simply to wander its labyrinth of streets and alleys.

The Bāzārīs

In Iran a bazaar is much more than just a place to stock up on a few essential shopping items. The *bāzārīs*, the men who run the stalls in the bazaar, are frequently very wealthy and wield enormous political power, most of them being politically and religiously conservative. In an attempt to weaken their power the last shah bulldozed new roads through parts of the bazaar, gave subsidised credit to competing supermarkets, and set up state purchasing bodies to handle sugar, meat and wheat. Not surprisingly, the Tehrān bāzārīs hit back during the Islamic Revolution by closing the bazaar and wreaking havoc on the economy.

It has been estimated that the Tehrān Bazaar controls a third of Iran's entire retail and trade sector. The carpet dealers and other merchants have access to foreign currency and are able to supply loans as readily as the banks to those they favour. Inevitably they tend to put their short-term commercial interests before the long-term investment needs of the country.

Even today it's hard to separate politics from the day-to-day life of the bazaars. Because of the conservatism of the bāzārīs it's here that the opponents of President Khatamī's reforms find much of their support (just as it's in the universities that Khatamī finds most of his supporters). When President Khatamī visited the supposedly liberal town of Orūmīyeh in 2000, some of the bāzārīs there opted to keep their shops open, only to have their windows smashed by people who obviously couldn't grasp that 'freedom' includes the right *not* to do something.

Try and visit in the morning – by the mid-afternoon work will have ceased and you'll be left looking at the litter. From late afternoon on Thursday through to Saturday morning the bazaar resembles a ghost town.

Emām Khomeinī Mosque

Tehrān has surprisingly few interesting mosques and mausoleums but one that's well worth visiting is the Emām Khomeinī Mosque (still sometimes known as the Shāh Mosque), right inside the bazaar. This is very much a working mosque, one of the largest and busiest in Tehrān. The building itself, though dating from the very early 18th century, is not the attraction; rather, you come here to see Islam in action. Since the courtyard is not cut off from the surrounding area and hundreds of people crisscross it on their way to and from the bazaar, it's no problem for non-Muslims to stand and watch the faithful performing their ablutions and praying. Entry is free, but taking photos could get you into hot water.

Sepahsālār Madraseh & Mosque

At the eastern end of Jomhūrī-yé Eslāmī Ave is the Madraseh va Masjed-é Sepahsālār

(Commander-in-Chief's Theological College and Mosque), built between 1878 and 1890. This complex is one of the most noteworthy examples of Persian architecture of its period, as well as one of the largest. The poetry inscribed in several ancient scripts in the tiling is famous. At the time of writing it was closed to visitors but restoration was in progress which might mean it will be open by the time you read this. Unfortunately, crossing Mostafā Khomeinī St to get to the madraseh is a nightmarish business – if you can get a taxi to drop you off there, jump at the chance.

Āzādī Monument

Way out west at the end of Āzādī Ave is the inverted Y-shaped Āzādī Monument, also known as the Freedom Monument, built in 1971 to commemorate the 2500th anniversary of the Persian Empire. If you arrive at either of the airports or at the western bus station you can hardly help but notice it. If you can manage to cross the road to reach it, the **Āzādī Museum** (☎ 602 3951) upstairs in the 45m-high monument contains a small collection of art and archaeological finds. Take the lift up to the top for a lofty view of Tehrān, smog permitting.

The museum is open from 9 am to noon and from 3 to 6 pm daily except Saturday. The nearby park with a lake might be nice were it not for the appalling noise of the traffic rushing by.

Pārk-é Shāhr

If you're staying in southern Tehrān and need a break from the traffic, head straight for Pārk-é Shāhr where you can go ice skating (in winter), take a boat trip on the tiny lake (in summer) and enjoy tea or a *qalyan* (water pipe) at the fantastic Sofre Khane Sonnati Sangalag teahouse year-round.

Tehrān University

If you're walking along Enqelāb Ave east of the square there's nothing to stop you strolling around the grounds of the impressive Tehrān University, though none of the buildings are old or particularly interesting. The prayers held here every Friday morning are especially fascinating to watch because of the sheer number of men who attend them. It won't take more than a few minutes to meet someone wanting to practise their English who can show you around.

Be aware, however, that universities are often the focus of political discontent. At times of tension it's best to keep away.

CENTRAL TEHRĀN

The sites of central Tehrān are rather more spread out and take more trouble to get to if you're staying around Emām Khomeinī Square. On the other hand the Carpet Museum is a must for anyone at all interested in Persian carpets, while the Rezā Abbāsi is one of Tehrān's most impressive small museums. The US Den of Espionage also holds a certain fascination, given the starring role it played in the events immediately following the Islamic Revolution.

Rezā Abbāsī Museum

Named after one of the great artists of the Safavid period, the Rezā Abbāsī Museum (☎ 863 001) is one of the best in Tehrān, but sadly ignored by most visitors, which is hardly surprising given that it's tucked away in the northern reaches of Dr Alī-yé

Sharīatī St, near the junction with Resālat Hwy (see the Tehrān map).

The museum is organised chronologically starting with the top-floor Pre-Islamic Gallery, where you'll find a stunning collection of **Achaemenid gold** bowls, drinking vessels, armlets and decorative pieces, often decorated with exquisite carvings of bulls and rams. Here, too, you'll find fine examples of **Lorestān bronzes** (for more information, see the boxed text 'Lorestān Bronzes' in the Khorram Ābād section of the Western Iran chapter).

The middle-floor Islamic Gallery exhibits a collection of ceramics, fabrics, brassware etc, while the ground-floor Painting Gallery shows samples of fine calligraphy from ancient Qurans and illustrated manuscripts, particularly copies of Ferdōsī's *Shāh-namah* and Sa'dī's *Golestān*.

The museum is open from 9 am to 5 pm daily except Monday. Despite a sign high up on a side wall it's not easy to identify the museum from the outside; if in doubt, ask. Entry costs IR25,000. There's a small shop in the lobby but nowhere to buy food or drink.

To reach the museum you could try taking a shared taxi from the junction of Dr Alī-yé Sharīatī and Enqelāb Ave, but not all of them continue as far north as this so you may be better off going private.

Museum of Contemporary Art

On north Kārgar Ave on the west side of Pārk-e-Lāleh, Tehrān's Museum of Contemporary Art (☎ 655 411) is housed in a striking spiral building vaguely reminiscent of the Guggenheim Museum in New York. It contains an interesting collection of paintings by modern Iranian artists, as well as regular temporary exhibitions featuring Iranian and foreign photographers and calligraphers. The museum is popular with locals, not least because of the cheap entry fee and the wonderfully comfortable seats around the corridors. The cafe inside ought to be a popular hang-out for arty types, but isn't.

The museum is open from 9 am to 7 pm every day except Friday, when it opens at 2 pm. Entry costs IR2000.

TEHRĀN

CENTRAL TEHRĀN

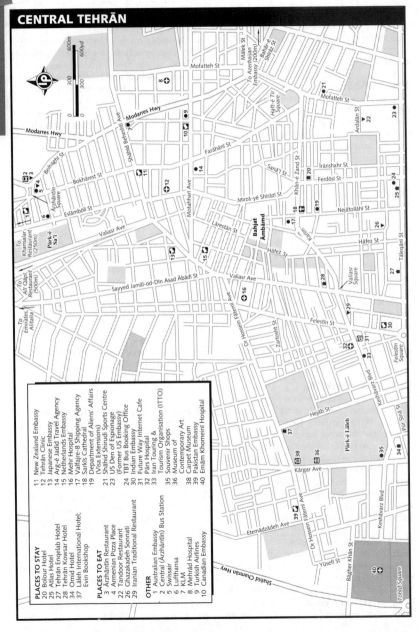

PLACES TO STAY
20 Bolour Hotel
25 Atlas Hotel
27 Tehrān Enqelāb Hotel
28 Tehrān Kowsar Hotel
34 Omid Hotel
37 Lāleh International Hotel;
   Evin Bookshop

PLACES TO EAT
3 Arzhāntin Restaurant
4 Armenian Pizza Place
22 Tandoor Restaurant
26 Ghazakadeh Sonnati
29 Iranian Traditional Restaurant

OTHER
1 Australian Embassy
2 Central (Arzhāntin) Bus Station
5 Swissair
6 Lufthansa
7 KLM
8 Mehrād Hospital
9 Turkish Airlines
10 Canadian Embassy
11 New Zealand Embassy
12 Tehrān Clinic
13 Japanese Embassy
14 Arg-é Jadid Travel Agency
15 Netherlands Embassy
16 Mehr Hospital
17 Valfajre-8 Shipping Agency
18 Sarkis Cathedral
19 Department of Aliens' Affairs
   (Visa Extensions)
21 Shāhid Shirudi Sports Centre
23 US Den of Espionage
   (Former US Embassy)
24 TBT Bus Booking Office
30 Indian Embassy
31 Future Way Internet Cafe
32 Pars Hospital
33 Iran Touring &
   Tourism Organisation (ITTO)
35 Souvenir Shops
36 Museum of
   Contemporary Art
38 Carpet Museum
39 Pakistan Embassy
40 Emām Khomeini Hospital

Carpet Museum

Just north of the Museum of Contemporary Art, the two floors of the Carpet Museum (☎ 657 707) house more than 100 pieces from all over Iran, dating from the 16th century to the present day; the older pieces are mostly upstairs. This is a spectacular place to visit and you should certainly come here if you have even the slightest interest in Persian carpets – although seeing the quality of these pieces will make it much harder to settle for buying something more affordable.

The museum is open from 9 am to 6 pm (to 5 pm in winter) daily except Monday. Entry costs IR25,000. Inside, a shop sells postcards and books and there's a pleasant cafe selling drinks (IR3000 for tea) and snacks. To protect the carpets from damage inflicted by flashes, cameras are not allowed.

US Den of Espionage

At the junction of Tāleqānī and Shāhīd Mofatteh Sts is the old US embassy, which played such an important part in events immediately following the return of Āyatollāh Khomeinī to Iran and the fall of the shah. Right on the corner where the two roads meet you'll see the predictable 'Down with the USA' sign, and further along Tāleqānī St you'll be able to see the old embassy insignia, its details methodically hacked out but still distinguishable. The former embassy is now known as the US Den of Espionage.

All along the wall overlooking Tāleqānī St are striking **murals** illustrating events in recent Iranian history (including the downing of the Iran Air plane over the Persian Gulf with the loss of more than 250 lives) and stating the government's hatred of the USA and Israel in unequivocal terms ('The US is the most hated nation after the occupier of Qods [Jerusalem]'; 'When the US praises us, we should mourn'). There's no sign saying you can't take pictures of these highly photogenic murals but be warned that the embassy is now occupied by the military; even if you get away with taking pictures near the road junction, to take them anywhere near the watchtower near the old entrance to the embassy is asking to be pursued by gun-toting soldiers who may rip your film from your camera.

Until recently a shop on the corner, called the Centre for the Publication of the US Espionage Den's Documents, used to sell anti-American propaganda in English, including copies of secret incriminating documents painstakingly pieced together from the shredder after the Islamic Revolution. Sadly, it's closed down and nothing has taken its place.

Sarkīs Cathedral

In case you assume that Islam has a monopoly on Iranian life, go to the north end of Nejātollāhī St to the junction with Khān-é Zand St, and visit this surprisingly large Armenian cathedral. Built between 1964 and 1970, it's wondrous not so much for any great age or beauty but because of what it is and where it is. It's by far the most visible and important non-Islamic religious building in Tehrān.

It's open free of charge to visitors daily except Sunday, and you can often find an Armenian who speaks English and is willing to show you around. The area immediately to the south is the Armenian quarter of Tehrān, the centre of a still-thriving community.

Although most of the Christians in Iran are Armenians, there's also a sprinkling of Protestants, Assyrians, Catholics and Orthodox Christians, all of whom have churches in Tehrān, most in the same district as the Sarkīs Cathedral.

Iranian Photographers' Centre

The Iranian Photographers' Centre, north of Enqelāb Ave, exhibits the work of local photographers, and is open from 9 am to 7 pm daily except Fridays, when it is open from 3 to 7 pm; admission is free.

NORTH TEHRĀN

With more time to explore, it's worth heading north for Tajrīsh Square in the suburb of Shemīrān, from where you can visit two separate palace complexes that are open to the public: Sa'd Ābād and Niyāvarān. From Tajrīsh Square you can also reach several popular walking trails into the foothills of the Alborz Mountains at Darband and Darakeh. Although serious walkers can head off into the wilds here, most people – including most Iranians – will be content with patronising the many places to eat and drink along the first stages of the trails. Finally, there's also the cable car to Tōchal at Velenjak, which is particularly popular with young Iranians looking for something to do on a Friday.

Sa'd Ābād Museum Complex

The park surrounding what used to be the shah's summer residence between Shemīrān and Darband now houses a complex of 10 or so museums (☎ 228 2031), some of them more interesting than others. The park is hilly and spread out, and there's a lot to see, so it may be wise to use the free minibus that trundles round the grounds at regular intervals.

What is now called the **White Palace** (Palace of the Nation) was once the last shah's palace, with 54 rooms. The two bronze boots outside are all that remains of a giant statue of Rezā Shāh Pahlavī. Upstairs in the Ceremony Hall, the 143-sq-metre carpet is said to be one of the largest ever made in Iran. Unfortunately, though, the palace is a modern building filled with a hodge-podge of overblown furnishings and paintings, some of them European, some of them Iranian. The shah is revealed as a man of no taste. If you're pushed for time, you won't have missed much if you don't make it here.

Uphill from the White Palace, the prettier **Green Palace** (Shāhvand Palace) was the office of the shah and contains a collection of carpets, furniture and other oddments, not dissimilar to that in the White Palace but rather more cohesively displayed.

Other small, specialist museums in the complex include the **Abkar Miniature Museum**, displaying miniatures by the artist Clara Abkar; the **Behzad Museum** containing paintings by the artist Behzad; the **Museum of Ethnological Research** with a few waxworks and ethnological artefacts; and the **Mir Emad Calligraphy Museum**, with samples of Iranian calligraphy from different periods.

At the time of writing the **Museum of Fine Arts**, which houses some charming Persian oil paintings dating back to the 18th century and some beautiful inlaid furniture, was closed for restoration. The **Military Museum**, housed in another palace belonging to the shah's nephew Shāhrām, was also closed for restoration. Also closed was the **Mother's Palace**, or Reversion & Admonition Museum, partly used for film archives, partly for more antique furniture.

The grounds are quite extensive, so allow plenty of time for wandering around. Near the entrance, there's an excellent tea garden, where you can smoke a qalyan and listen to the parrots screeching in the trees while reclining on carpet-covered *takhts* (thrones). Unfortunately you must buy a ticket to at least one of the museums before you can visit the tea garden. It's not a bad idea to combine a visit to the garden complex with lunch at a nice restaurant in nearby Tajrīsh or Niyāvarān.

The complex is open from about 8 am to 6 pm daily, but each museum has slightly different opening hours; it's best to visit in the morning, when most are likely to be open.

It's likely that all the museums that were closed at the time of writing will reopen during 2001. Unfortunately the charge for entry to each museum is IR25,000 or IR30,000; were you to visit them all you would wind up paying IR230,000 – way in excess of what they're worth. If pushed for time or money, stick with the White and Green Palaces. Tickets are on sale only at the booth in front of the complex entrance so you have to decide in advance what you want to see or keep going backwards and forwards.

Make sure you drop into the bookshop, which boasts one of the best ranges of tourist-oriented and English-language books about Iran in the country.

Getting There & Away To get to the museum complex, take a shared (or private) taxi from Tajrīsh Square, or walk about 1.5km from Tajrīsh Square, along Shāhīd Ja'farī St.

Niyāvarān Palace Museum

About 6km east of the Sa'd Ābād Museum complex, along Shāhīd Bāhonar Ave, is what used to be the last shah's second palace. It has been converted into the Niyāvarān Palace Museum (☎ 228 2012), set in five hectares of landscaped gardens and with four separate museums to visit.

The actual **Niyāvarān Palace** is an austere, functional building, stuffed full of elaborate furniture and carpets unlikely to appeal to many people's tastes. On the other hand it's worth seeing the magnificent Kermān carpet in the main hall, which shows all the Iranian kings right back to the Achaemenids, as well as some European sovereigns, including Napoleon Bonaparte. Admission costs IR30,000.

Just across from the palace is the **Treasure Room**, an attractive two-storey kiosk used to house assorted not especially interesting gifts to the shah. Admission costs IR25,000.

Across the park and through a gate in the wall is the **Sahebqerameh** or King's Special Office, which contains a fine collection of paintings, photographs and calligraphy, as well as some very attractive rooms, including a private basement teahouse and a bar resembling an overdone British pub. Unfortunately, the custodians will try and make you join a guided tour which, since it's in Farsi, will not be much use to foreigners. Admission costs IR30,000.

Through another wall beside the Sahebqerameh is the **Ganjineh** or Queen's Private Museum. Two main rooms and a few offshoots are filled with a mishmash of items including Iranian archaeological artefacts alongside finds from sites in Mexico and Egypt and icons alongside contemporary Iranian paintings. They're beautifully displayed but it won't take you long to look round and you'll probably feel the admission charge of IR25,000 was way too high.

The complex is open from 9 am to 5 pm daily except Monday. As at Sa'd Ābād you buy tickets for all the museums at the main gate. Unfortunately the cumulative IR110,000 to visit all four of them is way too much. If you can only manage one museum, the Sahebqerameh is the most interesting. Except in the Ganjineh, all captions in the museums are in Farsi.

Getting There & Away Take a shared taxi east of Tajrīsh Square (IR750), and ask to be dropped off at the end of Shāhīd

Bāhonar Ave, about 100m from the entrance to the museum.

DARAKEH & DARBAND
درکه
دربند

On a sunny day few things could be nicer than fleeing the traffic fumes of the town centre for the foothills of the Alborz Mountains and the **walking trails** of Darakeh and Darband.

Both the trails strike north, bypassing waterfalls and crossing streams. At Darband you need to walk for 45 minutes to get past the development, at Darakeh for 30 minutes. The trails are very crowded on Thursday afternoons and Fridays. Unfortunately the number of people visiting Darband, in particular, means that the paths and streams tend to be strewn with litter. Several times a year university students organise a clean-up-Darband campaign but it doesn't take long for the rubbish to accumulate again.

Both trails are lined with cafes, kabābīs (kebab shops) and drink stalls, some of which close midweek and in winter. A dish of ābgūsht (a stew-soup combination), a kebab or two, a cold drink or a huff and a puff on a qalyan at a cafe by the stream will soon help you forget the Tehrān traffic. Among other tasty treats to sample on the way up are dates, apricots, pickled walnuts, lavashak (sheets of pressed dried fruit), fresh mulberries and steamed lima beans.

Darband also has a ski lift, which is open in winter from 5.30 am to 7.30 pm daily. Tickets cost a reasonable IR1500/2000 one way/return to the only station.

Getting There & Away

The start point for getting to either trail is the north side of Tajrīsh Square. For Darband, either walk uphill north along Darband St from Tajrīsh Square (or take a shared taxi), or leave the grounds of Sa'd Ābād from the rear, cross Meydān-é Darband and continue uphill to where you see the ski lift on the left. The walking trail veers off to the right. A visit to Darband can easily be combined with a visit to Sa'd Ābād unless you're too worn out after all those museums.

To get to Darakeh take a shared taxi from Tajrīsh Square (IR2000). At the end of Darakeh St you'll be dropped in a square; the trail leads off from the north-east corner. A private taxi costs around IR7500.

TŌCHĀL TELECABIN تلهکبین توچال

Tehrān's popular telecabin (cable car; also called Velenjak Telecabin) runs from a station at the far north of Velenjak Ave up part of Mt Tōchāl (3957m), 7.5km away, stopping at two stations along the way. Some local optimists talk of linking this telecabin with the one near Chālūs on the Caspian Sea, thereby joining Tehrān with the Caspian Sea by telecabin.

You can walk some or all of the way up the mountain (plenty of masochistic locals walk it on Friday), and use the telecabin when your legs have given up. From the top station there's still a good two-hour walk to the summit. Teahouses at both stations, and at the start, will help to ease your recovery, and there's a restaurant a short walk from the last stop. The views of smog-laden Tehrān are superb, though the mountains are astoundingly barren and quite ugly. The forests start near Mt Damāvand (see Mt Damāvand later in this chapter) and extend north towards the Caspian Sea.

The telecabin operates only from 7 am to 11 pm daily (until 5 pm on Thursday and Friday), but you can walk along the trails up the mountain any time you want. A return trip to the middle station costs IR24,000, to the top station IR28,000, and you can get on and off as you like – part of your ticket is ripped off each time. One-way tickets cost IR18,000.

Getting There & Away

From the northern side of Tajrīsh Square, ask for a shared taxi (IR1500) to Tōchāl Telecabin. From where the taxi drops you off, a short walk leads through a car park to a stop where you catch a bus (IR500) to the telecabin ticket office.

PLACES TO STAY

Decent accommodation is sometimes hard to find, so if you haven't booked a room be-

forehand, try telephoning your chosen hotel from the airport or bus or train station on arrival. It's hopeless to arrive in Tehrān without a reservation within 10 days either side of Nō Rūz, the Iranian New Year (about 21 March). In view of the distance between hotels, and the possibility of problems finding a decent room in your price range, it may be worth hiring a taxi when you first arrive in Tehrān.

In Tehrān you certainly get what you pay for. It's worth splashing out a bit more to ensure greater comfort, peace and safety. The cheapest hotels listed here have very little going for them except low cost.

Unless stated otherwise, all places listed here have their names in English near the door. Finding somewhere with, or near, a decent restaurant is a good idea, especially if you're staying in a seedy area.

PLACES TO STAY – BUDGET
Camping

There is a *tourist camp site* (☎ 802 8625, fax 800 8423) at Jaddeh-yé Saveh, Kasemabad, behind the Nour Baterie factory and near the construction site that will eventually become the Emām Khomeinī international airport, but it's 28km south of Tehrān and hardly convenient. Food is available at the site.

Hotels

Just about every cheap place to stay is in the southern part of the city, within about a 1km radius of Emām Khomeinī Square. In particular there are about a dozen cheap places to stay near the corner of Amīr Kabīr and Mellat Sts, with more on and around Amīr Kabīr St itself. Unfortunately this is a noisy, grubby area full of car workshops and spare-parts shops. There are only a few decent restaurants nearby and to reach most of them you need to negotiate hair-raising traffic. Lone women should think carefully before heading here – it's not that anything will happen to you, necessarily, but it's hardly a female-friendly environment. There are a few more cheap hotels in the Tehrān Bazaar area and more along the streets heading north from Emām Khomeinī Square.

If you're staying along Amīr Kabīr St and your hotel doesn't have a shower, walk along the road (heading away from Emām Khomeinī Square) until you reach the turning to the Hotel Khazar Sea on the left. Keep going along Amīr Kabīr and take the first right (an alley without cars). You should see a teahouse on the left and then an alley on the right with stairs leading down to a public bathhouse with lots of hot water for showers.

The cheapest place in town has to be the *Hotel Shams* (☎ 390 0446, Bāzār-é Marvī St) in the bazaar district. The staff are friendly, but the rooms are very basic, as you'd expect for IR14,000 a double. Also in the bazaar area are the cheap, friendly and rudimentary *Hotel Piroz* and *Misaq Hotel* for about the same price.

The basic but clean *Sadaf Hotel* (☎ 392 6109, 15 Sour Esrāfīl St) offers three-bedded rooms with shared toilets for IR90,000. Don't expect a lot of sleep anywhere in the bazaar, however, except on Friday.

Aria Hotel (☎ 311 3011, 48 Katane St, Nazem-al-Atebba St) is behind a mosque so it's likely to be noisy. Rooms are tiny but reasonably clean for IR14,000/21,000 a single/double; one reader described the beds as 'appalling' though. There are a couple of other similar places a few metres away but with no signs in English. Someone working at one of them will probably find and guide you.

Some budget travellers like the *Hotel Khazar Sea* (☎ 311 3860), others think it 'pretty awful'. Beds in basic rooms with shared toilets and no showers cost about IR12,000. Look for the small sign in English at the second lane on the left as you head east of the intersection of Amīr Kabīr and Mellat Sts. A few metres away, the *Mosāferkhūneh Tabrīz* (no signs in English) is similarly basic for IR12,000/15,000.

Along the southern end of Mellat St, and in laneways off Amīr Kabīr St, there are several other equally nondescript places for about IR10,000/15,000. They are often quieter, but may not want to take foreigners. Look for a sign with the word 'hotel' in English hanging off any part of any building.

Moving up a notch, *Hotel Khayyam* (☎ 311 3757, fax 391 1497, 3 Navidy St) is off the main road and therefore much quieter. The rooms are small, but nicely furnished, and cost US$10 per person with bath. The restaurant doesn't open until 9 pm.

The friendly *Hotel Mashhad* (☎ 311 3062, 281 Amīr Kabīr St) has clean, cell-like rooms for IR19,000/34,000. It's very popular with Japanese visitors. Don't confuse this Mashhad with the more expensive Mashhad Hotel, near the former US embassy.

In the same area, the *Hotel Tehrān Gol* (☎ 311 3477, Amīr Kabīr St) is often full, although its rooms are very noisy. Singles/doubles cost IR40,000/60,000 with bathroom. There's also a handy restaurant, which saves trying to cross the road too often, and a pleasant lounge.

Farvardin Guest House (☎ 391 2777, 654 Emām Khomeinī Square, First Ferdōsī St) is just back from the main road – look for 'Hotel Hotel' written in English above a bright doorway. Clean, simple but noisy rooms with fan and shared bathroom cost IR50,000/60,000, or there are dorm beds for a little less. There's also a small restaurant.

Hotel Gilanow (☎ 311 8264, Ferdōsī Ave, opposite Sabt Ave) is almost permanently full of traders from Russia and other former Soviet states. Quiet rooms overlooking an internal courtyard cost a reasonable IR27,000 a head, including breakfast and tea.

A better choice is perhaps the homely *Hotel Arman* (☎ 311 2323, fax 392 0600, Sa'dī St, Ekbātān St). Beds in big, clean rooms with bathroom and air-con, in a fairly quiet area, cost a reasonable US$10 a head. The restaurant downstairs is very good. It's just a few metres down a lane off the southern side of Ekbātān St.

Nearby is the recently renovated and welcoming *Asia Hotel* (☎ 311 8320, Mellat St) with clean, simple rooms for US$10/15.

Another good, central option is *Hāfez Hotel* (☎ 670 9063, fax 670 1367, Ferdōsī St, Kūcheh Bank Melli), just down the appropriately named Bank Alley. The large, modern rooms are quiet, clean and have fridges, fans and showers, but the shared toilets are a bit grubby. Rooms cost IR50,000/85,000. The hotel has a small restaurant too.

A bit further north, **Hotel Naderi** (☎ 670 1872, fax 672 0791, Jomhūrī-yé Eslāmī Ave) offers spacious rooms with fan and bathroom for US$10 a head. Those at the back overlooking the garden are quietest. There's a big TV lounge downstairs but the place could do with a bit of modernisation.

Readers have enjoyed staying at the **Hotel Markazi** (☎/fax 391 4798, Lālehzar St), also known as Hotel Central, which charges a reasonable IR35,000 a head for small, simple rooms with bathroom.

The nearby **Hotel Sa'di** charges IR45,000/ 50,000 but is hardly geared up for Western visitors to judge by the difficulty we had even getting to look at a room.

PLACES TO STAY – MID-RANGE

Most of the mid-range hotels are in central Tehrān which means walking further to get to most of the museums but having a slightly more desirable environment to come back to afterwards. For roughly twice the price of the cheaper places you can find somewhere with five times the comfort level, which is well worth considering; Tehrān is exhausting enough without having to cope with a dismal hotel as well. Just about every mid-range hotel has a restaurant. Double rooms almost always have bathrooms.

One of the better places in south Tehrān is the **Ferdōsī Grand Hotel** (☎ 671 9991, fax 671 1449, Ferdōsī Ave, 24 Sabt St). It's stylish and central, and service is good, although the hotel is often packed with traders from Russia and other former Soviet countries. Singles/doubles cost IR260,000/360,000 with TV, fridge and air con.

Also in south Tehrān, the new **Shīrāz Hotel** (☎ 392 5342, fax 392 7548, Sa'dī St) has attractive rooms for US$20/30 including breakfast.

The **Parsa Hotel** (☎ 646 9211, fax 646 5482, Tāleqānī Ave) is a clean, presentable choice, near the junction with Valiasr Ave. Rooms have fridge, TV and air-con; English-language newspapers are available in the lobby. They cost US$40/50 including breakfast, making this a good choice for couples, but not such a good one for solo travellers.

The **Mashhad Hotel** (☎ 882 5145, fax 882 2681, Tāleqānī Ave, 190 Shāhīd Mofatteh St) is popular – look for the huge word 'restaurant' on the roof. The rooms are large and pleasingly furnished (although the pillows are far too hard), and they have TVs and decent bathrooms. Singles/doubles cost US$25/40. Note that this place should not be confused with the much cheaper Hotel Mashhad in Amīr Kabīr St.

One block south is the **Āzādī Hotel** (☎ 882 9542, Somayyeh St), which calls itself 'Liberty Hotel' on the facade. Clean rooms with spacious bathrooms cost US$30/40 and you'd be best off trying to get one at the back.

North of Ferdōsī Square, the **Marmar Hotel** (☎ 830 0083, Ferdōsī St) has rooms with reasonably modern decor, TV, fridge and air-con for US$23/37. There's a big restaurant and a separate breakfast room – one reader wrote to complain that breakfasts were on the pricey side.

A good choice in central Tehrān is the **Atlas Hotel** (☎ 890 6058, fax 880 0407, 206 Tāleqānī St) where rooms cost US$25/35. The rooms are quiet, with TV, fridge and air-con, and have huge bathrooms. Some have views over a courtyard.

Also apparently good is the **Bolour Hotel** (☎ 882 3080, 191 Qaranī St), near Sarkīs Cathedral. The rooms are large with pleasant bathrooms and it has a choice of two restaurants, but we have had complaints about disinterested staff. Rooms cost US$30/40, but it's best to ask for one away from the main road.

Just north-west of Tehrān University is the **Omid Hotel** (☎/fax 641 4564, 20 East Nosrat St). The friendly staff speak English, it's in a quiet location; and the large modern rooms, with kitchen, fridge, TV, video and stove, cost US$30/40, including breakfast. It is highly recommended and often full; booking ahead is advisable.

Not far away, the **Iranshāhr Hotel** (☎ 883 4976, fax 882 1924, Iranshāhr Ave) offers rooms with air-con, kitchen and TV for US$30/45, including breakfast. A handy shop in the lobby sells things such as toothpaste and soap.

PLACES TO STAY – TOP END

Tehrān has quite a few four- and five-star hotels, most of them in the north and hopelessly inconvenient for the rest of the city. Most are also useless if you want to get about by public transport. All demand US dollars, and plenty of them. Following is a selection of places that are comparatively central and reasonable value.

The 16-floor *Tehrān Enqelāb Hotel* (☎ 646 7251, fax 646 6285, 50 Tāleqānī St) is within walking distance of Pārk-é Lāleh and boasts a revolving restaurant. Comfortable rooms with such luxuries as a minibar (no alcohol, of course) and satellite TV cost US\$73/97 a single/double. The outdoor swimming pool is a big plus in summer if you're male, although female visitors to the hotel are greeted by a sign reminding them of the need to wear hejab so there's not much chance of mixed bathing.

At the north-eastern corner of Pārk-é Lāleh is the big *Lāleh International Hotel* (☎ 655 021, fax 655 517, Dr Hossein Fatemī Ave), once the InterContinental, which offers comfortable modern rooms in an excellent location. The ground floor boasts a good bookshop, several restaurants and a travel agency. All this can be yours for US\$99/112 plus tax of 19%.

Near Valiasr Square, the *Tehrān Kowsar Hotel* (☎ 890 8121, fax 889 1615, 8 Shāhīd Malaee Alley) offers pleasant, if not luxurious, rooms for US\$50/65 plus 21% tax. There's a Chinese restaurant on the premises and a stuffed lioness on the porch. One reader, describing the hotel as a 'depressing behemoth of a place', took particular exception to what he called the lackadaisical staff.

The *Shāhr Hotel* (☎ 770 041, fax 770 047, Damāvand Ave) is the extraordinarily elaborate, palace-like building opposite the eastern bus station, with what looks like a UFO on the roof. Elegant rooms cost US\$50/70 and offer pleasant modern decor in not too bad a location. The UFO houses a good restaurant with fine views.

Recently a few apartment hotels have started to open. Most of them are in the north and too expensive for most travellers' budgets. The *Tehrān Apartment Hotel* (☎ 880 4180, fax 880 4200, Hāfez St), south of Enqelāb Ave, is fairly central and offers very attractive modern self-catering apartments with one/two bedrooms for US\$48/85. The squat toilets are a shame but otherwise this place is an excellent choice, even though Hāfez St is not remotely picturesque.

Iran Air owns and operates the *Homa Hotel* (☎ 877 3021, fax 879 7179, 51 Khoddami St), which charges US\$65/75 per single/double in a none-too-central location.

As for the similarly priced *Āzādī Grand Hotel* (☎ 207 3021, fax 207 3038, Evin Crossing, Shahīd Chamrān Hwy), readers have reported that it is almost inaccessible on foot. It's close to the International Trade Fair Ground, but nothing else. You can do better.

PLACES TO EAT

While most hotels have signs in English, most restaurants that aren't part of a hotel, or don't serve Western-style fast food, don't. Many places close on Friday evenings, and just about *everything* in the whole city closes over public holidays, when eating at a hotel restaurant may be your only option.

Away from Tehrān the choice of food is much more limited so you may want to splash out a bit to sample special dishes before you move on.

Kabābīs & Fast Food

Kebabs are the standard fare at most of Iran's cheaper restaurants, and Tehrān is no exception. If you're staying in central or south Tehrān you won't have to look far; even the richer Tehrānīs head south if they're looking for a good kebab. There are dozens of almost identical restaurants in and around Emām Khomeinī Square, along Ferdōsī St, and near the corner of Jomhūrī-yé Eslāmī Ave and Mellat St. The same streets play host to dozens of snack bars where you can pick up a filling sandwich or eat chicken, tongue, brain or felafel as a change from kebab.

One old favourite kabābī is the downstairs *Ferdōsī Kabābī* where some staff speak English. A full chicken kebab meal, including salad, rice, drinks and bread, should cost around IR15,000. Much further afield is the *Lāleh Restaurant* on the north side of Tajrīsh

Square where, for IR15,000, you can have a pleasant meal of kebab and rice with a soft drink.

If you're near Ārzhāntīn Square, call in at the *Arzhāntīn Restaurant*. There's no sign in English but it's the green place next to the huge supermarket and it offers one of the best Western-style hamburgers in town for IR5000. Tasty Chinese food, or steak with vegetables, costs about IR12,000. It's deservedly popular with locals, as well as diplomats working in the area.

If you fancy a Western-style pizza the best place to head is north Tehrān where there are several good places to choose from on Shāhīd Bāhonar Ave near the Niyāvarān Palace Museum. Recommended is the *Chāman Pizzeria* which attracts a young crowd not just for pizzas but also for doorstep-sized sandwiches. Or there's the *Niyāvarān Pizza Place* where excellent pizzas cost about IR10,000.

Another favourite is the *Elma Tajrīsh Restaurant*, which serves scrumptious pizzas, salad and a drink for around IR9000. Other tasty treats include real hamburgers, half-decent lasagne and deep-fried chicken, all at reasonable prices.

Heading up Shahīd Ja'farī St towards Darband you'll pass a branch of *Dar-B-Dar Pizza* (☎ 270 8185), a stylish chain-pizzeria which does takeaways.

Other popular choices include the *Armenian Pizza Place*, next door to the Argentin Bookshop, and *Chela Pizza Bar* in Manūchehrī St, which features a rare English menu. It offers fried chicken and chips for IR4750, and Iranian-style hamburgers for IR2100.

Thousands of places around Tehrān sell tasty Iranian-style hamburgers, but if you search about you can also find places serving Western-style hamburgers and fried chicken. The best of these fast-food restaurants can be found along the upper reaches of Valiasr Ave, on Tajrīsh Square and near the corner of Valiasr and Enqelāb Aves.

To try some finger lickin' chicken go to the *Ultimate Fried Chicken Joint* on Ferdōsī St, just north of the junction with Jomhūrī-yé Eslāmī Ave. The food is excellent, if a little pricey at IR15,000 for fried chicken, chips, salad, bun and cola.

Restaurants

Recently a number of classy, traditionally decorated restaurants serving fairly limited but good quality Iranian menus have opened. The cheaper ones serve ābgūsht (a soup-stew combination) and double as teahouses for both sexes between meal times. Others are relatively pricey, but deservedly popular with locals and tour groups, for both their food and their ambience. Very often they're tucked away in basements so you need to keep your eyes peeled.

One of the easiest of these restaurants to find is the *Iranian Traditional Restaurant* (☎ 890 0522, 28 Keshāvarz Blvd) in central Tehrān, close to the Future Way Internet cafe, but with no English sign. Here you can sample excellent ābgūsht for IR10,000. In winter a musician performs from 9 pm.

Also easy to find is the *Bābā Tāher Restaurant* (Jomhūrī-yé Eslāmī Ave) in south Tehrān, which also serves as a new-look teahouse. This is another place to try out ābgūsht or bādenjūn (a popular pureed-aubergine dish). The beautifully decorated room is dominated by a tile picture of Babataher and by a pair of stuffed pied eagles. To find it peer into the doorways west of Ferdōsī St until you see a tiled picture of a qalyan.

If you're visiting the museums around Emām Khomeinī Square, a good place to stop for lunch (or a cup of tea) would be the *Sofre Khane Sonnati Sangalag* teahouse at the southern end of Pārk-é Shāhr. This is another good place to sample ābgūsht in attractively decorated surroundings (not underground for a change), and if you're lucky you'll find musicians entertaining the diners between noon and 3 pm.

One of the nicest new-look restaurants is *Ghazakadeh Sonnati* (☎ 880 2044, Karīm Khan-é Zand St, 7 South Aban St) in central Tehrān, which serves dishes such as zereshk polau (chicken and rice with barberries) for IR17,500, and aubergine porridge with mint and buttermilk for IR7500. If you haven't tried fesenjān (a meat stew made with pomegranate juice, walnuts, aubergine and cardamom) this is a good place to do so, but only at Monday lunch time (IR18,500). If you want to sample sturgeon it'll cost you IR28,000.

Tour groups are often taken to the *Alī Qāpū Restaurant* (☎ 226 7803, *Gandhi St*) near Vanak Square, where similar meals can be eaten to an accompaniment of traditional music.

At the *Bāgh-é Saba Restaurant* (☎ 753 9684, *Sharīatī St, opposite Mālek St*) you can sit on a platform over a stream or at tables around it where tasty nibbles (dates, cheese, walnuts and batter balls) will be served before the main course. With no English menu it's not easy to be sure what exactly is cooking, but chicken kebabs and *chelo* kebabs (with rice or bread and tomatoes) are staples. Expect your bill to come to around IR30,000 a head. A rather doleful musician plays here at lunch times.

Even more popular with locals is *Khansalar Restaurant* (☎ 878 0454, *Alvand St*), across from the Kasra Hospital. As well as a standard menu of perfectly cooked kebabs it has a big salad bar. Expect your bill, including soft drinks, to come to about IR38,000. It's advisable to book for dinner.

At weekends you will have trouble getting near the Stone Garden in Pārk-é Jamshidiyeh, north-west of the Niyāvarān Palace, off Amīr Arsatān St. Here there are three *themed restaurants* bestride a steeply sloping landscaped park with wonderful views back over the city; the Turkmen restaurant is housed in a cluster of yurts. More conventional are the Turkish and Kurdish restaurants; the food at the Kurdish is regarded as especially good although the menus are not as imaginative as you might hope. Don't expect much change from IR30,000 a head though.

On balmy evenings in summer half of Tehrān (or so it seems) heads for the hills at Darband and Darekeh where the walking trails are lined with cafes and restaurants serving everything from full kebab meals to generous helpings of ābgūsht or just snacks. Prices tend to be a bit higher than in town for the same thing – you're paying for the setting, of course – but it's worth it for the experience.

Most other places calling themselves restaurants serve Western food at tourist prices.

Hotel Restaurants

Anyone can eat in the hotel restaurants, whether they're a guest or not. Contact details for all the following places can be found in Places to Stay earlier, unless otherwise specified.

One of the best hotel restaurants in south Tehrān is the *Zeitoon Restaurant* on the ground floor of the Ferdōsī Grand Hotel. The menu is in English, although the staff don't speak anything but Farsi. Prices range from IR9000 to IR15,000, which seems a lot, but the meals are large and tasty, and worth paying a few extra rials for. One of the very few decent places to eat around Amīr Kabīr St is the *Hotel Khayyam* which offers Iranian dishes priced at about IR10,000 from 9 pm every evening.

In central Tehrān, check out the *Bolour Hotel* where the restaurant on the 6th floor offers excellent service plus a menu in English. Meals such as chicken and rice cost a surprisingly reasonable IR7500. There's also a Korean restaurant, the *Seoul Garden* on the first floor, with a much more extensive menu.

Also very good, with dishes from IR10,000 to IR15,000, as well as excellent service and a menu in English, is the *Omid Hotel*.

The restaurant on the 6th floor of the *Mashhad Hotel* is so-so, with dishes priced at IR12,000 to IR16,000 plus 15% tax (watch for a tendency to approximate the tax upwards). What could be superb views are blocked by an annoying row of shrubs.

The Lāleh International Hotel has several restaurants where you'll need to pick carefully from the menu to avoid running up a big bill. The *Tiare* serves Polynesian food, and the *Rotisseri* French cuisine, while in the intimate little *Namakdoon*, with its mirrored walls, you can sample fesenjān for IR32,500 or sturgeon kebab for IR38,500. The total bill is likely to come to around IR50,000 with tax of 15% on top.

The *Sahra Restaurant* (☎ 882 9095, *341 Tāleqānī Ave*) is in the basement of the

Hotel Sahra and very popular with middle-class women, who come here in droves. A set menu costing IR37,000 includes soup, salad, main course, a drink and dessert. The salad bar boasts such delicacies as stuffed tomatoes, raita, pickled onions and potato salad, and excellent French-style bread is also available.

If you're desperate to tuck into something other than Iranian food, the *Tandoor Restaurant* (☎ 882 5705, Ardalan St) under the Hotel Tehrān Sara is generally regarded as the best place in town for a curry. A delicious two-course meal, with all the trimmings, costs about IR30,000, supposedly including service although you'd be advised to leave a tip if you're coming back. There are a few vegetarian dishes for IR14,000 each.

Bakeries, Cafes & Teahouses

Tehrān has lots of excellent cake shops and confectioneries, many of them owned by Armenians. The greatest concentration is along Nejātollāhī St, and around the corner of Jomhūri-yé Eslāmī and Sa'dī Sts.

One of the best is the *Café Naderi* cafe and patisserie next to (and belonging to) the Hotel Naderi. Here you can enjoy small but delectable pastries for about IR500 each, with great iced coffee or Iranian nonalcoholic beer, alongside an intellectual set who seem to eat, drink and chat here for hours. Unfortunately lone women are not welcome unless they're prepared to sit in the empty, atmosphereless 'restaurant' at the rear.

There's another very pleasant place for tea and cakes, the *Koswar Restaurant*, along the eastern reaches of Enqelāb Ave before it joins Mofatteh St. There's no English sign but it's right on a corner and easy to spot. A pot of tea and a plate of cakes costs IR4000, and women are more welcome here than at the Naderi.

Central Tehrān has surprisingly few traditional teahouses although one or two can be tracked down along the eastern reaches of Jomhūri-yé Eslāmī Ave and on Hāfez St. The best places to go in search of tea on a sunny day are along the walking trails at Darband and Darakeh.

Self-Catering

If you're staying in Tehrān for long, or if you're a vegetarian, you may want to cater for yourself at least some of the time. If you're staying around Amīr Kabīr St this will mean venturing some way away from your hotel to find suitable shops; you'll be much better off if you're staying around Ferdōsī St or Jomhūri-yé-Eslāmī Ave where there are a few groceries and greengroceries. In the groceries you can usually pick up tinned fish, Iranian fetta cheese in tubs, strawberry-flavoured yogurt, fruit juices, cold meat, rice and a few other staples. Just east of the junction of Ferdōsī St and Jomhūri-yé-Eslāmī Ave there are also several meat and fish shops.

Bread other than *lavāsh* (a cardboard-like flat bread) is not always easy to come by; look for segregated huddles of men and women around holes in the wall and you'll usually find they're queuing for fresh bread. Manūchehrī St has a bakery selling French sticks and more unusual types of bread. Nearby there's a shop selling cornflakes and other types of cereal.

Rumour has it that there's a shop in northern Tehrān selling Camembert but you'll probably need an expatriate to guide you to it!

ENTERTAINMENT

Although the rigid social constraints of the Khomeinī brand of Islam have undoubtedly loosened recently, there's still very little to do of an evening in Tehrān. There certainly aren't any nightclubs, bars or discos. All those nightclubs and discos lovingly described in guidebooks published before the Islamic Revolution have long since gone, and are unlikely to reappear in the foreseeable future. Bring a big book with lots of words.

The one time when there *is* quite a lot of organised entertainment is over the 10 Days of Dawn (1–11 February) when you will be able to attend concerts of traditional Iranian music and music from around the world, plays and films, some of them with English subtitles. The one problem is likely to be finding out what's on where – see if your hotel can help.

Cinemas

A few carefully chosen foreign films are occasionally shown in cinemas in remote parts of north Tehrān, but they will all be censored and badly translated into Farsi. If you want to see an action flick, Iranian-style, head for one of the cinemas along southern Lālezār St or eastern Jomhūrī-yé Eslāmī Ave, in south Tehrān. Every day, films are shown about every two hours between 10 am and 8 pm. Screenings cost IR3000.

Given the recent international success of Iranian films you may be lucky and catch one of them showing in town. However, the dialogue will be in Farsi.

Theatre

Foreign-language students at the universities occasionally perform plays by writers such as Shakespeare in the original script and in period dress. If you're interested you will have to ask one of the English-language students who are bound to approach you if you spend much time in Tehrān, particularly around Tehrān University.

Other theatre productions (in Farsi) are staged at the huge, circular *Tezātre Shāhr* (City Theatre) on Valiasr Ave where it meets Enqelāb Ave. The easiest way to find out what's on is simply to visit and ask. Performances are normally nightly at 7 pm and seats cost IR5000.

Music

Organised public performances of Iranian music are rare. Again, your best bet is to rely on the guidance of an Iranian friend, or to talk to the staff at your hotel to find out what is going on. Special festivals, such as the Iranian Epic Music Festival, which is held in April, may be advertised in the English-language press, but don't count on it. Until Iran is ready for something different, most concerts will be extremely traditional: a solo male performer plucking at a *tar* (a traditional stringed instrument), with or without singing, for example.

Increasingly, the newer restaurants are employing musicians to entertain their guests. See Restaurants in Places to Eat earlier for some possibilities.

What to Do in Tehrān on Friday

If you're not prepared for it, Tehrān can seem eerily quiet on a Friday, with most of the shops closed and even the traffic madness temporarily stilled. Make sure you've done any essential shopping by Thursday lunch time since after that it's hard to predict what will and will not be open.

Still, provided you don't equate weekends with a wild time, there *are* plenty of things to keep you occupied:

• Take a ride on the Tōchāl telecabin.
• Join the crowds walking at Darband or Darakeh.
• Visit one of the museums.
• Watch a football match.
• Go to the cinema.
• Get an early night.

Concerts are sometimes held in the Bahman Cultural Centre in a converted slaughterhouse south-east of Bahman Square (south of the train station). To find out what's going on you may well have to go there and ask.

SPECTATOR SPORTS

Iran's most favoured sport is football (soccer), which is played at 10 major stadiums around the city. The most important games are played at the Āzādī Sports Stadium, which can hold up to 125,000 screaming fans, way out in the western suburbs. The English-language newspapers rarely carry advance information about games, so you will have to make inquiries. Matches are usually played on Thursday and Friday. If Esteqlal (blue shirts) or Persepolis (red shirts) are playing, tickets will be in short supply.

In the Āzādī Sports Stadium complex (☎ 942 014) you may also be able to see some wrestling, or motor racing with six categories of cars – all Paykans with different-sized engines. Save yourself time and money, and just sit in the middle of any main square in Tehrān.

You can watch a variety of sports at the Haft-é-Tīr Sports Stadium (☎ 673 365); the Chamrān Sports Centre (☎ 263 031); and the Shāhīd Shirudi Sports Centre (☎ 8822 110), where many sports clubs have their head-quarters.

SHOPPING

On the whole, souvenir shopping is easier and more fun in places like Esfahān or Shīrāz. For souvenir shopping in Tehrān you're best off heading straight for the bazaar (see Tehrān Bazaar earlier). Otherwise there are a few souvenir shops around town that offer an excellent choice. Prices are generally fixed, but if you buy a couple of things, or are good at bargaining, you should be able to get a discount without too much trouble.

Ferdōsī St is a good place to start looking for carpets, miniatures, lacquerware etc; check out the place with the snappy title of the Fair and Shop for Products of Self Sufficiency Plan of Emām Khomeinī's Relief Committee, just south of the square. Also worth a trawl are Tāleqānī St (especially opposite the US Den of Espionage) and Nejātollāhī St. Otherwise, try the various branches of the Iran Handicrafts Organisation all over town; or the shops to the south-west corner of Pārk- é Lāleh.

Locals claim that Valiasr Ave is the world's longest thoroughfare and it's one of Tehrān's major shopping districts. For many Tehrānīs the perfect night out means window-shopping, and the northern part of Valiasr Ave is one of their favourite places to do it. You may not want to buy much but it's fun watching what people like and seeing what's available.

If you need to buy a suitably Islamic overcoat, there is a cluster of shops around the junction of Jomhūrī-yé Eslāmī Ave and Hāfez St. A lightweight coat should cost less than IR80,000. For an even bigger choice, try Haft-é Tir Square.

Print film is easy to buy in Tehrān, slide film much less so; try Foto Asia at the junction of Valiasr Ave and Enqelāb St.

Several shops around town sell cassettes of Iranian music, which make good souvenirs. Often they have just one original and will duplicate it for you while you wait. Cassettes generally cost around IR2000.

If you've been admiring the posters of tourist attractions that you've seen around the country, it's worth knowing that there's a basement shop on the south side of Enqelāb St, in one of the arcades just east of Enqelāb Square, which stocks these posters along with some decent postcards and old magazines about Iran.

GETTING THERE & AWAY

The problem with travel in Iran is not how to get to Tehrān, but how to avoid it. Tehrān is the hub of almost all bus, train and air services. Every town and city of any size is directly linked to Tehrān; always by bus, usually by air and sometimes by train. Generally it's easier to get a ticket into Tehrān than out of it; it's always a good idea to book a ticket out of Tehrān as soon as you possibly can.

Air

Every day there are flights between Tehrān and every major city you are likely to want to visit, on one of the two main domestic airlines – Iran Air and Iran Asseman. Less often there are flights to and from Tehrān on the smaller airlines, which include Mahan Air, Saha Air, Caspian Air and Kīsh Airlines.

For details of schedules and costs of internal flights to and from Tehrān, see Getting There & Away under your destination later in this guide. For information on international flights to and from Tehrān, see the main Getting There & Away chapter.

If you need to know anything about any domestic or international flight to or from Tehrān it's usually easiest to ask a travel agent (many of those in Tehrān speak English). Alternatively you could try contacting the airline offices listed here, or ringing tourist information at Mehrābād international airport (☎ 646 7785) or the special airport information number (☎ 199).

Airline Offices Most airline offices in Tehrān are along, or near, Nejātollāhī St. They're well signed in English and easy to find so are not all shown on the maps in this guidebook. Staff usually speak good English. Airline offices are generally open from about 9 am to 4 pm, Saturday to Thursday.

The following international airlines are represented in Tehrān:

Aeroflot (☎ 880 8480) 23 Nejātollāhī St
Air France (☎ 670 4111) 882 Enqelāb Ave, near Ferdōsī Square
Alitalia (☎ 871 1512) Ārzhāntīn Square
British Airways (☎ 204 4552) Sayeh St, Valiasr Ave
Emirates (☎ 888 6467) Valiasr Square
Iran Air (☎ 979 011) Nejātollāhī St
KLM (☎ 204 4757) Sayeh St, Valiasr Ave
Kuwait Airways (☎ 225 3284) 86 Nejātollāhī St
Lufthansa (☎ 873 8701) Beheshtī Ave, Sarafraz St
Saudi Arabian Airlines (☎ 875 3100) Beheshtī Ave, Mahnaz Junction
Swissair (☎ 874 8332) Ārzhāntīn Square, 69 Bokhārest St
Syrian Arab Airlines (☎ 889 5584) Fallāh Pūr St, Nejātollāhī St
Turkish Airlines (☎ 874 8450) 239 Motahharī Ave

It is often just as easy to buy a ticket at a reputable travel agency (see Organised Tours in the Getting Around chapter); if you do that the agent will probably help you reconfirm your onward booking as well.

For the smaller internal airlines (ie, Kīsh, Saha, Mahan and Caspian), it's easiest to buy a ticket at a travel agency, or at the crowded counters in the domestic airport. You can contact the domestic airlines in Tehrān as follows:

Iran Air (☎ 600 1011) Nejātollāhī St
Iran Asseman (☎ 889 5567) Nejātollāhī St
Caspian Airlines (☎ 8807 633) 3 Karīm-Khān-é Zand St
Kīsh Airlines (☎ 466 5644) Babak Alley, Ekbatan Complex
Mahan Air (☎ 877 2605) 31 East Jahan-é Koodak Ave, Vanak Square
Qeshm Air (☎ 877 0593) #17, 11th Alley, Gāndi St.
Saha Air (☎ 699 4450) Terminal 4, Mehrābād international airport

International Arrivals Though the crowds and noise may be intimidating to anyone who has not travelled in this part of the world before, customs and immigration procedures at Mehrābād international airport are not much of a hassle although they do take a long time. Immigration is painless, as long as your visa is in order. (You probably won't be allowed on the plane to Iran in the first place if it isn't.) The only log jam might be at customs, but these days tourists are more or less waved through. Provided it's open, the tourist information counter is staffed by friendly, helpful people who will happily book hotels and flights for you, though they may not always be able to rustle up a map. The tourist information booth at the domestic airport, nearby, is also very helpful.

Despite the sign in English at the Bank Melli office immediately after immigration, you do not have to fill out a currency declaration form unless you're importing huge sums of money (US$1000 may seem a lot to you but doesn't to bank officials). This small bank can change major foreign currencies in cash, and, usually, travellers cheques; cash advances on MasterCard but not Visa are also possible. These days the rate at the bank is much the same as anywhere else. Still you may prefer to change just enough money to get transport to your hotel, and then to change more once you've checked the going rate the next day.

International Departures Leaving Tehrān on an international flight is not particularly traumatic, although you should allow plenty of time to get to the airport, clear customs and check in. If you leave your hotel about four hours before departure, you will be fine. Make sure you go to the correct airport; the international and domestic airports are about 1km apart. If you have changed money legally at a bank, and have a receipt to prove it, you can convert unused rials into US dollars cash at the bank in the international departure lounge. There are a couple of reasonable, but pricey, souvenir shops in the international departure lounge where you can offload any remaining rials.

Bus

Masses of buses leave Tehrān every few minutes to just about every city, town and village throughout the country, but as the city has four bus stations you will need to know which one your bus leaves from. To add to the confusion, some buses leave from two or more stations.

There is only one specific bus ticket office in the city: the TBT bus booking office on Tāleqānī St in central Tehrān. Generally speaking you will need to go to the stations to check times and prices. A good place to check bus schedules and buy advance tickets for any of seven major bus companies is the office marked in English 'The Union of Countries Travelling Companies' at the central (Ārzhāntīn) bus station at Ārzhāntīn Square. You will be lucky to find any English-speaking staff at the bus ticket offices.

The following tables show services to all major destinations on direct buses from Tehrān. Where two prices are given, the higher will be for travel on a Volvo bus. However, prices are very competitive so it's wise to shop around for tickets on popular routes.

For details of international bus services to/from Tehrān, see the Land section in the Getting There & Away chapter earlier in this book.

Western Bus Station The western bus station (*termīnāl-é gharb*, ☎ 606 2854) is the busiest terminal, catering, naturally, for the Caspian and places to the west of Tehrān, as well as for a few other destinations, including Ankara and İstanbul (Turkey), Baku (Azerbaijan) and Damascus (Syria). It's well set up with dozens of bus company offices, and a restaurant, post office, police station and information booth. To get there, take a shared taxi heading west from Emām Khomeinī Square, or catch anything going to Āzādī Square, and walk north-west to the huge station.

destination	price (IR)	duration (hrs)
Ardabīl	17,000	10
Āstārā	10,800	9
Chālūs	9,000	5
Hamadān	8,500	6
Kermānshāh	13,500	8½
Orūmīyeh	21,000	12
Qazvīn	3,500	2
Rāmsar	10,800	6
Tabrīz	14,000	10

Note that buses to Qazvīn leave from a separate station at the back of the main one every 15 minutes.

Central Bus Station The central bus station (☎ 873 2535), also known as the Ārzhāntīn or Sayro Safar station, is off Ārzhāntīn Square, accessible by shared taxis and local buses from most places in the south.

destination	price (IR; lux/super)	duration (hrs)
Bandar-é Anzalī	22,000	6
Esfahān	15,000/30,000	10
Kermān	23,000/43,000	15
Kermānshāh	27,000/30,000	10
Mashhad	31,000/40,000	14
Rasht	17,000/20,000	14
Shīrāz	40,000	5
Tabrīz	25,000/30,000	10
Yazd	30,000	14

Southern Bus Station The southern bus station (*termīnāl-é jonūb*, ☎ 559 163) has buses to the south and south-east of Tehrān. It's a huge circular building, well set up with a restaurant and information booth. To get there, take a shared taxi heading south from Emām Khomeinī Square. Try to avoid the expensive taxi agency that operates from this station.

destination	price (IR; lux/super)	duration (hrs)
Ahvāz	20,500/40,000	15
Bam	25,000/40,000	20
Bandar-é Abbās	31,500/55,000	20
Būshehr	28,000/55,000	17
Esfahān	10,500/20,000	7
Kāshān	5,800/9,000	4
Kermān	23,000/43,000	15
Qom	3,000/6,000	1½
Semnān	6,500	3½
Shīrāz	20,500/35,000	14
Yazd	15,000/30,000	10
Zāhedān	36,000/65,000	24

Eastern Bus Station The eastern bus station (*termīnāl-é shargh*, ☎ 786 8080) has buses to Khorāsān province and the Caspian region. It's a small station that's easy to use. Take a shared taxi to Emām Hossein Square, and then another shared taxi, or try the trolleybus directly to the station.

destination	price (IR; lux/super)	duration (hrs)
Gonbad	10,800	9
Gorgān	10,000/22,000	8
Mashhad	19,000	17
Sārī	8,000/13,000	5

Train

All train services around the country start and finish at the impressive train station in southern Tehrān. The destinations arrival and departure times are listed in English on a huge board at the entrance. The staff at the tourist information booth (☎ 565 1415) speak English, and are walking timetables, which is just as well as the only written timetables they have are in Farsi. If you ask nicely they may help you buy a ticket at an office upstairs in the main building.

Schedules The prices and days of departure in the timetable listed here are liable to change; in particular, what are daily services in summer may become much less frequent in winter. Remember that while there are no trains just to Semnān, for example, the very frequent trains to Mashhad call in there on the way. Qazvīn is served by train services to Sārī, Tabrīz and Zanjān.

destination	one-way fare (IR; 1st/2nd class)	no of trains daily
Ahvāz	31,050/12,250	3
Bandar-é Abbās	54,250 (1st class only)	1
Esfahān	16,150/6900	2
Gorgān	20,300/7500	1
Kermān	36,150/20,200	1 (Mon, Wed & Fri only)
Mashhad	76,000/18,350	12
Qom	4900	3
Sārī	16,150/6000	1
Tabrīz	31,100/20,650	1
Yazd	24,250/12,600	1
Zanjān	13,650/5300	1

Buying Tickets Although you can buy tickets a week or more in advance, buying them at the ticket office is such a hassle that you'll probably want to give up and head for the nearest bus station. The place to buy train tickets is unmarked in English; it's a small building behind a blue gate, 200m east of the train station. Go through the gates, and turn immediately to your left – just look for the chaos. Nothing is signed in English, so you will have to ask someone which line to join for a ticket to your destination. Avoid the first line as you come in the main entrance unless you want a job on the railways. The office is open from 7 am to 7 pm daily.

The 20% surcharge for advance tickets is well worth paying to ensure a seat on a train you want.

The train station and ticket office are easy to reach on any shared taxi heading south from the south-west corner of Emām Khomeinī Square – ask to be dropped at Rāh-Āhan Square.

Fortunately, these days some travel agencies are happy to organise train tickets for you in return for a small service charge (see Organised Tours in the Getting Around chapter for a list of travel agencies in Tehrān). Alternatively, you could try going direct to Raja, the train booking office in town from which the agencies buy their stocks.

Minibus

A few towns in central Iran and nearby parts of the Caspian provinces are linked to Tehrān by minibus. Minibuses are generally a little more expensive than buses, but leave more regularly because they have fewer seats to fill. They leave from specially designated sections within the eastern, southern and western bus stations, depending on the destination – see the Bus section earlier.

Shared Taxi

Most towns within about three hours' drive of Tehrān are linked to it by shared taxi, eg, Āmol, Sārī, Semnān, Kāshān, Qom, Zanjān and Rasht – and anywhere along the way. Prices are two to three times the price of the cheapest bus tickets, but are often worth paying to enjoy some comfort and speed.

For day trips from Tehrān, use a shared taxi, if possible. Shared taxis leave from specially designated sections inside, or just outside, the appropriate bus stations, depending on the destination – see the Bus section earlier.

GETTING AROUND
To/From the Airport

Taxi If you are arriving in Tehrān for the first time, and have some luggage, it's wise to bite the bullet and pay for a private taxi to your hotel, especially as you may be doing a bit of looking around to find a suitable hotel. Some English-speaking taxi drivers may want to take you to a hotel of their choice, but stick with your own preferences until you're sure they're all full.

Avoid drivers who work for the official Airport Taxi Service who loiter around waiting for naive foreigners. They want at least IR40,000 from either airport to the city centre. Find a normal private taxi, and don't pay more than IR30,000 to get to south Tehrān. (The tourist information booth at the domestic airport will be able to tell you the current taxi fare into the city.) When heading back to either airport, the driver will want to avoid paying the car park entrance fee by dropping you off about 200m from the international airport or 50m from the domestic one.

If you want a shared taxi (about IR7000 from the airport to the city centre), ask around or tell a taxi driver you want to share, and he will look for other passengers going the same way.

Alternatively, take a taxi or bus to Āzādī Square, and then catch another shared taxi to your destination.

Bus If you're confident, and don't have much luggage, public buses (IR200) leave every 15 to 20 minutes from immediately outside the domestic airport – but not from the international airport, about 1km away. Ask the friendly women at the tourist information booth at the domestic airport about the current timetables. Bus Nos 511 and 518 travel between the domestic airport and Enqelāb and Vanak Squares.

Bus

Extensive bus services cover virtually all of Tehrān, but as they're often crowded and slow, most travellers end up using taxis. Buses run from roughly 6 am until 10 or 11 pm, finishing earlier on Friday and public holidays. Tickets cost IR100 or IR200; as a guide, expect to pay IR100 for any trip covered by this book's Central Tehrān or South Tehrān map and IR200 for anywhere further afield. You must buy them from ticket booths along the main streets or at the bus stations, and give them to the driver when you board the bus.

Buses normally travel from one local bus station to another, so you may need to take more than one. Bus stations you are likely to use include Emām Khomeinī Square, for the south of the city; the station on the opposite side of Emām Khomeinī Ave from the National Museum of Iran, for the west; Ārzhāntīn, Vanak and Valiasr Squares, for the north; Āzādī Square, for further west; and Rāh-Āhan Square, for the far south.

The buses often have numbers, but never the destinations, in English. The buses listed in the following table should suit most travellers. Each number applies to buses going in both directions, eg, bus No 219 travels from Enqelāb Square to Ferdōsī Square and vice versa.

bus no	from	to
126	Ārzhāntīn Square	Tajrīsh Square
127	Valiasr Square	Tajrīsh Square
128 & 144	Valiasr Square	Emām Khomeinī Square
145	Emām Khomeinī Square	Tajrīsh Square
219	Enqelāb Square	Ferdōsī Square
511 & 518	Domestic Airport	Enqelāb & Vanak Squares

Minibus

There are a few very crowded public minibuses in the suburbs, but most travellers are unlikely to need them. If you do, finding the right minibus going your way is not easy, so ask, ask and ask again. A few private minibuses have irregular schedules: one, for instance, travels between Enqelāb and Tajrīsh

Squares. Tickets cost from IR300 to IR600, depending on the distance.

Trolleybus

One excellent but, sadly, unique innovation is the electric trolleybus. Currently, the one line runs between the eastern bus station and Emām Hossein Square. It's useful for getting to or from the bus station but not for anything else.

Metro

Tehrān's nine-station metro runs underground from the west side of Emām Khomeinī Square to the Karaj train station at the junction of Jenah Fwy and Tehrān Karaj Fwy. At the moment it's of limited use to tourists although you could use it to get within short shared-taxi distance of the western bus station and the airports. You could also use it to connect with the express trains to Karaj, from where you can get onward transport to Chālūs on the Caspian by a picturesque route. Trains run at half-hourly intervals and tickets cost a flat IR500 (the onward train to Karaj costs another IR1000). Station announcements are in Farsi only. Trains are nonsmoking and nonsegregated.

Taxi

Tehrān taxis come in a variety of colours. Blue and green taxis officially operate just to the airport and say 'Shuttle Service' on their roofs. However, on the return journey they often pick up fares as normal shared taxis. Orange taxis with a white stripe belong to taxi organisations; they're usually the newer vehicles and sometimes run on LPG. The privately owned white taxis are often the most clapped out.

Shared Taxi Taxi fares in Tehrān are higher than in the rest of Iran and the minimum fare of IR500 won't get you very far. For longer distances, expect to pay between IR1000 and IR2000. Always watch what other passengers are paying: you'll soon get a good idea what the current rates are.

Using shared taxis is especially hard in Tehrān partly because of the sheer volume of people but also because the one-way systems

make it very hard for an outsider to be sure where they will be going. It's easy to use the shared taxis plying the main roads between the following squares: Emām Khomeinī, Vanak, Valiasr, Tajrīsh, Ārzhāntīn, Āzādī, Ferdōsī, Enqelāb, Haft-é Tīr, Rāh-Āhan and Emām Hussein. However, even these squares may have several mini-stations for shared taxis heading in different directions, so you usually have to ask around a bit. You may be lucky and get a shared taxi all the way from, say, Emām Khomeinī Square to Tajrīsh Square (IR2000), but often you will have to change in Valiasr or Vanak Square.

When trying to hail a shared taxi don't bother with anything in any language along the lines of 'Iran Hotel, on the corner of…': the driver will have lost interest after the word 'hotel', picked up someone else and be halfway there before you know it. Use a major landmark or a town square as a destination, even if you are getting off before then. Shout it quickly and loudly: '…DŌS…!' will do for Ferdōsī St or square; similarly, '…HESHT…!' for Beheshtī St or Square; and so on. The driver will either completely ignore you, or give you a quick beep on the horn and pull over for half a second while you leap in. It's best to practise outside Tehrān and build up to the big city.

Private Taxi Unless you're going to be in Tehrān long enough to get the lay of the land you may find it hard using the shared taxis, in which case theoretically any taxi can also be hired privately. In practice, chartering a private taxi on the street is not as easy as you might expect since most of the taxis roaring around town are looking for shared fares; you may have to stop several and ask before you hit the jackpot.

The alternative is to get your hotel to call a taxi for you or to call one yourself (☎ 133 or 840 011), although this costs more than flagging a cab on the street.

Once you've found a taxi prepared to take you, you must agree on a price before setting out. Most taxi drivers seem to demand IR10,000 even before they know where you want to go. Sometimes this will turn out to be an extortionate sum for a short trip; at other times they'll be grumbling and complaining when they realise what a bargain you've landed.

To get from Emām Khomeinī Square to Valiasr Square should cost about IR8000; from Emām Khomeinī Square to Tajrīsh Square will cost about IR15,000. To hire a taxi for an hour or so to visit several sites shouldn't cost much more than IR15,000. To get from south Tehrān to the north even in a private taxi usually takes about half an hour.

In the northern suburbs, and at the airport and the southern bus station, avoid the smart-looking taxis with 'Taxi Service' written on top. Their prices are often higher than usual and non-negotiable.

Car & Motorcycle

The traffic in Tehrān is homicidal and heedless of rules. Traffic lights, indicators, footpaths etc go completely ignored. Most foreign drivers give up soon after arriving and quickly assimilate the lawless aggression of the locals. Drive with 100% attention at all times. Better still, don't drive at all. See Dangers & Annoyances earlier in this chapter for more information on how to avoid an ugly death in Tehrān traffic.

Car Rental Any of the travel agencies listed under Organised Tours in the Getting Around chapter will be able to lease you a car with driver. The cost depends on many variables, not least whether you want an English-speaking driver who can double as a guide, but reckon on paying between US$40 and US$65 a day.

To charter one of the airport shuttle taxis for the day would probably cost about US$30; to charter a Paykan in worse condition about US$15.

Around Tehrān

If you can manage to escape the capital, Tehrān province also offers barren hills to scramble around, lush valleys to explore and even a majestic mountain to climb. Most visitors to Tehrān will want to visit the Holy Shrine of Emām Khomeinī and the adjacent military cemetery to the southwest of the city. Using Tehrān as a base it's also possible to visit the towns of Rey and Vārāmīn, which were capitals of Iran before Tehrān. Enthusiastic mountaineers will want to head for the slopes of Iran's highest mountain, Mt Damāvand (5671m), while skiers may want to sample the delights of Dīzīn and other resorts in the Alborz Mountains.

HOLY SHRINE OF EMĀM KHOMEINĪ   حرم قم

Once completed, the resting place of His Holiness Emām Khomeinī will be one of the greatest Islamic buildings of modern times. For the time being, however, it resembles a half-built aircraft hangar set in a vast sprawl of half-completed structures.

It's fine for non-Muslims to enter the shrine provided they've removed their shoes. Men enter to the right, women to the left. You will be frisked, and although cameras are allowed in they seem to cause the people on duty at the entrances quite unnecessary concern. Inside you'll find the actual shrine tucked into a corner of what looks a bit like an ice-skating rink minus the ice. This vast empty space will be full of families having picnics, kids rolling coins along the floor and homeless men sleeping. Apparently the ayatollah wanted his shrine to be a public place where people could enjoy themselves, rather than a mosque where they must behave with reverence.

At the moment the complex contains several *restaurants* and *snack bars*; shops, where you can pick up tacky souvenirs; a post office; a bank (not for foreign exchange); and a branch of the nationwide Refah department store. When completed it will have its own university campus. Tehrān's international airport will also be relocated here.

The shrine is open daily, and entry is free. Whatever you do, don't visit on an official mourning day, when the shrine will be a seething mass of humanity (for more information on mourning days, see Public Holidays & Special Events in the Facts for the Visitor chapter).

TEHRĀN

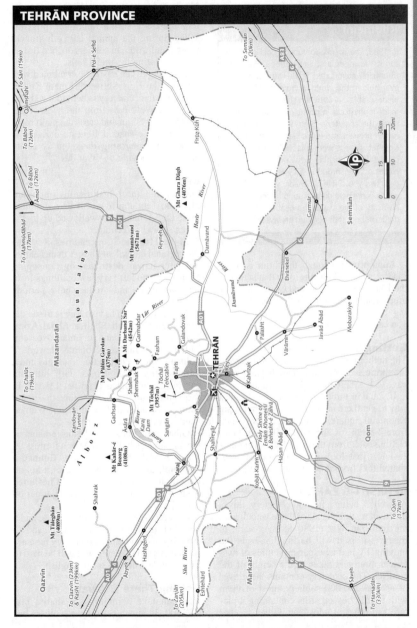

TEHRĀN PROVINCE

To Qazvin (23km) & Rasht (199km)

To Mahmūdābād (17km)

To Chālūs (19km)

To Qazvin (23km) & Rasht (199km)

To Zanjān (205km)

To Babol (12km)

To Āmol (12km)

Qā'emshahr

To Sāri (15km)

Pol-e Sefīd

To Babol (12km)

To Semnān (20km)

A83

Fīroz Kūh

Mt Ghara Dāgh (4076m) ▲

Ḥaṇir River

Reyneh

Mt Damāvand (5671m) ▲

Damāvand

Damāvand River

Garmsār

Evānekei

Semnān

M o u n t a i n s

Lār River

Mt Darband Sar (4542m) ▲

Mt Pālūn Gardan (4375m) ▲

Garmabdar

Fasham

Galandovak

Galandak

Javād Ābād

Mobarakiye

Mt Kahār-é Bozorg (4108m) ▲

Gachsar

Kandovan Tunnel

Shaleh

Shemshak

Āstā

Karaj River

Mt Tōchāl (3957m) ▲

Tōchāl Telecabin

Tajrīsh

Pālasht

Varāmīn

Mazandarān

A l b o r z

Kanal

Karaj Dam

Sangān

Kan

TEHRĀN

Rey

Kahrīzak

Qom

Mt Tālēghān (4089m) ▲

Shahrak

Abyek

Hashtgerd

Shīa River

Karaj

Shahrīyār

Robāt Karīm

Holy Shrine of Emām Khomeinī & Behesht-é Zāhā

Hasan Ābād

Eshtehārd

Markazi

Sāveh

To Qom (17km)

To Hamādān (330km)

Qazvin

0   15   30km
0   10   20mi

The Funeral of Āyatollāh Khomeinī

In 1989, the Islamic Republic's final send-off for its founder and inspiration, Āyatollāh Khomeinī, culminated in the largest funeral ever held in the world, a crush of 10 million inconsolable mourners. The crowd twice made it physically impossible for the hearse to reach the cemetery. Even when a helicopter hastily pressed into service landed, the armed Komīteh guards were unable to prevent the crowd from pushing forward and ripping pieces off the shroud as holy relics.

Unless you thrive on chaos, you're advised not to come here on or around 4 June, the anniversary of the ayatollah's death, when hundreds of thousands of mourners visit the shrine.

Appropriately enough, the shrine is on the road between Tehrān, the town that launched the Islamic Revolution, and Qom, where the great man underwent his theological training. It's right in front of Behesht-é Zahrā, so you can see both on one trip.

Getting There & Away

The authorities plan to extend the metro to the shrine eventually, but until they do you'll have to get there by bus or shared taxi.

If you don't mind a squeeze, the cheapest way to get there is to take a bus from Emām Khomeinī Square. You could charter a taxi from Tehrān for about IR10,000 per hour. Getting back from the complex to Tehrān is easier – just look for a minibus, bus or shared taxi from around the main car park.

BEHESHT-É ZAHRĀ   بهشت زهرا

As well as being a normal cemetery, this is the main resting place for those who died in the Iran-Iraq War (1980–88). As such, to many visitors it will be familiar from the moving TV and newspaper pictures of hysterical mourners taken at the height of the conflict. The cemetery contains the graves of around 200,000 soldiers, most of them with a little box on stilts containing a picture and relics of a lost son, father, brother

or husband. Right at the heart of the cemetery there's a shrine to Iranian pilgrims killed during the annual haj (pilgrimage) when Saudi Arabian soldiers opened fire on a crowd during the mid-1980s.

A visit here can easily be combined with a trip to the Holy Shrine of Emām Khomeinī since the cemetery is behind the shrine complex. Walk east from the back of the complex for 500m and cross the main road. The pine-tree-shaded Behesht-é Zahrā is packed on mourning days but is eerily empty and moving on other days.

REY   ری

One of the most historically important places in Tehrān province is Rey, although these days it has been swallowed up by the urban sprawl of Tehrān.

In the 11th and 12th centuries, Rey was the regional capital and larger than Tehrān, but later it was destroyed by rampaging Mongols, who left very few buildings from the Sassanian and Achaemenid periods standing.

The main reason to visit Rey is to see the lovely **Emāmzadeh Shāh-é Abdal-Azim**, built for a descendant of Emām Hossein. This mausoleum has elaborate tilework, a golden dome, a pool in the courtyard and a 14th-century sarcophagus with intricate carvings, constructed from betel wood. In the same complex is a shrine to Emām Hamzeh (brother of Emām Rezā). Women need to wear a chador here.

Other attractions include the remains of the Sassanian **Ghal'-é Tabarak**, a fortress on a nearby hill; the 12th-century **Gonbad-é Toghoral**, the 20m tomb tower of a Seljuq king in the town centre; and the **Cheshmeh Ali** mineral springs with some Qajar period carvings nearby.

Finding these sites without a guide and a vehicle is likely to prove frustrating, and although you could hire a taxi in Rey for a negotiable IR10,000 per hour it will be hard to find a guide who can speak English.

Getting There & Away

You can take a minibus or shared taxi (IR1500, 30 minutes) from the southern bus station in Tehrān. Alternatively you can take a tour organised by a Tehrān travel agency (see Organised Tours in the Getting Around chapter). This will allow you to visit Rey and Vārāmīn in the same day but is likely to cost from US$30 depending on the number of people you can get together.

VĀRĀMĪN   ورامین

More interesting than Rey, and easier to get around in, Vārāmīn is still designated as a village, though it will soon become part of southern Tehrān. Many of its historical buildings have been destroyed by earthquakes, but the town is important as much of what remains was built by the Mongols (who destroyed much of Rey).

Worth a look is the **Borq-é Aladdin**, a tomb, next to the main roundabout. It is more than 17m tall, and has been dated back to the 13th century. Nearby (ask for directions) is the famous **Jāmeh Mosque**, built during the 13th century. The dome, tiling, inscriptions and symmetrical iwans (*eivāns*; halls) are renowned.

Getting There & Away

Trains from Tehrān to Gorgān stop in Vārāmīn but it's probably easier to take a minibus or shared taxi from Tehrān's southern bus station (IR2000, 30 minutes). Alternatively you can take a tour that will include Rey as well (see Getting There & Away in the Rey section earlier).

KARAJ   کرج

Karaj, 42km west of Tehrān, is primarily a dormitory town for people working in the capital. It's also the starting point for a pleasant drive along a spectacular road forced north through the Alborz Mountains to Chālūs on the Caspian Sea by Shāh Rezā Khān. The drive takes you past the Karaj Dam where you can either walk and enjoy the scenery or take part in a variety of water sports. Heading north towards Chalūs you pass over the mountains with their breathtaking scenery. In summer, there's an astonishing shift from the hot, dry atmosphere of the mountains' southern face to the humidity of the north.

Karaj is easily accessible by express train from southern Tehrān (IR1000). To get to the dam you will need to find a shared taxi, which is likely to be easiest on Fridays.

MT DAMĀVAND   کوه دماوند

Shaped like Mt Fuji, Mt Damāvand (5671m) is the highest mountain in Iran and easily accessible from Tehrān, although it is actually in Māzandarān province. Damāvand is a volcano still belching sulphuric fumes which are strong enough to kill stray sheep. It was first climbed by a westerner in 1837. The usual starting point is Reyneh, where there is a mountaineering club at the junction where the main road enters the village.

Tragically, the manager of the club, an expert local mountaineer, and his sons died a few years ago while trying to climb the mountain. This gives you some idea of the potential danger.

You can see Mt Damāvand on the IR10,000 note, on bottles of Damarvand spring water and from the air as you fly into Tehrān, smog permitting. Don't confuse the mountain of Damāvand with the village of Damāvand to its south.

Reyneh   رینه

One possible starting point for exploring the mountain and the nearby countryside is the pretty village of Reyneh. From Reyneh, there are fine views of other picturesque villages on the far side of the valley. Even if you don't want to climb the mountain, there are plenty of other local walking trails to enjoy.

There is no hotel, but if you ask around, especially if you want to climb the mountain, someone will put you up in their home for about IR25,000 per person. There are a couple of kabābīs and other shops in the village.

A reader has recommended Reyneh-based Ahman Faramarzpour as a mountain guide. Ask around the village and someone will direct you to him. If you stay at his house for the night before ascending the mountain you will be able to read climbing reports going back to 1964.

Climbing the Mountain

From Reyneh, it's possible to take an ordinary vehicle as far as Gusfand Sara (3200m), where you can sleep in the mosque. However, if you want to acclimatise before climbing the mountain it may be better to walk up, taking perhaps four or five hours to get there. In summer local families will be able to provide simple food for small groups of people but for most of the year you must bring your own food.

From Gusfand Sara, you can walk, or ride a donkey, for about four hours to Barghahé-Sevvom (4150m), where you can stay overnight in a mountaineers' hut and clean water is available. There's no water en route so you should bring some up with you. The hut may be full, so bringing a tent (and leaving it there during the final ascent) is a good idea. You will also need to bring a sleeping bag, warm clothes and perhaps a gas camping stove for making hot drinks. A reader has pointed out that you should fill your water bottle in the evening since the water will be frozen when you get up before dawn.

Next morning you should get up at about 3 am to make the tough seven-hour climb to the summit in time to enjoy the views before clouds cover the peak and the sulphur fumes become overpowering. The path is fairly clear although it can be obscured by snow. In August you should be able to get up without special equipment. It's another four to five hours back to the hut from the peak.

Bear in mind that the weather can change suddenly and that snowfalls are a possibility, even in high summer. What's more, many of the rocks are loose and treacherous. For safety's sake you should take a guide.

As for what women should wear:

> I was wearing a scarf and my Moroccan *djellaba* (flowing cotton garment) up to 4150m. After that I sewed a kind of jacket from my djellaba, leaving my trousered legs free for anybody to see. This was accepted by all.
>
> **Marie-José Wijntjes**

Hot Springs

After expending all that energy climbing Mt Damāvand you'll be pleased to know that just 4km east of Reyneh, at **Ab Karm**, several hotels have been built around hot springs. You can rent a room for the night for around US$6, including breakfast, tea and a dip in one of the baths. Be aware that bath times at the shared baths have to be assigned by staff at reception.

Getting There & Away

Reyneh is not particularly easy to reach. Take a shared taxi or minibus from Tehrān's eastern bus station towards Āmol and get off at the junction to Reyneh, which is not signed in any language but is not far after the 'Amol 75' sign. (You will have to pay the full Tehrān-Āmol fare.) At the junction, where there is a decent restaurant, a shared taxi should be waiting for passengers going to Reyneh. Either wait for it to fill up, or charter the taxi up the hill to the village. You may want to walk back from Reyneh to the highway, but the road *up* is very steep.

Getting back to Tehrān from the highway, especially on a public holiday, may take some time.

One excellent option if you have a few rials up your sleeve, or if you are travelling in a group, is to charter a taxi from and to Tehrān for about IR50,000, plus a negotiable extra payment for waiting. This allows you to stop along the way for a picnic, or for lunch at one of the many restaurants along the road; take photos of the majestic mountains; explore streams and caves along the way; and to drive further up the mountain beyond Reyneh.

ALBORZ SKI RESORTS

Because the Alborz Mountains are so close to the capital, a dozen or so ski resorts have developed, mainly catering for wealthy Tehrān residents. Unfortunately, only three of them are easily accessible and have reliable facilities and equipment for hire. Darbansar Resort, near the village of Shemshak, is best for those who are still learning, while many experienced skiers base themselves at the Shemshak Resort nearby. Most swanky of all is Dīzīn, which is the largest and most popular ski resort, and *the* place to be seen. Near the village of Shaleh, it is sometimes overcrowded. Along with the ski slopes, Dīzīn boasts summer activities such as grass skiing, hiking, horse riding and tennis, and a children's playground.

A lift pass costs IR25,000 for the day, an instructor (should you want one), IR30,000.

Information

One of the few recognised ski agencies in Iran is Iran Khudro (☎ 276 701, fax 265 555) at 33 Sadābād St, Tajrīsh Square, Tehrān (PO Box 19615/519). The office is closed in summer. The Iranian Skiing Federation (☎/fax 881 1785) is on the 4th floor, 14 Varzandeh St, Tehrān, across the road from the Mountaineering Federation of Iran.

Places to Stay & Eat

All the resorts have upmarket *hotels*, with prices ranging from about US$25/35 per single/double to US$100 for a room in the main resort at Dīzīn. A few *restaurants* serve Western and Iranian food at reasonable prices, though if you're just coming up from Tehrān for the day, it's probably a good idea to bring a picnic.

Getting There & Away

With access to a vehicle, you can pick and choose between any of the resorts along the main road north of Tehrān, and stay wherever you want (or just take a day trip from Tehrān). For example, Dīzīn is roughly 2½ hours from Tehrān on a good road, although you'll need chains on your wheels or a 4WD for the last 10km or so.

If you are relying on public transport (ie, shared taxis or minibuses from the eastern bus station in Tehrān), you will be limited to the three major resorts mentioned earlier. You will also need to do a bit of hitching to get from the main road to the slopes.

Hitching a ride between resorts with some fellow skiers is easy if you have the cheek to ask. An alternative is to take an all-inclusive ski and accommodation package. A few overseas tour operators have started to sell these, but at frighteningly high prices. It's better to look for trips advertised in the English-language newspapers, or to ask at the more upmarket hotels.

Though you will probably be charged 'foreigner prices' in US dollars, they are low compared with what you'd pay at home.

Western Iran

ایران غربی

There is evidence of settlement in western Iran as early as the 6th millennium BC, and many of the earliest empires and kingdoms of Persia had their capitals here. Standing at the frontiers with Mesopotamia and Turkey, much of the region has been vulnerable to incursions from the west throughout its long history.

During the Iran-Iraq War western Iran was thrown into turmoil; its towns were bombed and in some cases occupied by Iraqi forces. Refugees from Iraq fled to western Iran throughout the Iran-Iraq War and, to an even greater extent, following the Gulf War and the widespread oppression of the Iraqi Kurds. Although you'll come across plenty of roadblocks, they're intended to dissuade Kurdish refugees and separatists rather than because of the region's proximity to Iraq.

Only a small proportion of the western Iranian population is Persian. Kurds predominate in the Kordestān and Kermānshāh provinces; Lors in Īlām and Lorestān; and Āzarīs in Āzarbāyjān-é Sharqī, Āzarbāyjān-é Qarbī and Ardabīl. In the remoter regions tribal dress is still the norm and nomadism still widely practised.

Outside the main towns there are few facilities for visitors and only a few places are linked to the rest of Iran by air; nor will the railway system get you very far. The ancient royal highways connecting the central plateau with Mesopotamia and Turkey are still very much in use, and you'll see the remains of many ancient caravanserais along the roads.

This chapter is organised on the assumption that most people will be coming from Turkey to Bāzārgān and Mākū and heading on to Tabrīz. It then looks at the alternative route into Iran from Turkey which leads through Serō to Orūmīyeh and onto Tabrīz. Next it looks at Tabrīz and its surrounds, before considering the route from Tabrīz to Zanjān and Qazvīn. It then describes the route from Tabrīz to the Azerbaijani border at Āstārā via Ardabīl. Finally, it looks at the towns you will pass through if you travel

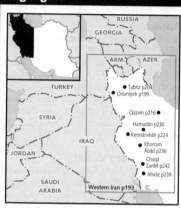

Highlights

- Admiring the tiles and stuccowork on the Oljeitu Mausoleum (Gonbad-é Soltānīyeh) near Zanjān
- Driving to Qareh Kalīsā near Mākū
- Inspecting the details of the Sassanian carvings at Tāq-é Bostān and the Qajar tiles on the Takieh at Kermānshāh
- Exploring the ruins at Takht-é Soleimān
- Soaking up the scenery on the road to the Castles of the Assassins near Qazvīn
- Getting lost in the bazaar at Tabrīz
- Watching the Ardabīl Carpet being re-created inside the shrine in Ardabīl city
- Visiting the ancient Elamite civilisation at the ziggurat of Choqā Zanbīl

south from Tabrīz to Shīrāz, Esfahān or Ahvāz.

BĀZĀRGĀN
بازرگان
☎ 04638

Despite its fine setting in the lee of the twin peaks of Mt Ararat on the Turkish side of the border, Bāzārgān is no more than a frontier settlement, existing solely to service people

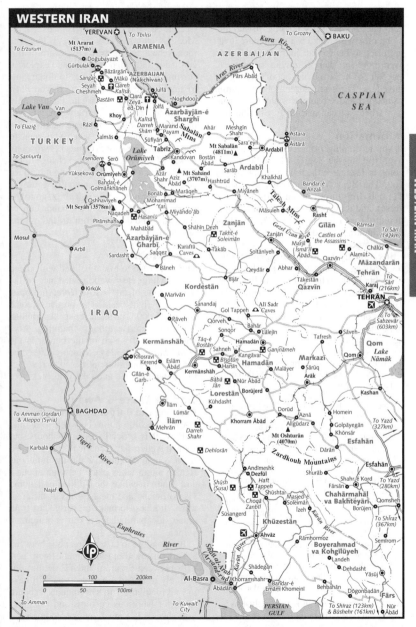

WESTERN IRAN

To Erzurum
YEREVAN
To Tbilisi
Mt Ararat (5137m)
Doğubayazıt
ARMENIA
AZERBAIJAN
To Grozny
BAKU
Kura River
Gürbulak
Bāzārgān
AZERBAIJAN
(Nakhichvan)
Pārs Ābād
Aras River
CASPIAN
SEA
Sangar
Mākū
Qāreh
Seyah
Cheshmeh
Kalīsā
Qara
Zeyā
ed-Dīn
Julfā
Jolfā
Noghdooz
Bastām
To Elaziğ
Lake Van
Van
Rāzī
Khoy
Azarbāyjān-e
Sharghī
Kalīsā
Darreh
Shām
Marand
Payam
Ahār
Meshgīn
Shahr
Astara
Āstārā
Salmās
Sūfīyān
Sabalān
Mtns
Mt Sabalān
(4811m)
Sara'eyn
Ardabīl
TURKEY
Tabrīz
Kandovan
Bostān
Ābād
Sarāb
Ardabīl
To Sanlıurfa
Esendere
Serō
Lake
Orūmīyeh
Āzar
Shahr
Aziz
Ābād
Mt Sahand
(3707m)
Hashtrūd
Khalkhāl
Bandar-e
Anzalī
Yüksekova
Orūmīyeh
Bonāb
Marāgeh
Miyāneh
Tālesh Mtns
Rasht
Rāmsar
To Sārī
(142km)
Bahdar-e
Golmānkhāneh
Mohammad
Yar
Māsuleh
Gīlān
Oshnavīyeh
Naqadeh
Hasanlu
Miyāndo Āb
Zanjān
Gezel Uzan River
Chālūs
Mt Seyah (3578m)
Pīrānshahr
Mahābād
Āzarbāyjān-e
Gharbī
Shāhīn Dezh
Takht-é
Soleimān
Zanjān
Marjīl
Ismā'īl
Ābād
Castles of
the Assassins
Alamūt
Māzandarān
Mosul
Arbīl
Sardasht
Bāneh
Saqqez
Karaftū
Caves
Tākāb
Soltānīyeh
Abhar
Qazvīn
Qazvīn
Tākestān
Tehrān
To
Sārī (216km)
Karaj
TEHRĀN
Kirkūk
Marīvān
Bījār
Kordestān
Qeydār
To
Sabzevār
(603km)
Sanandaj
Gol Tappeh
Alī Sadr
Caves
Bāhār
Sāveh-
I R A Q
Rāveh
Qorveh
Sonqor
Lālejīn
Tafresh
Qom
Lake
Namāk
Tāq-é
Bostān
Sahneh
Hamadān
Ganjnāmeh
Qom
Khosravī
Kerend
Eslām
Ābād
Bīsotūn
Kangāvar
Harsīn
Hamadān
Sārūq
Markazī
Malāyer
Arāk
Kermānshāh
Kermānshāh
Gīlān-e
Garb
Bābā
Jān
Nūr Ābād
Borūjerd
Lorestān
Kūhdasht
Kashan
BAGHDAD
Īlām
Lūmār
Khorram Ābād
Dorūd
Aznā
Alīgūdarz
Homein
Golpāyegān
Khōnsār
Esfahān
To Yazd
(327km)
To Amman (Jordan)
& Aleppo (Syria)
Īlām
Mehrān
Darreh
Shahr
Mt Oshturān
(4070m)
Dārān
Karbalā
Dehlorān
Zardkouh Mountains
Esfahān
To Yazd
(280km)
Andīmeshk
Dezfūl
Haft
Tappeh
Shūrāb
Shahr-é Kord
Fārsān
Najaf
Shūsh
(Susa)
Shūshtar
Masjed-é
Soleimān
Chaharmahāl
va Bakhteyārī
Qomsheh
Choqā
Zanbīl
Izeh
Borūjen
To Shīrāz
(367km)
Sūsangerd
Khūzestān
Kārūn River
Euphrates
River
Ahvāz
Rāmhormoz
Boyerahmad
va Kohgīlūyeh
Semirom
Tigris River
Shādegān
Landeh
Yāsūj
Dehdasht
Al-Basra
Khorramshahr
Bandar-e
Emām Khomeinī
Behbahān
Dogonbadān
Fārs
To Amman
Ābādān
PERSIAN
GULF
To Shīrāz (123km)
& Būshehr (161km)
Nūr
Ābād

0 100 200km
0 50 100mi

To Kuwait City

crossing to and from Turkey. If you arrive here late, it's perfectly possible to stay the night; otherwise Mākū is a much more inviting place to break your journey, and Tabrīz even more so. Many Bāzārgān locals speak English and make a living out of catering for travellers. There are dozens of uninspiring hamburger and kebab places along the main road where you can snack before heading on.

Information

If you're coming from Turkey it's hard to overestimate the degree of hassle you're going to face once the moneychangers spot you. The Bank Melli branch may change Turkish lira into Iranian rials (or vice versa), and will certainly offer Iranian rials in return for cash US dollars, UK pounds or deutschmarks, but don't expect it to be a speedy process.

It's perfectly possible to change money before arriving in Iran and you're well advised to do this, not least because fake IR10,000 are said to be circulating in the border region. Try Tehran Tur, 268 Ordu Caddesi, Laleli, İstanbul, if you're coming on a long-distance bus, or Mesfer Tur in Doğubayazıt, round the corner from the otogar.

> [At Bāzārgān] we were first quoted IR5000 to US$1, but were eventually offered the correct rate. We were supposed to get 168 IR10,000 notes. That takes a long time to count in the dark at 4.30 pm. The first bundle we were offered had only 100 notes, the second only 160. They then tried to say the '8' in the 1.68 notes was IR8000. We assured them it meant IR80,000 whereupon they snatched the whole lot from us, put it down on our bag and counted out 8 more IR10,000 notes. We insisted on recounting the bundle of 160 notes (for the third time) and found there were now only 142. They'd slipped back IR180,000 (more than US$20). Only then did they count out the missing 26 notes. The whole process took over an hour. The moneychangers then congratulated us on not falling for their tricks and showed us a few of their sleight-of-hand favourites.
>
> **Sean Cameron Lindsay &**
> **Sean Wayman**

An added complication is the confusion between the rials written on Iranian bank notes and the tomans people commonly talk about (see the boxed text 'Rials or Tomans?' in the Money section of Facts for the Visitor). The moneychangers are perfectly aware of this confusion and will do their best to exploit it, stirring in random references to dollars just to muddy the water further. If you *must* change money at Bāzārgān, change only enough to get you to Tabrīz where you will be able to sort things out more calmly.

It's not much easier when you want to leave Iran. The moneychangers will deny all knowledge of the rate of exchange of the Turkish lira to the dollar, making it hard for you to work out whether you're getting a good deal or not. While in Tabrīz, go to the Internet cafe and check www.oanda.com or www.turkishdailynews.com to find out the latest rate.

Places to Stay

The main road to Mākū is lined with cheap hotels within easy walking distance of the border. One of the best is *Hotel Jafapour* (☎ 2058) right beside the border. Rooms cost IR25,000. The manager speaks English and can organise money changing. Also within a camel's spit of the border is the *Hotel Sahar* (☎ 3284), which charges the same. If neither suits, just walk a few metres down the road and take your pick.

Getting There & Away

Crossing the Border Bāzārgān is the main border-crossing point between Iran and Turkey. It is officially open 24 hours, but some travellers have reported being stranded for a couple of hours, while the infamous Iranian siesta takes place between about 1 and 3 pm, or while the Turkish police and visa officials take meal breaks at different times. It's best to make an early start from either side, particularly if you're bringing a vehicle.

It's possible to take a direct bus between a Turkish town and an Iranian town, perhaps between Erzurum and Tabrīz, but this is likely to be slow because you will have to wait for all the Turks or Iranians on board to suffer laborious customs and immigration checks. It's much quicker to cross the border yourself and in stages; alone, you might, with a bit of luck, breeze through both borders in an hour or so.

On the Turkish side of the border the nearest sizeable town is Doğubayazıt where there's a good choice of places to stay at all budget levels. There you can pick up a minibus to Gürbulak at the Iranian border from outside the petrol station at the junction of Ağrı and Büyük Ağrı Caddesis (it's possible that the buses will leave from the main *otogar* or bus station in future). Expect a few checkpoints along the road to Iran, but these are normally painless for foreigners.

At the border you must walk or take a pick-up truck to the Iranian side, so hang onto some small change for the fare. Some travellers have reported demands for bribes on the Iranian side, but this is unusual and if it happens to you, just ignore them.

Unfortunately, on a bad day things may not progress so smoothly:

> After 45 minutes I got to the Turkish side…I and lots of Iranians waited for hours just to show our passports because Turkish customs were not working…The little room got totally crowded and it became chaotic. After seven hours I succeeded in giving my passport to one Turkish official, but after another hour or so, he gave it back and told me I should get my Turkish visa from the Turkish bank…That turned out to be quite difficult because the whole building was locked. In the end I found one man who was willing to sell me a visa only for dollars (at more than what it should cost!). Now I was told I should go back and start the whole thing again. I got really upset and insisted they process me immediately…and so after eight hours I was allowed to leave…Entering Iran this way is not so bad…but leaving is only for the adventurous.
>
> **Anonymous**

Minibus & Shared Taxi To get to Mākū, you can take a shared taxi from right in front of the border for IR1000 (but watch for overcharging); or walk about 1km down the road to the Bāzārgān station for a minibus (IR500). A shared taxi is quicker and easier.

If you want to bypass Bāzārgān and Mākū, there are often shared taxis all the way from the border to Tabrīz (IR20,000 per passenger).

On the Turkish side of the border, *dolmuşes* (minibuses) run to Doğubayazīt during the day. However, if you arrive after 5 pm you will probably have to hitch or pay for a pricey private taxi.

QAREH KALĪSĀ

قره کلیسا (کلیسای تادی مقدس)

The main reason not to race straight from Bāzārgān to Tabrīz is the chance to visit what is perhaps the most famous and remarkable Christian monument in Iran. Often called Qareh Kalīsā (Āzarī for 'Black Church'), the church is more accurately known as the Kalīsā-yé Tādī, the Church of St Thaddaeus. It's clearly visible long before you reach it, sitting on the edge of a promontory, behind a fortified wall with buttresses.

A chapel was erected on this site in AD 371 and expanded into a church in the 7th century, only to be destroyed by an earthquake in the early 14th century. Reconstruction began in 1319 and was completed in just 10 years. Some older parts, perhaps from the 10th century, survive around the altar. The church is roughly divided into two sections; most of the eastern part was built with black stone (hence the name), and dates from the 14th century; the western section was built with white stone in the early 19th century, and has distinctive columns and arches.

There's only one service a year, on the feast day of St Thaddaeus (around 19 June), when s pilgrims come from all over Iran and camp for three days while attending the ceremonies. This pilgrimage is an incredible sight and well worth being a part of should you happen to be in Iran at the time. Accommodation is likely to be very scarce, but if you bring a tent you can camp nearby like the pilgrims.

The church is officially open from 8 am to 7 pm daily, although it's wise to assume it may close earlier than that. Admission costs IR20,000. A leaflet in English gives details of other restored churches in the area.

Getting There & Away

It's possible to travel from Bāzārgān to Mākū visiting Qareh Kalīsā on the way.

WESTERN IRAN

Freya Stark in Iran

Freya Stark was one of those indomitable Edwardian women travellers who roamed around parts of the world where few men were prepared to go, in complete defiance of convention. Born in Paris in 1893, she grew up in Austria and was a nurse during WWI. From 1928 she spent much of the rest of her life travelling, predominantly in the Middle East, although later she also went to China, Nepal and Afghanistan.

Her early visits to what was then Persia took her to Alamūt, Māzandarān and then Lorestān, where she ransacked ancient graves in the hope of finding some of the famous local bronzes. Later visits took her to Qom, Hamadān and Esfahān. When arrested in Lorestān she was told by a local governor 'No wonder that yours is a powerful nation. Your women do what our men are afraid to attempt'.

Freya Stark wrote many books including the instant bestseller *The Valleys of the Assassins* and *Beyond Euphrates*. Although they are no longer easy to find, it's worth scouring second-hand bookshops since they contain vivid, if idiosyncratic, descriptions of Iran in the first half of this century before the towns became choked with cars.

Freya Stark died in Italy in 1993, aged 100.

Chartering a taxi for the purpose shouldn't cost much more than IR25,000, including waiting time, although you may have trouble persuading taxi drivers to take you for that price.

They may also take a circuitous route, claiming the direct road is 'very bad'; whether it is or not the detour will certainly bump up any price agreed per hour.

Alternatively, catch a bus or shared taxi from Mākū to Bāzārgān and get out at a junction when you see a sign to 'Kandi Kelisa'. There are usually one or two shared taxis waiting at the junction, and you can charter them for about IR10,000 per hour. Or you could try flagging a lift, although there's little shade and it could be a long wait.

MĀKŪ   ماکو
☎ 04634

The small town of Mākū (Makou), 22km from the Turkish border, is spectacularly situated in a rocky mountain gorge. It's certainly a more inviting place to spend the night than Bāzārgān and makes a good alternative base for visiting Qareh Kalīsā. Mākū attracts mosquitoes in summer – they presumably cross illegally from Turkey.

Orientation & Information

Everything in Mākū is along one very long street, Emām Khomeinī Ave, which continues all the way to the border in one direction and to Tabrīz in the other. The Bank Melli branch should be prepared to change US dollars, Turkish lira and Iranian rials into any of the other two currencies. Be wary of changing too much money with the freelance moneychangers.

Things to See

There are a few Urartian sites around Mākū, and on either side of the road between here and Orūmīyeh. You could charter a taxi to the small Urartian citadel of **Sangar**, about 10km west of Mākū, just off the road to Bāzārgān.

Baqcheh Juq Palace (☎ 36 455) is an impressive Qajar period building, which served as the private residence of the local governor until 1974. It's now a museum displaying some carpets and local handicrafts. It's open from 9 am to 1 pm and from 3 to 5 pm daily except Tuesday; admission costs IR20,000. It's about 6km out of Mākū, off the Bāzārgān road; get there by taking a Bāzārgān bus or shared taxi and then walking, or by chartering a taxi.

From Mākū, you can also visit Qareh Kalīsā (see earlier in this chapter). If you charter a taxi it should be possible to visit all three of these attractions in one day.

Hiking

It's very tempting to explore the readily accessible rocky hills around Mākū, but if you decide to do that, be extremely careful and stay within sight of the town. This area is very close to the border and trigger-happy guards may not understand your intentions.

Places to Stay & Eat

Beware of unscrupulous hoteliers and restaurant owners who will assume you have just arrived from Turkey and don't know the normal prices for food and accommodation.

You'd have to be feeling pretty desperate to stay at the very basic *Iran Tourist Hotel*, on the main road east of the square; however, just west of the square the *Hotel Alvand* (☎ 23 491, *Emām Khomeinī Ave*) has a variety of reasonable rooms with shared bathroom for IR25,000; ask for one at the back to avoid street noise. Directly opposite, the similarly priced rooms at the *Hotel Laleh* (☎ 23 441, *Emām Khomeinī Ave*) are not quite as good, but are larger than those at the Alvand.

Classier and pricier is the Iranian Touring & Tourism Organisation's (ITTO) *Mākū Inn* (☎ 23 212, *fax 23 184, Emām Khomeinī Ave*), west of the main square as you head out towards Bāzārgān. It's set back from the main road in a garden so is likely to be quieter than the other places. Clean singles/doubles with squat toilets cost IR70,000/90,000 (including a 15% service charge and 2% for 'Islamic guidance').

The Mākū Inn has a decent *restaurant* where you can admire a photo of the annual pilgrimage to Qareh Kalīsā while you tuck into a supper of kebabs for around IR25,000, including soft drink. Otherwise you will have to make do with the simple *kabābīs* along the main street. A few *cafes* also serve *ābgūsht* (a combined soup and stew – see the boxed text 'Eating Ābgūsht' in the Tabrīz section if this is your first encounter with the dish).

Getting There & Away

Buses to Tabrīz (IR6,000) usually leave about every two hours until about 2 pm. If the buses are full, and you don't want to hang around Mākū, take a shared taxi to Tabrīz (IR20,500). To Orūmīyeh, the buses are often heavily booked. If you can't get a seat, take a minibus to Khoy, and then another on to Orūmīyeh. If you're staying in Mākū, it's wise to pre-book an onward ticket as soon as possible at one of the bus company offices along the main street.

The station for buses, minibuses and shared taxis is about 3km from the town centre, at the eastern end of town (towards Tabrīz); take a shared taxi to get there. It's easy to pick up a shared taxi to Bāzārgān (IR1000) on the main road through Mākū. A bus or minibus to Bāzārgān should cost about IR500.

BASTĀM   بسطام

Bastām is probably the most important of Iran's many Urartian sites. Archaeologists have unearthed a mighty citadel, the largest discovered in Iran, along with great stone walls, two large gateways and the remains of a hall, together with some interesting ceramics and other finds. The settlement is believed to have lasted until a Median attack in about the 5th century BC. Much later it became the site of an Armenian village.

You can get there by driving from Mākū to Qareh Zeyā'-ed-Dīn and then taking the

The Urartians

The Urartians were a tribal people living in the region straddling what is now the Turco-Iranian border from around the 13th century BC when they first appear in the records of the Assyrian kings. By the 8th century BC north-western Iran seems to have been part of a vast kingdom stretching as far west as Elazığ in modern Turkey.

Between battling the Assyrians, the Urartians appear to have been great builders whose citadels, complete with cisterns and toilets, top many hills in the region. They had their own pantheon of gods and traded in precious metals with countries as far away as Greece and Italy. Their capital was at Tushpa, now Van in Turkey.

In 714 BC King Sargon II of Assyria determined to crush the Urartians and sent an army to attack their settlements round Lake Orūmīyeh; in the ensuing affray the ground was 'dyed with their blood like a robe'. Soon the Scythians were harrying the Iranian Urartians, but they seem to have held their ground until 585 BC when the Medes crossed through their territory en route to battle the Lydians. From then on, we read no more about the Urartians.

first turn to the left on the road west to Seyah Cheshmeh. Drive straight ahead for 6km along a rough road until you come to the tall hill on which Bastām stands.

KHOY   خوى
☎ 0461

There's nothing much to detain you in the junction town of Khoy, but if buses between Mākū and Orūmīyeh are full, you can catch a connecting minibus to either town from here.

If you do stay, have a look at the **Motalleb Khan Mosque**, dating from the Mongol period. The local **museum**, open from 8 am to 2 pm daily except Friday, contains a small collection of archaeological and ethnological items. Probably the most fascinating thing in town is the statue of two huge flamingos, joined at the side like Siamese twins, in the town square.

For places to stay, there's the cheap *Hotel Amīr*, opposite the Bank Melli, on the main road; or try the central *Jahāngardī Inn* (☎ 40 351), which costs US$15/25 for a single/double.

SERŌ   سرو

The nondescript settlement of Serō is the second border-crossing point between Iran and Turkey. There's nowhere to stay, although there are snack bars and plenty of freelance moneychangers.

The drive from Orūmīyeh to Serō is gorgeous, but if you decide to pop down it just for the scenery be sure to bring your passport with you for the roadblocks on the way.

Getting There & Away

Although the mountainous area on the Turkish side of the border used to be potentially dangerous, it is much more relaxed since the arrest of the Kurdistan Workers' Party (PKK) leader, Abdullah Öcalan. There's no longer any reason not to cross here.

From the Turkish side of the border, there may be dolmuşes direct to the regional centre of Van where there's plenty of accommodation in all price ranges. Or you can hitch or take a dolmuş to Yüksekova (40km from the border) where you can pick

up onward transport to Van. Allow a good four hours to get from the Esendere border post to Van (and vice versa).

Although there are a couple of places to stay in Hakkari, which is closer to the border than Van, we were not advised to go there, as that was one of the few parts of south-eastern Turkey still under martial law; the two hotels are usually full with refugees and/or construction workers.

On the Iranian side of the border, a few shared taxis wait patiently for passengers going to Orūmīyeh (IR3000, 45 minutes, 55km). If you don't want to wait for the taxi to fill up, charter one for around IR20,000. If you leave Orūmīyeh early in the morning, you should be able to get to Van the same day, or vice versa.

ORŪMĪYEH   اروميه
☎ 0441

Orūmīyeh (Ormia, Ūrmīyeh, Urmieh, Urmia) straddles a large and fertile plain to the west of the lake of the same name. Despite its relatively remote position, cut off from the interior by the vast salt lake, it lies on a trade route to Turkey that is increasing in importance. The city is more Turkish and Āzarī than Persian.

There's not a lot specifically to see in Orūmīyeh although it's a pleasant enough place to break your journey from Turkey and start to get to grips with Iran; the bazaar will certainly repay some exploration. If you're leaving Iran via Orūmīyeh it's a good place to buy last-minute souvenirs, although sadly you can't buy any of the pretty guidebooks available at historic attractions elsewhere in the country.

History

Orūmīyeh may date back to the middle of the 2nd millennium BC. It's one of the many places that claims to have been the birthplace of Zoroaster, but evidence of its early history is very scant. It fell to the conquering Arabs in the mid-7th century, and subsequently came under the control of the Seljuks and the Mongols. From then on, its history has been less eventful and more peaceful than that of Tabrīz.

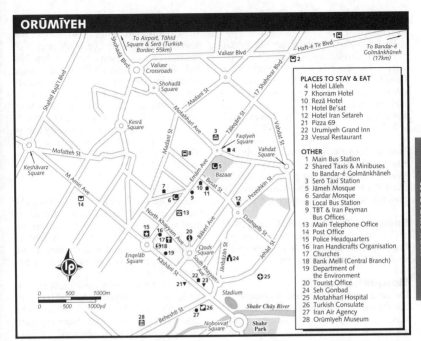

ORŪMĪYEH

To Airport, Tôhîd
Square & Serô (Turkish
Border; 55km)

To Bandar-e
Golmānkhūneh
(17km)

Valiasr Blvd

Haft-é Tir Blvd

Valiasr
Crossroads

Shohadā
(Square

Madani St

Faqīyeh
Square

Vahdat
Square

Kesrā
Square

Mofatteh St

Keshāvarz
Square

M Amīri Ave

Bazaar

Besat St

Pezeshkin St

North Khayyam Ave

Bakeri Ave

Dashqelb St

Jehād St

Engelāb
Square

Kāshāni St

Qods
Square

South Khayyam

Jānbāzān St

Stadium

Shahr Chāy River

Beheshti St

Nobovvat
Square

Shahr
Park

PLACES TO STAY & EAT
4 Hotel Lāleh
7 Khorram Hotel
10 Rezā Hotel
11 Hotel Be'sat
12 Hotel Iran Setareh
21 Pizza 69
22 Urumiyeh Grand Inn
23 Vessal Restaurant

OTHER
1 Main Bus Station
2 Shared Taxis & Minibuses
    to Bandar-é Golmānkhāneh
3 Serô Taxi Station
5 Jāmeh Mosque
6 Sardar Mosque
8 Local Bus Station
9 TBT & Iran Peyman
    Bus Offices
13 Main Telephone Office
14 Post Office
15 Police Headquarters
16 Iran Handicrafts Organisation
17 Churches
18 Bank Melli (Central Branch)
19 Department of
    the Environment
20 Tourist Office
24 Seh Gonbad
25 Motahharī Hospital
26 Turkish Consulate
27 Iran Air Agency
28 Orūmīyeh Museum

0   500   1000m
0   500   1000yd

The city is the centre of a large and long-established Christian community. Christians make up something like one-third of the population, probably the highest proportion in any Iranian town. In the 19th and first half of the 20th century, foreign missionaries were particularly active here and many of the locals were converted to Protestantism or Catholicism, but the largest churches belong to the Chaldeans, Armenians, Assyrians and Nestorians.

In 1918, most of the Christian population fled Orūmīyeh in the face of an Ottoman invasion, mindful of the appalling massacre of the Armenians in Turkey. Most of those who stayed were brutally slaughtered, but the Christian community soon re-established itself, free of the Turkish threat.

Orientation

Orūmīyeh is flat and easy to get around on foot. Most streets have signs in English, although none of the squares do. Most of the shops, restaurants and hotels are along Emām Ave, or near Faqīyeh and Enqelāb Squares. Unfortunately, most streets in Orūmīyeh have been renamed in the last three years, making most maps of the city out of date; ask at the tourist office for the latest version.

Information

Visa Extensions You're unlikely to have much success extending your visa in Orūmīyeh. It's better to head on to Tabrīz, where visa extensions are particularly painless and quick.

Tourist Offices The tourist office (☎ 227 722), 2/38 Danesh St, just off South Khayyam Ave, is open from 8 am to 4 pm Saturday to Thursday. Some of the staff speak English and should be able to advise you about visiting the lake.

Money Staff in an unmarked office to the left when you go inside the central branch of Bank Melli will change cash dollars, but not Turkish lira.

They can also manage a (non-American) travellers cheque, but charge US$10 per cheque for the privilege. If you're after Turkish lira ask around the Turkish consulate, but make sure you know the current exchange rate before making any transaction (check on the Web at the Internet cafe in Tabrīz).

Post & Communications The main post office, at the north-western end of M Amīri Ave, is inconvenient to get to on foot, so take a shared taxi from Enqelāb Square. The main telephone office is much closer.

Emergency The Motahharī Hospital (☎ 37 077) is quite close to the centre of town. The police headquarters (☎ 110) are on the north side of Enqelāb Square.

Mosques & Tombs

The large sand-coloured **Jāmeh Mosque**, inside the bazaar, has some fine plaster mouldings decorating its 13th-century mihrab (niche indicating the direction of Mecca), and a dome of very generous proportions. Although the kernel of the mosque dates from the Seljuk period, it has been extensively rebuilt and modernised over the centuries since. You may need help to find it.

The Qajar period **Sardar Mosque** used not to look much from the outside, but restoration work was in progress at the time of writing so it will probably look much perkier by the time you read this. Look for the truncated minaret just off Emām Ave.

Of fairly minor interest, the late 12th-century **Seh Gonbad** is a two-storey tower tomb, notable for its stucco and stalactite decorations. Some local historians claim it was either a Sassanian fire-temple or an early type of lookout, but it seems more likely to be a replica of one of the towers in Marāqeh. At the time of writing restoration was under way here too.

To find the tower take the second lane on your left along Jānbāzān St, south of the intersection with Dastgheib St; it's behind a fence at the end of the lane.

Museum

The Orūmīyeh Museum (☎ 46 520), in Beheshti Faculty Ave, has a small display of cultural costumes, some rocks, a few bits and pieces of ancient pottery and a huge basalt tablet, moved from an important archaeological site near the Iraqi border to escape destruction during the Iran-Iraq War. All captions in the museum are in Farsi.

It's open from 9 am to 6 pm daily except Monday, but admission costs a steep IR20,000, only worth it if you're very keen on archaeology.

Churches

The Assyrians, Armenians, Protestants, Orthodox and Roman Catholics (Chaldean Rite) all boast their own places of worship, and Orūmīyeh is the seat of a Chaldean archbishopric. Several of these churches are huddled together and accessible from Sosuth Khayyam St.

The most noteworthy church is **St Mary's**, the Kalīsā-yé Maryam-é Moqaddas. This low-roofed old building of white stone stands on the site of a much older church and has some interesting tombs inside, one of them inscribed in Russian and Persian. Next to St Mary's is a large modern church built in the 1960s and used by the Orthodox community, most of whom are descendants of a White Russian influx earlier this century.

Places to Stay

Orūmīyeh has several pleasant places to stay, although none of them will suit rock-bottom budgets. There's nowhere to stay close to the bus station, but buses and long-distance shared taxis, especially ones arriving after dark, often drop passengers off at Faqīyeh Square, within walking distance of most places.

One of the cheapest hotels to take foreigners is the **Hotel Iran Setareh** (☎ 354 454, Jānbāzān St), which says only 'hotel' in English. Clean, comfortable rooms, with a separate sitting area and private bathroom, cost IR15,000/18,000/25,000 for a single/double/triple.

The best value in town is probably the **Khorram Hotel** (☎ 225 444, Sardar Mosque

Alley), behind the Sardar Mosque and well away from the busy main road; look for the sign in English along Emām Ave. The friendly manager speaks English and charges a reasonable IR40,000/50,000 a single/double. The lobby is a great place if you want to chat up a Turkish truckie in the hope of a lift.

The *Rezā Hotel* (☎ 226 580, Besat St) is another good option. Though often full, it offers large singles/doubles with private facilities for IR40,000/60,000. In a good spot, but a little noisy, is the *Hotel Be'sat* (☎ 236 128, Besat St), with a large sign in English. Rooms with private bathroom cost a negotiable IR40,000.

The *Hotel Lāleh* (☎ 352 740, Shahīd Montazeri St) costs a negotiable US$10. The rooms are small and you'll need to ask for one at the back to be sure of a quiet night.

The upmarket place in town, the ITTO-run *Urumiyeh Grand Inn* (☎ 223 080, fax 226 478 Kāshānī Ave), also known as the Mehmūnsarā or the Jahāngardī Inn, is quite comfortable, though heavily indebted to Soviet architecture. It charges US$40/55 a modernish single/double with TV, fridge and air-con, but this is hopelessly bad value compared with what is on offer elsewhere.

Places to Eat

Orūmīyeh is western Iran's centre for citrus fruits, and many bottles and cartons of fruit juice are produced around here. If it's the right season, be sure to try some grapes, watermelons, oranges or peaches.

Baked potatoes wrapped in crumbly bread are a snack unique to Orūmīyeh. They're sold from stalls in the town centre.

For a decent meal it's probably best to visit a hotel restaurant. The large restaurant beside the *Rezā Hotel* is worth a visit; a tasty *chelō morq* with bread and a cola costs about IR17,000. Similar food at similar prices is on sale in the basement restaurant at the *Khorram Hotel*.

The restaurant in the *Urumiyeh Grand Inn* is huge, but in this case size doesn't necessarily equate with quality. You'd be better off going for a pizza at *Pizza 69*, across the road or to the nearby *Vessal Restaurant*,

which serves Turkish food in a basement dining room; an Urfa kebab costs IR15,000.

The *cake shops* along Emām Ave also sell fruit shakes and ice cream for afters.

Shopping

Orūmīyeh is a good place to pick up some last-minute souvenirs before you head on to Turkey. Cheap clothes and trinkets can be picked up in the bazaar, but they've often been imported from Turkey. Local souvenirs include decent woodcarvings, rugs and other handicrafts, and miniatures and picture frames. There are a few souvenir shops to be found along Emām Ave, including a big branch of the Iran Handicrafts Organisation.

Getting There & Away

Air The Iran Air office (☎ 40 530) is upstairs next to the Turkish consulate. Iran Air flies to Tehrān twice a day for IR125,000. There are no flights to anywhere in western Iran.

Bus Several bus companies, including Iran Peyman and TBT (Bus Cooperative No 15), have handy booking offices along Emām Ave. Some useful daily bus services from Orūmīyeh are listed in the following table.

destination	distance (km)	duration (hrs)	cost (IR)
Kermānshāh	582	11	16,000
Mākū	286	5	5,300
(on Iran Peyman; lux class only)			
Marāqeh	224	4	6,000
(lux class only)			
Sanandaj	460	9	14,000
Tabrīz	322	5	6500
Tehrān	894	15	21,000/
(lux/super)			35,000

The main bus station is to the east of town; catch a shared taxi (IR500) heading north from Faqīyeh Square or from anywhere along Emām Ave.

For places further afield (for example, to the far east or far south of Iran), you will have to change buses at Tabrīz, Kermānshāh or Sanandaj.

Note that buses to Tabrīz take the long way north around the lake.

Minibus There are four minibus stations in Orūmīyeh. If in doubt, just charter a taxi to the station handling the destination you need. However, the only minibuses you are likely to want are to Tabrīz (from the main bus station); and to Bandar-é Golmānkhāneh, from the corner of Valiasr Blvd and Haft-é Tir Blvd.

Shared Taxi Shared taxis for Tabrīz leave from outside the main bus station (IR12,500). Taxis and minibuses (but not buses) can use the bridge and ferry across Lake Orūmīyeh, a quicker and much more enjoyable way to get from one city to the other. Shared taxis also make the journey to Bandar-é Golmān-khāneh, departing from the same place as the minibuses.

Getting Around
To/From the Airport There's no airport bus service, so you'll have to take a taxi, which will probably prove expensive. From the airport (about 20 minutes from town), the taxi agency will ask IR20,000 per passenger in a shared taxi. To the airport, chartering a taxi should cost no more than IR14,000 per vehicle, but bargain hard. Shared taxis to the airport leave infrequently from Tōhīd Square.

Shared Taxi Most of what you'll want to see is within easy walking distance of Emām Ave, but shared taxis run along the main roads, with the greatest concentration along Emām Ave, and around Enqelāb and Faqīyeh Squares.

LAKE ORŪMĪYEH   دریاچه ارومیه
This huge (6000 sq km) lake has an average depth of between 6m and 16m, depending on the season. It's far too salty for anything but the most primitive creatures (such as the artimasalenya worm) to live in, but it does attract plenty of migratory water birds, including about 50,000 flamingos each year.

With its jagged, rocky islands and barren shores, the lake is not the most enticing of places. Nor is it especially easy to explore under your own steam. Most travellers will only see it while on a minibus or shared taxi whizzing between Tabrīz and Orūmīyeh. There are a few ports, several hotels and some low-key resorts along the shore, but you need your own transport to find them; the lakeshore is surprisingly undeveloped. The waters are believed to be therapeutic, especially for rheumatism.

Kabūdī Island   جزیره کبودی
The second largest of the hundred or so islands in the lake, Kabūdī is 32 sq km in area, has a high point of almost 1600m and is almost completely covered in trees. Also known as Jazīreh-yé Koyūn Dāqī or Sheep Mountain Island, it has a spring, which supports a small village and, naturally, a few wild sheep. The island also hosts a wide variety of migratory birds, including flamingos (in spring), wild ducks and pelicans.

On this island, Hulagu Khan, grandson of Genghis Khan, the sacker of Baghdad and founder of the Mongol dynasty, set up his treasury. In 1265 he was buried on the island, a ritual accompanied by the slaughter of virgins, as was demanded by the Mongol custom of the day.

Kabūdī Island is a conservation area of considerable interest to local naturalists and Unesco. If you want to visit, the easiest way is on a tour organised by ALP Tours & Travel Agency in Tabrīz (see Travel Agencies in the Tabrīz section for more information).

Bandar-é Golmānkhāneh   بندر گلمانخانه
The main port on the western side of the lake is not signposted but it's unmistakable. There's a jetty used by trans-lake ferries, but there's no regular transport to Kabūdī Island. The port makes a reasonable spot for looking at the lake and a base for **hiking** in the area. It's 17km from Orūmīyeh by minibus or shared taxi.

Getting Around
A causeway reaches about three-quarters of the way across the lake starting from the western shore, but is unlikely to be com-

pleted because of the depth of the water; you have to finish the journey by ferry. The ferry costs IR5000 per car, and another IR5000 per person, but this should be included in the fare for any through trip from Orūmīyeh to Tabrīz. The ferries travel between 7 am and 8 pm daily, and leave when there are enough passengers and/or vehicles – about every 30 to 40 minutes. It's a 20-minute crossing.

HASANLŪ   حسنلو
An important Iron Age settlement and later a citadel, Hasanlū was first settled as early as the 6th millennium BC. At the beginning of the 1st millennium BC the centre of the site became a hefty citadel with walls of great thickness and height. Despite its impressive fortifications, the skeletons of people who died here under violent circumstances suggest that the town was destroyed by the Urartians in the 9th century BC. It is perhaps best known for a priceless golden chalice dating from the 11th century BC uncovered during excavations here.

You can still see the outer walls of the citadel and the outline of the original town, with its alleys, mud-brick houses, storerooms and various administrative and other buildings, dating from four distinct periods.

Getting There & Away
Hasanlū is about 5km west of the village of Mohammed Yār, just south of the southern-tip of Lake Orūmīyeh, along the main road between Marāqeh and Orūmīyeh. You can get off any bus heading that way and walk to the site, or charter a taxi from Orūmīyeh. There are no set opening hours and at the time of writing there was no entry fee.

TABRĪZ   تبریز
☎ 041
Once a pretty oasis city in an enclosed valley, Tabrīz had a spell as the Persian capital and was until quite recently Iran's second biggest city. For many travellers it will serve as their introduction to Iran, and a fascinating one it is likely to prove too, with the restored Blue Mosque and the Azerbaijan Museum just two of the formal attractions to supplement the pleasure of exploring the enormous bazaar.

Because of the harshness of the climate, it's possible to ski near Tabrīz (at Payam and Mt Sayand) from October through to mid-May, sometimes even into June. Ask at the tourist office for details.

History
Although Tabrīz's early history is shrouded in mystery, it's believed to date back to distant antiquity, perhaps even to before the Sassanian period. Tabrīz was the capital of Azerbaijan in the 3rd century AD and again under the Mongol dynasty, although for some time Marāqeh supplanted it in importance.

In 1392, after the collapse of Mongol rule, the town was sacked by Tamerlane. It soon recovered under the rule of the Turkmen Qareh Qoyūnlū tribe, who established a short-lived local dynasty. Under the Safavids, it briefly rose from regional to national capital, but the second of the Safavid kings, Shāh Tahmāsb, moved the capital to Qazvīn because of Tabrīz's vulnerability to Ottoman attack. The town then went into a decline, fought over by Persians, Ottomans and Russians, and stricken by earthquakes and disease.

Tabrīz was the residence of the crown prince during the early Qajar period, but didn't recover its prosperity until the second half of the 19th century. In 1908, it was the centre of a revolt against Mohammed Alī, which was only put down by the brutal intervention of the Russians. The Russians occupied the city several times in the first half of the 20th century, including during most of the two world wars. Their main legacy was the train line to the Azerbaijani border (not currently in use for passenger services).

Orientation
The main street is predictably called Emām Khomeinī Ave, and it's a good idea to stay somewhere near it since there's a wide choice of places to stay and eat within walking distance of each other. The bazaar and the tourist information office are on Qods St; to reach them from Emām Khomeinī, walk north along Ferdōsī St. Government departments and transport stations are spread around town, the airport to the north, the train station

WESTERN IRAN

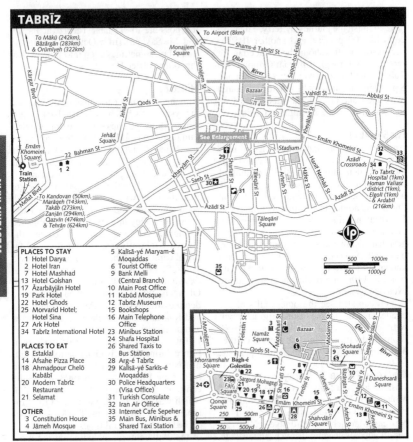

TABRĪZ

To Mākū (242km),
Bāzārgān (283km)
& Orūmīyeh (322km)

To Airport (8km)

Monajjem
Square

Shams-é Tabrīzī St

Saqqa-tol-Eslām St

Qūrī

River

Monajjem St

Bazaar

Vahīdī St

Abbāsī St

Kārgar Blvd

Qods St

Jehād St

Jehād
Square

See Enlargement

Emām
Khomeinī
Square

22 Bahman St

1 2

Train
Station

Mellat Blvd

To Kandovan (50km),
Marāqeh (143km),
Takāb (273km),
Zanjān (294km),
Qazvīn (474km)
& Tehrān (624km)

Khayyām St

Shariātī St

Saeb St

30

31

Āzādī St

Tāleqānī St

Stadium

Emām Khomeinī St

Ḥarīf Nezhād St

Artesh St

Āzādī St

Tāleqānī
Square

Āzādī
Crossroads

32

33

34

To Tabrīz
Hospital (1km),
Homan Valiasr
district (1km),
Elgolī (1km)
& Ardabīl
(216km)

Khāqānī St

Abbāsī St

35

0   500   1000m
0   500   1000yd

PLACES TO STAY	5 Kalīsā-yé Maryam-é	6 Tourist Office
1 Hotel Darya	Moqaddas	9 Bank Melli
2 Hotel Iran		(Central Branch)
7 Hotel Mashhad		10 Main Post Office
13 Hotel Golshan		11 Kabūd Mosque
17 Āzarbāyjān Hotel		12 Tabrīz Museum
19 Park Hotel		15 Bookshops
22 Hotel Ghods		16 Main Telephone
25 Morvarid Hotel;		Office
Hotel Sina	23 Minibus Station	
27 Ark Hotel	24 Shafa Hospital	
34 Tabrīz International Hotel	26 Shared Taxis to	
	Bus Station	
PLACES TO EAT	28 Arg-é Tabrīz	
8 Estaklal	29 Kalīsā-yé Sarkīs-é	
14 Afsahe Pizza Place	Moqaddas	
18 Ahmadpour Chelō	30 Police Headquarters	
Kabābī	(Visa Office)	
20 Modern Tabrīz	31 Turkish Consulate	
Restaurant	32 Iran Air Office	
21 Selamat	33 Internet Cafe Sepeher	
	35 Main Bus, Minibus &	
OTHER	Shared Taxi Station	
3 Constitution House		
4 Jāmeh Mosque		

Monajjem St

Felestin St

Namāz
Square

Motahhari St

3   4

Bazaar

Madares St

Saqqa-tol-Eslām St

Qomi St

6

Shohadā
Square

Otin
River

Khorramshahr
Square

Bāgh-é
Golestān

5

7 8

Sargord Mohaqeqi

Teribat St

9

10

Daneshsarā
Square

24

23
22

21 20 19 18 17

Fajr
Square

16

Bāzārbāsī St

12   11

Qonqa
Square

25

26

27

Emām Khomeinī St

28

15

Shahrdārī
Square

14

13

Emām Khomeinī St

Anvari St

0   250   500m
0   250   500yd

---

to the west. Note that on some older maps of Tabrīz the bus station is shown in the wrong place; it recently moved into the southern suburbs.

One useful landmark is Fajr Square with the Bāgh-é Golestān (Rose Garden) in the middle. Several minibuses leave from here.

If you want to see how Tabrīz's other half live, head due east along Emām Khomeinī (which eventually becomes 29 Bahman St), and then strike north along Valiasr Ave to find a maze of shopping streets, some of them pedestrianised, a great place for promenading in the evening.

Information

Visa Extensions At the time of writing, Tabrīz was one of the best places in the country to get a visa extension. The easiest way to get to the police headquarters in Saeb St is to take a shared taxi heading south along Sharīatī St and then walk. Once there, you'll need to look for the *yabaci polis* office (☎ 477 6666) upstairs in the main building dealing with 'Foreign Subjects Affairs'; if in doubt, ask at the information booth just inside the gate. It's open from 7 am to 1.30 pm daily except Friday. You'll be told to pay IR10,000 into a specified branch of

Bank Melli and you will need a couple of passport photos (women wearing headscarves) and copies of the most important pages of your passport. If you're lucky, it should all be over in a matter of hours.

Tourist Offices Tabrīz has one of the best tourist offices (☎ 526 2501) in the country, conveniently situated in Qods St right in front of the bazaar and above reasonably clean public toilets – there's a banner across the front announcing its presence. Staff don't speak English, but can hand out the decent *Tourist Map of East Āzarbāyjān* produced by the ALP Tours & Travel Agency. They will also phone Mr Nasser Khan for you. Mr Khan speaks eight languages and is a mine of useful information even for budget travellers. If he has time, he may be able to show you round the bazaar and make sure you don't miss its highlights. To find Mr Khan for yourself, either ring ☎ 522 9151 (cell ☎ 0911-416 0149) or call into the Watch Timer shop just to the east of the tourist information office along Qods St.

Money You can change money (including non-American travellers cheques) at the central branch of the Bank Melli, but it may be quicker to dip into the bazaar and find a goldsmith or carpet dealer who wants to do it.

Post & Communications The main post office is on the eastern side of Shohadā Square, and the main telephone office is in Miyar Alley, just across from the Azarbaijan Hotel (with a very traditional teahouse immediately opposite, perfect for relaxing in after a fraught connection). The Sepeher Internet Cafe is near the Tabrīz International Hotel on Emām Khomeinī St.

Travel Agencies One of the best travel agencies in town is ALP Tours & Travel Agency (☎ 331 0340, fax 331 0325, Bozorg Square), which organises regular day trips to nearby attractions such as Takht-é Soleimān and the Kalīsā Darreh Shām (Church of St Stephanos). Typically these tours cost IR30,000 for the day including breakfast and tea. The cheapest option is a trip to Kandovan (IR28,000), the most expensive is to Kabūdī Island (IR43,000; if you want to visit Kabūdī this is by far the easiest way to do so since it doesn't involve having to get personal permission). For the more adventurous, ALP organises ski trips to Payam and Mt Sahand, and rock-climbing trips to Mt Sabalan. It also arranges swimming trips to Eslām Island on Lake Orūmīyeh in summer.

ALP is on Bozorg Square, in the Valiasr district, which is way out to the east, but it advertises its tours on posters along Emām Khomeinī Ave.

Bookshops Along the eastern part of Emām Khomeinī Ave, there are several bookshops worth popping into. If you're lucky you'll find maps of regional cities in western Iran and of neighbouring countries such as Armenia and Azerbaijan, as well as current editions of *Time* and a few German magazines.

On the southern side of Emām Khomeinī Ave, near the Arg-é Tabrīz, there are often pavement bookstalls. Most of what's available is in Farsi, but you may find the odd book in English/French/German.

Emergency There is a general emergency number (☎ 115). The most central hospital is Shafa Hospital (☎ 807 168); the main Tabrīz Hospital (☎ 35 053) is near the Gateway to Tehrān building in the southeastern part of the city. The police headquarters (☎ 327 397) are along Saeb St.

Bazaar

A highlight of any trip to Tabrīz will be exploring the labyrinthine bazaar. Work on it probably began more than 1000 years ago, but most of what remains today dates back to the 15th century. The bazaar is a scary 3.5km long, and inside it there are 7350 shops and 24 separate caravanserais. It's a great place for getting hopelessly lost amid dusty architectural splendour, but come early since some shops (especially in the carpet sections) close in the afternoon.

The bazaar is divided into five main areas dealing with carpets, spices, gold, shoes and general household goods, but it also crosses the river to the north and there you'll find a section devoted to copperware and food-stuffs – cheese, dates, honey, helva and fresh butter.

Carpet making is still a major industry and if you poke about for long enough you'll be able to observe all sorts of different procedures; from straightforward weaving and repair work, to trimming the threads and hoovering the finished products. These days the spice bazaar is mostly given over to stationery although you should still be able to find shops selling herbal remedies and natural perfumes as well as spices for cooking.

A few shops sell old Russian samovars for as much as US$350. Look out also for a couple of shops selling traditional Āzarī hats, tall lamb's wool crowns in grey or black costing around IR75,000 each.

You may also be able to track down the odd shop where sugar is being made. Certainly you should be able to find pit ovens in which *sangak* bread is being baked.

It's easiest to get into the bazaar by ducking behind the shops along Qods St, east of the tourist office.

Blue (Kabūd) Mosque

Built in 1465, the Blue Mosque on Emām Khomeinī Ave has been badly damaged by earthquakes over the centuries, but after loving (and ongoing) restoration work it's still a strikingly beautiful building, notable for its extremely intricate tiles. The blue tiles of the portal repeat the name of Allah over and over again in some of the 1001 possible variations. Entering, you find a gorgeous open space beneath a 17m-high dome, the columns adorned with the names of Allah, Mohammed and Ali in masonry calligraphy. Don't fail to look into the room to the rear, which served as a private mosque for the shah; its lower walls are cloaked in marble, the vaults decorated with gold and lapis lazuli tilework. Steps lead down to the tomb of Jahan Shāh of the Qareh Koyūnlū tribe.

The mosque is open from 8 am to 8 pm daily. Admission costs IR20,000. Eventually there will be a handicrafts centre immediately in front of it.

Tabrīz Museum

The museum (☎ 66 343), 50m west of the Blue Mosque on Emām Khomeinī Ave, is a two-storey building with no sign in English – look for the wooden door and two stone sheep outside. Inside, it contains archaeological items taken from regional excavations – don't miss the so-called 'lovers', two skeletons excavated side by side at Hasanlū. Other exhibits include Sassanid silverware, Achaemenid drinking vessels, minor Lore-stān bronzes, pottery from Neishābūr and a copy of the Chelsea Carpet, thought to be one of the best ever made and so-called because it was last sold in King's Rd, Chelsea, London, some 50 years ago (the original is in the Victoria & Albert Museum in London). More curious are what look like stone versions of the handbags British prime minister Margaret Thatcher used to lug around. In fact they're symbols of the wealth of various Azerbaijani tribes, decorated with snakes and crocodiles as emblems of security, and used to be carried by provincial treasurers.

The museum is open from 8 am to 8 pm daily except Friday when it closes at 1 pm. Admission costs IR25,000.

Arg-é Tabrīz

This huge brick citadel (known as 'the Ark') was built in the early 14th century, on the site of a massive mosque, which collapsed more than 500 years ago. In earlier times criminals were hurled from the peak of the citadel into a ditch below, but, according to local legend, one woman was saved from death by the parachute-like effect of her chador. Well, it makes a good story.

While this remarkable building serves as an ideal landmark, it is not especially exciting and takes no more than five minutes to look round. A vast new **Jāmeh Mosque** should be taking shape in the space immediately to the east by the time you read this.

Churches

From the earliest days of Christianity Tabrīz has had a sizeable Armenian community, and the city boasts several churches, including one mentioned by Marco Polo on his travels. Probably the most interesting is the old, but substantially rebuilt, **Church of St Mary** (Kalīsā-yé Maryam-é Moqaddas) near the bazaar. Three other churches, including the cathedral or Kalīsā-yé Sarkīs-é Moqaddas, are close together in the southern part of town.

Elgolī

This pleasant park in south-eastern Tabrīz makes a great place to escape the city traffic fumes. Not surprisingly it's often full of young couples discreetly courting. It's possible to hire paddle boats for a splash on the Shahgolī Shāh Lake in the middle of the park, but most people will be happy just wandering and soaking up the views. It's especially pleasant to come here as the sun is setting at the end of a long, hot day.

There are a few *kabābīs* dotted about the gardens, or you can splash out to eat in what was once a 19th-century palace, then a 20th-century disco and is now an elegant restaurant in the middle of the lake.

To get to the gardens, take a shared taxi from Shahrdārī Square; you may need to change along the way.

Other Attractions

Keen historians might want to drop into **Constitution House** in Motahharī St. This pleasant house in a walled garden dates from the Qajar period and served as a base for revolutionaries who rebelled against the shah in 1906, furious at the influence Russia had over him (see History in the Facts about Iran chapter). Unfortunately, since all the signs are in Farsi you'd have to know a lot about the episode to make much of the exhibits without assistance. Some people will also find the photographs of massed hangings distressing. Despite the lack of English labelling you'll still have to pay IR20,000 to go in. The museum is open from 9 am to 1.30 pm and from 4.30 to 7.30 pm daily except Friday when it closes at 1 pm.

Tabrīz's **Jāmeh Mosque** was badly damaged by earthquakes and is due to be replaced by a bigger, better version next to the Arg-é Tabrīz. It's tucked away behind the bazaar, off Motahharī St.

The **Poets Mausoleum** is a modern memorial to several poets built after the death of the much-loved Tabrīzī poet Shahriah. There's an ancient **mosque** and a pleasant **park** right beside it. It's just to the west of the bazaar.

There's a **hammam** (bathhouse) with a sauna charging IR7000 for two hours along the eastern stretches of Emām Khomeinī Ave. It's open to men and women (although not together).

During daylight hours **Bāgh-é Golestān** in Fajr Square is a pleasant place to while away a few hours, watching people messing about on the boating pool and drinking tea. However, after dark some parts of it are distinctly shady – it's best to keep well away.

If you're feeling especially flush it's possible to take a **helicopter ride** over Tabrīz. It costs IR100,000 for 15 minutes and can only happen with a minimum of 20 participants. Several travel agencies about town can make a booking for you.

Places to Stay – Budget

Tabrīz is one of the best places in Iran for finding a cheap place to stay; there are no less than 17 cheap hotels and *mosāferkhūnehs* just along Ferdōsī St.

Camping There are pre-erected tents for hire overlooking the lake in *Elgoli Park* to the east of the city. To rent a two-bedded tent costs IR60,000; a three-bedded one costs IR70,000. Parking is an extra IR30,000. With a bit of persistence you just might persuade the managers to let you pitch your own tent. There are reasonable toilets, but no showers on site.

Mosāferkhūnehs & Cheap Hotels One of the best places to stay is the friendly *Morvarid Hotel* (☎ 553 1433, fax 556 0520), at the junction of Emām Khomeinī St and Fajr Square. Clean singles/doubles with private facilities, fridge and TV cost IR38,900/ 54,700; try and get a room away from the main road, otherwise you'll never get any sleep. This place seems especially popular with cyclists and motorcyclists.

Another good choice is *Hotel Mashhad* (☎ 555 8255, Ferdōsī St), which charges just IR10,000 per person in clean, simple rooms with shared facilities; showers are available after 9 pm for IR4000. The cafe downstairs serves breakfast and *ābgūsht* (stew) for lunch which is a distinct plus.

Along Emām Khomeinī St the ***Park Hotel*** (☎ *555 1852*) is reasonable value for IR30,000/40,000 for a single/double with shower (but shared toilet) and fridge. However, the nicely painted hall belies the musty rooms and the front rooms would be unbearably noisy.

Near the train station, but hardly convenient for the rest of the city, is the friendly ***Hotel Iran*** (☎ *459 515, Bahman St*), which charges a reasonable IR35,000 per person. The ***Ark Hotel*** (☎ *555 1277, Ark Alley, Southern Sharīatī St*) – named after the castle nearby, not Noah – is also recommended and charges IR24,000 a double. The pleasant ***Hotel Golshan*** (☎ *556 3760*) has singles/doubles for IR12,000/30,000; it's reasonably quiet, there's a restaurant, and some rooms have views of the Blue Mosque or the Aynali Mountains. Finally there's the ***Hotel Ghods*** (☎ *555 0898, Sargord Mohagegi St*) which charges IR45,500/68,500 for clean singles/doubles with decent bathrooms. Unfortunately the area can be a little dodgy at night so this is unlikely to be the best choice for women.

There are other very basic mosāferkhūnehs all along Emām Khomeinī Ave and Ferdōsī St. Some are more welcoming than others. A few have no showers on the premises, in which case men can use the Ferdōsī Hamam off Ferdōsī St for IR3000. Men and women can use the Moulin Rouge public baths off Fajr Square for IR3000 (they don't have signs in English, but a local should be able to point you in the right direction).

Places to Stay – Mid-Range

All Tabrīz's mid-range hotels have their own restaurants and rooms with private bathrooms. Next to the Morvarid Hotel, the popular ***Hotel Sina*** (☎ *556 6211, Golestān Garden Square*) charges IR85,000/160,000 for quietish singles/doubles with fridges and TVs. The ***Āzarbāyjān Hotel*** (☎ *555 9051, fax 553 7477, Ferdōsī St*), recognisable by

the violet columns on the outside, is the best in this range. Big singles/doubles with spotless bathrooms (squat and sit-down toilets) cost a very reasonable IR80,000 per person; those on the third floor have spyholes in the doors and safety chains.

Close to the train station, but nothing else, the ***Hotel Darya*** (☎/fax *445 9501, Bahman St*) charges IR174,000/243,000 for singles/doubles, but it's no better than the cheaper Hotel Iran nearby. Readers have also reported that when the wind is in the wrong direction you're forced to keep your windows closed to keep out the smell from the factories on the outskirts.

Places to Stay – Top End

The only place currently open in this category is the four-star ***Tabrīz International Hotel*** (☎ *334 1082, fax 334 1080, Daneshgah Square, Emām Khomeinī Ave*) which charges US$53/77. There are decent views and a ground-floor coffee shop, but frankly the rooms are not much more exciting than those for half the price.

At the time of writing two five-star hotels (the ***Shahryar*** and ***Elgolī International***) were nearing completion. A third new hotel, the ***Negin***, was being built beside the bus station, handy for early departures, but little else. Contact the tourist office for an update on the progress of these projects.

Places to Eat

There are plenty of simple ***kabābīs*** and ***hamburger joints*** along Emām Khomeinī Ave, mainly in the vicinity of the Park Hotel. In the evenings ***stalls*** are set up around Fajr Square selling tea, boiled eggs and tasty baked potatoes in their jackets. You can wash it all down with a delicious fruit juice at one of the many shops along Emām Khomeinī Ave, especially towards Mansor Square.

The large ***Modern Tabrīz Restaurant***, in a basement along Emām Khomeinī Ave, serves fairly standard Iranian fare; the 'modern' of the title refers to the pumping music, which hardly matches the traditional decor! A chicken kebab meal will come with salad, soup, bread and cola, thrown in as 'service', all for an inclusive IR16,000.

PAT YALE

MARTIN MOOS

SIMON RICHMOND

Top: Qareh Kalīsā, near Mākū, is Iran's most important pilgrimage site for Armenian Christians.
Bottom Left: The image of Āyatollāh Khomeinī graces a pool in the Bāgh-é Golestān, Tabrīz.
Bottom Right: Kandovan's cave houses, hollowed out from the deposits of the Mt Sahand volcano

Top: The outer facade of Emāmzādeh-yé Hossein, in Qazvīn, is covered in small, shining mirrors.
Bottom Left: Some of the superb, geometric tile mosaics of the Emāmzādeh-yé Hossein, in Qazvīn
Bottom Right: A dazzling turquoise tower within the Sheikh Safī-od-Dīn Mausoleum, Ardabīl

Close by is the *Ahmadpour Chelō Kabābī*; it's not signposted in English, so look for the words 'Chicken Kebab, Chicken Rice' and 'Chelo Kebab' on the window. *Chelō morq* (chicken and rice) with soup, salad, bread and a cola, costs IR12,000.

Vegetarians should head straight for tiny *Selamat* (no sign in English) at the junction of Emām Khomeinī Ave and Felestīn St, facing Fajr Park. Here you can buy potato cutlets with tomatoes and chips, felafels and *āsh* (yogurt and barley soup).

Not surprisingly for a town famed for its ābgūsht, Tabrīz also has lots of places where you can try this filling, nutritious stew (see the boxed text for tips on how to eat ābgūsht). One of the best is *Estaklal*, upstairs on the corner of Ferdōsī and Qods Streets. There's no sign in English, but someone should be able to point the way.

Tabrīz is well stocked with pizzerias. One of the easiest to get to is the *Afsahe Pizza Place* on Emām Khomeinī Ave, east of the Arg. There's an English menu and pizzas cost around IR12,000. Watch out for the low ceilings.

If you're prepared to venture further afield there are lots of other places to eat pizza in the Valiasr district to the east. One recommended place is *Balūch Pizza* in Valiasr St, which also serves Kentucky-fried-style chicken for around IR15,000 a head.

Most of the hotels have restaurants offering standard Iranian fare.

Teahouses

There are several inviting traditional teahouses in the bazaar; the best is tucked in among the copper shops in the westerly extension and you'll probably need help to find it. Another good one is upstairs, just inside the modern shopping mall opposite the bazaar in Qods St. Once again, you'll probably need to ask to find it. Both are guaranteed to be full of men puffing away on their *qalyans* (water pipes).

Shopping

The pedestrian-cum-shopping mall along Tarbeyat St is so unusual for Iran that it's worth walking up and down a few times to

---

Eating Ābgūsht

Tabrīz is the best place in Iran to sample *ābgūsht* (also known as *dīzī*), a combined soup and stew made out of beef or mutton so tender it melts in your mouth, chickpeas, potatoes, tomatoes, onions and a large chunk of fat. It's traditionally served in a dīzī (a small, upright container) and eaten with a spoon.

Once you've been served, you should pour the soup at the top of the dīzī into the separate bowl provided and drink it with bread (use a piece of bread to hold the dīzī while you pour). Once you've done that, take the pestle provided and pound the other ingredients left in the dīzī into a thick paste, which can be scooped up with more bread. You may need to get the waiter to show you how to do it the first time.

---

window-shop and enjoy the lack of traffic – except for the inevitable motorcyclists, of course.

The bazaar is by far the most exciting place to do your shopping. Some sections of the bazaar deal only with wholesalers so you may not always be able to buy just the one scarf you fancy.

If you're leaving Iran via Tabrīz don't assume you'll be able to buy all the lovely souvenir booklets you've seen elsewhere. At the time of writing no-one was selling them here, although this may change once the handicrafts centre outside the Blue Mosque is completed.

Getting There & Away

Air There are few flights to or from Tabrīz. Iran Air (☎ 343 515), on Emām Khomeinī Ave more or less opposite the Tabrīz International Hotel, flies to Mashhad twice weekly (but schedules change regularly) for IR225,000; Rasht on Saturday (IR92,000); and Tehrān at least four times a day (IR115,000). Iran Asseman also has flights to Tehrān three times weekly; you can book them through travel agencies about town.

Bus The huge, modern bus station (☎ 57 134) is in the far south of the city. When arriving in Tabrīz, get off somewhere in the city, probably near the train station, if you get the chance; then you can take a shared or private taxi to your hotel. However, going to the station when you arrive allows you to pre-book a ticket to your next destination.

Between the bus offices and the bus lanes, there's an information office in a squat, brick building; try coming here for help before relying on the annoying touts working for the buses and shared taxis. The offices for buses to local destinations can be found at the front of the main booking hall; those to places further away are at the back.

To get to the station, take a private taxi (IR5000) or a shared taxi (IR1500) from the southern corner of Emām Khomeinī Ave and Sharīatī St. At the station, avoid using the overpriced Terminal Taxi Service, though you can share them with other passengers.

Within Iran, there are frequent bus services to the following destinations:

destination	distance (km)	duration (hrs)	cost (IR)
Ardabīl	216	4	6500
Bandar-é Anzalī	416	7	13,000
Esfahān	1038	16	22,500
Jolfā	137	3	3340
Kermānshāh	578	11	16,500
Mākū	242	4	5000
Marāqeh	143	2	2800
Orūmīyeh	322	5	6500
Qazvīn	474	8	14,000
Rasht	481	8	12,000
Sanandaj	452	8	15,000
Shīrāz	1519	24	36,500
Tehrān	624	9	14,000
Zanjān	294	5	8000

Note that buses to Orūmīyeh travel the long way north round the lake. You're better off taking a shared taxi.

There are also twice-weekly bus services to and from Baku in Azerbaijan (IR50,000); and four times weekly to İstanbul (IR22,000) and Ankara (IR24,000) in Turkey. The days of departure change regularly, so check at the main station, and try and book ahead.

Minibus The minibuses that leave from along Felestīn St are handy for transport to regional towns, such as Kandovan. Ask around for the one that you want.

Train Tabrīz is connected, via places such as Marāqeh, Zanjān and Qazvīn, to Tehrān. Although the line continues to Jolfā, on the Azerbaijani border, passengers can't travel on this part of the line.

Tabrīz is one of the few places in Iran where it is worth using the train, particularly to go to Tehrān. The scenery is often picturesque, departures are regular and reliable, tickets are not too hard to obtain, the 1st-class sleeper carriage is comfortable and has a restaurant car, and the station is easy to reach.

Two 'express' trains and one 'regular' train leave every evening for Tehrān; tickets cost IR20,000/30,000 for 1st/2nd class. The station (☎ 444 4419) is at the far western end of town, and easy to reach by shared taxi along Emām Khomeinī Ave/22 Bahman Ave. The ticket office opens at about 4 pm for bookings for trains leaving that evening.

Shared Taxi Tabrīz is well connected to many places in western Iran by shared taxi. They all leave from a special section in the main bus station, which is unfortunately a big hassle to have to negotiate. Shared taxis from Tabrīz to Orūmīyeh (IR14,000) use the bridge and ferry across the lake, a much better way to go than the bus. There are also regular shared taxis from the main bus station to Mākū and Bāzārgān (for the Turkish border).

Getting Around

To/From the Airport If you don't have much luggage, you can catch a public bus between the airport and thse local bus station in front of the bazaar. Private taxis from the airport are very reasonably priced – about IR7500 – but it should cost less *to* the airport. The drivers who work for the Terminal Taxi Service at the airport will naturally want more, so look for an ordinary taxi or ask about sharing. A shared taxi to the airport is hard to find, but try looking around Khorramshahr Square.

Bus & Minibus Plenty of buses and minibuses ply up and down Emām Khomeinī Ave, but you are better off taking a shared taxi.

Shared Taxi Getting around is mostly a matter of saying *mostaqīm* (straight ahead) to shared taxi drivers, and covering short distances on foot. From the centre of town it's easy to get a shared taxi in any direction, even as far as to the train station, bus station or Elgolī.

AROUND TABRĪZ
Payam   چیام
Around 55km to the north-west, Payam has pistes suitable for beginners and more advanced skiers, and there's a restaurant at the *Payam Inn*. The season here lasts from mid-December through to mid-March.

Mt Sabalān   کوه سبلان
ALP Tours & Travel Agency (see Travel Agents in Tabrīz earlier) also organises short tours to Mt Sabalān (4811m), due east of Tabrīz, where it's possible to climb rocks and visit four glaciers in two or three days. A two-day tour inclusive of transport, full board and lodging in a mountain hut costs around US$22. A one-week tour taking in all the glaciers on the mountain is likely to cost around US$55 provided you've managed to assemble a group of at least 10 people. You can also climb Mt Sabalān from Sara'eyn (see Around Ardabīl later in this chapter).

Mt Sahand   کوه سهند
This majestic mountain (3707m), about 35km to the south-east of Tabrīz, dominates the area between Tabrīz and Marāqeh. It has ski slopes to suit all levels of ability as well as hot mineral springs and an ice lake for skating. Because Sahand is much higher than Payam, the ski season here is much longer.

ALP Tours & Travel Agency (see Travel Agents in Tabrīz earlier) offers day trips to the ski slopes inclusive of all necessary equipment for IR110,000 per person.

Despite its proximity to Tabrīz, very few people seem to climb Mt Sahand, so it's not easy to arrange guides (who are not essential anyway) or transport. The best idea is to visit the Tabrīz tourist office first, then ask around

Aziz Ābād for guides, donkeys or porters. This village, about halfway up the mountain, is the starting point for local treks, and is accessible by minibus from Marāqeh.

Kandovan   کندجان (کندوان)
One of the surprises of western Iran is to discover a 'mini Cappadocia' at Kandovan ('Chandovan' to the locals), 50km south-east of Tabrīz. Just as with the more famous Cappadocia in central Turkey, the landscape around Kandovan has been shaped by volcanic eruptions in prehistory; the soft materials thrown out by the Sahand volcano were gradually moulded by wind and rain into cones which locals found easy to hollow out and turn into cave houses. It's believed that people first started living in the Kandovan cones around 800 years ago. Even today around 600 people continue to live in them.

The water in the stream flowing through Kandovan is reputedly good for rheumatism.

Kandovan is a very popular place for Tabrīzīs to visit on Friday when the narrow streets between the cones will be crowded with visitors. At other times of the week you may have the place to yourself. The best time for photographs is early morning.

Although most come here on a day trip, it is possible to sleep in a *room* above the Dairyman shop. There are a couple of simple *cafes* beneath the cones, and a couple of decent *teahouses* serving ābgūsht across the stream which runs in front of them.

Getting There & Away To get to Kandovan, take a minibus to Osku (IR800) from one of the side streets off Felestīn St in Tabrīz (ask someone to direct you there). At Osku you can pick up another minibus on to Kandovan (IR2000), although you may have a long wait except on Friday. Sometimes you may be able to pick up a minibus straight back to Tabrīz for IR5000. To charter a taxi there and back with one hour's waiting time should cost around IR40,000.

Marāqeh   مراغه
☎ 0422
Another possible day trip is to the small, pleasant town of Marāqeh, a former capital of

the Mongol dynasty, 150km south-east of Tabrīz. The name Marāqeh means 'wallowing place for a beast', probably because the Mongols favoured this site for pasturing their horses. In the 13th century, Hulagu Khan established a famous **observatory** in a cave outside Marāqeh, but despite the optimistic signs pointing to it, almost nothing remains today and what does is closed to the public.

The centre of town stretches a few hundred metres between Mosallā Square (with something that looks like two huge tuning forks in the middle) and Fajr Square (the one without the tuning forks).

Tower Tombs Four interesting tower tombs have survived from Mongol times. The pretty **Gonbad-é Ghaffārīyeh**, overlooking the Safī Chai River, dates from the early 14th century, and is notable for the glazed tiles used to decorate its brick exterior.

There's nothing to look at inside any of the tombs, but you won't even be able to see the exteriors of the others without first finding the keyholder to open the gates. To do so, call in at **Marāqeh Museum**, tucked away down an alley off Daneshara St. It's open from 9 am to 1 pm and from 5 to 8 pm daily except Friday and although it's very small and hardly worth spending time in, one of the staff will come with you to unlock the gates to the tombs. You'll need to pay IR30,000 for a combined museum and tombs ticket.

To find the museum, come out of the bus station and turn right towards the Darya Hotel and Qazi Square (the one with a hand holding up a flame that's got lost). Cross over the river and turn left, then look for the museum down an alley on the right.

The **Gonbad-é Kabūd** (Blue Dome, also known as the Tomb of Hulagu's Mother) is a two-storey building with Kufic inscriptions in a cemetery that was being landscaped at the time of writing. The **Borj-é Modavvar** and **Gonbad-é Sorkh** (Red Tower) tombs, side by side in the grounds of a school, date from the 12th century AD.

A taxi driver will run you round the sites for around IR10,000 an hour, including waiting time.

Places to Stay & Eat Given the limited accommodation choices you're much better off visiting Marāqeh on a day trip. About 300m west of the bus station, the **Darya Hotel** (☎ 252 220, fax 250 533) is pleasant, but overpriced at US$27/35 for an air-con single/double with TV, but rather old-fashioned decor.

The only other alternative is the appalling **Aria Hotel** (☎ 222 294), halfway between the train station and Mosallā Square. Beds in grungy rooms with disgusting shared toilets cost IR12,000 each.

Although the restaurant at the **Aria Hotel** doesn't look too bad, that at the Darya is the best in town, an ideal place to relax if you're just here for the day.

Getting There & Away From Tabrīz, buses leave every 30 minutes (IR2800, two hours); there are also regular buses from Orūmīyeh (IR6000). The Marāqeh bus station is on the Tabrīz side of town, about 1.5km from Mosallā Square.

A shared taxi to Marāqeh from Tabrīz should cost IR8000; a chartered one about IR40,000.

Marāqeh is also on the train line from Tabrīz to Tehrān, although times are hardly convenient. The impressive train station is about 300m south of Mosallā Square.

JOLFĀ   جلفا

The border town of Jolfā was the main settlement for Armenians in Persia, until Shāh Abbās I moved them to New Jolfā, now part of Esfahān.

These days the main reason to come here is to visit the Church of St Stephen, Kalīsā Darreh Shām. The church is around 16km west of the town.

At the time of research, it appeared that foreigners with the appropriate visas could cross the Iran-Azerbaijan border at Jolfā. However, if they do so, they end up in the exclave of Nakchivan, separated from the bulk of Azerbaijan by Armenia; the only way to reach the capital Baku is to take an expensive flight (see the Getting There & Away chapter for more details about getting to Azerbaijan).

Places to Stay & Eat

Jolfā has a few nondescript hotels, but nothing to get excited about; the best is probably the ITTO's *Jolfā Inn* (☎ 492 302, Eslām St), along the western end of the main road, Emām Khomeinī Blvd. So-so rooms for a flat IR106,000 would be OK for one night if you've just arrived from Azerbaijan, and there's a reasonable restaurant.

Getting There & Away

Five buses a day link Jolfā with Tabrīz (IR3350). See the following section for more details on getting to the Church of St Stephen.

AROUND JOLFĀ
Church of St Stephen   كليسا دره شام

The Church of St Stephen (Kalīsā Darreh Shām) is a spectacular and remote Armenian monastery in the hills 16km west of Jolfā, at the point where the Aras and Āq Chāy Rivers meet. The road there follows the river, allowing you to observe the watchtowers and fencing. On the right you'll pass the ruins of an ancient **caravanserai**, then shortly after on the left, the tiny **Shepherd's Church**. The further you drive, the more craggy and dramatic the scenery becomes until finally you pull up in a car park just below the church.

The earliest surviving part of the building dates from the 14th century but a church is said to have been founded on the site by St Bartholomew (one of the earliest Christian apostles to Armenia) around AD 62. This well-preserved, hauntingly isolated stone building is remarkable for its fine exterior reliefs, which include Armenian crosses, angels and other Christian motifs, but it's worth coming here just for the views.

Getting There & Away If you don't want to stay the night in Jolfā, ALP Tours & Travel Agency in Tabrīz (see Travel Agencies in the Tabrīz section earlier) sometimes organises day trips to the monastery on Fridays. For IR30,000 a head, they're not at all a bad idea, especially considering the remoteness of the site.

If you travel by bus to Jolfā and then try to take a taxi to the monastery you may well be told you should have got official permission to visit in Tabrīz before setting out; several readers have written to say they were prevented from visiting when they tried to come this way. To get this permission, go to the police headquarters in Tabrīz (see Visa Extensions in that section above) and ask them to fax your details to their counterparts in Jolfā. Theoretically you are then free to take a bus.

Perversely, if you charter a taxi to run you from Tabrīz to the monastery and back no such permission is required. You'll be lucky to get away with IR75,000 including waiting time. It takes a good two hours to get to Jolfā from Tabrīz.

Noghdooz   نوردوز

If you want to cross the border into Armenia, you can take a taxi to the border at Noghdooz from Jolfā for about IR20,000; if you take a taxi from Tsabrīz for the 200km trip it will cost about IR120,000. Since very few westerners cross this border, you should expect very thorough baggage checks. In Yerevan you can pick up a bus to Noghdooz and Tehrān from outside the Hotel Erebuni.

> For US$45, a bus leaves from Yerevan at 9 am and arrives the next day in Tehrān at 1 pm. The bus is old and full of people. It takes about 12 hours to reach the border…the bus goes so slow that at a certain point even a man on a horse passed us while climbing the mountain! At the border there are no problems (two hours waiting).
>
> **Anonymous**

Another reader wrote to recommend taking the bus direct from Tehrān to Yerevan (US$45, 12 hours), to avoid getting slugged for around US$85 for the spectacular taxi ride to Yerevan (400km).

ZANJĀN   زنجان
☎ 0241

Zanjān is the capital of the province of the same name. Although it's not nearly as interesting or pleasant as the larger city of Qazvīn, it's not a bad place to break the journey between Tehrān and Tabrīz. It also makes a good base for visiting the magnificent ruins at

Takht-é Soleimān and the impressive Soltānīyeh Mausoleum. Otherwise, there's a large and busy **bazaar**, built during the Qajar period, the Rakhtsheekhaneh (a restored laundry) and a few **mosques** of little note. For some reason, Zanjān is a centre for knife-making, and hundreds of shops sell all sorts of household and ornamental knives. Even the service stations on the roads out of town sell knives, just in case you managed to resist the temptation while exploring the bazaar.

Orientation & Information

The centre of town is Enqelāb Square, about 1km south of the train station. In the south of the city, along the main road between Tabrīz and Qazvīn, there is a junction where buses and minibuses stop; shared taxis also gather at the corner of this road and Ferdōsī St.

Places to Stay & Eat

Zanjān is not great when it comes to places to stay or eat. The *Khayyam Hotel* (*Ferdōsī St*) charges IR10,000/15,000 for basic singles/doubles which some readers have complained were not clean. Right on Enqelāb Square, the *Hāfez Hotel* (☎ 24 731) has so-so rooms for IR40,000 above a restaurant. The lights are too dim to read by.

The *Hotel Sepid* (☎ 26 882, *Emām St*), just off Enqelāb Square, is overpriced in dollars, but readily sold our author a comfortable single with shared toilet for IR50,000. Luck? The restaurant is good, but doesn't open for dinner until 8.30 pm. Soup, a kebab and a cold drink is likely to cost around IR20,000.

On the main road to Soltānīyeh, the *Zanjān Inn* (☎ 771 910, fax 772 062, Khorram Shahr Blvd) charges US$17/20 for singles/doubles in cabins set in gardens, which might be pleasant were it not for the rushing traffic on the main road. Three rooms have fridges and TVs. It's hardly a convenient situation unless you have your own car, and the steps up to the rooms make it out of the question for anyone with mobility problems.

It's probably best to eat at a hotel restaurant, or you could try one of the ubiquitous *kabābīs* along the main streets. Several shops around Enqelāb Square sell milk shakes and cakes, including excellent macaroons.

Getting There & Away

There are daily buses to Takāb, as well as several daily to Tehrān, Tabrīz, Qazvīn, Rasht and Hamadān. Most leave from the main bus station, about 2km east of the city centre. You can also hop on any bus, minibus or shared taxi heading your way along the Qazvīn-Tabrīz road, particularly at the junction of this road with Ferdōsī St.

Zanjān is also on the train line from Tehrān to Tabrīz, but the departure times are lousy and tickets hard to get.

SOLTĀNĪYEH   سلطانیه

Destroyed by Tamerlane in 1384, the once great Mongol city of Soltānīyeh (meaning 'Town of the Sultans'), created in the early 14th century, is now no more than a large village with just one important Mongol building remaining intact. But what a building that is! Even with scaffolding inside and out, the Oljeitu Mausoleum (Gonbad-é Soltānīyeh) easily repays a couple of hours of anyone's time.

Oljeitu Mausoleum (Gonbad-é Soltānīyeh)

The building for which Soltānīyeh is deservedly famous is the Gonbad-é Soltānīyeh, the great mausoleum of the Mongol Sultan Oljeitū Khodābandeh, which has one of the largest domes in the world – up there with the Blue Mosque in İstanbul and St Paul's in London. Grandiose plans to repatriate the remains of Ali, the son-in-law of the Prophet Mohammed, from Iraq and rebury them in this mausoleum were abandoned after Oljeitu converted to the Sunni branch of Islam. Left with a vast mausoleum and no body to occupy it, the Mongol sultan had the building converted to serve as his own tomb. He was buried here in about 1317.

Visible from far across the surrounding plain, the mausoleum's striking dome is 48m high, and nearly 25m in diameter. Little remains of the eight minarets or the vast portals, but the main entrance on the east side leads to a chamber decorated with exquisite newly restored plaster mouldings, brickwork, inscriptions and early 14th-century mosaic tiles. The intricate, raised inscriptions on the stucco mihrab are among the finest in

Iran. An upstairs gallery lets you look more closely at the details of the decoration.

The mausoleum is open from 7 am to 8 pm daily, and entrance costs IR30,000. Be sure to walk round the outside of the building as well; if you do, you may spot 'chaikhūneh' painted on a wall amid the on-going excavations; this basement teahouse has been highly recommended by readers.

Getting There & Away

The mausoleum is just off the main road between Zanjān and Qazvīn, and very easy to spot. Catch an irregular minibus from Zanjān to the village of Soltānīyeh, or catch any bus, minibus or shared taxi between Qazvīn and Zanjān. You can get off at the junction (signposted in English), and catch another shared taxi to the village. If you want to walk from the main road (a pleasant 5km), don't get off at the junction, get off instead at the point where the mausoleum looks closest to the road and walk across the fields from there.

If you're having trouble persuading a taxi to take you to Soltānīyeh from Zanjān, ask your hotel to arrange something for you; expect to pay about IR40,000 return, including an hour's waiting time. It takes 45 minutes to drive there.

QAZVĪN   قزوین
☎ 0281

Famous for its carpets and seedless grapes, the large town of Qazvīn has always been an important transit centre, and today it makes a useful and pleasant stop between places like Tabrīz and Hamadān in the west and the Caspian region. It's far more interesting than the provincial capital, Zanjān; but if you don't want to stay it's just about visitable on a day trip from Tehrān, if you start early.

History

Founded by the Sassanian King Shāpūr I in the 3rd century BC, Qazvīn prospered under the Seljuk rulers who erected many fine buildings. It had a second, much later burst of prominence when the Safavid Shāh Tah-māsb I, a great patron of the arts, transferred the Persian capital here from Tabrīz. He embarked on an ambitious architectural plan

for Qazvīn, but the fine buildings founded here were only a dress rehearsal for Esfahān, where his successor, Shāh Abbās I, set up court in 1598. Qazvīn has been devastated by earthquakes more than once, and what remains is only a shadow of what it once was, although there are still some fine Safavid and Seljuk structures to admire.

Orientation & Information

The recommended hotels and restaurants are all within a few hundred metres of the town centre, Āzādī Square. Most of the attractions are also an easy stroll from this square. No streets are signposted in English, which makes getting around a little difficult.

Be a bit careful what you photograph in Qazvīn. When we were visiting we nearly ended up under arrest for snapping the tiles on what turned out to be a police station signposted only in Farsi off Ansārī St. It turned out there was a sign saying 'No Photos' – but only *inside* the building!

Mosques

The 12th-century **Jāmeh Mosque** retains some features dating from the early Arab period, but was extensively remodelled during the reign of Shāh Abbas the Great. Don't miss the fine marble mihrab, beautiful inscriptions and geometric plaster mouldings. The two minarets (currently undergoing restoration) and the imposing southern *iwan* (hall opening onto a courtyard) were added in the Safavid period. The pretty courtyard – so big it has its own street lights – is very busy on Fridays and religious holidays.

The largely Qajar **Nabī Mosque** (Mosque of the Prophet), down a flight of stairs in the middle of the bazaar, is also worth a visit.

Emāmzādeh-yé Hossein

This mausoleum was built in the 16th century, then renovated during the Qajar period. It is particularly beautiful, and particularly revered. Hossein was the son of the Eighth Imam and either died after a roof collapsed on top of him just after he performed a miracle, or as he accompanied his father to Khorāsān. You must take your shoes off to enter the shrine; men enter on the right,

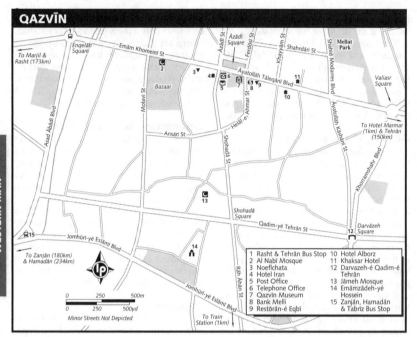

QAZVĪN

To Marjīl & Rasht (173km)

To Hotel Marmar (1km) & Tehrān (150km)

To Zanjān (180km) & Hamadān (234km)

To Train Station (1km)

Minor Streets Not Depicted

1 Rasht & Tehrān Bus Stop
2 Al Nabī Mosque
3 Noeflchata
4 Hotel Iran
5 Post Office
6 Telephone Office
7 Qazvīn Museum
8 Bank Melli
9 Restōrān-é Eqbī
10 Hotel Alborz
11 Khaksar Hotel
12 Darvāzeh-é Qadim-é Tehrān
13 Jāmeh Mosque
14 Emāmzādeh-yé Hossein
15 Zanjān, Hamadān & Tabrīz Bus Stop

women on the left. Try to avoid visiting on Fridays or religious holidays when it's very busy and foreigners may not be so welcome.

Qazvīn Museum

Qazvīn's museum is housed in the Safavid-era Chehel Sotun Palace, a two-storey kiosk reminiscent of the Hasht-Behesht Palace in Esfahan, set in a lovely park, just off Āyatollāh Tāleqānī Blvd. The upstairs houses a small, eclectic collection of ceramics and woodcarvings, only interesting if you won't be visiting any of Iran's bigger museums.

It's open from 8 am to 1 pm and from 5 to 8 pm daily except Monday. Admission costs IR10,000. In the grounds at the rear there's a small, pleasant teahouse.

Mustawfi's Mausoleum

Tucked away in the backstreets south of Āyatollāh Tāleqānī Blvd is the 14th-century mausoleum of the Qazvīn historian Hamdollah Mustawfi (c. 1281–1350). His *Nuz'hat*

ol-Qulub (Heart's Delight), written in 1340, describes the towns of Iran as they were in his lifetime.

Darvāzeh-é Qadim-é Tehrān

The Darvāzeh-é Qadim-é Tehrān or Gateway to Tehrān is in fact 140km from Tehrān, but it's an impressive sight with lovely tiles dating from the Qajar period. It has been repaired many times over the centuries. You can walk there, or take a shared taxi from Āzādī Square (changing taxis at Shohadā Square).

Places to Stay

There are very few hotels in Qazvīn, which doesn't really matter because the ones it does have are some of the best-value places to stay in the region. The *Hotel Iran (☎ 228 877, Shohadā St)* is central, and has clean singles/doubles, with a private shower (but shared toilet) for IR20,000/42,000. It's friendly, has a restaurant across the alley and staff who don't discriminate against foreigners.

The *Khaksar Hotel* (☎ 224 239, *Āyatollāh Tāleqānī Blvd*) has simple, clean rooms with shared bathroom for IR30,000/40,000; look for the small sign in English on a light-blue building along Tāleqānī Blvd.

The snazzy *Hotel Alborz* (☎/fax 226 484, *Āyatollāh Tāleqānī Blvd*) offers excellent modern rooms with fridge, TV, bath and air-con. Rooms cost US$23/35; breakfast is another IR8500.

The newer *Hotel Marmar* (☎ 555 771, *fax 555 774, Khameneh Blvd*) is inconveniently far out, but offers clean, presentable rooms for US$25/35 plus 17% tax.

Places to Eat

Some people regard the *Restōrān-é Eqbalī*, upstairs along Tāleqānī St and with a sign in English, as one of Iran's better restaurants, although others hotly dispute this. As a change from kebabs you can try the tasty beef *khōresht* (meat stew) with yogurt, rice and a cold drink for IR10,000.

The restaurant on the 1st floor of the *Hotel Alborz* caters mainly for guests, but if you ask nicely they will probably let you in. That at the *Hotel Marmar* caters for passing groups so the food is pretty reliable if not especially original.

The *Noeflchata* on Emām Khomeinī St looks promising, with its mirrored walls, chandeliers and mosaics of waterfowl; however, when we dined there the food – grey chicken and rice – was pretty mediocre. Otherwise, there are always the *kabābīs* and *cake shops* along Tāleqānī Blvd or Shohadā Sts.

Getting There & Away

Bus & Shared Taxi There are daily buses and shared taxis to Zanjān, Tehrān, Hamadān, Rasht and Tabrīz. The main bus terminal is just north-east of the Gateway to Tehrān. However, you can also pick up most buses from one of the main squares in the suburbs. For transport to Zanjān, Hamadān and Tabrīz, go to the junction of Asad Ābādī and Jomhūrī-yé Eslāmī Blvds; for Rasht and Tehrān, go to Enqelāb Square.

Train Qazvīn is on the Tabrīz to Tehrān line, but arrival and departure times are antisocial and hardly conducive to a restful night – use road transport instead. The train station is directly south of Āzādī Square.

Getting Around

Everything you want to use or see is within walking distance, except the roundabouts for onward transport. These are well connected by shared taxis (about IR400 a trip) from Āzādī and Shohadā Squares.

AROUND QAZVĪN
Alamūt & الموت
the Castles of دژهای حشیشیون
the Assassins

Tucked away in the remote valleys of the southern foothills of the Alborz Mountains, north-east of Qazvīn, lie the historic fortresses known as the Dezhā-yé Hashīshīyūn (Castles of the Assassins). It was returning Crusaders who first alerted Europeans to their existence, and they were made famous in the 20th century in Dame Freya Stark's classic travel book *Valleys of the Assassins*.

The castles were the heavily fortified lairs of the adherents of a bizarre religious cult, based loosely on the precepts of Ismailism. The word 'assassin' originates from the name of this sect (see the boxed text 'The Original Assassins'). As one might expect, the outlaws' mountain hideaways were designed to be impregnable and inaccessible. Sadly, these days no more than rubble remains, although the views and the countryside are attractions in their own right.

All but one of the castles are accessible to well-equipped, experienced trekkers only. If you're determined to see the others, hire a guide and donkeys in a nearby village, but be warned – this is no stroll in the countryside (the saddles will be uncomfortable, the donkeys stubborn, the trails tough, and the weather changeable). A complete tour of all the castles would take about six days.

The one accessible castle is Alamūt (Hasan Sabah), still known in the local dialect as 'Old Man of the Mountains' and dedicated to the founder of the Assassins. It was originally

The Original Assassins

The Ismaili cult of the Assassins was founded in the 11th century by Hasan Sabah (1040–1124), known in Western folklore as the 'Old Man of the Mountains'. At its height, the cult boasted adherents from Syria to Khorāsān province. However, in 1256 the Mongols captured its castles and consigned it to history.

This heretical and widely feared sect despatched killers to murder leading political and religious figures. Its followers, the Hashīshīyūn (assassins), were so called because of the cunning ruse used by their leaders of taking them into beautiful secret gardens (filled with equally enticing young maidens), getting them stoned on hashish, and then sending them on homicidal assignments believing that Hasan Sabah had the power to transport them to paradise.

However, some scholars think that the Assassins' reputation for carnage – and the extent of their reach – has been greatly exaggerated.

built in about AD 860, but captured in 1090 by the Assassins, who occupied it until 1256. Sadly only scant traces of walls and rooms remain at the top of a steep hill.

Getting There & Away Alamūt Castle is reached by a paved road heading 73km northeast from the outskirts of Qazvīn to the village of Alamūt, also known as Mo'allem Kalāyeh. From Alamūt, head north along a rough road to the village of Gāzor Khān (another 21km) and take the right turn out through the village square; the start of the path up to the castle is a little further along this road. Take sturdy shoes because the 20-minute climb up to the castle can be slippery (there are steps most of the way so it's not that difficult). Allow at least seven hours for the return trip from Qazvīn. Except in wet weather the start of the path is accessible by normal car.

One of the easiest ways to take a quick look at Alamūt is by hiring a 4WD car with driver from the Hotel Iran in Qazvīn. This should cost around IR150,000 return, including waiting time. The superb mountain

scenery along the road is enough to justify the trip even without the views from the ramparts of the castle.

It is possible to get by minibus from Qazvīn to Gāzor Khān, although as the bus goes in the early afternoon and the bus back leaves at 6 am you would probably have to stay two nights in the simple *Hotel & Restaurant Kouhsara* in the village. A bed on the floor here costs just IR8000 and public baths are available in the village.

Marjil

Heading north-west towards Rasht you'll pass through Marjil, notorious as one of the windiest places in Iran. Not surprisingly, it is home to the country's biggest **wind farm** and you won't be able to miss the great white sails slicing the air around the town. Just a little further north-west is **Rudbar**, famous for its olives.

ARDABĪL   اردبيل
☎ 0451

Ardabīl city, capital of the province of the same name, is a really long way from anywhere; unless you make a special trip you're only likely to pass through en route to or from Azerbaijan, or if you're heading for the Caspian via Āstārā. The main reason to come here is to visit the magnificent Sheikh Safī-od-Dīn Mausoleum, although poking about in the bazaar should keep you occupied for a few hours. Perhaps because it's so cut off, Ardabīl is especially friendly and welcoming to outsiders. Unfortunately, the choice of accommodation is poor. You could just about visit on a day trip from Tabrīz, but it would be a very long day.

Ardabīl is sufficiently high up in the mountains to be chilly for much of the year. If you come up from Tabrīz, even in September, you'd be wise to bring some warm clothing, however hot it was lower down.

Orientation & Information

The centre of the city is the triangle between Emām Hussein, Emām Khomeinī and Alī Qāpū Squares. Modarres St heads south-east from Emām Khomeinī Square to the river, which has pleasant parkland along its banks. The labyrinthine bazaar is south of Emām Hussein Square. The whole town can easily be explored on foot.

Sheikh Safī-od-Dīn Mausoleum

Dedicated to Sheikh Safī-od-Dīn, founder of the Safavid dynasty (1502–1722), this recently restored complex is a wonderful place to while away a few hours. A pretty flower garden leads to a courtyard, in the corner of which stands the charming octagonal Allah-Allah tower covering the tomb of Safī-od-Dīn. The walls of the courtyard are completely covered with beautiful tiles, so astonishing you almost miss seeing the entrance into the shrine itself.

Once inside you'll be able to inspect the beautiful wooden sarcophagi of Safī-od-Dīn and other lesser notables. You can also visit the Khān-é Chini, or House of Porcelain, especially designed to display the shah's collection of ceramics and now used as a ceramics museum; and the Candil Khandeh, or Chandelier House, where a chandelier hangs rather incongruously amid the frescoed iwans.

According to the notice outside the entrance, 'smoking and edible amusements are forbidden strictly' inside the complex. You must also take your shoes off before going in. The entrance is on Alī Qāpū Square, right in the middle of town.

The shrine is open from 8 am to 8 pm daily; admission costs IR20,000. For much of the lifetime of this book visitors will have the added pleasure of watching a team of men inside the shrine meticulously recreating the famous Arbadīl Carpet (see the boxed text), a task they expect will take two years.

Places to Stay

Unfortunately, most cheap places won't accept foreigners. One dismal place that will is the *Ojahan Inn* (☎ 22 481), right on Emām Khomeinī Square (look for a small sign above the door in English). It is noisy and depressing, but cheap at IR17,000 a room. The best middle-range option is the *Shaykhsafī Hotel* (☎ 224 2210, fax 224 2722, Sharīatī St), which charges US$15/25 for a clean if basic single/double.

The Ardabīl Carpet

Of all the famous Persian carpets in the world, perhaps the most famous is the Ardabīl Carpet, one of a pair woven for Sheikh Safī in 1568. Although the medallion design is typical of Tabrīz carpets, the Ardabīl Carpet was almost certainly woven in Azarbāyjān province or possibly in Kāshān. Measuring an astonishing 10.7m by 5.34m and containing nearly 30 million knots, it has two lines from Hāfez woven into the border:

> Except for thy heaven there is no refuge for me in this world
> Other than here there is no place for my head.
> **Work of a Servant of the Court, Maqsud of Kāshān, AD 946**

The design of the carpet is slightly asymmetrical although to the eyes of men seated at one end of it, it would have seemed symmetrical. Maqsud was probably its designer.

The original Ardabīl Carpet is on display in the Victoria & Victoria Albert Museum in London; its pair is in the Los Angeles County Museum of Art.

Mosāferkhūnehs that don't like the look of you may direct you to the *Sabalān Grand Hotel* (☎ 223 2910, fax 223 2897, Sheik Safī St). Although convenient for the mausoleum, it is hugely overpriced at IR100,000 for an indifferent room with bathroom.

The new *Darya Grand Hotel* (☎ 445 0055, fax 444 6977, Basij Square) is welcoming enough, but nowhere near anywhere you'll want to be. This makes the US$25/45 a single/double hard to take, even though the rooms are clean and quiet.

Places to Eat

There are a few *kabābīs* along Emām Khomeinī St and around the entrance to the mausoleum, but the thing to do while in Ardabīl seems to be to tuck into a bowl of *ash*, a thick, warming yogurt and barley soup sold in lots of shops along Emām Khomeinī St.

The huge restaurant on the 1st floor of the *Hotel Sabalān* is easily the best place to eat. The menu is limited, but they can rustle up a decent chicken kebab, with soup, salad, bread and a drink for IR20,000. You can round off the meal with a pot of tea in the foyer.

A couple of places near Emām Khomeinī Square sell yummy ice cream in crunchy cones, but while you're here make sure you try *helva siyah*, a thick pudding, rather like Christmas pudding, sprinkled with coconut, grated nuts and/or cinnamon. You can buy it in shops along Āyatollāh Kāshāni St opposite the mausoleum.

The Ardabīl region is also famous for the purity of its Sabalān hone:, try and buy some in the bazaar (around IR20,000 a kilo).

Getting There & Away

Air Saha Air and Iran Asseman supposedly fly between Ardabīl and Tehrān, but no information about their schedules was available when we were there. It's better to stick with Iran Air, which has daily flights from Ardabīl to Tehrān for IR100,000.

Bus Regular buses (IR6500), minibuses and shared taxis take the road from the main bus station in Tabrīz to Ardabīl via Bostān Ābād, meandering past some rare forest; at certain times of year the trip is worth it just for the scenery.

There are also daily buses to Rasht (IR7500), but to get to Zanjān you will first need to head for Tabrīz.

You may need to charter a taxi to and from the distant bus/minibus station in Ardabīl. Arriving in Ardabīl, get out of the bus before it heads for the station and take a shared taxi (IR500) into the centre.

AROUND ARDABĪL

There are several things to see within easy reach of Ardabīl, but for most places you will need your own transport.

Khalkhōrān   خالكوران

Sheikh Safī-od-Dīn's father, Sheikh Jebrā'īl, is buried in a 16th-century **mausoleum** in the village of Khalkhōrān, 3km north-east of Ardabīl. The mausoleum contains two porches, a pretty tiled dome and many tombs of Safavid-era generals. The village is surrounded by forest, which might tempt you into walking. Charter a taxi to get there for about IR7000.

Meshgīn Shahr   مشكين شهر

About 60km north-west of Ardabīl, this handsome village is famous for its hot springs (though those at Sara'eyn are more accessible), its nomadic population and the 9th-century **Arshoq Castle**.

Sara'eyn   سرعين
☎ 0452 222

For a long soak and bath it is hard to beat the hot mineral springs at Sara'eyn (Sareyin), nestling under the majestic Mt Sabalān, 27km due west of Ardabīl. The springs contain sulphur and other minerals said to be able to cure anything from baldness to syphilis. Sara'eyn is a funny little place with something of the feel of a British seaside resort (all beach balls and bathing costumes) about it. In 1997 it earned unwanted fame as the virtual epicentre of a devastating earthquake; over 500 people died and 50,000 were made homeless.

Hot Springs If you charter a taxi from Ardabīl, the driver will drop you at one of nine hot springs around the village; otherwise, it's easy enough to take your pick of the ones in the village centre. The cheaper, communal baths can be a bit grubby so you may want to pay marginally more to use the cleaner and more modern Hydrotherapy Complex, the main baths in the village. Naturally, the baths are segregated. Prices depend on the length of your visit.

Mt Sabalān Sara'eyn also makes the best starting point for climbing Mt Sabalān (4811m), which is visible from most parts of Ardabīl province. It's not a difficult climb as long as you have brought camping and cooking equipment with you. A guide is not essential, and even if you ask around in Sara'eyn you probably won't find anyone with much experience. Better to ask at Kassa Mountaineering & Tourism (☎ 751 0463, fax 751 0464, e KASSA@inte limet.net), 9 Maghdi Alley, Sharīatī St in Tehrān.

Places to Stay & Eat It's easy enough to take a day trip from Ardabīl, but given that the accommodation there is pretty lousy and that you might want to go for a few walks in the surrounding countryside, you could choose to stay at Sara'eyn instead. One possibility is the *Roz Hotel* (☎ 2366, *Valiasr Ave*), which has its own restaurant. Judging by the utter confusion of the receptionist when asked the price, they don't get many foreigners here, but the rooms are quite attractive for US$10/16 a single/double.

The flashiest place in town (indeed, one of the flashiest places in Iran) is the huge *Lāleh International Hotel* (☎ 2750, fax 2322) with inviting modern rooms with fridge, TV and air-con for US$65/95 a single/double plus 19% for service.

There are plenty of other places in town and all price ranges are covered.

Getting There & Away You can charter a taxi to Sara'eyn from Ardabīl's main bus station for about IR30,000 return, including waiting time while you bathe. If you need longer to soak off the dirt, or want to explore the village or countryside more thoroughly, minibuses leave Ardabīl for Sara'eyn about every hour or so.

TAKĀB   تکاب
☎ 04837

With its tree-lined streets and wooden-fronted shops, Takāb is a pleasant, if sleepy, medium-sized town, and the best place to base yourself if you want to explore the impressive ruins of Takht-é Soleimān and visit the Karaftū Caves.

Places to Stay & Eat
The only real hotel in town is the *Rangi Hotel* (☎ 23 179, *Enqelāb St*) where the rooms are large, comfortable and have a private bathroom. Some even have a fridge. The US$25 price for bed and breakfast may well get dropped to US$20, but you need to watch for 'taxes' and 'service charges' of around 20%, which get lumped on top. The English-speaking manager can help you arrange transport to the Karaftū Caves and other local attractions.

The only other alternative is a *mosāfer-khūneh* (☎ 22 119) with 'Pansiun' written on its windows, fairly close to where the buses from Bījār drop you off. A bed in a simple room without access to a shower will cost IR20,000. There's a handy *cafe* downstairs.

There are a few *kabābīs* along the road down from the Rangi and around the market. Otherwise the *Rangi Hotel* has a decent restaurant where a fish supper costs around IR25,500 including a soft drink.

Getting There & Away
To get to Takāb from Tabrīz you'll need to take the half-hourly bus (IR3000) to Miyāndoāb, then take a regular, but often crowded, minibus to Sā'in Qal'eh, and then another crowded minibus to Takāb. To find the departure points for the minibuses in Miyāndoāb and Sā'in Qal'eh, you will have to ask for directions. Allow the best part of a day to get from Tabrīz to Takāb.

It's easier to reach Takāb via Bījār which is midway between Zanjān and Sanandaj (IR3500, 2¾ hours). From Zanjān, there's at least one direct bus to Takāb daily.

Buses and minibuses from Takāb leave from three different mini-stations around town so you'll probably have to ask directions to find the right one. From Takāb, daily buses leave early in the morning for Tehrān, via Bījār (from where you can carry on to Hamadān) and Zanjān.

TAKHT-É SOLEIMĀN   تخت سلیمان
Takht-é Soleimān (Throne of Solomon) is one of the most interesting archaeological sites in western Iran, a vast disc rising up from the surrounding plain. Although the site is not as extensive as Bam or as spectacular as Persepolis, the setting is absolutely superb and well worth a detour. The drive there takes you through pretty mud-brick villages where, in autumn, the houses will be almost hidden from sight behind lofty haystacks.

The remains of a large fortified settlement (12 sq km) are built around a beautiful small lake which, despite its depth, makes a popular outdoor swimming pool for local boys. The original 38 towers along the wall – which probably dates from the 3rd century AD – have worn away to the same height as the wall, which is largely intact. There are remains of buildings from the Achaemenid, Parthian, Sassanian and Arab periods, many of them rebuilt or enlarged several times. The city was expanded again during the Mongol period but later abandoned for reasons unknown. The oldest remaining structures are the ruins of a **Sassanian palace** and substantial **fire temples**, which once formed part of a temple complex, now largely in ruins.

The entrance is remarkable in itself – a stone gate, with Kufic inscriptions and a tiny creek running through it. The site is open from 9 am to noon and from 1 to 7 pm daily – try to get there early or late for the best photos. Admission costs IR25,000. You can pick up a site plan (IR2500) at the ticket office. There's nowhere to buy food or drink at the site so bring something with you if you're anticipating a long visit – most people will want at least two hours here. At the time of writing restoration work was in progress, which could mean a teahouse gets added eventually.

Zendan-é Soleimān
زندان سلیمان

About 2.5km west of the ruins, a conical mountain known as Zendan-é Soleimān (Solomon's Prison) dominates the landscape. Inside some caves, ancient implements dating back more than 1000 years have been found. It's easy to walk up and you are rewarded with stunning views of the countryside, the village below and the ancient city in the distance.

Getting There & Away
From Takāb, it's possible to take a minibus (IR1000) to the tiny village of Nosratabad, 42km from Takāb which allows you plenty of time to explore the ruins and climb the nearby mountain.

The easiest, but most expensive, way is to charter a taxi from Takāb. Just hail any empty taxi, and then expect to pay about IR40,000 for the return trip, including about one hour's waiting time, the bare minimum you'll need for the site.

With your own car, leave Takāb heading towards Miyāndoāb and keep driving until you come to a sign on the right, reading Takht-é Soleimān, 37km.

KARAFTŪ CAVES
غار کرفتو

If you take a powerful torch (flashlight) you can explore the labyrinthine chambers and passageways of the Karaftū Caves, 25km south-west of Takāb. Among other traces of what must once have been a sanctuary carved out of the cliff, there is a Greek inscription mentioning Heracles (Hercules), who had a cult following in this region during the period. You will need to charter a 4WD vehicle to get there from Takāb. Ask at the Rangi Hotel and they should be able to arrange something for about IR60,000 return, including waiting time.

BĪJĀR
بیجار

The small junction town of Bījār, midway between Sanandaj and Zanjān, and between Takāb and Hamadān, is one of the highest in the country, so it's appallingly cold in winter. There is nowhere to stay, but if you are camping, or want to take a day trip from Takāb, there's some wonderful **hiking** and **rock climbing** in the area. If you have a vehicle and a local guide, you can also explore the remains of nearby ancient cities, such as **Qom Choga**, which retains some castle walls dating back about 3000 years.

Minibuses to Takāb (IR2500) and Sanandaj (IR4000) leave from a small station near Tāleqānī Square. Shared taxis also wait at the turn-off north to Takāb.

SANANDAJ
سنندج

☎ 04321

Although Sanandaj dates back to at least the Middle Ages, it is not of any great architectural or historical interest. Instead, most travellers come to what is now Iran's most Kurdish settlement for a glimpse of the Kurdish way of life. Here you'll find men dressed in traditional boiler suits and cummerbunds, and women in colourful dresses, a world away from the dreary conformity of Tehrān.

Sanandaj makes a pleasant enough place in which to while away a day or so although politics is never far from the surface in a town with unemployment of about 18%. If you've arrived from Turkey, don't be surprised if the first question you get asked is about Abdullah Öcalan, the jailed leader of the Kurdistan Workers' Party (PKK), revered here, as elsewhere in the Kurdish world, as a freedom fighter rather than a terrorist.

Orientation & Information

The two main squares are the northern Enqelāb Square (with giant white sculpted faces) and Āzādī Square (with fountains and a statue of a figure with an arm thrown up in the air) to the south. They are connected by the main shopping thoroughfare, Ferdōsī St. The bazaar district stretches east of Enqelāb Square.

The vast central branch of the Bank Melli is just east of Āzādī Square; the main post office 150m to the north-west; and the main telephone office 250m east of the same square. A few bookshops along Ferdōsī St sell the Gita Shenasi map of Sanandaj.

Things to See & Do

At the time of writing, the Sanandaj Museum (☎ 5455), housed in a fine early 16th-century building on the south side of Emām Khomeinī St, about 400m north-west of Enqelāb Square, was closed for restoration. When it reopens, expect to see archaeological exhibits and displays about the Kurds in lovely rooms set round a garden courtyard.

Nearby, the large Jāmeh Mosque dates from 1813 and has some attractive Qajar tiles, a dome, two pretty minarets and a shady courtyard with a small ablutions pool.

In the south-westerly district of Khosrow Abad a fine Qajar-dynasty private house is also under restoration. Once it's completed you will be able to stroll in a wonderful garden. To get there take a shared taxi along Bolvār-é Shebli from Āzādī Square and ask to be dropped off nearby.

About 4km east of Sanandaj is the impressive, though much reconstructed, Qeshlakh Bridge, reminiscent of the Sī-o-Seh Bridge in Esfahān, but not nearly as grand.

Approximately 10km north of the city is the enormous Vahdat Dam, which is great for fishing. You can also go hiking in the area.

Places to Stay & Eat

Most of the mosāferkhūnehs around the bazaar are reluctant to take foreigners, so you are really forced to stay at one of three places. Two are central, with signs in English, and offer clean doubles with bathrooms. The *Hedayat Hotel* (☎ 222 4117, Ferdōsī St), nearer to Enqelāb Square, has doubles for IR30,000, but may not be keen to take lone women. The friendly *Abidor Hotel* (☎ 324 1645, Ferdōsī St) charges IR55,000 for a small, clean double. The other alternative is the ITTO's *Sanandaj Inn* (☎ 63 525, Pasdaran St), which is overpriced at US$50 for a room with no single discounts. It's also inconveniently positioned, 2km away from Āzādī Square, so you'll need to charter a taxi.

There are a few *snack bars* and *kabābīs* around the two main squares, and a handful of smarter places along Abidor St, west of Āzādī Square; look for *Cactus* on the north side of the road if you fancy pizza or a burger, or for two classier eateries, no signs in English, on the south side. The *Abidor Hotel* has a pleasant ground-floor restaurant although the menu is restricted to kebabs.

There are lots of juice bars along Ferdōsī St, some selling ice cream as well.

Shopping

All along Ferdōsī St you'll see shops selling comfortable *givehs*, woven shoes similar to the *kalashs* of Kermānshāh, but especially popular in white instead of black.

Getting There & Away

Air Iran Air flies from Sanandaj to Tehrān three times weekly (IR94,000).

Bus & Minibus Some bus companies have booking offices around Enqelāb Square. The main bus and minibus station is in the south of the town (take a shared taxi to get there); the smaller station in the north has buses and minibuses to regional villages. The following table lists some useful daily minibus and bus services:

destination	distance (km)	duration (hr)	cost (IR)
Hamadān (minibus only)	176	3	3200
Kermānshāh (minibus only)	136	2	2600
Tabrīz	442	8	15,000
Tehrān (lux/super)	512	9	3,500/ 28,000

For places such as Īlām and Ahvāz you will probably have to change bus in Kermānshāh.

Shared Taxi Shared taxis to Kermānshāh (IR4400) and Hamadān (IR8000) leave from the southern bus/minibus station.

Getting Around
Everything except the bus station is within walking distance of the town centre. Shared and private taxis are available for longer trips. The airport is about 6km south of the city; charter a taxi to get there.

KERMĀNSHĀH   کرمانشاه
☎ 0431
An important station on the ancient trading route to Baghdad, s is by far the largest and busiest city in this part of Iran. With a beautiful setting, framed by permanently snow-clad mountains, it makes the perfect place to base yourself while exploring the surrounding area. Kermānshāh should be avoided in winter, but the climate is very pleasant for the rest of the year.

History
First built on a site a few kilometres from the present town, Kermānshāh probably dates from the 4th century AD. Its vulnerable position has always rendered it liable to invasion – it was captured by the Arabs in AD 649, assaulted by the Seljuks in the 11th century, and then sacked by the Mongols in the early 13th century. After several centuries of relative peace and prosperity, Kermānshāh's strategic position on the road to Baghdad brought it heavy missile and bomb attacks from Iraq during the Iran-Iraq War; new buildings are slowly going up in the spaces left.

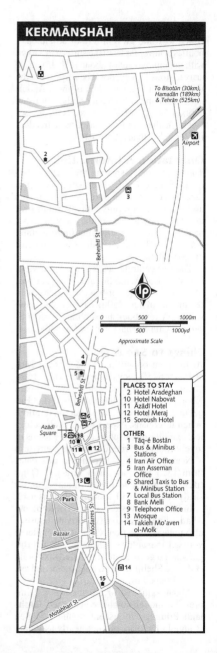

KERMĀNSHĀH

To Bīsotūn (30km), Hamadān (189km) & Tehrān (525km)

Airport

Beheshtī St

0   500   1000m
0   500   1000yd
Approximate Scale

Beheshtī St

Āzādī Square

Park

Bazaar

Modarres St

Motahhari St

PLACES TO STAY
2 Hotel Aradeghan
10 Hotel Nabovat
11 Āzādī Hotel
12 Hotel Meraj
15 Soroush Hotel

OTHER
1 Tāq-é Bostān
3 Bus & Minibus Stations
4 Iran Air Office
5 Iran Asseman Office
6 Shared Taxis to Bus & Minibus Station
7 Local Bus Station
8 Bank Melli
9 Telephone Office
13 Mosque
14 Takieh Mo'aven ol-Molk

Orientation & Information

Kermānshāh is one of the few major towns in Iran without street signs in English. Still, it's easy enough to get around, and most of what you want is along Modarres St, between the mammoth Āzādī Square and the junction with Motahharī St. Tāq-é Bostān is way out to the north, not far from the main bus station.

The enormous new Bank Melli building overlooking Āzādī Square is no more likely to want to change money than the nearby branches of Bank Mellat and Bank Sepah, although you could give it a whirl.

For medical emergencies call ☎ 20 050; for the police ☎ 834 404.

Tāq-é Bostān   طاق بستان

One of the highlights of any visit to western Iran, and the main reason for coming to Kermānshāh, are the bas-reliefs and carved alcoves at Tāq-é Bostān, which date back to the Sassanian dynasty and overlook a large pool and pleasant garden.

As you enter from the main gate you will see a large grotto, with a lower panel depicting an armoured figure seated on a horse and holding a lance, looking for all the world like a medieval knight jousting. The upper panel shows a royal investiture. Both are believed to represent Khosrō II, a contemporary of the Prophet Mohammed and a famous hunter. The walls of the grotto are decorated with wonderful reliefs of royal hunting parties; to the right men on horses and elephants hunting stags and deer, to the left more wild boars than you could possibly imagine. Two winged angels, representing victory, adorn the facade. Originally decorated in bright colours, the figures here are more formal and stylised than those on the Darius relief at Bīsotūn (see the Around Kermānshāh section later).

Next to this main grotto, a small arched recess carved out of the cliff in the 4th century AD shows Shāpūr II and his grandson, Shāpūr III. It was created by the latter as testament to his own dynastic credentials.

Further along are carvings depicting the investiture of Ardeshīr II by the deities Ahura Mazda, to the right, and Mithras, to the left (holding a symbolic sacred bunch of twigs). At the same time it celebrates a victory over the Romans.

The gardens are open from 8 am to sunset daily; entrance costs IR20,000. After visiting them you can relax over a meal or pot of tea in a nearby tea garden. Try to avoid coming here on a Friday or public holiday, when the place will be wall-to-wall picnickers.

To reach the gardens, take a shared taxi from the huge square next to the bus station – there are signs to the gardens in English. Afterwards, you could stroll the 4km back to the square, and take a shared taxi back to the city centre. A private taxi from the bus station to the gardens costs about IR5000.

Takieh Mo'aven ol-Molk

تکیه معاون الملک

The other reason for visiting Kermānshāh is to see the Takieh Mo'aven ol-Molk, which is not far from the Soroush Hotel. The Takieh is a Qajar-period Hosseinieh, one of those distinctively Iranian buildings commemorating the martyrdom of Hossein and used for rituals during the mourning period of Moharram. This is a particularly impressive example, the walls of the main chamber and all three of its courtyards completely covered in tiles, which repay detailed examination.

In the courtyard after the ticket office a large tiled panel on the right shows men flagellating themselves during Moharram. In the domed chamber the tiles mainly depict the story of Hossain's martyrdom at Karbala (the imam has the halo and green face veil), but you'll also find one showing an early attempt at flying. Finally, in the courtyard at the back there are tiles showing the wide range of clothing worn in late 19th-century Iran; a magnificent panel on the left shows dervishes with all their paraphernalia (see the boxed text 'The Dervishes of Iran').

The Takieh is open from 8 am to noon and from 4 to 8 pm daily except Friday. Admission costs IR20,000.

Places to Stay

Kermānshāh has a passable choice of places to stay. Most cheapies don't want foreigners, but you should still find something suitable.

The Dervishes of Iran

As in neighbouring Turkey, Iran's dervishes are viewed with suspicion by the religious establishment. Not unlike the wandering holy men of India, they are mystics whose religious practices include 40-day retreats during which they slowly reduce their food intake until they can reputedly survive on one date a day.

As is often the case, much anguish is caused over what might seem to an outsider like minor variations on a theme. All Shiite Muslims revere Emām Ali, Mohammed's son-in-law and the fourth caliph who they believe was wrongly dispossessed of his inheritance. However, the dervishes place such emphasis on Emām Ali that the ulema (religious leaders) think they come close to venerating him as a god.

Like Buddhist monks, the dervishes rely on donations to keep them going, and they carry round a special kashkool container full of rosewater with which to sprinkle those who give. (Unfortunately, these days some of them have become active beggars.) Many dervishes also carry a small ornamental axe. Iran's ethnography museums often contain complete sets of dervish accoutrements, including robes with Quranic texts handwritten all over them.

The dervishes have their own places of worship called khūneh-qahs. These are rectangular halls, with carpets and sheepskin rugs on the floor and pictures of Ali around the walls. It's not easy to identify these places (images of kashkools and axes are pointers) and you would really need an invitation to go inside one.

There is a particularly strong dervish presence in far western Iran, perhaps because it is on the road to Najaf in Iraq where Ali is buried.

The best of the budget range is the friendly **Hotel Nabovat** (☎ 831 018, Modarres St) which charges IR20,000/30,000 for cleanish if noisy singles/doubles. It's about 10m down a lane, just off Āzādī Square; look for the English sign, 'A Hotel An Inn'. The nearby **Āzādī Hotel** (☎ 833 076, Modarres St) offers cleaner, more modern rooms for IR50,000.

Across the road, the **Hotel Meraj** (☎ 833 288, Modarres St) charges IR80,000/140,000

for clean singles/doubles with shower, but shared toilet.

The **Soroush Hotel** (☎ 27 001, Modarres Crossroad) is a bit out of the way, although the location is likely to be quieter and is handy for the Takieh and bazaar. Comfortable rooms with decent bathrooms cost IR160,000.

The new **Hotel Aradeghan** (☎ 99 666, fax 93 503) is pleasant enough, but way overpriced at US$65 for a room (no single discounts) way out in the suburbs. It has all the trappings you'd expect of an upmarket hotel – fridge, TV, air-con – but you'll be paying a *lot* more for very little extra comfort.

Places to Eat

There are plenty of **kabābīs** and **cake** and **sweet shops**, around the southern parts of Āzādī Square and along Motahharī St. Both the **Soroush Hotel** and the **Hotel Aradeghan** have decent restaurants.

Easily the best places for lunch and a relaxing pot of tea are the restaurants and teahouses at Tāq-é Bostān. Around the entrance and along the main roads to the site there are dozens of pleasant *restaurants* where fried chicken, kebabs and sometimes fish are available for lunch. Our favourite was the place with the shady courtyard across from the site entrance, with 'Beef Chicken Kebab' written on the side wall; a really good, large chicken kebab and soft drink cost IR16,000. Even if time is short, you should at least stay for a pot of tea and a puff on a qalyan.

Shopping

The large bazaar spreads out on either side of Modarres St, but the ramshackle covered area on the east side is the most interesting. Here you can pick up a few items unique to the province, including a kind of woven shoe known as a *giveh* (IR20,000), sweets called *nān-é berenjī* (rice bread) and a type of guitar known as a *tar*.

Getting There & Away

Air Iran Air (☎ 848 814) has daily flights to Tehrān for IR98,000, and weekly flights to Mashhad for IR150,000. Iran Asseman (☎ 831 255) flies to Tehrān four times a week for the same price. The airport is small, chaotic and hopelessly inadequate, so allow plenty of time to check in.

Bus & Minibus Some daily bus and minibus services are listed in the following table:

destination	distance (km)	duration (hrs)	cost (IR)
Ahvāz	509	9	13,000
Esfahān	665	9	14,000
Hamadān	189	3	4000
Īlām (minibus only)	208	4	6000
Khorram Ābād (minibus only)	197	5	7500
Orūmīyeh	582	11	16,000
Sanandaj (minibus only)	136	2	4000
Shīrāz	1077	18	24,500
Tabrīz	578	11	18,500
Tehrān	525	9	13,500

The main bus and minibus stations are side by side, a long way north-east of Āzādī Square – take a shared taxi from the junction near the walkway, or bus No 2 from the local bus station. The locals in the station are very helpful, and if you look lost or helpless, someone – probably a bus tout – will show you where to go. If you haven't pre-booked a ticket and just turn up at the station, you will probably find something going your way in less than 30 minutes.

Note that queues for minibuses to Sanandaj can be particularly long, demand clearly outstripping supply.

Shared Taxi To get to major regional centres such as Hamadān, Īlām, Khorram Ābād and Sanandaj, take one of the shared taxis which leave from the main bus/minibus station.

Getting Around
To/From the Airport You may be lucky enough to find a local bus going between the airport and the local bus station on Āzādī Square, but you'll probably end up having to take a shared taxi to/from the taxi junction at Āzādī Square for about IR2000. A private taxi between your hotel and the airport should cost no more than IR10,000.

Bus The local bus station is next to the walkway on Āzādī Square. Bus No 2 is the one you're most likely to use since it links Āzādī Square with the Iran Air/Iran Asseman offices and the bus station.

Taxi You will probably only need to use a shared taxi to travel down Modarres St (which is a one-way street heading south) or out to the bus/minibus station (IR500). Naturally, Āzādī Square is the station for shared taxis, and there are hundreds of them heading in all directions. If in doubt, ask and ask again to make sure you're going the right way. The taxi drivers at the main bus station are inclined to behave like a flock of rapacious vultures.

AROUND KERMĀNSHĀH
The most obvious day trip out of Kermānshāh would take in the bas-reliefs at Bīsotūn and the temple of Anahita in Kangāvar. However, at the time of writing the Bīsotūn carvings were completely hidden behind scaffolding which looked as if it would be there for some time to come. Since the temple is of rather specialist interest you might want to try to find out whether the scaffolding is still in place before setting out.

Bīsotūn بیستون
The village of Bīsotūn is 30km east of Kermānshāh. Overlooking the main road to Hamadān, and 1km west of the village, are famous bas-reliefs carved out of a dramatic mountain imbued with religious significance in pre-Islamic times. Carved in three languages, the inscriptions on these bas-reliefs did for Old Persian what the Rosetta Stone did for Egyptian hieroglyphs. Hanging on the end of a rope, the soldier Henry Rawlinson copied them down in 1838 and then painstakingly worked out what the Persian version said; later scholars followed on by translating the Neo-Babylonian and Elamite texts. What they read was a unique contemporary account of the events of his reign by the Achaemenid king Darius!

Bas-Reliefs Get out of the bus from Kermānshāh and walk back the way it came,

WESTERN IRAN

bearing right when the road curves so you follow the cliff-face behind the village. Before long you'll come to an unimpressive mid-2nd-century BC **sculpture of Hercules** (Heracles) reclining beneath a tacky tin shelter. Across the road is what may one day be a pleasant small lake once restoration work has been completed.

Just past Hercules, steps lead up the rock face towards the famous **tablet of Darius I** which shows his hard-won victory over several rebel princes, including the pretender Gaumata, who had passed himself off as Cyrus the Great's second son Bardiya. The figure of the king is taller than that of any of the other mortals and is overshadowed only by the symbol of the deity Ahura Mazda hovering above the whole group. To see what the tablet would look like without the scaffolding, go to the cafe across the road and inspect the photo of it on the wall there (be careful though, one of the men working there molested one of our authors when she tried to do just that).

Of the two other heavily eroded **Parthian bas-reliefs**, the one on the left shows King Mithridates standing before four supplicants. The one on the right depicts several scenes relating to Gotarzes II including one of him on horseback spearing an enemy, another of him at his investiture, and a third at a religious ritual. A much later Safavid inscription in Arabic has defaced these.

Continue walking past the cafe and you will see a vast, exceptionally smooth **stone panel** cut into the rock in what was once probably an ancient stone quarry.

Walk back through Bīsotūn village to see a 115m Safavid-period **bridge**, which was partly built from stone taken from structures dating back to the Sassanian era.

Getting There & Away To get to Bīsotūn you can take any bus travelling between Kermānshāh and Hamadān. Alternatively, from Kermānshāh minibuses (IR750) leave every 10 to 15 minutes for Bīsotūn village and will drop you on the main road in the village. You can save yourself some time by getting out before the village and walk-

ing across the fields to the carvings, if you're sharp-eyed enough to spot them before arriving. Coming in the opposite direction from Hamadān, you will certainly have to walk from the village to the carvings.

You can easily combine a visit to Bīsotūn with one to Kangāvar (see the following section).

Alternatively, since the area around Kermānshāh is begging to be explored on foot and the best hiking spots are along the road to Bīsotūn, you could just hop off the bus on the way back and strike out in whatever direction you like (remembering to be careful if you come across anything that looks like a military area, of course).

Kangāvar كنگاور

The city of Kangāvar was built during the Parthian period, and boasted a fine temple dedicated to Anahita, the water goddess. Although it is thought to have been influenced by Persepolis, what you see today is a somewhat disappointing collection of rocks and half-demolished columns, giving little idea of what the city may have looked like originally. None of the remains have been identified or restored, making it a site for serious archaeology buffs only.

The site is open from about 8.30 am to 6 pm daily; entrance costs IR20,000.

Getting There & Away Kangāvar is about halfway between Kermānshāh and Hamadān, and accessible by public transport travelling between them. From Kermānshāh, the ruins can be combined with a trip to Bīsotūn by taking a minibus or shared taxi 25km east from Bīsotūn village to the small, pretty town of Sahneh, and then another minibus or shared taxi 30km east to Kangāvar. The fare from Bīsotūn to Kangāvar shouldn't exceed IR3500.

Coming from Kermānshāh the ruins are on the left-hand side of the road; ask to be dropped off at 'Anahita' (there's a sign along the main road in English).

If you're lucky you'll find a direct minibus back to Kermānshāh from the Kangāvar minibus station (IR1900), which is on the western side of town.

ĪLĀM

ایلام

☎ 08495

Until just before WWII this city was the seat of the Vālī Khāns, the Lor chieftains of the region. Although remains of their palaces can still be seen in the north of Īlām province, the town itself is uninteresting and a bit too close to the Iraqi border for comfort.

The main street, Heidarī St, changes its name to Ferdōsī St as it heads west. Most of the offices and restaurants are around 22 Bahman Square.

Places to Stay & Eat

Īlām's best hotel is the ITTO's *Jahāngardī Inn* (☎ 32 470, Jonūbī Blvd), which charges foreigners US$20/30 for a pleasant single/double. Other cheaper places for around IR80,000 a double include the *Lāleh Hotel* (☎ 32 895, Heidarī St), and the *Hotel Dalahou* (☎ 36 898, Vasetī St). It's probably best to eat at one of the hotels.

Getting There & Away

Currently, there is no legal crossing into Iraq from Īlām province for independent travellers.

Iran Asseman supposedly flies between Īlām and Tehrān (IR119,000) four times weekly, but flights are not reliable. Tiny Saha Air also links Tehrān with Īlām, but is also unreliable. Book tickets for either airline at the airport or at a travel agency in Tehrān.

There are direct buses daily from Īlām to Ahvāz, Khorram Ābād, Sanandaj and Tehrān. Otherwise take a minibus to Kermānshāh (IR6500) and pick up a connection.

HAMADĀN

همدان

☎ 0261 • pop 400,000

Hamadān (Hamedān) has always been a major stop on the ancient royal road to Baghdad, and it remains an important trading and transit point. The population is largely Persian, with a significant Āzarī minority. A sizeable Jewish community has been here at least since the 5th century AD, and possibly as far back as the time of Xerxes I. Sadly the once-flourishing Jewish community is now down to just 35 souls.

Karbala & Najaf

As you pass along the road from Hamadān to Kermānshāh you may be surprised to see signs to Karbala, even though it's more than 500km away and not even in Iran. But Karbala is where the third imam, the revered Hossein, was martyred in AD 680.

After the murder of Ali, the caliphate had passed to Mu'awiyah, the governor of Syria. On his death, he was succeeded by his son Yezid. Yezid demanded that Hossein, Ali's son, declare allegiance to him, at the same time as the citizens of the Iraqi town of Kufa appealed to Hossein to rescue them from a villainous governor appointed by Yezid. Hossein set off towards the Kerbala Desert with 72 men, but was cut off by an army of 4000 of Yezid's followers. By the 10th day of Moharram, Hossein and all but two of his men had been slaughtered. Since then Kerbala has been a pilgrimage site of enormous importance to Shiite Muslims.

Of similar significance is the Iraqi town of Najaf (previously Kufa) where Emām Ali died and was buried. These two towns are so important, in fact, that despite the continuing fallout from the Iran-Iraq War special arrangements are in place to let Iranian pilgrims cross the border without visas to visit them.

Sitting on a high plain dominated by Mt Alvand (3580m), Hamadān is a popular retreat for Iranians during the summer months There are a few things to see and do in Hamadān itself, but many people come here as a base for visiting the nearby Alī Sadr Caves (see Around Hamadān later in this chapter).

History

According to one legend, Hamadān was founded by the mythical King Jamshīd. It has certainly been inhabited since at least the 2nd millennium BC and became the capital of the Median Empire. Later, under Cyrus the Great, it was also the summer capital of the Achaemenids, known as Ecbatana or Hagmatāneh (Meeting Place). At the height of its glory, Hamadān was described as one of the most opulent cities, with splendid

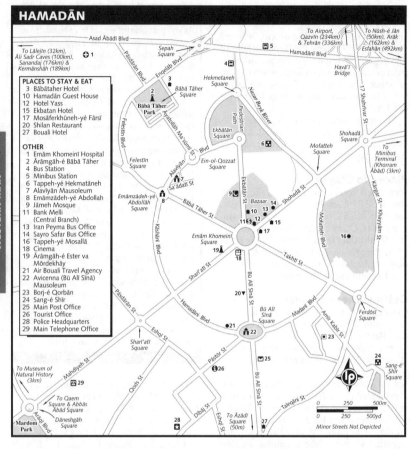

HAMADĀN

PLACES TO STAY & EAT
3   Bābātaher Hotel
10   Hamadān Guest House
12   Hotel Yass
15   Ekbatan Hotel
17   Mosäferkhüneh-yé Fārsī
20   Shilan Restaurant
27   Bouali Hotel

OTHER
1   Emām Khomeinī Hospital
2   Ārāmgāh-é Bābā Tāher
4   Bus Station
5   Minibus Station
6   Tappeh-yé Hekmatāneh
7   Alavīyān Mausoleum
8   Emāmzādeh-yé Abdollāh
9   Jāmeh Mosque
11   Bank Melli
      (Central Branch)
13   Iran Peyma Bus Office
14   Sayro Safar Bus Office
16   Tappeh-yé Mosallā
18   Cinema
19   Ārāmgāh-é Ester va
      Mördekhāy
21   Air Bouali Travel Agency
22   Avicenna (Bū Alī Sīnā)
      Mausoleum
23   Borj-é Qorbān
24   Sang-é Shīr
25   Main Post Office
26   Tourist Office
28   Police Headquarters
29   Main Telephone Office

Minor Streets Not Depicted

palaces, buildings plated with precious metals and seven layers of town walls, the inner two of which were coated in gold and silver.

These glorious riches naturally attracted invading armies. Hamadān faded in importance after the Arab conquest in the mid-7th century AD, but once again became the regional capital under the Seljuks for some 60 years in the late 12th century. The city was devastated by the Mongols in 1220 and again by Tamerlane in 1386, but soon returned to relative prosperity and remained so until the 18th century. Hamadān then fell into decline and was invaded by the Turks,

barely recovering again until the mid-19th century.

Valuable finds from the ancient city have come to light during this century, but the lower layers of settlement remain unexplored and must remain so unless the present city is uprooted.

Orientation

Despite its history, Hamadān is a rather drab town. In this century, it was rebuilt and designed around a main square, now predicably called Emām Khomeinī Square. From the square, six straight avenues radiate outwards;

most of the main offices and hotels are located along these avenues although some attractions are a little further out. The streets and squares mainly have signs in English.

Information
When it comes to extending your visa, changing money or seeking out tourist information, you're best off forgetting about Hamadān.

Post & Communications The main post office is about 150m south of Bū Alī Sīnā Square. You will need to take a shared taxi to get to the main telephone office, but there are booths for local calls outside the main post office.

Bookshops Hamadān is not somewhere you would expect to find a surfeit of English-language books, but the tiny bookshop at the Bouali Hotel has an outstanding range of titles about Iran, many of them published before the Islamic Revolution. They are mostly in English, with some in French and German. You will be able to pick up travel guides extolling the virtues of Tehrān discos and nightclubs, and books about Iranian carpets, cooking, history and language. Watch the prices, though, unless you think you're buying a hard-to-get gem. The shop is open from 7 am to 1.30 pm and from 3.30 to 8.30 pm.

Emergency For medical emergencies, go to the Emām Khomeinī Hospital (☎ 33 014), or ring the general emergencies number (☎ 28 88). The police headquarters (☎ 224 071) are in the southern part of town.

Ārāmgāh-é Ester va Mōrdekhāy
Iran's most important Jewish pilgrimage site, this shrine is believed to contain the bodies of Esther, the Jewish wife of Xerxes I, who is credited with organising the first Jewish emigration to Persia in the 5th century, and her uncle Mordecai. In fact, it's more likely to cover the grave of a much later Jewish queen, Shūshān, who is said to have persuaded her husband, Yazdgerd I, to allow a Jewish colony at Hamadān in the

early 5th century AD. The door is a vast granite slab, weighing 400kg.

Ring the bell and the caretaker will come and let you in, except on Saturday. He will suggest you make a donation to the shrine on top of the IR20,000 entrance fee, which has irritated some visitors. He's a keen collector of pens from around the world, should you happen to have any spare.

Gonbad-é Alavīyān
The well-preserved 12th-century mausoleum of the Alavī family, the pre-eminent family in the town during most of the Seljuk period, is interesting for its outstanding stucco ornamentation, with whirling floral motifs on the exterior walls and intricate geometric designs on its mihrab. The tombs are in the crypt, reached by a spiral staircase. The shrine stands in a small square at the end of a small lane, which leads east from Alavīyān Blvd; to find it follow signs to the Alavīyān dome. Admission costs IR15,000.

Avicenna Mausoleum
Obviously modelled on the magnificent Gonbad-é Kāvūs tower near Gorgān, this towering structure was built as recently as 1954 in memory of Bū Alī Sīnā (see the boxed text over the page). Inside, there's a **library** and a small **museum** (☎ 31 008) about the life and works of Bū Alī Sīnā which contains his original gravestone. In the gardens, you can also see the **tomb** of a 20th-century poet, Abolqasseim Aref.

Admission to the memorial will cost you IR20,000, but you may feel you don't need to do more than observe it from the outside. It's usually open from 8 am to 6 pm daily, closing at 4 pm in winter. This is a good place to buy assorted herbal remedies.

Ārāmgāh-é Bābā Tāher
It costs another IR15,000 to go inside the rather ugly mausoleum dedicated to the poet Bābā Tāher (known as 'The Naked'). Inside, the memorial slab is surrounded by fine modern tiles and alabaster panels. Of course it's perfectly possible to observe the tower for nothing from the park surrounding it.

Bū Alī Sīnā

Better known to the west as Avicenna, the great philosopher and physician Bū Alī Sīnā ('bū' means 'son of') was born in a Turkmenistan village near Bukhara in AD 980. Having practised medicine virtually from childhood, he left Bukhara at the age of 22 and spent several years as a traveller, before settling in Hamadān and becoming vizier to the Safavid emir whose ailments he had successfully treated. Unfortunately, when his patron died, Avicenna was caught out conspiring with a rival to the new emir and was thrown into prison. Eventually he managed to escape and fled to Esfahān where he spent the next 14 years working for the shah.

By the end of his life Bū Alī Sīnā had produced 250 books, including a widely respected medical encyclopaedia (*Canon Medicinae*) which was published in Europe and continued to be used in universities until the 17th century. His works showed the influence of both Greek and Islamic philosophers, and included several volumes of poetry. He died and was buried in Hamadān in 1037.

Tappeh-yé Hagmatāneh

The ancient Median and Achaemenid city of Hagmatāneh are slowly being excavated on an extensive plot of land, just north of the town centre. Small items found here and elsewhere in Hamadān are on display at the museum (☎ 224 005) in the centre of the site, but most are in the National Museum of Iran in Tehrān. As excavations progress so the site is becoming more interesting, although at the moment there are no signs to explain what you're looking at. You should be able to pick out stretches of ramparts 9m thick and assorted halls and courtyards though. The site is open from 9 am to 1 pm and from 3 to 8 pm daily (closing earlier in winter). Admission costs IR20,000.

Other Attractions

In the bazaar, the vast **Jāmeh Mosque** boasts some 55 columns. It was built during the Qajar dynasty and is worth a visit, not least because it's free to get in.

Also worth a look is the **Emāmzādeh-yé Abdollah**, in the middle of the square of the same name, but don't waste too much time tracking down the uninspiring 12-sided, 13th-century tower tomb, the **Borj-é Qorbān**.

The badly eroded 4th-century **Sang-é Shīr**, a stone lion in the square of the same name in south-east Hamadān, is the only surviving monument from the ancient city of Ecbatana. It originally guarded a city gate and may have been carved at the behest of Alexander the Great. It's not worth making a special trip to find it.

Some people really rate the **Museum of Natural History** (☎ 221 054) in the Bū Alī Sīnā University, which boasts the best collection of stuffed animals in the country, as well as (live) fish in tanks. This is the closest you are likely to get to the huge, horned Alborz red sheep. It's open from 8 am to 9 pm daily (closing at 6 pm in winter), but is poorly signposted and hidden behind a green fence, 5km from the town centre at the end of Azadegan Blvd. You will probably need to charter a taxi to get there and back for about IR7000, including waiting time.

Places to Stay

Many of the mosāferkhūnehs won't take foreigners and will direct you straight to the Hamadān Guest House. Most of the other places are overpriced, grubby or noisy.

One of the few real cheapies ready to accept foreigners is the friendly *Mosāferkhūneh-yé Farsi* (☎ 224 895, Shohadā St), directly opposite the Hotel Yass and up some stairs on the 1st floor. It costs IR25,000 per twin (or less per person in a four-bed dorm), but the shared bathrooms have no showers.

The most popular place for travellers, and deservedly so, is the friendly *Hamadān Guest House* (☎ 223 465, Ekbātān St), a two-storey building with a blue sign in English. Clean singles/doubles with shared bathroom cost IR40,000/60,000. If you haven't brought industrial-strength earplugs, try to get a room away from the main road.

There's not much to be said for the *Hotel Yass* (☎ 23 464, Shohadā St), which insists on US$50 for rooms worth perhaps IR25,000. To add insult to injury it's also in a noisy location, very close to Emām Khomeinī Square.

One of the nicest places to stay is the **Bouali Hotel** (☎ *825 2822, fax 825 824, Bouali Ave*). The rooms are excellent, with fridge and TV (showing BBC), but it's overpriced at US$50 a room (no single discounts). Even if you don't stay, it's worth coming here for the bookshop and restaurant.

Otherwise, you'll need your sunglasses to cope with the glare from the mirrors decorating the lobby of the newer **Babātaher Hotel** (☎ *422 6517, fax 422 5098, Babā Tāher Square*), a welcoming place to stay in a great location, but even more pricey at US$60 a double with fridge, TV and aircon. The buffet breakfast here is pretty good though.

Places to Eat

All the best *kabābīs* are on or around Emām Khomeinī Square, but none distinguish themselves. One of the best restaurants in town is the **Shilan Restaurant**. Signposted in English, it offers a decent selection of Iranian food for about IR8000 per dish, but only at lunch time.

Of the hotel restaurants, the **Hotel Yass** is OK, but the best restaurant in town, and one of the best in western Iran, is at the **Bouali Hotel** where you can dine alfresco in summer. A meal of shrimps, schnitzel, tongue and trout shared with others is like to cost you about IR40,000. Afterwards you can eat ice cream from the adjoining **Italian Ice Cream Stall**, also owned by the Bouali Hotel.

The restaurant in the **Babātaher Hotel** is also good, with places to eat inside or out. A fairly standard kebab dinner with soft drink is likely to come out at about IR25,000.

Shopping

Hamadān is justly famous for its carpets, as well as the ceramics, leather and copper products made in the region. You can buy these in nearby village markets, or at the bazaar in Hamadān. The nearby village of Lālejīn is the place to go for pottery and ceramics, and is worth a day trip for some souvenir hunting (see the Around Hamadān section following). You can also stock up on ceramics from a few shops around Bābā Tāher Square, but much of what is produced is likely to appeal to Iranian tastes more than those of foreigners.

Getting There & Away

Air Hamadān is too close to Tehrān for the airlines to bother flying here on a regular basis. Iran Asseman used to fly here infrequently; inquire at the Air Bouali Travel Agency (☎ 241 125, fax 229 999, Khajeh Rashidedin Blvd) if you're really keen to fly back.

Bus Hamadān is about five hours by bus from Tehrān by either the expressway via Tākestān or the more direct road via Sāveh.

A few bus companies have offices in the bazaar. The main bus station is within walking distance of the bazaar and most hotels, though a shared taxi will save your legs if you have heavy luggage. If you take the bus to Hamadān from anywhere between Tehrān and Kermānshāh, you will often be dropped off at the corner of Pāsdārān and Abbās Ābād Blvds. From here you can get a shared taxi to your hotel. This is also a good place to catch a passing bus going in either direction.

Some useful bus services are listed in the following table:

destination	distance (km)	duration (hrs)	cost (IR)
Ahvāz	465	7	15,000
Esfahān	492	7	11,500
Kermānshāh	189	3	4000
Shīrāz	918	15	19,500
Tehrān	336	5	8500/
(lux/super)			17,000

Minibus From the chaotic minibus station, not far from the main bus station, there are minibuses to Arāk, Sanandaj, Alī Sadr and Lālejīn. Men will probably crowd round you shouting 'Qar, qar' (cave), assuming you want to go to Alī Sadr. For minibuses to Khorram Ābād, there is a special minibus station in the eastern part of town; take a shared taxi from Emām Khomeinī Square. One minibus a day goes to Qazvīn; otherwise you may well have to take the Tehrān bus and risk being dropped 5km outside the city.

Getting Around
Hamadān is easy enough to walk around. Otherwise, take a shared taxi along any of the main streets, or to the bus or minibus stations, for about IR200 a trip.

AROUND HAMADĀN
See also the Around Kermānshāh section earlier in this chapter for other places that can be visited on a day trip out of Hamadān.

Ganjnāmeh
We used to recommend Ganjnāmeh as a great place to go **hiking** since it has a waterfall and rock carvings, and is easy to reach. However, a reader recently wrote that it reminded them more of an open sewer than a charming little piece of greenery. Another one bites the dust?

The misleadingly named **Treasure Book** is actually a pair of Achaemenid rock carvings of Darius I (on the left) and his son Xerxes I. Inscribed in the Old Persian, Elamite and Neo-Babylonian languages, these tablets list the kings' titles and hence the extent of their empires at the time. Nearby is a sign with the translation in English.

More enticing is the **waterfall**. Climb to the top for views of the Abbās Ābād valley. The area is popular with Hamadānīs for **skiing** in winter, and picnicking and **hiking** in summer.

Ganjnāmeh is crowded with *kabābīs* and *snack bars* where you can buy food and drinks. Even better, bring some food from Hamadān and enjoy a picnic.

Getting There & Away Ganjnāmeh is only about 8km from Hamadān. You can charter a taxi from the city centre for about IR8000 return, including about 30 minutes' waiting time. It's better to spend a few hours hiking around, however, and you can charter a taxi for IR5000 one way and maybe walk back (downhill) to Hamadān. Shared taxis to Ganjnāmeh are not easy to find except perhaps on Fridays and holidays; try at either Qaem or Abbās Ābād Squares in the south-west of the city.

Nūsh-é Jān
نوش جان

This mound, about 50km south of Hamadān, contains the remains of one of the earliest **fire-temples** discovered in Iran, dating back perhaps to the 8th century BC. It lies between the tiny villages of Nakmīl Ābād and Shūshāb, 20km north-east of Malāyer, and is most easily reached by chartering a taxi from Hamadān.

Lālejīn
لالجين

This village, 32km north of Hamadān, is famous for its **pottery** and boasts several dozen workshops producing all kinds of ceramics, particularly with the turquoise glaze for which the region is known. You can simply walk around and admire (or buy) the goods, or ask to visit a small factory to watch the experts at work. Bear in mind this is a bit like walking into a carpet showroom in Esfahān – you may find it hard to leave without some large, expensive item which you may not really have wanted. Some people love the pottery here, others think it tacky.

Minibuses to Lālejīn leave from the minibus station in Hamadān about every hour; a one-way trip costs IR3000.

Alī Sadr Caves (Qar Alī Sadr)
قار علی صدر

☎ 08262

Discovered 40 years ago by a local shepherd out looking for a lost goat, these remarkable caves, about 100km north of Hamadān, are up to 40m high. A river with clear water up to 14m deep flows through the middle. Nothing lives in the water – surprisingly even bats don't find it worth hanging around here – and there are no signs of any inhabitants from past centuries. Although it's possible to stay overnight most people visit the caves on a day trip from Hamadān.

The IR20,000 entrance fee includes a tour in a boat; you sit in a small rowing boat, attached to a paddle boat, which the guide steers. The commentary is only in Farsi, but there's little to explain anyway. The guide paddles away, while towing your boat, for about 20 to 30 minutes, then you walk around the middle of the cave for another 20 to 30 minutes – there are nearly 1km of walkways, and plenty more under construction. Then it's another 20- to 30-minute paddle, along a different route, back to the cave entrance.

Along the way you'll see labelling on some of the stalactites and stalagmites identifying them as the 'Statue of Liberty' etc. Texts from the Quran suspended above the water also help you while away the time. But it's the majesty and eeriness of the caves themselves which is the main attraction.

It can be cool inside the cave, so a light jumper (sweater) is a good idea. The caves are mostly well lit, but if you have a really strong torch (flashlight), bring it. Very few camera flashes will be good enough to take decent photos. The *Guide Map of Hamadān City & Road Map of Alisadr Wonderful Cave*, available in Hamadān, gives some useful information about the caves in English – though you will be glad to know there are no roads (yet) in the caves.

If possible, try and avoid visiting on a Friday or public holiday when the caves will be crawling with Iranian families and hundreds of screaming school kids. Foreigners are often whisked to the front of the queue for boats, but at such times the wait could be a long one. Outside the caves there is a real carnival atmosphere, with playgrounds and souvenir shops. How much you'll enjoy the caves probably depends on whether you come from a country with its own watery cave systems or not.

Places to Stay & Eat Staying near the caves or in the nearby village would allow you to see the caves in the afternoon and again the following morning.

Near the entrance to the caves is the ITTO's *Alī Sadr Hotel* (☎ 2099), which charges IR140,000/180,000 for a clean single/double with a bathroom. It's worth booking ahead and double-checking the price before carrying your luggage out there (or leave it in Hamadān). There are also some wooden *huts* (rather optimistically called 'suites') for hire, as well as some pre-erected tents, mainly used during the day by Iranian picnickers.

Several *stalls* around the cave entrance sell cold drinks and pots of tea, and some *kabābīs* and a decent *restaurant* serve standard Iranian fare. There is even a *teahouse* just inside the cave, serving tea, chocolate and – of all things – ice cream!

Getting There & Away Minibuses travel from Hamadān minibus station to Alī Sadr village whenever there are enough passengers, usually every hour or so but more frequently on holidays. Alternatively, if you want to stay at the caves and you don't have much luggage, you can always take a bus between Hamadān and Bījār, and get off at Gol Tappeh, from where you can hike (14km) or hitch a ride to the caves.

If you are in a hurry, or have some spare cash, chartering a taxi from Hamadān should cost about IR40,000 return, plus about IR10,000 an hour waiting time, but you'll need to bargain hard.

Parking at the site costs IR3000. It takes the best part of two hours to drive there.

KHORRAM ĀBĀD   خرم آبد
☎ 0661

Khorram Ābād makes a decent stopover between Hamadān and Kermānshāh, or between Ahvāz and Esfahān, and there is some good rock climbing available in the area. However, some commentators have been less kind in their assessment of the place:

> Picturesque at a distance beyond any Persian town that I have seen…Khorram Ābād successfully rivals any Persian town in its squalor, dirt, evil odours, and ruinous condition. Two-thirds of what was 'the once famous capital of the Atabegs' are now 'ruinous heaps'. The bazaars are small, badly supplied, dark, and rude; and the roads are nothing but foul alleys, possibly once paved, but now full of ridges, holes, ruins, rubbish, lean and mangy dogs, beggarly-looking men, and broken channels of water, which, dribbling over the soil in the bazaars and everywhere else in green and black slime, gives forth pestiferous odours in the hot sun.
>
> **Isabella Bird**
> *Journeys in Persia and Kurdistan (1889)*

While the redoubtable Ms Bird's description of late 19th-century Khorram Ābād was no doubt accurate, the town is now a perfectly pleasant place to while away a day. The fact that it's set in a rocky defile helps offset the impression that the main street is one long car workshop, and there's a magnificent fortress right in the middle of town.

Despite its air of lethargy Khorram Ābād was the setting, in August 2000, for one of those incidents that suggests how deep-rooted is the resistance to President Khatamī's gradual reforms. Two reform-minded politicians had arrived to address students, but were prevented from leaving the airport. In the ensuing fracas, a policeman was killed and a local politician assaulted.

Orientation & Information

All the hotels are along Sharīatī St, the main road heading north-east towards Hamadān and south towards Ahvāz. Tree-lined Alavī St is the main shopping district, one block west of Sharīatī St. The Falak-ol-Aflak fortress dominates the town and acts as the most important landmark; the bazaar is immediately to the west. The staff at the Bank Melli will probably have a fit if you ask to change money, so do it before you arrive. As for extending your visa…it's not even worth trying.

Falak-ol-Aflak

This impressive 12-towered fortress stands on a rocky promontory, dominating the city. There has probably been a fort on this site since Sassanian times, but this one was the citadel of the Atabegs, the powerful rulers of the Lorestān province from the 12th century until about 1600 when the last Atabeg king was defeated and killed by Shāh Abbās I.

The fortress stands about 40m high and covers 5300 sq metres. An ancient **well** inside it still draws fresh water from a spring 40m below the ground. The rooms around the rear courtyard now house a **museum** (☎ 24 090) with magnificent photographs of traditional life in Lorestān. There are also some fine examples of the famous Lorestān bronzes, together with a display of silverware from Kalmakarrah, including deep bowls and rhytons (horn-shaped drinking vessels) with delicate ibexes carved on them.

The fortress is open from 9 am to noon and from 3 to 7 pm daily except Friday. Ad-

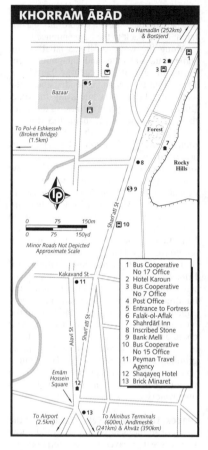

KHORRAM ĀBĀD

To Hamadān (252km) & Borūjerd

Bazaar

To Pol-é Eshkesseh (Broken Bridge) (1.5km)

Forest

Rocky Hills

0   75   150m
0   75   150yd
Minor Roads Not Depicted
Approximate Scale

Kakavand St

Alavī St

Sharīatī St

Emām Hossein Square

To Airport (2.5km)

To Minibus Terminals (600m), Andimeshk (241km) & Ahvāz (390km)

1   Bus Cooperative No 17 Office
2   Hotel Karoun
3   Bus Cooperative No 7 Office
4   Post Office
5   Entrance to Fortress
6   Falak-ol-Aflak
7   Shahrdārī Inn
8   Inscribed Stone
9   Bank Melli
10 Bus Cooperative No 15 Office
11 Peyman Travel Agency
12 Shaqayeq Hotel
13 Brick Minaret

mission costs IR20,000. A pleasant teahouse allows you to relax after inspecting the views from the ramparts.

Other Attractions

Khorram Ābād's other sights are of minor importance, but worth watching out for as you stroll round town. Along Sharīatī St is an **inscribed stone** dating from Seljuk times and setting out details of local grazing rights etc. Unfortunately at the time of writing it had been defaced with graffiti.

Overlooking Emām Hossein Square is a truncated **brick minaret** dating back to the

The Lorestān Bronzes

Way back in prehistory this part of western Iran was inhabited by the Kassites (also known as the Kussites), an agricultural, horse-breeding warrior tribe who eventually worked out how to produce decent bronze. Having done this, they proceeded to manufacture exquisite items whose fine decoration belied their often mundane purposes. You can see these horse bits, daggers, cups and tools on display in the National Museum of Iran and Rezā Abbāsī Museum in Tehrān and here, much closer to their origin, in Khorram Ābād. Most of them date back to around 1000 BC.

11th century. Although there are stairs inside you are not allowed to climb them.

About 2km west of town the graceful arches of the ancient **Broken Bridge**, Pol-é Eshkesseh, are stranded in a field.

For anyone who likes exploring rocky hills, those near Khorram Ābād, east of the road towards Hamadān provide some of the best and most accessible **rock climbing** in the whole country – just pick a spot and start scrambling.

Places to Stay

One of the better places to stay, as long as you can get a room away from the main road, is the *Hotel Karoun* (☎ 25 408). Large, clean rooms cost IR50,000 although the plumbing is a little iffy. The friendly manager has some books in English about local sites, which he'll let you look at. The *Shaqayeq Hotel* (☎ 432 648), on the corner of Emām Hossein Square, has similar rates, but could be a bit noisy.

The ITTO's *Shahrdārī Inn* (☎ 22 227) is tucked away in a quiet location behind a small forest with awesome views of the city and fortress. The rooms are pleasant, with fridge, TV and air-con, and some have balconies and views, but it's way overpriced at IR249,000 a room (no single discounts).

Places to Eat

Khorram Ābād is not a place to start dreaming of fine dining. There are nothing but basic *kabābīs* along the two main streets, so eating at a hotel is the best idea. The *Karoun* has a pleasant ground-floor restaurant where a kebab supper will cost about IR18,000 including a soft drink; breakfasts here – with fresh cream and jam – are good too. The *Shaqayeq Hotel* also has a decent restaurant, with meals for about the same price. The best place is the *Shahrdārī Inn*, though the views are better than the meals or service.

Getting There & Away

Air Iran Asseman has flights to Tehrān three times a week for IR92,000. Book at the airport (about 3km south of the bazaar); or at Peyman Travel Agency (☎ 432 222), the local agent for Iran Air and Iran Asseman.

Bus Getting out of Khorram Ābād by bus isn't especially easy. There is no bus station, but you can catch a direct bus to selected destinations from outside the appropriate bus company office along Sharīatī St. You can also hail a passing bus at the roundabout near the Hotel Karoun to anywhere immediately east, (Hamadān or Arāk), or to places further south. To get to many places, you will need to take a bus to Kermānshāh and change.

The road between Borūjerd and Khorram Ābād is winding and steep, and populated by suicidal truck drivers; if you're driving, take care; if you're in a bus, close your eyes. The road to Andīmeshk is similarly attractive, but choked with lorries.

Some useful bus services are listed in the following table:

destination	distance (km)	duration (hrs)	cost (IR)
Ahvāz	390	6	10,300
Andīmeshk	241	4	5000
Esfahān	368	6	10,000
Kermānshāh	629	5	7500
Shīrāz	852	12	20,700
Tehrān (lux/super)	491	8	13,000/ 20,000

There's only one bus a day (at 2 pm) to Kermānshāh, so if you're heading in that direction be sure to book a seat in advance at the Bus Cooperative No 7 office.

Minibus In this part of Iran minibuses are a common form of transport. From special stations 600m south of Shaqayeq Square, minibuses head for Andīmeshk (IR5000) whenever they have enough passengers.

Shared Taxi For many nearby destinations like Andīmeshk (IR15,000) it may be quicker to take a shared taxi than to wait for a bus. To get to Hamadān, take a shared taxi to Borūjerd and change.

Getting Around
Khorram Ābād is small enough to walk around, and you can reach the transport stations on foot. Shared taxis speed along the two main streets and are available for about IR250 a trip.

AROUND KHORRAM ĀBĀD
Borūjerd   بروجرد
The town of Borūjerd, on the main road between Hamadān and Khorram Ābād, has an interesting **Jāmeh Mosque** in Ja'fari Ave, which has a Seljuk-era dome and mihrab containing an inscription from the same period. The portico and minarets were added in the 18th century. The Qajar **Soltānī Mosque** and the fine Seljuk **Emāmzādeh-yé Ja'far** are also worth visiting, the latter for its wooden doors.

To get to Borūjerd, simply get off any bus travelling between Khorram Ābād and Hamadān, or take a shared taxi from either town.

Bābā Jān   بابا جان
Among the many pre-Islamic sites uncovered in the province, the most interesting is Bābā Jān.

Occupied from at least the 3rd millennium BC, this large mound shows the indistinct remains of a town, partly burnt in the 7th century BC and abandoned 200 years later. However, there's not much for the nonspecialist to see.

The ruins are accessible from the village of Nūr Ābād, about 90km north-west of Khorram Ābād. You will have to charter a vehicle from Khorram Ābād, Hamadān or Kermānshāh.

Dokhtar Bridge   پل دختر
If you're heading to Khorram Ābād from Andīmeshk you can hardly fail to see the remains of this fine Sassanian-era bridge, partly straddling the main road, partly collapsed into the river beside it. Originally it was 270m long and its name is believed to be a corruption of Kor-o-Dot (Boy and Girl). It's near the village of Baba Zeyd.

Mt Oshturān   کوه اشتران
Mt Oshturān (4070m) is the highest peak in the mighty Zāgros Mountains. It's in Lorestān province, a few kilometres south of Aznā, and about 80km east of Khorram Ābād. If you take the train from Arāk to Dezfūl, the first tunnel south of Aznā goes under part of Oshturān. To start a trek, charter a taxi to Aznā from Khorram Ābād.

Even if you don't want to climb the mountain, it's perfectly possible to trek in the region, admiring luscious waterfalls, two pretty volcanic lakes (Upper and Lower Gahar), and thousands of hectares of forests and wildflowers, including bright red tulips in spring.

AHVĀZ   اهواز
☎ 061 • pop 826,380
This industrial city on the banks of the Kārūn River owes its prosperity to the discovery of oil at nearby Masjed-é Soleimān in 1908. Much of Ahvāz was devastated by unremitting Iraqi bombing during the Iran-Iraq War. Subsequent redevelopment has turned it into a sprawling, featureless city.

Ahvāz is pleasant in winter, but hideous in summer (April to October) when the heat (regularly over 50°C) makes it impossible to leave your hotel between 10 am and 5 pm. Although Andīmeshk is a better base for visiting Shūsh or Choqā Zanbīl, Ahvāz has good bus and air connections and is thus a useful staging post between western Iran and southern cities such as Būshehr and Shīrāz.

A word of caution. Unfortunately for a city so blighted by the heat, Ahvāz's water is definitely not safe to drink.

Orientation
The main square is Shohadā Square just to the east of the suspension bridge, the

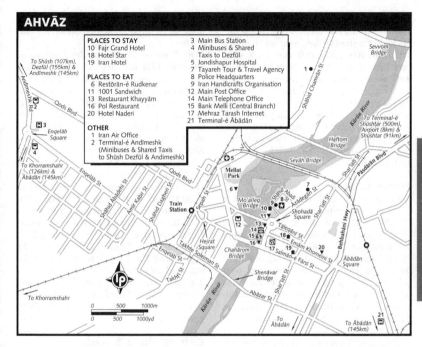

AHVĀZ

PLACES TO STAY
10 Fajr Grand Hotel
18 Hotel Star
19 Iran Hotel

PLACES TO EAT
6 Restōrān-é Rudkenar
11 1001 Sandwich
13 Restaurant Khayyām
16 Pol Restaurant
20 Hotel Naderi

OTHER
1 Iran Air Office
2 Terminal-é Andīmeshk
(Minibuses & Shared Taxis
to Shūsh Dezfūl & Andīmeshk)
3 Main Bus Station
4 Minibuses & Shared
Taxis to Dezfūl
5 Jondishapur Hospital
7 Tayareh Tour & Travel Agency
8 Police Headquarters
9 Iran Handicrafts Organisation
12 Main Post Office
14 Main Telephone Office
15 Bank Melli (Central Branch)
17 Mehraz Tarash Internet
21 Terminal-é Ābādān

Mo'alleq Bridge. The main shopping district and new bazaar are south-east of this square.

Information

The officers at the police headquarters seemed completely nonplussed as to why anyone would want to stay longer than they had to in Ahvāz; get your visa extension elsewhere.

You can change money at the central branch of the Bank Melli, although the foreign-exchange counter is only open in the morning.

Post & Communications The main post office is inconveniently located on the western side of the river; the main telephone office is not far from Shohadā Square.

Mehraz Tarash Internet (☎ 223 681) is more expensive than others elsewhere in Iran (IR1000 per minute, IR48,000 per hour), but you'll have to take what you can

get in Ahvāz. Walk south-east from Āzādegān St along Emām Khomeinī St. After about 50m, take the staircase leading up on the right immediately after the small bank (Bank Keshavarzi) with a green sign in Farsi above its door. At the top of the stairs, turn right; it's the third door on your right (look for the red sign).

Travel Agencies The friendly and efficient Tayareh Tour & Travel Agency (☎ 226 108, fax 224 134 467), Āzādegān St, handles international and domestic air tickets, and train tickets, and acts as agents for Valfarje-8 Shipping Company. It can also arrange tours to sites around Khūzestān province, including Choqā Zanbīl.

Emergency The police headquarters (☎ 110 or ☎ 222 231) can be found alongside the river. There is a medical emergencies number (☎ 115) or you can ring the Jondishapur Hospital (☎ 228 075).

WESTERN IRAN

Things to See & Do

There's very little to do in Ahvāz. It's possible to take a short **cruise** along the river in a small motorboat, from in front of the Restaurant Khayyām. It's also quite pleasant to walk along the riverside in the evening when the bridges are illuminated and the fierce sun has disappeared for a while. There are kiosks selling drinks and hiring out qalyans.

If the heat gets too much, visit the **swimming pool** at the Fajr Grand Hotel which is open to nonguests for IR10,000 – Ahvāz's best bargain.

Places to Stay

Some cheap places around the new bazaar district refuse foreigners, but the *Hotel Star* (☎ 224 640 Emām Khomeinī St) won't. The clean if basic singles/doubles with shared bathroom for IR30,000/ 35,000 are perfectly habitable for a short stay, although the air-con blows in through an open window, which is hardly ideal; most rooms also have a fan. It's a white, three-storey building on the corner of an unmarked lane and Emām Khomeinī St; there's a small sign in English above the door.

If the *Iran Hotel* (☎ 217 201, fax 217 206, Sharī'atī St) was anywhere else in Iran, it would be full of budget travellers. Its very comfortable and clean singles/doubles/triples are a steal at IR54,447/77,778/80,000; each one has a fridge, air-con, TV, bathroom and Western toilet. The double-glazed windows in the front rooms work wonders in keeping out the traffic noise. The staff is friendly, and there's a well-stocked snack bar and excellent restaurant.

The luxury *Fajr Grand Hotel* (☎ 220 091, fax 218 677, Shahīd Abedi Ave) has excellent, quiet rooms, most of which have views of the river for US$54/78/147 a single/double/suite. There's a very pleasant coffee shop in the lobby and the swimming pool could be the highlight of your time in Ahvāz.

Places to Eat

Around the Iran Hotel, a couple of unnamed *kabābīs* serve the usual fare, but with a difference because the bread is baked just inside the front door, and is really fresh. *1001 Sandwich* in an arcade off Shohadā Square does, surprisingly enough, reasonable sandwiches.

Both times we visited the *Restaurant Khayyām* (*Tāleqānī St*), the cook seemed to have succumbed to the heat and it was only serving ice cream, which in the heat of August is not such a bad idea. It's worth checking, though, as it has nice views and used to serve good, cheap meals. The *Restōrān-é Rudkenar* (☎ 332 421) also has a lovely riverside setting, but getting there involves a long walk across the river (especially as the Mo'alleq Bridge was closed for repairs at the time of research); a taxi costs around IR2000. For fish, it's hard to go past the *Pol Restaurant*, under the Chāhārom Bridge.

Of the hotels, the meals at the overpriced *Hotel Naderi* are better value than their rooms and the Karoun Restaurant in the *Fajr Grand Hotel* is pricey, but the service and food are excellent – the ice cream sundae (IR4300) is spectacular. The restaurant on the 1st floor of the *Hotel Iran* does consistently good food, with a particularly good khōresht.

Getting There & Away

Air To avoid an excruciatingly long and hot bus ride, it's worth flying to or from Ahvāz. Iran Air flies from Ahvāz to Tehrān twice daily (IR118,000), to Mashhad twice a week (IR220,000), to Esfahān daily (IR92,000) and to Shīrāz once a week (IR102,000). Iran Asseman flies regularly to Tehrān and even has a weekly international flight to Dubai for IR890,000; contact the Tayareh Tour & Travel Agency (☎ 226 108, fax 224 134), 467 Azādegān St.

The Iran Air office is located in the north of town on Shāhid Chamrān St. The airport is 7km north-east of town on Pāsdārān Blvd and accessible by shared taxi.

Bus, Minibus & Shared Taxi The main bus station is off Enqelāb Square in the far west of town. Although you could catch a shared taxi, you'd probably have to change a couple of times – take a private taxi.

Some useful daily bus services from Ahvāz are listed in the following table:

SIMON RICHMOND

HUGH WATTS

MARTIN MOOS

Top: The Castles of the Assassins, near Qazvīn, once protected adherents of a feared Ismaili sect.
Bottom Left: Looking out towards a shrouded Caspian Sea from high in the Alborz Mountains.
Bottom Right: A young goatherd and his flock pass the gateway to Takht-é Soleimān, near Takāb.

A crater lake, in the midst of the ruins of Takht-é Soleimān (Soloman's Throne), near Takāb

One of several statues guarding ancient Shūsh

An old stone bridge near Bījār

The 3000-year-old ziggurat of Choqā Zanbīl is the best preserved Elamite monument.

Cuneiform tablets at Choqā Zanbīl testify to the sophistication of Elamite culture.

destination	distance (km)	duration (hrs)	cost (IR)
Bandar-é Abbās	1169	19	21,500
Būshehr	626	7	10,500
Esfahān	765	14	19,000
Hamadān	465	7	13,500
Kermānshāh	509	9	13,500
Khorram Ābād	390	6	10,500
Shīrāz	568	10	14,000
Tehrān	881	15	14,000
Yazd	1008	20	23,500

For Ābādān and Khorramshahr, take a minibus (IR3000) or shared taxi (IR5000) from the Terminal-é Ābādān, south of town on Behbahani Highway.

Buses to Andīmeshk (2 pm, IR3000) and Shūsh (1 pm, IR2400) leave from the Terminal-é Andīmeshk 500m north of the main station. The departure times are not much use, and waiting for a shared taxi (IR10,000 to Andīmeshk, IR8000 to Shūsh) to fill can be like waiting for a cold spell in Ahvāz; you may have to pay for the whole taxi to yourself (IR50,000 and IR40,000, respectively). Occasionally, a bus will go from here to Dezfūl, but they also go from the yard on Enqelāb St, 50m south-east of Enqelāb Square.

It will cost you more in taxi fares to get to the chaotic Terminal-é Shūshtar than it will to get to the town of Shūshtar (1 pm, IR2300) itself. Some long-distance buses also leave from here, but the main station is far more user-friendly.

Train There are three daily trains to Tehrān; schedules change, but there's always one in the mid-afternoon and one in the early evening; first-/second-class tickets cost IR31,500/17,200. Express trains take 15 hours, while at least train a day stops at all stations and takes a full 18 hours. Occasionally a train will only go as far as Qom (IR26,000/14,500).

Taxi All shared taxis leave from outside the bus and minibus stations.

Chartering a taxi to Shūsh (Shūsh) and Choqā Zanbīl costs IR600 per kilometre in a Paykan, or IR1200 in an air-con Peugot from the Fajr Hotel Taxi Service (☎ 228 271). This adds up to between IR120,000 and IR150,000 for a day trip to Choqā Zanbīl and Shūsh for the non-air-con option. You should be able to negotiate a little less from ordinary taxi drivers; outside the Terminal-é Andīmeshk is a good place to start.

Boat The Valfarje-8 Shipping Company's ferry sails from nearby Khorramshahr to Kuwait on Sunday, Monday and Wednesday (five to six hours) for IR500,000/600,000 1st/2nd class. For tickets and current schedules, contact Tayareh Tour & Travel Agency (☎ 226 108, fax 224 134), 467 Azādegān St.

Getting Around

To/From the Airport There's no airport bus service, but you can take a private taxi to the city centre for a reasonable IR5000. From the airport, you should be able to share a taxi for about IR1000.

Taxi Shared taxis cost about IR500 for short trips, but this is one city where you should preserve your sanity and pay extra for a private taxi.

CHOQĀ ZANBĪL   چقا زنبيل

The remarkably well-preserved ziggurat (pyramidal tiered temple) of Choqā Zanbīl is the best surviving example of Elamite architecture anywhere, and is now one of Iran's three World Heritage Sites. Originally it had five concentric storeys, but only three remain. They reach a total height of some 25m, considerably less than the original 60m, but still impressive. It's hard to believe that such an imposing landmark could have been lost to the world for more than 2500 years, which was the case until it was accidentally discovered in 1935 during an Anglo-Iranian Oil Company aerial survey.

History

In ancient times the inhabitants of Iran attached great religious importance to mountains, and where they had no mountains, they made their own imitations, thereby creating the distinctive pyramidal style of building known as a ziggurat. This ziggurat was the *raison d'etre* of the town of Dur Untash, founded by King Untash Gal in the

WESTERN IRAN

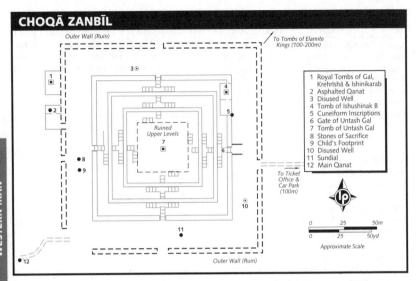

CHOQĀ ZANBĪL

Outer Wall (Ruin)

To Tombs of Elamite
Kings (100-200m)

3 ⊙

1
4
2
5

Ruined
Upper Levels
7

6

8
9

10

11

12

Outer Wall (Ruin)

To Ticket
Office &
Car Park
(100m)

1 Royal Tombs of Gal,
   Krehrīshā & Ishinikarab
2 Asphalted Qanat
3 Disused Well
4 Tomb of Ishushinak B
5 Cuneiform Inscriptions
6 Gate of Untash Gal
7 Tomb of Untash Gal
8 Stones of Sacrifice
9 Child's Footprint
10 Disused Well
11 Sundial
12 Main Qanat

LP

0   25   50m
0   25   50yd

Approximate Scale

middle of the 13th century BC. It reached its peak towards the start of the 12th century BC, when it had a large number of temples and priests, but was later sacked by the Assyrian king Ashurbanipal around 640 BC.

The ziggurat, the most imposing structure of Dur Untash, was dedicated to Inshushinak, the chief god of the Elamites and patron of Shūsh; there was originally a quadrangular temple to him on the summit of the ziggurat, accessible only to the elite of Elamite society. The ziggurat was built on a square plan, with its sides measuring 105m, and its five storeys were erected vertically from the foundation level, as a series of concentric towers, rather than one on top of another as was the custom in Mesopotamia. It was built on a low base as a precaution against flooding, as this was once a fertile and forested area.

There was originally a complex of chambers, tombs, tunnels and water channels on the lowest level, as well as two temples to Inshushinak on the south-eastern side. The ziggurat was surrounded by a paved courtyard protected by a wall. Outside were the living quarters of the town and 11 temples dedicated to various Elamite gods and goddesses.

Many of the artefacts found here are now on display in the National Museum of Iran in Tehrān.

The Ziggurat

Choqā Zanbīl's setting is bleak, barren and windswept, all of which is part of its charm. The three storeys that remain are remarkably well-preserved and restoration work is continuing. On each of the four sides, a steep staircase leads to the summit (25m high), providing a sense of proportion and symmetry.

As you approach the ziggurat from the tourist office and after passing through what remains of the **outer walls**, you'll come to the **Gate of Untash Gal**. Here the foundations are all that remain of two rows of seven columns where supplicants and worshippers used to approach the ziggurat and seek the pleasure of the king. To the right of the Gate of Untash Gal is a narrow opening, within which is the **Tomb of Ishushinak B**, one of 14 dotted around the site and surrounding hills. If these rooms are accessible (the area is roped off, but a guide may be able to get you permission), look for the perfectly preserved cuneiform **inscriptions** at eye level inside the door frame. If you can get close enough, there are more inscriptions around the base, about 1m above the ground.

At some points around the perimeter, particularly on the northern side, you can still see the (very) faint remnants of blue, white, black and gold ceramic tiles around the base. On the western side, built into inner walls which encircle the ziggurat are the **tomb chambers** of the Elamite kings Gal, Krehrīshā and Ishinikarab, as well as a small room containing an ancient asphalted *qanat* or water channel. Nearby, alongside the **stones of sacrifice** is the mysterious 3300-year-old **footprint** of an Elamite child, which is strangely moving, having remained untouched on this lonely plain for more than three millennia.

To the south-west, where the inner walls are least intact, there is a track leading off to the signposted **main qanāt**, which was used to channel water from ancient rivers as far as 45km away into the (now filled-in) wells that circle the base. There's also a huge **sundial** at the foot of the southern staircase.

There are no official opening hours and, theoretically, the site can be visited after dark when the ziggurat is floodlit. This may be a good option in summer when the temperature can reach 45°C by mid-morning, but bring a flash or tripod if you want to take photographs. Entry costs IR30,000.

One guide lives permanently at the site. Although not strictly necessary, he speaks reasonable English and is helpful in pointing out hard-to-find inscriptions and the footprint. He will also show you the **tombs** of the Elamite kings in the hills nearby. There is no set fee, but IR5000 is a reasonable amount to pay; IR10,000 if you've extracted him from his air-con haven in the heat of the day.

Like Shūsh, the virtually deserted site of Choqā Zanbīl makes a good spot for a bit of bird and lizard spotting.

Getting There & Away

Choqā Zanbīl is 45km from Shūsh, 65km from Andīmeshk and 122km from Ahvāz. Because it's off the beaten track, you should consider chartering a taxi (see Ahvāz Getting There & Away earlier for expected rates) and perhaps combining a visit with one to Shūsh. If you have your own vehicle, Choqā Zanbīl

is signposted in English (though easy to miss) along the Ahvāz-Andīmeshk highway. From the turn-off, it's 27km to the site. You could try and get off a bus at the turn-off and try to hitch a lift, but there's not much traffic so you might have to wait an hour or two – something definitely to be avoided in summer.

HAFT TAPPEH   هفت تپه

To the left of the road as you leave Choqā Zanbīl for Shūsh, look out for the remains of this 2nd millennium BC Elamite town. Haft once had several ziggurats as well as various royal buildings, tombs and temples. There's less to see here than at Choqā Zanbīl or Shūsh, because the site is much more spread out than the other two, but it's still worth a look if you're in the area.

SHŪSH (SUSA)   شوش
☎ 0642 252

Shūsh was one of the great cities of ancient Iran and one of the earliest to be explored by archaeologists. Unlike at nearby Choqā Zanbīl, you'll need quite an imagination to conjure up Shūsh's past grandeur.

History

Though best known as an Achaemenid capital, Shūsh was in fact a prehistoric settlement from at least the 4th millennium BC, and an important Elamite city from about the middle of the 3rd millennium. Around 640 BC, it was burnt by the Assyrian king Ashurbanipal, but it regained prominence in 521 BC when Darius I set it up as his winter capital. Darius fortified Shūsh and built palaces and other buildings suggesting that at one time Shūsh must have been similar in grandeur to Persepolis.

In 331 BC, Shūsh fell to Alexander the Great, and its days of splendour were over. It later became the Sassanian capital, and, during Shāpūr I's reign in the 4th century AD, an important centre of Christianity. The city had to be evacuated in the face of Mongol raids and didn't come back to attention again until 1852 when the British archaeologist WK Loftus became the first to survey the site. His work was continued by the French Archaeological Service from

1891 more or less until the Islamic Revolution of 1979.

Ancient City

Many fine examples of bronzes and pottery from various periods, showing the development of the typically Persian, highly stylised animal motif, have been found here. Most are now on display at the National Museum of Iran in Tehrān, while a famous bulls' head capital dating from the 4th century BC is in the Louvre in Paris.

As you enter through the gate from the street, you cannot fail to notice the **castle**. Quite unlike any other archaeological camp, it was built by the French Archaeological Service at the end of the 19th century as a defence against the Arab tribes of the region. It is now the most imposing structure at Shūsh.

The city was built on four small mounds. Next to the Acropolis, the largest mound contains the remains of the **Royal Town**, once the quarter of the court officials. North-west of this was the **Apadana**, where Darius I built his residence and two other palaces. Two well-preserved foundation tablets found beneath the site of **Darius' Palace** record the noble ancestry of its founder; they are now in the National Museum of Iran in Tehrān. All that remains of the Palace are the half-metre-high foundation floor plan. There are some impressive columns and a few elegant horses' head statues which give an enticing but ultimately frustrating hint of what it must have been like before Shūsh was dismantled and carted off to the museums.

The mound labelled as the **Artisans' Town** dates from the Seleucid and Parthian eras. The overgrown and sparse **Royal City** to the east is probably only of interest to archaeology buffs.

The entrance to the site is along the main street in the town. A ticket costs IR30,000, although to see inside the castle you'll be asked for another IR20,000. The site is open from 8 am to 7 pm daily, sometimes later in summer. Beside the gate you won't be able to miss a sign bearing one of Āyatollāh Khomeinī's pearls of wisdom: 'The School Which Has Martyrs Has No Captivity'.

Tomb of Daniel

Also in the modern village of Shūsh is the unusual Tomb of Daniel (Ārāmgāh-é Dānyāl), a short walk west of the entrance to the ancient city. Though not particularly old (it was built in 1870), the tomb is quite striking and has some good mirrorwork on the interior. Men and women must enter through different doors.

Places to Stay & Eat

Shūsh is one of the more pleasant towns in this part of the country with a canal running through its heart and a quiet, relaxed atmosphere. Now that there's a hotel in town, Shūsh is probably the best place to base yourself for exploring the ancient city and Choqā Zanbīl. The **Apadana Hotel and Restaurant** (☎ 3131) has very pleasant rooms with aircon and bathroom for IR50,000/80,000; some even overlook the canal and castle. It has received rave reviews from other travellers and is within walking distance of the ancient city and the Tomb of Daniel. The hotel restaurant is the best place to eat although there are plenty of **snack bars** and **kabābīs** scattered around town.

Getting There & Away

Shūsh is 116km north-west of Ahvāz and 38km south of Andīmeshk. It's rare to find a direct bus to Shūsh, but most buses en route to Andīmeshk or Ahvāz stop at the entrance to town on the main highway, about 1.5km from the ancient city and centre of town, from where it is easy to get a shared taxi along the main street. There is also a small minibus station halfway between the highway and the centre. Minibuses leave from time to time to Andīmeshk (IR1000) and Ahvāz (IR2400).

SHŪSHTAR   شوشتر

About 90km north of Ahvāz, along the old road between Ahvāz and Dezfūl, the pretty town of Shūshtar is famous for the ancient **Shadorvan** and **Band-é Qaisar Bridges**, both constructed during the Sassanian period, and for its **water mills**. The 9th-century **Jāmeh Mosque**, renowned for its minarets and inscriptions, is also worth a look. Shūshtar is probably not worth a special detour, but it's a reasonable alternative to the main Andīmeshk-Ahvāz road if you have your own vehicle. Buses (1 pm, IR2300) leave from the Terminal-é Shūshtar in the north-east of Ahvāz.

ANDĪMESHK اندیمشک
☎ 064 242

Andīmeshk makes a reasonable place to base yourself for trips to Shūsh and/or Choqā Zanbīl, or to break a journey between southern and western Iran. It's slightly cooler than Ahvāz although you'd have to have stood in the Ahvāz sun in August to notice it. Andīmeshk is mainly inhabited by Lors, who are keenly engaged in vegetable farming, courtesy of the incredible Dez Dam about 30km north of Dezfūl. If you're staying in Andīmeshk, a good place to watch the sunset is from the main bridge overlooking the mud-brick buildings along the river at Dezfūl, 10km to the south-east.

Places to Stay & Eat

The *Hotel Rostam* (☎ 22 818) has tidy singles/doubles with air-con and bathroom for IR30,000/50,000 and the friendly management speaks some English. There's a good restaurant downstairs. It's about 300m north of Beheshtī Square along the main shopping street. A further 200m on, *Hotel Eghbal* (☎ 22 437) looks like it is being gutted from the inside, but the rooms are comfortable enough for IR80,000/120,000 a single/double. Some travellers have reported a less than friendly reception, but we felt perfectly welcome. The upmarket *Hotel Andīmeshk* (on the right as you enter town from Ahvāz) was temporarily closed when we visited, but

it should be a good upper mid-range option when it reopens.

Andīmeshk is pretty much a culinary desert, with little beyond indifferent kebabs on offer around town. If you get to any restaurant before 8.30 pm there may be a panic and a rush to find the cook. Make sure you try the locally grown tomatoes, which are large and delicious.

Getting There & Away

Bus & Minibus Though there are some bus companies in Andīmeshk with direct services to Tehrān, it's easier to stand along the side of the highway, next to the major roundabout and flag down a bus going your way.

From the small station – 200m towards Ahvāz from the roundabout on the highway – minibuses go to Khorram Ābād (IR8000), Ahvāz (IR3000) and Shūsh (IR1000), Dezfūl (IR1000) and Shūshtar (IR1500). Shared taxis hover outside the station and cost a little more.

If you want to take a taxi tour of Shūsh and Choqā Zanbīl, there is a taxi rank outside the Hotel Eghbal. Expect to pay about IR120,000 for a four-hour tour, including waiting time.

Train Getting *to* Andīmeshk by train is a good idea because the station is right in the town centre, 150m west of the town square, but timing your arrival at the station to coincide with one of the three daily trains from Ahvāz to Tehrān and Qom is difficult. Trains from Tehrān will drop you off before dawn – and the conductor will probably wake you a good hour before you need to get off!

The Caspian Sea

دریای خزر

North of Tehrān, the main road skirts the Daryā-yé Khazar (Caspian Sea) from Astara and the Azerbaijani border in the far west to Gomīshān and the Turkmenistan border in the east. Despite unfettered development that has robbed the coastline of much of its charm, the Caspian region is particularly popular with Iranian tourists, especially Tehrānīs. Except over public holidays, finding decent accommodation is unlikely to be a problem although prices are higher than elsewhere in Iran.

The three Caspian provinces of Gīlān, Māzandarān and Golestān boast a varied terrain, with thick forests and the towering Alborz Mountains backing a coastal plain up to 100km wide. The northern slopes of the mountains are still densely forested and the forest remains rich in wildlife.

Although the modern Caspian coastline is densely populated, that hasn't always been the case. Small settlements have existed here since earliest times, but until this century malarial swamps and dense forests discouraged large-scale settlement. The southern parts of all three provinces are still thinly populated.

The wet Caspian littoral (it receives about 2000mm of rain a year) is ideal for growing rice and tea. Cotton and citrus fruits are also grown. Sturgeon, salmon, perch and pike are all caught here and caviar processing is extremely lucrative.

Independent until the 16th century, the largely rural western province of Gīlān still has its own distinctive dress and dialect (Gīlākī). The provincial capital of Rasht is the Caspian region's most important city, while its main port is Bandar-é Anzalī.

The central coastal strip of Māzandarān province is slightly drier. At its narrowest and most attractive point (roughly between Rāmsar and Sīsangān), the slopes of the Alborz Mountains roll almost to the sea.

To the far east, Golestān province is largely inhospitable steppe and marshland. The Torkamān Sahrā (the harsh Turkmen

Highlights

The Caspian Sea p248-9

- Relaxing in the hill village of Māsuleh, near Rasht
- Shopping in the Turkmen market at Bandar-é Torkamān
- Admiring the Gonbad-é Kāvūs tower, near Gorgān
- Bird-watching on the Anzalī Lagoon, near Bandar-é Anzalī
- Chilling out in friendly Rāmsar

desert) occupies the strip south of the Atrak River, which forms part of the border with Turkmenistan. The more fertile Dasht-é Gorgān (Gorgān plain), between the desert and the mountains, used to form the boundary between the settled and nomadic populations. The population is largely Turkmen, and the Gorgān plain is believed to contain some of west Asia's most important archaeological sites.

ĀSTĀRĀ
آستارا
☎ 1852

This small town to the far north-west of Iran is right on the border, which divides it from the town of Astara in the republic of Azer-

The Mighty Caspian Sea

The Caspian Sea (Daryā-yé Khazar) is the world's largest lake. Covering an area of 370,000 sq km and measuring 1210km from north to south and between 210km and 436km from east to west, the Caspian is five times bigger than the next largest lake (Lake Superior, on the border of the USA and Canada) and contains 44% of all the water in the world's lakes. The Caspian has many large tributaries, such as the Volga, Zhem and Ural Rivers, but no outlet to the ocean.

The Caspian is a salt sea, about one-third as salty as sea water, and its surface lies about 30m below sea level. However, the water level is rising by an average of 15cm to 20cm per year for reasons that are not entirely clear; it has risen a whole 2m since 1978. One theory is that the clearing of local land for agriculture has led to increased water run-off, and another is that it could be to do with the movement of tectonic plates. The Caspian has an average depth of 170m, making it nearly twice as deep as the Persian Gulf.

The countries bordering the Caspian Sea – Iran, Russia, Turkmenistan, Azerbaijan and Kazakhstan – are starting to realise the potential benefit of a joint regional economic zone, boosted by transport across the Caspian, and have formed the nascent Caspian Cooperation Organisation (CASCO). But argument continues to rage over whether the Caspian is a 'sea' (which means each country around its perimeter would have the right to exploit its own section of the seabed at will) or a 'lake' (in which case they must all share the benefits equally).

baijan. At the time of writing this appeared to be the only reliable and safe road crossing between Iran and its northern neighbour although we have received reports from travellers who have been turfed off the supposedly through bus to the Azerbaijani capital, Baku – check and check again before assuming you'll be allowed to cross.

Although devoid of historical interest, Āstārā is not unattractive, and there are worse places to spend the night. However, if you've come into Iran from Azerbaijan, it's probably better to keep heading towards Rasht or Ardabīl. With time to kill, you can visit the nearby Abbās Ābād gardens.

Places to Stay & Eat
There are a few mosāferkhūnehs around Shahrdārī Square, but some may not take foreigners; if they do, they charge about IR20,000 for a basic room. The best of the lot is the **Hotel Aras**.

The recognised 'tourist hotel' is the fading two-star **Āstārā Inn** (☎ 22 134, fax 60 65), which is set in a pretty garden only a few metres from the Azerbaijan border (go out of the gate, turn right and then left and you're there). It charges IR155,000 for a comfortable double room, with TV, fridge and decent bathroom. As at most Iran Tour-

ing & Tourism Organisation (ITTO) places, you won't have much luck negotiating a discount even for single occupancy.

There are a few **kabābīs** around Shahrdārī Square, but the best place to eat in town is the **restaurant** at the Āstārā Inn.

Getting There & Away
Every hour, minibuses head towards Rasht, Bandar-é Anzalī and Ardabīl (IR3000), where you can get onward connections. Shared taxis ply the same route for roughly twice the bus fare. An alternative way to get to Rasht, Bandar-é Anzalī or Ardabīl is to take a private taxi to the main road (3km from the town) and wave down any transport going your way.

Assuming your paperwork is in order and you're allowed to cross the Azerbaijani border, it is four hours to Baku by shared taxi compared with about 10 hours by bus as everybody's bags are given a complete going over. See the Getting There & Away chapter for more information about crossing the border into Azerbaijan.

RASHT رشت
☎ 0131 • pop 400,000 • elevation -7m
About 15km inland from the Anzalī Lagoon, Rasht is the largest city in the Caspian

THE CASPIAN SEA

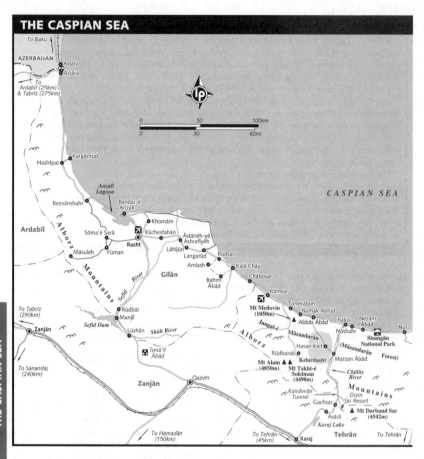

THE CASPIAN SEA

To Baku

AZERBAIJAN

Astara
Āstārā

To Ardabīl (25km) & Tabrīz (275km)

CASPIAN SEA

Hashtpar

Kargānrūd

Anzalī Lagoon

Rezvānshahr

Bandar-é Anzalī

Ardabīl

Khomām

Sōma'é Sarā
Kūchesfahān

Āstāneh-yé Ashrafiyéh

Rasht

Māsuleh
Fūman

Lāhījān
Langarūd
Rūdsar

Amlash
Kalā Chāy

Gīlān

Chābosar

Bahim Ābād

Rāmsar

To Tabrīz (290km)

Rūdbār
Manjīl

Mt Medovin (1050m)

Tonekābon

Zanjān

Sefīd Dam

Lūshān
Shāh River

Namak Abrūd
Nezām Ābād

Jangal-é

Māzandarān

Chālūs
Nōshahr

Nūr

Īsmā'īl Ābād

Abbās Ābād

Sisangan National Park (Māzandarān Forest)

To Sanandaj (240km)

Rūdbarak
Hasan Keif

Marzan Ābād

Zanjān

Qazvīn

Mt Alam (4850m)
Kelardasht

Mt Takht-é Soleiman (4490m)

Chālūs River

Kandovān Tunnel
Gachsar

Dizin Ski Resort

To Hamadān (150km)

To Tehrān (45km)
Karaj

Āsārā
Karaj Lake

Tehrān

Mt Darband Sar (4542m)

To Tehrān

provinces and the region's industrial centre. Only 324km north-west of Tehrān along a good motorway, Rasht makes a very popular weekend and holiday destination for Tehrānīs, for whom the change in climate and scenery makes up for an absence of interesting or historic buildings. In itself the city has little to offer travellers but it makes a good base for exploring other places nearby. Come prepared: Rasht is one of the wettest places in Iran, and can be uncomfortably humid in summer. The tap water is best avoided: Stick to bottled water if you can.

History

Rasht grew into a town around the 14th century AD, and soon became the major settlement in Gīlān province. The city has been occupied by Russians several times in its history, most ruinously in 1668 when almost the entire population was massacred by the forces of the Cossack brigand Stenka Razin. Razin had already destroyed the Persian navy in the Caspian Sea. His sole aim in life appears to have been to rape and pillage.

During WWI the city was again occupied by Russians, and in 1920 the Bolsheviks

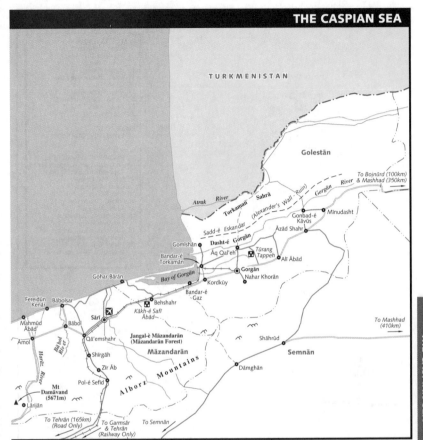

THE CASPIAN SEA

destroyed much of the bazaar, driving many of the townspeople into temporary exile.

Orientation & Information

The three main thoroughfares, Sharīatī, Sa'dī St and Emām Khomeinī Blvd, converge at the vast Shohadā Square, which, during summer, chokes up with something reminiscent of the worst traffic chaos of Tehrān. If you stay near this square you will find it easy enough to get around Rasht.

Visa Extensions Readers have reported some success in getting visa extensions at Rasht police headquarters. The only slight hitch appears to be that as well as paying the IR10,000 visa fee into Bank Melli, you must also pay a IR4,000 fee to Gaidwan Bank, inconspicuously located in a hut beside the visa office.

Money The three major banks should be prepared to change your money although not necessarily speedily. You might be better off patronising Mehrpouya Currency Exchange Service (☎ 40 016, fax 47 200), a safe and legal money exchange office, signposted in English at the end of the lane

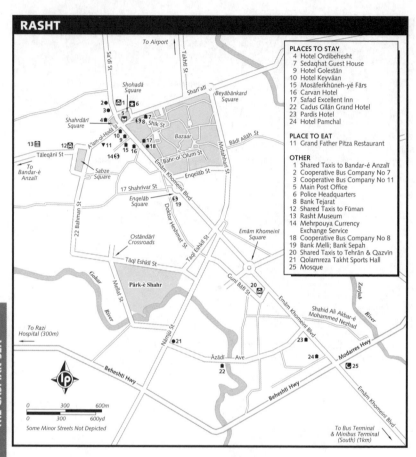

RASHT

To Airport

PLACES TO STAY
4 Hotel Ordibehesht
7 Sedaqhat Guest House
9 Hotel Golestān
10 Hotel Keyvāan
15 Mosāferkhūneh-yé Fārs
16 Carvan Hotel
17 Safad Excellent Inn
22 Cadus Gīlān Grand Hotel
23 Pardis Hotel
24 Hotel Pamchal

PLACE TO EAT
11 Grand Father Pitza Restaurant

OTHER
1 Shared Taxis to Bandar-é Anzalī
2 Cooperative Bus Company No 7
3 Cooperative Bus Company No 11
5 Main Post Office
6 Police Headquarters
8 Bank Tejarat
12 Shared Taxis to Fūman
13 Rasht Museum
14 Mehrpouya Currency
   Exchange Service
18 Cooperative Bus Company No 8
19 Bank Melli; Bank Sepah
20 Shared Taxis to Tehrān & Qazvīn
21 Qolamreza Takht Sports Hall
25 Mosque

Shohadā Square
Sharī'atī
Beyābānkard Square
Shahrdārī Square
Shīk St
Bazaar
Bādī Allāh St
A'lam-ol-Hodā St
Tāleqānī St
Bahr-ol'Olūm St
Motahharī St
To Bandar-è Anzalī
Sabze Square
Emām Khomeinī Blvd
Enqelāb St
17 Shahrīvar St
Enqelāb Square
22 Bahman St
Doktor Heshmat St
Emām Khomeinī Square
Ostāndārī Crossroads
Tāqī Eshkīl St
Gōhar River
Mellat St
Pārk-è Shahr
Taqī Eshkīl St
Nāmjū St
Gunī Bāft St
Emām Khomeinī Blvd
To Razi Hospital (300m)
Shahid Ali Akbar-é Mohammed Nezhad
Zarrūb River
Beheshtī Hwy
Āzādī Ave
Modarres Hwy
Beheshtī Hwy
Emām Khomeinī Blvd
To Bus Terminal & Minibus Terminal (South) (1km)

0   300   600m
0   300   600yd
Some Minor Streets Not Depicted

THE CASPIAN SEA

off Emām Khomeinī Blvd where the Hotel Golestān is located.

Post & Communications The post office is on the south side of Shohadā Square. You can also make phone calls from here.

Emergency There is an official emergency number (☎ 60 825). Alternatively, try directory inquiries (☎ 118). There are several hospitals; the best is the Razi Hospital (☎ 23 963) on Sardār Jangal St. The police headquarters (☎ 27 777) is on the north-east side of Shohadā Square.

Rasht Museum
Rasht Museum (☎ 27 979) on Tāleqānī St is only really worth a look if you've got the time. It contains a small collection of ceramics, pottery, traditional clothes and implements labelled only in Farsi so that it's difficult to learn much. It's open from 9 am to 6 pm daily except Monday; admission costs IR10,000.

Places to Stay
Most of the budget accommodation is around the bazaar district, which is the also the most convenient, if noisy, place to stay.

Rashtīs – Butt of Many a Joke

Political correctness has yet to touch the Iranian sense of humour. Rashtī jokes are as much part of the national culture of Iran as Irish jokes used to be in England. Much fun is made of the curiously lisping Rashtī accent, but most of the jokes home in on the popular belief that Rashtī husbands can't trust their wives to be faithful.

Other stereotypes have it that Āzārīs are slow-witted, Esfahānīs mean and cunning, people from Orūmīyeh too clever for their own good and Qazvīnīs sexually promiscuous.

However, some places will not take foreigners, and you may have trouble finding somewhere cheap in peak season (May to September). In summer a fan or air-con is essential as the humidity can be unbearable.

Places to Stay – Budget

Although Rasht has quite a few cheap places to stay, most of them have come in for criticism from readers, both for their standards of cleanliness (or lack of it) and for noise.

The most popular hotel among travellers is the *Carvan Hotel* (☎ 22 613), also signed as the Gesting House Karvan. The staff are friendly, speak some English and are used to foreigners. Beds in very basic rooms, with a fan and sink cost IR20,000 each; the shared toilets can be pretty whiffy in summer. It's easy to spot just off Emām Khomeinī Blvd.

Across Emām Khomeinī Blvd and inside a shopping mall is the new *Safad Excellent Inn* (☎ 42 407); look out for the neon sign and once inside the mall, turn right and look for a flight of stairs up on the left. Simple singles/doubles up lots of stairs cost IR30,000/ 40,000.

Another cheapie is the *Mosāferkhūneh-yé Fārs* (☎ 25 257), down a side alley off Emām Khomeinī Blvd, near a cinema. It's not signposted in English, so look for the manager, who is likely to be sitting on a chair at the foot of the stairs. Quiet rooms with a fan cost IR16,000/23,000 without/with bathroom but a reader complained that the showers were always cold.

Opposite the Fārs is the rambling *Hotel Golestān* (☎ 29 131). The rooms are quiet and cost IR15,000/20,000 for singles/doubles, but some have no outside window and there's no shower on the premises.

We used to recommend the centrally located *Sedaghat Guest House* (☎ 46 088) on Sharīatī St, up five flights of stairs – look for a tiny sign in English above the door. Unfortunately, although the manager is friendly and speaks reasonable English, the place is now dirty even by the often grungy standards of mosāferkhūnehs. A musty-smelling double costs IR30,000.

Places to Stay – Mid-Range & Top End

There are several decent mid-range places to stay and you may be able to negotiate a discount outside the busy summer period.

Many foreigners end up at the *Hotel Ordibehesht* (☎/fax 22 210) on Shahrdārī Square, immediately to the west of Shohadā Square. It's very convenient if you arrive in town by shared taxi and only too visible from the main square, but depending on who's staffing the desk you may or may not get a friendly reception. Large, clean rooms with air-con cost IR150,000/180,000.

At the *Hotel Keyvāan* (☎ 22 967) on Emām Khomeinī Blvd, dejected-looking rooms are noisier, the bathrooms less well-kept and the staff not especially friendly. A double costs IR106,000 (no discounts for singles).

Less conveniently located but still worth investigating are three other good hotels. Pleasant, if rather noisy, rooms with TV and air con cost US$30 at the classy *Pardis Hotel* (☎ 31 177, fax 30 997) on Emām Khomeinī Blvd; the *Pamchal Hotel* (☎ 666 3822), just off Emām Khomeinī Blvd, is far better value at US$15/20 for spacious singles/doubles, although the bathrooms have squat toilets only. The vast *Cadus Gīlān Grand Hotel* (☎ 39 071, fax 30 050) on Āzādī Ave caters mainly for tour groups but offers comfortable modern rooms with TV, fridge and air con for US$48/60/72 a single/double/triple. 'Extras' include a pool, coffee shop, pizzeria and a good restaurant.

Places to Eat

Chicken and fish are common ingredients in Rashtī cooking, as are pickles of various kinds. Many restaurants also serve *fesenjān* (meat stew with pomegranate juice, walnuts, aubergine and cardamom). There are several decent Western-style *hamburger joints* around Sabze and Shohadā Squares, but the cheapest places to eat are the *stalls* which are set up in the bazaar every evening; join the huddles of locals tucking into tasty lima beans mopped up with hunks of bread, with tea and boiled eggs.

The welcoming *Grand Father Pitza Restaurant* on A'lam-ol-Hodā St is a great place to go if you fancy a Western-style pizza; the chicken, cheese and mushroom version is well worth a splurge of IR15,000. Schnitzel and pasta cost about the same. Look out for a giant döner kabāb stand and peer down the corridor behind it.

The *Pardis Hotel* has an elegant restaurant, and the *Hotel Pamchal* is worth the short shared taxi ride from the town centre. The *Hotel Ordibehesht* also has a decent ground-floor restaurant, although when we were there, the chicken kabāb turned out to be cheap (IR12,000) because it was entirely made up of back bone! One reader wrote in to recommend the sturgeon kabāb for IR20,000. You pay an extra 15% for service, but since you get mayonnaise, a bucket of ice for your soft drink and – heavens! – fresh French-style bread, it's probably worth it.

As you'd expect, the restaurant at the *Cadus Gīlān Grand Hotel* is excellent, with nibbles of olives and walnuts preceding dishes such as tasty whitefish or kabābs. This is a good place to sample caviar but you should reckon on forking out around IR30,000 for a full meal with a cold drink.

For afters, look out for *stalls* about town selling hazelnuts and delicious nut brittle.

Getting There & Away

Air Iran Air (☎ 722 444) has daily flights from Rasht to Tehrān (IR91,000); and twice-weekly flights to Mashhad (IR173,000). The once-weekly flight to Tabrīz costs IR92,000.

The Iran Air office is in the suburb of Shahrak-é Golsār, just north of the city cen-

tre. Take a shared taxi from Shohadā Square to 'Golsār' (IR250), and look for the well-signposted building on the left-hand side of the main road. The airport is only a short distance north of Rasht on the road to Bandar-é Anzalī.

Bus The bus station (*termīnāl*) is some way out of town, so take a shared taxi from outside the Hotel Keyvāan heading south along Emām Khomeinī Blvd. You can buy tickets at one of several bus companies in the centre of town; one of the best is the Cooperative Bus Company No 7 (☎ 722 599).

There are several daily buses to the following destinations, among others:

destination	distance (km)	duration (hrs)	cost (IR)
Esfahān	737	12	17,000
Gorgān	511	9	10,500
Hamadan	407	9	8000
Mashhad	1075	18	23,000
Sārī	380	7	10,000
Tabrīz	481	9	12,000
Tehrān	324	6	18,000

To get to places east of Rāmsar, take a bus heading for Sārī, Gorgān or Mashhad and ask to be dropped off along the way. Note that there are no direct buses to Qazvīn from Rasht and that if you take a Tehrān bus you will be dropped at a roundabout a good 5km out of town; it's better to take a shared taxi.

Minibus The two minibus stations are in the outer suburbs. Minibuses leave from near the main bus station every 15 to 20 minutes to places as far east as Chālūs (IR7500). Minibuses to Bandar-é Anzalī (IR3000) and Āstārā (IR9000) leave from the small Īstgāh-é Anzalī – to get there take a shared taxi from Shohadā Square.

Shared Taxi Tracking down a shared taxi can be confusing as they leave from all over the place. Those going to Rāmsar (IR12,000) generally leave from around Shohadā Square; those to Fūman (IR1500; for connections to Māsuleh) from Sabze Square; and those to

Bandar-é Anzalī (IR2000) from around the post office corner of Shohadā Square. Shared taxis to Tehrān (about IR40,000) and Qazvīn (IR30,000) depart from near the Hotel Ordibehesht and a spot along Emām Khomeinī Blvd. For other destinations, try the Īstgāh-é Anzalī.

Getting Around

There's no airport bus service. You can try asking about shared taxis around Shohadā Square but you will probably end up paying about IR7500 for a private one.

Hundreds of shared and private taxis congregate around Shohadā Square and ply up and down the main roads for IR500 per trip.

AROUND RASHT

If the hustle, bustle, heat and humidity of Rasht is getting you down, then head up into the hills for some cooler weather and fantastic hikes.

Fūman   فـومن

If you're heading for Māsuleh you may want to pause in Fūman, a leafy junction town 33km to the east. Fūman's wide boulevards are lined with date palms, plane trees or an incongruous mixture of both, and it's known as the 'City of Statues' as a result of the sheer quantity of kitsch plaster-cast statues dotted about town. Many of these depict hunters; others show local inhabitants handing out the Fūman traditional cookies for which the town is also famed. If you'd like to try the cookies, look out for bakeries advertising them about town. They're outsize circular biscuits with patterns embossed on the top and a thin walnut paste inside, best eaten fresh from the oven.

Shared taxis to Fūman (IR1500, 30 minutes) leave from Sabze Square in Rasht. They will drop you off in Valiasr Square in Fūman. To find a minibus (IR1000, 30 minutes) or shared taxi (IR2000) on to Māsuleh, walk straight ahead through the shops to the main road and turn left. Minibuses ply up and down this road but for a shared taxi you will need to walk about 1km to the edge of town, or take yet another shared taxi (IR250).

Māsuleh   ماسوله
☎ 01864 • elevation 1050m

There are many traditional and unspoilt mountain villages throughout Gīlān province, but one of the most breathtakingly beautiful is Māsuleh, a perfectly preserved village that appears to have grown out of its surroundings like a limpet clinging to a rock. It's formed by several irregular levels of pale cream houses with grey slate roofs, interspersed with evergreen trees. So steep is the slope that the familiar Iranian network of narrow alleys is entirely absent; instead the flat roofs of many houses form a pathway for the level above.

Māsuleh has few specific facilities to offer the visitor, but its inspiring setting makes it a perfect antidote to travel in the dry and dusty central plateau. It's bitterly cold in winter, with snow sometimes 3m deep, but the climate in summer is extremely pleasant. In summer about 1600 people live here but this dwindles to around 600 in winter, which makes finding private accommodation much trickier. There are no established hiking trails, so just strike off in any direction that takes your fancy.

Places to Stay & Eat Although it's perfectly feasible to visit Māsuleh on a day trip from Rasht, the atmosphere is so pleasantly laid-back that you may want to stay put here for a few days. Currently the only proper hotel is the **Monfared Masooleh Hotel** (☎ 32 50, fax 43 19), easy to spot, next to the main bus and taxi stop. Spacious singles/doubles with TV, fridge, cooking facilities and bath cost US$20/30. It boasts two **restaurants**, with potentially wonderful views marred by roadworks at the time of writing. We had been receiving a lot of complaints about this place but after a change of management things look set to improve.

As you walk into the village you can hardly miss the building above a cafe on the left which calls itself **Cheap Hotel**. However, since all you'll get for your IR30,000 is floor space you're probably better off inquiring about renting a room in a private house.

If you ask about, you should be able to rent a *room* in a local home with your own kitchen and bathroom for as little as IR50,000 a double. Prices are likely to go up but should still be lower than in the hotel. A good place to start asking is the blacksmith's shop in the tiny bazaar.

The area around Māsuleh is probably one of the nicest places in Iran for *camping*, and there's nothing to stop you pitching a tent anywhere you want near the village. On the road up to Māsuleh from Fūman there are several *cabins*; they're aimed at domestic tourists, and without a car they'll be inconveniently far out, but there's nothing to stop you renting one.

Getting There & Away Getting to Māsuleh from Rasht (56km away) requires a change of transport in Fūman (see the Fūman section earlier). It's best to allow most of the day for a trip there and back, especially if you want to look around Fūman too. On Fridays and public holidays you may be lucky and find a shared taxi direct to Māsuleh from Rasht.

Alternatively, since the road up to Māsuleh is one of the prettiest in Iran, passing rice paddies, tea plantations, thatch-roofed houses and dense forest, it might be worth chartering a taxi from Rasht so you can stop to take photos. The trip should cost about IR40,000 return, including waiting time.

The Hotel Ordibehesht in Rasht also organises 'tours' with a two-hour stop in Māsuleh for IR70,000.

Note that if you drive up to Māsuleh you will be charged IR2000 to park in the village.

BANDAR-É ANZALĪ   بندر انزلی
☎ 0181

This town first came to prominence in the early 19th century as the Russians took a hold on trade in the Caspian Sea; while traders from Western Europe were most active in the region, the river port of Langarūd, 96km to the east, was the main outlet to northern Persia. Around 1800 the Russians established their trading post at Bandar-é Anzalī, taking advantage of its unrivalled natural harbour. Since then it has been the only major port along the southern Caspian coast, and today

it's the only one actively trading with the former Soviet states. The Russian influence over Anzalī has been strong, and the city bears a remarkable physical likeness to the Azerbaijani port of Baku, its main trading partner on the western Caspian Sea. Not surprisingly, you can pick up Russian produce in the bazaar, including the famous nests of wooden dolls.

Orientation & Information

Bandar-é Anzalī is divided in two by the outlet of the Anzalī Lagoon (Mordāb-é Anzalī); two bridges connect the town to the small and undeveloped Beheshtī Island, just inside the mouth of the lagoon. The docks and Customs House are on Gomrok Square, but the main commercial centre is around Emām Khomeinī Square, past the second bridge as you approach from Rasht.

A wide and often windswept promenade is situated along the west bank, facing the harbour; from there you can organise boat trips into the lagoon. Bank Melli and Bank Sepah, both on Emām Khomeinī Square, will change money.

Anzalī Lagoon

Although Anzalī is a pleasant town, the real reason to come here is the 450 sq km Anzalī Lagoon, one of the largest freshwater lagoons in the world and an internationally recognised haven for migratory waterfowl. In all, 70 species of migratory birds are recorded at Anzalī. The best time to visit is June when many of the birds will be nesting. At other times you should still be able to see terns, herons, cormorants and assorted birds of prey.

To take a boat out on the lagoon, head for the promenade near the Hotel Iran where you will be able to hire a boat for around IR40,000 per hour. Unfortunately all the boats are speedboats and although this makes for an exhilarating ride, keen birdwatchers may find it upsetting to see all the birds they've come to see flying away in terror. There are other places about town to hire boats (follow the painted waterlily signs on the walls to find them) but although the boats may be more comfortable, they're also more expensive (IR100,000 to IR175,000).

Blooming Algae

Unfortunately, at the time of writing the Anzalī Lagoon was being colonised by a fast-growing algae that threatens to smother all the other plant life. Why this is happening has not yet been confirmed, although some probable culprits will be obvious even to casual visitors: pollution seeping down from the Caspian Sea, household waste being emptied into the water from the homes lining its shore, and oil leaking from the boats that whiz visitors around the lagoon.

The United Nations Development Program (UNDP) has agreed to work with Iran to try to find a solution. However, once it has taken a grip, this algae is notoriously difficult to uproot.

Most boat rides whisk you past waterside houses, reminiscent of those you see in Bangkok, and out into the lagoon. Afterwards the boats whip you around the harbour where you can observe the rusting hulks of ancient Soviet ships, and out as far as the Caspian Sea itself.

Other Attractions

Although Anzalī has a big **caviar-processing factory**, managed by the state-run Iranian Fishing Company, the public is not currently allowed to visit it. (The secret process of caviar production is a serious and very competitive business, earning the country millions of dollars.) If you want to buy caviar, look for the fishy section of the daily **Shanbeh Bazaar**, which is particularly busy on Saturday.

Anzalī is the only Iranian Caspian port with a real promenade, and it's enjoyable to while away a few hours strolling along it and soaking up a bit of Iranian seaside *joie de vivre*.

There's a small **military museum** in Takavaran St and some mildly interesting, very Russian-looking 19th-century **ruins** around Emām Khomeinī Square.

Places to Stay & Eat

The only budget place to stay is the *Tehrān Hotel* (☎ 22 868), a charming place upstairs on Emām Khomeinī Square, with beds for IR12,000. It doesn't seem too keen to accommodate foreigners though.

The *Hotel Iran* (☎ 22 524, fax 28 060, Motahharī Ave), east of Emām Khomeinī Square towards the promenade, offers comfortable doubles, some of them with river views, for IR200,000 (no discounts for single occupancy). In summer it's often full anyway. It boasts a very good *restaurant*.

Perhaps the nicest place to stay (even though it's potentially noisy) is the quirky, attractive *Hotel Ancient Golsang* (☎ 23 910) on Emām Khomeinī Square. Big singles/doubles with high ceilings, fan and bathroom cost IR96,000/120,000.

If you'd rather stay near the sea *Grand Hotel Cadusan* (☎ 43 001, fax 41 482, Pasdaran Ave) has spacious, reasonably comfortable rooms with bath for an excessive US$45 (no single discounts); those at the back have sea views.

Around Emām Khomeinī Square there are several decent **snack bars** and upmarket **restaurants**. The *Yass* offers fish lunches for around IR30,000, or there's the restaurant under the *Hotel Ancient Golsang* that serves fish and rice for IR28,000, if you can bear to eat under the watchful eyes of assorted stuffed coots, herons, Caspian seals etc. If you're staying at the *Grand Hotel Cadusan* there's a rather soulless restaurant that can rustle up shrimps, whitefish and steak.

Getting There & Away

Shared taxis for Rasht (IR2000, 30 minutes) leave from Emām Khomeinī Square. Regular minibuses and shared taxis to Āstārā (IR5000) depart from the junction heading north from near the second bridge as you come in from Rasht. For most other destinations, you're better off going to Rasht and getting a connection there. A couple of bus companies offering services to Āstārā, Tehrān, Ardabīl and Tabrīz can be found on Emām Khomeinī Square.

At the time of writing it was impossible to confirm the timetable for passenger/cargo boats from Anzalī to Baku, the Azerbaijani capital. If they run at all, it seems to be to a very erratic schedule, which it may

Alarm Bells Ring for Caspian Wildlife

The Caspian has always been home to vast numbers of fish, including the caviar-producing sturgeon, migratory birds, turtles, and the unique Caspian seal. However, its ecology is under threat from shipping, the development of ports, industrial chemical waste, oil and gas exploration, and broken oil and gas pipelines. A recent report suggested that more than 11,000 seals and thousands of other marine animals had died in the first quarter of 2000.

Of all the threats to the Caspian one of the worst may come from illegal fishing and caviar smuggling. The number of sturgeon in the sea is already said to have shrunk by 25%. Environmentalists are talking of a disaster comparable to that which turned the Aral Sea into a lifeless cesspit unless urgent steps are taken to improve matters. But with five countries claiming a stake in the Caspian, it's hard to see an agreement coming easily.

be virtually impossible to ascertain in advance. Ask at the Azerbaijani embassy in Tehrān before setting out.

LĀHĪJŪN لاهیجان
☎ 0141

On the road between Rasht and Rāmsar, Lāhījūn, is a small town which tends to be a traffic bottleneck. There are still a few **traditional Caspian houses** with sloping, channelled brick roofs and pastel-coloured walls, but most have been superseded by modern houses of metal, plastic and cement.

Lāhījūn was once the only settlement of any size in Gīlān, but it fell into decline after the 14th century as Rasht grew up to eclipse it. It does attract a few tourists, but its main claim to fame is as a tea-growing area.

Mosque of the Four Guardians
The Mosque of the Four Guardians (Masjed-é Chahār Ōleyā') is on Sardār Jangal Square, in the west of Lāhījūn. Probably dating from the 13th century, it is dedicated to four members of the Sādāt-é Keyā family, though tombs are only visible for three of them. You can see some excellent examples of woodcarving inside the mosque. One of its carved wooden doors – among the finest surviving examples of its kind – is in the National Museum of Iran in Tehrān.

Mausoleum of Sheikh Zāhed
A short distance east of Lāhījūn, along the road to Langarūd, is this historic and typically colourful Caspian mausoleum, Boq'eh-yé Sheikh Zāhed. The square building has a tiled roof surmounted by a sculpted, pyramid-shaped painted roof, supported by white pillars on three sides. The inner vault is covered with colourfully tiled plaster mouldings and contains the tombs of Sheikh Zāhed and two other religious figures, Sayyed Rezā Keyā and Gholām Sheikh. The date on the carved wooden tomb of Sheikh Zāhed corresponds to 1419, although part of the original structure may have been built before this date.

Next door is a simple teahouse where you can buy home-made tea.

Tea History Museum of Iran
This museum (☎ 229 980) in East Kashef St was established around the mausoleum of Kashef ol-Saltaneh, who was credited with having introduced tea cultivation to Iran. It's open from 8 am to 6 pm daily except Monday.

Sheitān Kūh
Sheitān Kūh (Devil Mountain) is a tree-covered hill south of the eastern approach to Lāhījūn, with a natural pool and large park on its slopes. There are plenty of forested hills suitable for hiking around this eastern part of town.

Places to Stay & Eat
Lāhījūn is an easy day trip from Rasht so there's no need to stay. If you do stay, the only hotel is the pleasant *Chaharfasi Guest House*, signposted in English, on Shohadā Square – the main square with the unimpressive, oversized pot plant in the middle. Clean, comfortable if noisy rooms cost a negotiable IR25,000.

There are several *hamburger joints* and *kabābīs* along the main streets. Home-made

Roots of That Cuppa

Arguably Iran's best and most famous *chāy* (tea) comes from around Lāhījūn, in Gīlān province, where the climate is ideal for tea growing. More than 90% of Iran's tea comes from Gīlān province, a total output of about 60,000 tonnes per year, although still not enough to meet the demands of tea-loving Iranians.

The Indians and Chinese were busy cultivating and enjoying the tea leaf centuries ago, but tea didn't reach Persia until the 17th century and even then was only available to the Persian elite.

During the Qajar period, attempts to grow tea in Persia were unsuccessful, but in about 1900, an Iranian consul living in India somehow learnt the secret of good tea growing and brought home 4000 tea plants. Not surprisingly he's remembered in a mausoleum near Lāhījūn.

You will see plenty of plantations along the main road between Rasht and Gorgān.

tea is served in the *teahouse* behind the Mausoleum of Sheikh Zāhed.

Getting There & Away

Several bus companies have offices around Shohadā Square and buses from Rasht, Sārī and Gorgān also stop for passengers at Lāhījūn. From Shohadā Square you can also easily catch a shared taxi to towns east or west along the main coast road.

The Hotel Ordibehesht in Rasht offers taxi 'tours' to Lāhījūn for IR45,000, including two hours' waiting time.

RĀMSAR رامسر
☎ 01942

Since the mountains stop only a few hundred metres short of the coast at this point, is squeezed into little more than a couple of main streets, which has helped to make this one of Iran's more attractive seaside resorts. The last shah built a palace in the thickly wooded hills overlooking the town, and who can blame him, since the setting is one of the best anywhere along the Caspian coast.

Apart from visiting the Caspian Museum, there's not much to do here, but the scenery and laid-back atmosphere is usually enough for most visitors. It has to be said, though, that unrestrained development has started to spoil some of the erstwhile wonderful views. People here are very friendly and like to see foreigners, perhaps because they bring back memories of the boom years before the Islamic Revolution when women strolled around town in bikinis and blackjack was the game of choice in the casino.

Orientation & Information

Rāmsar stretches for many kilometres along the coast and for a few blocks either side of the coast road. The main thoroughfare is Motahharī St, but a lot of traffic bypasses the town and travels along the main road closer to the beach. Don't assume you'll be able to change money anywhere in town.

Caspian Museum

Just west of the Rāmsar Grand Hotel, what was once the summer palace built in 1937 for Reza Shāh is now open to the public as the Caspian Museum. The small, curvy, white kiosk is set amid sweet-smelling box hedges, with wooded mountains providing a spectacular backdrop. The richly furnished rooms once used by the Pahlavīs have been retained just as they were, and English-speaking guides are on hand to identify the origins of the chandeliers, gilded dinner service, carpets, paintings etc. Interestingly, the so-called bedroom has no bed in it because Reza Shāh was a soldier who preferred to sleep on the carpeted floor.

Walk around the back of the kiosk to see two **marble tigers**, their faces contorted in rage but their paws neatly crossed as if they were domestic cats in front of a fire. Here, too, you can see the shah's private **bathroom**, still under restoration at the time of research.

On the front porch don't miss a copy of Khomeinī's **edict** of 1979 authorising the confiscation of all the Pahlavīs' possessions.

The museum is open from 9 am to 1 pm and 4 to 8 pm (to 10 pm Thursday) daily. Admission costs IR20,000.

THE CASPIAN SEA

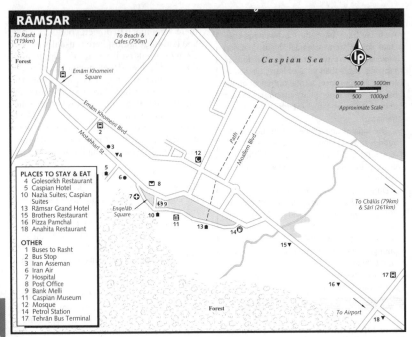

RĀMSAR

To Rasht (119km)
To Beach & Cafes (750m)

Forest

Caspian Sea

Emām Khomeinī Square

Emām Khomeinī Blvd

Moṭahharī St

Moʻallem Blvd

Path

0   500   1000m
0   500   1000yd
Approximate Scale

To Chālūs (79km) & Sārī (261km)

Engelāb Square

To Airport

Forest

PLACES TO STAY & EAT
4 Golesorkh Restaurant
5 Caspian Hotel
10 Nazia Suites; Caspian Suites
13 Rāmsar Grand Hotel
15 Brothers Restaurant
16 Pizza Pamchal
18 Anahita Restaurant

OTHER
1 Buses to Rasht
2 Bus Stop
3 Iran Asseman
6 Iran Air
7 Hospital
8 Post Office
9 Bank Melli
11 Caspian Museum
12 Mosque
14 Petrol Station
17 Tehrān Bus Terminal

THE CASPIAN SEA

Beach

Even if you don't, like one reader, come across the dead carcasses of any dogs, it's unlikely that you'll be much impressed with Rāmsar's beach. A once spectacular but now slowly fading palm-tree-lined promenade runs down from opposite the Rāmsar Grand Hotel to the beach, or you can take the seaward road from near the Iran Asseman office. Unfortunately all you'll come to is a few empty cafes and souvenir shops overlooking a dirty gravel beach, with some wretched horses waiting to be hired nearby. Men and women must swim in separate areas and women must keep their *hejab* (covering garments) on, which rather militates against having a fun time in the water.

Places to Stay

Rāmsar has some of the best accommodation along the Caspian coast. It may not be terribly cheap, but you can usually stay either in a suite or villa (a fully equipped self-

catering apartment); or a homestay (a room in the home of a friendly local). For a *homestay*, either ask at the snack bars near the Iran Asseman office, or just look lost around the Anahita Restaurant for a few minutes and someone will probably rush to offer you something. You will probably be asked for IR40,000 or IR50,000, although sometimes (especially in high summer) the only places on offer are large apartments suitable for groups and charging around IR150,000, regardless of whether you're alone or not. Take care that you're not accepting somewhere out in a remote part of town.

The best place to head for is the huddle of suites known collectively as *Nazia Suites* (☎ 66 00), not far from the Rāmsar Grand Hotel. The first place you see as you enter from the road costs a reasonable IR40,000 for an apartment with two beds, kitchen, fridge, TV, sitting room and bathroom. Next door the *Caspian Suites* (☎ 67 700) are sumptuous apartments, with everything but a bar, for IR70,000 a night; the price decreases for longer stays. The garden here is particularly inviting. Unfortunately, over high summer both sets of suites are likely to be fully booked for months in advance.

If the suites are full and you can't land a private room for a price you can afford, the friendly *Caspian Hotel* (☎ 22 457), just off Motahharī St, also offers glistening new self-catering apartments for which the owners ask a negotiable IR100,000 per person.

The impressive four-star *Rāmsar Grand Hotel* (☎ 23 592, fax 25 174) is set up on the hillside, overlooking the town. If possible, try to get a room in the older wing, which used to be the casino, rather than in the modern annexe. The older rooms costs US$40/60 a single/double, with the newer ones costing US$5 less (plus 21% tax). The views from all of them must have been spectacular until someone utterly insensitive authorised the construction of the huge, ugly, high-rise apartment blocks that stand unfinished nearby. If there are enough people, the hotel can sometimes organise tours to places like the mountain village of Javehar Deh, with a chance to do some hiking.

Places to Eat

There are several very reasonable *kabābīs* and *hamburger joints* along Motahharī St, mainly catering for passing traffic. To serve all the self-caterers in town there are also quite a few grocery and vegetable shops dotted along the main street.

The big *Golesorkh Restaurant* has tables indoors and out, and can even manage a menu in English; a local *tarsh kabāb* made with a pomegranate and walnut sauce costs IR18,000. Also good is the *Anahita Restaurant* serving other local dishes like *mirza-qasemi*, a stew made with meat, garlic and tomatoes (IR9500). A local broad bean stew costs IR14,000. For more standard kabābs and rice try the *Brothers Restaurant*; there's no sign in English but it's a vast building raised off the footpath and usually packed with happy Iranian diners.

The menu in the *Roz Restaurant* in the Rāmsar Grand Hotel is in English. Prices are mostly from about IR20,000 to IR30,500 a dish, plus 15% tax, but it also serves spaghetti bolognaise for IR14,000. If that's still too much, try a tea or coffee in the sumptuous lounge just for the experience.

If you fancy a pizza you could do much worse than head straight for *Pizza Pamchal* where delicious pizzas (about IR12,000) are served in a cafe with a stream running through the middle and two large aviaries and a big fish tank to keep diners entertained.

Getting There & Away

Air Although Iran Air (☎ 27 88) doesn't fly to or from Rāmsar, it does have a small office along the main street. Staff are helpful, perhaps because they don't have many customers. The nearest Iran Air flights are from Sārī and Rasht.

Iran Asseman (☎ 45 25) also has an office on the main street and offers twice-weekly flights between Tehrān and Rāmsar (IR92,000).

Bus & Minibus You can pick up a minibus to Rasht (IR2500, two hours) from Emām Khomeinī Square.

To get to Chālūs, Sārī and Gorgān, you can also catch any bus going through Rāmsar. Note that most public transport doesn't go along Motahharī St, but detours at the western entrance to Rāmsar and hurtles along the main street closer to the beach. Just stand at the unofficial bus stop indicated on the map and flag down something going your way.

Direct buses to Tehrān (IR10,600, six hours) leave from an office 100m north of the Anahita Restaurant.

Shared Taxi As elsewhere in the region, shared taxis offer the quickest, if not the cheapest, way to get around. To get to Rasht (IR7500), take a shared taxi from Emām Khomeinī Square. To get to Chālūs, ask around the Bank Melli in the centre of town or flag something going along the northern main road – but not along Motahharī St.

Getting Around

The airport is about 2km from Rāmsar, on the way to Chālūs. You should be able to get into town from the airport in a shared taxi for not much more than IR1000, but you'll probably need to charter one to get to the airport from Rāmsar (about IR2000).

Most places in Rāmsar are within easy walking distance of each other but if you do need to take a taxi just hail one and say *mostaqīm* (straight ahead). They all travel between the Rasht station and Bank Melli, and down the two main roads to the beach, for IR250 per trip.

AROUND RĀMSAR
Bahim Ābād   بهیم آباد

There isn't a lot to do around Rāmsar, but a visit to Bahim Ābād, 38km west of Rāmsar off the main road to Rasht, is a good idea. This friendly little village has been made popular by Rāmsarīs who flock here for the mineral hot springs. You will probably need to charter a taxi from Rāmsar, or take a shared taxi and ask to be dropped off in Kalā Chāy, from where you can walk the 5km north to Bahim Ābād.

NŌSHAHR &   نوشهر
CHĀLŪS   چالوس
☎ 0191

Once two of the quaintest villages along the Caspian coast, the twin towns of Nōshahr and Chālūs are now part of the horrid urban sprawl that stretches between Rasht and Sārī. Although they're readily accessible from Tehrān, the only reason to stay in either town is to explore the attractions nearby. Since there are good transport links between Nōshahr and Chālūs, even late at night, you can easily stay in one town and still take advantage of the restaurants etc in the other.

If you must stay, leafier Nōshahr is a nicer place to do so than Chālūs, a sprawling industrial and junction town, 5km to the west. There's also an impressive new mosque, the Jāmeh Mosque, in Nōshahr. Nōshahr port was enlarged recently, engulfing what used to be a popular bathing beach, but as there's little shipping business, the town still relies on domestic tourism for its livelihood.

Trekking
There's a relatively easy three- or four-day trek from Garmabdar to Nōshahr, although

you will need a guide to steer you through some of the dense forest along the way. To start the trek, take a minibus or private taxi to Garmabdar and then head north, detouring around Mt Darband Sar (4542m).

From Chālūs, it's also possible to trek to Karaj, near Tehrān, over the Alborz Mountains. The easy route takes the Kandovān tunnel, south of Gachsar, and bypasses the road from Gachsar to Āsārā. It skirts the picturesque Karaj Lake, but from then on the scenery is destroyed by the ugly urban sprawl of Karaj. This is a very popular driving route from Tehrān, taking the best part of a day to complete.

Places to Stay & Eat
Nōshahr The one place to stay in Nōshahr is the friendly *Shalizar Restaurant & Hotel* (☎ 34 264, fax 35 051) on Āzādī Ave. Tastefully decorated rooms, with air-con, fridge, bathroom and good views, cost a negotiable IR150,000 but can be a bit noisy because of the traffic roundabout outside. The basement *restaurant* is done up like a cave with jars of pickled vegetables on the tables. A plate of fish kabābs, though tasty, costs a pretty steep IR40,000.

Chālūs There are two comfortable, midrange places just at the point where Nōshahr and Chālūs meet. The *Hotel Malek* (☎ 24 107, fax 23 602) on Nōshahr Blvd asks IR123,000 for pleasant air-con rooms, some with a self-catering unit; while the *Hotel Kourosh* (☎ 23 104, fax 24 174) also on Nōshahr Blvd asks IR90,000/120,000 a single/double in a building set back from the main road and so possibly a bit quieter (one four-bedded room for IR200,000 is particularly good value).

A few decent pizzerias and hamburger joints are spread along the main road, and are easy enough to find using a shared taxi. One of the best is *Toranj Pizza*. The *Malek* and *Kourosh* hotels have good restaurants, although they don't open until 8 pm for dinner.

Getting There & Away
Air Iran Asseman flies to Nōshahr from Tehrān (IR92,000) once a week, and usually

more often in summer. Its office (rarely open) is on the main road into Nōshahr from Chālūs. The airport is north of the main road between the two towns; take a private taxi.

Bus & Minibus Most onward transport leaves from Chālūs rather than Nōshahr. Take a shared taxi along Nōshahr Blvd and get out at the big Moalan Square, before the road crosses a bridge into Chālūs shopping centre. The Number One bus station, for buses to Tehrān (IR8300, five hours, 205km), Mashhad (IR18,000/35,000, 14 hours, 877km) and Tabrīz (IR16,000, 11 hours, 679km), is a few hundred metres north of the square.

For buses and minibuses to other points along the Caspian coast you will have to go to the Tonekābon bus station, east of the Number One station. There are all sorts of vehicles heading towards Rasht and Rāmsar (minibuses to Rasht leave about every 15 minutes in summer); east to Sārī and Gorgān (about every hour); and every 30 minutes or so to Tehrān. There are also a couple of daily buses to Mashhad, Sārī and Tabrīz. Whatever you do, don't confuse the Tonekābon station with the town of Tonekābon, some 60km west of Chālūs.

To get to anywhere between Nōshahr and Nūr, take a minibus from the main square in Nōshahr.

Shared Taxi To get to Namak Abrūd, take a shared taxi from Moalan Square in Chālūs (IR2000). Shared taxis to Tehrān (IR20,000) leave from outside the Number One bus station in Chālūs. Regular shared taxis also run to Rāmsar and Āmol from the Tonekābon bus station.

Getting Around
There are minibuses between Nōshahr and the main square of Chālūs (IR250), every few minutes until about 6 pm. Alternatively you can take one of the many shared taxis (IR500 to IR700) that speed along the main road.

AROUND NŌSHAHR & CHĀLŪS
There are several quite good sandy beaches along the road between Nōshahr and Nūr,

and a surprising lack of development so far. If you want a plunge, just get on and off the shared taxis and minibuses that regularly screech along the highway.

Namak Abrūd نامک آبرود
In summer people flock to Namak Abrūd, 12km west of Chālūs, to ride the telecabin (cable car) up 1050m-high **Mt Medovin**. It's a magnificent ride, but very cold even in summer, and if you're unlucky the hill will be covered in low cloud, blotting out the magnificent views – make an early start before the clouds can set in. There are plans to build a second telecabin, and dreamers scheme to extend the original all the way to Tehrān.

A return trip on the telecabin costs IR20,000, and it's open from 10 am to 4 pm daily in summer. The entrance is off the main road between Rāmsar and Chālūs, but the telecabin itself is 2km further back; you could probably hitch a ride from the entrance, or just walk – it's easy enough to spot.

Places to Stay A posh European-style resort is planned for the village. Otherwise, it already boasts some upmarket holiday and retirement homes and the five-star *Caspian Āzādī Hotel* (☎ 22 001, fax 22 102), previously the Hyatt Regency and the Caspian Enghelāb, on Rāmsar Rd. Unfortunately, this temple to Western hedonism is largely the preserve of well-to-do Iranians and even wealthier tourists. Prices are US$95/120 for singles/doubles, but although the rooms are perfectly comfortable, you're paying mainly for the views, for the lovely gardens and for the outdoor pool.

Other motels along the road between Rāmsar and Chālūs cater mainly for holidaying Iranians. Foreigners are welcome but these motels are really only convenient if you have your own transport. There are also plenty of self-catering villas, although you are likely to have trouble tracking down their owners; ask at the entrance to the telecabin if anyone knows anywhere to stay, or try a taxi driver.

Getting There & Away Hop on any transport heading west from Chālūs and ask to be dropped at the telecabin. When waiting by the roadside for transport back, lone women can expect to be the object of far too much unwanted attention.

Kelardasht كلاردشت

Nicknamed the 'Paradise of Iran', Kelardasht is a fertile depression more than 1250m above sea level. Recent archaeological discoveries (the finds are in the National Museum of Iran in Tehrān) have uncovered habitation dating back to the 10th century AD. The main town in the region is Hasan Keif, on the road between Abbās Ābād and Marzan Ābād.

Although it's not very easy to reach without a car, Kelardasht is the place to head for if you are hankering after some outdoor activities. There are some great **hiking** trails, especially around the tiny and peculiarly shaped Valasht Lake; **trout fishing** spots in nearby streams; and even **cross-country skiing** in winter. Ideally, come for a few days and bring camping equipment with you. Unfortunately, Kelardasht has become so popular with the locals that litter is becoming a serious problem.

One possible longer **trek** runs from near Ābyek (about halfway between Karaj and Qazvīn), via the foothills of Mt Alam and Kelardasht to Abbās Ābād, just west of Chālūs. You shouldn't need a guide for this walk but if you want one, ask at Kassa Mountaineering & Tourism (☎ 751 0463, fax 751 0464, @ KASSA@intelimet.net), 9 Maghdi Alley, Sharīatī St, Tehrān. Kelardasht also makes a possible base for climbing up Mt Alam itself.

Mt Alam كوه علم

The best place to start climbing Mt Alam (4850m), or one of the dozens of peaks higher than 4000m in this part of the Alborz, is Rūdbarak, about 20km north-east of Mt Alam. At Rūdbarak, you can find somewhere to stay, and organise a guide and hire donkeys and porters for the ascent.

It generally takes two days to trek from Rūdbarak, via Vanderaban village, to the first hut at Sarchal (at 3900m), where you can stay and cook meals. There's another simple hut at 4200m. From Sarchal, the climb to the peak and back along the easiest route (ask directions if you have no guide) can be done in one day. You can also walk from Mt Alam to Mt Takht-é Soleimān (4490m) in one day along a thin ridge, but this is an experts-only route, so seek local advice before attempting it.

Sīsangān National Park پار کملی سی سنگ

This small national park, 31km east of Nōshahr, is a pocket of precious and rare forest, a sad reminder of how beautiful this part of Iran must once have been. In the park, there are a few paved roads and unmarked **trails** leading nowhere in particular, but hikers should find enough to keep them happy for a few hours. You can even hire **horses** for short trots around the park. Entrance to the park is free.

There's nowhere formal to eat, but you can cook for yourself at open (concrete) fireplaces, with tables and toilets to hand. No camping is allowed; Iranian families put up tents as shelters just for the day. Depending on your disposition you may want to avoid Fridays and public holidays in summer, when the park becomes bumper to bumper Paykans and picnic hampers.

From Nōshahr, take a minibus (IR1000, 45 minutes) or shared taxi (IR2000) towards Nūr and get off when you see a sign reading 'Jangali Park' (Jungle Park).

NŪR نور
☎ 1964

The town of Nūr retains some semblance of quaintness. A brief stop or an overnight stay would allow you to explore the nearby attractions, which include the tiny pocket of jungle known as the **Kajvil Forest**.

The two-star *Nūr Grand Hotel* (☎ 33 38) on Moallem Ave charges about US$25/35 for a single/double. Alternatively there's the pricier, classier *Darya-e Nūr Hotel* (☎ 38 14, fax 38 35), opposite the petrol station in nearby Izadshahr.

Nūr is easy enough to reach by minibus (IR1000) or shared taxi (IR2000) from Nōshahr, or you can just jump off any transport travelling along the Chālūs-Āmol road.

ĀMOL آمل

Āmol succeeded Sārī as the capital of the region of Tabarestān in the 9th century, and became renowned for a distinctive style of glazed earthenware pottery, which reached its peak of popularity between the 10th and 13th centuries. After the devastation of the Mongol invasions (AD 1220–1335), Āmol reverted to relative obscurity. In 1888, Edward Browne described it as 'one of the chief cities of Māzandarān, a picturesque straggling town divided into two parts by a large river, which is spanned by a long narrow bridge built of bricks.' Sadly, nobody could write lyrically of its beauty anymore.

You will probably bypass Āmol en route from Chālūs to Sārī, but if you want to climb mighty **Mt Damāvand** from the northern side, Āmol is the best place to look for transport. There's nowhere to stay in Āmol, so you must come here on a day trip from Sārī, Chālūs or Bābol.

Mashhad-é Mīr Bozorg

This mausoleum, built during the reign of Shāh Abbās I, is Āmol's most interesting sight. With its huge dome and brick construction, Safavid tiles and restored sarcophagus (dated AD 1623), this sanctuary of the martyred Mīr Bozorg is situated a short distance north of Āmol on the west bank of the river.

Getting There & Away

There are four main roads out of Āmol, all served by regular shared taxis; Āmol is also the junction for regional transport to and from Tehrān. The north road takes you to the small coastal town of Mahmūd Ābād (20km); the east to Bābol (29km); the south to Tehrān (174km); and the west to Nūr (45km), from where you can get connections to Nōshahr and Chālūs. From Tehrān, shared taxis (IR30,000) and minibuses (IR5000) leave from the Eastern bus station.

BĀBOL & BĀBOLSAR بابل بابلسر
☎ 01291

Founded in the early 16th century on the main east-west route through the Caspian

provinces, Bābol was once a busy and pleasant town with its harbour at Bābolsar. Nowadays it's a sprawling, drab commercial centre and transport junction, with only a few isolated ancient buildings. The small **Archaeology & Ethnology Museum** (☎ 92 877) in Modarres St is usually open from 9 am to noon and 5 to 7.30 pm daily.

Bābolsar port was once the province's main international trading outlet. More recently it has become a fashionable resort town with a luxury seaside hotel complex. Nowadays, however, the dock is dry, tourism is virtually nonexistent and Bābolsar is no longer particularly inspiring, although Iranian tourists still come here. If you can't get enough of mausoleums, ask for directions to the **Emāmzādeh-yé Ibrahim**, dating back to at least the early 15th century. With time up your sleeve, a walk along the **river** is a pleasant diversion, and boats are available for hire.

Beach

The main part of Bābolsar is 4km inland, and the walk between it and the coast is lonely and disappointing. The beach area isn't inspiring, consisting of a dead-end road looking over a short and usually deserted stretch of sand, with a small children's playground at the junction of the road back into the centre. To get there, you can take a shared taxi north-east from Bābolsar's main square.

Maqbareh-yé Soltān Mohammed Tāher

This late 15th-century tower tomb stands in an old cemetery in the village of Soltān Mohammed Tāher, 4km from Bābol on a road to the east (not the main road to Qā'emshahr). The exterior features a simple arched frieze beneath its polygonal tiled dome, shallow arched recesses on each outer wall and a tall portal over the original carved wooden door. A carved wooden sarcophagus dating from AD 1470 remains inside the mausoleum.

Places to Stay & Eat

The *Hotel Michka* (☎ 24 656, Saheli Blvd), in Bābolsar is a good modern hotel in a pleasant garden, unusually built in the style of a Mediterranean villa. It charges US$34.50 per room with sea view and air-con but it's often full, which makes it difficult to negotiate a discount. The hotel *restaurant* is good but quite expensive. Otherwise, try a few of the *fish restaurants* along the beach, or, as a last resort, the *kabābīs* in town.

Getting There & Away

Shared taxis and minibuses for Chālūs (IR3000, two hours, 128km) and Qā'emshahr (IR1500, 15 minutes, 20km) leave from the Chālūs station in the far western part of Bābol. From there, you can also get immediate connections by shared taxi or bus to Sārī. To Rasht and Tehrān, you're better off going to Āmol and finding a connection.

Bābolsar is linked by frequent shared taxis and minibuses (IR1500) to Bābol.

SĀRĪ
☎ 02431

ساری

Much smaller and less developed than Rasht, Sārī has three distinctive *emāmzādehs* (mau-

soleums) and some typical Māzandarānī houses with sloping timber roofs but is not an otherwise attractive city. It makes a reasonable stopover between Gorgān and Chālūs or Rāmsar, and a good base for exploring towns like Āmol, Bābol and Bābolsar.

History

The origins of Sārī are lost in the mists of time, but it's known to have been the first capital of Māzandarān province (then known as Tabarestān) perhaps from as early as the Sassanian period until the 8th or 9th century AD. This was the last part of Iran to yield to Islam following the Arab invasion. Some centuries after the capital was moved to Āmol, Sārī was sacked, first by the Mongols and later by Timur. In 1937, it once again became the provincial capital.

Orientation & Information

The main square is the small Haft-é Tīr Square, commonly known as Clock (Sā'at)

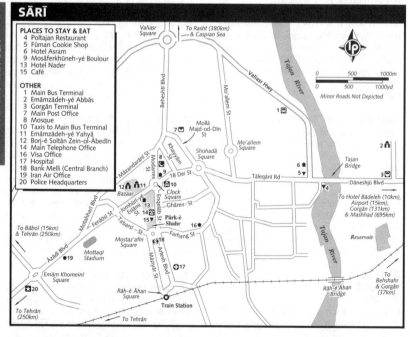

SĀRĪ

PLACES TO STAY & EAT
4 Poltajan Restaurant
5 Fūman Cookie Shop
6 Hotel Asram
9 Mosāferkhūneh-yé Boulour
13 Hotel Nader
15 Café

OTHER
1 Main Bus Terminal
2 Emāmzādeh-yé Abbās
3 Gorgān Terminal
7 Main Post Office
8 Mosque
10 Taxis to Main Bus Terminal
11 Emāmzādeh-yé Yahyā
12 Borj-é Soltān Zein-ol-Ābedīn
14 Main Telephone Office
16 Visa Office
17 Hospital
18 Bank Melli (Central Branch)
19 Iran Air Office
20 Police Headquarters

Square because of the clock tower in the centre. The bazaar, the old part of Sārī and most other points of interest are within walking distance of this square.

The main post office is 500m north-west of Shohadā Square, and the main telephone office is 400m south of Clock Square.

You're unlikely to have success either extending your visa or changing money in Sārī.

In an emergency, dial the general directories number (☎ 118) or try the special emergencies number (☎ 20 31). The main hospital (☎ 34 56) is near the train station. The police headquarters (☎ 30 20) is just past Emām Khomeinī Square.

Mausoleums

To find the Emāmzādeh-yé Yahyā and the Borj-é Soltān Zein-ol-Ābedīn mausoleums, duck down the lane leading into the bazaar immediately opposite the Hotel Nader.

Built in the 15th century, **Emāmzādeh-yé Yahyā** is in a small square inside the bazaar district, close to some fine old wooden houses. This simple, vaguely Rhenish building with its tiled pyramid-shaped roof is highly regarded for its original wooden doors and sarcophagus. You can normally go inside only on Thursday afternoon and Friday, but if you ask around at other times someone may let you in.

Beside Yahyā's mausoleum, the **Borj-é Soltān Zein-ol-Ābedīn** is a small, square, early 15th-century brick tomb tower, with a tiled octagonal dome. Apart from some plain, arched brick friezes below the lower and upper roof levels, the exterior is unadorned. The main interest is in the fine wooden sarcophagus inside. This tomb is more often open than Yahyā's.

The largest of Sārī's historic mausoleums, the **Emāmzādeh-yé Abbās** is situated apart from the others, about 500m east of the Tajan River; to get to it take a shared taxi from Clock Square. The brick tower rises to a conical dome but the exterior decorations are only simple. The tower is attached to a low rectangular modern annexe. According to the date on the tomb (which Abbās shares with two others), the wooden sarcophagus was carved in AD 1491.

Places to Stay

Sārī has a handful of cheap but not especially cheerful hotels in the centre of town, some of them barely adequate even for one night. Just off Clock Square, *Mosāferkhūneh-yé Boulour* on Modarres St is noisy and dirty – sheets don't appear to always be changed between guests. Beds, many of them in dorms, cost IR22,000, with another IR2,000 for a shower and the same for tea. To find it, glance up the stairwells at the start of Modarres St until you see grapes and melons painted on the wall, then head upstairs.

The marginally better *Hotel Nader* (☎ 22 357) is on Jomhūrī-yé Eslāmi St 200m south-west of Clock Square; look for a four-storey place with the word 'Nader' on top, visible only from the other side of the road. Noisy singles/doubles with sinks but no curtains cost IR15,000/25,000.

Much better but considerably more expensive is the unmissable red and white, three-star *Hotel Asram* (☎ 55 090, fax 55 092, Valiasr Hwy), convenient for the bus station but nothing else. It's large, modern and has a good restaurant, but singles/doubles cost US$35/45. At night the different floors are lit up in the colours of the Iranian flag!

With a car you might want to head 10km out on the road to Gorgān in search of the *Hotel Bādeleh* (☎ 25 49, fax 25 48, Gorgān Rd). Pleasant modern singles/doubles with TV, fridge and air-con cost US$35/52, but you'll often find it full in peak season. Getting from the hotel into town by shared taxi (IR500) is easy enough, although crossing the highway isn't much fun: just stand opposite the hotel and flag something down.

Places to Eat

The same places that are decent accommodation options are also the best to eat in. The *Hotel Bādeleh* has a reasonable restaurant that is worth the shared taxi ride to get to but it doesn't open until 8 pm. Also popular is the restaurant in the *Hotel Asram* where a decent chicken kabāb with rice and a soft drink (soda) should cost about IR25,000. The *Poltajan Restaurant* has a nice terrace overlooking the river but was closed at the time of research.

For cheaper eats there are plenty of *snack bars* and *kabābīs* around Clock Square. A small *cafe* overlooking Shahr Park on the way to the train station serves delicious banana milk shakes at IR2000. You can buy lovely fresh *Fūman cookies* at a shop on Valiasr Highway just before the Hotel Asram.

Getting There & Away

Air Sārī is a stopover on Iran Air's thrice-weekly flights to Tehrān (IR93,000) and Mashhad (IR124,000), but if you're going to or from Mashhad and have the time, the scenery is good enough to justify the long bus ride. The Iran Air office (☎ 69 400) is on the way to Emām Khomeinī Square from the town centre.

Bus & Minibus The main bus station is on the ring road, near the west bank of the river, accessible by shared taxi from Clock Square (IR200). Touts will show you where to buy your ticket.

Buses leave Sārī for Ardabīl (IR14,000, 11 hours, 645km); Mashhad (IR15,000, 12 hours, 695km); Rasht (IR10,000, seven hours, 380km); and Tehrān (IR8000, five hours, 250km) every day.

There are also minibuses, from the special Gorgān station east of Emām Tajan Bridge to Gorgān (IR4000), Bābol (IR2500) and other local destinations.

The Gorgān station can be reached by shared taxi from Clock Square. To get to Rasht, take a minibus to Rāmsar and change there; to Chālūs, take a minibus to Bābol first.

Train Trains to Tehrān leave on Thursday, Friday and Sunday at 9.30 pm (IR16,000/6000 for 1st/2nd class). A train to Gorgān (three hours), via Behshahr and Bandar-é Torkamān, leaves Sārī at 2.30 pm daily but only 2nd-class tickets (IR2000) are available and the train is often very full. Try getting a 1st-class ticket on the direct Tehrān-Gorgān train.

The train station (☎ 21 082) is about 1km south of Clock Square and easy to reach on foot or by shared taxi.

Shared Taxi The quickest way from Sārī to Gorgān and any place in between is by shared taxi (IR10,000 rials). They leave every 15 minutes or so from outside the Gorgān station. Shared taxis from the stand in the Eastern bus station in Tehrān go all the way to Sārī (IR25,000), or you can get a connection in Āmol.

Private Taxi If you're depressed by the unrelenting urban sprawl along the main Caspian road, you will be pleased to know that the Sārī to Gorgān road is still quite pretty, flanked by sunflower plantations, rice paddies and stunning mountains. It is worth chartering a taxi to enjoy the scenery. Expect to pay about IR50,000 between Sārī and Gorgān if you bargain hard.

Getting Around

The airport is 15km from Sārī, off the main road to Gorgān. You will probably have to charter a taxi there for about IR10,000. From the airport, jump on anything heading into town.

Shared taxis around Sārī are some of the cheapest in the country (it currently costs IR200 from Clock Square to the train station) but Sārī is quite small enough to walk around.

BEHSHAHR   بهشهر
☎ 01572

Behshahr is a small sleepy town on the main road between Sārī and Gorgān, and is one of the more pleasant places along the main Caspian road. The Bay of Gorgān lies 12km to the north and immediately south are hills and woodland where you can hike as long as you're careful about local military posts. You can easily spend an hour or two in the delightful **Shahr Park**, on the main road south of Emām Khomeinī Square. You can also hire a taxi to see the small **Abbāsābād Lake**, built by Shāh Abbās I, with a small fort in the middle.

Places to Stay & Eat

The best place to stay and eat if you want to break the journey between Sārī and Gorgān, or have a good look around the area, is the friendly *Miankaleh Hotel* (☎ 29 161, fax 22 800) on Emām Khomeinī Ave, a few metres north of Emām Khomeinī Square. The charge of US$25/35 a single/double is pretty steep, but may be open to negotiation. The decent *restaurant* is open for lunch and dinner.

Getting There & Away

You can pick up a shared taxi, minibus or bus to Gorgān (IR1500, 1¼ hours) or Sārī (IR1250, one hour) from anywhere along the main road. Alternatively transport to nearby towns leaves from the bus station, on the southern side of the main road, near the western edge of Behshahr. Behshahr is on the main Tehrān-Gorgān train line. The train station is about 1.5km north of Emām Khomeinī Square.

Coming into Behshahr from Gorgān you will probably be dropped in Qods Square and have to take a shared taxi into the town centre.

AROUND BEHSHAHR
Kākh-é Safī Ābād کخ صف آبد

On Mt Kākh, a tall hill thick with trees south-west of Behshahr, are the remains of a Safavid palace. In about 1612, Shāh Abbās I set about building a palace in a royal water garden, the Bāgh-é Shāh, on this idyllic woodland perch. Many palaces and other buildings for the king and his court grew up on the same site, which gradually expanded to become the town of Ashraf (present-day Behshahr), but over the centuries they fell into ruin and today the only remaining structure is the Safī Ābād Palace.

While the palace stands majestically on the hill as you approach from Sārī, the area is currently part of a military complex and strictly off-limits to foreigners. If you go hiking, be very careful not to trespass on military property.

Prehistoric Caves قار هاى

Prehistoric pottery dating back perhaps to the 10th millennium BC, as well as evidence of unusual ancient burial rites, have been found in two interesting caves near Behshahr. To get to the caves, take a shared taxi from Behshahr and ask to be dropped at the Serāh-é Torūjan-é Bālā, about 3km west of Behshahr on the main road to Sārī. From

there walk south for about 300m until you come to a small village, Torūjan-é Bālā, where you will see the Hōtū Cave overlooking the road. The Kamarband Cave is a short distance south of here.

GORGĀN & گرگان
NAHAR KHORĀN ناهار خوران
☎ 0371 ● pop 220,000

Squeezed between the northern edge of the Alborz Mountains and the southern edge of the north-eastern steppe, Gorgān (formerly known as Aster Ābād) has, for much of its long history, been the last secure outpost of Persian civilisation. Settled since ancient times, it has, with the exception of a series of incursions in the last century, been geographically positioned to resist the threat of Turkmen raids, unlike Gonbad-é Kāvūs and other towns to the north and east. The Turkmen started to give up their nomadic and pillaging ways at the turn of the 20th century, and it's one of the twists of history that

GORGĀN

1 Bus & Minibus Station	7 Bank Melli
2 Gorgān Museum	8 Taxis to Gonbad-é
3 Taxis to Bus Station	Kāvūs Terminal
& Train Station	9 Taxis & Buses to
4 Emāmzādeh-yé Nūr	Nahar Khorān
5 Jāmeh Mosque	10 Tahmasebi Jadid Hotel
6 Taslimi Hotel	11 Hotel Maroof

To Gonbad-é Kāvūs Terminal (3km),
Tourist Home (3km) &
Gonbad-é Kāvūs (93km)

Train Station

Shahrdārī
Square

To Nahar
Khorān (6km)
& Mashhad
(553km)

Pasdaran St

Shohada St

Pārk-è Melli

Khakh
Square

Bazaar

Emām
Khomeinī St

Emām
Khomeinī
Square

To Sārī (37km)
& Tehrān
(387km)

Jomhūrī-yé Eslāmī St

0   1   2km
0   0.5   1mi
Approximate Scale
Minor Streets Not Depicted

they eventually conquered Gorgān not by violence but by peaceful settlement.

Gorgān became the new railhead for the Caspian provinces after a branch line was constructed from Bandar-é Torkamān in the 1970s, but it's still little more than a provincial market town. Sadly, some of its individuality has now been replaced by Iranian uniformity, and very few women still wear the distinctive Turkmen dress.

About 6km east of Gorgān is a pocket of unspoilt forest known as Nahar Khorān. Though there are some holiday cabins and a children's playground nearby, the concrete mixers and bulldozers that have ploughed through the rest of the Caspian region have so far left this part of Iran almost pristine. There are plenty of hiking trails through dense forest that are easy to find and just begging to be explored.

Though Nahar Khorān can be crowded in summer, especially on Fridays and public holidays, you may have the forest to yourself at other times. One reader has written to complain that the paths were hard to find and dirty, and we recently received another letter from a reader who had been followed into the forest and attacked by a man armed with a knife. Maybe it's no longer such a good idea to come here on your own.

You come to Gorgān more as a base for exploring nearby sites, such as Gonbad-é Kāvūs and Bandar-é Torkamān, than because there's much to see in the town itself.

Orientation & Information

Most of the main thoroughfare, Emām Khomeinī St, is flanked to the west by the bazaar, a network of narrow winding kūchés (alleys) dotted with examples of traditional Māzandarānī houses, with tiled sloping roofs and charming wooden balconies. The centre of town is Shahrdārī Square but there are few English street signs to help you find your way around Gorgān.

Things to See

Built around a quadrangle in the bazaar, the **Jāmeh Mosque** is a single-storey mosque with a traditional sloping tiled roof and an unusual minaret. It dates from the 15th century but has been repaired numerous times because of the many devastating earthquakes that have struck this area.

The **Emāmzādeh-yé Nūr**, about 200m west of the mosque, is a small 14th- or 15th-century polygonal tower tomb, its outer walls decorated with simple brickwork designs. The mosque and tower are normally locked, but if you ask around someone will probably open it for you.

Gorgān Museum (☎ 24 53), not signposted in English along the western part of Shohadā St, is worth a visit for some archaeological and ethnological displays, including tombstones, from Tūrang Tappeh and other nearby sites. It is open from 8 am to 6 pm daily but admission costs IR20,000, which is a lot to pay for a dusty local collection.

Trekking

It's possible to trek to Nahar Khorān from Shāhrūd in Eastern Iran (see the Eastern Iran chapter for details on Shārūd), taking about four days to do it. You don't have to have a guide, although one might prove useful for finding your way through some pockets of dense forest. It's also possible to walk to Gorgān from Shāhrūd along the road via Āzād Shahr, although if you choose to do this you may want to use public transport at least part of the way.

Places to Stay

It can't be said that the choice of places to stay in Gorgān is anything other than dismal. If you can afford it and have private transport you'd be better off staying in the eastern suburb of Nahar Khorān. Few places will countenance a discount for single occupancy of rooms.

The only really cheap place in town is the unlikely sounding *Tourist Home* (no phone), an ugly building inconveniently and noisily situated near the station for minibuses to Gonbad-é Kāvūs. Clean but uninspiring singles/doubles with shared bathrooms cost IR15,000/25,000.

Up a notch is the *Taslimi Hotel* (☎ 24 814, Emām Khomeinī St), which charges IR50,000/60,000 for a spacious, if charmless, single/double with fan and bathroom.

In summer the water supply is likely to be sporadic.

On a very busy corner along the main road to Tehrān is the ITTO *Hotel Maroof* (☎ 25 591, *Jomhūrī-yé Eslāmī St*), which asks US$20 for indifferent rooms with a fan.

The only decent hotel in the town is *Tahmasebi Jadid Hotel* (☎ 23 780, fax 40 575, *Jomhūrī-yé Eslāmī St*) where clean rooms with fridge, TV and air-con cost US$20.

At the end of the road from Gorgān to Nahar Khorān is the *Hotel Shahrdārī Gorgān* (☎ 0171-552 4077), a grand old place that has seen better days. It is understandably busy from June to August when you'll be lucky to find a room. Clean, comfortable rooms with pleasant views cost US$30/40 a single/double.

Across the road is a hotel and a collection of brightly coloured cabins collectively called the *Nahar Khorān Inn* (☎ 0171-552 0034) where you'll be charged US$36 per person, with another IR3,000 for breakfast.

There's nothing to stop you *camping* discreetly in the forest but see the warning at the start of this section.

Places to Eat

The range of restaurants in Gorgān is as disappointing as the range of hotels. In town only the *Hotel Maroof* has a restaurant and it looked pretty dispiriting but you could try the *restaurants* in the two hotels at Nadar Khorān. Otherwise you will have to make do with a hamburger or kabāb at one of the places around the main squares or in the bazaar. There are also several *cake shops* if you crave something sweet. Self-catering is the other obvious alternative; you can easily pick up picnic ingredients in the bazaar.

Getting There & Away

The road east to Mashhad makes for a spectacular drive through dramatic forest scenery but you must expect some thorough baggage checks because of drug trafficking from Turkmenistan. There are not currently any flights to Gorgān.

Bus & Minibus The main bus station is north-west of Shahrdārī Square and easy to reach by shared taxi (IR250) from Shohadā St. Daily buses and minibuses head for the following destinations, among others:

destination	distance (km)	duration (hrs)	cost (IR)
Mashhad	564	10½	12,000
Rasht	511	9	12,000
Sārī (minibus only)	37	2	4000
Shāhrūd	124	4	6300
Tehrān	387	7	10,000/
(lux/super)			25,000

Note that the journey from Gorgān to Tehrān via Shāhrūd is especially beautiful.

The minibus station for Gonbad-é Kāvūs is to the north of town and easily reached by shared taxi from Shohadā St. Buses to Mashhad sometimes travel via Gonbad-é Kāvūs.

Train The 497km train ride from Tehrān to Gorgān passes through spectacular scenery but as the direct trains travel overnight you're unlikely to see much of it.

From Gorgān, there's a daily train to Sārī (IR2000) that travels via the junction of Pol-é Sefīd, from where you can get a connection to Tehrān. However, the train leaves from Gorgān at the ungodly hour of 4.30 am.

It's better to try to get a seat (not always easy) on the Gorgān-Tehrān train that leaves at 7.30 pm daily in summer, arriving in Tehrān at 6.40 am; to Gorgān it leaves Tehrān at 6.50 pm. Tickets cost IR8000/20,300 for 2nd/1st class.

The train station (☎ 27 911) is a few hundred metres west of the bus station and easily reached by shared taxi from Shohadā St.

Shared Taxi There are frequent shared taxis to Sārī from the main bus station. The fare should be around IR10,000 but one reader wrote to complain of a driver asking IR50,000 and then demanding IR500,000 on arrival!

Getting Around

You can easily walk around the centre of town, and there are plenty of shared taxis to the bus and train stations for a standard IR250.

The cheapest way to get to Nahar Khorān is to catch the half-hourly bus from Khakh Square (IR200); the lazy way to do it is to charter a taxi for about IR4000. Nahar Khorān is at the top of a steepish road, so if you want to walk one way, get a bus or taxi there and then walk back again – it is easy to follow the main road back into Gorgān.

AROUND GORGĀN

While Gorgān may not be the most exciting place in Iran, there are plenty of great day trips out of it to justify coming here.

Bandar-é Torkamān   بندر ترکمن

A coastal town just south of the narrow inlet to the Bay of Gorgān, Bandar-é Torkamān is, as the name suggests, the Turkmen port of Iran. For a long time it was a major channel for trade with Russia, despite the attentions of Turkmen pirates who preyed on shipping until the 19th century. With the establishment of the trans-Iranian railway in the 1930s, Bandar-é Torkamān also became the sole railhead on Iran's Caspian coast. The decline in the shipping trade has left it a small, largely Turkmen settlement with the air of a frontier town. There's nowhere to stay but it's an easy day trip from Gorgān.

The region is most famous as Iran's caviar production centre. In 1997, almost 50% of the country's caviar came from near here. About 150 ships are based at the port, trailing up and down the coastline in search of those fast-vanishing sturgeon and their valuable little fish eggs (see the boxed text 'Caviar Anyone?' for more details). Unfortunately the port is too far from the town centre to walk to.

If you can time your visit for a Monday morning, it's worth visiting the weekly **market** where you'll see the local Turkmen women in their brightly coloured shawls and shift dresses, a striking contrast to the ubiquitous black *chadors* (cloaks) worn elsewhere. At the market you can buy local produce and handicrafts, including brightly coloured Turkmen shawls and typical maroon-coloured Turkmen rugs.

Caviar Anyone?

That quintessential luxury food item, caviar (the roe of the sturgeon and especially of the Beluga sturgeon), is caught from large wooden boats trailing huge nets at many points along the Iranian part of the Caspian coast and particularly around Bandar-é Torkamān. Caviar may be a delicacy in the West but it's not much enjoyed in Iran (too salty, perhaps?) and you'll probably have to ask around in hotel restaurants if you want to try it.

The quantity of caviar produced for export is falling sharply as the Caspian becomes more and more polluted; in 1996 about 150 tonnes of caviar was exported but by 1999 this was down to about 100 tonnes.

In recent years hatcheries have been established to try and ensure continuing supplies and in 2000, 25 million sturgeon fingerlings were released into the Caspian. Fine-net fishing was also outlawed to try and give young sturgeon a chance to reach maturity. The state monopoly on the production of caviar was also lifted in another effort to boost production.

Sadly, the high price that caviar commands on world markets – at the time of writing it was fetching about US$680 per kilogram – continues to encourage illegal fishing.

Getting There & Away Bandar-é Torkamān is on the train line between Gorgān and Tehrān although the times of arrival are hardly convenient in either direction.

There are regular minibuses straight to Bandar-é Torkamān from Gorgān's main bus station (IR750, 40 minutes). If you're feeling energetic you could get out at the junction for Kordkūy and walk the 8km to Bandar-é Torkamān along a pleasant road flanked by small Turkmen farms. Bandar-é Torkamān's minibus station is a small yard off Seyed St.

Gonbad-é Kāvūs   گنبد کاووس

The featureless but pleasant Turkmen town of Gonbad, 93km north-west of Gorgān, is famous for just one thing but this alone makes it worth a day trip from Gorgān. The Gonbad-é Kāvūs is a spectacular **tower tomb** (known locally as Mīl-é Gonbad) built by Qābūs ebn-é Vashmgīr ('Kāvūs' is a corruption of 'Qābūs'), a prince of the local Ziyarid dynasty who was also famous as a poet, scholar, general and patron of the arts. Qābūs ruled the surrounding region of Tabarestān at the turn of the 11th century and decided to build a monument to last forever. The monument was completed in 1006, six years before he was slain by an assassin. It's a remarkable memorial to a remarkable man.

This earliest of brick skyscrapers is 55m tall (though surprisingly the statistics vary) and rests on a large earth mound formed around foundations, which are at least 12m deep. The circular structure has 10 buttresses rising from the base to the pointed dome, which measures 18m in height. Two inscriptions ring the tower, one on a moulded cornice below the dome, the other 1m above the doorway. It's believed that the glass coffin of Qābūs originally hung from the dome of the tower but it vanished long ago (nobody knows how) and there's no longer anything to see inside. Robert Byron's *The Road to Oxiana* gives more details about the tower's history.

Entrance to the park surrounding the tower is free but to walk up the ramp and go inside costs IR10,000. Unfortunately you may find peaceful enjoyment of the tower marred by the attentions of small boys selling chewing gum.

Immediately opposite the park there's a good *cake shop* with photos of a cake baked to celebrate the 1000th anniversary of the tower's erection. It weighed 65kg and was enough for 250 people. The park itself makes a pleasant place for a picnic.

Getting There & Away From Gorgān, minibuses to Gonbad (IR1750, 1½ hours) leave hourly from the special Gonbad station. You'll be dropped off some way from the tower and will have to take a shared taxi to reach it; ask for the Mīl-é Gonbad, as the tower is known locally. There are also daily buses from Gonbad to Mashhad and Tehrān.

The urban sprawl along the Caspian coast stops east of Gorgān, and the Gorgān-Gonbad road passes through lovely scenery. You might want to charter a taxi between

the two towns for about IR20,000 per hour which would let you stop in Alī Ābād where there are two waterfalls, reached only by private transport – they're signposted off the road with paintings of the falls. Also along this stretch of road are two small forest parks, Gologh Park and Park Deland, both of them ideal for short walks.

Tūrang Tappeh   تورنگ تپه
Destroyed by the Mongols, Tūrang Tappeh was once a major regional caravan station and town dating back to the 6th millennium BC. The lapis lazuli beads and ceramic pieces found here indicate that it was a major pottery-producing centre especially in the 2nd and 3rd millennia BC. The best pieces of pottery are now on display in the National Museum of Iran in Tehrān, and it's really only worth coming here if you're very keen on ancient archaeology.

Tūrang Tappeh is 22km north-east of Gorgān, accessible by road and dirt track. It's impossible to reach by public transport, and even by private car it becomes cut off in bad weather. In summer, you should be able to hire a taxi to get there from Gorgān for around IR40,000, including waiting time.

Sadd-é Eskandar   سد اسکندر
The remains of the so-called Sadd-é Eskandar or Alexander's Wall stretch for more than 160km from about 25km west of Gonbad-é Kāvūs to within about 5km of the sea. Probably built in the 6th century (and therefore not by Alexander the Great) as a bulwark against warring tribes to the north, this Iranian equivalent of Hadrian's Wall has crumbled and been comprehensively cannibalised for building materials. Only the foundations are still clearly visible, so you'll need a good imagination to make much of what's left.

The wall is difficult to get to and, since it's near the Turkmenistan border, you should really get written permission from the *farmāndārī* (district administrative headquarters) in Gorgān before setting out. Armed with this permit, you should be able to charter a taxi for around IR20,000 per hour to get to the wall. It isn't safe to walk there.

Central Iran

ایران مرکزی

Central Iran has been fought over for centuries; it's a place where the contest of great civilisations has yielded the country's richest concentration of architectural wonders. From the unrelenting splendour and majesty of Esfahān and the refined elegance of Shīrāz to the mud-brick antiquity of Yazd and Abyaneh, the towns of Iran's central provinces are where you'll probably spend the most time. Close to Shīrāz, the evocative city of Persepolis speaks of an even more ancient inheritance and is the most stunning of Iran's many ruins. Although Kāshān's claim to a share of the tourist dollar is drowned out by the better-known sights to the south – reason enough perhaps to go there – it too is home to splendid mosques and gardens, not to mention the town's magnificent traditional houses now painstakingly restored.

Central Iran's people are also surprisingly diverse, from the religious conservatives of Qom to the reform-minded Esfahānīs, while the relaxed Yazdīs seem willing to keep the peace. That Shīrāz owes much to its heritage of Persian kingdoms and enlightened dynasties is reflected in the sophistication of its people and the architectural reminders of a time when Persian rulers rubbed shoulders with the greatest poets of the age.

The two great deserts of Iran, the Dasht-é Kavīr and the Dasht-é Lūt, occupy the east of the region. Even in the more hospitable parts to the west most of the settlements began as oases and largely remain so today. If you travel by land across this mostly barren heartland, you will begin to appreciate the appeal to ancient travellers of these settled oases with their caravanserais. Throughout history their inhabitants have sought to give them an air of security and stability, echoed in the many sturdy monuments that survive as a testament to their builders.

Highlights

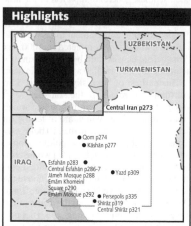

- Immersing yourself in the majesty of Esfahān's blue-tiled mosques and restful bridges

- Ambling through Esfahān's Great Bazaar

- Picking your way through the ancient ruins of Persepolis

- Savouring the poetry of Hāfez, relaxing in the gardens and exploring the Bāzār-é Vakīl in Shīrāz

- Getting lost in the wonderful old city of Yazd

- Stepping back in time in the quiet, ancient village of Abyaneh

- Seeing how the other half lived in the traditional houses of Kāshān

ARĀK

اراک

☎ 0861 • elevation 1759m

Arāk is not a city known for its great cultural or historical legacy, but it can be a convenient place to break the journey between Hamadān and Qom. It's a little cooler than other places in the region, which is certainly an advantage in summer.

One archaeological site of interest is in Sārūq, 50km north of Arāk. The ruined 12th-century **Astan-é Haftādo-o-Do-Tan**, or Mausoleum of the 72 Martyrs, has two domes and contains some very old wooden sarcophagi; there's also a cemetery in the courtyard. It's

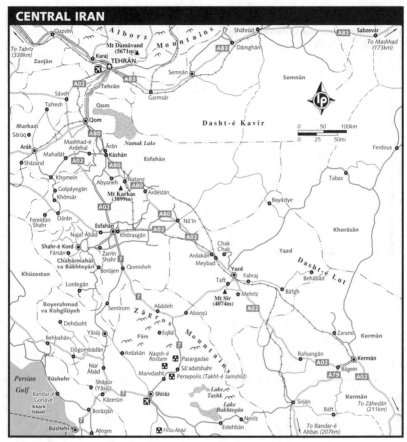

CENTRAL IRAN

accessible from Arāk – infrequent minibuses leave from the main bus station and cost around IR2000.

Accommodation options in Arāk are limited. Try the **Hotel Kheibar** (Khordād St), as you come into Arāk from Tehrān. It charges about IR70,000 a double. The rooms at the **Hotel Lādan** (☎ 47 354, Qodousi St) are pleasant and cost US$20/30 a single/double.

There are direct daily buses to Shīrāz, Esfahān, Hamadān and Tehrān, among other destinations. Several daily trains pass through for Qom, Tehrān and Ahvāz.

QOM
☎ 0251 • pop 270,000

قم

Qom is Iran's second holiest city after Mashhad, home to the magnificent Hazrat-é Masumeh shrine. The city was the heartland of the Islamic Revolution and remains one of the most conservative places in the country. Qom attracts Shiite scholars and students from all over the world. Although non-Muslims are not permitted to enter the shrine, Qom is worth visiting for the fleeting insight it offers into those sections of Iranian society most resistant to the reforms introduced by President Khatamī and his

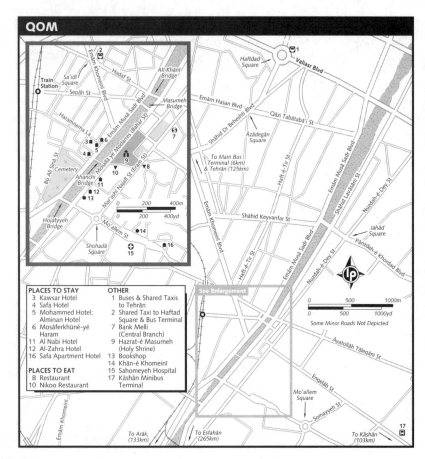

QOM

PLACES TO STAY
3 Kawsar Hotel
4 Safa Hotel
5 Mohammed Hotel;
  Alminan Hotel
6 Mosāferkhūné-yé
  Haram
11 Al Nabi Hotel
12 Al-Zahra Hotel
16 Safa Apartment Hotel

PLACES TO EAT
8 Restaurant
10 Nikoo Restaurant

OTHER
1 Buses & Shared Taxis
  to Tehrān
2 Shared Taxi to Haftad
  Square & Bus Terminal
7 Bank Melli
  (Central Branch)
9 Hazrat-é Masumeh
  (Holy Shrine)
13 Bookshop
14 Khān-é Khomeinī
15 Sahomeyeh Hospital
17 Kāshān Minibus
  Terminal

supporters. Its streetscape owes much to the high concentration of mullahs and religious students, as well as women wearing the head-to-toe chador (black covering garment) in contrast to the tentative relaxation of dress codes taking place elsewhere in Iran.

As a consequence, travellers should be discreet and dress conservatively, particularly around the Hazrat-é Masumeh.

Very little English is spoken in Qom.

Note that the tap water is salty. Drink bottled water, which is readily available around town.

Orientation & Information

The main 'river' through Qom is so dry that it has been concreted over and is now used as a car park, market and playground. Most of the hotels and restaurants are along the banks of the 'river' in the blocks around the shrine.

You can change money at the Bank Melli but they love their paperwork so you might be better off getting your cash in another town – ie, Kāshān or Tehrān.

The bookshop near the Al-Zahra Hotel has a surprising range of current and old magazines in English (*National Geographic*,

Newsweek and even, incongruously, *Horse & Hound*) and French (*L'Express*).

Hazrat-é Masumeh

The town owes its eminence to the burial place of Fātemeh (sister of Imam Rezā), who died and was interred here in the 9th century AD. This extensive complex was built under Shāh Abbās I and the other Safavid kings who were anxious to establish their Shiite credentials and to provide a counterweight to the sect's shrines at Karbala and Najaf (see the boxed text 'Karbala & Najaf' in the Western Iran chapter for more details), then under Ottoman occupation. The magnificent golden cupola of the shrine was an embellishment built by Fath Alī Shāh. Along with the enormous tiled dome and exquisite minarets, it can only be admired from the outside – non-Muslims are not allowed to enter the complex.

While not as significant as Mashhad, Qom attracts hundreds of thousands of pilgrims every year and watching this convergence of devotees from around the world is fascinating.

Khān-é Khomeinī

Surprisingly little fanfare surrounds the simple brick former residence of Āyatollāh Khomeinī just east of Shohadā Square. It was here that Khomeinī lived – before being forced into exile in the 1960s – and where he first built his power base among conservative clerics. Apart from a not uncommon mural of him alongside his successor, Āyatollāh Alī Khameneī, there's little to distinguish it from the houses around it. Opposite the Sahomeyeh Hospital, the house is not open to visitors and is of more historic than aesthetic appeal.

Places to Stay

Qom is one of the few cities in Iran where foreigners are routinely charged the same prices for rooms as Iranians, although this may change. The best place to start looking is Haramnema Lane, a small alleyway just north of Ahanchi Bridge. The *Alminan Hotel* (☎ 49 640) is excellent value with good singles/doubles with bathroom for IR19,400/27,500; some overlook the shrine but also the very noisy Emām Musā Sadr Blvd. There's a kitchen where management can cook something up for guests.

Across the lane and up some stairs, the *Mosāferkhūneh-yé Haram* (not signposted in English) has OK rooms for IR30,000 per person. Although the owner is a man, all of the guests when we visited were Iranian women so this may be a good choice for lone female travellers.

The rooms are better at the *Mohammed Hotel* (☎ 614 861), in the same lane, and cost IR35,000/50,000 for a double without\with. It's popular with Iranian families so the quiet location is often drowned out by squealing children.

The *Safa Hotel* (☎ 617 370, Emām Musā Sadr Blvd) nearby is basic and noisy but has clean rooms with shared bathroom for IR22,000.

The manager at the *Al-Zahra Hotel* (☎/fax 744 004, Bahar St) has an inflated opinion about the quality of his rooms, something reflected in the US$23 he charges for a depressing single with bathroom. The larger doubles are marginally better for US$35, while US$70 for their suite is bordering on the ridiculous. This place is a favourite of local taxi drivers.

Better are the *Kawsar Hotel* (☎ 618 969, fax 55 000, Haramnema Lane), where spacious rooms cost US$20/30 (plus 18% tax), and the *Al Nabi Hotel* (☎ 744 270, fax 744 600, Bahar St), which costs the same and is a stone's throw from the shrine.

Best of all, the friendly *Safa Apartment Hotel* (☎ 732 499, fax 732 574, Mo'allem St) has doubles with bathroom for US$25 as well as lovely suites starting from US$30 – top-end quality at mid-range prices. The location's not the best but it's still within easy walking distance of the shrine.

Places to Eat

Fine dining is not exactly an option in Qom. Hotel restaurants are probably the best but still have fairly uninspired menus. The *Al-Zahra Hotel*, *Al Nabi Hotel*, *Kawsar Hotel* and *Safa Apartment Hotel* are all reasonable; the latter is arguably the best.

Alternatively, there are plenty of *kabābīs* around town. You could also try the no-name *restaurant* opposite the south-eastern entrance to the shrine or the *Nikoo Restaurant* in the lane to the south.

One thing you must try is the sinfully delicious pistachio brittle known as *sōhūn*, produced locally and available in almost every main street of Qom. Not as sickly sweet as some Iranian confectionery, sōhūn becomes an obsession once you've tasted it.

Shopping

Stalls around the shrine sell prayer rugs, small tablets of compressed earth used in Shiite prayers, inscriptions from the Quran, pictures of Mecca and many other religious items. Flails wielded by the devout during processions in the month of Moharram are also on offer, if not always on display. The Persian carpets made in Qom are famous for their classical designs, although good ones can be hard to find.

Getting There & Away

Try to avoid travelling to Qom on Friday, and certainly on any holy day, because most transport will be packed to the hilt.

Bus & Minibus Leaving Qom can be surprisingly difficult. The main bus station can be found in the bleak northern suburbs of town. It has daily buses to Shīrāz (IR16,000), Kermān (IR16,000), Hamadān (IR8000), Tabrīz (IR15,500), Esfahān (IR6500), Mashhad (IR21,600), Kermānshāh (IR11,500) and Yazd (IR10,500). However, each time we visited, the desks of the bus company offices were either unmanned or their were occupants asleep. Most activity takes place in the early morning or late afternoon, as well as two apparently regular departure times for Esfahān at 8 am and 4 pm. Unless you're prepared for a potentially long wait, you'd be better off heading for the minibus station for buses to Kāshān (east end of Enqelāb St; IR3000, two hours) or to Tehrān (Haftad Square; IR3000, two hours) and making a connection from there. For the Kāshān terminal in the east of the city, you'll need to charter a taxi; ask for Termināl-é Kāshān.

The other alternative for most places to the south and west is to hail one of the many passing buses at Haftad Square in the northern part of the city, although some buses are full so you'll have to compete with other frustrated passengers for a seat.

Shared Taxi Shared taxis cost a little more but are generally quicker. They leave from Haftad Square and the main bus terminal.

Train The only convenient thing about catching a train to or from Qom is the central location of the station. Departures are not kind – usually in the middle of the night – unless you can get a train originating in Qom (for Mashhad and occasionally Ahvāz and Kermān). A weekly train leaves Qom at 4.30 pm arriving in Mashhad at 9 am the following day. The day changes depending on the season. Train buffs aside, buses are infinitely preferable.

KĀSHĀN   کاشان

☎ 0361 • pop approx 120,000

This attractive small oasis city was once a favourite of Shāh Abbās I who beautified it and asked to be buried here. Kāshān is also home to some of the best traditional houses in the country as well as beautiful gardens and some splendid Islamic buildings. The covered bazaar is deceptively large and one of the most atmospheric outside the major cities. Kāshān is an ideal place to stop for a day or two (or even longer if the choice of accommodation was wider) between Tehrān and Esfahān and as a base for visiting the nearby village of Abyaneh.

History

Recent excavations date the original settlement of the area to the Achaemenid period, while some buildings have been dated as early as the Sassanian period. Kāshān was all but destroyed during the Arab invasion of AD 637 and by various earthquakes although, thankfully, a few ancient relics and buildings have survived. One popular local myth claims that the city was founded by the Sultaness Zobeida, wife of the famous Abbasid caliph, Harūn ar-Rashīd (AD 786–809) of

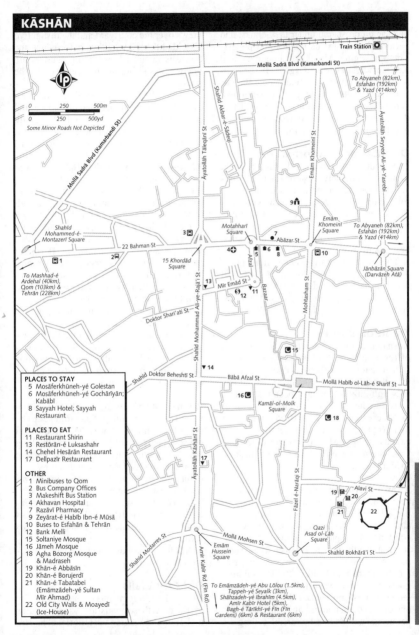

KĀSHĀN

Train Station

Mollā Sadrā Blvd (Kamarbandi St)

To Abyaneh (82km),
Esfahān (192km)
& Yazd (414km)

0   250   500m
0   250   500yd

Some Minor Roads Not Depicted

Molla Sadra Blvd (Kamarbandi St)

Shahid Akbar-é-Sādeqi St

Ayatollah Tāleqāni St

Emām Khomeini St

Ayatollah Seyyed Ali-yé-Yasrebi

Shahid
Mohammed-é-
Montazeri Square

22 Bahman St

Motahhari
Square

Abāzar St

Emām
Khomeini
Square

To Abyaneh (82km),
Esfahān (192km)
& Yazd (414km)

15 Khordād
Square

To Mashhad-é
Ardehal (40km),
Qom (103km) &
Tehrān (228km)

Afzal St

Bāzār

Mohtasham St

Jānbāzān Square
(Darvāzeh Atā)

Mir Emād St

Shahid Mohammad Ali-ye-Rajā'i St

Doktor Shari'ati St

Shahid Doktor Beheshti St

Bābā Afzal St

Mollā Habib ol-Lāh-é Sharif St

Kamāl-ol-Molk
Square

Ayatollah Kāshāni St

Fāzel-é-Naraqi St

Alavi St

Qazi
Asad ol-Lāh
Square

Shahid Modarres St

Amir Kabir Rd (Fin Rd)

Mollā Mohsen St

Emām
Hussein
Square

Shahid Bokhārā'i St

To Emāmzādeh-yé Abu Lôlou (1.5km),
Tappeh-yé Seyalk (3km),
Shāhzādeh-yé Ibrahim (4.5km),
Amir Kabir Hotel (5km),
Bagh-é Tārikhi-yé Fin (Fin
Gardens) (6km) & Restaurant (6km)

PLACES TO STAY
5 Mosāferkhūneh-yé Golestan
6 Mosāferkhūneh-yé Gochāriyān;
   Kabābi
8 Sayyah Hotel; Sayyah
   Restaurant

PLACES TO EAT
11 Restaurant Shirin
13 Restōrān-é Luksashahr
14 Chehel Hesārān Restaurant
17 Dellpazir Restaurant

OTHER
1   Minibuses to Qom
2   Bus Company Offices
3   Makeshift Bus Station
4   Akhavan Hospital
7   Razāvi Pharmacy
9   Zeyārat-é Habib Ibn-é Mūsā
10 Buses to Esfahān & Tehrān
12 Bank Melli
15 Soltaniye Mosque
16 Jāmeh Mosque
18 Agha Bozorg Mosque
    & Madraseh
19 Khān-é Abbāsin
20 Khān-é Borujerdi
21 Khān-é Tabatabei
    (Emāmzādeh-yé Sultan
    Mir Ahmad)
22 Old City Walls & Moayedi
    (Ice-House)

CENTRAL IRAN

The Thousand and One Nights fame. Kāshān once again prospered under the Seljuks, and became famous for its textiles and pottery. The rampaging Mongols came next and Kāshān was devastated again. It regained some of its former glory under the Safavids, when some rulers and kings preferred to live here rather than in the capital, Esfahān. These days, Kāshān is overshadowed by Esfahān, but it retains some real charm and history.

Orientation & Information

The centre of town is Kamāl-ol-Molk Square, from where most of Kāshān's sites can be reached on foot. For sites along the road to the Fīn gardens (variously known as Fīn Rd and Amīr Kabīr Rd), you'll probably need a taxi.

The Bank Melli just west of the bazaar changes money.

The medical emergencies number is ☎ 115. The Akhavan Hospital (☎ 443 000) is the most central, and the Razāvī Pharmacy (☎ 444 554) is opposite the Sayyah Hotel. If you need the police, call ☎ 554 038.

Traditional Houses

Kāshān is home to the richest concentration of restored traditional houses anywhere in Iran. The tourist authorities claim that there are over 600 such houses in Kāshān alone, although only a few have been restored. A word of caution: Since entrance to most of the houses costs IR20,000, visiting all of them (plus the other sites) can make for an expensive stay. Most of the sites are open from 8 am to 8 pm, often closing an hour earlier in winter.

Khān-é Borujerdī Originally built as a private residence in the early 19th century, it has a lovely courtyard, flanked by summer and winter houses. At the southern end of the courtyard, the splendid motifs carved into stone above the arched entrance to the summer house indicate that this was the home of a rich merchant of handicrafts. The summer guest room has beautiful stalactite work, faded murals and sunken doorways, while one of the smaller adjoining rooms has a carpet design carved in relief on the ceiling.

It is possible to climb to the roof for good views over the courtyard and the distinctive six-sided domed windtowers for which the house is famous. More living quarters are being restored but are not yet open to the public.

To get there, walk east along Alavī St, turn right opposite another old house and pool currently being restored, then walk about 80m along a tiny lane. If in doubt, ask for directions; locals will know where it is.

Khān-é Tabatabei Built in 1834 by Seyyed Ja'far Tabatabei, a wealthy carpet merchant, the Khān-é Tabatabei is renowned for its intricate relief designs carved into stone as well as for its wonderful mirror and stained-glass work. All the windows open onto the main courtyard and the house is entirely concealed from the street. Larger than the Borujerdī house, it covers 4700 sq metres, has 40 rooms and over 200 doors. It consists of three sections – the internal area (*andarūnī*) where family members lived, the external area (*birūnī*) used for entertaining guests, and the servants' quarters (*khadameh*).

The entrance is next to that of Emāmzādeh-yé Sultan Mīr Ahmad, the conical tower of which is visible from all over this part of town, including from outside the entrance to Khān-é Borujerdī.

Khān-é Abbāsīn Although restoration work is still continuing, this promises to be one of the finest of Kāshān's traditional houses. There are at least two breathtaking two-storey courtyards flanked by elegant arches, enticing stairways and rooms containing the usual plaster reliefs, fine mirror work as well as some exceptionally beautiful and detailed stained-glass windows. Entrance only costs IR10,000 but expect that to increase when the restoration work nears completion.

Ask for directions from the Khān-é Borujerdī, 300m away.

Old City Walls

One of the few remnants of the ancient city of Kāshān, these walls are worth a quick look if you're visiting the traditional houses in the area. Some of the ramparts have been restored and there's a large pointed *moayedī* (ice-house) now used as a rubbish dump. The walls are sometimes floodlit at night.

Agha Bozorg Mosque & Madrassa

This mosque and theological school is arguably the finest Islamic complex in Kāshān. More understated than the mosques of Esfahān, it is famous for its unusual sunken courtyard. It also has a lovely portal and a nice mihrab (niche indicating the direction of Mecca) at the back. The imposing, austere dome is flanked by two squat minarets adorned with beautiful tiles and geometric designs. The fine Quranic inscriptions and mosaics throughout are brought out by the predominance of sand-coloured brick used for much of the construction. The magnificent wooden door at the entrance is said to have as many studs in it as there are verses in the Quran. Above the entrance are, unusually, two four-sided windtowers.

Entrance costs IR20,000.

Zeyārat-é Habīb Ibn-é Mūsā

The revered Shāh Abbās I would be disappointed with the comparative size of his unimpressive tomb, the Zeyārat-é Habīb Ibn-é Mūsā, just north of Emām Khomeinī Square off Emām Khomeinī St. The building around it was little more than a shell when we visited as reconstruction work was under way. Entrance is likely to be free for some time to come.

Soltānīyeh Mosque

Lost in the midst of the labyrinthine bazaar is the Soltānīyeh Mosque, dating back to the Seljuk period. The current structure was built in 1808 by Fath Alī Shāh and now houses a *madraseh* (theological school) which is not open to women.

Jāmeh Mosque

The much-restored Jāmeh Mosque, just south of Bābā Afzal St in the centre of town, is relatively unimpressive. It dates from the Seljuk and Timurid periods, and has a mihrab from the 11th century.

Emāmzādeh-yé Abu Lōlou

On the road from Kāshān to Fīn, Emāmzādeh-yé Abu Lōlou probably dates back to the Mongol period, although it has been heavily renovated many times since. The shrine has a fine, slender dome and two turquoise minarets, all visible from the road.

Shāhzadeh-yé Ibrahīm

This delightful shrine was built in the Qajar period (1779–1921), and boasts beautiful tiles, two colourful minarets and a pretty courtyard. The conical, tiled roof over the dome is distinctive to this part of the country and chances are you'll have seen it on posters long before you arrive. It's just off the main road to the gardens at Fīn and is clearly visible from the road, so simply follow your nose from there. Although chartering a taxi in combination with a visit to the gardens at Fīn is the easiest way to get there, it isn't too difficult to jump on and off the minibuses that run the length of the road. Entrance is free.

Tappeh-yé Seyalk

This is probably the richest archaeological site uncovered so far in central Iran, although the most interesting finds have been moved to various institutes and museums, including the National Museum of Iran in Tehrān, and the Louvre in Paris. A large number and variety of pottery and domestic implements, made from stone, clay and bone from as early as the 4th millennium BC, have been discovered at the site but there's little of interest for the average visitor.

Seyalk is 4.5km to the north-west of Fīn, on the right-hand side of the road from Kāshān.

Bāgh-é Tārīkhī-yé Fīn

This famous garden with its pools and orchards is quite beautiful, although some travellers have found it a disappointment after the gardens of Māhān and Shīrāz. Designed for Shāh Abbās I, this classical Persian vision of paradise has always been prized for its natural springs and still contains the remains of the shah's two-storey palace. The garden has other Safavid royal buildings, though they have been substantially rebuilt, and others were added in the Qajar period. The palace is also infamous for being the site of the murder in 1851 of the revered Mirza Taghī Khān, commonly known as Amīr Kabīr (see the boxed text 'Who's That Man?' in the Tehrān chapter).

Inside the grounds, a mildly interesting **museum** contains archaeological items from Tappeh-yé Seyalk and Choqa Zanbīl, among other sites, but unless you're a student of archaeology, it's probably not worth the additional IR10,000. There's a picturesque teahouse at the back of the gardens and an expensive shop in the grounds sells postcards of the gardens and other attractions in and around Kāshān.

The gardens, in the village of Fīn about 8km south-west of central Kāshān, are open from about 8 am to about 7 pm daily and entrance costs IR30,000. You can get there by shared taxi (IR3000) or minibus (IR200) from central Kāshān (see Getting Around later). A private taxi costs about IR10,000 per hour and enables you to explore some of the other sights nearby more easily.

Places to Stay

There's a handful of *mosāferkhūnehs* (basic lodging houses) in Kāshān, particularly around Motahharī Square near the entrance to the bazaar.

Mosāferkhūneh-yé Golestan (☎ 446 293), upstairs in a building to the south-east of the square, is probably the best, charging IR40,000 per person for simple but clean rooms with shared shower and toilet. Some of the rooms at the back have windows looking down on a minor leg of the bazaar – a great vantage point, if a little noisy at times. Sadly, foreigners are not allowed to join the locals who sleep under the stars on the roof.

The *Mosāferkhūneh-yé Gochārīyān* (☎ 445 495), above a *kabābī* (snack bar) a few doors east of the bazaar entrance, is a little more reluctant to take foreigners and charges the same as the Golestan for rooms that are more basic.

Most travellers stay at the *Sayyah Hotel* (☎ 444 535, Abāzar St), which has pleasant rooms (some are a little cramped) for US$15/20 without/with a spotless shower

and Western toilet. The price also includes breakfast, which is served between 7 and 9 am, although the waiter knocks on all doors around 7.30 am if business is a little slow. There is off-street parking for those with their own vehicle.

On the main road, about 1km before the gardens at Fīn, the *Amīr Kabīr Hotel* (☎ 30 091, fax 30 938) has pretensions to luxury but the rooms are decidedly plain and overpriced at US$35/55 for a single/double with bathroom. The wonderful views from the upper rooms are a redeeming feature and there's a reasonable restaurant downstairs. It's a long way from the centre of Kāshān (around 8km) so they have an expensive taxi service (IR3000); much cheaper minibuses run past the front door (IR200).

Places to Eat

The *Dellpazīr Restaurant* (☎ 272 276, Āyatollāh Kāshānī St) is almost worth the trip to Kāshān on its own as it has one of the most extensive and varied menus in Iran. There's a full page of starters ranging from chicken (with sauces to dip it in) to marinated chicken pieces with green pepper and mushroom. The excellent choice of main dishes includes three types of *khōresht* (meat stew), steak and kebabs, and this is one of the best places in Iran to try *fesenjān* (chicken in a rich walnut and pomegranate sauce). The service is friendly and English is spoken. Look for the 'Wellcome' sign in a small arcade.

Another good choice is the *Chehel Hesārān Restaurant* (☎ 22 118, Shahīd Mohammad Alī-yé Raja'ī St). Although the menu is not as varied as Dellpazīr's, they do a good *ābgūsht* (stew of potatoes, meat and lentils), and the lovely underground setting includes cane mats on the floor, soft lighting and tinkling fountains. The restaurant is signposted in English two storeys above the footpath.

On the same street, *Restōrān-é Luksashahr* (☎ 454 745) is popular with local Iranians. Although it lacks the atmosphere of the other two, most tables overlook the street. The food isn't bad either.

The *Sayyah Restaurant*, attached to the hotel of the same name, is a bit inconsistent and the service can be a little distracted – all of which is a pity because the servings are a decent size and the prices are cheap. A good khōresht, crunchy rice, a decidedly ordinary salad, a soft drink and delicious *mâst* (yogurt), which arrived just as we were leaving, cost altogether around IR15,000.

Elsewhere, there are several kabābīs along Abāzar St. *Restaurant Shirin* in the bazaar is a little run-down but cheap, and there's an OK *restaurant* outside the entrance to the Fīn gardens.

Getting There & Away

Bus & Minibus Not a lot of buses originate in Kāshān and there's no real terminal. Buses and minibuses leave regularly for Esfahān and Tehrān (both around IR7000) from the bus company offices east of Shahīd Mohammed-é Montazerī Square or from around Emām Khomeinī Square. The makeshift terminal at 15 Khordād Square caters for buses passing through Kāshān on the way to Tehrān as well as Yazd and Esfahān, and is a good place to pick up a bus to these destinations.

Minibuses to Qom (IR3000) leave from just east of Montazerī Square about every hour.

Shared Taxi Less regular shared taxis leave from around 15 Khordād or Emām Khomeinī Squares and cost a touch more than the buses and minibuses.

Train There is a train from Kāshān to Tehrān (IR9250) at around 4 pm daily, arriving in the capital sometime after 8 pm. Trains to Yazd (IR15,700) and Kermān (IR27,900) roll out on Monday, Wednesday and Friday at 9 pm. The train station is in northern Kāshān but is within walking distance of the city centre.

Getting Around

A shared taxi from the centre of town to Bāgh-é Tārīkhī-yé Fīn costs IR3000, a lot more than the minibus which runs at regular intervals between 15 Khordād Square and the gardens for IR200. Chartering a private taxi costs IR10,000 an hour.

AROUND KĀSHĀN
Mashhad-é Ardehal مشهد اردهال

About 40km west of Kāshān, there is a magnificent **Seljuk tomb** with two courtyards and two balconies, built for Alī ibn Mohammed Bagar on the slope of a hill. The village of Ardehal (more often called Mashhad by the locals) is more famous for its annual carpet-washing ceremony.

Abyaneh ابيانه

One of the most fascinating villages in the country has to be Abyaneh. Its twisting, climbing lanes of mud and stone pass predominantly ochre-coloured houses with lattice windows and fragile wooden balconies. There are also some magnificent views across the valley. Recognised for its antiquity and uniqueness by Unesco, the village provides the perfect antidote to the bustling cities of modern Iran, particularly as there are few motorised vehicles to disturb the quiet.

Most of what has remained intact from the ravages of time and invading armies dates from the Safavid period. Most of the inhabitants were Zoroastrians, who later converted to Islam.

The Carpet-Washing Ceremony of Ardehal

In the first week of October every year, the *qali shuran* is held at Ardehal. Developing more than 1200 years ago, the ceremony commemorates the legend of a son of an imam from the holy city of Medina who lived in Ardehal. The imam's son had a premonition in his sleep that a local governor planned to assassinate him. He and his supporters thwarted the initial assassination attempt, but the son was later killed while praying on a mat. His followers later placed the body on the carpet, and washed it in accordance with tradition before burying him.

On the anniversary of his murder, thousands of locals, joined by visitors from Kāshān, Qom and as far away as Yazd, carry the same carpet (or what's left of it) from the shrine, beat it to symbolise their hatred of the murderers, and then wash it in a local stream.

Serenely situated at the foot of Mt Karkas, Abyaneh is cool in summer and frightfully cold for the rest of the year. The village faces east for maximum sun and was built high to minimise the effects of floods and howling gales in winter; the houses were built in a huddle to increase their security against frequent raids by marauders and are on the rocks rather than on valuable farmland. Most of the homes were built from mud brick and clay; like in Māsuleh, near Rasht, many lanes and the front yards of some homes were built on the roofs of homes below.

Although Abyaneh is best appreciated by exploring slowly in whichever direction takes your fancy, there are some specific buildings to watch out for. Try to look for the 14th-century **Emāmzādeh-yé Yahya**, with its conical, blue-tiled roof, and the **Zeyaratgāh shrine** with its tiny pool and views of the village. Probably the most beautiful building is the 14th-century **Jāmeh Mosque** with its walnut-wood mihrab and ancient carvings. On top of the rocky hills are the remains of a couple of **castles**, known locally as *haman*. By following the steep paths between the houses up the hillside, it is possible to reach one of these small castles with spectacular views onto the town and across the valley.

Abyaneh has nowhere to stay. The *Abyaneh Restaurant & Supermarket*, on the main road as you descend the hill into town, is the only place to eat or buy drinks.

Getting There & Away Abyaneh is 82km from Kāshān, and not easy to reach. The cheapest way is to take a regular minibus from Kāshān towards Natanz (make sure the bus is not taking the road to Nā'īn) and get off at the signposted turn-off. Then wait for another lift for the remaining 22km.

Alternatively, chartering a taxi for a half-day from Kāshān should cost about IR100,000 after some bargaining. Chartering also allows you to stop along the way and admire the magnificent scenery.

Natanz نطنز
☎ 0362 424
The attractive town of Natanz, on the lower slopes of Mt Karkas (3899m), is a good place to break the journey between Kāshān and Esfahān. The **Jāmeh Mosque** and **Emāmzadeh-yé Abd al-Samad** are next to each other in what was an important early Islamic complex. The tomb belongs to a renowned local Sufi mystic of the 11th century; the mosque is believed to date from the early 14th century. The beautiful portal of the (now closed) shrine has some unusual turquoise ceramics and sparing use of calligraphy while the entrance to the mosque has an intricately carved wooden door. Entrance is free.

There was much discussion at the *Hotel Saraban (☎ 2603, fax 2604)* before we arrived at the price of US$20/30 for a pleasant, airy single/double with bathroom, fridge and balcony; after some more discussion you may be able to get it for a little less. There's also a *restaurant* in the hotel as well as others right outside the front door. The hotel is on the main road into town from Esfahān, on the left.

Most buses from Esfahān to Kāshān pass through Natanz and there is a direct daily minibus from Esfahān's Kāveh Terminal at 2 pm.

ESFAHĀN اصفهان
☎ 031 • pop 1,220,595
Esfahān (Isfahan) is Iran's masterpiece, the jewel of ancient Persia and one of the finest cities in the Islamic world. The exquisite blue mosaic tiles of Esfahān's Islamic buildings, its expansive bazaar and the city's gorgeous bridges demand as much of your time as you can spare. It's a city for walking, getting lost in the bazaar, dozing in beautiful gardens, and drinking tea and chatting to locals in the marvellous teahouses. More than anything else, though, Esfahān is a place for savouring the high refinements of Persian culture which are most evident in and around Emām Khomeinī Square – the Emām Mosque, the Sheikh Lotfollāh Mosque, the Ali Qāpū Palace and the Chehel Sotūn Palace. Such is Esfahān's grandeur that it is easy to agree with the famous 16th-century half-rhyme *Esfahān nesf-é jahān* (Esfahān is half the world).

That said, there is quite a lot of heavy industry on the outskirts of the city and the air

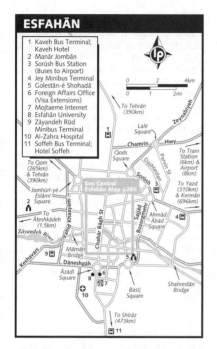

ESFAHĀN

1 Kaveh Bus Terminal;
  Kaveh Hotel
2 Manār Jombān
3 Sorūsh Bus Station
  (Buses to Airport)
4 Jey Minibus Terminal
5 Golestān-é Shohadā
6 Foreign Affairs Office
  (Visa Extensions)
7 Mojtaeme Internet
8 Esfahān University
9 Zāyandeh Rūd
  Minibus Terminal
10 Al-Zahra Hospital
11 Soffeh Bus Terminal;
  Hotel Soffeh

The power and breadth of Shāh Abbās' vision is still very much in evidence. During his rule, Esfahān produced some of the most beautiful and inspiring architecture, art and carpets seen anywhere in the Islamic world.

Orientation

The main street, Chahār Bāgh (Four Gardens), was built in 1597, and was once lined with many palaces. Although it's over 5km long, most travellers base themselves along the middle section of the street, called Chahār Bāgh Abbāsī St, between Sī-o-Seh Bridge (Pol-é Sī-o-Sé) and Takhtī Square. Most of the sights, shops, offices and hotels are within easy walking distance from this part of Esfahān and it's a pleasure to wander along the tree-lined avenues; Chahār Bāgh Abbāsī St has a pedestrian boulevard in the middle of the road. The few outlying attractions are easily visited by shared or private taxi.

The Zāyandeh River starts in the Zāgros Mountains, flows from west to east through the heart of Esfahān, and then peters out into the Dasht-é Kavīr. It separates the northern part of the city from the Armenian quarter in Jolfā, south-west of Sī-o-Seh Bridge.

Information

Visa Extensions Esfahān is a great place to get a 10- or 14-day visa extension, often within the hour. Those on transit visas are unlikely to be given more than an additional five days, although multiple extensions are often possible. Go to the 2nd floor of the Foreign Affairs Office (☎ 688 166), opposite Esfahān University. You'll need two photos, photocopies of the relevant pages of your passport and IR12,500. Mercifully, the usual inconvenience of depositing the money at a Bank Melli branch is replaced by a sensible system of the officers themselves collecting the money. To get there take a shared taxi from the southern end of Sī-o-Seh Bridge (IR600).

Tourist Offices Esfahān boasts one of the best tourist offices in the country (☎ 228 541, fax 618 660). The office is centrally located (on the ground floor of the Alī Qāpu Palace) and staffed by helpful English-speaking personnel. They can usually

pollution and traffic congestion can give Tehrān a run for its money on a bad day.

Note that there are a lot of things to see in Esfahān. You can easily get through US$20 in admission fees alone here.

History

Esfahān did not rise to national prominence until the early 1500s when the first rulers of the Safavid dynasty drove the Mongols from the country. When Shāh Abbās I (also revered as Shāh Abbās the Great) came to power in 1587, he extended his influence over rivals within the country and then pushed out the Ottoman Turks who had occupied a large part of Persia. With his country once more united and free of foreign influence, Shāh Abbās I set out to make Esfahān a great city. However, its period of glory lasted for little more than a century: An invasion from Afghanistan hastened the decline and the capital was subsequently transferred to Shīrāz and then to Tehrān.

provide a reasonable free map of the city. Opening hours are from 8 am to 12.30 pm and 5 to 7 pm daily. Some travellers have reported getting prompt replies to faxes, even those sent from outside Iran.

Money The central branches of the big three banks – Bank Melli, Bank Tejarat and Bank Mellat – have foreign exchange facilities. Many hotels and shops (particularly those around Emām Khomeinī Square) will also gladly (but discreetly) change money. Some have even been known to give change in US dollars for larger purchases.

Post & Telephone The main post office is along Neshāt St, east of Emām Khomeinī Square, but there are more convenient offices on Enqelāb-é Eslāmī Square and the western side of Emām Khomeinī Square. The central telephone office is easy to find along Beheshtī St. The useful Amīr Kabīr Hostel (see Places to Stay later in this section) has a reasonably priced international fax and telephone service.

Email & Internet Access Internet places are springing up all over town, although there are few dedicated Internet cafes. Many shops in the bazaar and in the complex opposite the Abbāsī Hotel run single-computer operations, usually as a lure for their handicrafts or carpets. One shop that lets you check your emails without the hard sell is the Internet Cyber Café (☎ 212 627, ⓔ ghalizadeh@hotmail .com) in the Ali Quapoo Carpet Shop in the first lane off Emām Khomeinī Square as you go north from Sheikh Lotfollāh Mosque. Another option is Silk Road Carpets (☎ 201 137, fax 202 721, ⓔ irajdelta@hotmail.com), around the corner from Ali Quapoo. The Amīr Kabīr Hostel also has Internet access. A bit further from the centre of things, Mojtaeme Internet (☎ 711 750) in the Mojtaeme Shopping Complex about 2.5km south of the river is also good. Expect to pay from IR25,000 to IR30,000 per hour.

Travel Agencies Mina-yé Naghsh-é Jahān Tour & Travel Agency (☎ 222 193, fax 228 060) handles international and domestic air tickets, and train tickets and can arrange sightseeing tours around Esfahān; it also has periodic Internet access. Iran Travel & Tourism Tour (☎ 223 010, fax 228 060) is similar and can also arrange car rental; it also represents of the Touring & Automobile Club of Iran. Both agencies are in the shopping complex opposite the Abbāsī Hotel.

There are surprisingly few agencies offering tours around Esfahān for budget travellers, possibly because many carpet shops and hotels offer these services as an adjunct to their main business. Highly recommended and offering a relatively soft sell on carpets is the experienced Nomad Carpet Shops which has two branches around Emām Khomeinī Square. These places can arrange overnight trips to some of the nomad communities in the surrounding countryside, as well as tours within Esfahān. Iraj Riahi (☎/fax 21 536, ⓔ iraj_riahi@yahoo.com) is a knowledgable and engaging local guide who offers a similar service. The Ali Quapoo Carpet Shop has bikes for hire.

Bookshops Esfahān is one of the better places in Iran for browsing in bookshops, with most selling a good range of coffee-table books in English and European languages as well as postcards and posters. One of the best is the bookshop on Emām Khomeinī Square, a few doors north of the Alī Qāpū Palace. There are also bookshops at the Kowsar International Hotel and in the gardens of the Chehel Sotūn Palace. The Farhangsara-yé Esfahān Bookshop on Chahār Bāgh Abbāsī St sells *Newsweek*, *Time* and *National Geographic*. Look for the *Time* sticker on the door.

Photography Dozens of quite professional shops in Esfahān sell film (including slide film) and photographic equipment; some also develop films. The best place to start looking is along Chahār Bāgh Abbāsī St or in the complex opposite the Abbāsī Hotel.

Emergency The best hospital for travellers is the Al-Zahra Hospital (☎ 692 183) which has several English-speaking doctors who are relatively used to dealing with foreign travel-

Esfahān Walking Tour One

Starting on the south-eastern side of Takhtī Square, head south along Chahār Bāgh St for about 200m, where a small lane leads east. Here, you'll leave the clamour of modern Esfahān behind and enter the quiet, attractive lanes which are concealed from view if you stick to the main thoroughfares. Winding your way east, you'll come across the **Hakīm Mosque**, the oldest mosque in Esfahān. Continuing east, you'll pass through the quieter alleys of the **Bāzār-é Bozorg** where souvenir shops are greatly outnumbered by places where Esfahānīs buy their household goods. The bazaar veers to the north-east and gradually becomes busier. As you wander you will find shops that sell almost every imaginable item, as well as mosques, madrasehs, teahouses, banks, bathhouses and even the occasional garden.

Madraseh-yé Nimurvand, just north of the main thoroughfare, is one theological school where the students normally welcome visitors and is thus a good place to see a working madraseh. The bazaar branches out and feeds into the area around Qiyam Square, just north of which lies the **Jāmeh Mosque**, one of Esfahān's most important mosques.

Plunging back into the bazaar after your visit to the mosque, there are a number important sites just off the main bazaar thoroughfare. The octagonal **Emāmzādeh-yé Ja'afar** (1325) and the **Mausoleum of Harūn Vilayet (Bogh-é Harūn Vilayet)** – built in the early 16th-century and containing some good frescoes – are probably the most worthwhile of the tombs dotted around the area. Nearby, the **Minaret of the Mosque of Ali (Manar-é Masjed-é Alī)** has a towering brick minaret which has some attractive geometric designs and, at 48m high, is visible from many points around town on a clear day.

Rejoining the main bazaar (which may involve doubling back to the north in some places), you'll find yourself in covered lanes with filtering sunlight and surrounded by the aroma of spices as you head back towards Emām Khomeinī Square. En route, the Madraseh-yé Sadr has a large, green courtyard which can provide a momentary respite from the bustle of the bazaar. Following a southwesterly path (and the call of a growing number of traders with an interest in your business), you should arrive at the northern end of Emām Khomeinī Square. After pausing in the Gheysarieh Tea Shop, which overlooks the square, to get your bearings, launch into the square by either following the covered bazaars which circle the square behind the facades or by setting off to explore the jewels of Esfahān – the **Emām Mosque**, the **Sheikh Lotfollāh Mosque** and the **Alī Qāpū Palace.**

When you can finally tear yourself away from the splendour, head east for about 500m along Sepāh St with its carpet shops and moneychangers to the **Chehel Sotūn Palace** with its glorious frescoes. Continuing east and then south along Chahār Bāgh Abbāsī St takes you to the **Hasht Behesht Palace**, another architectural jewel set in lovely gardens. Rejoining Chahār Bāgh Abbāsī St – at its best here with trees lining the footpaths – you'll pass the restful **Madraseh-yé Chahār Bāgh**. Finally, turn east into Amadegh St where, after about 150m, you find yourself at the Abbāsī Hotel – the perfect place to sip tea and rest those tired feet.

---

lers. The Esfahān Hospital (☎ 230 015) is also recommended. The medical emergencies number is ☎ 275 555. Although the main police office (☎ 247 921) is behind the Alī Qāpū Palace, the police section of the Foreign Affairs Office (☎ 680 047; see Visa Extensions earlier in this section) is set up to handle any difficulties experienced by tourists.

Dangers & Annoyances Most hotels have signs in English warning foreigners to watch out for the surp risingly frequent scam of young men in cars posing as policemen by quickly flashing a bogus identity card and asking to see your passport. Simply walk away or offer to go with them to the nearest police station; they'll soon disappear. The police (who claim that no genuine policeman will stop a foreigner unless they've committed a crime) advise you to leave your passport in the safe at your hotel. If this happens to you, try and get the registration number of the car and report the matter to the police (☎ 680 047).

CENTRAL ESFAHĀN

To Train Station (10km)
& Airport (12km)

Forūghī St

Shohadā
Square

Ebn-é Sīnā St

See Jāmeh Mosque Map p288

Majlesī St

Chahār Bāgh-é Pa'īn St

To Kaveh Bus Terminal,
Kaveh Hotel (5km)
& Tehrān (390km)

Qiyām
Square

Takhtī
Square

Jamāl-od-Dīn Abdolrazāgh St

1

Masjed-é
Sayyed St

10

START OF
WALKING
TOUR 1

2

Bāzār-é
Bozorg

3

Hātef St

Masjed-é Sayyed St

12

11

9

5

Shahīd St

4

Walking Tour 1
Walking Tour 2

Stadium

8

13

7

6

Ahmad Ābād St

Golbahār St

See Emām Khomeinī
Square Map p290

To Jey Minibus
Terminal (4km)

To Manār
Jombān (7km) &
Āteshkādeh (8km)

Tāleqānī St

14

15

16

Bāzār-é
Bozorg

Sepah St

17

Hāfez St

18

21

Emām
Khomeinī
Square

19

Shams Ābādī St

Chahār Bāgh Abbāsi St

Emām
Hussein
Square

27

26

Beheshtī St

22

23

20

Bahā'ī St

Fathīyeh St

24

25

28

29

Shahīd Medānī St

30

31

34

33

32

36

37

35

Abūzar St

Abbās Ābād St

38

39

40

41

44

42

Sayyed Alī Khān St

43

START OF
WALKING
TOUR 2

Engelāb-é
Eslāmī Square

Motahharī St

Sī-o-Seh
Bridge

45

46

To Khājū Square
(1km)

Allāmeh Amini St

Bozormeghr
Bridge

Salmān-é Fārsī St

Bāzārcheh St

Ābshār St

Zāyandeh River

0   400   800m
0   400   800yd

Sa'di Blvd

Mellat Blvd

48

Pānzdah-é Khordād St

Shahrestān
Bridge

To Mārnān
Bridge (1.5km)

47

Ferdōsī
Bridge

Hazrat-é Qāem St

Ābshār St

Sajjād St

Sajjād St

To Zāyandeh Rūd
Minibus Terminal (2km)

Jolfā

Ā'īneh Khūneh Blvd

Chūbī
Bridge

Chahār Bāgh-é Sadr St

Khājū
Square

Moshtāgh St

To
Shahrestān
Bridge (3km,
see inset)

50

Nazar St

Khājū Bridge

Zāyandeh River

Chahār Bāgh-é Bālā

Nazar
Crossroads

51

53

52

Mīr Fendereskī St

Feiz
Square

Qoddūsī St

54

To Shīrāz (473km)

0   250   500m
0   250   500yd

PLACES TO STAY
- 9 Persia Hotel
- 10 Pardis Apartment Hotel; Sandwich Shop
- 11 Āzādy Hotel
- 12 22 Bahman Hotel
- 13 Amīr Kabīr Hostel; Pizza Hamburger Joint
- 14 Naghsh-é Jahan Hotel; Piroozy Hotel; Nobahar Restaurant
- 20 Hotel Apartments Mehr; Kīsh Airlines
- 29 Shad Hotel
- 31 Abbāsī Hotel; Chehelstotoun Restaurant; Naghsh-é Jahan Restaurant
- 32 Aria Hotel; Safīr Hotel
- 34 Pars Hotel
- 36 Hotel Alī Qāpū
- 38 Saadi Hotel
- 39 Tourist Hotel
- 40 Tous Hotel; Pizza Restaurant
- 44 Sahel Hotel; Bame Sahel Teahouse
- 47 Pol and Park Hotel

- 48 Kowsar International Hotel
- 54 Julfa Hotel

PLACES TO EAT
- 8 Restōrān-é Sa'dī
- 15 Candida Pizza Hamburger
- 37 Restaurant Shahrzad
- 41 Iseman
- 42 Maharaja Restaurant
- 49 Pizza Homa
- 50 Restōrān-é Khayyām

OTHER
- 1 Jāmeh Mosque
- 2 Mausoleum of Harūn Vilayet
- 3 Manar-é Alī Mosque
- 4 Emāmzādeh-yé Ja'afar
- 5 Madraseh-yé Nimurvand
- 6 Madraseh-yé Sadr
- 7 Hakīm Mosque
- 16 Bank Mellat (Central Branch)
- 17 Natural History Museum
- 18 Bank Melli (Central Branch)
- 19 Main Post Office
- 21 Police Headquarters
- 22 Decorative Arts Museum of Iran; Museum of Contemporary Art

- 23 Chehel Sotūn Palace; Teahouse; Bookshop
- 24 Main Telephone Office
- 25 Local Bus Station
- 26 Farhangsara-yé Esfahān Bookshop
- 27 Esfahān Hospital
- 28 Hasht Behesht Palace
- 30 Madraseh-yé Chahār Bāgh
- 33 Iran Air Office; Iran Handicrafts Organisation; Mina-yé Naghsh-é Jahān Tour & Travel Agency; Iran Travel & Tourism Tour; DHL; Photography Shops
- 35 Iran Air Office
- 43 Train Ticket Office; Bank Tejarat (Central Branch)
- 45 Shuttle Bus to Train Station
- 46 Paddleboat Hire
- 51 Church of Bethlehem (Kelīsā-yé Bethlehem)
- 52 Church of St Mary (Kelīsā-yé Maryam)
- 53 Vank Cathderal (Kelīsā-yé Vānk) & Museum

The water in Esfahān is a little polluted; the locals tend to drink mineral water so it's a good idea if you do too.

Hakīm Mosque

This large Safavid mosque contains a beautiful portal believed to date from the late 10th century, making it the oldest surviving structure in Esfahān. The mosque itself is fairly unremarkable but is worth a quick visit to see one of the last relics of the Buyid dynasty.

Jāmeh Mosque

This mosque is a veritable museum of Islamic architecture, displaying styles from the 11th to the 18th centuries, from the stylish simplicity of the Seljuk period, through the Mongol period and on to the more baroque Safavid period. Although more sober in its decorations than the Emām Mosque or Sheikh Lotfollāh Mosque, the Jāmeh Mosque provides a fascinating bridge between some of the most important periods of Persian history. At 30,000 sq metres, it is also the biggest mosque in Iran.

The first large mosque was built on this site in the 11th century. The two large domes above the north and south *iwans* (halls) have survived intact, with most of the remainder destroyed by fire in the 12th century. The mosque was rebuilt in 1121, with later rulers adding their own refinements, although the Safavids contributed little more than superficial decoration. The mosque was hit by an Iraqi bomb 16 years ago but suffered only minimal damage which has since been repaired.

In the centre of the main courtyard, which is surrounded by four contrasting iwans, is an attractive **ablutions fountain** designed to imitate the Kaaba at Mecca; would-be haj pilgrims would use it to practise the appropriate rituals. The two-storey porches around the courtyard's perimeter were constructed in the late 15th century.

The **south iwan** is the most elaborate, with two minarets showing geometrical designs,

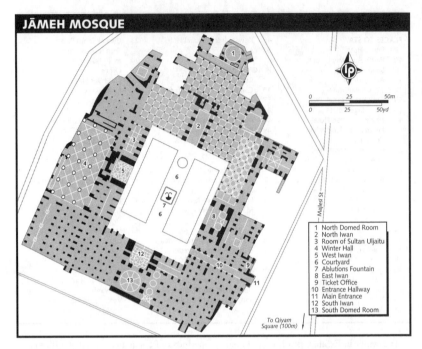

JĀMEH MOSQUE

1 North Domed Room
2 North Iwan
3 Room of Sultan Uljaitu
4 Winter Hall
5 West Iwan
6 Courtyard
7 Ablutions Fountain
8 East Iwan
9 Ticket Office
10 Entrance Hallway
11 Main Entrance
12 South Iwan
13 South Domed Room

To Qiyam
Square (100m)

some Mongol-era stalactite mouldings – which are less intricate than those from the Safavid period – and some splendid mosaics on the side walls dating from the 15th century. The **north iwan** has a wonderful monumental porch with Kufic inscriptions dating from the Seljuk period, and austere brick pillars in the sanctuary.

On the western side of the courtyard, the **west iwan** has Safavid mosaics which are more geometric than those of the southern hall. The courtyard is topped by a small raised platform with a conical roof from where the faithful used to be called to prayer.

You may need to ask the gatekeeper to let you into some of the fine interior rooms. The **Room of Sultan Uljaitu** (a 14th-century Shiite convert) has a wonderful stone mihrab awash with dense Quranic inscriptions and floral designs flanked by two slender pillars. Next door is the Timurid-era **Winter Hall** (Beit al-Sheta) built in 1448 and lit by alabaster skylights. The two **domed rooms** to

the north and south of the complex are Seljuk (11th century) in origin and are the oldest parts of the building.

The mosque is open from 7 am to 7 pm daily; entrance costs IR25,000. The main entrance is the only one with a ticket office; there are three other entrances which are used by locals.

Bāzār-é Bozorg

Esfahān's Bāzār-é Bozorg or Great Bazaar is one of the highlights of Esfahān, linking Emām Khomeinī Square with the Jāmeh Mosque, several kilometres away. The covered bazaar, one of the largest and most labyrinthine in the country, was mostly built during the early 16th century, although some of it dates back almost 1300 years. Excellent use of light is made by placing large windows in the high domed and vaulted ceilings.

[Continued on page 296]

CENTRAL IRAN

JOHN BORTHWICK

JOHN BORTHWICK

ANTHONY HAM

HUGH WATTS

Some of the highlights of Esfahān: the dome and minaret of the Emām Mosque (top); the magnificent Sheikh Lotfollāh Mosque (bottom left); one of the famous Shaking Minarets (middle right); the moving Golestān-é Shohadā, memorial to those who died during the Iran-Iraq War (bottom right)

Qashqā'ī nomads trek down from the Zāgros Mountains.

A Qashqā'ī woman from Shahr-é Kord

Goats graze with the snow-covered Zāgros Mountains as their dramatic backdrop.

The tilted summit of Mt Bijan rises to over 4000m.

View towards the desolate Dasht-é Kavīr

EMĀM KHOMEINĪ SQUARE

The magnificent Emām Khomeinī Square (Meydān-é Emām Khomeinī; still known as Naghsh-é Jahān Square by many locals) is home to some of the most majestic buildings in the Islamic world. Built in 1612 and measuring 500m by 160m, this huge, open square owes much to the vision of Shāh Abbās the Great. Flanked by the incomparable Emām Mosque, the supremely elegant Sheikh Lotfollāh Mosque and the indulgent Alī Qāpū Palace, it's a place you'll come back to again and again.

Before the Alī Qāpū Palace was built the square was even bigger than it is now. However, the shops were moved forward to align them with the palace, so reducing the area. Traditionally, the square was closed to men for one day a week so women could shop; male shop-keepers were obliged to stay indoors out of sight.

The square is best visited in the late afternoon and early evening when local families flood in to outnumber the Iranian and foreign

Inset: Moonlit minaret of the Emām Mosque (photo by Phil Weymouth)

Right: Sunlight highlights the ornately tiled archways of a hallway within the Emām Mosque

HUGH WATTS

289

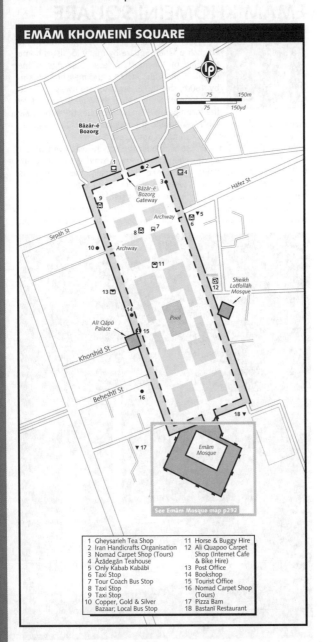

EMĀM KHOMEINĪ SQUARE

Bāzār-é Bozorg

Bāzār-é Bozorg Gateway

Háfez St

Archway

Sepáh St

Archway

Pool

Sheikh Lotfollāh Mosque

Alī Qāpū Palace

Khorshid St

Beheshtí St

Emām Mosque

See Emām Mosque map p292

1 Gheysarieh Tea Shop
2 Iran Handicrafts Organisation
3 Nomad Carpet Shop (Tours)
4 Āzādegān Teahouse
5 Only Kabab Kabābī
6 Taxi Stop
7 Tour Coach Bus Stop
8 Taxi Stop
9 Taxi Stop
10 Copper, Gold & Silver Bazaar; Local Bus Stop
11 Horse & Buggy Hire
12 Ali Quapoo Carpet Shop (Internet Cafe & Bike Hire)
13 Post Office
14 Bookshop
15 Tourist Office
16 Nomad Carpet Shop (Tours)
17 Pizza Bam
18 Bastanī Restaurant

tourists. This is also when the fountains in the rectangular pool in the centre are turned on, the light softens and the splendid architecture of the perimeter is illuminated.

Emām Mosque

The Emām Mosque (Masjed-é Emām) is one of the most beautiful mosques in the world. The richness of its blue-tiled mosaic designs and its perfectly proportioned Safavid-era architecture form a visually stunning monument to the imagination of Shāh Abbās I. The lavish decoration of the mosque perfectly complements the architectural elegance, the two combining to foster an air of tranquillity.

Work started on the magnificent entrance portal in 1611, although it took four years to finish – look for mismatches in its apparent symmetry, intended to reflect the carver's humility in the face of Allah. It was not until 1629, the last year of the reign of Shāh Abbās and some 18 years after construction commenced, that the high dome, and therefore the mosque, was completed. Although minor additions were later made, unusually for Iran most of what remains dates from that 18-year period. This explains the fact that although each of the mosque's constituent parts is a masterpiece in itself, the unity of the overall design is what leaves the lasting impression.

The original purpose of the **entrance portal** had less to do with the mosque's spiritual aims than its location on the square. Indeed its function was primarily ornamental in providing a counterpoint to the entrance to the Bāzār-é Bozorg at the northern end some 500m away. The foundation stones are of white marble from Ardestān and the portal itself, some 30m tall, is decorated with magnificent geometric designs, floral motifs and calligraphy by some of the most skilled calligraphers of the age. The splendid niches contain complex stalactite mouldings in a honeycomb pattern, each panel with its own intricate design.

Right: Mosaic calligraphy on the wall of the Emām Mosque

PATRICK SYDER

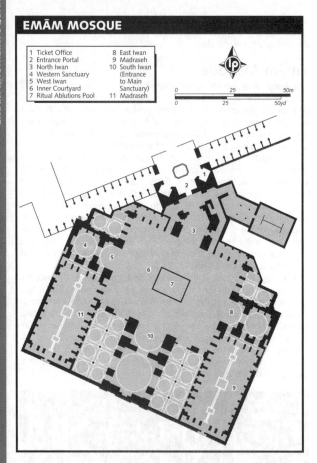

EMĀM MOSQUE

1 Ticket Office
2 Entrance Portal
3 North Iwan
4 Western Sanctuary
5 West Iwan
6 Inner Courtyard
7 Ritual Ablutions Pool
8 East Iwan
9 Madraseh
10 South Iwan
   (Entrance
   to Main
   Sanctuary)
11 Madraseh

0   25   50m
0   25   50yd

Although the portal was built to face the square, the mosque itself is angled so as to point in the direction of the holy city of Mecca. A short, winding corridor leads into the **inner courtyard**, which has a large pool for ritual ablutions in its centre and is surrounded by four **iwans**. The walls of the courtyard contain the most exquisite sunken porches, framed by mosaics of deep blue and yellow, the intensity of which is breathtaking.

Each iwan leads into a vaulted sanctuary. In the **east sanctuary**, a few black paving stones under the dome create clear echoes when stamped upon; although scientists have measured up to 49 echoes, only around 12 are audible to the human ear. The **west sanctuary** has some particularly fine floral motifs with the usual blue and white combined with softer pinks and mauves to stunning effect.

The **main sanctuary** is entered via the south iwan. Find yourself a quiet corner in which to sit and contemplate the richness of the domed ceiling with its golden rose pattern (the flower basket) surrounded by concentric circles of busy mosaics on a deep blue background. The interior ceiling is 36.3m high, although the exterior reaches up to 51m due to the double-layering used in construction. The marble **mihrab** (niche facing Mecca) and **minbar** (pulpit) are also beautifully crafted.

The main sanctuary provides wonderful views back to the two turquoise **minarets** above the entrance portal. Each is encircled by projecting balconies and white geometric calligraphy in which the names of Mohammed and Ali are picked out over and over again. Each is also topped by an elegant dome.

To the east and west of the main sanctuary are the courtyards of two madrasehs. Both provide good views of the main cupola or **dome** with its tiles alternately every shade of turquoise depending on the position of the sun.

The mosque is open from about 7.30 am to 1 pm and from 2.30 to 7 or 8 pm daily except Friday morning. Entrance costs IR25,000 and cameras are allowed. The tents that fill the courtyard to protect worshippers in the summer months can wreak havoc with your photos.

Sheikh Lotfollāh Mosque

While the appeal of the Emām Mosque owes much to the majesty of its grand design, the smaller Sheikh Lotfollāh Mosque (Masjed-é Sheikh Lotfollāh) is a study in harmony. This mosque, on the eastern side of the square, is the perfect complement to the overwhelming richness of the Emām Mosque.

The Sheikh Lotfollāh Mosque was built between 1602 and 1619, also during the reign of Shāh Abbās I. The ruler dedicated it to his father-in-law, Sheikh Lotfollāh, a revered Lebanese scholar of Islam who was invited to Esfahān to oversee to oversee the king's mosque (the present day Emām's Mosque) and theological school and theological school.

The pale **dome** makes exensive use of delicate cream-coloured tiles which change colour throughout the day from cream to pink, depending on the light conditions; they are at their best around sunset. The signature blue and turquoise tiles of Esfahān are evident only around the dome's summit.

Right: The entrance to the Sheikh Lotfollāh Mosque

PATRICK SYDER

The pale tones of the cupola stand in contrast to the remainder of the facade around the **portal** where you'll find some of the best surviving Safavid-era mosaics. The exterior panels contain some wonderful arabesques and other intricate floral designs; those displaying a vase framed by the tails of two peacocks are superb. The portal itself contains some particularly fine stalactite work with rich concentrations of blue and yellow motifs.

The Sheikh Lotfollāh Mosque is unusual because it has neither a minaret nor a courtyard, and because steps lead up to the entrance. The **sanctuary** or prayer hall is reached via a twisting, enclosed **hallway** which, although purely functional in purpose, is itself attractive with its subtle shifts of light.

The sanctuary is another place to sit and marvel at the complexity of the mosaics that adorn the walls and ceiling. The latter is extraordinarily beautiful with the intensity of its shrinking, yellow motifs drawing the visitor's eye into the exquisite centre. The shafts of sunlight that filter in through the few high, latticed windows produce an interplay of

MARTIN MOOS

Left: The magnificent dome of the Sheikh Lotfollāh Mosque

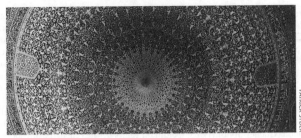

PATRICK SYDER

light and shadow which can bring a whole new perspective to the motifs and calligraphy around the walls.

The mihrab is one of the finest in Iran and has an unusually high niche, filled with lovely mosaic tilework, stalactite mouldings of simple design and a wonderful calligraphic montage which contains the name of the architect and the date 1028 AH.

The mosque is open from 7 am to noon and from 3 to 7 pm daily; entrance costs IR25,000. Photography is allowed, but you'll need a powerful flash or tripod inside.

Alī Qāpū Palace

This unusual six-storey palace was built in the early 17th century initially as a monumental gateway (Alī Qāpū means the 'Gate of Alī') to the royal palaces which lay in the parklands between the square and the Chahār Bāgh thoroughfare. It later served as a seat of government where the king received notables and ambassadors.

The highlight of the palace is arguably the **elevated terrace** with its 18 slender columns, which affords a wonderful perspective over the square and one of the best views of the Emām Mosque. If you make the climb you'll be in good company – the Safavid kings and the rest of the royal party used to sit here to oversee races, an ancient form of polo (*chogrān*) and other entertainments performed in the square for the royal pleasure. If you look up, you'll see an attractive wooden ceiling with intricate inlay work and exposed beams, reminiscent of the nearby Chehel Sotūn Palace.

Many of the valuable murals and mosaics which once decorated the small rooms, corridors and stairways were destroyed during the Qajar period and since the Islamic Revolution. However, some lovely paintings remain in the **Throne Room**, which leads off the terrace. There are also mosaics throughout the palace, although these are kept to a relatively simple minimum.

On the upper floor, the **music room** is definitely worth the climb. The plaster ceiling is riddled with the shapes of vases and other household utensils cut to dramatic, almost eerie effect and almost certainly copying those in the shrine of Sheikh Safī-od-Dīn in Ardabīl. This distinctive craftsmanship, considered by some to be one of the finest examples of secular Persian art, is also said to have enhanced the acoustics.

The palace is open from 7 am to noon and 3 to 7 pm daily; entrance costs IR20,000.

Right: The domed ceiling of the Sheikh Lotfollāh Mosque. Lemon-shaped mosaics are surrounded by unglazed bricks, creating a remarkable, shimmering effect.

[Continued from page 288]

Chehel Sotūn Palace

Standing in a pretty garden, this palace is another of the highlights of Esfahān; its frescoes are as beautiful as any you'll see elsewhere. Chehel Sotūn was originally built as a pleasure pavilion and reception hall by Shāh Abbās II with one inscription dating the completion of construction to 1647. The name Chehel Sotūn (Forty Columns) refers to the fact that with their reflections in the garden's rectangular pool, the 20 columns on the palace terrace become 40, which is synonymous with respect and admiration in the Persian language. The columns stand on lion-shaped bases, the lion being an age-old symbol for the Safavids and, by extension, for Iran. At the height of the palace's glory, a kiosk facing it would have housed musicians whose music would have wafted across the pool to the people inside.

The palace is entered via an elegant terrace, which perfectly bridges the transition between the Persian love of gardens and interior splendour. Its slender, ribbed wooden pillars rise to a superb wooden ceiling with crossbeams and exquisite inlay work.

The Great Hall contains a rich array of frescoes, miniatures and ceramics. The upper walls are dominated by historical frescoes on a grand scale, sumptuously portraying court life and some of the great battles of the Safavid era. From right to left, above the entrance door, the armies of Shāh Ismail do battle with the Uzbeks; Nāder Shāh battles Sultan Mahmūd (astride a white elephant) on an Indian battleground; and Shāh Abbās II receives King Nāder Khān of Turkestan complete with musicians and dancing girls.

On the opposite wall, also from right to left, Shāh Abbās I presides over an ostentatious banquet; Shāh Ismail battles the janissaries of Sultan Suleiman; and Shāh Tahmasp receives in his court Humayūn, the Hindu prince who fled to Persia in 1543.

These extraordinary works of art survived the 18th-century invasion by the Afghans, who coated the paintings with whitewash to show their disapproval of such extravagance. Even more surprisingly, a fresco showing a man kissing the foot of a half-naked dancing girl survived the Islamic Revolution, thanks to the palace caretakers who stood heroically between the masterpieces and fundamentalists intent on their destruction.

More intricate but less expansive are the paintings – which owe much to the skill of Persian miniaturists – and ceramics that adorn the lower walls. The two smaller rooms off the main hall contain what are believed to be the portraits of ambassadors, some delicate china work and a beautiful stained-glass window dating from 1453.

The palace grounds are open from 8 am to 1 pm and from 4 to 8 pm daily (they sometimes close on Friday); entrance costs IR20,000. There is a small teahouse serving ice cream, and a bookshop near the entrance. The gardens are a lovely place for a picnic. Early morning is the best time for photos; you'll need a tripod for the interior.

The Conservation Game

Wherever you go in Iran you will see the most painstaking and expert restoration of historic monuments taking place. There hardly seems to be a Safavid bridge that has not been lovingly restored. The government body in charge of this renaissance is the Cultural Heritage Organisation, which also publishes decent guides to many of the historic monuments.

Much of the motivation for all this restoration must lie in the hope of attracting more tourists to the country. However, some of the work is being done out of simple pride in the great history of Iran, dismissed by the Pahlavīs in their rush to modernise but which has now acquired new value as the Islamic clerics look back to what previous Islamic dynasties achieved. Throughout the long years of the Iran-Iraq War, heritage had to take its place in the queue behind the demand for guns and tanks. Now that money no longer needs to be wasted on fighting, it can be redirected to the more positive business of rebuilding.

When I commented on the expense, my guide simply shrugged. 'Labour is cheap', he said. 'And time means nothing in Iran!'

Pat Yale

Esfahān Walking Tour Two

The **Sī-o-Seh Bridge (Pol-é Sī-o-Seh)** is one of Esfahān's most recognisable landmarks and a great place to start a walk. To get a good idea of the bridge's elegance and scale, walk south-east along the river-bank, away from the noise of Enqelāb-é Eslāmī Square. The path leads past grassy verges descending to the river and affords wonderful views back towards the Sī-o-Seh Bridge and the mountains which provide its backdrop. Passing the Ferdōsī Bridge, you'll come to the **Chubī Bridge (Pol-é Chubī)**, with its superb teahouse – the perfect place to linger with a chāy and a qalyan. With energy levels replen-ished, follow the riverbank to the **Khājū Bridge (Pol-é Khājū)**, Esfahān's most elegant bridge and home to another good teahouse; Khājū Bridge is about 3km from Sī-o-Seh Bridge.

The energetic can continue eastwards to the **Shahrestān Bridge (Pol-é Shahrestān)** – a round trip of around 7km along a quiet stretch of riverbank. If that doesn't appeal, share taxis run along the roads by the river. From Khājū Bridge, follow the southern riverbank back towards the southern end of Sī-o-Seh Bridge, perhaps stopping off along the way in your favourite teahouse. You could also take a picnic lunch and join the Esfahānīs in one of their favourite pastimes – the southern bank of the river has plenty of shade and is a great place to while away a summer's afternoon.

East of the bridge, follow the shady Mellat Blvd for about 500m before heading south into Jolfā – an area where you're as likely to hear Armenian being spoken as you are Farsi. Any of the streets will do as they all lead south to Nazar St. The **Church of Bethlehem (Kelisā-yé Bethlehem)** is a good place to start with its lovely dome and fine frescoes, while **Vānk Cathedral (Kelisā-yé Vānk)** is sim-ilarly impressive and also has a good museum. The **Church of St Mary (Kelisā-yé Maryam)** is also within striking distance of the cathedral.

Take your pick about which way you return to the riverbank – there are other churches scattered around Jolfā and you're likely to come across some of them in the narrow lanes of the Armenian Quarter. Just for something different, tea in one of the teahouses at the Sī-o-Seh Bridge is a great place to relax from the day's exertions.

Hasht Behesht Palace

Although it lacks the frescoes of Chehel Sotūn, the exquisite Hasht Behesht (Eight Paradises) Palace, built in 1669, will seem even more attractive to some travellers. Like Chehel Sotūn, it has a terrace sup-ported by soaring wooden columns that seem to mirror the trees in the surrounding park.

Inside, it boasts some charming mosaics and stalactite mouldings, but it is the garden setting and the ceilings cut into a variety of shapes (similar to those in the music room of the Alī Qāpū Palace) for which the palace is famous. Look out for the marble panel at the side of the house, over which water used to flow, and try to imagine just how beautiful a setting this would have been then. Ongoing renovation work was nearing completion at the time of writing. The palace is open from 8 am to 8 pm; en-trance costs IR20,000.

Madraseh-yé Chahār Bāgh

You will probably pass the Madraseh-yé Chahār Bāgh (previously known as the Madraseh-yé Mādar-é Shāh or Theological School of the Shāh's Mother) many times while walking along Chahār Bāgh Abbāsī St. The courtyard, which is surrounded by the two-storey porches leading to the rooms of the students, is extraordinarily beautiful and restful. Built between 1704 and 1714, the whole complex contains a prayer hall with a lovely mihrab, two of the finest Safavid-era minarets in Esfahān and some exquisite mosaics. It is usually closed to the public, but if you can find the gatekeeper he may let you have a quick look around for a small token of your appreciation.

Bridges

There are 11 bridges across the Zāyandeh River, five of them old, six of them new. One of your lasting impressions of Esfahān will undoubtedly be the old bridges. Try to spend as much time as you can exploring the bridges, enjoying the teahouses underneath them (see Places to Eat later in this section), and strolling along the river banks – a favourite pastime of Esfahānīs. This is especially pleasant at sunset and early evening when most of the bridges are illuminated. Sadly, at the time of research the Zāyandeh River had all but dried up as a result of the drought that devastated the country in 2000. Apart from the serious consequences for humans, the lack of water also ensured that the normally fast-flowing river merely trickled, if at all, through the arches, thereby diminishing the appeal for a time. All the more interesting bridges lie to the east of Chahār Bāgh St, with the exception of the shorter Mārnān Bridge (Pol-é Mārnān) which is to the west. Like most of the bridges, it was built in the Safavid period.

Sī-o-Seh Bridge The 160m-long Sī-o-Seh Bridge (Pol-é Sī-o-Seh or Bridge of 33 Arches) was built in 1602 and links the upper and lower halves of Chahār Bāgh St. Although less elegant than the Khājū Bridge, the Sī-o-Seh is still a great place to wander – there are no vehicles except recalcitrant motorcyclists. The teahouses are marvellous, although at busy times you may not be allowed to linger in them for more than 15 minutes at a time.

You can also hire a paddleboat from the banks of the river just south-east of the bridge, although at IR5000 for 20 minutes the novelty may soon wear off.

Chubī Bridge Nearly 150m long, with 21 arches, this bridge was built by Shāh Abbās II in 1665, primarily to help irrigate palace gardens in the area; it was once connected to a canal which ran to the north. This bridge is often ignored, which is a shame because it houses what some consider the best teahouse in the city.

Khājū Bridge This is the finest of Esfahān's bridges. Built by Shāh Abbās II in about 1650 (although a bridge is believed to have crossed the waters here since the time of Tamerlane), it doubles as a dam, and has always been as much a meeting place as a bearer of traffic.

Its 132m length has two levels of terraces overlooking the river; the lower ones contain locks regulating the flow of the river. At many places along the bridge you can catch glimpses of the river and mountains

The Sī-o-Seh Bridge, a great place for a cup of tea

CENTRAL IRAN

KELLI HAMBLET

through the 23 arches. If you look hard, you can still see original paintings and tiles, and the remains of stone seats built for Shāh Abbās II to sit and admire the views. In the centre, a pavilion was built exclusively for his pleasure. This is one of the best places in Iran to enjoy a chāy, although the actual teahouses are not the prettiest.

Shahrestān Bridge This is the oldest of the bridges spanning the river. Although it's about 3km east of the Khājū Bridge, it's worth visiting, and the walk there is very pleasant, although recent development has robbed it of much of its setting. Most of the 11-arched stone and brick structure is believed to date from the 12th century, although it stands on the foundations of a much earlier Sassanian bridge.

Armenian Quarter

Jolfā is the Armenian quarter of Esfahān. It dates from the time of Shāh Abbās I, who transported this colony of Christians from the town of Jolfā (now on Iran's northern border) en masse, and named the village 'New Jolfā'. The skills of these industrious merchants and entrepreneurs were coveted and their religious freedom respected, but the Armenians were restricted to one area and kept away from the Islamic centres. The community had a population of 60,000 inhabitants at the time of the massacres carried out by the Afghans after the downfall of the Safavid dynasty. As Esfahān expanded, Jolfā became another suburb, but the inhabitants have always been predominantly Christian. There are now 13 Armenian churches and an old cemetery scattered around Jolfā. If you want to see the others churches, ask at Vānk Cathedral Museum for directions.

Vānk Cathedral Built between 1606 and 1655 with the encouragement of the Safavid rulers, Vānk Cathedral (Kelīsā-yé Vānk) is the historic focal point of the Armenian church in Iran. The exterior of the church is unexciting, but the interior is richly decorated and shows the curious mixture of styles – Islamic tiles and designs alongside Christian imagery – which characterises most

churches in Iran. The frescoes are magnificent, if sometimes gruesome. There's a detached **bell tower**.

The attached **museum** contains more than 700 handwritten books, including what is claimed to be the first book printed in Iran, and other ethnological displays relating to Armenian culture and religion. There's even a small drawing by Rembrandt. Church and museum are open to visitors from 8 am to noon and 3 to 6 pm Saturday to Thursday and 8 am to 12.30 pm on Friday. Entrance costs IR20,000, although some travellers have managed to see the cathedral for free by skipping the museum.

In the grounds look out for a **memorial** to the Armenian genocide of 1915 when thousands of Armenians were forced out of Turkey, many of them dying in the Syrian desert.

Other Churches The frescoes on the walls and ceilings of the **Church of Bethlehem** (Kelīsā-yé Bethlehem) are arguably more intricate and impressive than those in Vānk Cathedral. The interior of the high dome is decorated with swirling black motifs on a golden background, while the base is surrounded by paintings of Biblical scenes. The **Maryam Church** (Kelīsā-yé Maryam) is the least impressive of the three, but does have some nice frescoes.

Manār Jombān (Shaking Minarets)

In Kaladyn, about 7km west of the city centre, is the tomb of Abu Abdollah, a revered dervish of the 14th century. The tomb is normally known as Manār Jombān (Shaking Minarets) because if you lean hard against one minaret it will start to sway back and forth followed by its twin. Although by no means unique, these Safavid-period shaking minarets are probably the most famous of their kind. If you come here on a Friday when it's crowded, you may have to wait to climb to the top.

The title of Iran's most unlikely occupation must surely go to the Official Minaret Shaker, who ascends one of the minarets every half hour, calls on Allah and then

A Shake Too Far?

Ask a guide why the shaking minarets shake and they are likely to embark on a lengthy explanation of vibration theory. It's a bit of a disappointment, therefore, to find out that a mundane building error may really be responsible for this astonishing phenomenon. In a recent report geologists suggest that the wrong kind of sandstone was used to build the minarets. This sandstone contains felspar which dissolves over time, leaving the stone flexible and liable to shake. In support of their argument, geologists point out there are no historic references to the minarets shaking.

Luckily for romance, not everyone agrees. At the City Museum, Yatin Pandya points out that other buildings in the city were constructed from the same sandstone and yet show no propensity to shake.

shakes it, causing its opposite number and then the whole roof to shake (see the boxed text 'A Shake Too Far?' in this section).

You can take Bus No 236 from the city centre along Chahār Bāgh St (IR300), from anywhere along Tāleqānī St or from the bus station near Emām Hussein Square. Chartering a taxi for an hour or so as to include the nearby Āteshkādeh-yé Esfahān fire temple is another alternative (IR10,000). Several readers have commented that the surrounding area is rather poor and may not be the safest to walk in alone.

Āteshkādeh-yé Esfahān

This disused fire temple, perched conspicuously on top of a small hill, is another 1.5km further west from the Manār Jombān, along the same road. Dating from Sassanian times, these ancient mud-brick ruins give you a good view back to the city and of the Zāyandeh River. It costs IR10,000 to scramble to the top (10 minutes).

A very pleasant, quiet country road follows the river back to the town centre from near Āteshkādeh-yé Esfahān; follow the signs of the Bird Garden if you want to walk or cycle it. Along the way you'll pass quince orchards and stretches of the river where

tablecloth-makers come to wash their wares. There's a pleasant tea-garden roughly halfway back to the centre and there are plenty of places to join Iranians picnicking on the banks of the river.

Museums

Esfahān's museums are conveniently located between the Chehel Sotūn Palace and Emām Khomeinī Square. Although not as interesting as the other sights, they are worth a quick look if you have some spare time.

The **Natural History Museum** (☎ 29 700) is housed in a Timurid-era building which is quite interesting in itself, although the plaster dinosaurs outside somewhat detract from the effect. It's open from 9 am to 9 pm daily and entry costs IR2000.

Of the two nearby art galleries, the **Museum of Contemporary Art** (open from 8 am to noon and 3.30 to 6 pm daily except Friday; IR5000) next door won't take up much of your time, unlike the impressive **Decorative Arts Museum of Iran** a couple of doors further on. Open from 8 am to 1 pm daily except Friday, it contains some wonderful miniatures, lacquer work, ancient Qurans, calligraphy, ceramics, brass work, woodcarvings and traditional costumes. Entry costs IR20,000 and photos are not allowed, which is a pity because the building is itself a historic monument, originally built as stables for the nearby Chehel Sotūn Palace.

Golestān-é Shohadā

The Rose Garden of Martyrs is a cemetery for those who died in the Iran-Iraq War. The rows and rows of photographs on the tombstones are an unforgettable sight. By the entrance there is also a modern, domed mausoleum to Āyatollāh Shams Ābādī, said to have been assassinated by the last shah's secret police – the dreaded Savak – shortly before the Islamic Revolution. Please be discreet: this is not a tourist attraction as such but a moving insight into the grief caused by the Iran-Iraq War.

The cemetery is about 1.5km south of the Khājū Bridge. To get there take a shared taxi from the southern side of the bridge to Basīj Square, and then walk east for about 400m.

Places to Stay

It's best to find somewhere central to stay – ie, within walking distance of Chahār Bāgh Abbāsī St – although most places directly on the main road will be very noisy. Unless stated otherwise, every hotel has a sign in English and most places in the middle and upper price range who quote their prices in US dollars will accept rials.

For those with their own vehicle, there is a car park about 200m south of Takhtī Square along Chahār Bāgh Abbāsī St which charges IR12,000 per night for a car and IR10,000 per motorbike. There's a guard on duty around the clock.

Places to Stay – Budget

Deservedly the most popular place in this range is the *Amīr Kabīr Hostel* (☎/fax 227 273, **e** mrziaee@hotmail.com, Chahār Bāgh Abbāsī St). It's a very friendly place and the brothers who run it speak good English and are used to travellers. You can sleep in the dorm for IR20,000 while a simple, clean single/double/triple goes for IR25,000/40,000/60,000. All showers and toilets are shared. It also offers Internet access, an international fax and telephone service, laundry, a book exchange of sorts, a well-stocked fridge with a wide range of drinks that can be purchased, a traveller's information board and a fascinating guest book. It can also arrange taxis, bus and train tickets, and help out with applications for visa extensions. This is not the place to go if you want to avoid other travellers – the hostel is often full and you'll need to book ahead in peak times. The internal courtyard is a lovely place to pass the evening surrounded by the languages of the world.

The *Shad Hotel* (☎ 236 883, Chahār Bāgh Abbāsī St) is another good, central option. Small, clean two-/three-bed rooms that cost IR40,000 aren't bad although rates are sometimes increased in high season. The elaborate ceiling decoration in the reception area suggests this place was once a lot grander.

Other reasonable choices along Chahār Bāgh Abbāsī St include the *Pars Hotel* (☎ 260 018) which has singles/doubles with shared bathrooms for IR60,000/100,000; and

the *Tous Hotel* (☎ 260 068) which has nice, airy rooms for the summer/winter price of IR60,000/50,000. In both places the rooms at the front are hideously noisy.

A stone's throw from Enqelāb-é Eslāmī Square at the southern end of Chahār Abbāsī St, the *Sahel Hotel* (☎ 234 585) has pretty good rooms without/with bathroom for US$8/15; although they prefer US dollars you can pay in rials.

At the upper end of the budget range and sheltered from the main road, the *Saadi Hotel* (☎ 236 363, Abbās Ābād St) has been recommended by some travellers. When we visited they were full and wouldn't show us the rooms, suggesting either an admirable approach to security or that they had something to hide – most likely the former. Doubles cost IR75,000.

Also away from the main thoroughfare *22 Bahman Hotel* (☎ 203 953, fax 204 546, Masjed-é Sayyed St) north of the centre is quite good value, charging US$10/20/24 for a single/double/triple with bathroom (you can pay in rials).

Places to Stay – Mid-Range

One of the better choices in the mid-range is the *Aria Hotel* (☎ 227 224, Shahīd Medānī St). It's in a good, quiet location and the manager speaks English. Single/double rooms, with a private bathroom and maybe a balcony, are great value for US$15/20, especially as breakfast is included in the price.

The *Naghsh-é Jahān Hotel* (☎/fax 219 518, Chahār Bāgh Abbāsī St) is centrally located but a touch overpriced at IR118,500/158,000 for rooms that are nothing special. They do, however, accept MasterCard and offer considerable discounts for pre-booked groups.

The *Tourist Hotel* (☎ 263 094, fax 263 228, Abbās Ābād St) is quieter and is decent value at US$20/30.

South of the river, rooms at the *Pol and Park Hotel* (☎ 612 785, fax 612 788, Ā'ineh Khūneh Blvd) are a little jaded but most have a balcony. It's a fantastic location for exploring the bridges and parkland along the Zāyandeh River. Rooms cost US$20/30 and you can pay in rials.

In the Armenian quarter, around the corner from Vānk Cathedral, the *Julfa Hotel* (☎ 244 441, fax 249 446, Kelīsā St) charges US$20/30 for simple, quiet rooms with bathroom.

Close to Takhtī Square at the northern end of Chahār Bāgh Abbāsī St, the *Persia Hotel* (☎ 223 274) has been recommended by several travellers; nice, large rooms with bathroom cost IR120,000/160,000.

Also good for a little more is the *Āzādy Hotel* (☎ 204 011, fax 203 713, Masjed-é Sayyed St) where very good rooms with TV, fridge and bathroom cost IR210,800/319,600 – considerably less in real terms than you'll be charged if you pay the dollar rates of US$30/45 plus 4% tax. There's also a small gift shop and a good restaurant here.

Though hopelessly inconvenient for the city, both the main bus terminals have hotels which are handy for late night arrivals and early morning departures. *Hotel Soffeh* (☎ 686 462, fax 652 990), upstairs in the Soffeh bus terminal, has rooms which are clean and quiet (courtesy of double-glazing), and come with TV and bathroom. Rooms cost US$20/30, but management has a strange if welcome policy of offering a 50% reduction up front, making it great value. At the northern Kaveh bus terminal, the *Kaveh Hotel* (☎ 420 531, fax 245 441) charges US$20/30 for large rooms with TV and bathroom.

Places to Stay – Top End

The recently refurbished *Abbāsī Hotel* (☎ 226 009, Shahīd Medānī St), luxuriously created in the shell of an old caravanserai, is undoubtedly the most romantic place to stay in Esfahān, if not Iran. The rooms are surprisingly ordinary but the setting is superb if you can get a room overlooking the courtyard (the rooms in the dingy annex at the back are no cheaper). If you are contemplating a splurge somewhere during your trip, seriously consider this place, but book ahead to get a good room. Rooms cost US$100/120. The hotel is certainly worth visiting to see the extravagance of the decorations, the magnificence of the courtyard with its views of the Madraseh-yé Chahār Bāgh, or just to linger over a pot of tea in

its teahouse (afternoons only). There's an excellent bookshop in the lobby too. (We have received one complaint from an Iranian woman travelling with her foreign husband who was forced to go to the police to have her wedding certificate verified before she was allowed to check into a mediocre room at the Abbāsī.)

The *Kowsar International Hotel* (☎ 240 230, fax 249 975, Mellat Blvd) is Esfahān's other five-star place with a five-star price: US$70/100, plus 19% tax. The elegant rooms are tastefully furnished and those on the upper floors have splendid views over the river or the mountains. Sadly this view comes at the cost of everyone else's – it's the big concrete monstrosity which provides the backdrop to the southern end of the Sī-o-Seh Bridge. The gardens at the back are nice with a lovely teahouse and a men-only swimming pool.

The centrally located *Piroozy Hotel* (☎ 231 182, fax 239 519, Chahār Bāgh Abbāsī St) offers overpriced rooms (US$45/65) with rather alarming 1970s decor and poor service (no tea available after 10 pm, surely a first in Iran).

The *Hotel Alī Qāpū* (☎ 231 282, fax 239 519, Chahār Bāgh Abbāsī St) has more luxurious rooms (and a swimming pool and sauna) for US$52/75 plus 15% tax, while rooms at the pleasant *Safir Hotel* (☎/fax 219 931, Shahīd Medānī St) cost US$45/65.

Esfahān also has at least two apartment hotels which are surprisingly good value and worth considering for a longer stay. The cheaper of the two is the *Pardis Apartment Hotel* (☎ 200 308, fax 227 831, Takhtī Square) where spacious suites start from IR215,000. Even better, and worth considering as an alternative to the other top-end places, is the *Hotel Apartments Mehr* (☎/fax 222 625, Ostāndārī St). The location is brilliant – a couple of hundred metres from Emām Khomeinī Square – and the luxurious, modern apartments comprise a kitchen, spacious sitting room and bedrooms. There's also secure underground parking for those with their own vehicles. Four-bed apartments cost US$60 – definitely worth a splurge.

Places to Eat

There's a good selection of eateries in Esfahān, from the cheap and cheerful to the sophisticated and expensive – a chance to get away from kebabs for a while. And don't forget to visit a teahouse (or two) under one of the bridges.

Kabābīs & Fast Food If you're after another kebab or Iranian-style hamburger, there are plenty of places all over the centre of town. *Only Kabab Kabābī*, just east of Emām Khomeinī Square, isn't bad and there is a good *sandwich stall* on the southwest side of Takhtī Square.

If you're wandering around Emām Khomeinī Square and find yourself suddenly craving a pizza, those at *Pizza Bam* (☎ 202 323, Ostāndārī St) are pretty good and have been recommended by several travellers. The four kinds (Mexican, special, seafood with a few token shrimps and vegetarian) share the menu with schnitzels, sandwiches and spaghetti. They cost IR13,000 for a decent-sized serving. Sadly for coffee lovers, the espresso and cappuccino advertised on the menu weren't happening when we visited – hopefully you'll have better luck. Pizzas are also good at *Pizza Homa (Mellat Blvd)*, just along from the Kowsar International Hotel, and at the *shop* underneath the Tous Hotel. The pizzas at the *Candida Pizza Hamburger (Chahār Bāgh Abbāsī St)* are not as sinister as the name suggests.

Restaurants One of the best cheap Iranian restaurants in town is the *Nobahar Restaurant*, signposted in English and next to the Naghsh-é Jahān Hotel. The khōresht with rice is particularly good value at IR7650, as is the *māst sīr* (yogurt with garlic, for IR1000). Most kebabs with rice cost around IR12,000 to IR15,000. The menu is in English and it's popular with Iranians – always a good sign.

Also good for cheap Iranian food is the *Restōrān-é Sa'dī*, downstairs and immediately opposite the Amīr Kabīr Hostel. It's not marked in English, but the menu is and owes a lot to a preoccupation with kebabs. Expect to pay around IR10,000. The service can be a little slow in busy periods.

Another good cheapie is the *Maharaja Restaurant*, just north of Enqelāb-é Eslāmī Square, where the meals are a bit inconsistent although the curries are usually good.

For a little more money, the popular *Bastanī Restaurant* (☎ 200 374) off the southeast corner of Emām Khomeinī Square has a lovely underground setting and excellent food at mid-range prices. The menu has a tempting array of stews, although check what is available before setting your heart on one. The service is also good.

One place heartily recommended for a splurge is the classy *Restaurant Shahrzad* (☎ 234 474), on Abbās Aābād St, just west of Chahār Bāgh Abbāsī St, with its beautiful period wall-paintings, stained-glass windows and mirror work. Western meals such as schnitzel with the trimmings are available, as are fish and other kebab dishes. They also serve a good fesenjān. This place is very popular and you may even have to wait in peak season, which may also explain the small army of black-suited waiters hovering with intent between the tables during the quieter lunch times. The food is of the highest quality; no colas here, only *dūgh* (a sour-milk drink).

In Jolfā, the *Restōrān-é Khayyām* is very popular with locals and is cheaper than places in the centre of town with an OK kebab, yogurt, bread and drink costing IR7000. It's on Nazar St opposite Church of Bethlehem.

Hotel Restaurants The *Chehelsotoun Restaurant*, in the glorious Abbāsī Hotel, is one of the few top-end places in Iran with prices to match – you won't get much change from IR80,000. You are paying more for the elegance of the decor than the quality of the food, but prices are not unreasonable by Western standards, especially considering the service and unabashed splendour of the dining area. It's a great place for a special occasion.

The *Julfa Hotel* puts on very good buffet lunches (about IR25,000) from time to time but the restaurant is also worth a visit at other times. One traveller claimed that they serve 'the best *chelō kabāb* in Esfahān' – a grand claim given the number of competitors.

Surprisingly reasonable value can also be found at the restaurant at the *Piroozy Hotel*, and some readers have raved about the French cuisine and pizzas served at the restaurant in the *Hotel Alī Qāpū*. Other hotels with decent restaurants include the *Āzādy Hotel* and *Safīr Hotel*, while the top-floor restaurant of the *Kowsar International Hotel* has superb views over the floodlit Sī-o-Seh Bridge and the rest of Esfahān, although it's sometimes understandably booked out by wedding parties.

Teahouses There are few things more enjoyable than sipping a pot of tea in the teahouses underneath the bridges of Esfahān. It is very easy to spend an entire morning or afternoon sauntering along the riverbank, stopping every few hundred metres for a chāy and a qalyan. Unfortunately you won't be able to savour the atmosphere for too long – most of the teahouses have placed limitations on how long you can stay, which can amount to just 15 minutes in peak season.

The *Sī-o-Seh Bridge* has teahouses at either end where you can enjoy a pot of tea, or a cooked breakfast for about IR10,000. Some people prefer the gorgeous little teahouse in the middle of the *Chubī Bridge* with its idiosyncratic decoration and views of the river. One English traveller wrote to say that the 'teahouse under the *Khāju Bridge* is worth the round-trip to Iran'. The setting is indeed superb and the tea and local biscuits are delicious. Much quieter, except when a tour bus rolls in, is the cosy little teahouse on the *Shahrestān Bridge*.

Overlooking Emām Khomeinī Square, the outdoor tables at the *Gheysarieh Tea Shop* make a great vantage point from which to watch the changing moods of the square. When it gets too hot, the traditional decor of the interior is also nice. To get there, take the steep staircase to the left of the entrance to the bazaar at the northern end of the square; the sign reads 'Qeysarieh Tea Shap Sherbet'. There are also other *teahouses* in the bazaar.

The *Bame Sahel Teahouse*, on the top floor of the Sahel Hotel, may be a little rough at the edges but it's a great place for ābgūsht, tea and a qalyan. There's not much

floor space left, what with all the traditional benches and rugs, and there are sketches all along the wall. This place should not be confused with the more upmarket Sahel Restaurant around the corner.

In a lane off the north-east corner of Emām Khomeinī Square, the cosy *Āzādegān Teahouse (Chāykhūneh-yé Āzādegān)* houses an astonishing collection of old weapons, photographs and other memorabilia. The atmosphere is better if you don't go in as part of a group.

If your budget doesn't stretch to a night in the majestic Abbāsī Hotel, have a pot of tea or coffee at the *Naghsh-é Jahān Restaurant*. Dress reasonably nicely or the doorman may not want to let you in.

Tasty Treats Many places along Chahār Bāgh Abbāsī St serve ice cream; others sell delicious fruit shakes (try *Iseman* on Chahār Bāgh Abbāsī St for one of the best) for about IR2000.

Esfahān's famous speciality is *gaz*, a delicious kind of nougat usually mixed with chopped pistachios or other nuts. It isn't generally served in restaurants other than the Shahrzad, but you can easily pick it up in the *confectionery shops* along Chahār Bāgh Abbāsī St or around Emām Khomeinī Square.

Shopping

With the possible exception of Tehrān, Esfahān has the widest selection of handicrafts anywhere in the country. However, it's also the one town where you will almost certainly be approached by men whose sole objective is commercial.

The best buys are carpets (from all over Iran), miniatures hand-painted on camel bone (many of the artists run the stores themselves and are happy to give demonstrations) and intricate copper work. You can also pick up locally produced, hand-printed tablecloths and bedspreads and other metalwork (brass and silver). Esfahān can be more expensive than elsewhere but you're more likely to find what you like amid the vast range on offer here – and it's certainly more pleasurable to shop here than amid the traffic chaos of Tehrān.

A good place to get an idea of prices is the Iran Handicrafts Organisation shop at the northern end of Emām Khomeinī Square, or their other branch in the complex opposite the Abbāsī Hotel.

There are plenty of handicrafts shops in the bazaar and around the square. Competition is fierce (and sometimes nasty) among the various carpet shops in particular, so don't pay too much attention to what one shop owner says about his competitor down the lane. Although some places employ high-pressure sales tactics, most are friendly and willing to chat over a chāy without twisting your arm too much. It can actually be quite enjoyable, as long you don't go in with an attitude or forget that you don't actually have to buy anything. Nevertheless, bargain hard wherever you go.

Getting There & Away

Air The two most convenient Iran Air offices are on Chahār Bāgh Abbāsī St (☎ 228 999) and in the shopping complex opposite the Abbāsī Hotel on Shahīd Medānī St (☎ 228 200). Both offices are open from 7 am to 7.30 pm Saturday to Thursday, sometimes closing an hour earlier in winter.

Iran Air flies once a week between Esfahān and Kuwait City for US$122/244 one way/return, and to Bahrain once a week in summer for the same price.

Kīsh Airlines (☎ 204 477) has twice-weekly flights to Dubai for US$96/175, as well as a relatively expensive daily flight to Kīsh Island for IR298,000.

Iran Air flies from Esfahān to the following places in Iran:

destination	frequency	cost (IR)
Ahvāz	daily	92,000
Bandar-é Abbās	four times a week	161,000
Būshehr	once a week	119,000
Kermān	twice a week	120,000
Mashhad	daily	169,000
Shīrāz	daily	92,000
Tehrān	several daily	92,000
Zāhedān	twice a week	182,000

Bus There are two main bus terminals – the Soffeh bus terminal (☎ 688 341) in the far south, and the Kaveh bus terminal (☎ 413 124) in the inner north. Both the terminals are clean and well organised with an information counter; some bus companies have a computerised advance-booking system, and some also list their destinations in English. Both have buses to most destinations outside Esfahān Province, although the Kaveh terminal is more convenient from the centre of town and has slightly more bus company offices.

From both terminals, buses leave Esfahān several (often many) times a day to:

destination	distance (km)	duration (hrs)	cost (IR)
Ahvāz	765	14	19,000
Bandar-é Abbās	1082	18	21,500
Hamadān	492	7	10,500
Kāshān	192	4	7000
Kermān	703	12	14,500
Kermānshāh	665	9	14,000
Rasht	737	12	16,000
Sanandaj	672	10	17,500
Shīrāz	473	8	11,000
Sirjān	657	11	14,900
Tabrīz	1038	16	22,500
Tehrān	390	7	10,500
Zāhedān	1244	21	25,500

Note that buses to Yazd leave from the Jey minibus terminal (see Minibus, following).

Most of the long-distance buses travel overnight. You can usually get a bus to a major destination within an hour or so, although buses to Shīrāz often leave only in the evening or before 10 am. None of the bus companies have booking offices in the town centre, although if you're staying at the Amīr Kabīr Hostel management can arrange tickets for most destinations to save you the long ride out to the terminals.

For the Kaveh terminal take a shared taxi north along Chahār Bagh St for IR2000; to get to Soffeh, take one from just south of the Sī-o-Seh Bridge (IR1400). A private taxi to either terminal will cost around IR10,000.

Minibus For destinations within Esfahān Province, there are two minibus terminals. For Shahr-é Kord (IR2500, 1¾ hours, 107km), head for the Zāyandeh Rūd minibus terminal (☎ 759 182) from where minibuses leave when full, usually every hour or so. To get to Zāyandeh Rūd terminal, take a shared taxi west from just south of the Sī-o-Seh Bridge (IR1500).

From the Jey minibus terminal (☎ 510 003), there are five departures throughout the day to Yazd (IR7000, six hours, 316km). Minibuses also go to Nā'īn (IR2500, 138km) and Ardestān (IR2800, 232km). To get to the Jey minibus terminal, take a shared taxi from Takhtī Square (IR1000).

Train Daily trains leave Esfahān for Tehrān (via Kāshān and Qom) at 11.50 am and at 10.20 pm, arriving in Tehrān about eight hours later. Only 1st-class tickets (IR18,900) are available. All trains from Esfahān go north towards Tehrān; to get to Kermān or Bandar-é Abbās you'll have to change trains in Kāshān or Ardakān.

Thankfully, you don't have to go all the way to the train station to book a seat. The ticket office (☎ 224 425) is wedged between the Bank Mellat and Bank Tejarat buildings on Enqelāb-é Eslāmī Square. Although it's not signposted in English, the picture of a train above the door should be enough. The staff are helpful and speak some English. Tickets can be bought up to one week in advance and the office is open Saturday to Thursday from 8 am to 4 pm. Mina-yé Naghsh-é Jahān Tour & Travel Agency (see Travel Agencies earlier in the section) also sells tickets.

The train station (☎ 688 001) is way out to the east of the city, near the airport. Passengers with pre-booked train tickets can catch a special bus from opposite the Kowsar International Hotel. In theory, the bus leaves an hour before the train departs although it is far more erratic in practice – check with the ticket office. A private taxi (IR15,000) can cost almost as much as the train ticket. Alternatively, take a shared taxi from Qods or Lāleh Squares.

Shared Taxi Shared taxis leave from outside the four bus and minibus terminals. From the Soffeh bus terminal, shared taxis head to places to the south while Kaveh bus

terminal is the place to head for destinations to the north. Zāyandeh Rūd minibus terminal handles destinations to the west and Jey minibus terminal the ones to the east. Shared taxis are quicker but less regular and more expensive than the buses.

Getting Around

Esfahān has long had the justifiable reputation as home to some of the most curmudgeonly taxi drivers in the country. Most have no compunction about overcharging any foreigner silly enough to pay too much.

If you want a shared taxi, never get into an *empty* vehicle, because unless you can speak Farsi, the driver will assume you want to charter it and will charge you accordingly. And even if you have agreed to charter the entire taxi to the Kaveh bus terminal, for example, don't be surprised if the driver picks up a few other paying passengers along the way anyway.

To/From the Airport The airport is way out of town and there is no airport bus service. To get *to* the airport take any bus (IR150) heading east along Jamāl-od-Dīn Abdolrazāgh St from Takhtī Square. Get off the bus at Ahmād Ābād Square where the small Sorūsh bus station has buses to the airport (IR300). *From* the airport, ask around for any shared taxis heading into the city, from where you may need to get another to your hotel. If you charter a private taxi in either direction, don't expect too much change from IR20,000. The Airport Taxi Service will no doubt ask for more.

Bus & Minibus Buses and minibuses leave the local bus station, near the Chehel Sotūn Palace, to every direction every few minutes. Just ask – and keep asking – for one heading your way. Elsewhere in town simply jump on any bus heading your way and jump off when it deviates. Tickets cost from IR150 to IR300 depending on the distance and are available at the local bus station or the booths along Chahār Bāgh Abbāsī St.

Shared Taxi The long Chahār Bāgh St is the main thoroughfare through the city, and every couple of seconds a shared taxi goes *mostaghīm* (straight ahead) for about IR400; don't be surprised if you have to debate the price. To outlying destinations such as the transport terminals, look for taxis heading in the right direction from the following places: Lāleh, Qods and Ahmād Ābād Squares (for anywhere to the east); Emām Hussein and Shohadā Squares (for the north); and the southern side of Sī-o-Seh Bridge and Āzādī Square (for the south and west). Note that locals heading for Emām Khomeinī Square just say 'meydān' to the driver.

Private Taxi Depending on the distance – and, more importantly, your negotiating skills – a fare in a private taxi around town costs from IR3000 to IR7000, although getting to the terminals, train station or airport is likely to cost considerably more. Luckily there are so many taxis that it's easy to negotiate by threatening to find another one. Unless you're desperate, avoid the taxi drivers who hang around Emām Khomeinī Square who spot tourists coming a mile off.

To hire a private taxi for an hour costs IR10,000 within the city limits – a good way to see the Āteshkādeh-yé Esfahān and Manār Jombān. You'll have to bargain hard or get your hotel to arrange it.

SHAHR-É KORD   شهر كرد
☎ 0381
Nestling in the mountains, this sleepy provincial capital has little to offer tourists, although the setting is pleasant and it can be a good place to unwind. The major sight of interest is the Atabakan Mosque, which was undergoing renovation at the time of research. When Isabella Bird travelled around this region in 1890, she painted a picture of a wild and inhospitable terrain inhabited by fiercely independent and warlike tribespeople (principally Lors and Bakhteyārīs) governed by feudal chieftains. It's a lot more hospitable these days.

Places to Stay & Eat
The *Hotel Enghelab* is the cheapest option at about IR40,000 a double, but it's sometimes reluctant to take foreigners.

The best of the mid-range places is the *Shahr-é Kord Āzādī Hotel* (☎ 30 020) which charges US$25/45 a single/double; the rooms are nothing special but you'll be willing to forgive that if you get a room with a view.

There are plenty of *kabābīs* and *hamburger joints* along the main street, but you are better off eating at a hotel.

Getting There & Away
Shahr-é Kord is close enough to Esfahān to visit on a day trip, and its only link by public transport is with Esfahān. About every hour, minibuses (IR3000) and shared taxis (IR8000) travel between the Zāyandeh Rūd terminal in Esfahān and the terminal in Shahr-é Kord, about 3km out on the Esfahān side of the town centre. Share taxis (IR400) run into town from the terminal at regular intervals.

ARDESTĀN   اردستان
☎ 03242
Ardestān is an ancient city dating back to the Parthian period, but it is famous also as the birthplace of the Sassanian king, Khosro Anushirvan.

The town is worth visiting on your way from Esfahān to Yazd for the 10th-century Jāmeh Mosque, with its brick dome, beautifully ornamented prayer hall, mihrab and simple brick minaret. The Seljuk Pā Manār Mosque is nearby and once formed part of a much larger complex which contained a madraseh, *hammam* (bathhouse) and caravanserai. It has what is believed to be the second oldest minaret in Iran (dating from AD 1068).

The only hotel that will take foreigners is the Iran Touring & Tourism Organisation's (ITTO's) *Ardestān Inn* (☎ 3501), which is a little run-down and costs US$15 a double (plus 17% tax); sometimes, usually in high season, the owners see fit to bump the price up to an unreasonable US$25. It has an OK *restaurant*.

Take any bus travelling between Yazd and Kāshān or Qom and get off in Ardestān, or take a direct minibus from Esfahān's Jey minibus terminal.

NĀ'ĪN

ناﺌین

☎ 03267

Slumbering Nā'īn, an important transit point at the geographical centre of Iran, makes a good stop between Yazd and Kāshān or Esfahān. The town is also known for its carpets with classical designs, and the 10th-century **Jāmeh Mosque**. This mosque has no iwan and dates from the early Islamic period. It still has some features from the 10th century, and is especially notable for its fine mihrab and its innovative yet simple use of stucco decoration which is remarkably well preserved. Watch out also for the **traditional houses** dotted around town that have been restored.

Places to stay include the *Guesthouse Islami Inn* (signposted in English) near Emām Khomeinī Square for IR21,000 a double; the *Nā'īn Hotel* (☎ 3081) for IR70,000 a double; or the ITTO's *Jahāngardī Inn* (☎ 3665) for US$15/25 a single/double.

Keliza Pizza, underneath a carpet shop on Emām Khomeinī Square, isn't bad.

To get to Nā'īn, take any bus travelling from Esfahān or Kāshān to Yazd or Kermān. There is also a direct minibus from Esfahān's Jey minibus terminal.

YAZD

یزد

☎ 0351 • pop 400,000 • elevation 1230m

Midway between Esfahān and Kermān, Yazd will be a highlight of any trip to Iran. Wedged between the northern Dasht-é Kavīr and southern Dasht-é Lūt deserts, Yazd boasts the best old – and still inhabited – city in the country. The town is still home to Iran's largest community of Zoroastrians. The combination of an ancient desert city and a multi-religious heritage gives Yazd its distinctive relaxed atmosphere. The proliferation of tree-lined streets doesn't hurt either.

Yazd can be quite cold in winter, but is very hot in summer. The city has always been a great weaving centre, known for its silks and other fabrics even before Marco Polo passed through along one of the Silk Routes in the late 13th century. Yazd is also famous for its *bādgīrs*, the windtowers designed to catch and circulate the merest breath of wind, which dominate the city's roofscape (see the boxed text 'The Bādgīrs of Yazd' later in this section).

History

Although Yazd dates from Sassanian times (AD 224–637), its history is fairly undistinguished. It was conquered by the Arabs in about 642, and subsequently became an important station on the caravan routes to Central Asia and India, exporting its silks, textiles and carpets far and wide. When Marco Polo passed this way in the 13th century, he described Yazd as 'a very fine and splendid city and a centre of commerce'. It was spared destruction by Genghis Khan and Timur, and flourished in the 14th and 15th centuries, yet its commercial success and stability were never translated into political status. Like most of Iran, the town fell into decline after the end of the Safavid era and remained little more than a provincial outpost until the last shah extended the railway line to Yazd.

Orientation

The centre of Yazd is Beheshtī Square (sometimes still known by its old name of Mojāhedīn Square). If you stay within walking distance of this square, most sights and restaurants can be visited on foot. To the north lies the old city which is bisected by the main Emām Khomeinī St, while most transport arrives and leaves from the far south of town. When walking around the old city, expect to get hopelessly lost – just ask for directions when you want to get out.

Information

Visa Extensions For visa extensions, visit the large building directly opposite the entrance to the bus terminal (not signposted in English) two days before your visa expires. It is open from 8 am to 2 pm Saturday to Wednesday and 7 am to noon on Thursday. From the entrance foyer take the third door on the right where there is a sign in English setting out the requirements: two photos, IR10,000 deposited in the Bank Melli and a photocopy of the relevant pages of your passport. There should be no problems getting a couple of weeks extra on a tourist visa and five to seven days on a transit visa.

YAZD

PLACES TO STAY
3 Āzādī Hotel
20 Nabavi Hotel
25 Hotel Amīr Chakhmāgh
28 Hotel Farhang
30 Beheshty Hotel; Internet
31 Aria Hotel
44 Jahāgardī Inn (Tourist Inn)

PLACES TO EAT
2 Restōrān-é Tehrānī
16 Persia Sandwich
19 Hamūm-é Khan Restaurant
    (Chāykhūneh-yé San'ati)
29 Melli Dinner House

33 Baharestān Restaurant
36 Pizza
46 Restōrān-é Hanar-yé Sabz

OTHER
1 Afshar Hospital
4 Main Telephone Office
5 Bāgh-é Doulat Ābād
6 Fortress of Lions
7 Tomb of the 12 Emāms
8 Alexander's Prison
9 Khan-é Larī
10 Husseinia
11 Main Post Office
12 Bogheh-yé Seyed Roknaddīn

13 Bank Melli
    (Central Branch)
14 Y@zd Internet Café
15 Jāmeh Mosque
17 Hazireh Mosque
18 Amīr Chākhmaq Mosque
21 Iran Air Office
22 Yazd Seyr Tour
    & Travel Agency
23 Saadat Seir Travel Agency
24 Bus Company Offices
26 Amir Chākhmaq Mosque
27 Amin Money Exchange
32 Āteshkadeh (Zoroastrian
    Fire Temple)

34 24-hour Pharmacy
35 Rānāmū Hospital
37 Jahaferī Bookshop
38 Telephone Office
    (Āzādī Square)
39 Police
    Headquarters
40 Iran Handicrafts
    Organisation
41 Tourist Organisation
42 Bus Terminal
43 Visa Office
45 Henna Grinding Mills
47 Oge International Tour
    & Travel Company

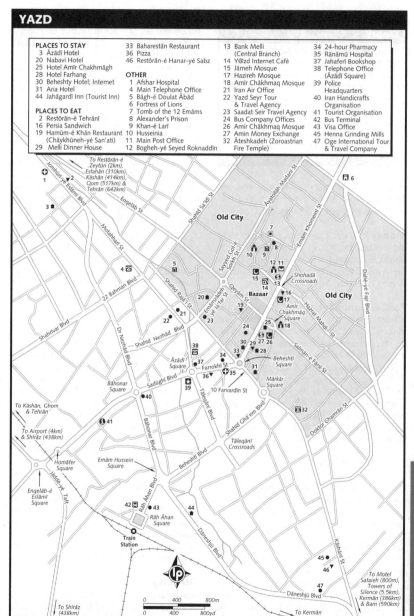

CENTRAL IRAN

Who's That Knocking At My Door?

As you wander around the narrow streets of old Yazd, look at the doors carefully. Most have two knockers, one round and fat, the other long and thin. These were designed to give off different sounds so that whoever was in the house would be able to tell whether a man or woman was knocking and so decide who should open the door to them, vital in a society where women lived in purdah.

If that all sounds easy, make sure you end up in the right office – see the boxed text 'Too Many Questions?', opposite.

Money You can change money upstairs at the central branch of Bank Melli at the Shohadā Crossroads or, far more quickly, at the Amin Money Exchange, just south of Amīr Chakhmaq Square.

Post & Communications The main post office is right next to the Bank Melli. The main telephone office on Motahharī St is a little inconvenient, but there are plenty of private telephone offices dotted around town.

The Y@zd Internet Café (☎ 23 832, e Touristicplace@yahoo.com), 50m east of the Jāmeh Mosque, is one of the best in the country. It's a very relaxed and friendly place where you can get a tea, a soft drink and snacks while you send your emails (IR30,000 an hour). It also doubles as a very savvy travel agency.

'Internet' (☎ 23 505, e honaf@mail.yazd. co.ir), near the Beheshty Hotel, is another good central place which charges IR30,000 and is open from 9 am to 1 pm and 5 to 9 pm Saturday to Thursday. Other places are springing up out in the suburbs.

Travel Agencies Y@zd Internet Café (see Post & Communications earlier in this section) can arrange tours around Yazd and to the various sights around Yazd Province, including overnight trips into the desert. They also have bicycles for hire, which are a great way to explore the old city. The indefatigable

Hossein and Alī operate as a de facto tourist office and are helpful in finding accommodation and buying bus tickets. It's probably *the* place in Yazd to meet other travellers.

For longer and more upmarket tours, Oge International Tour & Travel Company (☎ 848 148, fax 848 593) can arrange trips to anywhere in Iran and they have plans for three-day camel treks into the Dasht-é Kavīr starting in spring 2001. Oge is located a fair way south-east of the town centre on Dāneshjū Blvd.

Strangely for a city which has few air links, Yazd is home to two highly professional travel agencies specialising in domestic and international air tickets; they also sell train tickets. Yazd Seir Tour & Travel Agency (☎ 745 116, fax 744 632, e yazdseir@mail.yazd.co.ir, Motahharī St) and Saadat Seyr Travel & Tour Agency (☎ 666 599, fax 23 603, 21/1 Emāmzadeh-yé Ja'far St) are both exceptionally helpful, have English-speaking staff and are open from 8 am to 9 pm Saturday to Thursday and 8 am to 1 pm Friday.

Bookshops The Jahaferī Bookshop offers an amazing range of maps for most major cities in the country, including Yazd. It's not signposted in English but look for the newspapers displayed outside on the street just west of Āzādī Square. The shop in the foyer of the Motel Safaieh has a small but pricey collection of interesting handicrafts, maps and English-language books.

Emergency For general emergencies dial the directories number (☎ 118). There's a medical emergencies number (☎ 115) or you can contact the Rānāmū (Emergency) Hospital (☎ 66 002) on Farrokhī St just west of Beheshtī Square; there's a 24-hour pharmacy opposite. For less urgent ailments, the Afshar Hospital (☎ 556 011) is in the north-west of town. The police headquarters (☎ 119) is on Āzādī Square.

Old City

According to Unesco, Yazd is one of the oldest towns in the world, so it's well worth spending a few hours getting completely

Too Many Questions?

As the questions piled up in the name of research, the uniformed official behind the desk became suddenly unsmiling and suspicious, interrupting my questions with those of his own: What was I doing in Iran? If I didn't want a visa extension, why did I need so much information? My explanation about Lonely Planet's benign aims in gathering so much detail, even my letter of accreditation, were summarily brushed aside. Just as suddenly, he stood up and briskly informed us that we were not permitted to leave. An Iranian friend who had accompanied me said simply: 'I think we're under arrest'.

After what felt like hours, I was told to return to my hotel to retrieve my passport while my friend would be held as an insurance against my return. By the time I made it back, filled with visions of imminent deportation, my friend had found the right office, the information had been given freely and I was told with a smile and no apparent sense of irony to enjoy my time in Yazd.

After I made an informal complaint, the officer in question was reprimanded and I was assured that applicants for visa extensions were welcome in Yazd. Although such an experience is highly unlikely to be replicated for other travellers, please be careful about taking Iranian friends along to government offices – this can put them (and you) under suspicion and the consequences for them are likely to be far worse than for you. Whatever you do, though, don't ask too many questions.

Anthony Ham

lost in this living museum. The town is the colour of clay, from the sun-dried bricks, and the skyline is dominated by the tall windtowers, or bādgīrs, on every rooftop (for more details, see the boxed text 'The Bādgīrs of Yazd' later in this section). The residential quarters appear almost deserted because of the high walls, which shield the houses from the narrow and labyrinthine kūchés (alleys) crisscrossing the town.

Just wander around, and you'll doubtless discover simple courtyards, ornate wooden doors and some lovely adobe architecture. In the meantime you'll be discovered by countless children who will help lead you out of the maze when you are ready. The best place for this type of wandering is north and northeast of the Jāmeh Mosque. At some point, it is also worth taking a friend or guide who can point out the **Husseinia** (a small shrine north-west of the mosque which has incomparable views over Yazd and the desert fringe from the roof and is a perfect place to watch the sunset) or the traditional houses which lie hidden from public view.

Jāmeh Mosque

The mosques of Yazd are like no others and the magnificent Jāmeh Mosque dominates the old city. Its remarkably high, tiled entrance portal, flanked with two magnificent minarets and adorned with an inscription from the 15th century, is simply superb. The beautiful mosaics on the dome and on the mihrab are also exquisite, while the tiles above the main western entrance to the courtyard are particularly stunning.

Constructed in the 14th century under the direction of Bibi Fātemeh Khatoun, the redoubtable wife of a former governor of Yazd, Amīr Chakhmāq, the mosque was built on the site of a 12th-century building believed to have itself replaced an earlier fire temple. In the courtyard of the mosque there is a narrow stairwell leading down to a qanāt (underground water channel; see the boxed text 'The Qanāt' later in this section) used these days for ritual ablutions.

The caretaker will allow you to climb the stairs above the entrance for breathtaking views of the old city, for which a small tip is appreciated. Otherwise, entrance is free.

On Friday morning between 9 am and noon you could see a strange thing – unmarried women go to the top of the minarets. They wear a kind of padlock on their scarf and throw the key down into the courtyard of the mosque. If a man picks it up, the woman will come down, let him open the lock and offer him cakes and sweets. The popular belief is that they will get married promptly.

Véronique Yacan & Leó Gaill

The Bādgīrs of Yazd

Any summer visitor to Yazd can hardly fail to appreciate the need for cool air and for the proliferation of *bādgīrs*, or windtowers, constructed to fulfil just that need. These ancient systems of natural air-conditioning, which are also a feature of the architecture along the shores of the Persian Gulf, are designed to catch even the lightest breeze and direct it to the rooms below.

All but the simplest towers – which range from standard two-sided models to the more elaborate six-sided variety – consist of at least four parts: the body or trunk which contains the shafts; air shelves which are used to catch some of the hot air and prevent it from entering the house; flaps which redirect the circulation of the wind; and the roof covering. The currents that enter the house do so above a pool of cool water, thereby cooling the air, while the warm air continues its circular path, redirected upwards through a different shaft.

If you stand directly beneath a *bādgīr*, the air is indeed appreciably cooler, and while not quite as cold as modern air-con, they're a whole lot healthier.

Mausoleum of Seyed Roknaddīn

Near the entrance to the Jāmeh Mosque, the gilt-edged tomb (Bogheh-yé Seyed Roknaddīn) of local Islamic notable Seyed Roknaddīn Mohammed Qazi sits beneath a beautiful tiled dome which is visible from any elevated point around the city. There are some splendid golden geometric designs in and around the sanctuary portal. Constructed in the 14th century, this tomb and mosque used to be part of a complex that included an observatory, a madraseh and a library. The interior was being restored at the time of research and will be magnificent when finished; don't be surprised if an entrance fee is soon charged.

Khān-é Larī

This 150-year-old house is one of the best preserved houses of its kind in Iran, with traditional doors, stained-glass windows, elegant archways and alcoves as well as the ubiquitous bādgīrs. Once the home of a rich family of merchants, it was opened to the public after the last generation of the Larī family sold it to the government. Subsequent restoration work has yielded impressive results, and the interior courtyard now home to architecture students. Hidden behind a mud wall, the house is not signposted and is indistinguishable from those around it so you'll need to ask for directions; locals also know it as Khān-é Mahmūdī.

Alexander's Prison

Allegedly built by Alexander the Great, this prison was renowned throughout the region; even the poet Hāfez wrote from Shīrāz about the prison's less-than-salubrious conditions. Now renovated, the prison is mildly interesting, but is not a must. The small display on the old city of Yazd is probably just as interesting as the prison itself.

Entrance costs IR15,000. It is signposted in English, next to a garden in the old city.

Tomb of the 12 Emāms

This early 11th-century plain brick tomb is almost next door to Alexander's Prison. It has fine inscriptions inside, with the names of each of the Shiite Emāms (see the boxed text 'The 12 Emāms' in the Religion section of the Facts About Iran chapter), none of whom are buried here. Although the mausoleum is small, dusty and almost forgotten, it is nonetheless a well-preserved Seljuk building. Entrance costs IR15,000.

Amīr Chakhmāq Complex

The stunning three-storey facade of the *takieh* in the Amīr Chakhmāq Complex is one of the most recognisable and unusual sites in Iran. Its rows of perfectly proportioned sunken alcoves are at their best around sunset when the light softens and the towering exterior is discreetly floodlit to spectacular effect. Also designed by the wife of Amīr Chakhmāq, this complex contains a small set of buildings at ground level behind the facade including a small, decaying **bazaar**. At the entrance from Amīr Chakhmāq Square, look out for the huge wooden *palm nakhl*, an important centrepiece for the observance of the Shiites passionate Ashūra commemorations in the sacred month of Moharram.

For IR10,000 you can climb to the top of the facade via a series of staircases for wonderful views over Yazd. The last bit of the ascent might not suit anyone claustrophobic. Look for a wooden door facing the square and ask around if the custodian isn't there.

Across the street look out for the picturesque **Shesh Bāgdīr** – group of six windtowers.

Bāgh-é Doulat Ābād

This residence of the former ruler, Karīm Khān Zand, was built in about 1750 and consists of a small pavilion set amid quiet gardens. Although the gardens are a little neglected, the interior of the pavilion is superb with intricate lattice work and exquisite stained-glass windows throughout. It is also renowned for having the loftiest bādgīr in town, standing over 33m high.

The Qanāt

The traditional Iranian method of irrigating the land, first practised on the central plateau at least 2000 years ago, is the *qanāt* or underground water channel. To build a qanāt you first need to bore a well down to an underground water source, which may be more than 100m deep but must be at a higher level than the point at which the water is to be collected. Then you dig a tunnel just wide and tall enough to crawl along to carry the water along a very shallow gradient to that point. Narrow wells are dug down to the tunnel at regular intervals for ventilation and to dispose of the excavated soil.

Because of the hazards and expense of constructing a qanāt, complex laws govern every aspect of its use and maintenance. Iran is thought to have more than 50,000 qanāts, the longest more than 40km long. Although modern irrigation projects like the hydroelectric dam at Karaj now take priority, qanāts and other traditional methods of supplying water are still very important, and the highly skilled, well-paid qanāt builders of Yazd (which is where they traditionally come from) won't be picking up redundancy cheques for many years yet.

Entrance is IR10,000 and, apart from Fridays, you're likely to have the place to yourself. Sadly you are not allowed to walk among the orchards. It is open from about 8 am to 5 pm daily, although it may close in the middle of the day if the gatekeeper fancies a siesta.

It is easiest to reach the entrance from the western end of Shahīd Rajā'ī St, taking one of the narrow lanes and then following the direction of the tallest bādgīr you can see.

Zoroastrian Sites

Āteshkadeh This Zoroastrian temple in a small garden attracts followers from around the world. The sacred flame, behind a glass case and visible from the entrance hall has apparently been burning since about AD 470, and was transferred first to Ardakān in 1174, then to Yazd in 1474 and to its present site in 1940. The priests regularly stoke the flame with dry and durable wood (apricot or almond is preferred).

The entrance hall contains some quotations from Zoroaster, and the couple of paintings on display in the entrance hall include one of Zoroaster.

On the external facade of the building above the entrance you can see the symbolic bird-man symbol of Zoroaster. One hand holds a ring, which symbolises loyalty, while the other hand is held up to indicate respect. The wings have three layers of feathers, reflecting the Zoroastrian belief that you should think, speak and act decently.

Enter via a small gate in an alleyway north-west of Kāshānī St, not far from Mārkār Square. The temple is open from 7 to 11 am and 5 to 7 pm daily. There is no entrance fee, but a small donation is welcome.

Towers of Silence Set on two lonely, barren hilltops on the southern outskirts of Yazd are the evocative Zoroastrian Towers of Silence (Dakhmeh-yé Zartoshtiyūn). In accordance with Zoroastrian beliefs about the purity of the earth, dead bodies were not buried but left in these uncovered stone towers so that vultures could pick the bones clean. A priest would sit with the bodies, which were placed in a sitting position, and

Zoroastrianism

Zoroastrianism was the main religion across the Iranian plateau until the Arab Conquest brought Islam to the people. Zoroastrians are followers of Zoroaster (Zartosht, Zarathustra), who was probably born about 550 BC at Mazar-é Sharif in what is now Afghanistan (though several places in present-day Iran also claim the honour). Zoroastrianism was one of the first religions to postulate an omnipotent, invisible god. Zoroastrians worship fire as a symbol of God and keep 'eternally' burning flames at their temples.

Very little of what Zoroaster wrote has survived, but he preached dualism: the eternal battle of good and evil. He believed in two principles, Vohu Mano (Good Mind) and Ahem Nano (Bad Mind) which were responsible for day and night, life and death. These two opposing 'minds' coexisted within the supreme being, Ahura Mazda, and in all living things. Zoroastrianism became the state religion under the Sassanians.

Since Zoroastrians believe in the purity of the elements, they refuse to bury their dead (because it pollutes the earth) or cremate them (because it pollutes the atmosphere). Instead the dead were exposed in 'towers of silence', where their bones were soon cleaned up by the vultures, a practice rarely undertaken today. Nowadays, deceased Zoroastrians are usually buried in graves lined with concrete, to prevent 'contamination' of the earth.

Many Zoroastrian temples are adorned with bas-relief winged figures, with the layers of feathers on the wings symbolising purity of thought, word and action. These can also be seen at other sites around Iran, such as Ferdōsī's Tomb in Tūs and in Persepolis.

Zoroastrian men aren't easily distinguished from Muslims, but Zoroastrian women can be recognised by their patterned headscarves and embroidered dresses with white, cream or red being the predominant colours. They never wear chadors (black covering garments), although they follow the strict hejab laws governing women's dress.

Of the 150,000 or more Zoroastrians in the world, an estimated 30,000 still live in and around Yazd. Today the religion is going through a period of readjustment, as previously strict regulations on marriage resulted in a steep fall in the numbers of adherents.

Zoroastrianism is also known as Mazdaism from the name of its supreme god, Ahura Mazda, and as Magism from the name of its ancient priests, the magi. One of the largest communities of Zoroastrians lives in India (particularly the western state of Gujarat). Known as Parsīs, Indian Zoroastrians are descendants of the faithful who fled Persia in the 10th century in the aftermath of the arrival of Islam.

watch to see which eye the vultures plucked out first: the right eye and the soul faced a good future; the left and the future looked more grim. Such towers have not been used for almost four decades.

At the foot of the hills there are several other disused Zoroastrian buildings including a defunct well, two small bādgīrs, an *ashpāzkhūneh* (kitchen) and a lavatory. It is possible that the area will eventually be fenced off and an entrance fee requested.

To get there, take a shared taxi to Abāzār Square, about 4.5km south of Markar Square. From there, take another shared taxi, or bus, south-west along Shahīd Tīmsār Fallahī Rd, passing through two squares along the way. The second of these squares, Atlāsī Square is about 1.2km from Markar Square and 3.5km from the Towers of Silence. You may have to walk the last few kilometres.

Alternatively, charter a private taxi for about IR10,000 return, including waiting time. Ask for Dakhmeh-yé Zartoshtiyūn. Although there is no real need for a guide, you may want to contact Dinyar Shahzādī (☎ 20 404, fax 20 405), a local Zoroastrian archaeologist who works with the Cultural Heritage Office, before setting out.

Fortress of Lions

In the north-east of Yazd, the Fortress of Lions (Ghal'eh-yé Asadān) houses another

Zoroastrian eternal flame moved there some 20 years ago. It is often closed, however, unless you can get permission to see it from the Āteshkadeh.

Places to Stay

Accommodation in Yazd is generally of a reasonable standard, although there are few outstanding places, particularly at the budget end of the scale. Unfortunately, strict local planning regulations limiting the construction of new hotels mean that this is unlikely to change in a hurry.

If you have a problem with a hotel, contact the Tourist Organisation (☎ 747 100), a government watchdog set up to handle complaints.

Places to Stay – Budget

Often crowded with travellers, the *Aria Hotel* (☎ 660 411) gets very mixed reviews, particularly about the service which ranges from the off-hand to the deliberately unhelpful. Lone female travellers have also reported a decidedly casual approach to privacy. *Most* of the rooms are clean and quite pleasant if a little overpriced at IR60,000 for a double without bathroom. There's a nice internal courtyard. The hotel is up a lane 75m south-east of Beheshtī Square.

One reader described the accommodation at the *Beheshty Hotel* (☎ 24 717, *Emām Khomeinī St*) as 'the worst value room I was shown in Iran', but all of the rooms we saw (without revealing our identity) were tidy and spacious. A single/double with shared bathroom costs IR40,000/50,000, while a triple with bathroom costs IR80,000. It's in a good location and there's off-street parking. No English is spoken.

An increasing number of budget travellers are heading for the *Hotel Amīr Chakhmāgh* (☎ 669 823), which is arguably the best budget choice in Yazd. Some rooms could be a touch cleaner but the staff are friendly and get the thumbs up from many of the travellers we met. Rooms at the front are very noisy but have the spectacular compensation of views over the Amīr Chakhmāq Complex. At IR30,000/45,000 for a room with shared facilities they're not bad value, particularly

given the location. It's not signposted in English – look on the south-western side of Amīr Chakhmāq Square for a faded yellow awning above a stairwell leading to the 1st floor.

One place which opened after we visited and is definitely worth checking out is the *Yazd Backpackers Guesthouse* (☎ 30 494, e *touristicplace@yahoo.com*). Run by the same traveller-friendly people who run the Y@zd Internet Café, double rooms cost IR50,000 and meals (including vegetarian options) are available. They also have Internet access. It's signposted in English next to the Āteshkadeh.

Places to Stay – Mid-Range & Top End

The *Hotel Farhang* (☎ 665 011, fax 660 725) is probably the best in the mid-range with double rooms with bathroom – featuring Iranian *and* Western toilets – for IR150,000 including breakfast, rising as high as IR200,000 in the busier months. It's a little overpriced as the peeling wallpaper of the rooms contributes to an overall impression that the hotel is jaded and past its prime. Expect a (very) early wake-up call from the mosque out the back. The rooms are cleaned every day. The entrance is along a lane off Emām Khomeinī St, just north of Beheshtī Square and is signposted in English.

Nabavi Hotel (☎ 612 89) is central and charges IR200,000 for a pleasant, spacious double with a dining table and bathroom. Management will sometimes negotiate if things are quiet. Sadly, this is another place where the unfriendliness or diffidence of the staff has left a bad impression on readers. The hotel is in a quiet lane off Emāmzādeh-yé Ja'far St.

Among the top-end places, the *Jahāngardī Inn* (☎ 47 221, fax 47 222, Dāneshjū Blvd), also signposted as the Tourist Inn, seems particularly good value. Although inconveniently located (like all the top-end hotels), the rooms are very attractive, the management is friendly and there's a coffee shop and a gift shop in the lobby. Doubles with fridge and TV (with the possibility of satellite television soon) cost US$60 plus 20% tax.

Other good hotels in this range include the excellent *Motel Safaieh* (☎ 842 812, fax 842 811, Shahīd Timsar Fallāhī St) which has a lovely sheltered garden setting, a good restaurant and luxury rooms for US$79/109; and the *Āzādī Hotel* (☎ 553 111, fax 556 444, 🅴 AzadiHotel@hotmail.com, Meysam St), formerly the Enghelab Hotel, which charges US$60/103 for similar rooms. Male (but not female) guests may use the pool for free while nonguests pay IR5000.

Places to Eat

For a tasty cooked breakfast, a pot of tea and a qalyan, head straight for the unnamed *chāykhūneh*, near the Hotel Farhang. It's not signposted in English but is recognisable by, of all things, a picture of Donald Duck enjoying the qalyan in the sheltered doorway. Women are expected to sip their tea apart from the men here. A more salubrious but less atmospheric buffet breakfast at the *Āzādī Hotel* costs IR14,000.

The area around Beheshtī Square is crowded with places selling Iranian-style hamburgers and kebabs. Near the clock tower, *Persia Sandwich* is one of the better of the genre. *Baharestān Restaurant* is signposted in English (though little is spoken inside) and revels in its no-frills decor but the staff are friendly and a good meal of *kabāb-é kūbīdé* with tomatoes, bread, māst (yogurt) and a soft drink should set you back around IR10,500. A few doors up, the *Melli Dinner House* serves excellent barbecued chicken with rice, yogurt and drink for around IR11,500. They also do samosas.

There are plenty of pizzerias of varying quality around Yazd. One good place is *Pizza*, on Farrokhī St between Beheshtī and Āzādī Squares. It's spotlessly clean and while the servings could be larger, the small/large pizzas for IR5500/8800 are pretty good. Look for the red neon sign, 100m past the hospital.

Out in the west of town, both the *Restōrān-é Tehrānī* (☎ 551 743) and the *Restōrān-é Zeytūn* (☎ 525 566, Jomhūrī-yé Eslāmī Blvd) are recommended, if inconveniently located, and popular with middle-class Yazdīs. The Restōrān-é Tehrānī has a

particularly nice ambience. Expect to pay upwards of IR30,000 per person, to which must be added the taxi fare (IR3500 one way) from the centre of town.

The *restaurant* at Jahāngardī Inn has over 50 items on the menu and the cook promises to cook just about anything you want if given a day's notice.

There are two outstanding restaurants in Yazd. The first, *Hamūm-é Khān* (☎ 670 366), also known as the *Chāykhūneh-yé San'ati*, is deep in the heart of the old city and is undoubtedly the most romantic choice in Yazd. This elegantly restored underground hammam is entered via a lovely staircase underneath mud-brick arches, while the interior of the restaurant itself has tranquil pools and attractive tiles. If only the lighting could be a little softer. The food is pricey but good. To find it, walk away from Emām Khomeinī St along Qeyām St for about 500m where you'll see a lane signposted in English as 'Meydān-é Khān Bazaar'. Follow the alley for about 50m until it twists right into a large open courtyard; take the lane on the south-western corner of the square and the restaurant is about 50m on the left, just after the first cross street.

The other highlight is the *Restōrān-é Hanār-yé Sabz* (☎ 32 824), housed in an old henna grinding mill in the south-east of town. The food is good without being spectacular and the setting is lovely; make sure you pay a visit to one of the still-functioning henna mills across the lane where massive wheels spin deep into the night in Dickensian work conditions and where you can buy a small bag of Yazdī henna for IR3000. The restaurant is off Kashāni St on Mazarī Lane and you'll need a taxi (IR3000) to get there – ask for 'hanār sayeh sar' (henna grinding mills).

Shopping

The many bazaars in the old city and the Iran Handicrafts Organisation are probably the best places in Iran to buy silk (known locally as *tirma*), brocade, glassware and cloth – products which brought the town its prosperity in centuries gone by. Finding the best places to buy these goods in the old city can be difficult – try to take an Iranian friend with you. If you have a sweet tooth, don't forget to try some of the *pashmak* sweets, renowned in Yazd and available in many shops around Beheshtī Square.

Getting There & Away

Air Yazd airport (☎ 43 031) is not the busiest in Iran. Iran Air (☎ 28 030) only flies to Mashhad, (twice weekly, IR142,000) and Tehrān (daily, IR113,000). The office, on Motahharī St, is open from 7 am to 6 pm Saturday to Thursday and from 8 am to noon on Friday. Iran Asseman has an inconvenient daily post-midnight flight to Tehrān (IR113,000).

Bus & Minibus Many bus companies have offices along Emām Khomeinī St in the blocks north of Beheshtī Square. All buses leave from the main bus terminal, on Rāh Āhan Blvd, about 3km south-west of the town centre, accessible by shared taxi from Beheshtī and Āzādī Squares, or by bus No 27 from Beheshtī Square.

Some useful destinations are listed in the following table:

destination	distance (km)	duration (hrs)	cost (IR)
Bam	590	9	12,000
Bandar-é Abbās	671	11	17,000
Esfahān	310	6	7000
Kermān	386	6	8000
Mashhad	939	16	24,500
Shīrāz	438	7	10,000
Tabas	419	8	18,000
Tehrān	677	10	18,000
Zāhedān	928	14	19,000

For Bam, you may have to take anything going to Zāhedān and will sometimes have to even pay the full price.

Train There are daily trains from Yazd to Tehrān (IR20,000/35,000 for 2nd/1st class), via Kashān and Qom, which leave at 10 pm and arrive in Tehrān at 6 am the following morning. From Tehrān, trains leave at 8.30 pm and arrive in Yazd at 4 am. If heading south-east from Yazd, you could join this train (departs around 5 am) to Kermān,

(IR15,700 – one class fits all) or Bandar-é Abbās (IR27,000).

The train station (☎ 748 551) is next to the main bus terminal. Get there by shared taxi from Beheshtī or Āzādī Squares, or on bus No 27 from Beheshtī Square. Train tickets can be purchased in advance at both the Yazd Seir Tour & Travel Agency and the Saadat Seyr Travel & Tour Agency (see Travel Agencies under information earlier in this section).

Getting Around

To/From the Airport There is no airport bus service so you must take a shared taxi from Enqelāb-é Eslāmī Square for about IR1500, or you can take a private taxi for about IR7000.

Bus & Taxi There is really only one useful bus – No 27 – which goes between Beheshtī Square, the bus and train terminals and the visa office.

The standard fare in a shared taxi anywhere around town should be around IR500. For private taxis, the fare will be in the order of IR2000 and IR4000 as far as the bus and train terminals.

Taxis can be chartered for around IR11,000 per hour.

AROUND YAZD
Taft   تفت

Only 18km south-west of Yazd, and under the looming Mt Sīr, Taft is cooler than Yazd, and worth a quick look around if you have time. Huge pomegranates are the staple agricultural product, and qanāts provide water for pretty gardens.

The *Hotel Shīrkuh* charges a steep US$60 for a double. Take a minibus or shared taxi from the main bus terminal in Yazd.

Chak Chak   چک چک

This important Zoroastrian fire-temple is on a hill about 50km to the north-west of Yazd on the southern fringes of the Dasht-é Lūt. Many of the buildings that form part of the complex are modern and uninspiring. However, the **fire temple** cut into the cliffside at the top has a wonderful brass door that's embossed with the likeness of Zoroaster, and the location is suitably dramatic.

Chak Chak attracts thousands of pilgrims for an annual festival which lasts for 10 days from the beginning of the third month after the Iranian New Year, Nō Rūz (about 21 March).

The return trip by private taxi, along a difficult stretch of road off the main route to Tabas, will cost around IR90,000 including waiting time, but you'd be better off going with the guys at the Y@zd Internet Café (see Travel Agencies in the Yazd section earlier) since their price includes breakfast in the desert, a lunch of camel kabābs in Ardakān and a stop in Meybod en route back to Yazd. Prices depend on the number of people but shouldn't come to more than IR120,000. There is no public transport.

Ardakān   اردکان

In the middle of the desert, about 60km north-west of Yazd, Ardakān is a regional agricultural centre, courtesy of the amazing qanāt irrigation system (see the boxed text 'The Qanāt' in the Yazd section earlier). It has also come to prominence in recent years as the birthplace of President Mohammed Khatamī. Ardakān's desert setting, rather than any buildings, makes it worth a detour on the way back to Yazd from Chak Chak. There are some attractive old lanes and bādgīrs around the **Jāmeh Mosque**. Ardakān is famous for its camels, so for a distinctive taste, try a delicious **camel kabāb** from the store about 150m south of the mosque.

To get there, take a minibus, or any bus heading north-west along the main highway, from the main bus terminal in Yazd.

Meybod   میبد

With a rapidly growing population, Meybod is now almost joined to Ardakān to its north and worth a quick look if you're passing by. The thoroughly restored **old post office**, **caravanserai** with a splendid covered qanāt in the centre of its courtyard, and amazing Safavid-era **ice house** (*moayedī*) are adjacent to each other in the west of town. The **castle** in the centre of town is rarely open but it's attractive from the outside nonetheless.

SHĪRĀZ   شیراز
☎ 071 • pop 1,042,801 • elevation 1491m

Shīrāz is a city of sophistication and has always been celebrated as the heartland of Persian culture. In its heyday, the city was given the epithet of Dār-ol-Elm (House of Learning) and became synonymous with learning, nightingales, poetry, roses and wine. It was also one of the most important cities in the medieval Islamic world and was the Iranian capital during the Zand dynasty (1747–79) when many of its most beautiful buildings were built or restored.

The charms of modern Shīrāz are less immediately apparent, but vestiges of its glorious past remain. It is still a city of poets, and is home to the graves of Hāfez and Sa'dī. The town has an important university with a prestigious medical faculty – the combination of relaxed, highly educated inhabitants and wide tree-lined avenues makes it one of the more pleasant large Iranian cities. Shīrāz has one of Iran's most agreeable climates and is located in a fertile valley once famed for its vineyards. Its splendid gardens, exquisite mosques and whispered echoes of ancient sophistication reward those who linger longer than it takes to visit nearby Persepolis.

The attractions of Shīrāz range from exquisite mosques to mausoleums of great historical significance and tranquil gardens. No visit be complete without joining the thousands – literally – of locals in the very modern Friday night ritual of strolling and picnicking along the western reaches of Dr Chamran Blvd.

> To the three weeks which I spent in Shīrāz I look back with unmixed pleasure. The associations connected with it are familiar to every student of Persian; its natural beauties I have already feebly attempted to depict; its inhabitants are, amongst all the Persians, the most subtle, the most ingenious, the most vivacious, even as their speech is to this day the purest and most melodious.
>
> **Edward Browne,**
> *A Year Amongst the Persians (1893)*

History
There was a settlement at Shīrāz at least as early as the Achaemenid period, and it was

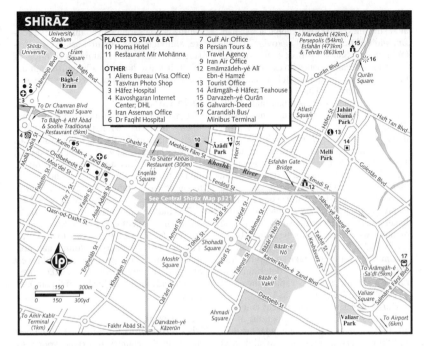

SHĪRĀZ

PLACES TO STAY & EAT
10 Homa Hotel
11 Restaurant Mīr Mohānna

OTHER
1 Aliens Bureau (Visa Office)
2 Tasvīran Photo Shop
3 Hāfez Hospital
4 Kavoshgaran Internet
  Center; DHL
5 Iran Asseman Office
6 Dr Faqīhī Hospital
7 Gulf Air Office
8 Persian Tours &
  Travel Agency
9 Iran Air Office
12 Emāmzādeh-yé Alī
   Ebn-é Hamzé
13 Tourist Office
14 Ārāmgāh-é Hāfez; Teahouse
15 Darvazeh-yé Qurān
16 Gahvarch-Deed
17 Carandish Bus/
   Minibus Terminal

already an important regional centre under the Sassanians. However, it did not become the provincial capital until about AD 693, following the Arab conquest of Estakhr, the last Sassanian capital (8km north-east of Persepolis, but now completely destroyed). As Estakhr fell into decline, Shīrāz grew in size and importance first under Arab rule and then under a succession of local dynasties. By the time Estakhr was eventually sacked in 1044, Shīrāz was said to rival Baghdad in importance.

The city grew further in the 12th century under the Atābaks of Fārs when it became an important artistic centre. Shīrāz was spared destruction by the invading Mongols when the province's last Atābak monarch offered tribute and submission to Genghis Khan. It was again spared in 1382, when the local monarch, Shāh Shojā', agreed to submit to Timur's armies, even offering the hand of his granddaughter in marriage to a grandson of Timur. Shāh Shojā' was fol-

lowed by a turbulent succession of rulers until Timur appointed his own son as ruler.

The period under the Mongols and the Timurids marked the peak of Shīrāz's development. The encouragement of its enlightened rulers, the presence of Hāfez, Sa'dī and many other brilliant artists and scholars, and the city's natural advantages helped Shīrāz to become one of the greatest cities in the Islamic world throughout the 13th and 14th centuries. Shīrāz was also known as a leading centre of calligraphy, painting, architecture and literature.

For several centuries, even after the end of the Mongol period, artists and scholars from Shīrāz sallied forth as cultural emissaries, both inside and outside the country, beautifying Samarkand and many of the Mogul cities of India. The most noteworthy was Ostād Īsā, a 17th-century Shīrāzī architect who provided the design for the Taj Mahal.

Under Shāh Abbās I, Imam Gholī Khān, the governor of Fārs, constructed a large number of palaces and other ornate buildings along the lines of the royal capital at Esfahān. But while Shīrāz remained a provincial capital during the Safavid period, even attracting several European traders who exported its famous wine, the city quickly fell into nearly a century of decline. This was worsened by several earthquakes, the Afghan raids of the early 18th century, and an uprising led by Shīrāz's governor in 1744, which was put down after a siege by Nāder Shāh.

At the time of Nāder Shāh's murder in 1747, most of Shīrāz's historical buildings were damaged or ruined, and its population had fallen to 50,000, a quarter of what it had been 200 years earlier. Shīrāz soon returned to prosperity under the enlightened Karīm Khān, the first ruler of the short-lived Zand dynasty, who made Shīrāz the national capital in 1750. Master of virtually all Persia, Karīm Khān refused to take any higher title than *vakīl* (regent). He was determined to raise Shīrāz into a worthy capital, the equal of Esfahān under Shāh Abbās I.

Karīm Khān was a benevolent and wise ruler, and one of the greatest patrons of the arts in Persian history. Employing more than 12,000 workers, he founded a royal district in the area of the Arg-é Karīm Khānī and commissioned many fine buildings, including the finest bazaar in Persia. However Karīm Khān's heirs failed to secure his gains. When Agha Muhammed Khān, the cruel founder of the Qajar dynasty, came to power, he wreaked his revenge on Shīrāz, destroying the city's fortifications and, in 1789, moving the national capital to Tehrān, taking with him the remains of Karīm Khān. Although reduced to the rank of provincial capital, Shīrāz managed to remain prosperous due to the continuing importance of the trade route to Būshehr.

The city's role in trade greatly diminished with the opening of the trans-Iranian railway in the 1930s, as trade routes shifted to the ports in Khūzestān. Much of the architectural inheritance of Shīrāz, and especially the royal district of the Zands, was either neglected or destroyed as a result of irresponsible town planning under the Pahlavī dynasty. Lacking any great industrial, religious or strategic importance, Shīrāz is now largely an administrative centre, although its population has grown considerably since the Islamic Revolution of 1979. It's also home to a large (though decreasing) population of Afghan refugees.

Orientation

The main street of Shīrāz is the wide, tree-lined Karīm Khān-é Zand Blvd (often shortened simply to Zand). This boulevard runs about as far east and west as you would want to go without leaving Shīrāz. Most of the things to see, and nearly all the hotels, are along here or within walking distance of it, so this is a street you'll keep coming back to.

The old city and the commercial centre of Shīrāz are south of the Khoshk River, while the smarter residential areas are to the north. The modern university buildings and dormitories are on a steep hill in the north-west of town. The city centre is Shohadā Square (still widely known as Shahrdārī Square), on Zand.

Information

Visa Extensions Shīrāz is one of the best places in the country to extend your visa. The genial staff at the Aliens Bureau are used to foreigners and the courtyard is well set up with a Bank Melli branch to buy your stamp (IR12,500) and a snack bar. A small shop 75m west of the compound does photocopies of the relevant pages of your passport and the Bank Melli stamp; if you don't have the requisite two photos, stop off at Tasvīran Photo Shop on Alam Square en route. Extensions are usually issued within the hour and they routinely give as much as one month extra on tourist visas.

The Aliens Bureau is a little hard to find. Take a shared taxi to the Hāfez Hospital or Alam Square then walk west along Dr Chamran Blvd. Take the first right (after the blue pedestrian bridge) and follow Abiverdi St (there is a sign in English) up a slight hill for 200m, then turn right at the small photocopying store – the bureau is through a gate 75m further on, on the left side of the road. A private taxi from the centre of town costs IR5000.

Yazd makes a welcome break from the desert wastes that surround it. *Bādgīrs*, wind towers that cool mud-brick homes (top) and the minarets of the Amīr Chakhmāq Complex (bottom) dominate the skyline. The evocative Zoroastrian Towers of Silence (middle) can be found on the city's outskirts.

The Bāgh-é Eram is one of Shīrāz's most popular gardens.

Reliefs depicting a victorious King Shapur I, Naqsh-é Rostam

Schoolgirls in hejab

The imposing Tomb of Cyrus II, Pasargadae

A mullah reads his Quran.

Tourist Offices The tourist office (☎ 20 791) hands out the odd brochure and occasional (free) map, but otherwise can provide only limited assistance. The office (not marked in English) is opposite Melli Park and is open from 7.30 am to 2.30 pm Saturday to Thursday.

Money The central branches of the major banks have foreign exchange facilities. The huge Bank Melli office, next to the Arg-é Karīm Khānī, is the most efficient. Their rates are displayed on a board in the main lobby, although the exchange office is in the

well-marked building out the back, which you can also enter from 22 Bahman St. They were also giving cash advances on Master-Card, but not Visa, at the time of research. Chahtoosi Exchange changes money more quickly and with less paperwork and similar rates. All along Zand you're likely to be approached by unofficial moneychangers, but there's no need to take the risk.

Post & Communications The main post office is behind the central branch of the Bank Melli; some travellers have reported that this is a good place to send parcels. The

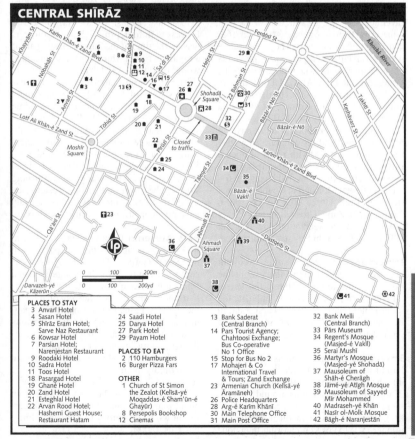

CENTRAL SHĪRĀZ

PLACES TO STAY
3 Anvarī Hotel
4 Sasan Hotel
5 Shīrāz Eram Hotel;
  Sarve Naz Restaurant
6 Kowsar Hotel
7 Parsian Hotel;
  Narenjestan Restaurant
9 Roodaki Hotel
10 Sadra Hotel
11 Toos Hotel
18 Pasargad Hotel
19 Ghane Hotel
20 Zand Hotel
21 Esteghlal Hotel
22 Arvan Rood Hotel;
  Hashemi Guest House;
  Restaurant Hatam

24 Saadi Hotel
25 Darya Hotel
27 Park Hotel
29 Payam Hotel

PLACES TO EAT
2 110 Hamburgers
16 Burger Pizza Fars

OTHER
1 Church of St Simon
  the Zealot (Kelīsā-yé
  Moqaddas-é Sham'ūn-é
  Ghayūr)
8 Persepolis Bookshop
12 Cinemas

13 Bank Saderat
  (Central Branch)
14 Pars Tourist Agency;
  Chahtoosi Exchange;
  Bus Co-operative
  No 1 Office
15 Stop for Bus No 2
17 Mohajeri & Co
  International Travel
  & Tours; Zand Exchange
23 Armenian Church (Kelīsā-yé
  Āramāneh)
26 Police Headquarters
28 Arg-é Karīm Khānī
30 Main Telephone Office
31 Main Post Office

32 Bank Melli
  (Central Branch)
33 Pārs Museum
34 Regent's Mosque
  (Masjed-é Vakīl)
35 Serai Mushī
36 Martyr's Mosque
  (Masjed-yé Shohadā)
37 Mausoleum of
  Shāh-é Cherāgh
38 Jāmé-yé Atīgh Mosque
39 Mausoleum of Sayyed
  Mīr Mohammed
40 Madraseh-yé Khān
41 Nasīr ol-Molk Mosque
42 Bāgh-é Naranjestān

main telephone office no longer handles international calls and its staff will direct you to the private office in the same building as Chahtoosi Exchange.

The Kavoshgaran Internet Center (☎ 684 221, Mollā Sadrā) has excellent connections and charges IR25,000 an hour. It's at the back of a small complex of computer stores 50m south of the western end of Zand. Pars Tourist Agency (see Travel Agencies following) is more central and charges IR30,000 per hour. You should have no trouble finding somewhere – Internet cafes are springing up all over town.

Travel Agencies There are several decent travel agencies along Zand. One of the best is the Pars Tourist Agency (☎/fax 23 163, e masoudn@farsnet.net). They run a range of tours (including eco tours) to the sights around Fārs Province, including Persepolis, Pasargadae and Firūz Ābād. All their drivers speak English and they can also arrange guides in German, French, Italian and Dutch. Expect to pay IR100,000 for a half day, and up to IR240,000 for a full day trip including guide and air-con car. They also offer Internet access (with plans to open a fully fledged Internet cafe) upstairs and can help with visa extensions and bus tickets.

For air tickets Mohajeri & Co International Travel & Tours (☎ 26 963, fax 26 366, 6 Karīm Khān Zand Cross Rd) and Persia Tours and Travel Agency (☎ 332 700, fax 338 627, 10 Dr Faqīhī St) are recommended.

Bookshops Shīrāz has some excellent bookshops, the best being the two in the grounds of the tomb of Hāfez, the Persepolis Bookshop on Rudāki St, opposite the Sadra Hotel (Harry Potter in Farsi!) and in the bazaar in a small alleyway south-east of Serai Mushīr.

Emergency Shīrāz is famous for the standard of its medical training, so this is probably the best place to fall ill outside Tehrān. Of the numerous hospitals around the city, the most central is Dr Faqīhī Hospital (☎ 51 091). There is also a medical emergency number (☎ 115) or you can ring telephone inquiries (☎ 118). The police headquarters (☎ 22 071) is on Shohadā Square.

Dangers & Annoyances Sadly, the influx of comparatively wealthy tourists has increased the temptation and opportunity for low-level crimes against foreign travellers. Although very rare, robberies have recently taken place in Shīrāz. We have also received several reports of travellers stopped and robbed by bogus police.

Museums & Castles

Arg-é Karīm Khānī The imposing structure of the Citadel of Karīm Khān dominates the city centre and served as a prison in Pahlavī times. This well-preserved fortress with four 14m-high circular towers was, in the time of the Zand dynasty, part of a royal courtyard which Karīm Khān hoped would rival that of Esfahān.

The sign inside proclaims that 'The exalted stature of the Karīm Khānī citadel amuses every new traveller for a long time who arrives in Shīrāz'. The IR20,000 admission fee is altogether less amusing as it only grants you access to the unimpressive courtyard, private prayer room and bathhouse. Save your money and admire the austere and squat exterior, particularly the disturbing slope of the tower on the south-eastern side – experts from as far away as Pisa in Italy have given up efforts to correct the slope.

Pārs Museum Opposite his Arg, Karīm Khānī built a small octagonal pavilion in the Nazar Garden. The building later became his tomb, until the vengeful Agha Muhammed Khān moved the royal remains to his new capital of Tehrān, out of spite for the dynasty he had overthrown. The magnificently restored interior has glorious sombre-toned stucco work on the ceiling although, sadly, photos are forbidden. The pavilion now operates as a museum with some mildly interesting Qurans in the Kufic script and Safavid-era marriage contracts.

The museum (☎ 24 151) is open from about 8 am to 8 pm (closing one hour earlier in winter) Saturday to Thursday. Entry costs IR20,000.

Mosques & Mausoleums

Regent's Mosque The beautiful Regent's Mosque (Masjed-é Vakīl), built in 1773 by Karīm Khān at one of the entrances to his bazaar, is beautiful. The mosque has two vast iwans to the north and south, a magnificent inner courtyard surrounded by beautifully tiled alcoves and porches, a wonderful vaulted mihrab with 48 impressive columns, and a remarkable 14-step marble minbar. Although the structure of the mosque dates from 1773, most of the tiling, with its predominantly floral motifs, was added in the early Qajar era.

The door is usually open during daylight hours. Entrance costs IR15,000. Some readers have written to recommend an elderly guide who shows people round this mosque. On the other hand, one reader complained of being asked for US$20 for such services. Who knows if they're all bumping into the same guy…

Martyr's Mosque The Martyrs' Mosque (Masjed-é Shohadā), at the end of a short lane leading west from Ahmadī Square, is one of the largest ancient mosques in Iran; its rectangular courtyard covers more than 11,000 sq metres. Founded at the start of the 13th century, the mosque has been partially rebuilt many times, and now has very little in the way of tiling or other decorations,

Lingering Magic

Despite the overwhelming presence of Islam everywhere in Iran, you will occasionally catch glimpses of beliefs that certainly don't stem from the Quran. You will, for example, sometimes see young boys going from shop to shop swinging tin cans of burning seeds that give off clouds of smoke. This is supposed to ward off the evil eye, although the foul smell is much more likely to drive customers away.

You will also see lots of people with caged budgies and finches that are supposed to be able to tell fortunes. You pay your money and the bird will pick out a piece of paper with something written on it, probably from one of the great poets.

though it does boast some impressive barrel vaulting. Sadly, it is closed for restoration and it may be some time before it reopens.

Mausoleum of Shāh-é Cherāgh The famous Mausoleum of Shāh-é Cherāgh or Mausoleum of the King of the Lamp (Bogh'é-yé Shāh-é Cherāgh) houses the remains of Sayyed Mīr Ahmad (brother of Imam Rezā of Mashhad fame) who died, or was killed, in Shīrāz in AD 835. A mausoleum was first erected over the grave in the mid-14th century and it has been an important Shiite place of pilgrimage ever since.

The shoe repository outside the doorway to the shrine is as hectic as that of any mosque in Iran, and the expansive courtyard is a great place to sit and discreetly observe the moving climax to what is an important religious rite for Shiites from all over Iran and further afield. Non-Muslims should ask for permission before entering – if you are polite and well presented, you'll be allowed in. The multicoloured reflections from the vast numbers of minute mirror tiles inside the shrine are quite dazzling and the golden-topped minarets above it are superb.

The bookshop between Ahmadi Square and the western entrance to the courtyard has a range of postcards, posters and the occasional book in English.

The mausoleum is open from about 7 am to 10 pm daily; entry is free. All visitors should dress very respectfully –women must put on a chador even if they are already wearing a coat and headscarf; you can borrow one from the bookshop outside the complex. Cameras are forbidden inside the shrine but permitted in the courtyard.

Jāmeh-yé Atīgh Mosque This ancient mosque, first built in 894, is in an alley south-east of the Shāh-é Cherāgh mausoleum. Virtually all the original structure has disappeared, as a result of various earthquakes, and most of the building dates from the Safavid period onwards.

It is mainly of interest for the very unusual turreted rectangular building in the centre of the courtyard. Known as the Khodākhūné (House of God), it was built in the mid-14th century to preserve valuable Qurans, and is believed to be modelled on the Kaaba at Mecca. Although most of it was very skilfully rebuilt in the early 20th century, the House of God still bears an original and unique inscription in raised stone characters on a tiled background.

Mausoleum of Sayyed Mīr Mohammad This mausoleum (Bogh'é-yé Sayyed Mīr Mohammad) was built for the brother of Mīr Ahmad, who also died in Shīrāz. The shrine has intricate mirror tiling and some inscriptions in the dome, but it is less interesting than the Shāh-é Cherāgh mausoleum.

Madraseh-yé Khān Imam Gholī Khān, governor of Fārs, founded this serene theological college for about 100 students in 1615. The original building has been extensively damaged by earthquakes and only a small part remains. The mullahs' training college (still in use) has a fine stone-walled inner courtyard set around a small garden. The building can be reached from a lane through a very impressive portal; watch for the unusual type of stalactite moulding inside the outer arch and some very intricate mosaic tiling with much use of red in contrast to the tiles used in Yazd and Esfahān.

Although the madraseh is often closed, the caretaker will sometimes open it; a tip is appreciated (locals also pay to have the door opened). If you can get in, make sure you climb to the roof for wonderful views over the bazaar.

Nasīr-ol-Molk Mosque Further down the bazaar from the Madraseh-yé Khān, this mosque is one of the most elegant in southern Iran. Built relatively recently, at the end of the 19th century, its coloured tilings (an unusually deep shade of blue) are exquisite. There is some particularly fine stalactite moulding in the smallish outer portal and in the northern iwan. The structure has survived numerous earthquakes, due in part to its construction using flexible wood as struts within the walls. There is a small museum and also some wonderful stone pillars. Entrance costs IR15,000.

Emāmzādeh-yé Alī Ebn-é Hamzé This tomb of the nephew of the seventh Shiite Imam has a bulbous dome which is quite stunning. The interior (no photos allowed) has mirror work as dazzling as you'll see anywhere, as well as beautiful stained-glass windows and an intricate, ancient wooden door. The tombstones around the courtyard, for which families of the deceased paid a small fortune, are also interesting; some date back to the 19th century. Virtually all the original 10th-century structure has disappeared, after several earthquakes and significant repairs and extensions, but unless you saw the original you're unlikely to be disappointed.

Churches
The Anglican Church of St Simon the Zealot (Kelīsā-yé Moqaddas-é Sham'ūn-é Ghayūr), built by R Norman Sharp in 1938, is very Iranian in character and even contains stone tablets with biblical stories incised on them in cuneiform, probably by Sharp. According to local tradition, St Simon was martyred in Persia together with St Thaddeus, another of the 12 Apostles. The great metal door bearing a Persian cross is usually closed; just walk along the wall and ring the doorbell to be let in.

The 17th-century Armenian Church (Kelīsā-yé Ārāmāneh), in an alley off Qā'ānī St, is worth a quick look if you're in the area.

Parks, Gardens & Tombs
Ārāmgāh-é Hāfez The tomb of the celebrated poet Hāfez is north of the river along Golestān Blvd. The charming garden with its two pools is very restful, especially in the warmer months when the flowers are in full bloom. The mausoleum itself is simpler and more attractive than that of Sa'dī.

The marble tombstone, engraved with a long verse from the poet's works, was placed here, inside a small shrine, by Karīm Khān in 1773. In 1935, an octagonal pavilion was put up over it, supported by eight stone columns beneath a tiled dome. Karīm Khān also built an iwan close to the shrine, which was enlarged at the same time as the pavilion was erected.

To fully appreciate Hāfez's significance to Iran, plan to spend a couple of hours sitting in a discreet corner of the grounds, at sunset if possible. If you've spent any time around Iran in teahouses frequented by locals, you're likely to have come across groups of Iranians reading excerpts of Hāfez's works. Iranians also have a saying that every home must have two things: first the Quran, then Hāfez. One popular belief is that if you wish to know your destiny, then open a volume of Hāfez and all will be revealed. Around the tomb itself, this deep respect for the greatest of Persian poets comes to life, with Iranians from all walks of life strolling through the gardens reading from his poetry in groups or alone and approaching the tomb with great reverence. After the sun sets, with the tomb floodlit and sung versions of the poetry of Hāfez piped quietly over the public address system, it is difficult not to feel transported back to the magic of ancient Persia.

While you may not be able to fully replicate the experience, it is easy in such surroundings to agree with Gertrude Bell, who, in the early 19th century asked, 'is it not rather refreshing to the spirit to lie in a hammock strung between the plane trees of a Persian garden and read the poems of Hafiz?'.

The grounds are open from about 8 am to 9 pm daily and entrance costs IR15,000. There's a wonderful teahouse in the private, walled garden inside the grounds (see Places to Eat later in this section) and two excellent bookshops.

You can take a shared taxi from Shohadā Square or bus No 2 from Sa'dī St. A private taxi from the centre of town should cost no more than IR3000.

Ārāmgāh-é Sa'dī The garden at the Tomb of Sa'dī is tranquil, with a natural spring in a valley at the foot of a hill and a fish pond fed by a qanat. The plain marble tomb with its Farsi inscription dates from the 1860s and is surrounded by an octagonal stone colonnade, inscribed with various verses from Sa'dī, supporting a tiled dome.

The entrance fee is IR15,000 and the gardens are open from 8.30 am to 11 pm.

The useful bus No 2 leaves from the city centre and stops at a terminal about 50m from the entrance to the tomb. There are plenty of places to buy food and drink near the entrance, so you can enjoy an impromptu picnic in the gardens. There's also an underground teahouse set around a fish pond which several readers have recommended.

Bāgh-é Eram Famous for its cypress trees, the delightful Garden of Paradise is the place where any budding botanist should head. Alongside a pretty pool is the charming 19th-century Qajar palace, the **Kākh-é Eram**, which has some wonderful paintings, plaster facades and mirror work. Unfortunately, visitors cannot enter the palace.

The gardens are easy enough to reach by taking any shared taxi going along Zand heading towards the university. They close at 7.30 pm. Entrance costs IR20,000. The best time for photos is early morning.

Bāgh-é Naranjestān Known as the Orange Garden, this recently restored house and garden makes a worthy rival to the Bāgh-é Eram. The main pavilion, Naranjestān-é Ghavam, was built between 1879 and 1886 as a reception hall for visitors, and was also used as the Governor's Residence during the late Qajar period. It was connected to the Zinat ol-Molk building, where the women and children resided, by an underground tunnel to enable them to pass without being seen. Shīrāz University runs an impressive **art gallery** in the vaulted rooms beneath the Zinat ol-Molk building.

Inside the pavilion, there is a dazzling mirrored entrance hall, while the surrounding rooms have a breathtaking combination of intricate tiles, inlaid wooden panels, plaster period painting and beautiful stained-glass windows. The facade also has some mock Persepolis bas-reliefs. The gardens are compact but very attractive with an orchard and a headstone dating from AD 150.

The gardens, open from 7.30 am to 6 pm, are behind a pale sandstone walled compound at the eastern end of Dastqeib St, about 300m beyond the Masjed-é Nasīr ol-Molk. Entrance costs IR20,000.

CENTRAL IRAN

Bāgh-é Afīf Ābād The pretty gardens around the Afīf Ābād Palace once belonged, like most things, to the shah. Built in 1863 in Qajar style, the lower floor of the palace is now a **military museum**. Also in the grounds are the remains of a Turkish bathhouse and a small but excellent teahouse. The gardens have odd opening hours – from 5 to 8 pm daily, closing a little earlier in winter. Entrance costs IR20,000.

The gardens are a fair way from the city centre; you'll probably have to charter a private taxi (IR4000). It's worth combining a visit to the gardens with a dinner at the excellent, but pricey, Soofie Traditional Restaurant, a few hundred metres away (see Places to Eat later in this section).

Darvazeh-yé Qurān On the outskirts of Shīrāz is the Darvazeh-yé Qurān or Quran Gateway, the burial tomb for Mir Alī, grandson of Imam Musā Kazem. The exact dates of construction are conflicting, but it is known that the great Karīm Khān added a room at the top of the gateway to house a holy Quran. An ancient Persian tradition, still observed by some, requires that all travellers pass underneath a Quran before undertaking any journey.

In the general complex, you can visit the **Tomb of Kharjū-yé Kermānī**, another famous poet and a contemporary of Sa'dī, where a bust of Kermānī is on display. Those with good leg muscles may want to look for some **bas-reliefs** further up the hill, from where the views of Shīrāz are breathtaking.

The teahouse is a perfect spot for a break. Next to it is an underground waterfall. The immense set of rusting girders on the hill is the framework of a hotel, abandoned (too late) after permission to build it was withdrawn.

If you have chartered your own vehicle to Persepolis or beyond, stop here on the way. Getting a shared taxi to the gateway is not easy, but you could combine it with a visit to the tomb of Hāfez, which is within walking distance – just head up Hāfez St, preferably in daylight as we have had reports of stones being thrown at foreigners around here. Entrance is free.

Gahvarch-Deed Directly opposite the Quran Gateway is a lookout, the Gahvarch-Deed, right at the top of a very steep trail. It was used to spot invading armies; a fire would be lit to warn of impending doom. The views over Shīrāz are worth the climb.

Bāzār-é Vakīl

This fine bazaar was constructed by Karīm Khān as part of a plan to make Shīrāz into a great trading centre. The vaulted brick ceilings ensure that the interior is cool in summer and warm in winter, and it has been described as the finest bazaar in Iran. In the best traditions of Persian bazaars, the Bāzār-é Vakīl is best explored by wandering without concern for time or direction, soaking up the atmosphere in the labyrinthine lanes.

Chances are you'll stumble across **Serai Mushīr**, off the southern end of the main bazaar lane coming from Zand. This tastefully restored two-storey caravanserai is a pleasant place to gather your breath and do a bit of souvenir shopping.

The bazaar has its own Zand-era bathhouse, the **Hamūm-é Vakīl**, dating from Karīm Khān's time, next to the Regent's Mosque. The hammam was undergoing renovation at the time of research and will be one of the best in the country when finished. In the meantime, one of the workmen may let you have a look around for a small tip.

Places to Stay

Shīrāz has plenty of hotels to suit all budgets, and the best place to base yourself is near Zand – but not too near, because it's a very noisy area. Almost without exception, every place is signposted in English.

Places to Stay – Budget

Unlike Esfahān, Shīrāz has few stand-out budget options. The *Esteghlal Hotel* (☎ 27 728, Dehnay St) is very laid-back and friendly. A tidy double with air-con and without/with bathroom costs IR35,000/40,000. Management can arrange tours to Persepolis and, being just off the main road, the rooms are quieter than most. Unfortunately, some readers have complained about the cleanliness (or lack of it) at this hotel.

Zand Hotel (*☎ 22 949, Dehnay St*) nearby is not far behind, charging IR30,000 for an OK double with bathroom. This is a good choice for those with their own vehicles as there is off-street parking. There is a kitchen available for use by guests.

There is a concentration of reasonable (if noisy) cheapies along Pīrūzī St. Of the dozen or more similar places, the **Hashemi Guest House** (*☎ 25 270*) has basic twin rooms for IR25,000; the **Darya Hotel** (*☎ 21 778*) is priced at IR25,000/35,000 for quite good rooms with attached shower (a bit grubby) and shared toilet; while the **Saadi Hotel** (*☎ 25 126*) is arguably the best value with clean two-/three-/four-bed rooms with shower going for IR20,000/40,000/60,000. They don't come much cheaper than the **Arvan Rood Hotel** (*☎ 42 041*), but the rooms (IR14,000/28,000 a single/double) are hard on the nose and it's all a bit creepy – lone women travellers should look elsewhere.

Toos Hotel (*☎ 47 261, Rūdakī St*) is another reasonable cheapie. The location is good, the service indifferent and the basic twin rooms are pretty good value at IR35,000 with a sink and shared bathroom.

Both times we visited the **Pasargad Hotel** (*☎ 44 919, Zand Blvd*), they were cleaning the rooms so we're not sure how far they got; it's on Zand and thus noisy, but the airy doubles with shared bathroom for IR25,000 should be reasonable value.

Several travellers have written to recommend the **Payam Hotel** (*☎ 27 994*) along the quieter 22 Bahman St. It's an eccentric place, but the double rooms with shared bathroom are pretty good at IR40,000. The upper floors have decent views.

At the upper end of the budget range, the **Anvarī Hotel** (*☎ 337 591, Anvarī St*) is deservedly popular. Staff are friendly and the simple, clean rooms with bathroom (some have a balcony) cost 45,000/50,000/60,000 a single/double/triple. If you pay an extra IR5,000, you can sometimes get a room with a fridge and TV. During the quieter months, they seem quite willing to negotiate; this is also a good place to make international phone calls. Travellers with their own transport can leave their vehicles in the car park opposite. There is a kitchen for guests.

Places to Stay – Mid-Range

By far the best in this range is the stylish **Shīrāz Eram Hotel** (*☎ 337 201, fax 335 292,* **e** *shirazeramhotel@payamava.com, Zand Blvd*). The spacious rooms are nicely finished with a huge fridge, sunny bathroom and enormous beds; some rooms have Persian carpets on the floor. At US$25/35/45 a single/double/triple including breakfast, it's very good value and they're happy to negotiate with budget travellers (rials are accepted). There's a 24-hour coffee shop in the lobby. Staff are very friendly and helpful, and can arrange tours to Persepolis and further afield; management may have Internet access up and running by the time you read this.

There are also a couple of decent places along the quieter Rūdakī St. The friendly **Sadra Hotel** (*☎/fax 24 740*) has clean, large rooms with a fridge and lovely bathroom for US$20/30/35 including breakfast. There are some older, musty singles/doubles for US$15/25. You can only pay in dollars.

The rooms with bathroom at the **Roodaki Hotel** (*☎ 29 594, fax 24 521*) are very clean and quiet but a little overpriced at US$20/25 a single/double; we were (mystifyingly) mistaken for Iranians and offered the Iranian price of IR60,000/80,000 which is excellent value if you can get it. Ignore the Visa/MasterCard symbol at reception – neither are accepted.

The **Kowsar Hotel** (*☎ 335 724, fax 333 117*), along the very noisy Zand, also has good, disinfected rooms for US$20/37/37. The restaurant is only open for breakfast.

The same is true at the **Sasan Hotel** (*☎ 337 830, Anvarī St*) where the rooms with bathroom and Western toilet (some rooms) aren't bad for IR120,000/150,000, although unusually for this range, the rooms have a fan only and no air-con.

Finally, one place definitely worth checking out is the pleasant **Ghané Hotel** (*☎ 43 210, fax 49 037, Tōhid St*). Set back from the main road, and quieter than most other places, it offers low-season rooms with bathroom for US$20/25, rising to US$25/33 in high season; you can pay in rials. No English is spoken.

Places to Stay – Top End

The ITTO's *Parsian Hotel* (☎ 308 450, fax 337 512, Rūdakī St) has semi-luxurious doubles for US$53 (plus 19% tax). The rooms have satellite TV, 24-hour room and laundry service and air-con. Secure parking is available, and there are two restaurants and a coffee shop. All very plush and professional.

The expensive and expansive *Park Hotel* (☎ 21 426, fax 21 429), along an alley north of Shohadā Square, is popular with upmarket tour groups and has a nice outdoor garden (with an empty pool). Rooms cost US$45/65 (plus 19% tax), but this is far too high considering the bargains elsewhere in town.

Part of the national chain, the *Homa Hotel* (☎ 28 000, fax 47 123, Meshkin Fām St) charges US$95 a double and is hardly convenient because most restaurants and attractions are not within walking distance.

Places to Eat

Shīrāz is one place where you may want to fork out a few more rials to enjoy some decent meals.

Shīrāzīs take the art of liquid refreshment very seriously, especially tea and fruit juices. Sadly, the world-famous Shiraz (Syrah) grape is no longer made into the wine that inspired Omar Khayyām to poetry – it's frustrating to be in the home of Shiraz wine and not be able to get any.

Fast Food Zand is lined with plenty of cheap *kabābīs* and *hamburger joints*. If you've been travelling in the far south for a while, the Western-style hamburgers in Shīrāz may seem bigger and tastier than what you're used to, although the effect may wear off after you've had one or two. One of the best places is *110 Hamburgers*, handy to the hotels along Anvarī St. You can get a large burger, chips (French fries) and cola for about IR8000. Also good is the *Burger Pizza Fars* on Zand which is popular with young locals. Individual pizzas (IR8000) aren't bad, and a meal of fairly good Western-style burger, side salad and drinks costs IR5500.

Restaurants Shīrāz has some excellent restaurants. The *Restaurant Mīr Mohānna* (☎ 45 590, Horr St) is a great choice north of the river. As befits the distinctly nautical interior, the seafood is a highlight. One reader described the shark kabāb as fantastic and it's certainly worth a try for only IR13,500. The service is attentive if eccentric – twins who dress as indistinguishable sailors.

Another good choice is the *Shater Abbas Restaurant* (☎ 661 573) with its cosy traditional atmosphere, waiters in old Iranian costumes and an open-sided kitchen where they bake their own (delicious) bread. They specialise in kabābs and though the servings could be bigger, the *larry kaba* (a speciality of southern Iran) was tender and beautifully cooked. The menu is in English but the prices are not – a meal of kabāb, māst (yogurt), salad, soft drink and bread adds up to around IR27,000. It can be difficult to find (75m west of Āzādī Blvd on Khakshenasī St, not signposted in English) but if it's all too hard, don't worry as they will even deliver to your hotel.

The upmarket *Soofie Traditional Restaurant* (☎ 661 573, Afīf Ābād St) has an attractive underground setting where you should dress up a little and expect to pay for the privilege. Apart from the usual dishes, they serve some good Persian Gulf fish and shrimps; don't expect much change from IR40,000 and watch for nifty bill fiddling.

If all of these are a bit out of your price range but you want a sit-down meal, *Restaurant Hatam* on Pīrūzī St, underneath the Hashemi Guest House, is a mediocre cheapie.

Hotel Restaurants Best among the hotel restaurants around Rūdakī is the one in the *Sadra Hotel*. The menu is in English and an excellent meal of a three-meat barbecue kabāb, māst, soup, good bread and a drink costs a bargain IR20,000. Service can be a bit indifferent when it's quiet though.

Just as good is the *Sarve Naz Restaurant*, on the 1st floor of the Shīrāz Eram Hotel. The Caucasian kabāb (small tender pieces of marinated meats with onion and capsicum) is not your ordinary kabāb. When you add an extensive buffet salad bar and drinks, all for less than IR30,000, chances are you'll be back. They also do *filet mignon* and shrimps.

Prices at the **Narenjestan Restaurant** in the Parsian Hotel are not as expensive as the room rates would suggest and it has been highly recommended by some readers.

Teahouses The most atmospheric *teahouse* in Shīrāz is the small outdoor one in the grounds of the tomb of Hāfez. You can sit on cushions, in one of the niches in each of its four walls, and drink pots of tea for IR1000, or puff at the qalyan to your heart's content. This is also a good place to try the local Shīrāzī speciality, *falūdeh*, a refreshing vermicelli-type ice cream drowned in either lemon juice or rose-water. A reader also raved about their lunch-time *ābgūsht* for IR6000.

You may stumble across a few other *teahouses* around the Bāzār-é Vakīl, and the ones at the Quran Gateway (Darvazeh-yé Qurān) and the Bāgh-é Afīf Ābād are lovely. There are also several makeshift *tea stalls* along the pavements on or around Zand.

Shopping

Most of the items you can buy in Tehrān and Esfahān are also available in Shīrāz, though not in the same quantity or variety. On the other hand, you are less likely to be over-charged. Good buys in the bazaar include metalwork and printed cottons, especially tablecloths and rugs woven by Fārs nomads. Some travellers have reported that Shīrāz is a good place to buy kilims and *gabbehs* (traditional carpets). For handicrafts, head to Serai Mushir in the Bāzār-é Vakīl, where you'll find some excellent shops (including the Iran Handicrafts Organisation and a good bookshop nearby). Along the streets off Zand, there are plenty of places to stock up on dates and pistachios.

Getting There & Away

Air Shīrāz is a great place to start or finish your trip to Iran. Gulf Air (☎ 335 030) has a weekly flight to Paris (via Bahrain) for US$350/550 one way/return.

Iran Air and Gulf Air each fly between Shīrāz and Dubai (US$109) four times a week, with Gulf Air flying via Bahrain. Iran Air also flies regularly to Doha (Qatar) and Bahrain for a similar price.

The airport has a handy flight information number (☎ 720 6543). The busy Iran Air office (☎ 33 001) is on the corner of Zand and Faqīhī St. Iran Air flies from Shīrāz to the following destinations within Iran:

destination	weekly flights	cost (IR)
Ahvāz	1	99,000
Bandar-é Abbās	4	105,500
Bandar-é Langeh	4	96,000
Būshehr	1	92,000
Esfahān	7	92,000
Mashhad	6	191,000
Tehrān	several daily	141,000

Iran Asseman (☎ 337 534) has three weekly flights to Tehrān (IR141,000) and daily flights to Kīsh (IR92,000), as well as twice weekly flights to Lāmard (IR92,000) and Lār (IR92,000) both of which are in Fārs Province.

Bus & Minibus The main bus terminal is the Carandish bus terminal (☎ 41 654), also known as the Termīnāl-é Bozorg, which handles all long distance destinations. Buses and the occasional minibus leave regularly for the following destinations:

destination	distance (km)	duration (hrs)	cost (IR)
Ābādān	615	10	16,000
Ahvāz	568	10	14,000
Bandar-é Abbās	601	10	15,000
Bandar-é Langeh	654	12	15,500
Būshehr	317	5	6,000
Esfahān	473	8	11,000
Hamadān	918	15	21,000
Kermān	545	8	13,500
Kermānshāh	1077	18	24,500
Tabrīz	1519	24	32,000
Tehrān	895	16	20,500
Yazd	438	7	10,000
Zāhedān	1088	17	28,000

Some of the bus companies have offices along, or just off, Zand, which is handy for booking tickets in advance.

CENTRAL IRAN

Buses to towns closer to Shīrāz leave from the Amīr Kabīr Terminal in the southern outskirts. Buses for Kāzerūn (IR4,000) depart regularly throughout the day. There are also buses to Būshehr (IR6,000), but it's easier to catch them from the more central Carandish terminal.

Shared Taxi Shared taxis for regional towns such as Kāzerūn, Fīrūz Ābād and Marvdasht (for Persepolis) go from Carandish on a semiregular basis (see the relevant sections later in the chapter for more details).

Getting Around

To/From the Airport
A ticket for the airport bus service costs IR3000 from the office in the arrivals lounge. The local bus No 10 also leaves from the airport and will drop you off behind the Arg. A private taxi between the airport and the city centre should cost about IR10,000, a shared taxi from Valiasr Square around IR1500.

Bus & Minibus Shared taxis are generally more useful in Shīrāz although one very handy bus is the No 2 (with Roman numerals, and sometimes marked 'Sa'adi' in English). It leaves from outside the Burger Pizza Fars and passes the tourist office, the corner of Golestān and Salmān-Farsi Blvds (from where you can walk to the Carandish bus terminal), Hāfez's tomb and finishes outside Sa'dī's tomb. Bus tickets cost IR100 for a short trip, IR200 for the longest trip around the city. Buy your tickets from the booths along Zand.

Taxi You can take a shared taxi around the city for IR500 to IR1000. They travel along the main streets, but you may need to take more than one. Chartering a taxi around the city will cost from IR2000 to IR5000 depending on the distance. However, watch out for the occasional 'tourist price' charged by taxi drivers; where possible, just pay what the locals pay. The Park Taxi Service (☎ 41 765) opposite the Park Hotel is expensive but has been recommended by several travellers.

FROM SHĪRĀZ TO KERMĀN

If you have your own transport (or a bike) and are heading towards Kermān or even Bandar-é Abbās, it's worth noting that the route south round Lake Bakhtegān (periodically home to thousands of flamingos, but made dry during the drought of 2000) from Kherāmeh to Neyriz is said to be very beautiful. Roughly 70km of it is still unsealed and quite mountainous as it passes through the southern reaches of the Zagros Mountains.

PERSEPOLIS   تخت جمشید

A visit to the ruins of the ancient city of Persepolis (Takht-é Jamshīd) will almost certainly be one of the highlights of any trip to Iran. See the Persepolis special section at the end of this chapter for details. Persepolis is the best preserved of Persia's ruined cities and the finest legacy of the great Achaemenid Empire which ruled Persia between 559 and 330 BC. The most impressive features of the ruins are the splendid bas-reliefs which adorn many of the staircases and palaces on the site and provide a rich treasure house of ancient history. See the Persepolis special section for more information.

Entry costs IR50,000 and this is one place where a student card *won't* get you a discount. The site is open from 7.30 am to 7.30 pm. Some people have been disappointed by the metal roof raised over the finest carvings to protect them, because this can throw shadows over the bas-reliefs and make them hard to photograph.

Places to Stay & Eat
Apart from the stall next to the museum, the only place to eat is the ***Takhté Tawood Restaurant***, about 1.5 km west of Persepolis on the road to Pasargadae, next to the petrol station. However, it caters to package tour groups and is a little expensive – you'd be better off bringing a picnic lunch. There is nowhere to stay at Persepolis so you'll need to take a day trip from Shīrāz.

Getting There & Away
Bus & Shared Taxi It is possible to reach Persepolis by public transport, at least in part. Take a minibus from the south side of

the Carandish bus terminal in Shīrāz to Marvdasht (IR3000, 42km, every hour or so). From outside the small bus park in Marvdasht, you might find a shared taxi heading for Persepolis but chances are you'll have to take a private taxi for the remaining 12 or so kilometres. Expect to pay around IR8000. Returning from the site, there are always plenty of vehicles lurking outside the entrance – either hitch a ride or take a taxi back to Marvdasht.

Alternatively, you could catch any bus from Shīrāz heading towards Esfahān and the north and ask to be let out at the turn-off to Persepolis. The walk from the second turn-off (both are signed in English) is shorter (about 2km). On the way back, walk to the main Shīrāz-Esfahān road and hail any passing bus heading all the way to Shīrāz.

Private Taxi The easiest way to get to Persepolis is to charter a taxi from Shīrāz which will also allow you to visit the other sites of Naqsh-é Rostam and even Pasargadae (see these sections later in this chapter) in one day. Just about everyone in Shīrāz has a friend just dying to take you to Persepolis; the advantage is that it should be a buyer's market when it comes to negotiating a price. However, one reader who arranged to hire a taxi was unimpressed with the service to Persepolis:

> There appears to be a rather annoying habit of ripping people off on taxi fares to Persepolis. ...two teenage boys asked if we were going to Persepolis the next day – their uncle had a taxi. We said we wanted to go to Persepolis, Naqsh-é Rostam and Pasargadae. They told us their uncle would take us for IR60,000 the next day...After visiting Persepolis they came out with the favourite line – Pasargadae is closed. We said we wanted to go and were told that we had to pay IR100,000...They came down to IR80,000 but we were fed up and ended up going to Persepolis and Naqsh-é Rostam and back to Shīrāz for IR40,000. This was a particularly annoying scam as they claimed they had not agreed to Pasargadae...In all my travels I have never agreed a price and then had the driver go back on it.
>
> **Emily Peckham**

Some travel agencies also run tours. One of the best is offered by Pars Tourist Agency (☎/fax 071-23 163, ✉ masoudn@ farsnet .net) in Shīrāz. All the drivers from this agency speak English, and the agency can arrange guides in German, French, Italian and Dutch.

Expect to pay IR100,000 for half a day taking in Persepolis and Naqsh-é Rostam, and IR180,000 for a full day trip including Pasargadae. Guides cost an extra IR60,000, which is worth while if you want to fully appreciate the ruins.

The drivers organised by the Shīrāz Eram Hotel (☎ 337 201, fax 335 292), on Zand Blvd in Shīrāz, are also reliable, and charge around IR150,000 for a full-day trip, or IR80,000 to IR100,000 for half a day. Of course, any private taxi owner will gladly make the trip and you may be able to bargain them down to less if they're having a quiet day, although you probably won't get it for much under IR80,000.

NAQSH-É ROSTAM & NAQSH-É RAJAB
نقش رستم
نقش رجب

The sites of Naqsh-é Rostam and Naqsh-é Rajab are definitely worth visiting as part of a trip to Persepolis. The rock tombs of Naqsh-é Rostam are magnificent. Hewn out of a cliff high above the ground, the four tombs of Naqsh-é Rostam are believed to be those of Darius I, Ataxerxes I, Xerxes I and Darius II (from left to right as you look at the cliff) although historians are still debating this. The tombs of the later Ataxerxes above Persepolis were modelled on those at Naqsh-é Rostam. The openings in the massive cross-shaped tombs lead to the funerary chambers, where bones were stored after the vultures had picked them clean, but you can't go inside them any more. The reliefs above the openings are similar to those at Persepolis, with the kings standing at Zoroastrian fire altars supported by figures representing the subject nations below.

The eight Sassanian **stone reliefs** cut into the cliff beneath the facades of the Achaemenid tombs depict scenes of imperial conquests and royal ceremonies. These include the investiture of Ardeshīr I (on the far left of the cliff), and a relief portraying Bahman II carved over the top of an Elamite carving dating from over a thousand years before (around the 8th century BC), of which only the figures on either end remain. It is believed that most of the reliefs were created to celebrate the victory of the Sassanian king, Shāpūr, over the Roman invader, Valerian, in the 3rd century. At one time it was thought that the pictures might represent stories of Rustam from the *Shāh-namah*, hence the name of the site.

Facing the cliff is what is believed to be an Achaemenid **fire temple**, the Kābā Zartosht, although the walls are marked with inscriptions cataloguing Sassanian victories.

Entry to the site costs IR15,000 and it's open from 8 am to 6 pm, sometimes later in summer.

The tombs of Naqsh-é Rajab are directly opposite the turn-off to Naqsh-é Rostam on the Shīrāz-Esfahān road and are worth a quick look on your way between Persepolis and Naqsh-é Rostam. These four fine Sassanian bas-reliefs are hidden from the road by the folds of the cliff face and depict various scenes from the reigns of Ardeshīr I and Shāpūr the Great. A man called Rajab once had a teahouse here, hence the name of the site.

Getting There & Away Both Naqsh-é Rostam and Naqsh-é Rajab can be easily combined with a trip to Persepolis (see the Persepolis special section at the end of this chapter for details). If you don't have a vehicle, you can easily walk the 6km from Persepolis to Naqsh-é Rostam, stopping at Naqsh-é Rajab en route. The latter is about 2km from Persepolis on the main highway. From here, follow the turn-off to Naqsh-é Rostam (signposted in English) for another 4km. If you're planning on doing this trip in summer, take plenty of water.

PASARGADAE   پاسارگاد

Begun under Cyrus (Kouroush) the Great in about 546 BC, the city of Pasargadae was quickly superseded by Darius I's magnificent palace at Persepolis. Some travellers have questioned whether Pasargadae is worth the effort of getting there, and the site is certainly not as well preserved as Persepolis, however these ruins are beautiful in a lonely kind of way. Hard though it is to believe it now, this hot, deserted plain was once surrounded by forest.

The first structure you'll come across is the six-tiered **Tomb of Cyrus**. Standing proudly on the windswept plain, this impressive stone cenotaph was originally much taller than it is now and is still the best preserved of the Pasargadae ruins. Legend has it that when Alexander the Great arrived at Pasargadae, he was greatly distressed by the destruction of the tomb and ordered its restoration.

Within walking distance of the tomb (though perhaps not in summer) to the north and north-east are the insubstantial remains of three **Achaemenid Palaces** – the Entrance Palace, the Audience Palace and Cyrus' Private Palace; the ruins of a tomb on a plinth, known as the **Prison of Solomon** (Zendān-é Soleimān); a large stone platform on a hill known as the **Throne of the Mother of Solomon** (Takht-é Mādar-é Soleimān; the views from the top over the surrounding countryside are superb); and two **stone plinths** which originally formed part of a pair of altars within a sacred precinct. Some local historians believe that the references to Solomon date from the Arab conquest, when the inhabitants of Pasargadae renamed the sites with Islamic names to prevent their destruction. In **Cyrus' Private Palace**, there is a cuneiform inscription which reads: 'I am Cyrus, the Achaemenid King'.

Pasargadae is open from about 7.30 am to 8 pm daily, although it often closes earlier in winter. It's better not to arrive later than about 3 pm if you are relying on public transport. Entrance costs IR15,000. By far the easiest way to get there is to charter a taxi from Shīrāz, where just about everyone knows someone with a car. Both the Pars Tourist & Travel Agency (see Travel Agencies in the Shīrāz section) and the drivers at the Shīrāz Eram Hotel (see Places to Stay in the Shīrāz section earlier) are highly recommended.

If travelling by public transport, you can take a bus (IR7000) from the Carandish bus terminal in Shīrāz to Sā'adatshahr (also known as Sā'adat Ābād), but from there you'll have to take a taxi or a very occasional minibus the remaining 30km or so. Even better, jump on any bus heading towards Yazd or Esfahān (you may have to pay full fare) and get out at the turn-off to Pasargadae which is signposted in English. From there, it's an 8km walk or hitch with any vehicle heading down the road.

FĪRŪZ ĀBĀD   فیروز آباد
☎ 07242

Two places often missed by those in a rush to get to Persepolis are the remains of the old cities of Fīrūz and Gūr, dating from the Sassanian period. If you are there around April or May, you will see plenty of nomads crossing the Zāgros Mountains.

About 6km before Fīrūz, along the road from Shīrāz, you'll see a chairlift, with cables stretching across the road, leading to the **Qal'eh-é Doktar** or Maiden's Palace. This is a three-storey fort with a courtyard, probably built by Ardeshir I. Sadly, the chairlift doesn't work, so you'll have to scramble up the rocky hill to see the remains of the palace. The views from the top are worth the effort. There are several **Sassanian bas-reliefs** in the area, not all of them easy to find.

About 4km further on, towards Fīrūz, an unsigned rocky trail leads to the best of the ruins of ancient Fīrūz: What was thought to be a fire temple, but is probably the ruins of Ardeshir's **palace** with the remains of a small fire temple beside it. Architecture buffs will be interested in what are thought to be the earliest examples of the squinch (what the dome rests on) and iwan.

In a taxi you'll have to take a lengthy 20km detour to avoid the Tang-Ab River. Alternatively, stride across the river, then walk about 800m along the rocky trail.

Places to Stay & Eat
The only place to stay in Fīrūz is the ITTO's *Jahāngardī Inn* (☎ 2105), where a single/double costs US$25/35. It's better to take a day trip from Shīrāz.

There are plenty of *hamburger joints* and *kabābīs* in town, but taking food and drink

from Shīrāz, and having a picnic by the tiny lake at the fire temple, is a great idea. Fīrūz is famous for the quality of its dūgh, a sour milk drink.

Getting There & Away
There is at least one bus every day from Shīrāz to Fīrūz (ask to get off where the broken chairlift crosses the road), but make sure you find out when it returns, otherwise you may be forced to stay the night in the expensive Jahāngardī Inn. Shared taxis do run back to Shīrāz but space in them is at a premium. To see most of the remains of both ancient cities, it's best to charter a taxi, which you can do either from Shīrāz or Fīrūz.

KĀZERŪN &   کازرون
SHĀPŪR   شاپور
Just off the main road between Shīrāz and Būshehr are the small but fascinating ruins of another two ancient cities: Kāzerūn and, about 25km to the west, Shāpūr. At Kāzerūn (the name comes from an ancient word meaning 'people who wash cotton clothes'), there are some mildly interesting **bas-reliefs** from the Sassanian period, though they are most interesting to archaeologists for their unique inscriptions.

Shāpūr is the larger and more interesting city to the casual visitor. The remains of this Sassanian city include the **Palace of Shāpūr** and a nearby **fire temple**. The Tand-é Chogan (or Shāpūr Cave) contains the mighty **Statue of Shāpūr I**, which stands 7m high, although you'll probably need a vehicle to reach it.

Along both sides of the river there are some excellent **bas-reliefs** which commemorate, among other historical moments, the victory of Shāpūr citizens over Roman invaders; it's a great spot for a picnic. Entrance to the site costs IR15,000.

The trip to this part of Fārs Province is pretty and worth dedicating a day to. Chartering a taxi is the easiest but most expensive way (at least IR120,000 from Shīrāz), but with an early start, it can be done by public transport.

Take the bus to Kāzerūn from the Amīr Kabīr terminal in Shīrāz (1½ hours, IR4,000) or from Būshehr. Keep an eye out en route for the 15-arch **Karīm Khan Bridge**, an ancient bridge built in the Zand period; it's about 40km west of Shīrāz. After the bus turns off the Shīrāz-Būshehr road, it's about 7km to the ruins, which are on the right-hand side of the road.

PERSEPOLIS (TAKHT-É JAMSHĪD)

The first capital of the Achaemenid Empire was at Pasargadae, further north, but in about 512 BC Darius I (the Great) started constructing this massive and magnificent palace complex to serve as the summer capital. Some historians believe that the site was chosen by Cambyses II, son of Cyrus the Great. It was completed by a host of subsequent kings, including Xerxes I and II, and Artaxerxes I, II and III, over a period of 150 years.

The ruins you see today are a mere shadow of Persepolis' former glory, even though they are much more revealing than the less well-preserved traces of the Achaemenid administrative capital capital at Shūsh or further north at Pasargadae. Incredibly, the ancient city was

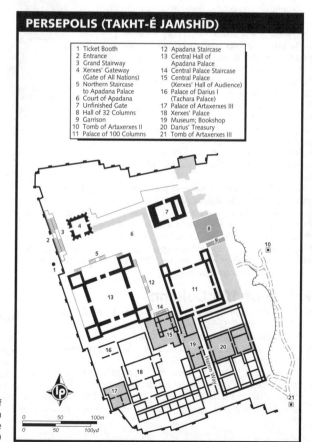

PERSEPOLIS (TAKHT-É JAMSHĪD)

1 Ticket Booth
2 Entrance
3 Grand Stairway
4 Xerxes' Gateway (Gate of All Nations)
5 Northern Staircase to Apadana Palace
6 Court of Apadana
7 Unfinished Gate
8 Hall of 32 Columns
9 Garrison
10 Tomb of Artaxerxes II
11 Palace of 100 Columns
12 Apadana Staircase
13 Central Hall of Apadana Palace
14 Central Palace Staircase
15 Central Palace (Xerxes' Hall of Audience)
16 Palace of Darius I (Tachara Palace)
17 Palace of Artaxerxes III
18 Xerxes' Palace
19 Museum; Bookshop
20 Darius' Treasury
21 Tomb of Artaxerxes III

Inset: Bas-relief of one of the tributary nations on the Apadana Staircase (photo by Patrick Syder)

lost to time for centuries, totally covered by dust and sand, before extensive excavations, began in the 1930s, revealed the glories of the city once more.

Entering the City

From the outside, much of the city is obscured by its high walls. Entrance to the site is, as it was during the days of Achaemenid Persia, via the monumental Grand Stairway, carved from massive blocks of stone but with shallow steps so Persians in long elegant robes could walk gracefully up into the palace.

Whenever important foreign delegations arrived, their presence was heralded by trumpeters at the top of the staircase (amazingly, fragments of these bronze trumpets are on display in the museum). Acolytes then led the dignitaries through Xerxes' Palace, also known as the Gate of All Nations, still a wonderfully impressive monument today. They wouldn't have seen the modern graffiti that scars some of the stone panels, although some of these scrawls have become footnotes of history themselves, with many left by British soldiers posted here in the 19th and 20th centuries; note in particular the mark left in 1889 by one Lieutenant-Colonel J Meade, Her Britannic Majesty's Consul General.

The gateway was built during the time of Xerxes I and is guarded by bull-like figures, which are strongly reminiscent of the statues of Assyria. Above these look for a cuneiform inscription in the Persian, Babylonian and Elamite languages. It delares, among other things, that 'I am Xerxes, Great King, King of Kings, King of lands, King of many races…son of Darius the King, the Achaemenid…Many other beautiful things were constructed in Persia. I constructed them and my father constructed them'.

Palace of 100 Columns

Visitors from nations of lesser importance were then sometimes led to the Palace of 100 Columns where the king would receive them. As you follow in their footsteps through the Court of Apadana, look for the Unfinished Gate, the Hall of 32 Columns and the impressive double-headed eagles or griffins.

The Palace of 100 Columns was the largest of the palaces at Persepolis; here delegates from subject nations came to restate their loyalty and pay tribute in a ritual reassertion of the power of the Achaemenid Empire. Light was provided by lamps placed in alcoves around the walls.

KELLI HAMBLET

Left: Artist's impression of a double bull capital from the Palace of 100 Columns. Mythical creatures, such as dragons and unicorns, were also intricately carved to adorn the columns of the main hall.

PATRICK SYDER

Top: The view over the ruins of Persepolis from the Tomb of Artaxerxes II is superb. Work on the city was begun in 518 BC by Darius I, king of the Achaemenids. In 330 BC it was burned to the ground during a visit by Alexander the Great. While it's easy to imagine Alexander wreaking havoc in retaliation for the Persian sacking of Athens, the burning of the city may have simply been an accident.

PHIL WEYMOUTH

MARTIN MOOS

Middle Left & Right: Persepolis' bas-reliefs are its great attraction. While they are exceptional works of art in their own right, they also provide insight into the city's social and political history.

Bottom Left: On this bas-relief Xerxes I is depicted with a retainer. Elsewhere on the site, inscriptions declare the monarch 'Xerxes, Great King, King of Kings, King of lands, King of many races'.

Bottom Right: One of several griffin-headed beasts that stand guard over the ruins.

MARTIN MOOS

PATRICK SYDER

BETHUNE CARMICHAEL

BETHUNE CARMICHAEL

BETHUNE CARMICHAEL

MARTIN MOOS

Top: A lion attacking a bull, as depicted on the Apadana Stairway. The bull was an object of worship during the New Year Festival, for which Persepolis was specifically built.

Middle Left: The eastern section of the Apadana Stairway depicts dignitaries of the realm paying tribute.

Middle Right: The northern section of the Apadana Stairway portrays members of the imperial guard carrying lances and wearing twisted headbands, loose-fitting robes and laced boots.

Bottom: Tourists are dwarfed by the rock-cut Tomb of Artaxerxes II on the hill above Persepolis.

Apadana Palace & Staircase

Important Persian and Median notables were more likely to be ushered to the Apadana Palace to the south. Constructed on a terrace of stone by Xerxes I, the palace was reached via another staircase. Although it can be difficult to picture the grandeur of the palace from what remains, the bas-reliefs along the northern wall evocatively depict the scenes of splendour that must have accompanied the arrival of delegations to meet with the king.

Most impressive of all, however, and among the most impressive historical sights in all of Iran, are the bas-reliefs along the **Apadana Staircase** of the eastern wall, which can also be reached from the Palace of 100 Columns. The northern panels recount the reception of the Persians in their long robes and the Medes in their shorter ones, and the three tiers of figures are amazingly well preserved. Each tier contains representations of the Imperial Guard or the Immortals. On the upper tier, they are followed by the royal procession, the royal valets and the horses of the Elamite king of chariots, while on the lower two tiers they precede the Persians with their feather headdresses and the Medes in their round caps. The stairs themselves are guarded by Persian soldiers.

The central panel of the staircase is dedicated to symbols of the Zoroastrian deity Ahura Mazda. God is symbolised by a ring with wings, flanked by two eagles with human heads and guarded by four Persian and Median soldiers; the Persians are the ones carrying the indented shields. An inscription announces to the world that the palace was started by Darius and completed by Xerxes and implores God to protect it from 'famine, lies and earthquakes'.

The panels at the southern end are for many visitors the most interesting, showing 23 delegations bringing their tributes to the Achaemenid king. This rich record of the nations of the time ranges from the Ethiopians in the bottom left corner, through a climbing pantheon of, among various other peoples, Arabs, Thracians, Indians, Parthians and Cappadocians, up to the Elamites and Medians at the top right. Of all the panels, those on the staircase's southern face most strongly evoke the great power of the Achaemenid Empire.

Inset: Bas-relief of a Persian guard with a fluted helmet and well-manicured beard. (Illustration by Trudi Canavan)

Right: Vassals presenting gifts to honour the ancient rulers of Persia

TAMSIN WILSON

Persepolis Reconstructed

In its heyday the city spread over an area of 125,000 sq metres and was the place where all the peoples of the empire came to pay homage to the kings over Nō Rūz (New Year); at other times of year it was probably deserted. For a city that stood at the heart of such a great empire, Persepolis was rarely mentioned in foreign records, fuelling speculation among some archaeologists that the existence of the

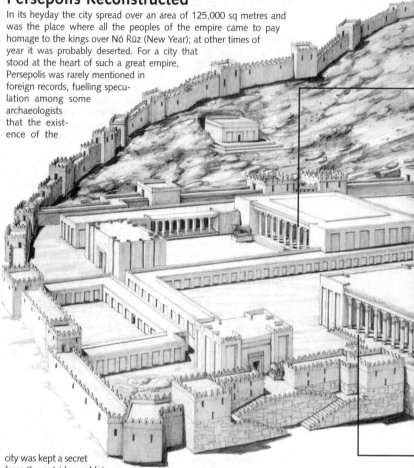

city was kept a secret from the outside world; in the records that remain, attention focused on the other Achaemenid cities at Shūsh and Baghdad.

Persepolis stands on the slopes of Mt Rahmat and was surrounded by an 18m-high wall. Its original name was Parsa; the first known reference to it by its Greek name of Persepolis – meaning both City of Parsa (City of Persia) and Destroyer of Cities – came after its sacking by Alexander the Great's army.

Persepolis was burned to the ground during Alexander's visit in 330 BC, although historians disagree about whether this was accidental or in retaliation for the destruction of Athens by Xerxes 150 years earlier.

The Palace of 100 Columns

ILLUSTRATIONS BY KELLI HAMBLET

The Apadana Staircase

Royal Palaces

The south-west corner of the site is dominated by the palaces attributed to each of the kings. The Palace of Darius I (known sometimes as the Tachara or Winter Palace) is probably the most striking, with its impressive gateways and bas-reliefs and cuneiform inscriptions around the perimeter. The palace opens onto a royal courtyard, which is also flanked by the unfinished Palace of Artaxerxes III and Xerxes' Palace.

BETHUNE CARMICHAEL

Left: Members of the imperial guard, wearing loose-fitting robes and twisted headbands, parade across the eastern portico of the Apadana Staircase.

Central Palace

This palace is also referred to as Xerxes' Hall of Audience or the Triplyon, and stands at the heart of Persepolis. Its location enabled the king to receive his notables in an area shielded from outside view and it was here that many important political decisions were taken. On the columns of the eastern doorway are reliefs showing Darius on his throne, borne by the representatives of 28 countries; the crown prince Xerxes stands behind his father.

Museum

Immediately to the east of the Central Palace lies the museum. Despite the depictions around the door of the king defeating evil, the original purpose of this structure is not known. The museum contains a stone foundation tablet and a range of artifacts discovered during excavations: alabaster vessels, cedar wood, lances and arrow tips. Look also for the small representation of a Sassanian king on a horse. Entry to the museum is included in the IR50,000 fee that you pay to enter the site. Note that the museum sometimes closes for an hour at lunch time. There is a great bookshop just to the right of the entrance and a stall selling some drinks.

Treasury & Tombs

The south-east corner of the site is dominated by Darius' Treasury, where archaeologists found stone tablets in Elamite and Akkadian detailing the wages paid to the unsung (and underpaid) labourers who built Persepolis. Little more than a few bas-reliefs and some of the foundations of the hundreds of columns strewn around the site remain. On the hill above the Treasury are the rock-hewn tombs of Artaxerxes II and Artaxerxes III, each with Zoroastrian carvings. The view from the tombs over Persepolis and the plain that extends to the west is quite beautiful.

Sound & Light Show

Inset: The image of a lion devouring a bull appears numerous times at Persepolis. (Illustration by Tamsin Wilson)

A sound and light show takes place intermittently at around 8.30 pm on Thursday and Friday. It can go on for hours but is only in Farsi and you're unlikely to be able to convince the gatekeeper that you deserve not to pay another IR30,000 to get back in. That said, if the grandeur of Persepolis has gripped you, it can be a great way to get another perspective on this most spectacular of sites, even if you don't stay right to the end. Before setting out from Shīrāz, ask your hotel if the show will be running, or, if you're in the vicinity, check with the gatekeeper.

Eastern Iran

ایران شرقی

Eastern Iran is frontier territory, dominated by the deserts that spread from the fringes of Tehrān to the border with Afghanistan. In the north-east, the sparsely populated Khorāsān province (a name which means 'Where the Sun Rises') covers one-fifth of Iranian territory, spanning the steppes of Central Asia with its echoes of the Silk Road and the immense salt wastes of the Dasht-é Kavīr. Mashhad, one of the holiest sites for Shiite Muslims, is a city of pilgrims steeped in historical and spiritual significance.

The south-east is more starkly beautiful, with Kermān and Māhān offering respite from the trackless wastes of the Dasht-é Lūt. Zāhedān is a town with a distinctively frontier character, determined by its proximity to the remote, inhospitable and sometimes lawless borders of Afghanistan and Pakistan. Here, in Sistān vā Balūchestān province, is an Iran you'll find nowhere else, with nomads sharing the desert with smugglers. In the middle of it all, is the breathtaking ancient city of Bam. Undoubtedly a highlight of any visit to Iran, the Arg-é Bam and the attractive modern town that surrounds it are definitely worth the long desert journey needed to reach them.

In many ways, the eastern part of the country is Iran in microcosm – dotted with the architectural landmarks of a rich historical, cultural and religious heritage, and populated by a friendly people well versed in the traditions of hospitality.

Highlights

- Rambling through the ancient city of Bam
- Strolling in the gardens at Māhān
- Downing a *chāy* (tea) at the Chāykhāneh-yé Vakīl in Kermān
- Observing the passion of the pilgrims at the Holy Shrine in Mashhad
- Lounging in the traditional restaurants of Torqabeh.

KERMĀN

کرمان

☎ 0341 • pop 340,000 • elevation 1755m

The desert city of Kermān is sheltered from the vast Dasht-é Lūt by the barren Pāyeh Mountains and is a pleasant place to visit, even in summer. Although an increasing number of travellers are using the city as a base for visiting Bam, Kermān is a worthy destination in its own right and you could easily spend a couple of days seeing the numerous sights in and around the town.

The town has a Zoroastrian minority population, though much smaller than Yazd's.

Kermānīs have a distinct accent, which is often hard to understand even if you've managed to pick up a bit of Farsi.

Modern Kermān is a centre for coal, copper and iron mining.

History

Kermān has had a long and turbulent history and has only enjoyed short spells of simultaneous peace and prosperity. Believed to have been founded in the early 3rd century AD by Ardeshīr I, founder of the Sassanian dynasty, from the 7th century it was ruled in turn by the Arabs, Buyids, Seljuks, Turkmen and Mongols, and then until the Qajar dynasty by a further succession of invaders and regional despots. Kermān obtained security

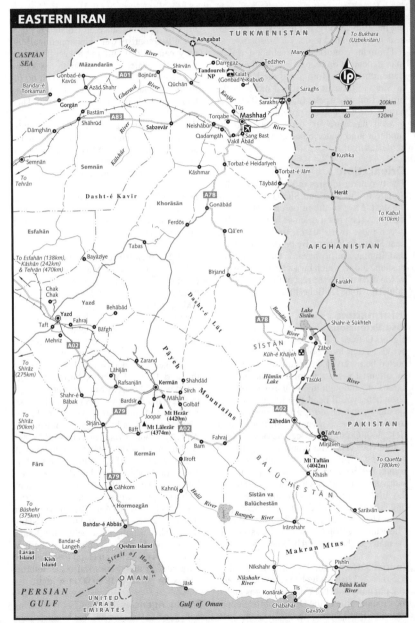

EASTERN IRAN

EASTERN IRAN

under the central government in Tehrān during the 19th century, but its relative remoteness has continued to deny it prosperity.

For many centuries the livelihood of Kermān depended on its place along the Asian trade routes, but from about the beginning of Safavid times it has relied more on the production of carpets. In view of its barren nature, the city and the province to which it gives its name are very dependent on *qanāts* (underground water channels), built many centuries ago.

Orientation

The two main squares in Kermān are Āzādī Square to the west and Shohadā Square to the east. Most of the important offices and things to see are on or close to the road between these two squares, or in the bazaar near Shohadā Square. Be on the lookout for that Iranian traffic hazard, the contraflow bus lane along which buses hurtle in the *opposite* direction to the rest of the traffic, particularly along Dr Beheshtī St.

Information

Visa Extensions The Management of Foreigners Office (☎ 268 293) is a good place to get visa extensions. Some travellers have reported being given an additional one month for a tourist visa, even for a second or third extension, although this is unusual. As with elsewhere, you'll need two photos (women should wear a chador), a photocopy of the relevant pages of your passport and IR12,500. Go to the office one or two days before your visa expires and if you get there when the office opens at 8 am, you can sometimes pick up your visa at 11 am the same day. The office closes at 1 pm and all day Friday. If you have any difficulties getting your visa extended and you're staying at the Akhavan Hotel (see Places to Stay – Mid-Range & Top End later in this section), the manager there should be able to help you.

Tourist Offices The tourist office (☎ 210 635, fax 212 013), which is open from 8 am to 2 pm daily except Friday, also goes under the ominous title of the Office for the Supervision of Foreigners. The staff take this title

seriously and, though polite, have become a little overbearing since an isolated incident when two tourists were kidnapped in 1999; they can be difficult to shake off. Inconveniently located in the far south-east of the city, the office can provide you with no information that you can't get elsewhere and there's little reason to track it down. Then again, if you can prise out of them some of their outstanding glossy brochures – good enough to take home as souvenirs – about the attractions in Kermān province, it might just be worth the trip. There are plans to move the office closer to the centre of town.

Money The central branch of Bank Melli on Adālat St, close to the post office, will change money. Some hotels can also help out if the bank isn't open.

Post & Communications The main post office is next to Bank Melli; the main telephone office is a little further north, between Adālat and Mo'allem Sts. The Akhavan Hotel is also useful for arranging international faxes and telephone calls.

At the time of research there were two offices set up for public Internet access and doubtless more will spring up. 'Internet' (info@kermoon.net, ☎/fax 237 023) is on the 2nd floor of a brick building, about 200m north of Qareny Square; there is a sign in English high above street level. It is open 8.30 am to 9 pm most days except Friday when they close a little earlier if business is slow. One hour of surfing costs IR25,000. At Internet Coffee (cyber@karmania.net, ☎ 23 900), the staff claim to have a satellite connection, which may be why you pay a little more (IR30,000). Although it was on Valiasr Square when we visited, the office was soon to move to Āzādī Square (between Bahmanyār St and Jomhūrī-yé Eslāmī Blvd). They usually close between 1.30 and 4 pm although this may change at the new premises. The Akhavan Hotel (see Places to Stay later in this section) also has Internet access for guests at IR30,000 per hour.

Travel Agencies Kermān is overflowing with good travel agencies that handle airline

EASTERN IRAN

KERMĀN

PLACES TO STAY
5 Amin Hotel
20 Mosāferkhūneh-yé Āzādī
21 Valiasr Hotel
25 Omid Inn
42 Akhavan Hotel;
   Guest House Milad
43 Naz Hotel
44 Guest House Saady
45 Kermān Hotel

PLACES TO EAT
4 Marmar Restaurant
12 Chāykhāneh-yé Vakīl
13 Chāykhāneh-yé Sardār
41 Chāykhāneh-yé Khayyam

OTHER
1 Iran Air Office
2 Kermān National Library
3 Moayedī Ice House
6 Mosque Pā Manār
7 Moshtarī-yé Moshtāq
   Alī Shāh
8 Jāmeh Mosque
9 Minibuses to Sīrch
   & Shahdād
10 Emām Khomeinī Mosque;
   Shared Taxis to Bus Station
11 Hamūm-é Ganjalī Khan
14 Hamām Ebrahīm Khan
15 Vatan Caravan Tours
   and Travel Agency

16 Management of
   Foreigners Office
   (Visa Extensions)
17 Bank Melli
   (Central Branch)
18 Shared Taxis to Joopar
19 Shared Taxis to Māhān
22 Main Post Office
23 Main Telephone Office
24 Police Headquarters
26 Internet
27 Bāhonnar Hospital
28 Sanati Museum Kermān;
   Khan-é Sayyah Kermān
   Restaurant
29 Kermān Gasht Travel Agency

30 Cinema Mahtab
31 Kermān Dāmān Hospital
32 Raya Travel Agency
33 Kermān Zamīn Travel
   Agency and Tour Services
34 Kermān Balan Tour and
   Travelling Agency
35 Māhān Air Office
36 Iran Handicrafts Organization
37 Shared Taxis to Bāzār-é
   Vakīl and Shohadā Square
38 Kermān Tours; Internet Coffee
39 Shared Taxis to Sīrjān,
   Rafsanjān & Train Station
40 Shared Taxis to Bus Terminal
46 Bus/Minibus Terminal

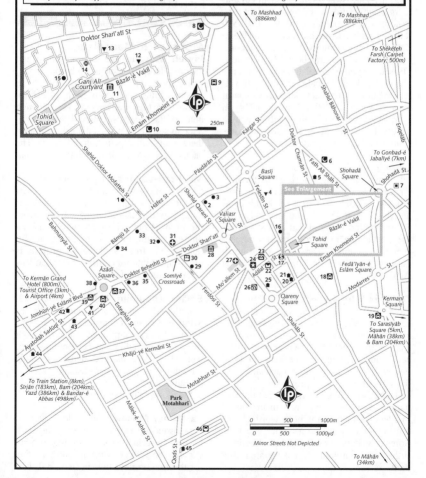

bookings. The more efficient ones include Raya Travel Agency (☎ 54 527) on Ferdōsī St; Kermān Zamīn Travel Agency & Tour Services (☎ 48 334), Bāmjū St; Kermān Balan Tour & Travelling Agency (☎ 41 192, fax 41 194), Bāmjū St; and Kermān Tours (☎ 50 465, fax 51 299) on Bahmanyār St.

For tours around Kermān and elsewhere in the province, it's hard to beat Vatan Caravan Tours and Travel Agency (☎/fax 226 793) on Ganj Alī St. Hossein Vatanī is a delightful one-man show who offers excellent cultural tours around Kermān and his overnight trips to nomad encampments in the desert (US$20 if there is only one person, reduced to US$10 if there are more than five) have been recommended by several travellers. There are also plans to organise camel treks from nearby Shahdād to Bam. Female (and male) travellers might want to check out Kermān Gasht Travel Agency (☎ 260 217, fax 260 214) on Ferdōsī St, where Elham Vakilī (elhamva hid@yahoo.com) offers Kermān city tours from a woman's perspective.

Emergency For general emergencies, dial telephone directories (☎ 118) or medical emergencies (☎ 115). Kermān Dāman Hospital (☎ 220 015) on Ferdōsī St and Bahonnār Hospital (☎ 235 011) on Shahīd Qareny St, are the most central and easiest to find, and the Bahonnār has an emergency number (☎ 411) for ambulances. The police headquarters (☎ 110 or ☎ 220 160) are along Adālat St.

Dangers & Annoyances In 1999 two foreign tourists were kidnapped and held hostage for a few weeks by drug smugglers seeking the release of several prisoners. They were eventually released unharmed, and since then the police have cracked down on smuggling and related activities throughout the eastern provinces.

There is nothing to suggest that the kidnapping was anything more than an isolated incident, although it might be worth checking the security situation before you visit. Some travellers have also reported feeling a little uneasy around the bazaar area after dark.

Jāmeh Mosques

Although every Iranian town has several mosques, the most important one is the so-called Jāmeh or Friday Mosque (masjed-é jāmeh). This is where men gather for prayers at noon every Friday and where they will listen to the Friday prayer leader preach. In small towns this prayer leader may be a simple imam (prayer leader) but in the bigger towns he may be an hojattol-Eslām or even an ayatollah, a religious expert who may have studied the Quran for 20 years or more.

Mosques & Mausoleums

Jāmeh Mosque The well-preserved and restored Jāmeh Mosque in the bazaar should definitely be on your itinerary. This large mosque, with its four lofty iwans and shimmering blue tiles, was built in 1349, although much of the present structure dates from the Safavid period or later. At the main entrance there is a useful explanation in English. The back entrance leads directly into the bazaar.

Moshtarī-yé Moshtāq Alī Shāh This attractive mausoleum to a renowned Sufi mystic dates from the Qajar period, although some parts of the structure are from the Mongol era. The stuccowork and the blue-and-white-tiled roofs are beautiful (and visible from Shohadā Square), as is the compact interior courtyard with gardens and octagonal pool.

Emām Khomeinī Mosque This quadrangular, domed mosque dates from the Seljuk period, and includes the remains of the original Seljuk mihrab and minaret, though much of the building has been rebuilt since then. The mosque has been under restoration for some years, but the painstaking work is revealing some splendid reliefs, particularly in the rooms high above the main iwan.

Pā Manār Mosque This mildly interesting mosque on Fath Alī Shāh St, dating back to the 14th century (or, according to other experts, the 12th century), is worth visiting for the fine original tiles in its portal. It is sometimes possible to climb one of the minarets for nice views over the old town.

Museums

Hamūm-é Ganj Alī Khān This fascinating museum (☎ 25 577), with wonderful frescoes of animals and humans around the entrance, is popular with Iranians though visited by surprisingly few foreign travellers. Originally built in 1631 for Ganj Alī Khān, the governor of Kermān, it's well worth visiting if you're passing. It contains a collection of wax dummies showing the viewer what happened in a traditional bathhouse. The reception area, for example, is divided up so that men practising different trades could all disrobe together.

The entrance, signposted in English, is directly opposite the Ganj Alī Khān Courtyard, in the middle of the bazaar. It is open from 9 am to noon and from 4 to 6 pm during winter daily except public holidays, and from 9 am to 1 pm and from 4 to 8 pm in summer; entry costs IR20,000.

Sanati Museum Kermān This interesting building contains a large collection of watercolours, mostly by the renowned local artist Sayyed Alī Akhbar Sanati who is famous for his stone inlay works. There is a small entrance fee of IR2000. The garden surrounding the museum is also pleasant.

Gonbad-é Jabalīyé

Just beyond the eastern edge of Kermān, this small and unadorned octagonal double-domed structure, called the Mountain of Stone, is of unknown age or purpose. Appearing to predate the 2nd century AD, it may have been a Zoroastrian building. It is remarkable because it's constructed of stone rather than the usual brick.

It's a fair way to come just to see two domes but the setting, at the foot of the Pāyeh Mountains, is picturesque. To get here, try to find a shared taxi from Shohadā Square, but you will probably have to charter one for about IR10,000 return.

Moayedī Ice House

This weird ice house, originally dating from the Safavid period, has been renovated so

well it is hard to think of it as old or important. Built and renovated with *khesht* (a common form of locally made brick, dried in the sun), the ice house is now used as a library and childrens' park.

Kermān National Library

If you happen to be walking past the library (which is also labelled as the Kermānology Centre) on Shahīd Qarani St, have a quick look at this interesting building, once a textile factory. The gardens are lovely and worth using for a picnic.

Bāzār-é Vakīl

The Bāzār-é Vakīl, which runs between Tohid Square and the Jāmeh Mosque, is around 1km long and is one of the best bazaars in this part of the country. Although the entire bazaar is called the **Bāzār-é Vakīl** for the sake of simplicity, each section dates from a different historical period. The area around the pretty **Ganj Alī Courtyard** is known as the **Bāzār-é Ganj Alī** and was built in the Safavid period; the courtyard is partially surrounded by the **Coppersmith's Bazaar**.

Leading west from the courtyard, the section known as **Bāzār-é Ekhtiarī** runs into the **Bāzār-é Vakīl**, which extends to the back gate of the Jāmeh Mosque. Both of these bazaars are around 150 years old. Running outside the southern wall of the mosque to Shohadā Square is the open-air **Bāzār-é Mosaffārī**, the oldest of Kermān's bazaars at over 700 years old, although there is little if any evidence of such antiquity.

One of the less-frequented minor bazaars is the **Gold Bazaar** (Bāzār-é Zārgārān), which runs from the north-eastern corner of the Ganj Alī Courtyard. Take the first lane to the left and after about 50m, you'll reach a small square with an attractive portal leading to an old (and now closed) madraseh. Follow the steps down into the **Hamām-é Ebrāhīm Khān**, a traditional bathhouse which is still in use. For the full scrub and massage, men (sadly the bathhouse is not open for women) pay around IR20,000. The hammam is open from 7 am to 7 pm, even when the rest of the bazaar is closed.

Shēkēteh Farsh

This carpet-making factory is one of the most accessible of its kind in the country and is set up to keep alive traditional carpet-weaving techniques. It is fascinating to wander through the two rooms where the all-female staff labour away at huge looms, weaving in a range of colours and styles. Entrance is free. The centre is in the north-east of town on Bausteny Piroozy Blvd and you'll need a taxi to get there.

Places to Stay – Budget

Kermān has few really good budget options that will accept foreigners.

To the south-west of the bazaar, *Valiasr Hotel* (☎ 224 912) on Felestīn St has basic twin/triple rooms for IR23,000/27,000. Check that the shared showers are in working order – there were promises of repair when we visited. A few doors up, *Mosāferkhūneh-yé Āzādī* (☎ 227 007) is slightly better for IR26,000/30,000 for a twin/triple room and has been recommended by some travellers. There's no sign in English.

A couple of blocks to the west, the *Omid Inn* (☎ 220 571) on Shahīd Qareny St seems unable to decide whether or not they'll accept foreigners, although lone women are always refused. The rooms and prices are similar to the Āzādī.

Two of the better budget places are west of Āzādī Square, but still within walking distance of the centre of town. *Guest House Milād* (☎ 50 617) on Āyatollāh Sadūqi St is good value with clean singles/doubles with shared bath for IR30,000/35,000. There are some doubles/triples with bath for IR50,000/60,000, although most of these seem to be at the front and therefore a tad noisy. The staff are friendly and there is a kitchen that may be used by guests.

Guest House Saady (☎ 43 802) off Āyatollāh Sadūqi St is another friendly choice with simple, quiet rooms ranging from IR20,000 for a single without bathroom to IR35,000 for a twin room with bathroom. No English is spoken but the staff can arrange meals if you give them enough notice. There is also a secure parking area for guests.

Places to Stay – Mid-Range & Top End

The *Akhavan Hotel* (☎ 41 411, fax 42 799 e akhavanhotel@yahoo.com) on Āyatollāh Sadūqi St is almost worth the trip to Kermān on its own. The family who runs the place is friendly, offering a perfect mix of Iranian hospitality and tourist savvy. The semi-luxurious rooms are great value at US$20/30 a single/double with bath, fridge and TV during high season – even more so during low season at US$10/15. These prices, which include breakfast, are open to negotiation and discounts are available for stays of longer than two days. The services available include tours around the city and further afield; reasonably priced Internet access; international fax and telephone services; assistance with visa extensions; bus, train (including from Zāhedān to Quetta) and airline tickets; and a range of postcards and books. There is secure off-street parking for those with their own vehicle and you can camp in the yard at the back and use their showers for US$1 per person per day.

If the Akhavan is full, *Naz Hotel* (☎ 46 786, fax 504 98) across the road is adequate at IR140,000/176,000 for a spacious but jaded single/double with bathroom. A few rooms were being refurbished when we visited so they should improve. Ask for a room at the back, away from the main road. Closer to the centre of town, the *Amin Hotel* (☎ 229 464) on Dr Chamran St has been recommended by several travellers. The good rooms are quiet, although their starting price of US$15/25 for a double with/without bathroom is a bit too much; negotiations are possible.

The *Kermān Hotel* (☎ 225 065, fax 232 285) is convenient for the bus station but not much else. For US$10/20 for a double with/without bath, you'd expect the rooms to be a little cleaner.

The best top-end place is the *Kermān Grand Hotel* (☎ 45 203, fax 44 087) on Jomhūrī-yé Eslāmī Blvd where tasteful doubles cost US$60 and enormous suites go for US$100. There is a 17% tax as well. There are three restaurants, a gift shop and a traditional teahouse scattered around the foyer, although, sadly, the swimming pool, which you might longingly overlook from your room, is only open to children.

One of the *caravanserais* in the Bāzār-é Vakīl is slated to become a hotel, and a very beautiful one it will be too.

Places to Eat

Eating out in Kermān is an unexpected pleasure. The nightly banquet dinners at the *Akhavan Hotel & Restaurant* are rapidly becoming the stuff of legend for hungry travellers from İstanbul to Kathmandu. The food is good and the quantities huge – five or six courses for IR25,000. A range of single dishes are also available if your appetite is less ambitious. Also good is the *Khān-é Sayyah Kermān Restaurant* in the grounds of the Sanati Museum Kermān. The pleasant, traditional atmosphere makes it popular with Iranians and the tasty meals are reasonably priced. There is also an excellent salad bar.

Two other places that have been recommended by travellers are the restaurant at the *Amin Hotel* and the *Marmar Restaurant* (no sign in English) on Felestīn St.

Teahouses

Without doubt the most atmospheric place to eat or drink in town is the architecturally magnificent *Chāykhāneh-yé Vakīl* (☎ 25 989), inside the Bāzār-é Vakīl. This subterranean teahouse and restaurant with its elegant brickwork arches and superb vaulted ceilings is known more for its traditional decor than its service or meals. It offers lunch (for around IR15,000 a dish) from about noon to 2 pm, and there is live music most days between noon and 3 pm. As this is a tourist attraction in its own right, you pay an entrance fee of IR6000, which includes a small pot of tea. It closes at 7 pm and all day Friday.

More popular with locals is the *Chāykhāneh-yé Sardār* (☎ 264 016) where you can sit on cushions either inside or in the garden while live traditional music is played on Thursdays and Fridays from 8.30 to 11.30 pm. This is an excellent place to sample the local speciality, *borsgoné*. The dish is a do-it-yourself mixture of ābgūsht, served in the

traditional stone pot (dīzī), and *kashkē bademjon*, an eggplant dish cooked in a milky sauce to a soup-like consistency. Each individual dish is delicious, and the combination is spectacular. If you have some drinks and the wonderful *māst sīr* (yogurt with garlic), two people should be well-fed for a bargain IR30,000. The place, which has no sign in English, can be difficult to find. Head east along the main Bāzār-é Vakīl. About 50m after the Chāykhāneh-yé Vakīl, take the first lane on the left; look for the Bank Sepah sign. Follow the lane for about 100m until you find yourself in an open parking area. Veer slightly left across the yard and then right; the arched entrance of the teahouse is on the right before you reach the main road.

Not far from Āzādī Square, the *Chāy-khāneh-yé Khayyam* is a little garish from the outside and the service could be better, but it's a pleasant place to eat nonetheless.

Shopping

Kermān is a good place to buy carpets for a bit less than in Esfahān or Tehrān. This is also the only place you're likely to see the beautiful *Kermān paté*, a brightly coloured square of cloth with intricate embroidered designs that is unique to Kermān. The Iran Handicrafts Organisation shop on Dr Behestī St is worth a look, but you are likely to get better prices in the bazaar.

Getting There & Away

Air Kermān has good air links to the rest of Iran. Currently, Iran Air (☎ 58 871), with an office on Shahīd Dr Mafatteh St, has flights to Esfahān (twice weekly, IR120,000); Tehrān (daily, IR159,000); Mashhad (twice weekly, IR154,000); and Zāhedān (twice weekly, IR93,000). Māhān Air (☎ 50 542), Dr Behestī St, also flies to Tehrān (twice daily except Friday) and Mashhad (twice weekly) for the same price as Iran Air.

Kermān's only international connection is the weekly flight to Dubai (via Kermānshahr) on Qeshm Air for around US$130 plus IR70,000 departure tax. For Qeshm Air tickets and schedules, contact the Kermān Balan Tour & Travelling Agency (see Travel Agencies earlier in the section).

Bus & Minibus The bus station is in the south-west of Kermān. The bus companies are only represented at the bus station. Some useful daily bus and minibus services are listed in the following table:

destination	distance (km)	duration (hrs)	cost (IR)
Bam	204	2½	4600
Bandar-é Abbās	498	8	11,500
Esfahān	703	12	14,500
Mashhad	886	16	25,500
Shahr-é Bābak	238	4	5500
Shīrāz	545	8	13,500
Tehrān	1064	18	23,000
Yazd	386	6	8000
Zāhedān	525	7	12,000

For Shahr-é Bābak, you'll need to go to Bus Cooperative No 4.

Minibuses (IR600) as well as shared taxis (IR1500) to Māhān leave from Kermānī Square and occasionally from Āzādī Square. For Shahdād, take a minibus from Emām Khomeinī St, just south of Shohadā Square.

Train The 1106km rail line starts in Tehrān and ends at Kermān, so if you are heading for Pakistan you will have to continue your journey by road. To Tehrān (IR38,000/20,000 for 1st/2nd class), trains leave Kermān at any time between 2 and 4 pm on Tuesday, Thursday and Saturday, and stop off at, among other places, Yazd, Kāshān and Qom, but *not* Esfahān. The journey to Tehrān is supposed to take 13 hours but may take longer – not such a bad thing if it means avoiding a 3 am arrival.

Train tickets can be purchased in advance from Kermān Tours (see Travel Agencies earlier in the section) or arranged through Akhavan Hotel, both of which save you the long trip out to the station (☎ 58 761) 8km south-west of town. Shared taxis (IR1500) leave from Āzādī Square, but you may have to charter a taxi for about IR7000. There will certainly be shared taxis available at the station when the train arrives.

Shared Taxi Shared taxis leave Kermān regularly for regional towns, but they all depart from different spots. Shared taxis to Bam (IR12,000) go from Sarasiyāb Square (about 5km east of Kermānī Square), and to Sīrjān from Āzādī Square for IR12,000. Shared taxis to Māhān (IR1500) leave from Kermānī Square and occasionally from Āzādī Square). Occasional shared taxis to Joopar (IR2000) run from just south of Emām Khomeinī St.

Getting Around

To/From the Airport There is no bus to the airport. You can try to get a shared taxi heading along Jomhūrī-yé Eslāmī Blvd from Āzādī Square, but you may have to charter a private taxi for about IR6000.

Bus & Minibus Buses travel between Āzādī Square and Shohadā Square for IR200.

Taxi The main stations for shared taxis around town are Āzādī and Shohadā Squares. From Āzādī Square, shared taxis run to the bus station (IR600), Bāzār-é Vakīl and Shohadā Square (IR500; for a private taxi, expect to pay IR3000) and the train station (IR1500). Prices are similar from Shohadā Square. Taxis all to yourself cost IR3000 to most destinations around town and IR10,000 per hour.

AROUND KERMĀN

There are some great places to visit in the vicinity of Kermān. Although most are covered by intermittent public transport, it might be worth chartering a taxi if you have limited time. The standard rate is calculated at IR600 per km, although you should be able to negotiate a full day for around IR100,000 to IR120,000 depending on the distance.

Māhān   ماهان
☎ 0346346

An increasing number of travellers are discovering the lovely town of Māhān, southeast of Kermān, which is another good base for exploring the region. Apart from the pleasant tree-lined streets and relaxed atmosphere, Māhān attracts visitors for its fine mausoleum, and beautiful palace and gardens.

Domes & Minarets

The development of the dome was one of the greatest achievements of Persian architects. The Sassanians (AD 224–637) were the first to discover a satisfactory way of building a dome on top of a square chamber by using two intermediate levels, or squinches – the lower octagonal and the higher 16-sided – on which the dome could rest. Later domes became progressively more sophisticated incorporating an inner semicircular dome sheathed by an outer conical or even onion-shaped dome. Externally the domes were often encased in tiles, with patterns so elaborate they had to be worked out on models at ground level first.

However elaborately some of them may be decorated now, the minaret started life as an entirely functional tower from the top of which the muezzin called the faithful to prayer. However, during the Seljuk period minarets became tall, tapering spires, which were far more decorative than practical. Since it was feared that someone standing at the top of one would be able to look into the private family areas of nearby houses, Shiite mosques often have a separate hut-like structure somewhere on the roof from where the muezzin makes the call to prayer (ezan). A light in the top of the minaret acted as a beacon to direct people coming from the fields to the town to pray.

Ārāmgāh-é Shāh Ne'matollāh Valī The splendid dome over the tomb of Shāh Ne'-matollāh Valī, a well-known Sufi dervish, is one of the most recognisable images of eastern Iran. The mausoleum dates from the early 15th century, but many of the other religious buildings in the small enclosed complex around it were built in the reign of Shāh Abbās I or in the 18th century. The mausoleum is renowned for its tiles, and for the seven ancient wooden doors throughout the building. Don't miss the small, tranquil prayer room, which is adorned with wonderful hand-painted Quranic verses and symbols such as the double-edged sword of Emām Alī.

Ask the caretaker to let you climb the stairs to the roof for a better look at the two slender Qajar minarets and the vast Safavid cupola. You can climb the minarets via one of two narrow staircases for spectacular views over the town and surrounding mountains.

The mausoleum is in the middle of Māhān, and the minibuses and shared taxis from Kermān will take you straight to it. Entrance costs IR10,000.

Bāgh-é Shāhzāde One reader described these charming gardens, dating back to 1873, as 'a jewel of my visit to Iran'. The beautifully maintained grounds contain a series of split-level fountains leading to a large palace, once the residence of Abdul Hamīd Mīrza, one of the last princes of the Qajar dynasty. To the left of the palace, there is a well-preserved bathhouse that the caretaker will open for you; a tip is appreciated. The palace itself has been partially converted into a restaurant that serves a decent lunch and drinks, but is also a great place for tea. As the sun disappears, the fountains and palace are floodlit – a wonderful sight. Occasional music festivals are held in the grounds.

The gardens are a 5km walk up the main road through the village from the mausoleum, and the turn-off is signposted in English. Entrance is IR10,000, although expect this to rise.

It is easy to get a private taxi between the two main attractions in town.

Places to Stay & Eat Staying in Māhān makes a lovely alternative to Kermān. The *Māhān Inn* (☎ 27 00) is one of the few places in Iran where prices have actually gone down since the last edition, making it excellent value especially if you pay in rials. The tidy rooms with bathroom and Western toilet cost US$11 plus 15% tax. The staff are friendly and there's a good restaurant. The hotel is at a roundabout, a few blocks west of the mausoleum and public transport from Kermān takes you past the hotel.

One of the most romantic places to stay in all of Iran is the *Hotel Garden Shāhzādeh*

The Wonder of Water

In a country largely made up of desert, water was such a precious commodity that past rulers went in for conspicuous displays of water where modern rulers might go in for conspicuous displays of jewellery. The gardens of Shāhzāde were just one of the places where they could show off their access to water. The long lines of defiant fountains are forced up from the ground by the pressure of gravity rather than by pumps.

Even today, one easy way for a philanthropist to show off their benevolence is by supplying a public drinking fountain.

(☎ 21 03) inside the walls of the gardens of the same name. All the rooms open onto the gardens, which you're likely to have all to yourself, particularly after the sun sets. Prices range from IR80,000/120,000 for a single/double up to IR300,000 for a small suite with traditional decor and beautiful arched windows at the front. Not all the rooms have a bathroom but even without they are fantastic value. As the restaurant does not always open in the evenings, you may want to bring your own food; to that end there are a few small grocery shops opposite the entrance to the mausoleum, back in town.

Avoid the restaurant behind the mausoleum. It serves average food and charges an entrance fee; the architectural merits of the building, which are the supposed reason for the fee, are not at all obvious.

Getting There & Away About every hour, shared taxis (IR1500) and minibuses (IR600) travel the 38km between Kermānī Square in Kermān (they can also occasionally be found at Āzādī Square) and Nem'-atollāh Square in Māhān, right in front of the mausoleum.

Joopar   جوپار

A visit to Joopar, 30km south of Kermān, is also worthwhile. The main attraction is the **Emāmzādeh-yé Shāhzāde Hossein**, built in the Safavid period, and similar in design to the mausoleum in Māhān. The mirrored ceiling inside the room that contains the shrine is exquisite.

Occasional shared taxis to Joopar (IR2000) run from just south of Emām Khomeinī St in Kermān, but it's easier to charter a taxi from Māhān or Kermān. The mausoleum is off the main roundabout in the village.

Shahdād   شهداد

Shahdād is a quiet town to the north-east of Bam wedged between the Pāyeh Mountains and the south-western fringe of the Dasht-é Lūt and is fiercely hot in summer. The oranges from Shahdād (harvested in October) are reputedly the best in Iran.

About 5km east of town is a prehistoric mound, known as the **Tappeh-yé Kohné** where archaeologists discovered many fascinating metal implements with animal motifs and clay figurines of humans dating from 3000 BC. Some are on display at the National Museum of Iran in Tehrān.

Another kilometre further on along a dirt track is **Shāhrak-é Kotūlūha** (City of the Little People); the excavated remains are of unknown origin although the name refers to a local Lilliputian legend. Both sites are probably of interest only to archaeology buffs, although their location at the edge of the desert is interesting.

In the town of Shahdād itself there is an impressive mausoleum, the **Emāmzādeh-yé Mohammed Ebn-é Zeid**, dating back to the Safavid period.

There is no hotel in Shahdād, so you'll have to come from Kermān for the day. Semi-regular minibuses travel between Shahdād and Emām Khomeinī St, just south of Shohadā Square, in Kermān. You can also charter a taxi for half a day for around IR100,000 from Kermān.

Around Shahdād

If you're feeling energetic, a good option is to take the Shahdād minibus as far as Sīrch, an attractive, cool, green town surrounded by barren mountains, and then walk back to Kermān. At the far eastern end of town are some hot springs (ask for Abgārm Sīrch). Due to the absence of accurate topographical maps for the region, it is best to follow the narrow,

The Gonbad-é Sabz Mausoleum, Mashhad, was built during the Safavid period.

Kalat viewed from its towering, natural fortress

A tablecloth seller in Kermān's bazaar

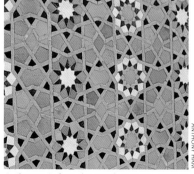
A tile mosaic from the Jāmeh Mosque, Kermān

Scenes from Bam: the flat ground outside the city, perfect for football (top left); a farmer harvesting dates (top right); view of the Arg-é Bam from the citadel (centre); a Baluchī musician in mid-song (bottom left); the entrance to the old city illuminated at night (bottom right)

picturesque valley through which the quiet road to Kermān passes. There are numerous narrow side valleys that are worth exploring and are good places to pitch a tent, as long as you keep the road within striking distance to avoid getting lost. At regular intervals, there are wells surrounded by plane trees as well as cherry and apricot groves, not to mention the likelihood of frequent encounters with friendly nomads and shepherds. In winter the mountains are often capped with snow.

After a gentle climb of about 17km, the road to Kermān cuts through a 2km-long tunnel under the mountains. While it is possible to hitch a ride to the other end, you can also follow one of the shepherd's trails up over the top for a challenging climb and wonderful views. On the other side, follow the wider valley for about 5km to the magnificent mud-brick village of Bolbolū a few hundred metres north of the road.

The tarmac continues down to the plains where it joins the main Bam-Kermān highway and it would be easy to hitch a lift to wherever you're heading. It is theoretically possible to walk north, then east from Bolbolū all the way to Kermān through the Sarasiyāb district over the Pāyeh Mountains. We were unable to follow this route but some of the tour companies in town assured us it was possible; there are no organised trekking routes, although nomads and other villagers have been walking to the markets of Kermān across these trails for centuries. If you want to take this route, let someone in Kermān know what you're planning and make sure you're self-sufficient in food and water.

FROM YAZD TO KERMĀN
Rafsanjān رفسنجان
☎ 03431

Rafsanjān is famous for its pistachios, which can be bought here more cheaply than anywhere else in Iran, and as the birthplace of the ex-president Rafsanjānī. There is nothing much else of interest to the visitor, but it is an OK place to break the journey between Kermān and Yazd or Sīrjān.

The ITTO-run *Mehmūnsarā-yé Rafsan-jān* (☎ 20 50) charges US$15/25 for a single/double. The cheaper and more negotiable

Pariz Hotel (☎ 58 33) on Tāleqānī Blvd costs about IR40,000 a double.

Shared taxis from Kermān's Āzādī Square cost about IR8000, or jump on any bus on the way to Yazd. Iran Asseman has weekly flights between Rafsanjān and Mashhad; contact any one of the travel agents listed in the Kermān section for prices and current schedules.

Meimand ميمند

If you're driving from Kermān to Yazd or Sīrjān it's well worth taking the route via Shahr-é Bābak and diverting 27km northeast to Meimand, a pretty village with houses carved out of the hillside, similar to Cappadocia in Turkey, albeit on a small scale. The scenery en route certainly warrants a day trip, if you have some time up your sleeve. It's usually deserted in summer and there's nowhere to stay. However, you can stay at the *Motel-é Bābak* in Shahr-é Bābak where a double costs US$25.

To get there, you will have to take a shared taxi from Shahr-é Bābak, accessible by bus from Kermān (IR4000); or you can charter a taxi from Kermān or Shahr-é Bābak.

SĪRJĀN سیرجان

Sīrjān is probably not worth a detour, but it's a useful place to break a journey from Kermān to Bandar-é Abbās or Shīrāz. If you do stay, there are a few attractions: the **Mir-é Zobair**, which contains some ancient calligraphy; the **Emāmzādeh-yé Alī**, which is mildly interesting; the ancient **Firuz Fire-Temple**; and **Ghal'eh-yé Sang**, the limited remains of a walled town on the northern and eastern flanks of a small hill.

Places to Stay & Eat

There is not a great choice. The only cheap hotel is *Hotel-é Kasra*, down a lane between the main branches of Bank Mellat and Bank Melli, in the centre of town. They charge a negotiable IR14,000 per person in basic but adequate rooms. *Hotel Suroosh* (☎ 37 388), on the main road and opposite the petrol station, is decent if you can get a room away from the highway. It charges IR80,000 per double with bathroom. You could also try the *Kakeshān Tourist Inn* for US$15/20 a single/double.

Hotel Suroosh has a decent *restaurant* downstairs; otherwise you will have to make do with a local *kabābī*.

Getting There & Away

Sīrjān is easy to get to by shared taxi (IR12,000) from Kermān's Āzādī Square, or by direct bus from Kermān, Yazd, Shīrāz or Bandar-é Abbās. There is no bus station, and the individual bus companies are spread all over town. It is best to take a private taxi and ask, for example, for the *termīnāl-é Yazd* (or wherever you want to go). There's a train to Tehrān, leaving mid-morning.

BAM

☎ 03447 • pop 80,000

If Esfāhān is the jewel in Iran's considerable crown, Bam, due west of Zāhedān, comes a close second. What makes Bam truly special, and undoubtedly one of the highlights of a visit to Iran, is the incredible, ancient mud-brick city. The modern town of Bam is also attractive with predominantly mud-brick buildings, water from desert springs running through roadside channels, and a relaxed pace of life. Stretching out behind the citadel are miles of enclosed date gardens full of birds and with irrigation streams running through them – a great place for wandering, especially at sunset.

Although it's a long way east if you are not travelling to Pakistan, Bam is worth the long detour and the sort of place where you're likely to stay longer than planned.

Orientation & Information

Bam is easy enough to walk around, and the ancient city is only about 2km from the centre of town, which is Emām Khomeinī Square. Both Bank Melli and Bank Sepah on Shahīd Sadoqī St will change money at a much better rate than in the bazaar. The main post office is only a few metres east of Emām Khomeinī Square. It is not possible to extend your visa in Bam.

Travel Agencies Arian Tourist & Travel Agency (☎/fax 56 04) on Emām Khomeinī St runs several day-long tours into the desert surrounding Bam, as well as an overnight stay with one of the nomadic tribes of the region. By the time you read this, they may also have Internet access up and running. Setar-é Nakhl Travel & Tourism Agency (☎ 75 00, fax 99 500) on Shahīd Sadoqī St can also book a range of domestic air tickets for Iran Air and Iran Asseman.

Emergency For medical emergencies, call ☎ 115 or the Aflā Touniyan Hospital (☎ 90 006). There's also a 24-hour medical clinic and pharmacy (☎ 91 699). If you're in need of police help, contact the Criminal Investigations Department (☎ 21 31) in Emām Khomeinī St, just north of the bazaar.

Things to See

Bam is a pleasant place just to wander around, with most streets lined by eucalypts, citrus gardens and the prolific date palms for which the area is famous (see the boxed text). The small **bazaar** is worth a quick look, especially in the quieter lanes leading off busy Emām Khomeinī St. At the northern end of the bazaar is the blue-tiled **Emāmzādeh-yé Āsīrī**, the tomb of one of the colleagues of Emām Rezā who was martyred along with his brother en route to Iraq. His brother's tomb, **Emāmzādeh-yé Zeid** on Zeid St, also dates from the 15th century and can be visited on the way to the old city.

Places to Stay – Budget

The best place in town, and one of the best budget accommodation options in Iran, is *Akbar Tourist Guest House* (☎ 58 42) on Sayyeh Jamal od-Din St. Within minutes of arriving, Akbar, the obliging owner, makes a mockery of myths of Iranian hostility towards the West. Rooms range from a dorm bed for IR20,000, to a spotless double with/without bathroom for IR80,000/50,000. Even better, for a negotiable IR20,000 you can sleep under the stars and palm trees in the enclosed courtyard, which is also a wonderful place to relax and meet other travellers. There is a secure parking area for those with their own vehicles and the rates for international phone calls are reasonable.

EASTERN IRAN

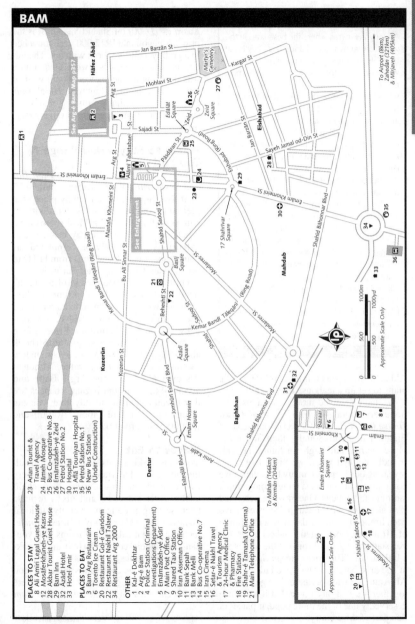

BAM

To Airport (8km),
Zahedan (321km)
& Mirjaveh (405km)

See Arg-é Bam Map p357

Jan Barzān St

Martyr's Cemetery

Mohlavi St

Kargar St

Edālát Square

Zeid Square

Eishabad

Sajadi St

Sayeh Jamal od-Din St

Jan Barzān St

Emām Khomeini St

Allámi Tabatabaei

17 Shahrivar Square

Shahid Sadooji St

Shahid Bāhonmar Blvd

Mahdab

See Enlargement

Bu Ali Sinnar St

Basij Square

Beheshti St

Kemar Bandi Tālegāni (Ring Road)

Kuzerún

Kuzerún St

Azādi Square

Shahid Bahonmar Blvd

Baghkhan

Jomhuri Eslami Blvd

Emām Hosein Square

Amir Kabir St

Deztur

Esteqlal Blvd

To Māhān (166km)
& Kermān (204km)

Emām Khomeini St

Modarres St

Modarres St

Approximate Scale Only

0   500   1000m
0   500   1000yd

Bazaar

Emām Khomeini St

Emām Khomeini Square

Shahid Sadooji St

Modarres St

Approximate Scale Only

0   250

PLACES TO STAY
8 Ali Amiri Legal Guest House
18 Mosáferkhuneh-ye Kasra
28 Akbar Tourist Guest House
29 Bam Inn
32 Azādi Hotel
33 Hotel Amir

PLACES TO EAT
3 Bam Arg Restaurant
6 Torento Ice Cream
20 Restaurant Gol-é Gandom
22 Restaurant Nakhil Talaey
34 Restaurant Arg 2000

OTHER
1 Kal-é Dokhtar
2 Arg-é Bam
4 Police Station (Criminal
   Investigations Department)
5 Emāmzādeh-yé Asiri
7 Main Post Office
9 Shared Taxi Station
10 Iran Asseman Office
11 Bank Sepah
12 Bank Melli
14 Bus Co-operative No.7
15 Iran Cinema
16 Setar-é Nakhil Travel
   & Tourism Agency
17 24-hour Medical Clinic
   & Pharmacy
18 Fire Station
19 Shahr-é Tamashá (Cinema)
21 Main Telephone Office
23 Arian Tourist &
   Travel Agency
24 Jāmeh Mosque
26 Bus Co-operative No.8
26 Emāmzādeh-yé Zeid
27 Petrol Station No.2
30 Hospital
31 Aflā Touniyan Hospital
35 Petrol Station No.1
36 New Bus Station
   (Under Construction)

The Date Palms of Bam

Ask anyone in Iran where the best dates in the world are grown and chances are they'll say Bam. In summer, the enormous bunches weighing down the straining palm trees must be tied to prevent wind damage. September, when the dates ripen, is a great time to visit as the bunches are untied and the dates shaken into a cloth ready to eat or export. The people of Bam have a saying that if you are the owner of 40 date palms, you'll never have to work again and indeed the dates of Bam are one of eastern Iran's most lucrative exports. Even the Prophet Mohammed recommended them and they are often the food of choice for breaking the fast of Ramadan throughout the Islamic world. The dates, used for producing date juice, delicious date honey *(shireh)* and even date vinegar, are also seen as a symbol of strength and virility to the extent that brides will often feed them to their husbands on their wedding night. While frozen dates are available year-round, if you have the good fortune to be in Bam in late September, ask around the bazaar for a bowl of Mozafati dates, which are the sweetest and most famous, but which cost a bargain IR6000.

Akbar, who speaks impeccable English, plans to set up a teahouse on the premises.

We have received more complaints from travellers about *Ali Amiri's Legal Guest House* (☎ 44 81, fax 90 085), south-east of Emām Khomeinī Square, than any other place in Iran. Although we found the staff friendly enough when we visited (without revealing our identity), many travellers have complained about everything from temper tantrums to bedbugs. One traveller described it as akin to a 'prison camp'. Showers have been limited to one per day with a maximum of 10 minutes permitted – take longer and you start paying – and some of the rooms are a little airless. The prices are similar to those at Akbar's, but it may be a good idea to give Ali Amiri's a wide berth until he gets his act together – a real pity given that it was once deservedly one of the more popular places in this part of the country.

The only virtue of *Mosāferkhūneh-yé Kasra* (☎ 37 00) on Shahīd Sadoqi St is the price. A negotiable IR12,000 gets you a bed in a grubby, cell-like room with fan. The toilets are shared and, when we visited, a hose was doubling as the shower. South-west of town out on the main highway, *Hotel Amir* (☎ 50 91) is similarly only for real shoe-stringers for whom price (IR10,000) is everything.

Places to Stay – Mid-Range & Top End

The only mid-range place is the *Bam Inn and Restaurant* (☎ 33 23), 50m south of 17 Shahrīvar Square. It's a friendly place with pleasant, spotless doubles with/without bathroom for US$24/20. Most rooms have a balcony. These prices may change (and extensions may finally be completed) as management was due to shift from ITTO to private hands not long after our visit.

On the south-western edge of town, the *Āzādī Hotel* (☎ 90 091) is a four-star luxury hotel with prices to match. Its rooms are very comfortable with a fridge, TV, balcony and marble bathroom. Prices range from US$60/70 for a single/suite (book ahead) down to US$48/56 for a room in low season, which is not bad value. Although it's over 6km from the Arg-ē Bam, and around 4km from the bazaar, chances are that if you can afford to stay here, you can afford the taxi fare (about IR4000 and IR3000, respectively).

Places to Eat

Years ago, Akbar took as a personal insult the inference that Iranian cooking rarely transcended the boundaries of a chelō kabāb. Ever since, he and his wife have been serving a delicious variety of local dishes at the *Akbar Tourist Guest House*, including great salads and mains. All-you-can-eat dinners cost IR10,000 and breakfasts are available for IR5000.

There can be no complaints about the food at *Ali Amiri's Legal Guest House* where guests can eat well for the same price. *Bam*

[Continued on page 361]

ARG-É BAM

ارگ بم

Unlike many ancient sites, the old city of Bam demands no leap of imagination to visualise a time when it was a living city. Its remarkable state of preservation, coupled with careful restoration work, ensure that the eerily silent and ramshackle mud lanes are a place in which to get lost, surrounded by the echoes of a history possibly spanning 2000 years. As the Iranian writer Abdolreza Salar-Behzadi observed:

Watch and pass very gently by these ruins, because every spot that you put your foot on, there may lie a king, a swordsman, an old sage, a lover, a mother.

History

According to local legend, the ancient city of Bam dates back to the Parthian period, although the citadel and city were probably founded later, in Sassanian times. With the arrival of Islam, the character of the city changed from a multicultural mix of Zoroastrians, Christians and Jews to a predominantly Muslim town. During the Safavid period, around 70% of the population lived inside the current walls, which were surrounded by a moat. There were 36 towers, over 400 houses and a population of some 11,000 people living in what was a thriving desert centre used as a staging post along the trade routes from India

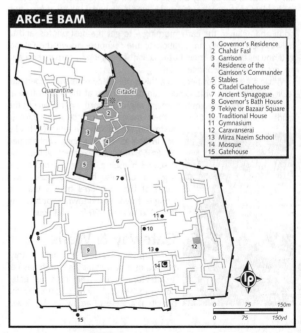

ARG-É BAM

1 Governor's Residence
2 Chahár Fasl
3 Garrison
4 Residence of the Garrison's Commander
5 Stables
6 Citadel Gatehouse
7 Ancient Synagogue
8 Governor's Bath House
9 Tekiye or Bazaar Square
10 Traditional House
11 Gymnasium
12 Caravanserai
13 Mirza Naeim School
14 Mosque
15 Gatehouse

Quarantine

Citadel

Inset: The main bazaar (photo by Anthony Ham)

and Pakistan to the Persian Gulf. The greater part of what remains dates from this period.

The Arg-é Bam (Arg means a citadel surrounded by fortified walls) was first abandoned following an invasion by the Afghans in 1722. The final nail in the coffin came in the early days of the Qajar dynasty when Lotfallī Khān, the last Zandian prince was arrested by the Governor of Bam on the order of Agha Muhammed Khān. With Qajar rule thus extended to Bam, many of the inhabitants of the Arg left the old city for fear of reprisals. Although it was inhabited by townsfolk until the mid-19th century, the Arg-é Bam fell into decline.

The old city was used as a barracks for soldiers until 1931, after which it was finally abandoned. With no-one watching over the site, the old city was damaged by looting and general neglect. In the early 1970s, the Iranian government began the task of restoration. When the then-president Rafsanjāni came to the Arg in 1993, he was so impressed that he urged every Iranian to visit it at least once in their lives. Thus returned to national prominence, the Arg's future protection appears assured, although debate continues to rage as to whether, through the very act of restoration, the ancient character of the city has been lost forever.

Information

The Arg-é Bam is open from 7 am to 7 pm daily, although if you are already inside, you will be allowed to remain until the sun sets. After dark, much of the old city is floodlit. Entrance costs IR30,000 (IR15,000 for holders of student cards), and is worth every rial. Allow *at least* two hours to look around. It is worth going twice – once in the late afternoon and again in the early morning – to get the best photos, and to fully explore the city. In addition to the teahouse above the Citadel gatehouse, there is a small but excellent bookshop, a carpet shop and an international telephone booth.

While a guide is not necessary, this is one place where an expert can really enhance your visit. Guides can be arranged at the ticket office as you enter. If you have limited time, it might be worth ringing one of the guides and arranging to meet them there. This can be done through

Arian Tourist and Travel Agency (☎/fax 56 04) in Bam or the engaging Mohammed Alī (☎ 78 42), an excellent guide who describes himself as being 'married to the Arg'. He can also help you track down some of the traditional houses that are being restored around town. Expect to pay IR30,000 to IR50,000 for a full tour.

Gateway & Walls

Not surprisingly given its varied history, the Arg as it now stands is a mishmash of architectural styles. The imposing **gatehouse** to the south where you enter the old city is a series of archways. The lower

Left: Mud-brick making is an important part of Arg-é Bam's restoration process.

PATRICK SYDER

arches are built in Sassanian style, while the higher ones owe more to the Islamic period and were built to support the structures added above the gateway.

From here you can climb the steep stairway on the right to the **outer walls**. From directly above the gatehouse, the views are spectacular; from here it is possible to fully appreciate the scale of the old city and the citadel that dominates it. The walls, made of a mixture of clay and sun-dried mud-brick, almost circle the city and date from the 9th century, although they have been considerably restored. The 2km length of the ramparts, broken only by the citadel itself, offers vantage points for every conceivable angle within the old city and the 30 or so small towers provide good views over the oasis of modern Bam beyond the walls.

The Bazaar

Back at ground level, the ancient bazaar cuts a straight line through the western sector of the old city. Once 115m long and covered by a roof, the bazaar is one of the most evocative areas of the site. Much of the framework of the 42 shops (which included bakeries as well as spice, date and textile shops) remains, in the form of arched entrances, sunken ovens and display shelves around the entrance for attracting passers-by. The location of the bazaar was a deliberate component of the security strategy of the town; because it was close to the entrance, outsiders could enter the city for the purposes of trade without infiltrating the residential areas.

While it is possible to branch off into the old city from many points along the bazaar, most first-time visitors head straight for the **citadel** at the far end. The **Tekiye or Bazaar Square**, most of which dates back to the Safavid period, was used for ritual ceremonies during Moharram; at other times its courtyard served as an extension to the bazaar.

The Citadel

Flanked by the inner walls, the Citadel **gatehouse** is an attraction in itself, with a wonderfully atmospheric teahouse above the entrance. The climb to the top of the citadel is quite steep but there are plenty of attractions along the way. In the garrison, shout something and listen to the extraordinary echo – archaeologists consider this to be deliberate, an ancient loudspeaker system. Nearby, are the 14th-century **stables**, which once held up to 300 horses and a **well** that made it impossible for anyone to cut off the citadel's water supply.

On the way up to the Governor's Residence, look into the very dark and scary dungeons, built to hold those who displeased the governor. The **Residence of the Garrison's Commander** provides awesome views of the ancient town. In some places on the climb, the walls have eroded a little, revealing the struts of palm trunks that serve the dual purpose of flexibility during earthquakes and ensuring resistance to termites. The four different chambers on each side were used for the four different seasons; the one with no chimney was for summer.

At the top, a small open courtyard provides some shelter from the wind. This upper part of the citadel is home to a fortified 17th-century residence known as the **Chahār Fasl** (Four Seasons), which offers wonderful

ANTHONY HAM

vantage points over the desert to the north and west of Bam. From here, you can see the **Kal-é Dokhtar** to the north-west, a mud-brick military garrison that predates the Arg. Also visible are two distinctive hills a few kilometres due west, known locally as the Twins and thought by some to be the remains of the Zoroastrian Towers of Silence, where the dead were taken. It is also the best place from which to see the north-western corner of the city that has been left untouched by restoration and is clearly separated from the remainder of the city – this was the quarantine area.

A **tower** marking the highpoint of the citadel offers more marvellous views over the old city and surrounds.

The Eastern Sector

After climbing back down and pausing for tea, head left from the Citadel Gatehouse to the covered corridor about 50m away. The first door on your right is the **ancient synagogue** which is under restoration and not always open. The narrow lanes that lead south into the heart of the old city are places for exploring without direction, particularly on your first visit.

The old **gymnasium** is worth a look, as is the unlabelled **traditional house** 50m to the west. This former aristocratic residence has domed waiting rooms, expansive stables, summer and winter pavilions (look for the ceiling with 28 shafts as a reminder of ancient air-conditioning systems unique to Bam), kitchens and guest quarters. Like most houes in the old city, this one faces towards the citadel enabling the ancient inhabitants to see the approach of danger or a royal event as indicated by smoke rising from the tower. It also signals the invisible starting point of the eastern part of the city, which was home to the town's more aristocratic and wealthy residents.

A little to the south, the **Mirza Naeim School** is now closed to visitors, and used as a base for an archaeological research unit. Try the door knockers on the front door. The one on the right is only used by women, the left by men; their different pitch indicated to the women inside the house whether it was safe to open the door to a visitor. The main **mosque** nearby was originally constructed in the 9th century, but has been rebuilt numerous times since. The domed cupola on the roof suggests that the mosque was built on the site of a Zoroastrian fire temple.

Left: View of Chahār Fasl from the citadel

[Continued from page 356]

Inn and Restaurant is another good option where a full meal including drinks shouldn't cost more than IR28,000. The restaurant at the *Āzādī Hotel* is expensive but good.

Beyond the hotels, there are several *kabābīs* and *hamburger joints* around the centre of town and *Torento Ice Cream* is a cheerful place to finish off a meal.

Restaurant Gol-é Gandom on Shahīd Sadoqī St does reasonable *khoresht* (meat stew) for IR9500 and a range of kebabs for IR15,000. Further afield, *Restaurant Nakhil Talaey* on Beheshtī St isn't bad but not worth making a special detour for, and you can't miss the *Restaurant Arg 2000*, with its kitsch castle design, on the main roundabout as you enter town – the food and service are patchy.

Opposite the entrance to the Arg, is the more attractive garden setting of the *Bam Arg Restaurant*. It offers a traditional breakfast and Iranian food for lunch, but it's not open for dinner.

Don't forget to visit the *teahouse* in the old city for something really special – perfect views over the old city, wonderful decor and date cookies (IR500) to die for.

Getting There & Away
Air A small airport, just east of Bam, is mainly used by the KAIC Development Company, but Iran Asseman (☎ 25 26), which has an office in Shahīd Sadoqī St, flies between Bam and Tehrān twice a week for IR198,000. Although there are a limited number of flights to Bam, tickets for further afield with Iran Air can be purchased at Setar-é Nakhl Travel & Tourism Agency (see Travel Agencies earlier in the section).

Bus & Minibus If you start really early you could take a day trip here from Kermān, but it's worth staying in Bam to allow at least two visits to the old city. At the time of research, buses were departing from the bus company offices around town, although a new bus station is under construction in the southern outskirts of town and may be operational by the time you visit. Some regular services are listed in the following table:

destination	distance (km)	duration (hrs)	cost (IR)
Bandar-é Abbās	449	8	10,800
Esfahān	703	11	25,000
Irānshahr	352	7	8000
Kermān	204	2½	4600
Tehrān	1258	21	26,200
Yazd	590	9	12,550
Zāhedān	321	4½	7900

The bus to Zāhedān leaves at 6.30 am, enabling you to cross the border in one day.

It may be difficult to get a direct bus to some longer-haul destinations as few originate in Bam, so you may have to change in Kermān or Zāhedān. It is also possible to catch onward transport in either direction at the main roundabout along the road between Kermān and Zāhedān (ie, next to the Restaurant Arg 2000). You may be dropped off at the roundabout when you arrive. Try to stay alert when travelling on the bus as many simply speed past Bam unless you ask the driver to stop.

Getting Around
Bam is small enough to walk around, and the old city is only about 2km from the centre of Bam. Private and shared taxis are available, but only necessary to get to or from the roundabout on the Kermān-Zāhedān road (IR1500 from the centre of town), or from the old city (IR1000) if you are tired after walking around there for a few hours.

ZĀHEDĀN   زاهدان
☎ 0541 • pop 400,000
Zāhedān, capital of the desolate and near-lawless Sīstān va Balūchestān province, is a frontier town that offers little respite from the desert. The town has few attractions, although its proximity to the only legal crossing point between Iran and Pakistan makes it a reasonable place to break the journey if travelling to or from Pakistan. Keep an eye out for camel races (*mosābāgheh-yé shotor-é davānī*), a traditional Balūchī activity. They can be difficult to track down but at least one important race meeting is held here each year. Unless you're invited by a Balūchī, you're more likely to see it on

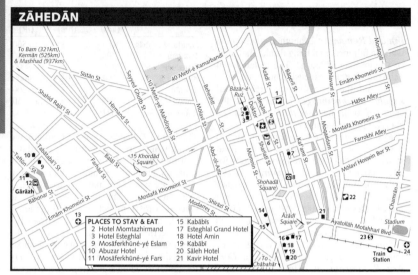

ZĀHEDĀN

To Bam (321km),
Kermān (525km)
& Mashhad (937km)

PLACES TO STAY & EAT
2 Hotel Momtazhirmand	15 Kabābīs
3 Hotel Esteghlal	17 Esteghlal Grand Hotel
9 Mosāferkhūné-yé Eslam	18 Hotel Amin
10 Abuzar Hotel	19 Kabābī
11 Mosāferkhūné-yé Fars	20 Sāleh Hotel
	21 Kavir Hotel

television – the races receive nationwide television coverage.

Orientation

Zāhedān is a flat, dusty, featureless town. Though the main offices are spread all over the place, most visitors will only worry about getting from the airport terminal or bus station to their hotel and back, which is easy to do. Although the whole of Zāhedān seems to be one huge marketplace with no particular focus, Bāzār-é Rūz is best considered the centre of town.

Information

Visa Extensions The Police Department of Alien Affairs is in the east of town on Motahharī Blvd on the way to the airport. Downstairs is the chaotic preserve of Afghans and Pakistanis, but visa extensions are handled in greater serenity by the Police Department of Foreign Affairs on the 1st floor. Little English is spoken in the office, which is open from 8.30 am to noon daily except Friday. You'll need two photos and IR10,000, which you'll need to deposit at the central branch of the Bank Melli, although the branch just west of the train station sometimes accepts them.

You're unlikely to be given more than a week's extension and it may take a few days to rustle something up; Kermān is more user-friendly as well as being a more pleasant place to wait.

Money The central branch of Bank Melli on Āzādī St changes US dollars at the prevailing market rate between 8.30 am to 2 pm (closed Friday). There is little reason to seek out the small black market in the bazaar as you'll run the risk of attracting the attention of Zāhedān's considerable police presence. For Pakistani and Afghan currency, the bazaar is the only option in town. The Taftan bus station on the Pakistani side of the border offers the best rates for Pakistani currency.

Post & Communications The main post office is along Dr Sharīatī St. At the time of research, the customs officer, whose presence is necessary for sending parcels, was only in attendance on Wednesday and Saturday mornings. The main telephone office is further south, along Tāleqānī St.

Emergency There is a general emergencies number (☎ 224 000). The main hospi-

ZĀHEDĀN

OTHER
1 Consulate of India
4 Police Headquarters
5 Bank Melli
    (Central Branch)
6 Main Post Office
7 Khaterat Zāhedān
    Travel & Tours
    (Iran Asseman
    Agency)
8 Main Telephone
    Office
12 Bus Terminal

13 Hospital
14 Iran Handicrafts
    Organization
16 Iran Air Office
22 Consulate
    of Pakistan
23 Bank Melli
24 Hospital
25 Pik-ups to Mīrjaveh
26 Police Department
    of Alien Affairs
    (Visa Office)
27 Gate to Airport

Airport ✈

27 ●

Motahhari Blvd ✚ 26

Montazeri St

0   400   800m
0   400   800yd

To Mīrjaveh
(84km)   Some Minor Roads Not Depicted

Forūdgāh
Square   ✚ 25

tal (☎ 224 991) is just to the east of the train station. The police headquarters (☎ 222 092) is next to the bazaar, but hard to find, so ask directions.

Dangers & Annoyances Because there's so much drug smuggling in the area, it is a little unsafe around some parts of Zāhedān at night, and you don't see many people out on the streets after dark. Car theft is also a problem so if you have a vehicle, it's a very good idea to find a secure place to leave it overnight. Do not venture west of Zāhedān in the area known as the Black Mountains – the jagged hills visible from Zāhedān – unaccompanied or on foot; gun law is in force there and they're not known as the Black Mountains for their colour alone.

Places to Stay

An increasing number of travellers are bypassing Zāhedān, choosing instead to break the long overland journey in Bam or Kermān. If the prospect of another few hours on the bus is too much to bear, Zāhedān has a range of reasonable options to suit most budgets. The cheapest places to stay are around the grimy bus station area in the west of town; if

you're staying longer than overnight, the centre of town is much more pleasant.

Places to Stay – Budget

In the noisy vicinity of the bus station, **Abuzar Hotel** (☎ 512 132) on 40 Metri-é Kamarbandī St is convenient and very good value at IR22,000 for a room with a fan and shared bathroom; some rooms are cleaner than others. Directly opposite, the **Mosāferkhūneh-yé Eslam** is sometimes reluctant to take foreigners and has abysmal toilets, but basic, cell-like singles/doubles/triples are generally clean and not bad for IR12,500/ 16,500/19,500. A bed in an insecure dorm goes for even less. The grotty **Mosāferkhūneh-yé Fars** costs the same but is impossibly noisy. Neither mosāferkhūneh has a sign in English.

Hotel Momtzahirmand (☎ 224 351) in the bazaar in the centre of town is the best in the budget range. Its rooms are a little spartan but excellent value at IR15,000/19,000/23,000. Most rooms have a (cold water) sink and a fan (make sure it works); rooms with windows are a little less claustrophobic. The showers and toilets are shared. It's a good place to meet other travellers who have just come from, or are going to, Pakistan. The hotel is a little hard to find; head north along Doktor Sharīatī St from the corner with Emām Khomeinī St, the hotel is 80m along the first lane on your left.

On Emām Khomeinī St, the **Hotel Esteghlal** (☎ 222 250) charges IR15,000 for grubby rooms with two beds, regardless of how many of them you fill. Toilets and showers are OK but a long way up the hall.

Places to Stay – Mid-Range & Top End

Best value in the mid-range is the **Kavir Hotel and Restaurant** (☎ 224 010, fax 220 059, Āyatollāh Motahharī Blvd), which has recently reopened. Tidy, pleasant singles/ doubles with air-con and bathroom go for IR75,000/100,000. It's at the eastern end of Āzādī Square and within easy walking distance of the bazaar.

The drab rooms at the **Sāleh Hotel** (☎ 231 797, Momnin St) don't quite live up

From 'Thieves' to 'Ascetics'

Not so long ago Zāhedān (meaning 'Ascetics') went under the far less-inviting name of Dozdā (Thieves). The locals offer several explanations for the original name. The more obvious of the two is that the village of Dozdā first developed as a place where bandits came to rest, but the more romantic version has it that rain used to soak straight through the soil, thereby effectively 'stealing' it. Passing through one day, Rezā Shāh was astonished that, despite its name, the town appeared no more full of thieves than its neighbours. At once he had the name changed to Zāhedān in a nod of recognition to the more conspicuous collection of straggly-bearded, ascetic-looking men living there.

to the grandeur of the marble pillars and gold frames in the lobby. The usual asking price of US$20/30 (they do accept rials) for a single/double with bathroom can usually be negotiated down to around half that without too much trouble. The lacklustre rooms are more than compensated for by the friendliness of the staff.

Rooms at the nearby *Hotel Amin* (☎ 239 892) are similarly disappointing, especially as some of the toilets smell far worse than you'd expect for the price of US$20/30 a tatty single/double with bathroom. Bargaining is possible but there is less room for manoeuvre than at the Sāleh.

Zāhedān's finest is the *Esteghlal Grand Hotel* (☎ 238 052, fax 222 239) on Āzādī Square. The beautifully appointed rooms are worth every one of their four stars and contain spotless bathrooms, fridge, air-con and satellite television. Rooms on the upper floors have good views over the city. The prices are excellent value at IR246,200/350,800/500,000 a single/double/suite. If you can afford it, it's worth a splurge in advance, or in the dusty and exhausting aftermath, of the long desert journey to or from Pakistan.

Places to Eat

There are several *restaurants* in the bus station area; the one in the *Abuzar Hotel* (see

Places to Stay) is the most popular and hygienic. In the centre of town, along Momnin St, around Hazrat Emām Alī Square, there are a couple of decent *kabābīs* that are worth trying.

The best places to eat are in the hotels. The restaurant in the *Hotel Momtzahirmand* is basic but the best in the budget range of hotels. *Sāleh Hotel* also has a good restaurant, serving a range of nicely cooked main dishes (chelō kabāb, fish, chicken) with soup, rice, yogurt and a soft drink, all for around IR18,000. The *Kavir Hotel and Restaurant* is also good.

Shopping

Zāhedān is famous for its low prices on all manner of goods, especially cigarettes, which are imported (and smuggled) from Pakistan under Western brand names. If you want to pick up a last-minute souvenir before heading into Pakistan, the Iran Handicrafts Organisation shop on Momnin St is worth a look.

Getting There & Away

Air Given Zāhedān's isolation from much of the rest of Iran, flying makes a good alternative to long hours of overland travel. It is also a good idea for northwards journeys to Mashhad as long as the troubles continue in Afghanistan, and drugs continue to be smuggled into Iran.

Iran Air (☎ 220 813), with an office near Āzādī Square, flies from Zāhedān to Chābahār (five times weekly, IR100,000), Esfahān (twice weekly, IR178,000), Kermān (twice weekly, IR91,000), Mashhad (three times weekly, IR153,000) and Tehrān (up to three times daily, IR208,000).

Iran Asseman also has twice weekly flights to Tehrān (IR208,000) and Irānshahr (IR91,000). The representative for Iran Asseman is Khaterat Zāhedān Travel & Tours (☎ 225 001) on Āzādī St, which is open 8 am to 8pm Saturday to Thursday, as well as Friday mornings.

This efficient travel agency also sells tickets for Zāhedān's only international flight, which is to Dubai every Saturday for US$130 on Māhān Airlines.

Bus For those with the constitution of a camel, roads go north to Mashhad and Zābol (expect an inordinate number of checkpoints along the way), and south to Chābahār. Most travellers, however, are only interested in roads east to the Pakistani border and west to Bam and Kermān.

The sprawling bus station area in the west of Zāhedān, generally known as the 'Gārāzh', is a noisy repository of diesel fumes and careening vehicles, but there is a system amid the chaos. The bus company offices line Taftūn St in the block north of Bāhonar St. Next to each office is a driveway leading to a parking area from where the bus leaves. For shorter distances, there's little difference between the various companies; those seeking overnight buses may want to check out Bus Cooperative No 9, which seems to have the most air-con buses. Buses leave Zāhedān several times a day for the following destinations:

destination	distance (km)	duration (hrs)	cost (IR)
Bam	321	5	8000
Bandar-é Abbās	1039	17	24,000
Chābahār	691	12	20,000
Esfahān	1244	21	25,500
Kermān	541	7	12,000
Mashhad	937	15	26,000
Shīrāz	1088	17	28,000
Tehrān	1605	22	36,000
Yazd	928	14	19,000
Zābol	216	4	4500

If you're heading to Bam, it might be easier to take any bus heading west (to Kermān or Yazd) and get off at Bam.

To/From Pakistan Currently, there are frequent buses (IR3000), minibuses (IR4000) or 'pik-ups' (utility-style shared taxis) for IR6000 from Zāhedān to Mīrjāveh (96km). Most buses leave from the bus station, but it isn't too difficult to hail a passing pik-up or minibus at Forūdgāh Square in the far east of town. Remember that Pakistan time is either a half or 1½ hours ahead of Iran.

The Iran-Pakistan border is 15km further east of Mīrjāveh village, so clarify whether

Refugees

Although Iran hosts more refugees than almost any other country in the world, it has only recently received any international aid to help it cope. Iran is in an unfortunate geographical position, surrounded by ethnic and political strife in all directions. To the west, Kurds, who are persecuted in Turkey and Iraq, flock to Iran; 600,000 Kurds, Lōrs and other ethnic minorities have fled Iraq for Iran since the start of the brutal Iran-Iraq war in 1980.

An estimated 1.4 million Afghan refugees live in Iran, mainly in Tehrān and Mashhad, with perhaps another 700,000 living elsewhere in the country illegally. Many originally fled the Soviet invasion but stayed because of the endless fighting in Afghanistan. Male refugees often end up leading short, tough lives as labourers in the construction industry. Many Iranians view the Afghan refugees as parasites and blame them for all sorts of social and economic woes. Since early 2000 the United Nations High Commissioner for Refugees has been running a program to return many of the Afghans to their homeland but with limited success.

your vehicle is going to the village or border. It is easy enough to get something between the village and border. Once you are at the border, cross it on foot (see the Mīrjāveh section later in this chapter for more details) and then take whatever form of transport is heading your way on the other side.

From Taftan, there are regular buses to Quetta for Rs250 (Pakistani rupees) – about US$4.80, although most leave in the morning or late afternoon.

If you are travelling from Quetta, buses for Taftan leave from the New Bus Stand (about 1.5km south of the train station), although you can buy tickets from the bus company offices along Jinnah Rd, just along from the Muslim Hotel. Most companies have at least three afternoon departures between 2 pm and 6 pm. Make sure your bus has air-con and that you have a seat to yourself; the sturdiness of the road (and the buses) can be patchy. Count on a minimum of 14 hours.

Train Plans to build a new line between Kermān and Zāhedān are still a long way from being realised.

To/From Pakistan While the train between Zāhedān and Quetta has plenty of character and you meet some fascinating people, it is painfully slow, and leaves only once a week. Also it takes three to five hours to clear both borders. It is much quicker to get to Mīrjāveh by bus, minibus or *pik-up*, cross the border on foot and then link up with the train there (or take any form of transport leaving for Quetta from Taftan).

In April and May, when the rains are more prevalent, delays can stretch to eight or 10 hours, making the trip unbearably long. One official in Quetta told us that the journey has been known to take up to a week in summer if sand blows across the track; 24 to 36 hours is more usual. The normal passenger/cargo service leaves Zāhedān's station for Taftan and Quetta at 8.30 am on Monday.

The 700km trip between the Iran-Pakistan border and Quetta…will forever be remembered as 'The Pakistani Nightmare'. Everybody told us to take the train. It's more comfortable, everybody said. We did it and we regretted it. After twenty hours, we got about halfway…something was broken on the rails, so we had to wait another 10 hours. How it ended up we don't know, because after those 10 hours we jumped on a bus that stopped by the train station and went to Quetta.

David Kucera

Tickets from Zāhedān to the border (IR1700/ 1200 for 1st/2nd class; one to two hours), and sometimes another ticket for the onward leg to Quetta (Rs686/310 – about US$13.20/5.95) are available at the impressive little train station in Zāhedān. The ticket officer told us simply to turn up the morning of the trip and 'no problem for ticket'. We suggest that you try the day before departure or at the very least ring inquiries (☎ 224 142) to check ticket availability.

Coming from Quetta, the train leaves at 11.45 am on Saturday, arriving, *in sha'Allah*, in Zāhedān the following evening. It may be quicker to get off the train in Taftan. It's worth getting to Quetta a few days before departure (or booking your ticket in advance elsewhere) as sleepers fill up quickly; don't leave Quetta without one. Take plenty of food and water with you and in winter take a sleeping bag or you will be very, very cold.

There is no bank in Taftan, so you will have to get some Pakistani rupees or Iranian rials from the moneychangers at the train (or bus) station.

Taxi Between Zāhedān and the border, a private taxi shouldn't cost more than IR50,000 and is a good way to avoid the log jam at the checkpoint between Mīrjāveh and the border.

Car & Motorcycle Drivers who are travelling between Turkey and India often describe the trip between Zāhedān and Quetta, across the vast Balūchestān desert as the worst leg of their journey. The road from Quetta to the Iranian border is barren and lonely, with virtually no facilities and there is a (decreasing) risk of bandits. If you're travelling in your own transport, it's advisable to travel in a convoy.

The clearly signposted road between Zāhedān and Kermān is good but short on facilities. Take plenty of water with you if you are driving, and make sure your vehicle is in good order or risk a long and unpleasant wait for repairs. Petrol is available in Mīrjāveh, Zāhedān, and Fahraj (between Zāhedān and Bam).

Getting Around

To/From the Airport A private taxi between the airport and town should be no more than about IR3000 for a single passenger, but unscrupulous drivers may demand more than double this – bargain hard. Alternatively, look for some fellow passengers to share a taxi. There is no airport bus service.

Taxis Vans and private cars often duplicate the services of the official (orange) taxis and buses in Zāhedān. Private taxis are reasonably priced at about IR2000 for shorter trips; from the bazaar to the bus station, expect to pay IR3000. Shared taxis are available along the main roads for about IR500 a trip.

MĪRJĀVEH   ميرجاوه
☎ 05448

If you're travelling between Iran and Pakistan by road or train, you'll pass through the Iranian village of Mīrjāveh. A typical border settlement with nothing much to interest travellers, it's still a reasonable place to stay overnight and regain your energy.

Places to Stay & Eat

The cheapest place in town is the *Montaza-hirmand Hotel* with basic but OK singles/doubles for IR15,000/18,000. For a place run by the ITTO, the *Mirjaveh Inn (☎ 43 86)* is a surprisingly good option where large, clean doubles cost IR50,000, although it has become a little jaded in recent years. Look for the sign in English 'Room Resturant' at the main roundabout. The attached restaurant is also good. There's a host of cheap grocery shops along the main street.

Getting There & Away

From the Iranian border, wait outside the large border compound for any form of transport to fill up and leave for Mīrjāveh or Zāhedān. From Mīrjāveh, there is always something about to go to the border or to Zāhedān, from where you will probably need another connection if continuing east.

To/From Pakistan Foreign travellers crossing the border are often whisked through customs and immigration on both sides. The Pakistani customs officers often wave travellers through the scrum, stopping only long enough to record your passport details (you may have to go through a similar process at the checkpoint 10km before Taftan) and warn you about the strictness of the Iranian customs checks. It's very prudent for men and women crossing this border into Iran to dress appropriately and be polite. Don't carry any drugs, or anything that remotely looks like drugs. Occasionally either side of the border closes at odd times, but it's generally open during daylight hours to coincide with the arrival of buses from Quetta; some travellers

coming this way have completed all formalities by 9 am.

Taftan, on the Pakistani side, is a depressing, fly-blown den of smugglers, and you can expect to spend an hour or two waiting for onward transport. In summer this can be murder. The only accommodation in town is the depressing Taftan Hotel run by the Pakistan Tourism Development Corporation (PTDC). The rooms are basic and the air-con is problematic, but you're not exactly spoilt for choice.

To enter Iran, walk through the gate of the ominously named Mīrjāveh Terminal Corporation, fill out the entry card the guard will hand you and then hand it with your passport through the appropriate window inside the arrivals building (women have a separate window to the right). American travellers usually have to undergo a brief but polite interview about their itinerary in Iran. A sign in English promises that Iranian rial amounts in excess of IR200,000 will be confiscated and deposited in a government bank account, although this is rarely enforced. Make sure you keep the customs declaration slip as you *will* be asked for this when you leave Iran.

With all the formalities completed (usually in under an hour depending on the crowd), there is a free shuttle bus service from outside the customs hall to the gate of the border compound. Buses and other vehicles leave from this gate to Mīrjāveh and Zāhedān.

People with their own transport have reported a similarly relaxed approach to baggage searches. Crossing into Iran, the vehicle driveway is obvious, to the left of the main immigration gate. After completing immigration formalities, drive past the main customs hall and turn right at the first roundabout where the car will be searched.

Buses from Quetta conveniently unload their exhausted human cargo right outside the border crossing. The moneychangers who will quite openly approach you the second you step from the bus can change Pakistani rupees or US dollars into Iranian rials or vice versa. While you should try to ask someone crossing the border the other way for the current exchange rate, most offer close to the market rate without too much hassle. You'll need to change at least enough to get you to Zāhedān, because Bank Melli on the Iranian side was, strangely, not changing money when we were there. Alternatively, check around the Kandahari Bazaar in Quetta where traders offer rials along with Kalashnikovs.

CHĀBAHĀR
چابهار

☎ 05423

South of Zāhedān, on the Gulf of Oman, the isolated town of Chābahār (the name means Four Springs) is known to most Iranians as the Chābahār Free Zone (CFZ), a duty-free port along the lines of Kīsh Island. Here, thousands of Pakistanis and Balūchīs line up for days in the searing heat to buy duty-free goods. Unaccompanied foreigners won't normally be allowed into the customs yard to witness the entire bureaucratic nightmare and indeed there's little reason for travellers to visit Chābahār. The largely uninhabited coastline east and west of town will be worth exploring if smuggling activities and police suspicions of everyone ever subside.

Chābahār is very hot in summer and very expensive all the time.

Places to Stay & Eat

Along the main street, the dingy *Mosāfer-khūneh-yé Mohammedi* (no sign in English) charges IR22,000 for a bed in a two-bed room with few concessions to personal hygiene, and no air-conditioning. *Mosāfer-khūneh-yé Āzādī* is in the same class.

At the main roundabout, the *Mehmūn-sarā-yé Jahāngardī (☎ 24 444)* is run by the ITTO and won't budge from US$30 per room – way too much. One bizarre upmarket place is the *Marian Hotel (☎ 34 84)*, a converted South Korean barge full of apartments that cost a negotiable US$15 a double, with TV, fridge and air-con. It is near the main jetty.

As you might expect, fish dishes are common in this part of Iran. There are several *snack bars* and *chelō kabābīs* along the main road. The restaurant in the *Mehmūnsarā-yé Jahāngardī* is fairly good and inexpensive.

Getting There & Away

Air Chābahār is very isolated by land, and the most sensible way to get there is by air. Iran

Air flies most days to Zāhedān (IR100,000) with connections to Tehrān, and to Bandar-é Abbās (three times a week, for IR102,000). There is also a weekly flight to Mashhad (IR226,000). The Iran Air office (☎ 33 83) is on Sayad Blvd. Consider also Iran Asseman which flies to Tehrān.

Bus The only regular buses connect Chābahār with Zāhedān (IR20,000, 12 hours) via Irānshahr. Roads to/from Chābahār are improving, but it is still a long, hot trip.

There is no legal route between Iran and Pakistan except at Mīrjāveh. The land crossing into Pakistan through Pīshīn is not open to foreigners, and this is wild and desolate drug-smuggling territory where foreigners should be neither seen nor heard.

Getting Around

The airport is 46km away in the desolate village of Konārak, and the runway is another 12km from the station. Take whatever vehicle is going from the airport to Chābahār; and ask the airline office in Chābahār about sharing transport *to* the airport. You may get lucky.

ZĀBOL
زابل

Heading north from Zāhedān, this dusty overgrown village, dangerously close to the border with Afghanistan, is of no interest to travellers except as a stepping-off point for Kūh-é Khājeh. Zābol has earned a name as a town where only two things matter – guns and money. Before heading to Zābol check the current situation with the visa-extension-cum-foreigners' registration office in Zāhedān. At the time of research, we were advised that travel to Zābol was unsafe due to ongoing skirmishes between smugglers and the huge police presence in the border areas.

Places to Stay & Eat

Try the *Mosāferkhūneh-yé Valī-yé Asr*, 1km from the bus station, where rooms should cost around IR15,000. There are also several grotty mosāferkhūnehs around the bazaar, which is also where you are most likely to find the largest concentration of *kabābīs*.

Getting There & Away

Iran Asseman flies between Zābol and Mashhad. Buses link Zābol with Mashhad (IR22,000, 14 hours, 1149km) and Zāhedān (IR4500, four hours, 216km).

KŪH-É KHĀJEH   کوه خواجه

Kūh-é Khājeh is a small hilly island with several ancient ruins on its peak, rising out of the seasonal Lake Hāmūn. The area is especially beautiful between early spring and early autumn when the level of the lake rises and the causeway to the island becomes impassable; in winter and late autumn it is usually possible to walk across, but at other times you will probably have to take a *tūtan* (a tiny wickerwork punt) at a negotiable fare.

The village of Kūh-é Khājeh is 1.5km east of the island, and this is where you will be dropped off if you arrive by bus or shared taxi from Zābol. There is no accommodation and nowhere to eat, and since you should count on at least 2½ hours to see the remains on the island and get back to the village bus stop, it is best to leave Zābol (or Zāhedān) in the morning.

TABAS   طبس

An oasis poised between two deserts, the Dasht-é Lūt and the Dasht-é Kavīr, Tabas is the only town of any size for hundreds of kilometres in any direction, and no visitor can fail to appreciate its special relationship with the desert. When you arrive at Tabas with its palm trees, paved roads, bazaar and public gardens, you'd be forgiven for thinking you had stepped into a mirage.

The city is one of the more attractive towns in the Iranian desert, and none of its fertile land is wasted. It is easy to understand the Iranian passion for gardens if you visit the **Bāgh-é Golshan** with its lush variety of tropical trees, pools and cascades, and its utter defiance of the desolate conditions at its edge. The ruined 11th-century citadel, the **Arg-é Tabas**, is also worth a look.

Places to Stay & Eat

The best place to stay and eat in town is the *Hotel Bahman* (☎ 535 422), near the petrol station. A decent apartment, complete with kitchen, costs a reasonable IR50,000. If this is full, or more than you want to spend, ask around the bus station for cheaper alternatives.

Getting There & Away

Iran Asseman has occasional flights to Mashhad via Tehrān.

Buses originating in Tabas travel daily to Yazd (IR18,000, eight hours, 419km) and Mashhad (IR10,000 or IR11,500 via Bīrjand, 10 hours, 521km). Alternatively, flag down any bus heading your way.

MASHHAD   مشهد

☎ 051 ● pop 1,964,500

Mashhad is Iran's holiest city and its name literally means 'Place of Martyrdom' or 'Place of Burial of a Martyr'. The city is extremely sacred to Shiites as the place where the eighth Shiite imam and direct descendant of the Prophet Mohammed, Emām Rezā, died in AD 817. What had been a small village called Sanābād has since grown to become Iran's most important pilgrimage centre.

The population of Mashhad ballooned during the Iran-Iraq War, simply because it was the furthest Iranian city from the Iraqi border. Many people stayed, and the city has become huge and unwieldy. Mashhad can get very cold in winter and there is often snow on the ground for four or five months of the year.

Around Nō Rūz (the Iranian New Year; about 21 March) and the height of the pilgrimage season (June to September) the population can triple in the space of a few days. More than 12 million pilgrims visit Mashhad each year. There is little in the city to detain you longer than it takes to visit the Holy Shrine, though there are a few attractions near Mashhad, and the city is a natural staging post if you're travelling to or from Turkmenistan.

History

Mashhad grew up around the legend of Emām Rezā, heir to the Abbasid caliphate and eighth of the Shiite imams, and the city's history is inextricably linked with that of his shrine. According to popular belief,

MASHHAD

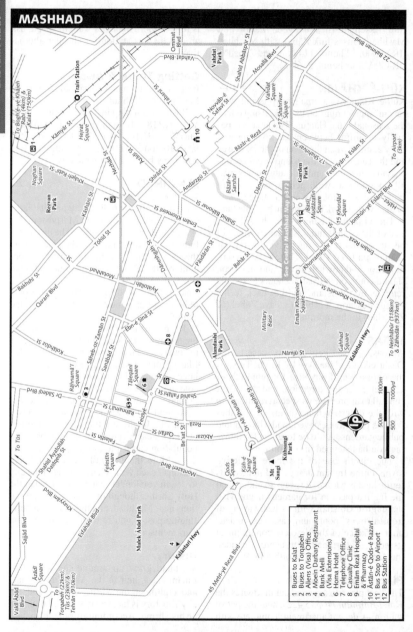

1 Buses to Kalat
2 Buses to Torqabeh
3 Aliens (Visa) Office
4 Moein Darbary Restaurant
5 Bank Melli
   (Visa Extensions)
6 Homa Hotel
7 Telephone Office
8 Casualty Clinic
9 Emām Rezā Hospital
   & Pharmacy
10 Āstān-é Qods-é Razavi
11 Bus Stop to Airport
12 Bus Station

Rezā was poisoned on the orders of the Caliph Ma'mūn (see the boxed text 'The Martyrdom of Emām Rezā'). Ma'mūn buried him in a tower in Sanābād next to the tomb of his own father, the famous Hārūn-ar-Rashīd. Although this burial place began to attract Shiite pilgrims, it remained of regional importance only for many centuries.

In the centuries after it was built, the shrine was destroyed, restored and destroyed again as invaders plundered the area. In the dark years of the Mongols, however, Mashhad grew to become the capital of Khorāsān, in succession to the nearby town of Tūs, and the mausoleum of Emām Rezā was restored.

In the early 15th century, Shāh Rokh, son of Timur, enlarged the shrine, and his extraordinary wife, Gōhar Shād, commissioned a mosque on the site. Even during this remarkable reign, the city was troubled by Uzbek invasions, and the population fell dramatically.

Mashhad did not become a pilgrimage centre of the first order until the coming of the Safavid dynasty at the turn of the 16th century. Having established Shiism as the state creed, the most brilliant of the early Safavid rulers, Shāh Esma'īl I, Shāh Tahmāsp and Shāh Abbās I, gave the city and shrine the prominence they have held ever since, frequently making pilgrimages to Mashhad themselves and generously endowing the sacred complex.

The city's location put it at constant risk of invasion, and Mashhad suffered Uzbek attacks on several occasions in the 16th and 17th centuries (though they respected the shrine enough to leave it unscathed). In 1722 it was also attacked by the Afghans. In the 18th century the shrine was again firmly established as the greatest Shiite pilgrimage centre in Iran. Nāder Shāh, though a Sunni of missionary zeal, generously endowed the shrine and restored Mashhad to stability. Several uprisings during the 19th century were severely put down by the ruling Qajars, but Mashhad returned to peace under the reign of Nasr-od-Dīn Shāh, and the city was modernised under Rezā Shāh. Since the Islamic Revolution, massive construction work and the government's prominent support for the holy cities has ensured Mashhad's position as one of the world's most visited pilgrimage sites.

The Martyrdom of Emām Rezā

Emām Rezā, a direct descendant of the Prophet Mohammed, was born in AD 765 in Medina. When his father, the seventh imam, died in 799 in the Baghdad prison of the Abbasid caliph, Hārūn al-Rashīd, the 35-year-old Rezā became the eighth Shiite imam. Successive caliphs were troubled by the growing popularity of the imams, who they saw as a threat to their own spiritual and temporal power. Caliph Ma'mūn was no exception. He 'invited' Emām Rezā to travel from Medina to his capital at Marw; when the imam refused, the caliph's troops took him into exile. After a journey taking him through Basra (now in Iraq), Khorramshāhr, Ahvaz and Neishābūr to popular acclaim, the imam arrived in Sanābād. Caliph Ma'mūn kept him under close guard, but his presence at the royal court generated huge popular support for the charismatic Rezā, not to mention great discomfort for Ma'mūn. Finally, the caliph imprisoned the imam before poisoning his grapes and pomegranate juice. The imam's body was buried at night to avoid a popular outpouring of grief over his death, a grief still keenly felt to this day.

Orientation

As you might expect, all the main roads in Mashhad lead to the Holy Shrine of Emām Rezā. Almost everything of interest is within walking distance of this most unmistakable of landmarks, and all the public transport radiates from its perimeter. Away from this physical and spiritual centre, the city, though pleasant, is largely flat and featureless.

Information

Visa Extensions The Aliens Office is just south of Rāhnamāi'ī Square in the northwest of the city. First visit the downstairs section of Bank Melli about 750m south along Rāhnamāi'ī St (don't use the main entrance – it's a small door further along the main road) and join the crowd of Afghans and Central Asians filling out deposit slips

EASTERN IRAN

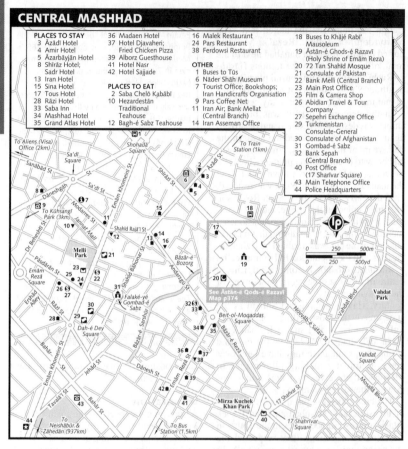

CENTRAL MASHHAD

PLACES TO STAY
3 Āzādī Hotel
4 Amir Hotel
5 Āzarbāyjān Hotel
8 Shīrāz Hotel;
   Sadr Hotel
13 Iran Hotel
15 Sina Hotel
17 Tous Hotel
28 Rāzi Hotel
33 Saba Inn
34 Mashhad Hotel
35 Grand Atlas Hotel

36 Madaen Hotel
37 Hotel Djavaheri;
   Fried Chicken Pizza
39 Alborz Guesthouse
41 Hotel Nasr
42 Hotel Sajjade

PLACES TO EAT
2 Saba Chelō Kabābī
10 Hezardestān
   Traditional
   Teahouse
12 Bagh-é Sabz Teahouse

16 Malek Restaurant
24 Pars Restaurant
38 Ferdowsi Restaurant

OTHER
1 Buses to Tūs
6 Nāder Shāh Museum
7 Tourist Office; Bookshops;
   Iran Handicrafts Organisation
9 Pars Coffee Net
11 Iran Air; Bank Mellat
   (Central Branch)
14 Iran Asseman Office

18 Buses to Khājé Rabī'
   Mausoleum
19 Āstān-é Ghods-é Razavī
   (Holy Shrine of Emām Reza)
20 72 Tan Shahīd Mosque
21 Consulate of Pakistan
22 Bank Melli (Central Branch)
23 Main Post Office
25 Film & Camera Shop
26 Abidian Travel & Tour
   Company
27 Sepehri Exchange Office
29 Turkmenistan
   Consulate-General
30 Consulate of Afghanistan
31 Gombad-é Sabz
32 Bank Sepah
   (Central Branch)
40 Post Office
   (17 Sharīvar Square)
43 Main Telephone Office
44 Police Headquarters

and paying the requisite IR10,000. The form is only in Farsi so take a local with you or plead ignorance. Back at the visa office, take an application form from the small office on your left as you enter, and hand over a further IR2500 (for a folder in which your application will be filed) and two photos. Follow the sign to the Foreign Affairs counter where you'll be fingerprinted and can lodge the application. The staff may tell you it takes five days to process, but if you plead an emergency it's not too difficult to get a one- or two-week extension within 24 hours.

Getting to the office via shared taxi can be time-consuming, so you may want to charter your own; ask for Edārī-yé Atbāreh Khārijī (Aliens' Office) and expect to pay around IR3000 one way. Adibian Travel Agency (see Travel Agencies later in the section) can take care of the process for around US$10. If you have to wait about, come out of the office, turn left, walk to the main road, turn right and at the first junction cross diagonally to a drinks shop that sells excellent banana milk shakes with slices of banana and honey in them for IR5000. Very soothing.

Tourist Offices The tourist office (☎ 717 057) caters almost exclusively to pilgrims; no-one speaks English and they can't even provide any maps. The only reason for travellers to visit is to pick up the free official permission slip *(mojāvez)* needed for visiting the border areas around Sarakhs and Kalat.

Money The central branches of Bank Melli and Bank Sepah are among those with foreign exchange counters. There is also one at the departure (but not arrival) lounge at Mashhad airport. The Sepehri Exchange Office on Pāsdarān St is more speedy than the banks and changes at market rates.

Post & Communications The main post office (not marked in English) is near Bank Melli; there's a smaller branch on 17 Shahrīvar Square. The telephone office is easier to recognise, but is inconveniently located in the southern part of the city.

Pars Coffee Net (e Parscoffeenet@ Persiannet.net, ☎ 221 5383, fax 221 1599) on Dāneshgāh St is open from 9 to 11 am and it costs IR20,000 per hour to go online. There is a pleasant garden setting if you have to wait.

Travel Agencies Mashhad is full of travel agencies (85 at the last count), most of which attend solely to the needs of pilgrims.

Undoubtedly the best agency in town, and one of the best in the country, is the highly professional and efficient Adibian Travel Agency (☎ 98 151, fax 854 2373) on Pāsdarān St. In addition to selling domestic and international air tickets, and train tickets, and providing assistance with visa applications, it offers a range of tours around Mashhad and further afield. Their half-day tours include the Holy Shrine (US$20) and Tūs (US$30), and full-day trips go to Neishābūr (US$45), Kalat and the caravanserais of the Silk Road around Sarakhs (both U$50, although this can drop to as little as US$10 per person depending on the size of the group). With a little notice, they can arrange guides who speak English, French, German and Italian. They are also the representatives of the Touring & Automobile Club of Iran.

Photography & Film Mashhad is one of the best places outside Tehrān or Esfahān to purchase films or get them developed, with a particular concentration of shops in the streets leading to the shrine. For films (including slide) and photographic equipment, there are a couple of excellent stores along Pāsdarān St.

Emergency For general emergencies, telephone the directories number (☎ 118). Of the many hospitals in Mashhad, the Emām Rezā Hospital (☎ 43 031) is probably the best and most accessible and there is a pharmacy attached (☎ 98 466). There is also an ambulance service (☎ 197). The police headquarters (☎ 22 001) can be found south-west of the Holy Shrine near Emām Khomeinī Square; the police emergencies number is ☎ 110.

Dangers & Annoyances Be particularly careful not to upset Muslim sensibilities in this most holy of Iranian pilgrimage sites. Dress must be extremely conservative and clean: ideally men should not wear short sleeves in or near the shrine although if you're accompanied by an Iranian man this is unlikely to be a problem. Women *must* wear a chador inside the Holy Shrine, even if it is over the top of what they are already wearing. Remember; it is a privilege for non-Muslims to visit the shrine. Any incidents involving non-Muslims are likely to make the situation more difficult for subsequent visitors.

Āstān-é Qods-é Razavī

The Holy Shrine of Emām Rezā and the surrounding buildings of the *haram-é motahhar* (sacred precincts), known collectively as the Āstān-é Qods-é Razavī, make up one of the marvels of the Islamic world. There is so much to see in such a confined area that it is impossible to take in everything in one visit.

As well as the shrine itself, this large circular walled island in the centre of Mashhad contains mosques, museums, lofty iwans or halls (two of them coated entirely with gold), theological colleges (madrasehs), numerous courtyards, several libraries, a small post office, bookshop, and many other religious and administrative buildings. Beneath

ĀSTĀN-É QODS-É RAZAVĪ

1 Sahn-é Rezvan (Rezvan Courtyard)
2 Bookshop (Postcards and Qu'rans)
3 Sahn-é Ghadīr (Ghadir Courtyard)
4 Sahn-é Jomhūrī Eslāmī (Islamic Republic Courtyard); Sundial
5 International Relations of Āstān-é Qods-é Razavī (Foreigners Registration Office)
6 Gōhar Shād Library
7 Bast-é Sheikh Bahā'ī (Sheikh Bahā'ī Transitional Courtyard)
8 Parizād Madraseh (Theological College of Parizād)
9 Bast-é Sheikh Tossī (Sheikh Tossī Transitional Courtyard)
10 New Library
11 Bast-é Sheikh Tabarsī (Sheikh Tabarsī Transitional Courtyard)
12 Sahn-é Enqelāb (Enqelab Courtyard)
13 Holy Shrine
14 Azīm-é Gōhar Shād Mosque (Great Mosque of Gōhar Shād)
15 Sahn-é Qods (Qods Courtyard)
16 Sahn-é Emām Khomeinī (Emām Khomeinī Courtyard)
17 Mūzé-yé Markazi (Main Museum)
18 Mūzé-yé Qu'ran (Quran Museum)
19 Sahn-é Āzādī (Āzādī Courtyard)
20 Bast-é Sheikh Horre Amelī (Sheikh Horre Amelī Transitional Courtyard)
21 Mehmūnsarā-yé Āstān-é Qods (Hotel of the Holy Threshold for official guests only)
22 Emām Rezā Islamic Sciences University
23 Sahn-é Hedayat (Hedayat Courtyard)
24 Sahn-é Kosa (Kosa Courtyard)
25 72 Tan Shahīd Mosque

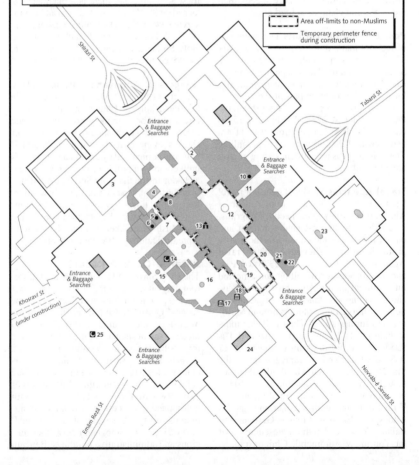

- - - - Area off-limits to non-Muslims
———— Temporary perimeter fence during construction

Shirāzī St

Tabarsī St

Entrance & Baggage Searches

Entrance & Baggage Searches

Khosravī St (under construction)

Entrance & Baggage Searches

Entrance & Baggage Searches

Entrance & Baggage Searches

Emām Rezā St

Navvāb-é Safavī St

0   50   100m
0   50   100yd

the shrine complex is a vast cemetery – to be buried near the Emām is a great honour. Unlike Mecca and Medina in Saudi Arabia, which are completely off-limits to non-Muslims, the holy precincts at Mashhad (although not the shrine itself) are open to nonbelievers.

Since the Revolution, the foundation that manages the shrine of Emām Rezā has become one of the biggest business conglomerates in Iran, managing an empire containing nearly 60 diverse companies ranging from bread-making factories to transport companies. Most of the money comes from donations, bequests and the selling of gravesites beneath the shrine itself, although the government also contributes significant amounts. The proceeds are used for the extensive charity activities of the foundation, which include hospitals, pharmacies, housing for the underprivileged, building mosques and developing poorer areas of Khorāsān province.

Information The shrine itself is closed to non-Muslims and there are strict rules about which other parts of the complex can be visited. Access is largely restricted to the courtyards (Sahn-é Emām Khomeinī, Sahn-é Jomhūrī Eslāmī and Sahn-é Qods), the Great Mosque of Gōhar Shād and the museum. Although there are no signs to warn you, the Sahn-é Āzādī and Sahn-é Enqelāb are strictly off-limits, as is the shrine itself.

Please dress neatly and conservatively and behave with the dignity the site deserves. Women *must* wear a full chador over the top of their normal hejab. You may feel more comfortable (and find the whole experience more rewarding) if you take a guide. Some travel agencies around town can provide guides in a range of languages (see Travel Agencies earlier). Non-Muslims should not attempt to visit on a Friday.

We had a guide who made sure we didn't stray. Of course it's a holy shrine and Muslim sensibilities have to be respected. But the amount you can see inside is limited. I think many travellers will feel like we did, that having arrived at 'the Vatican', we weren't able to see the 'Sistine Chapel'.

Mark Nicholls & Sharon Peake

An alternative is to take a (free) guide from the office of the International Relations of Āstān-é Qods-é Razavī (☎ 223 474, fax 59 090; also signed in English as 'Guidance for Foreign Pilgrims'). Regardless of whether you wish to use one of their guides, all visitors should visit their office to register their presence. The friendly, professional staff speak English and will show you a short video about the shrine (there is also another video about the bombing but they prefer not to show this to non-Muslims who, they say, find the images of severed body parts gross). This is also the place to ask for an up-to-date map, which will reflect the dizzying pace of construction around the perimeter of the complex.

For those with more interest in the history of the complex, Emām Rezā or Shiite theology, the office has a range of books and other resources, free of charge, in response to the thousands of queries the office receives from around the world. The staff are responsible for ensuring that you don't stray onto holy ground, but they also promise to 'answer any questions, solve any problems'. The office is open from 7 am to 4 or 5 pm daily except Fridays.

A fatal bombing in the shrine complex in 1994 killed 27 people and since then there has been significantly heightened security in and around the shrine, with strict baggage searches upon entering. No cameras are allowed inside the main gates, all bags must be left at the main entrance, and you will be frisked on the way in.

There are several entrances, although the most accessible are adjacent to Shīrāzī and Emām Rezā Sts. All the rebuilding work around the shrine makes it a bit difficult to find the way in.

The Holy Shrine The original tomb chamber was built by the Caliph Hārūn-ar-Rashīd in the early 9th century. In AD 944 the shrine was destroyed by the fervently Sunni Saboktagīn, founder of the Qaznavid dynasty, only to be rebuilt by his son Mahmūd in 1009. Both the shrine and the city were ransacked when the Mongols invaded in 1220. The present structure in the centre of the complex was built for Shāh Abbās I at the beginning of the 17th century.

The actual tomb in the Holy Shrine is 10m long with stunning gilt edges and is enclosed in a gold latticed cage. Pilgrims touch and kiss the cage in a moving climax to the pilgrimage. The shrine built over the tomb has a shimmering gilded cupola, single minaret and a vast tiled iwan.

The magnificent golden dome *(gonbad)* over the tomb has a circumference of 42.1m and about 7m, and above the tomb are some beautiful Quranic inscriptions by the renowned 16th-century calligrapher, Alī Rezā Abbāsī. The interior ceiling has some dazzling stalactite stuccowork decorated with multicoloured glass.

The two golden minarets attached to the shrine appear at first to lack symmetry. And yet, their unusual distance from each other is deliberate in order that pilgrims entering the complex from Emām Rezā Ave will see the dome between two perfectly aligned minarets.

Do *not* attempt to enter the actual shrine unless you are a Muslim. Non-Muslims are excluded not because of their faith (or lack thereof), but because there are special cleanliness rituals and prayers to be performed before entering.

The Pilgrimage to Mashhad

A pilgrimage *(ziyarah)* to Mashhad is one of the most important acts in the life of a Shiite Muslim. Although less significant than the haj pilgrimage to Mecca and Medina, or to the holy cities of Najaf and Kerbala in Iraq, a pilgrimage to Mashhad remains a deeply significant expression of faith. In the same way that haj pilgrims are known as *haji*, a title of great respect, pilgrims to Mashhad are entitled to attach the prefix *mashti* to their names. Scholarly opinion is divided over the spiritual value *(thawab)* of the ziyarah; some equate it with the haj, others even claim that a pilgrim to Mashhad ensures a place in paradise. Whatever the answer, no non-Muslim visitor can fail to be moved by the powerful outpouring of devotion visible here.

Great Mosque of Gōhar Shād This fine mosque, which is accessible to non-Muslims, is one of the best surviving examples of Timurid architecture in Iran. Queen of a mighty empire, wife of Timur's eldest son Shāh Rokh, patron of the arts and a powerful personality in her own right, Gōhar Shād was one of the most remarkable women in Islamic history. Although most of her major architectural commissions were at her capital Herat (in present-day Afghanistan), this mosque is the best-preserved testament to her genius. Constructed between 1405 and 1418, it has four iwans, two minarets, and some extraordinarily beautiful stalactite mouldings, calligraphic inscriptions and exquisite floral motifs. Its blue dome and cavernous golden portal are also exceptional. The minbar (pulpit) next to the mihrab is, according to Shiite tradition, the place where the Mahdi (the Hidden Emām) will sit on the Day of Judgement (for more information about the Mahdi, see the boxed text 'The 12 Emāms' in the Religion section of the Facts about Iran chapter).

Museums The museums, which are effectively combined into one, are excellent and certainly worth visiting. On the ground floor, there is a 16th-century gold bas-relief door that originally belonged to the Holy Shrine. A recent addition is the Carpet of the Seven Beloved Cities, which is said to have taken 10,000 weavers 14 years to make, and has a staggering 30 million knots. There is also an evocative mural depicting key scenes from Ashura, commemorating the event in which the third Shiite imam, Hossein, was martyred (see the Religion section in the Facts About Iran chapter).

Another highlight is the display of paintings by the renowned modern artist Mahmood Farshchian including the gorgeous *Fifth Day of Creation* and the intensely moving *Afternoon of Ashura*, which captures the grief-stricken aftermath of the martyrdom of Emām Hossein as his horse returns to camp. A part of the museum also houses some historical photos of Mashhad, the shrine complex and the damage caused by the bomb blast in 1994. Other features include an intricate stone mihrab dating from

1215, a huge 800-year-old wooden door and a one-tonne stone drinking vessel made in the 12th century. There are also displays of carpets, examples of calligraphy in Arabic and Farsi and a collection of more than 100 hand-inscribed Qurans – probably the largest public display in Iran. Some are written on deerskin, paper and wood, and are in Arabic as well as the ancient Kufic script.

On the top floor, there is an interesting architect's model of the shrine complex, while immediately downstairs from the museum entrance is a display of stamps and coins.

Most captions in the museum are translated into English. The museum is open from about 7.30 am to 1.30 pm daily, and from 7.30 am to noon on Friday. Entrance costs IR2000.

Boq'eh-yé Khājeh Rabī'

This fine 16th-century octagonal mausoleum 4km north of central Mashhad is worth a visit. It contains several famous 16th-century inscriptions by Alī Rezā Abbāsī, one of the greatest Persian calligraphers. The mausoleum stands in the midst of a large four-walled Martyrs' Cemetery known as the Ārāmgāh-é Khājeh Rabī', which contains thousands of tombstones with the usual photo displays of martyrs killed in the Iran-Iraq War. To get there, take bus No 38 from Kūhsangī Park or a shared taxi (IR400) from outside the train station or just north of the Holy Shrine. Entrance is free.

Nāder Shāh Museum

This unattractive concrete building, housing the tomb of Nāder Shāh and topped with his statue, is in a small park not far from the shrine. The Nāder Shāh Museum (☎ 24 888) is largely devoted to a collection of guns, swords and other militaria, mostly from the time of Nāder Shāh. Outside the museum stands a solitary bronze Spanish cannon, dated 1591 and later inscribed in Farsi with the Persian date 1180. How it came to be here is a mystery.

The museum and park are open from 8 am to 7 pm daily. Entrance costs a steep IR20,000.

Other Attractions

The blue dome of the 15th-century **Mosque of the 72 Martyrs** (Masjed-é 72 Tan Shahīd; previously the Shāh Mosque) in the Bāzār-é Bozorg can be seen from the shrine.

The **Gonbad-é Sabz** (Green Dome) in the centre of its own small square is Mashhad's most interesting and best-preserved historical building outside the shrine. It is a small quadrangular mausoleum, once used by Naghshbandī dervishes, and originally built in the Safavid period. The gonbad is often closed, but if you are lucky and can get inside, it contains the tomb of Sheikh Mohammed Hakīm Mo'men, author of a famous book on medicine, and lots of fine metal standards, or *alamats*.

As an alternative to the many religious attractions, little **Kūhsangī Park** is being developed and should be quite attractive when it's finished. There will be a fountain or two, a huge restaurant overlooking a tiny lake, and some small hills behind it to explore on foot. You can catch bus No 38 from the northern side of the shrine, or hop on a shared taxi heading west from the city centre.

Places to Stay

Mashhad is bursting with hotels, most of which are bursting with pilgrims. The majority are within a few minutes' walk of the Holy Shrine. For about 10 days before and after the Iranian New Year (about 21 March), and during the summer pilgrimage season, finding a room can be a real problem. At other times, most hotels will be virtually empty, so, if you bargain hard, you may get a decent mid-range place for a budget price. All prices listed in this section are for high season, so expect to pay less at other times. All the places in the middle and top-end price range have rooms with bathrooms.

Places to Stay – Budget

Despite the proliferation of mosāferkhūnehs around the shrine, getting into one as a non-Muslim is not always easy. Remember that a sign in English does not necessarily mean the management wants foreign guests and rarely means that the staff speak English.

One good option and quieter than most, though often full, is **Hotel Nasr** (☎ 854 2554) off Emām Rezā St – look for the word 'Nasr' in English above the door. It charges IR17,000 per person for a clean room, although we have received a complaint about the poor quality of the service.

The noisy **Hotel Sajjade** (☎ 45 238, Emām Rezā St) is in a central location and is good value. It charges IR15,000 per room.

The **Alborz Guesthouse** (☎ 825 097, Emām Rezā St) is not interested in foreigners during high season but at IR18,000/23,000 for passable doubles in a good location, it might be worth a look at other times.

Not far from the shrine, the **Saba Inn** (☎ 222 3515, Andarzgū St) is worth its IR21,500/29,300 for good singles/doubles; the rooms at the back are quieter. For a little more, **Tous Hotel** (☎ 222 4385) off Shīrāzī St is one of the best in the budget range. The rooms (IR33,000/41,000) are tidy and quiet despite being a mere stone's throw from the shrine.

Places to Stay – Mid-Range

Rāzi Hotel (☎ 854 5333, fax 44 099, Rāzi St) is great value, with comfortable singles/doubles with bath, TV and fridge for US$10/20 including breakfast (you can pay in rials). The location is also good, within walking distance of the shrine but away from its crowds. Similarly recommended is the friendly **Sina Hotel** (☎ 222 8543, Bahonnār St), where the IR60,000 for a reasonable double also includes breakfast.

Emām Rezā St is lined with mid-range hotels in the blocks south of Beit-ol-Moqaddas Square. **Madaen Hotel** (☎ 96 031) is particularly good value at IR120,000/180,000 for good rooms, and the staff are helpful. Another popular place is the **Hotel Djavaheri** (☎ 99 817), which charges IR100,000/150,000 for attractive doubles/triples with a fridge and TV.

The cluster of upper mid-range places opposite the Nāder Shāh Museum on Āzādī St operate as a cartel. All have identical prices and are aimed squarely at the pilgrim market, but aren't bad value in low season when there are significant discounts to be had.

Āzarbāyjān Hotel (☎ 54 001) is the friendliest of the bunch, the lobby of the **Āzādī Hotel** (☎ 51 927, fax 222 5389) is busier than the bazaar, and the **Amir Hotel** (☎ 222 1300, fax 222 0442) would prefer not to have to deal with foreigners. All charge US$25 for quite comfortable doubles.

Although quite a walk from the shrine, the **Shīrāz Hotel** (☎ 839 717, Dāneshgāh St) is definitely worth considering. The staff are friendly, the rooms are spacious and pleasant and a steal if you can, as some travellers have managed, get the Iranian price of IR111,000/142,000.

Places to Stay – Top End

The **Iran Hotel** (☎ 222 8010, fax 222 8583, Andarzgū St) is a touch of accessible luxury. Some rooms on the upper floors have great views and the management are refreshingly welcoming for a top-end place. At IR240,000 for a lovely double, it's a great place for a splurge.

Another good option in the lower top-end range is the **Sadr Hotel** (☎ 836 801, fax 816 020, Dāneshgāh St) where the rooms are of similarly high quality (US$35) and the staff don't make you feel like an imposter if you arrive looking a bit dishevelled.

The **Mashhad Hotel** (☎ 222 2666, Emām Rezā St) is not as good as it used to be. The rooms are the same but the increased asking price is a little steep at US$30/40 (including breakfast) a single/double. It's often filled with group bookings so the manager has little reason to negotiate but you could try and get the Iranian price of IR166,000/213,500. The rooms are quiet, especially further upstairs and away from the main road.

The **Grand Atlas Hotel** (☎ 854 5061, fax 854 7800, Beit-ol-Moqaddas Square) couldn't be more centrally located and charges IR215,000/250,000 in the high season and IR170,000/212,500 in the low. Either way it's good value, particularly if you get a room on an upper floor at the front where you should have an uninterrupted view over the shrine.

The recognised top-class tourist hotel is the **Homa Hotel** (☎ 832 001, Feizīyé St) which is, typically for this chain, inconveniently located in the west of town. Prices are US$75/100 for a single/double.

Places to Eat

Ābgūsht (a soupy meat stew) is popular and fairly cheap in Mashhad and neighbouring Torqabeh. The stone dish, or *dīzī*, in which ābgūsht is served around the country originates from Mashhad. For great ābgūsht in traditional surroundings, head for one of the teahouses listed in the following section.

There are plenty of cheap eating houses along Emām Rezā St and also the length of Emām Khomeinī St. Next door to the Hotel Djavaheri, *Fried Chicken Pizza* does reasonable fast food and is popular with a young crowd. *Saba Chelō Kabābī*, just up from the Nāder Shāh Museum isn't bad either and is handy for the chain of hotels opposite.

Pars Restaurant on Emām Khomeinī St is excellent for tasty Iranian food at Iranian prices of about IR15,000 a plate. It's packed out for lunch and dinner – always a good sign – but don't bother turning up for dinner before 8.30 pm. Another cheap but good choice is the friendly *Malek Restaurant* on Andarzgū St, as is the *Ferdōsī Restaurant* on Emām Rezā St.

You'll need a taxi to reach the more up-market *Moein Darbary Restaurant* on the Kālantarī Hwy in the west of town, but it has been highly recommended by several travellers.

Most of the dozens of hotels along Emām Rezā St have restaurants that serve good food in pleasant surroundings. Expect to pay about US$2 a dish, including soup, salad and drinks. The *Mashhad Hotel* is probably the best and serves excellent breakfasts for guests. The lunch and dinner menu is limited but good value; a *chelō kabāb* (kebab with rice), cola and soup comes to IR15,000.

Teahouses

Mashhad has at least two traditional tea-houses. *Hezardestān Traditional Tea House* (☎ 222 2943) rivals the best Iran has to offer and may just be a highlight of your visit to Mashhad. The underground setting is beautifully decorated with carpets, samovars, an-

tique water pipes, cushions and wooden benches while the walls are adorned with scenes and calligraphy from Ferdōsī's *Shāh-namah*. There is live music most nights and even an artisan who sketches the night away, including your portrait if you ask nicely. The teahouse also serves good ābgūsht. It can be difficult to find; look for the green urn at the top of a discreet staircase in Jannat Mall or ask any local for the Sofrakhāneh Sonati Hezardestān.

Bagh-é Sabz Tea House, on the 1st floor above the busy corner of Emām Khomeinī and Shahīd Rajā'ī Sts, also has a great atmosphere. The cushions provide the perfect vantage point from which to watch Mashhad's crush of people and vehicles on the streets below. It's a lovely place to relax with a *qalyan* (water pipe), and the ābgūsht isn't bad either.

Shopping

When they are not busy visiting the shrine, Iranian tourists love to shop, and there are several bazaars and shopping arcades to choose from.

Mashhad used to be famous as a place to buy turquoises, although many tourists went away more sold on the sales pitch of the dealers than the quality of their turquoise. Not much has changed over the last century since Curzon wrote:

> It would be quite a mistake to suppose that by going either to Meshed (Mashhad) or to Nishapur (Neishābūr), or even to the pit mouth (of the turquoise mine), the traveller can pick up valuable stones at a moderate price. Fraser tried several years ago, and was obliged to desist from the attempt by the ruthless efforts made to cheat him. Every succeeding traveller has tried and has reported his failure. All the best stones are bought up at once by commission agents on the spot and are despatched to Europe or sold to Persian grandees. I did not see a single good specimen either in Meshed or Teheran, though I made constant inquiries…
>
> **GN Curzon,**
> *Persia and the Persian Question (1892)*

The mine at Neishābūr is still one of the largest in Iran. Buy only if you have a clear idea of the international market value of the turquoises and can recognise a fake.

The **Bāzār-é Rezā** is 800m long and is open mornings and evenings, except Friday. You can buy gorgeous fabrics and rugs, as well as nuts, honey and saffron. Saffron is cheap in Mashhad; a 10g box costs about IR12,000 and makes a great souvenir (see the boxed text 'Saffron'). Try and resist the considerable temptation to buy an oversaturated photograph of yourself superimposed upon the Holy Shrine or a scene from the Swiss Alps.

Getting There & Away

Air Mashhad has regular flights to most major centres in Iran. Given its isolation from the rest of the country, consider taking a relatively cheap flight to/from Mashhad – but book early. Iran Air flies directly from Mashhad to the following places:

destination	flights per week	cost (IR)
Ahvāz	2	221,000
Bandar-é Abbās	2	208,000
Būshehr	2	222,000
Esfāhān	7	169,000
Kermān	2	154,000
Kermānshāh	1	224,000
Rasht	2	176,000
Shīrāz	1	191,000
Tabrīz	2	225,000
Tehrān	2	153,000
Yazd	2	142,000
Zāhedān	3	155,000

The number of flights is often reduced during the quieter winter months.The Iran Air office (☎ 52 080; airport office ☎ 99 955) is open from 7.30 am to 6.30 pm Saturday to Thursday and from 7.30 to 11.30 am on Friday. The office in town is on Emām Khomeinī St.

Most other domestic airlines also fly to Mashhad. Iran Asseman (☎ 58 200), which has an office on Andarzgū St, shadows many Iran Air routes but also flies to Zābol, Rafsanjān and Bīrjand, although both schedules and prices were in a state of flux at the time of research.

Tiny Māhān Air links Mashhad with Kermān twice a week for IR154,000; and Saha Airlines (☎ 221 9294, fax 221 9293), An-

Saffron

Saffron is a spice containing stigmas of the crocus plant, used for the natural flavouring and colouring of dishes such as Iranian chelō (rice) and Spanish paella. Extracts from the plant can also help with digestive problems and nervous disorders, and there are unproven claims that saffron boosts energy and improves memory.

Saffron was imported from ancient Persia by many regional empires, and used for pharmaceutical purposes, also as a spice, in religious ceremonies and as a dye for the paint used in decorating holy manuscripts. Cleopatra apparently used to bathe in a mixture that included saffron. By the 18th century, seeds were successfully taken to Spain, which supplied the increasing European market.

Though Spain still dominates the international market for saffron, the plant is still grown extensively in southern regions of Khorāsān, as well as Fārs, Kermān and Yazd provinces. Saffron seeds are planted in May or August, then irrigated with care, before the bright pink or violet flowers bloom for about three weeks from mid-October. The stigmas are separated and left to dry in sheds, or hung from the roof in special containers, and then crushed into powder. It takes a staggering 2000 to 3000 flowers to make about 15g of saffron powder.

darzgū St, flies daily to Tehrān, three times a week to Esfāhān and twice weekly to Shīrāz for the same prices as Iran Air.

If you arrive in Mashhad by air, there is a useful hotel reservation counter inside the arrivals hall. Although it handles only midrange and top-end places, this can save you from driving all over town in a taxi, especially in peak season when many hotels are full. You pay a small percentage of the nightly rate, which should theoretically be deducted from your bill later by the hotel.

The airport can be pretty chaotic and there are no flight announcements in English so you must pay close attention.

International Flights Mashhad has some handy international connections, particularly to Central Asia and the Arabian Peninsula.

Iran Asseman (☎ 58 200) has three flights per week to Ashghabat in Turkmenistan for US$85/105 one way/return; two flights a week to Dushanbe in Tajikistan (US$165/247); and weekly flights to Bishkek in Kyrgyzstan (US$200/325), Dubai (US$125/230) in the UAE and Quetta in Pakistan (US$105/175). The latter is an excellent alternative to two or three days' dusty road travel.

Iran Air (☎ 52 080) has some flights from Mashhad to Kuwait (US$124 one way) and Bahrain (US$215) during peak pilgrimage season although seats are hard to come by as most are booked out by travel agencies in the Gulf countries. Kuwait Airways also flies twice a week to Kuwait (US$124).

Bus & Minibus The bus station (☎ 99 001) is at the southern end of Mashhad, but easy to reach by any shared taxi (IR400) heading south along Emām Rezā St. Getting there is the easy part though.

> I think it would be worth considering an LP Travel Survival Kit to the bus station in Mashhad. Always plenty of people screaming in Farsi, nobody speaking English, no destination written in English – hell for the non-believer! The magic object of desire is…the Sayro-Safar office and an advanced computer printed ticket…Some companies start to sell tickets only if and after the bus came from the opposite direction. It means that you have a good chance of spending some unforgettable nights and days at this place. Mashhad bus station is probably the only place in the whole of Iran where I felt really lost and desperate.
>
> **Pawel Mroczkowski**

For Tabas, it is quicker to take a bus to Yazd, although you may have to pay the full fare; similarly, you may have to pay the Tehrān price even if you're only going to Shāhrūd.

Check the security situation before travelling overland from Mashhad to Zāhedān or Kermān due to the ongoing troubles in Afghanistan, and constant smuggling of drugs along the border. Expect frequent baggage searches along the way. It can be a *very* long and hot trip.

To catch a minibus to Tūs (IR450), go to Shohadā Square. For Torqabeh (IR200),

buses leave from the kerbside 100m north of Shohadā Square on Khājeh Rabī' St.

Useful daily services are listed in the following table:

destination	distance (km)	duration (hrs)	cost (IR)
Chālūs	877	14	18,700
Esfahān	1338	22	29,000
Gonbad-é Kāvūs	471	8	10,300
Gorgān	564	9	12,400
Kermān	886	16	26,900
Neishābūr	114	3	3000
Qom	1049	16	22,300
Rasht	1075	18	23,100
Sarakhs	185	3	4200
Sārī	695	12	13,500
Shāhrūd	517	10	10,600
Tabas (via Bīrjand)	521	10	11,500
Tāybād	224	3	4800
Tehrān	924	14	19,500
Yazd	939	16	24,500
Zābol	1149	14	22,000
Zāhedān	937	15	26,900

To/From Turkmenistan The border to Turkmenistan is at Sarakhs (see the Sarakhs section later in this chapter for detailed information about crossing the border). To get to Sarakhs from Mashhad, take a bus (IR4200, three hours, 185km) from the bus station; at the time of research, Bus Cooperative No 10 had 17 buses daily. From Sarakhs, simply take whatever is going to Mashhad. Shared taxis from Sarakhs to Mashhad shouldn't cost more than IR8000.

Train The 926km train journey to Tehrān makes an interesting alternative to the plane or long hours of bus travel. The train station (☎ 51 555) is easy to reach by shared taxi (IR1000 from the centre of town). A bus often links the train station with Beit-ol-Moqaddas Square.

This is the busiest train line in the country, and there is a good chance you will get a ticket at either end. Currently, there are as many as 11 trains daily between Mashhad and Tehrān in peak season, some express (ie, stopping at only a few main cities), the rest stopping at all stations. Prices range from IR34,250 for a bunk in a six-sleeper compartment to IR38,900 for one shared with three others and IR76,000 for a deluxe service including dinner and breakfast.

There's also a Tuesday service to Qom at 8.10 pm that arrives at 1.25 pm the following day. A 2nd-class-only ticket costing IR23,100 is available. Twice a week, the train rolls out to Tabrīz; 1st-class sleeper tickets cost IR56,500.

To/From Turkmenistan Although there are plans to connect Turkmen and Iranian trains to allow passengers to take the train across the border, don't hold your breath. The opening of the line was delayed in 1996 when it was realised that the trains in Iran and Turkmenistan run on different gauges. This realisation is as far as they've got.

In the meantime, a train leaves Mashhad daily at 5.10 pm, arriving at Sarakhs around 8 pm. The train returns the following morning, leaving Sarakhs at 6.30 am, arriving in Mashhad four hours later. Tickets cost IR3650.

Getting Around

To/From the Airport The Mashhad Taxi Agency, with its new Peugot 405s, holds a monopoly on taxis from (but not *to*) the airport and has a counter right outside the station. You might be able to find a stray Paykan hanging around outside the departure hall but don't count on it. The official agency price to the centre of town is about IR10,000. Far cheaper, but inconvenient if you have a lot of luggage, is the public bus that travels regularly between the airport terminal and Basīj Mustāzafin Square.

Bus Most hotels are within walking distance of the shrine so local buses are not normally needed. One useful bus (but check the number when you arrive in Mashhad) is No 38, which travels between Kūhsangī Park, the shrine and the Boq'eh-yé Khājeh Rabī'.

Taxi Fares for shared taxis around Mashhad are reasonably low, costing about IR400 for a short ride, or IR1500 right across town. But be careful – some drivers overcharge all visitors, Iranian or foreign.

AROUND MASHHAD

You can visit most places around Mashhad by public transport, but it's worth chartering a private taxi for about IR15,000 per hour if you want to see as much as possible in one day. Otherwise, hop on a guided tour – see Travel Agencies in the Mashhad section earlier for more information.

Torqabeh   طرقبه
☎ 05287

This particularly pretty tree-lined village is appreciably cooler than Mashhad and a quiet alternative to the bustle of the city. It is famous for handicrafts, carpets, baskets and carvings, and it's a fantastic place to stroll around and do a bit of souvenir hunting. Although its population is small, the village stretches for several kilometres through low valleys overflowing with cherry, apple, apricot and walnut trees, the produce of which is highly sought after in Arab countries. The blossoms in spring are spectacular.

No trip to Mashhad would be complete without an evening visit to Torqabeh. Every night until 1 or 2 am, the wonderful traditional garden restaurants for which Torqabeh is famous are filled with Mashhadīs sitting under the stars, smoking qalyans in a delightfully relaxed and festive atmosphere. There are few better ways to spend a summer's evening.

Places to Stay & Eat If you are longing to escape the clamour of Mashhad, consider the ***Grand Hotel*** (☎ 20 09, fax 22 52) on the main road into Torqabeh. This enormous hotel has semi-luxurious singles/doubles for IR193,200/315,000 in the high season, with prices dropping by as much as 20% during the quieter months. Minibuses shuttle guests to and from the hotel in Mashhad at regular intervals. It's a pleasant 4km walk to the centre of Torqabeh.

The ***restaurants*** begin about 500m beyond the main roundabout and continue for almost 5km. Choose whichever setting takes your fancy – the ābgūsht is consistently good wherever you go. Also don't leave without trying the local ice cream (*bastānī*) available from the *sweet shops* along the main street.

Getting There & Away Torqabeh is 25km east of Mashhad. Buses to Torqabeh leave from 100m north-east of Shohadā Square in Mashhad every half-hour or so.

Tūs (Ferdōsī)   توس

Sacked in AD 1389 and abandoned in the 15th century, Tūs (also now known as Ferdōsī) was the regional capital before Mashhad. Parts of the walls of the citadel of the great city remain, but the present-day village is best known to most Iranians as the home town of the epic poet Ferdōsī, whose mausoleum lies over what is believed to be his exact place of death. It is a lovely place, and an easy trip from Mashhad.

Ferdōsī's Tomb Set in its own park and dominating the village of Tūs, the pale stone mausoleum of Ferdōsī was built in 1933 in preparation for the celebration of the 1000th anniversary of the poet's death.

It was rebuilt in 1934 because the first version was thought too plain, and again in 1964 after it started to sink on its weak foundations. It was partially destroyed during the earliest and most violent throes of the Islamic Revolution because Ferdōsī was thought then to be anti-Islamic. He is now revered once again, his tomb being one of Iran's most popular domestic tourism drawcards.

The tomb's structure is strongly reminiscent of the Tomb of Cyrus at Pasargadae, and the upper panels have winged carvings of Zoroastrian motifs.

The interior is beautifully set out with stone reliefs depicting scenes from the *Shāh-namah* along the walls. In the centre stands the simple marble tomb with a eulogy to the poet on the top.

There is a marble statue of Ferdōsī in the garden and, behind the tomb, some mud-brick remains of the city walls of ancient Tūs, which are labelled in English. The small **Tūs Museum** (☎ 25 180) inside the park contains a collection of ceramics and pottery inspired by Ferdōsī and a 73kg copy

of the *Shāh-namah* but most captions are in Farsi only.

A **restaurant** in the gardens serves cold drinks and simple meals for lunch. Inside the room containing the tomb there's a bookshop selling books (with surprisingly few copies of the *Shāh-namah* in English) and postcards.

Entrance to the mausoleum will set you back IR25,000, plus another IR30,000 for the museum, which is far too much; you'll probably be in and out again in 15 minutes. The park, mausoleum and museum are open daily from 8 am to 8 pm, closing an hour earlier in winter. The best time to visit is late afternoon, but don't stay too long after dark because getting back to Mashhad by public transport can be difficult.

Boq'é-yé Hordokieh' Also known as the Gonbad-é Haruniyeh, this 14th-century brick mausoleum, about 1km south of Ferdōsī's Tomb and on the road to Mashhad, is popularly associated with Hārūn-ar-Rashīd (whose earthly remains are, however, generally accepted to have been buried near those of Emām Rezā in Mashhad). Theories about the origin of the mausoleum are varied: it is either (a) the home of an unknown poet; (b) a previous place of worship for an unknown religious cult; or (c) a prison for the killer of Emām Rezā. On the exterior of the north wall, the remains of an ancient mihrab suggest that it was also a mosque at some stage in its history.

Between Ferdōsī's tomb and Boq'é-yé Hordokieh' the ancient citadel of Tūs, the **Arg-é Tūs**, is visible across the windswept plain to the west. You can also see the foundations of walls and buildings from the ancient city in the fields.

Getting There & Away Tūs is 23km from Mashhad on a turn-off east of the road to Gorgān. Minibuses direct to the mausoleum (IR400, 30 to 40 minutes) leave about every 20 to 30 minutes during the day from Shohadā Square in Mashhad. Shared taxis (about IR1250) leave from the same square in Mashhad, and hover outside Ferdōsī's Tomb in Tūs alongside the private taxis.

NEISHĀBŪR نیشابور
☎ 0551

Due west of Mashhad, Neishābūr was the earliest known capital of Khorāsān. Originally established during the Seljuk period, and at one time a thriving literary, artistic and academic centre, Neishābūr is now most famous as the birthplace and resting place of the poet, Omar Khayyām.

Omar Khayyām's Tomb
Omar Khayyām's very simple tombstone sits in uneasy contrast with the questionable modern structure towering above it. Several very tall and narrow tiled concrete lozenges are linked at the edges and redeemed only by inscriptions from the works of the great man. The gardens surrounding the tomb, Bāgh-é Mahrūgh, are probably more of an attraction. Also in the same

MARTIN HARRIS

Listening to recitations of Omar Khayyam's poetry constitutes a big night out in Iran.

grounds is the Emāmzādeh-yé Mohammed Mahrūgh, a fine 16th-century domed mausoleum. The gardens and tombs are about 1km south of Neishābūr, but if you are walking there from town, you will need to ask directions. Entrance costs IR25,000.

Caravanserai
The partially restored caravanserai, on a roundabout on the main road between the town and Omar Khayyām's Tomb, dates back to Safavid times and is worth a quick look. It contains a couple of souvenir shops and a small museum.

Places to Stay & Eat
Next to the city park in the centre of town is the unmarked ITTO *Tourist Hotel* (☎ 33 445), also known as the Neishābūr Inn. It charges US$20/30 for a single/double, and rials are accepted. The restaurant is excellent, and worth visiting if you are coming from Mashhad for the day. There are plenty of *hamburger joints* and *kabābīs* along the main street.

Getting There & Away
Several minibuses leave every morning from Mashhad to Neishābūr (IR3000, 2½ hours, 114km), or you can just hop on any bus heading along the main road towards Semnān, and get off at Neishābūr.

For a private taxi to/from Mashhad, expect to pay about IR15,000 per hour, but bargain hard.

FROM NEISHĀBŪR TO MASHHAD
Hiring a private taxi for the journey between Neishābūr and Mashhad is a good idea because it allows you to visit several historical places between Neishābūr and Mashhad, including the ruins of the 15th-century Mosallā-yé Torāq (14km from Mashhad), the Qaznavid minaret and dome at Sang Bast (37km from Mashhad), Boq'eh-yé Qadamgāh and the parkland at Vakīl Ābād.

Boq'eh-yé Qadamgāh بقعه قدمگاه
This charming 17th-century octagonal mausoleum doesn't look much from the outside,

but it's in a small, pretty garden in the otherwise dreary village of Qadamgāh. Qadamgāh means 'Place of the Foot' and it is so-called because inside the mausoleum there is a stone slab with what are believed to be the (very large) footprints of Emām Rezā. While the gardens are worth a trip, sadly the mausoleum is full of modern graffiti and badly needs renovation. Some steps inside the mausoleum lead to the source of a mountain spring, apparently created by the great Emām Rezā himself.

This place is on the busy itinerary for pilgrims who want to see everything to do with Emām Rezā. The mausoleum and village are just off the main road between Neishābūr and Mashhad. Take a shared taxi (about IR4000) from Neishābūr or get off any bus heading west from Mashhad and walk south for 5km from the main road.

Vakīl Ābād   وكيل آباد

About halfway between Mashhad and Neishābūr is this lovely bit of parkland. There is plenty of fresh air and scenery to enjoy, and a couple of *cafes* and *kabābīs* sell cold drinks and kebabs. If you have chartered a taxi, you could visit this park on the way to/from Mashhad or get off the minibus between Neishābūr and Mashhad.

SARAKHS   سرخس

The town of Sarakhs, once an important staging post along the famous Silk Road, is right on the Turkmenistan border 185km north-east of Mashhad by road (but only 120km by train). Watch out for the **Rubat Sharaf Caravanserai**, one of the biggest and finest of Iran's Silk Road caravanserais, just before Sarakhs. Adibian Travel Agency (see Travel Agencies in the Mashhad section) organises tours that take in Rubat Sharaf.

Gonbad-é Sheikh Loghmān Bābā

Sheikh Loghmān Bābā was a famous 10th-century teller of fables, and this vast domed monument on the outskirts of Sarakhs was constructed as his mausoleum in the 14th century. For the scale and quality of its interior and exterior decorations in brick and plaster, this mausoleum is one of the most impressive surviving structures of its period in Iran, despite its ruined condition.

Getting There & Away

Shared taxis from Sarakhs to Mashhad should cost about IR8000, otherwise, just take whatever's going in your direction. From Mashhad, take a bus (IR4200, three hours, 185km) from the bus station.

To/From Turkmenistan The border crossing here is the newest and most modern crossing in Iran, and after decades of closure, it is now open to foreigners. Foreigners must cross the border on foot (there are no direct buses in either direction), or hitch a ride on a truck. Some cyclists have reported a slow, but generally trouble-free crossing.

The border posts are at Sarakhs (Iran) and Saraghs (Turkmenistan). Keep some *manat* (Turkmenistan's currency) or rials in case you have to pay for the minibuses between control points. Both sides of the border close at 5 pm, so make an early start. If you take the train between Sarakhs and Mashhad, you'll have to stay overnight in Sarakhs and it can be difficult getting any sort of road transport after 5 pm. Expect long delays on the Turkmenistan side of the border, partly because of persistent requests for bribes; the Iranian side of the border is a relative model of efficiency.

You can stay in a small unnamed *hotel* on the Iranian side of the border for IR21,000 per person; or at the *Saraghs District Hotel* on the other side of the border in Saraghs for the manat equivalent of about US$3; it's better to get from Mary (Turkmenistan) to Mashhad (or vice versa) in one day. From Saraghs you can get onward transport to Mary (the bus leaves at noon, four hours) or Ashghabat (8 am, six hours) through one or two checkpoints where Turkmen customs officers may request some small additional 'fees'.

QUCHAN & BAJGIRAN   قوچان بجگیران

People heading to Turkmenistan via the Bajgiran (Iran) and Howdan (Turkmenistan) border crossing will need to take a bus from Mashhad central bus station to Quchan and then pick up onward transportation. If you arrive too late to head on, the centrally located *Hotel Khayyam* offers rooms for IR20,000 and has a restaurant too.

At Bajgiran there are buses to take you to the border. The Iranian and Turkmen borders are roughly 30km apart but there are buses to ferry you between them. On the Turkmen side taxis wait to run you to Ashghabat.

Crossing into Iran here, you may be lucky and find a shared taxi going direct to Mashhad for around IR30,000 per person. The journey will take about 8 hours, although there may be a wait in Quchan.

KALAT   كلت

This dramatic natural fortress, also known as Gonbad-é Kabud (Blue Dome), is 150km north of Mashhad. The valley is 36km long and 12km wide at its widest point. Surrounded by the steep-sided ridges that protect the valley from the outside world, it is easy to see why Kalat has gained such a reputation for being a redoubt of rebels.

The legend of Kalat is formidable – it was never captured by Tamerlane despite his vice-like grip over much of Iran and it was made famous as the stronghold of Nāder Shāh as he retreated from the battlefield and sought protection from his considerable band of enemies. It was first mentioned in Ferdōsī's epic, the *Shāh-namah*, where the ruler tells his army commander that of the two routes to Turkmenistan – via the harsh desert or through Kalat – the desert is the far less dangerous.

To fully appreciate Kalat's natural impregnability, ask to be let out at the entrance to the tunnel which runs beneath the towering cliffs. Follow the creek and unpaved track that twists through the 500m-long, narrow canyon, one of only two entrances to the valley. High on the cliff face to the right is an unfinished stone tablet carved with poetry praising Nāder Shāh. A few fortified watchtowers sit on rocky outcrops from where there are spectacular views and where a small number of troops could control access to the valley.

The modern inhabitants of the valley trace their origins to the Germanj sect of Kurdish tribes who were transferred to Kalat during the Safavid dynasty to keep guard against northern invaders.

Spring is a the best time to visit, when the countryside turns green, fields of flowers transform the countryside and the tents of nomads dot the surrounding plains. It can also be beautiful in winter after a light snowfall. Make sure you stop off at the tourist office in Mashhad for a free permission slip (*mojavez*) to allow you to visit this border area.

Khorshīd Palace

About 5km from the western entrance to the valley in the village of Kabud Gonbad lies the Khorshīd Palace (Sun Palace) with its distinctive circular stone tower on an octagonal base. Set amid lush lawns, the palace is thought by local historians to have been built by Nāder Shāh as a mausoleum rather than a palace.

The exterior panels are decorated with intricate carvings of fruit (pineapples and pears) not found in Khorāsān, suggesting that they were completed by artisans Nāder Shāh brought with him from his Indian conquests. The interior, currently under typically painstaking and precise restoration, will be magnificent when finished. The Quranic calligraphy and 16 perfectly proportioned sunken alcoves are a particular feature.

Entrance is free. There is a small kiosk that sells drinks at the entrance and a stall inside sells a reasonable range of postcards, maps and books.

Kabud Gonbad Mosque

The beautiful blue dome is the main highlight of this small mosque. It was built under the supervision of Nāder Shāh during 1736–47, although there is some brickwork on the left as you enter which dates from Seljuk times. The main road running 5km beyond the mosque to the ancient dam, **Band-é Nāderī**, offers some of the best scenery in the region.

Places to Stay & Eat

There is nowhere to stay in town so you'll need to take a day trip from Mashhad or camp somewhere en route. *Restōrān-é Khorshīd* does nice, reasonably priced meals though kebabs are a recurring theme. There's no sign but it's 400m west of Khorshīd Palace on the south side of the road. There is also a smattering of grocery stores along the main street.

Getting There and Away
The cheapest option is to take a semi-regular bus (IR3000, three hours) from Mashhad although it's a long day that won't allow you much time to explore the valley and you'll need a very early start. At the time of research, buses were leaving from the intersection of the Fajr Highway and Khājé Rabī' St in the north of Mashhad, although you might find the occasional bus leaving from the bus station. Check the best location a day ahead to get the most from your time. Also, get your free permission slip to visit this border area in advance.

Far better if you can afford it is to charter a private taxi that allows you to stop off along the way to admire the rolling hills and poplar groves of Central Asia's southern steppes. You could also take a picnic lunch and stop at one of the many shady roadside streams en route. A private taxi will cost a minimum of IR240,000 including waiting time. Adibian Travel Agency (see Travel Agencies in the Mashhad section) runs expensive but professional tours for US$50 per person for the full day. The price drops considerably if you can get a group together.

TANDOUREH NATIONAL PARK پار کملی تندوره
This national park is home to the Oreal ram and ibex and, if you're exceptionally lucky, you may even come across a snow leopard. The park is inaccessible by public transport but talk to the Adibian Travel Agency in Mashhad (see Travel Agencies in the Mashhad section) who can arrange ecotours to the region, including the park.

TĀYBĀD تایباد
Tāybād, 224km south-east of Mashhad, is the nearest town to the border post with Afghanistan. There is an interesting 14th-century mosque, the **Mōlānā Mosque**, but otherwise this is definitely not a town you want to visit unless you're heading for Herat across the border – a foolhardy undertaking given the situation in Afghanistan.

There are regular buses to Mashhad (IR4800, three hours, 224km).

SHĀHRŪD شاهرود
☎ 0273
Shāhrūd is a very pleasant town wedged between the northern fringe of the Dasht-é Kavīr and the eastern Alborz Mountains. Its tree-lined streets, pleasant climate and relaxed atmosphere make it an excellent place to break the long journey between Tehrān and Mashhad or to commence an exploration of the eastern Caspian region. Shāhrūd also makes a good base for a visit to the pretty village of Bastām. You could even travel to Gonbad-é Kāvūs (see The Caspian Sea chapter for more details) from here.

The main road through town is 22 Bahman St, which stretches from the bus station in the south to Āzādī Square in the north of the town.

Places to Stay & Eat
The cheapest places are around Jomhūrī-yé Eslāmī Square. Of these, the *New Islami Inn* (☎ 22 335), a few metres east of the square, is one of the few places in Iran where prices have actually gone down and is now as cheap as you'll get anywhere – IR9000/10,000 for a basic single/twin room. The shared showers don't always work and there's no English spoken but it's still an OK choice.

Hotel Rezā (☎ 26 525) has singles with bathroom that are pretty good value at IR85,000 although the doubles are a little overpriced at IR170,000. The rooms are very clean but the furniture can be a bit on the spartan side and some beds sag atrociously. It's 300m south of Āzādī Square along 22 Bahman St and there's a reasonable restaurant.

On the south side of Āzādī Square in the north of town, there is a good choice of places to eat from *kabābīs* to something a little better – the pleasant *Kohpayeh Restaurant* comfortably straddles the two. The only authentic things about the *Pizza Hut* are the

EASTERN IRAN

posters inside, although the pizzas aren't bad for around IR14,000 and they also do kebabs; it's a short block north of Hotel Rezā. There are a few decent *snack bars* and *cake shops* around Jomhūrī-yé Eslāmī and Emām Squares.

Getting There & Away

Bus & Minibus The main bus station is 5km south of Jomhūrī-yé Eslāmī Square; a shared taxi there costs IR1000. The bus companies have convenient offices around Jomhūrī-yé Eslāmī Square where you can buy tickets in advance. There are several direct buses a day to Tehrān (IR9300), Gorgān (IR6300), Mashhad (IR10,300), Sārī (IR8500) and Semnān (IR5000), as well as less frequent buses to Rasht (IR15,000) and Esfahān (IR18,000).

Buses and minibuses for Gorgān also leave from the small and well-organised Termīnāl-é Shimāl on Hussein Square; ask at the bus company offices for the best place to go. Some travellers even use Shāhrūd as a base for visiting Gonbad-é Kāvūs (around IR5000), 142km to the north-east. To do this you may need to take a bus for Gorgān (make sure it doesn't go via Dāmghān) and change in Āzād Shahr for the final 18km.

Hourly minibuses also go from the main bus station to Dāmghān (IR1500) and Semnān (IR4000) but it may be more convenient just to hail something at Āzādī Square, through which all transport passes.

Train Shāhrūd is on the line between Tehrān and Mashhad, but nearly everyone uses the quicker and more reliable bus or minibus. The train station is about 3km south-east of Jomhūrī-yé Eslāmī Square.

BASTĀM   بسطام

The village of Bastām is lovely and tree-lined and certainly worth a look if you are in this part of the country. It's a pleasant place to wander around, with quiet streets and the occasional caravanserai, but the highlight is undoubtedly the beautiful **mosque** that was possibly started in the 11th century AD. The main part that you can see today was built during the Seljuk period of the early 13th century. It is decorated with some wonder-

ful swirling stucco reliefs, especially in the mihrab. The stone minaret, which was under scaffolding when we visited, is particularly fine, as is the circular **tower tomb** about 100m south of the main complex, which dates from the Mongol era. These buildings once formed part of a larger monastery complex, the Sōme'é-yé Bāyazīd Bastāmī.

Non-Muslims are welcome to look around and can enter the mosque (remove your shoes first). It is open during daylight hours daily except Friday morning. Entrance is free.

Getting There & Away

Bastām is about 7km north of Shāhrūd, just off the main road to Gorgān. Regular minibuses run north along 22 Bahman St from Jomhūrī-yé Eslāmī Square in Shāhrūd to Bastām for IR500. They pass right outside the entrance to Bastām mosque, from where there are plenty of shared taxis also making the return journey. Alternatively, for a private taxi, pay about IR10,000 return, including waiting time. It's even better to walk back to Shāhrūd.

DĀMGHĀN   دامغان
☎ 02233

This sleepy (almost comatose), historic town, settled at least since the 8th century, contains what may be Iran's oldest surviving mosque. There are also several ancient minarets and tomb-towers in Dāmghān, similar to those built in Māzandarān province, across the Alborz Mountains to the north.

Things to See

Dating from about AD 760, the **Tārīkhūneh Mosque** is the oldest surviving mosque in Iran. The small four-iwan mosque has a square inner courtyard, and a towering 25m minaret. It is about 500m to the south-east of the main square, Emām Khomeinī Square, and is open daily except Friday.

The only remaining feature of the long-vanished Jāmeh Mosque is the **minaret** (Manār-é Masjed-é Jāmeh), probably dating from the mid-11th century. To get there, turn left outside the Tārīkhūneh mosque and walk straight ahead for 300m, cross the road and turn into Kūcheh-yé Masjed.

The round **Ārāmgāh-é Pīr Alamdār** tower, 100m north of the Jāmeh mosque, dates from AD 1026. It was originally domed, and is remarkable for its innovative use of brick patterns, and its inscription, visible beneath the roof level.

There are some prehistoric ruins at **Tappeh Hissar**, about 200m east of the train station along the tracks, as well as a Qajar era **caravanserai** inhabited by shepherds and their flocks sheltering from the elements.

About 10km west of town, on the south side of the road, is **Doulat Ābād**, one of many impressive caravanserais along this road, which follows the ancient Silk Road.

Places to Stay & Eat

The ITTO's *Dāmghān Inn* (☎ 20 70) on Āzādī Blvd is next to a pretty park and designed to resemble a caravanserai, although the rooms are not as interesting as the exterior suggests; it's arguable whether the rate of US$30 per room is too much. You could also try the *Bābak Hotel* (☎ 41 64) on Emām Khomeinī St for about IR24,000/28,000. The best places to eat are the hotel restaurants.

Getting There & Away

Dāmghān is an easy day trip by hourly bus from the nicer town of Shāhrūd (IR1500), or a little further by minibus every hour from Semnān (IR2500). From Shāhrūd, get off the minibus at Emām Khomeinī Square in the centre of town rather than at the distant minibus station. But to go *from* Dāmghān, you'll have to get a private taxi to the minibus station. Long-distance buses often bypass Dāmghān, so you may need to get a connection in Shāhrūd or Semnān for onward travel.

The train station is 2km south-east of Emām Khomeinī Square. Trains pass through regularly but it's less convenient than travelling by bus.

SEMNĀN
سمنان
☎ 02231

Dating back to Sassanian times, Semnān lies on the northern edge of the Dasht-é Kavīr, and owes its origins and mixed fortunes to its location on the ancient trading route between Tehrān and Mashhad. The town was occupied by a long succession of invaders, including the Mongols and the Timurids, neither of whom did anything to enhance it. The attractive older part of Semnān city hasn't been modernised too much and there are still a few interesting historic buildings, although the outskirts are more industrial.

Orientation & Information

Most points of interest are in, or near, the central bazaar. The main east-west street, Emām St, is an extension of the road from Tehrān and goes past the bazaar, while the north-south Qods St joins the road to Mashhad.

The police headquarters are on the corner of Tāleqānī and Shohadā Sts; Bank Melli is along Emām St, just east of the bazaar; and the telephone and post offices are north of the bazaar, along Tāleqānī St.

Jāmeh Mosque

The present structure of the Jāmeh Mosque in the bazaar (which was closed at the time of research) dates from 1424, and has an impressive entrance portal and some interesting stuccowork around its mihrab. The magnificent 21m brick minaret dominates the town. It probably dates from the 11th century AD, and has a charming octagonal balcony with an inscription slightly below it.

Emām Khomeinī Mosque

Founded under Fath Alī Shāh in the 1820s, this mosque is one of Iran's finest surviving buildings from the Qajar period. It has a very fine tiled mihrab with stalactites. The high entrance portal is also very attractive; it's in the same clay colour as the rest of the old city, with the ribs of the stalactites delicately picked out in contrasting colour, and some understated geometric motifs and inscriptions on the facade. It is about 200m east of the Jāmeh Mosque.

Places to Stay & Eat

Easily the best place to head for is the friendly and central *Hotel Kormesh*, next to the park on Emām Square. Rooms without/with a bathroom cost IR21,000/ 28,000.

The *Jahāngardī Inn* (☎ 27 028) on Shāh-mirzād St is run by the Iranian Touring & Tourism Organisation (ITTO) and charges US$20/30 for pleasant singles/doubles.

Besides the usual *kabābīs* and uninspiring hamburger joints, the best restaurant in town is the *Mohel Restaurant*, next to the Emām Khomeinī Mosque – but don't turn up for dinner until after 8.30 pm.

Getting There & Away

Bus & Minibus Daily buses to Tehrān (IR6000) leave from the main bus station *(termīnāl)*, about 3km west of the bazaar;

take a shared taxi from Motahharī Square. To Mashhad, and anywhere east of Semnān, it's best to hail any bus heading your way along the main road outside the station.

Minibuses go from the minibus station (on the corner of Qods and Haft-é Tīr Sts, 1.5km north of the bazaar) to Dāmghān about every hour (IR2500) and to Shāhrūd (IR4000) every one to two hours.

Train Regular trains pass through Semnān en route from Tehrān (IR9250) to Mashhad (IR27,000). The train station is 1.5km south of Emām Square.

Persian Gulf

The Persian Gulf coast is one of the least visited areas of Iran. It is, however, a diverse region, and a place where distinctive historical and geographical influences are evident in the variety of people who inhabit it.

The communities along the Persian Gulf have always earned their living through trade (legal and illicit) and fishing, thereby bringing them more often into contact with traders and pilgrims from across the sea than mainland Iran. As a result, their heritage is a rich hybrid of ancient Persia and 'Arabia' across the water, and the area still contains pockets of a way of life almost vanished from elsewhere in the country. Hormoz Island, the evocative old cities of Būshehr, Mīnāb and Bandar-é Langeh are fascinating places to experience this legacy.

Some words of warning: Think twice about visiting in summer when temperatures anywhere close to the Gulf's shoreline are fierce and the humidity debilitating.

This chapter covers Būshehr and Hormozgān provinces.

BŪSHEHR
بوشهر
☎ 0771 • pop 200,000

The old city of Būshehr, with its elegant Bandārī architecture, twisting mud-brick lanes and location on a peninsula in the Persian Gulf is a gem, one of Iran's best-kept secrets. The modern town is also the most pleasant of the larger towns along the Iranian shores of the Persian Gulf. It lacks the frantic bustle of Bandar-é Abbās and is mostly free of the lethargy of Bandar-é Langeh. The Būshehrīs have time to talk to foreigners and the pace of life is relaxed.

Būshehr is impossibly hot and humid in summer (April to October), but is definitely worth a detour from Shīrāz at other times of the year.

History

The original settlement at Rīshahr, 12km south of modern Būshehr, may have been founded in the time of Ardeshīr, or even as

Highlights

- Sitting on the ramparts of the Portuguese castle on Hormoz Island in the middle of the Persian Gulf
- Getting lost in the old Bandārī city of Būshehr
- Joining traders from miles around at Mīnāb's Thursday market

early as the Elamite era. From the early Arab period in the 7th century until at least the 16th century, Rīshahr was one of the chief trading centres of the Persian Gulf, but it lost its importance after Bandar-é Abbās was established in the early 17th century.

In 1734, Nāder Shāh chose the site of Būshehr, then only a small fishing village, to become Persia's principal port and naval station. Its prosperity was assured when in 1759 the British East India Company, then the dominant power in the Persian Gulf, moved its base to Būshehr after the destruction of its factory at Bandar-é Abbās by the French. By the end of the 18th century Būshehr became the chief port of Persia.

Under the rule of Karīm Khān Zand, Būshehr remained peaceful and prosperous within the domain of the hereditary Arab

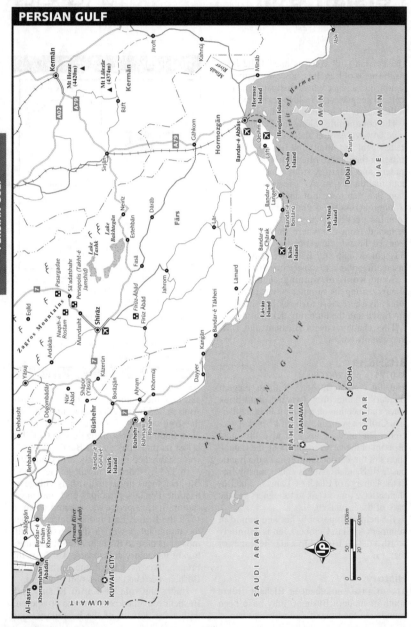

PERSIAN GULF

ruler, Sheikh Nasr, who maintained trading relations with Muscat and India. However, when Sheikh Nasr's son succeeded to the throne he ushered in a long period of tension and misrule; the area subsequently returned to central Persian control in the mid-19th century. At about the same time, Būshehr became the seat of the British Political Residency on the Persian Gulf. The town was briefly occupied by the British in the 1850s and again during WWI.

In the 1930s the new trans-Iranian railway bypassed Būshehr in favour of the ports in Khūzestān province, and the town began to decline. The British moved their Political Residency to Bahrain in 1946, and the British consulate closed in 1951, after the nationalisation of the Anglo-Iranian Oil Company. The town was quite important to the navy during the Iran-Iraq War, but most of its commercial activities collapsed, much to the benefit of the less-exposed Bandar-é Abbās to the east.

Orientation

The Old City is in the northern tip of Būshehr, while the town centre is Enqelāb Square. Unlike some Iranian ports, which stretch for kilometres along the coast, Būshehr is small and manageable enough to explore on foot. Most of the attractions and the hotels, restaurants and bus station (*termīnāl*) can be found in the northern part of Būshehr, which is circled by Khalīj-é Fārs St (the esplanade).

Information

Visa Extensions Some travellers have reported being able to get their visa extended at the Police Department of Aliens' Affairs, on Leyān St. More often the officials will refer you to Shīrāz.

Money You can change money at Bank Melli on Leyān St, just west of Enqelāb Square. The foreign exchange counter is on the 1st floor and the staff speak English.

Travel Agencies Setar-é Bandar Travel Agency (☎ 252 2826, fax 255 433) on Emām Khomeinī St handles domestic and

international air tickets as well as the various boat services across the Persian Gulf.

Post & Communications The post and telephone offices, along Valiasr St, are easy to spot.

Emergency For medical problems, dial the medical-emergencies number (☎ 115) or contact the main hospital (☎ 252 3564). The police headquarters (☎ 252 3035) is on Qods Square.

Old City

The old city is one of the largest living museums of traditional Bandarī architecture. Unlike so many other ports in the region, the old city of Būshehr offers glimpses of a way of life fast disappearing from the shores of the Persian Gulf. It is possible to lose yourself in the old city for hours and it's worth at least a couple of visits.

Most of the old houses in the narrow, winding *kūchés* (alleys) and blind alleys are still inhabited and many women are dressed in the traditional, brightly coloured layers of clothing unique to the Persian Gulf. The houses are made of mud brick covered with a thin layer of sand-coloured plaster. There is a faded grandeur about the tall facades, latticed stained-glass windows and arched balconies. Wrought-iron grilles adorn many windows and doors, not as protective measures but as a way of enhancing the rows of arched windows. The densely packed wooden struts that overhang some of the narrow lanes are also unique. Keep an eye out for the door knockers shaped like human hands in the north-western quarter of town.

After we had completed our research, we learned of a new **museum** that has since opened in the council building along the esplanade (the modern building with pillars across the front). There are ethnological and archaelogical displays downstairs and contemporary artworks by local artists upstairs. Entrance costs IR10,000 and it's open from 9 am to 2 pm Saturday to Thursday.

There are four **mosques** in the historical quarter and what's left of a small **Armenian church**. After loving restoration by the small

BŪSHEHR

PERSIAN
GULF

To Kuwait
& Bahrain

Docks

Old City

Enqelāb
Square

Bazaar

Stadium

Qods
Square

Komīteh
Enqelāb-é
Eslāmī
Square

To Airport
(4km) &
Rīshahr
(12km)

To Shīrāz (317km),
Ahvaz (634km) &
Bandar-é Abbās (903km)

PLACES TO STAY
8 Mosāferkhūneh-yé Pars
16 Hotel Saadī
17 Mosāferkhūneh-yé Hāfez
23 Jahāngardī Inn
26 Delvar Hotel
28 Hotel Rezā

PLACES TO EAT
2 Sahel Restaurant
4 Gab Goo
10 Lian Restaurant
11 Cafe
14 Āzādī Restaurant
24 Cafe

OTHER
1 Armenian Church
3 Museum
5 Customs Office
6 Cargo Ships to
  Kuwait & Bahrain
7 Port Entrance
9 Bank Melli
12 Hospital
13 Police Department of
   Aliens' Affairs
15 Local Bus Station
18 Minibus Station
19 Bus Station
20 Main Post Office
21 Main Telephone Office
22 Iran Air
25 Setar-é Bandar Travel
   Agency; Cinema
27 Police Headquarters

Armenian congregation, it was damaged by a burst water main and is now hard to find.

Although many crumbling houses of the Old City are in danger of suffering a similar fate and are in desperate need of restoration, the Old City is still sufficiently intact to have preserved the magic of old Būshehr. This is most evident just after sunrise, at sunset or later in the evening.

Walk in the old city after 9 pm, while dusk takes over the squalid decay, and wander, and wander and wander, as if you were without a compass... You will begin to walk through Moroccan squares, stare at Mexi-

can courtyards and pass by Peruvian mudwalls... And without knowing how, you are back in front of your *mosāferkhūneh*.

Massimo Giannini

Places to Stay

Būshehr's greatest drawback is the absence of good budget accommodation; some cheaper places will look the other way if you ask for a room. In winter, you may be struggling to find somewhere at all. On a really tight budget, you may wish to take an overnight trip from the cheaper Shīrāz. If none of the Būshehr cheapies will take you, get a letter from the police headquarters allowing you to stay at the mosāferkhūneh – this has worked well for several travellers, even those arriving late at night.

Around the bazaar area, a short walk from the bus station, the *Mosāferkhūneh-yé Hāfez* (☎ 252 2228) on Hāfez St is one place that may be willing to take foreigners, although not all travellers have been fortunate. The rooms with fan and shared facilities are as basic as they come, but they're clean and incredibly cheap at IR8300 per person. They're set around a courtyard and thus largely sheltered from the main street.

Among the others, some travellers have reported that both the *Hotel Saadi* (a few doors north of the Hafez) and the *Mosāferkhūné-yé Pars* on Enqelāb Square are OK cheapies. When we visited, however, they wouldn't give their prices or let us look in any rooms. These are two places where a letter from the police might be worthwhile as both are in a good, central location.

The same can't be said for *Hotel Reza* (☎ 252 7171, fax 252 7173), Emām Khomeinī St, which is a fair walk from the Old City and a long way from any decent restaurants. The double rooms with bath aren't bad (though a little overpriced by Iranian standards) at IR150,000. There's no restaurant, but it serves a decent breakfast for IR4000.

The quiet *Jahāngardī Inn* (☎ 252 2346, fax 252 2410) on Valiasr St has a lovely waterfront location and some rooms have views over the Persian Gulf. Sadly, it has Government Hotel written all over it with long, empty corridors, and musty, tired rooms. The water is as cold as the air-conditioning, which may not be such a bad thing in summer although less than you'd expect for the US$30 you must pay for a double. The restaurant menu is similarly uninspired (although the shrimps for IR20,000 almost save the day) and there's even a tacky gift shop selling Persian Gulf memorabilia.

The *Delvar Hotel* (☎ 252 6276, fax 252 5217) on Komīté-yé Enqelāb-é Eslāmī Square is the place to head if money is no object. The semiluxurious rooms are not quite as grand as the foyer suggests, but still the best in town. A twin room costs IR376,000 and, strangely for a top-end place, they don't accept dollars.

Places to Eat

One dish to keep an eye out for in Būshehr is *ghalyé māhi*, a very tasty fish stew.

The *kabābīs* are concentrated along Enqelāb and Leyān Sts, and around the bazaar. The interestingly named *Gab Goo* serves reasonable Iranian-style hamburgers (IR5000), fried chicken and kebabs.

For fresh air and great views go to the unnamed *cafe*, on the esplanade and directly opposite the Jahāngardī Inn. It serves Iranian-style hamburgers, cold drinks and ice creams, but its biggest drawcard is the setting with outdoor benches looking out to sea. Try to be there on a Thursday or Friday evening when the friendly Būshehrīs love to stroll along the waterfront. Another good spot to watch the sunset is the open-air *cafe* at the western end of Leyān St.

One of the cosiest places in town, with friendly staff and meals for about IR12,000, is the *Āzādī Restaurant* on Shohadā St. Also good is the *Lian Restaurant* on Leyān St where there's the usual preoccupation with kabābs (one with rice, tomatoes, yoghurt and a soft drink costs about IR11,000). The fish is also tasty and reasonably priced, although the occupants of the aquarium thankfully aren't on the menu.

A great place to finish off a wander around the Old City is the *Sahel Restaurant* on the esplanade near the northern end of Enqelāb St. Although indoors, the setting is pleasant with the waters of the Gulf visible through the windows. Meals are reasonably priced and the eating area is spotless. It's not signed in English.

Of the hotels, the restaurant in the *Jahāngardī Inn* is OK and the service is friendly once you get to know them, while the restaurant at the *Delvar Hotel* isn't bad for a splurge.

Getting There & Away

Air Iran Air (☎ 252 2041), located on Valiasr St, has one-way flights from Būshehr to: Tehrān (daily, IR171,000), Shīrāz (once a week, IR92,000), Esfāhān (once a week, IR92,000) and Mashhad (twice weekly, IR222,000). The office is open from 7.30 am to 6 pm Saturday to Thursday and 7.30 am to 1 pm Friday.

Though there are few internal flights, Būshehr has an international connection: Iran Asseman flies to/from Dubai in the United Arab Emirates (UAE) once a week for US$113 one way, plus the usual IR70,000 departure tax. Contact the helpful Setar-é Bandar Travel Agency (see Travel Agencies earlier in the section) for tickets.

Bus & Minibus The bus station is easy to reach on foot and it's here that the small number of bus companies who operate out of Būshehr maintain their offices. Buses leave the bus station at least daily to the following destinations:

destination	distance (km)	duration (hrs)	cost (IR)
Ahvāz	626	7	13,500
Bandar-é Abbās	903	16	22,000
Bandar-é Langeh	656	9	13,200
Esfāhān	790	16	17,000
Shīrāz	317	5	7000
Tehrān	1185	19	28,000

Boat A couple of times a month ships leave Būshehr en route to Bahrain (US$60), Qatar (US$56) and Kuwait (US$56), but schedules are unreliable and change from month to month.

While we were in Iran, newspapers reported the imminent inauguration of a high-speed ferry connecting the major ports of the Persian Gulf, including Būshehr. The new boats can carry up to 84 vehicles and 585 passengers, each of them with a luggage allowance of 100kg. Prices for passengers are expected to be around US$120 for most destinations (with Bahrain possibly as low as US$70) although neither schedules nor prices had been released at the time of research.

For all international boat departures, a departure tax of between IR15,000 and IR23,000 is payable. To find out what may be going from Būshehr, talk to the staff at the Setar-é Bandar Travel Agency (see Travel Agencies earlier in the section).

Getting Around

To/From the Airport A private taxi from Būshehr airport into town costs IR8000. There is no airport bus service. To get to the airport, you could try taking a shared taxi from Komīté-yé Enqelāb-é Eslāmī Square for around IR1000, but you may have to take a private taxi anyway unless you can find others to share.

Bus Local buses can be found at the bus station at the northern end of Mo'allem St. From here, you can also catch a bus to Rīshahr. You could also try the minibus station close to the bus station.

Taxi Būshehr is small enough to walk around, but there are shared taxis, for about IR500, for any trip around town.

AROUND BŪSHEHR
Rīshahr   ريشهر

The early history of Rīshahr is described in the Būshehr section. Despite its historical importance, very little remains of the ancient city of Rīshahr, built during the Elamite and Sassanian eras. In any case the ruins currently stand within sight of no fewer than three top-security military installations and are not very easy to explore.

Along the 12km stretch of road between Būshehr and Rīshahr, especially south of Bāhmanī, there are a few carved **tombstones** from the early Arab period. Excavations along the same road have revealed a more or less continuous line of buried earthenware vases, believed to contain the remains of Zoroastrians after the vultures had done their work.

Rīshahr can be reached by bus from the bus station in Būshehr.

FROM BŪSHEHR TO BANDAR-É LANGEH

There are some beautiful towns along Iran's central Persian Gulf coastline. You really need your own vehicle to fully explore the region and, as you'll probably be the first tourist the locals have seen for a while, you'll need to take whatever accommodation you can find or bring your own.

About 250km south-east of Būshehr, Kangān is a pretty little fishing village well worth exploring. Bandar-é Tāherī, a little further south-east, boasts the **ruins** of the 18th century **Sheikh's fortress**; the **views** from the wind-tower over the Gulf are superb. The town itself is quite picturesque. Nearby on the rocky coastline are the ruins of the **ancient town of Siraf** with some well-preserved stone graves. Bandar-é Bostānū, 18km west of Langeh has some great *bādgīrs* (windtowers).

Getting to these towns is not too difficult, but buses often pass through in the middle of the night and moving on can involve long waits. Take any bus or minibus travelling along the coastal road, then wave down any public transport to get to the other places.

BANDAR-É LANGEH بندر لنگه
☎ 0762

Bandar-é Langeh (or Langeh to the locals) is an infectiously lethargic place. It is also an excellent introduction to the mixed Arab and Persian communities of the southern Persian Gulf. The population is half Sunni and half Shiite, and both Arabic and Farsi are spoken, a diversity reflected in the hybrid architecture and clothing of the locals.

During the day, especially in summer, there's little to do except observe the obligatory five or six-hour siesta. By late afternoon, however, it's a lovely place to wander when the setting sun turns the town pale yellow. Things to see include several **pale stone mosques**, with single minarets decorated in the Arab style, and a few old and largely derelict **Bandarī buildings** made of mud brick with huge, squat bādgīrs. Conical **water reservoirs** are scattered all over town. They have small holes at the top of the dome, which let the rain in, two narrow doors, and pools from which the locals once gathered water for washing.

Langeh makes a pleasant overnight stop before or after visiting Kīsh Island, or a day trip from Bandar-é Abbās.

Orientation & Information
The main streets are Emām Khomeinī Blvd (the coastal road and esplanade) and Enqelāb St, which heads to Bandar-é Abbās. This is not a town where foreigners are expected; few signs are in English, but it would be hard to get lost. Don't arrive without any rials because Bank Melli won't change money and rates in the bazaar are low.

Places to Stay & Eat
Mosāferkhūneh-yé Golestan (☎ 24 006) seems reluctant to take foreigners and some rooms catch a lot of sun, but they're new, tidy and pretty good value at IR21,000/28,000 a single/double with air-con and shared bath. It's located up the flight of stairs just north of Pāsdāran Square.

Closer to the port, *Hotel Amir* (☎ 22 922) on Enqelāb St has a sign in English, and is equally pleasant and clean and, though the rooms are a little older, still good value for the same price as the Golestan.

Hotel Babu (☎ 22 170) on Pāsdārān St charges IR30,000 for basic triple rooms with peeling walls, Sassanid-era air-con and a ceiling fan that poses a serious danger to tall people. As in many places in this part of the country, think twice before taking a shower to cool off on a summer's afternoon – the overheated pipes will produce overheated water.

The *Bandar Lengeh Inn* (☎ 22 566), also known as the Mehmar Sara Jahāngardī, seems to operate on the principle that all of the money you save on nearby Kīsh should be spent here. For US$33 you get a pleasant but overpriced double with cooler and bath; most have views over the Gulf. It's difficult to decide whether the hotel's location 2km west of town down a lonely side road is hopelessly inconvenient or wonderfully serene; probably the latter as the manager can arrange taxis and its position, literally on the water's edge, means you can sip tea in the garden with your toes in the Persian Gulf. There's a very good *restaurant*, which means that you could be entirely self-contained here and never discover how pleasant Langeh actually is.

For food options, there are several *kabābīs* and surprisingly well-stocked supermarkets along Enqelāb St between Pāsdāran St and the entrance to the port. Among the sit-down cheapies opposite the port, *Restōran-é*

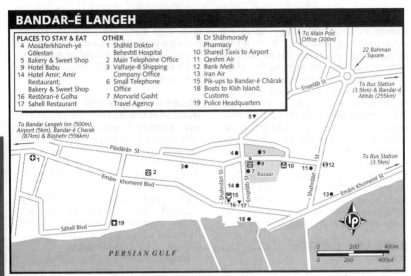

BANDAR-É LANGEH

PLACES TO STAY & EAT
4 Mosáferkhúneh-yé Gólestan
5 Bakery & Sweet Shop
9 Hotel Babu
14 Hotel Amir; Amir Restaurant; Bakery & Sweet Shop
16 Restóran-é Golha
17 Sahell Restaurant

OTHER
1 Shāhīd Doktor Beheshtī Hospital
2 Main Telephone Office
3 Valfarje-8 Shipping Company Office
6 Small Telephone Office
7 Morvarid Gasht Travel Agency

8 Dr Shāhmorady Pharmacy
10 Shared Taxis to Airport
11 Qeshm Air
12 Bank Melli
13 Iran Air
15 Pik-ups to Bandar-é Chārak
18 Boats to Kīsh Island; Customs
19 Police Headquarters

To Main Post Office (200m)
22 Bahman Square
Engelāb St
To Bus Station (3.5km) & Bandar-é Abbās (255km)

To Bandar Langeh Inn (500m), Airport (5km), Bandar-é Charak (87km) & Búshehr (556km)

Pāsdārān St

Emām Khomeinī Blvd

Shahrdāri St

Engelāb St

Bazaar

Shahrdāri St

To Bus Station (3.5km)

Emām Khomeinī St

Sāhelī Blvd

PERSIAN GULF

0   200   400m
0   200   400yd

Golha and *Sahell Restaurant* are arguably the best of an ordinary lot.

The best place to eat in the centre of town is the *Amir Restaurant* a few doors south of the hotel of the same name. The dining area is pleasant, they serve good *meigū* (battered prawns or shrimps) for IR20,000 and there's a small teahouse attached to follow up your meal with a *qalyan* – in Langeh they come without a pipe and the mouthpiece leads directly into the water jug. It's the perfect vantage point from which to watch the evening ritual of Iranians scrambling up the police-lined main street from the ferry, laden with huge boxes of electrical goods.

Finish your meal with a visit to one of the excellent little *sweet shops* along the main street.

Getting There & Away

Air Staff at the huge Iran Air office (☎ 22 799) on Emām Khomeinī St are hardly overworked – the only flight goes four times a week to Tehrān (IR206,000) via Shīrāz (IR92,000). The office is open from 7.30 am to 1.30 pm and from 4.30 to 6.30 pm Saturday to Thursday (from 8 am to noon Friday). You could also try Morvarid

Gasht Travel Agency (☎ 23 345, fax 22 352). Qeshm Air, opposite the Bank Melli, has three staff but only one weekly flight from Langeh to Qeshm for IR150,000. However, since the existence of this flight was denied by Qeshm Air staff on the island, it might be better not to count on it.

Bus The bus station is typically inconvenient, about 3.5 km east of town. Buses (IR6000) and shared taxis (IR8000) to Bandar-é Abbās (four hours, 255km) leave about every hour. Several buses to Búshehr (IR13,200, nine hours, 656km) leave daily. There are occasional buses to Shīrāz although you'll probably need to get a connection from Bandar-é Abbās or Búshehr.

If you're arriving from Búshehr, chances are you'll do so at 2 or 3 am. Although such an ungodly arrival time can be disorienting, if you ask to be dropped at the port entrance (other locals will get out here), it's easy to find your way up the main street opposite; there may even be the odd taxi around.

Boat Langeh has ferries (IR15,000) to Kīsh Island, the duty-free hot spot in the Persian Gulf, at 2 pm on Sunday, Tuesday and

Thursday and at 9 am and 6pm on Monday, Wednesday and Friday. The journey takes two hours, but ferries are often cancelled due to rough seas. Tickets can be bought at the Valfarje-8 office (☎ 23 448, which has a sign in English) on Pāsdāran St. The quicker alternative is to take a speedboat (IR20,000) from Bandar-é Chārak (89km west of Langeh). If you want to return to Langeh by nightfall you'll need to take an early morning (6 am) *pik-up* from Shahdāri St.

Getting Around

To/From the Airport From the airport, just take a shared taxi or pik-up (IR2000) to the bazaar. Getting to the airport, you'll need to charter a private taxi (IR10,000).

Taxi & Pik-Ups The town is small enough to walk (or saunter) around. The pik-ups that roam the streets are only necessary for longer trips.

KĪSH ISLAND   جزیره کیش
☎ 07653

Kīsh Island is a bizarre place; a little bit of Singapore with highways and towering apartment blocks, a quasi-Disneyland with theme parks, and a poor man's California with beaches and bicycle paths – all with a unique Iranian style. Iranians will tell you that you absolutely *must* visit Kīsh. The main attraction for them, however, is the availability of duty-free electrical goods so unless you're homesick for a colour TV with remote control there really is no reason to visit.

The glossy brochures extol the attractions of the 12 or more 'bazaars' on Kīsh Island but don't be fooled into expecting anything exotic – these bazaars are little more than concrete malls. **Bāzār-é Saffein**, a mud brick tunnel, is one of the more interesting malls-cum-bazaars.

Kīsh is *very* expensive; the theory is that if you can afford to come here, you can also afford to be overcharged for everything. Taking a day trip is a possible way of minimising costs as long as you get an early start.

Kīsh's popularity as a playground for the rich is nothing new – in the days of the last shah Concorde used to fly here from Paris.

History

In the Middle Ages, Kīsh Island became an important trading centre under its own powerful Arab dynasty, and at one time it supported a population of 40,000. The island was known for the quality of its pearls; when Marco Polo was visiting the imperial court in China, he remarked on the beauty of the pearls worn by one of the emperor's wives – he was told that they had come from Kīsh.

The island fell into decline in the 14th century and remained obscure until just before the Islamic Revolution, when it was developed as a semiprivate retreat for the Shāh and his privileged guests, with its own international airport, palaces, luxury hotels and restaurants, and even a grand casino. Shortly after the Revolution, the new government established Kīsh as a duty-free port, taking advantage of the facilities already in place.

Orientation & Information

There's no real centre to Kīsh Island, despite signs in English indicating a 'City Centre', and there are no addresses as such. The Arab settlements are the town of Saffein, on the north coast, and the small oasis village of Bāghū, in the south-west of the island. Most people live near the main roads along the northern and eastern coasts, and many of the offices, shops and hotels are along a small section of road in the northeast.

The best place to get information, as well as maps (in English and French), is the Kīsh Tourism Organisation. Staff are friendly, and some speak English. It is open from about 8 am to 5 pm, Saturday to Thursday. There are three branches of the main banks in the business heart of the island, including Bank Melli, where you can change money.

Hopefully, you won't need to call the police headquarters (☎ 21 43) or Kīsh Hospital (☎ 21 11).

Customs Regulations It's not worth buying anything on Kīsh. At the time of research, if you purchased duty-free goods totalling more than US$27, you had to line up in the chaos of the customs office at the boat terminal or airport and then wait to be

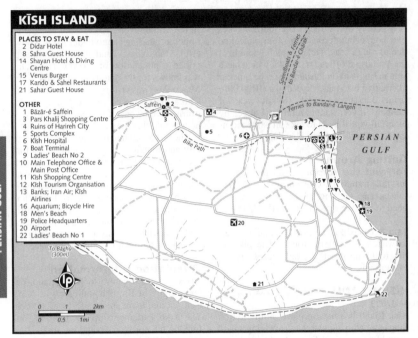

KĪSH ISLAND

PLACES TO STAY & EAT
2 Didar Hotel
8 Sahra Guest House
14 Shayan Hotel & Diving Centre
15 Venus Burger
17 Kando & Sahel Restaurants
21 Sahar Guest House

OTHER
1 Bāzār-é Saffein
3 Pars Khalij Shopping Centre
4 Ruins of Harireh City
5 Sports Complex
6 Kīsh Hospital
7 Boat Terminal
9 Ladies' Beach No 2
10 Main Telephone Office & Main Post Office
11 Kīsh Shopping Centre
12 Kīsh Tourism Organisation
13 Banks; Iran Air; Kīsh Airlines
16 Aquarium; Bicycle Hire
18 Men's Beach
19 Police Headquarters
20 Airport
22 Ladies' Beach No 1

processed. You'll soon wish you'd made your purchase elsewhere.

Before committing yourself to buying anything and taking it out of Kīsh, you're strongly advised to ring local customs (☎ 25 77) and find out what you have to do to be able to take it off the island.

Beaches

Kīsh is one of the very few places in Iran where swimming is actively encouraged. There are sandy, uncrowded beaches around most of the coast, but the authorities request that female swimmers use either **Ladies Beach No 1** or **Ladies Beach No 2**, while men have to use the **Men's Beach**.

Theme Parks

Efforts have been made to 'green' the island, and there are several small parks of tropical trees. Theme parks, such as the **Family Park** and **Deer Park**, are being completed; in the meantime tourists can visit the **Aquarium**.

Diving & Other Excursions

There is a wide range of colourful fish around the coral reefs off Kīsh, including the rare emperor fish. Kīsh is the only place in Iran that has a diving centre, though it's still in its infancy.

If you are keen to dive, make inquiries at the Diving Centre (☎ 27 71) which is located at the Shayan Hotel. For more professional standards, you might consider contacting the Iran International Diving Centre in Tehrān (☎ 021-881 0085, fax 889 2515), Unit 7, No 244 Ostād Nejātollāhī Ave, before setting out.

East of Kīsh is Farun Island, which many professional divers consider to be the best in the region; ask around the boat terminal to organise a boat or make inquiries at the Diving Centre.

Also ask around the boat terminal to see if you can hire a boat to the **turtle colony** (*dasté-yé lāk-é poshté ābī*), off the southern coast.

Places to Stay & Eat

The guesthouses are the best places to try. The **Sahra Guest House** (☎ 21 10) and the harder to reach **Sahar Guest House** (☎ 2067) are both as cheap as they get, charging around US$15 a double; but they are often full. You can sometimes arrange an apartment for as little as US$10 per person; ask at the tourist office.

Reasonable value by Kīsh standards is the **Didar Hotel** (☎ 27 06), which charges a negotiable US$25 for a huge air-con room with TV and fridge. There are many other top-end hotels and resorts along the northern and eastern coasts, and many more to come to judge by the number of cranes and bulldozers. One excellent, central place is the **Shayan Hotel** (☎ 27 71), which charges US$47 for a luxurious double room.

After we visited, some travellers wrote to recommend **Amīr Kabīr Hotel** (☎/fax 76 444), about 1km from Ladies Beach No 1. Bungalows with three beds, kitchen, air-con and television reportedly go for IR100,000.

Kīsh is the sort of place where you can buy 15 different types of 'steam/dry/spray irons (with detachable water tank)', but you can spend three days looking for somewhere to buy a cup of tea.

One place with decent prices is **Venus Burger**, a western-style hamburger joint where burgers, including a drink, cost from US1.25. For something tasty from about US$3, try the **Kando Restaurant** or the **Sahel Restaurant** nearby.

The only places to get food at a reasonable price are the handful of **cafes** and **restaurants** in Saffein village, about five minutes' walk north of the Didar Hotel. Here you can get a burger and cola for under US$1. The restaurant at the **Didar Hotel** is ridiculously expensive.

Getting There & Away

Day trips are possible by pik-up and boat from Bandar-é Langeh, as long as you start very early (see Bandar-é Langeh's Getting There & Away section earlier).

Flying in and out of Kīsh in one day is also possible if the schedules work in your favour.

Air Tickets to Kīsh can be difficult to get because demand is so heavy.

Kīsh Airlines (☎ 22 59) flies to Bandar-é Abbās at 8 am on Sunday, Tuesday and Thursday; the return flight departs from Bandran at 9.30 am. It also flies daily to Tehrān (IR215,000 one way) and Esfahān (IR298,000 one way) with occasional flights to Shīrāz and Mashhad. Iran Asseman flies to and from Bandar-é Abbās twice a week. Both airlines charge IR92,000/184,000 one-way return. Iran Air (☎ 22 74) also covers many of these routes. Book your return ticket before you arrive in Kīsh.

Boat Valfajre-8 sails to Kīsh from Bandar-é Langeh (IR15,000) at 2 pm on Sunday, Tuesday and Thursday and at 9 am and 6pm on Monday, Wednesday and Friday, returning on alternate days.

Easily the best way for travellers to visit Kīsh is to take the speedboat from Bandar-é Chārak – an easy ride from Bandar-é Langeh in a pik-up (IR8000, 1½ hours). The pik-up will take you to the beach at Chārak, where most of your fellow passengers will pile into a speedboat (IR20,000). To visit Kīsh in one day, start from Langeh at about 6 am, and allow enough time to get back. You should also factor in the time you will spend clearing customs checks; even if you haven't bought anything that needs declaring, chances are someone on your boat has.

Getting Around

To/From the Airport You will probably have to charter a taxi from the airport for about IR10,000.

Minibus & Taxi Excellent air-con minibuses (IR1000) cruise the northern and eastern roads. Standing is not allowed.

From the boat terminal, you can crowd onto a local minibus, but if you have some luggage it's better to take a private taxi. Be careful before chartering any taxi as they charge up to IR40,000 per hour.

Bicycle A welcome innovation is the well-marked Special Bicycle Route, which circles the island. This would be great if it

The Persian Gulf

The mighty Persian Gulf (Khalīj-é Fārs) stretches 965km from the Shatt al-Arab River (part of the border between southern Iraq and Iran) and the Strait of Hormoz, which becomes the Gulf of Oman to the east. The Persian Gulf is between 50km and 370km wide, is about 233,100 sq km in area and is quite shallow – no more than 90m deep. It is bordered by Iran, Iraq and the Gulf states of Kuwait, the UAE, Qatar, Oman and Saudi Arabia, while the island nation of Bahrain is to the south.

Since the Gulf is the world's major oil-producing region, it is not surprising that pollution is rife. In the early 1980s, dozens of catastrophic oil spills resulted from the Iran-Iraq War; 200,000 tonnes of crude oil from just one oil rig (near Khārk Island) spilled into the Gulf. During the Gulf War, an estimated one million tonnes of crude oil also poured into the Gulf, and leakages from oil tankers continue unabated today. Surprisingly despite the pollution, more than 200 varieties of fish and other marine life thrive in the Gulf.

Increasing industrialisation and unrestrained development of the Gulf islands have caused extensive damage to its fragile ecosystem. Problems include the dumping of rubbish and untreated sewage; industrial and agricultural chemicals seeping into rivers, and then into the Gulf; and the adverse affects of the dredging used to create and maintain deep channels for shipping.

Hopefully, the new Regional Organisation for the Protection of Marine Environment, created by the countries bordering the Gulf, will find some way of tackling these problems.

---

wasn't so damn hot most of the year and if bikes were easier to hire. You might be able to find some bikes for hire near the aquarium. Otherwise, ask at your hotel.

BANDAR-É ABBĀS   بندر عباس
☎ 0761 • pop 360,000

Overlooking the Strait of Hormoz, Bandar-é Abbās is the busiest port in Iran. Despite its links with Shāh Abbās I, who founded the town in 1622, about the only reminder of the origins of 'Port of Abbās is its name. The city's population is a diverse mix of Persian Bandārīs, Arabs and black Africans, with a large Sunni minority. The small but long-established Hindu community has a temple here.

Smuggling is big business here – don't stick your nose (or any other part of your body) anywhere it isn't wanted, particularly along the waterfront after dark. Depending on your perspective, Bandar-é Abbās – known simply as Bandar by the locals – is either delightfully seedy with the audible whispers of smugglers or a stepping-off point for the nearby islands.

History
Once the tiny fishing village of Gāmerūn, this strategically important site was chosen

as Persia's main southern port and naval dockyard after the decline of nearby Hormoz Island. The British East India Company was granted a trading concession, followed later by concessions to Dutch and French traders. By the 17th century, Bandar-é Abbās had become the chief Persian port and main outlet for the trade in Kermānī carpets.

The port went into decline following the end of the Safavid dynasty. Then in 1759 the British East India Company moved to the new port of Būshehr after its factory at Bandar-é Abbās was destroyed by the French. By 1793 Bandar-é Abbās had fallen into the hands of the Sultan of Oman. In 1868, the port returned to Persian control, but its role in maritime trade remained peripheral until the second half of the 20th century. Its hour of glory came during the Iran-Iraq War, when the ports to the northwest – Būshehr, Bandar-é Emām Khomeinī and Khorramshāhr – became too dangerous for regular shipping.

These days, Bandar-é Abbās is still the only truly active, international port on the northern shores of the Persian Gulf. The city has grown dramatically over recent years, and vast sums have been invested in expanding and improving its port facilities.

BANDAR-É ABBĀS

PLACES TO STAY
1 Homa Hotel
6 Hotel Amin
7 Hotel Hormozgān; Safa Hotel; Safa Kabābī
12 Atilar Suites Hotel No 1; Persian Restaurant
18 Sāhel Hotel
19 Hotel Ghods
23 Mosāferkhūneh-yé Bāzār
28 Mosāferkhūneh-yé Maharaja
30 Bolvar Inn
31 Hotel Hamze

PLACES TO EAT
2 Tānūrī Pizza; Pizza Restaurants
8 Felfely Pizza
11 Cheap Kabābīs; Shahrzad Cinema; Ladan Ice Cream; Private Telephone Offices
17 Shamshīr Restaurant
20 Kabābīs

OTHER
3 Customs and Foreign Parcels Post Office

4 Iran Air; Qeshm Air
5 Ani Taxi Service
9 Main Post Office
10 Private Telephone Office
13 Morvarid Money Exchange
14 Hindu Temple
15 Bank Mellī (Central Branch)
16 Police Headquarters
21 Bala Parvaz Travel Agency & Train Ticket Office
22 Mosque (unfinished)

24 Jetty for Boats to Islands
25 Open-Air Teahouse
26 Local Bus Station & Shared Taxi Terminal
27 Iran Asseman Office; Gameron Air Travel Agency
29 Shared Taxis to Mīnāb
32 Hava Gasht Air Travel Agency
33 UAE Consulate
34 Emergency Clinic

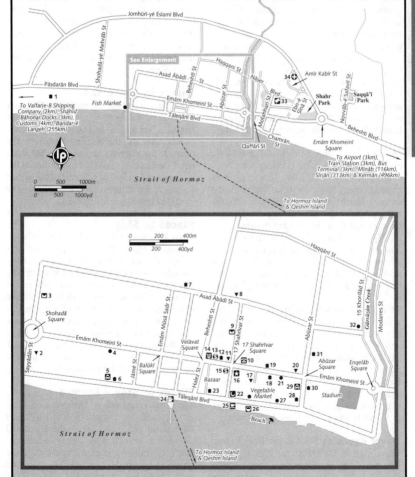

PERSIAN GULF

Orientation

Bandar-é Abbās stretches along an elongated, narrow coastal strip. The main east-west thoroughfare changes its name from Beheshtī Blvd (in the eastern suburbs), to Emām Khomeinī St (through the centre of town), ending as Pāsdārān Blvd (towards the docks to the west).

Information

Visa Extensions The police at the headquarters on 17 Shahrīvar Square are more than a little laid-back – the sun affects everyone in Bandar – but they'd prefer you went somewhere else for a visa extension.

The consul at the United Arab Emirates (UAE) consulate (☎ 38 262) Nasr Blvd is friendly and speaks English. A one-month visa costs IR250,000 and can take three days to issue. You'll need three photos and a genuine sponsor in the UAE; opening hours are from 8.30 am to 3 pm, Saturday to Thursday.

Money The central branch of Bank Melli on 17 Shahrīvar Square is the only bank to change money officially, but it's more chaotic than most in Iran, particularly around lunchtime. Most of the official money exchange offices around Bandar have closed their doors. One that hasn't is the Morvarid Money Exchange in an arcade just west of 17 Shahrīvar Square; its rates are marginally less than the bank's. There's a black market in UAE dirhams and other Gulf state currencies in the nearby bazaar.

Post & Communications The main post office is 150m north of 17 Shahrīvar Square. For international parcels go to the Customs and Foreign Parcels Post Office inconveniently located 100m north of Shohadā Square in the west of town. Like others in Iran the main telephone office has closed and you'll need to rely on hotels or private telephone offices, the largest concentration of which is around 17 Shahrīvar Square.

Travel Agencies Staff at the Bala Parvaz Travel Agency (☎ 29 881, fax 22 519, Emām Khomeinī St) are friendly, speak enough English to be of assistance and handle Iran Air flights as well as a small range of international airlines. Hava Gasht Air Travel Agency (☎ 20 774, fax 20 776) on 15th Khordad Ave is the place to go for Kīsh Airlines tickets, but it also acts as agent for Iran Air as well as selling train tickets. Gameron Air Travel Agency (☎ 20 274, fax 29 02) on Tāleqānī Blvd is little more than an adjunct to the Iran Asseman office.

Emergency One of several hospitals dotted around this sprawling city is the Emergency Clinic (☎ 31 001) in the north-east of the city. There's also a medical emergencies number (☎ 115). The police headquarters (☎ 27 676) is on the south-eastern side of 17 Shahrīvar Square.

Things to See & Do

A pleasant walk heading east along Tāleqānī Blvd takes you from the busy **beach**, with boatmen, smugglers and seaside attractions on one side and the bustling bazaar on the other, to the morning and evening **fish market**. Construction seems to have stalled at the huge **mosque**, a few metres east of the bazaar – a pity as it will have one of the tallest *iwans* (halls) in Iran when it's finished.

Places to Stay

There can be a shortage of accommodation in Bandar, especially in winter when nearly everyone wants to visit. None of the cheap *mosāferkhūnehs* (lodgings) are keen to take foreigners and, even if they do, they're not recommended for lone women. If you are desperate, try to get a letter of introduction (from the police headquarters) that allows you to stay at a mosāferkhūneh or head to Mīnāb (see later in this chapter). Make sure you have a fan or air-conditioning in your room during the summer months.

Places to Stay – Budget

The *Mosāferkhūneh-yé Maharaja* on Abūzar St (without a sign in English) went through the process of giving the prices and showing us several rooms, only to then say that they could not accept foreigners. Other travellers have had better luck. The rooms are pretty basic but cheap at IR13,000/20,000/

24,000 for a dorm bed/single/double. On the other side of the road, the ***Bolvar Inn (☎ 22 625)*** is similar. The area is a bit dodgy at night.

Above the bazaar, ***Mosāferkhūneh-yé Bāzār*** is noisy but certainly close to the action. The covered rooftop, which doubles as a dorm (IR10,000 per bed), is a wonderful vantage point from which to watch the smugglers and sunset over the Persian Gulf. The rooms are largely clean and cost IR13,000/16,000/18,000 for a single/double/ triple.

There are two decent places next to each other on Asad Ābādī St. Both are central and signed in English. The ***Safa Hotel (☎ 22 651)*** is pretty basic but certainly habitable at IR21,000/32,000 for a double with fan/aircon. Next door is the ***Hotel Hormozgān (☎ 571 259)***, probably the best in the budget range. Its pleasant and tidy rooms are good value at IR25,000/30,000 for a double with fan/air-con; a spacious four-bed suite with shower and toilet costs IR50,000 but is often full. The manager is a friendly woman and lone female travellers may feel more comfortable here.

Places to Stay – Mid-Range & Top End

The ***Hotel Ghods (☎ 22 344)*** on Emām Khomeinī St is popular with Russian traders, but the rooms are pleasant. Singles/doubles with bath are good value at US$10 per person. The rooms are set around an internal courtyard and surprisingly quiet for Bandar's main thoroughfare. Across the road, the staff at the ***Sāhel Hotel (☎ 22 603)*** would prefer it if you spoke Russian, but the rooms with shared bath are reasonable value for IR50,000 /100,000.

Hotel Hamze (☎ 23 771) is also quiet and friendly, and the rooms, though nothing special, aren't bad at US$10/20 a room with shared bath. The hotel is about 30m down an alley, just north of Abūzar Square.

At the ***Hotel Amin (☎ 574 309, fax 39 411)*** in the western part of the city, US$35 is way too much for doubles that are pretty similar to those at the Hotel Ghods.

Excellent value for a top-end place is the ***Atilar Suites Hotel No.1 (☎ 27 420, fax 27 121)*** off Emām Khomeinī St. Small/medium/large apartments with at least a large bedroom, sitting room, kitchen and bathroom are a bargain at US$30/35/40 plus 17% tax. Most rooms have nice views over the town; the ones with Persian Gulf views cost around US$5 extra. In low season, you should have little trouble getting the Iranian price of IR180,000 for a small suite – a steal. You'll need a reservation in winter and around Nō Rūz (Iranian New Year).

The ***Homa Hotel (☎ 554 080)*** off Pāsdārān Blvd has all the five-star amenities, including tennis court, swimming pool, coffee and pastry shop and gives the impression of being self-contained; just as well because it is a long way from anywhere. Singles/doubles/suites cost US$60/80/150 plus 19% service tax; the rooms with Persian Gulf views cost the same.

Places to Eat

Bandar is not a bad place to eat out, but is a bit short on fine-dining options.

There are hundreds of ***kabābīs*** along Emām Khomeinī St, particularly around 17 Shahrīvar and Abūzar Squares. ***Safa Kabābī***, directly under the Safa Hotel on Asad Ābādī St, is quite good. For IR12,000 you can get a plate of tasty beef kebabs, bread and tomatoes, as well as a cold drink. Not far away, ***Felfely Pizza*** does good hamburgers.

In the block between Shohadā Square and the waterfront are at least four surprisingly good ***pizza restaurants*** where the service is fast and friendly. Even in the name of comprehensive research, we couldn't eat at all four but the closest of these to Shohadā Square, ***Tānūrī Pizza***, did do the closest to Italian quality, with real mozzarella, that we tasted in Iran. There's a choice of six decent-sized pizzas each for IR15,000.

Two excellent cheap restaurants closer to the centre of town are ***Shamshīr Restaurant*** (in a small lane off Emām Khomeinī St, 75m west of Hotel Ghods on the south side of the street) and the ***Persian Restaurant***, a stone's throw west of 17 Shahrīvar Square. Just for something different, both specialise in kabābs, but they do them well.

PERSIAN GULF

They also do chicken, the service is friendly and the atmosphere relaxed.

The best of a limited choice of upmarket restaurants is probably at the *Atilar Suites Hotel No.1*. This is a good place to try out the local specialty, *chelō meigū* (battered prawns or shrimps with boiled rice) for IR21,000, although they do a good range of other dishes. The menu in English lists prices, to which must be added 15% tax. The atmosphere is a little strange – you feel like you're eating in the hotel lobby – but the service is attentive. The traditional teahouse is a lovely place to get out of the Bandar heat.

Against all the odds, *Ladan Ice Cream* on 17 Shahrīvar Square does profiteroles.

Teahouses
When the sting goes out of the sun, head to the waterfront opposite the unfinished mosque (see Things to See earlier in the section) where you can join the locals for tea and a hubble bubble at the open-air *teahouse*, without a sign, almost at the water's edge.

Shopping
All manner of imported (and smuggled) goods are traded here, many of them brought over from the UAE. If you're looking for some local souvenirs – traditional Arab clothes, coarse rugs and carpets, woollen blankets, and various implements woven from the fibres of the date palm leaf – visit the bazaar in Bandar or the market in Mīnāb (see later in this chapter).

Getting There & Away
Air Bandar is well connected by air, which is just as well, because overland travel to and from Bandar is tiresome. Iran Air (☎ 39 595) is open from 7 am to 7.30 pm Saturday to Thursday, and from 7 am to noon, Friday.

Iran Air, which has an office in Emām Khomeinī St, flies from Bandar-é Abbās to:

destination	flights weekly	one way (IR)
Chābahār	3	102,000
Esfahān	4	161,000
Mashhad	2	208,000
Shīrāz	4	105,000
Tehrān	7	214,000

Iran Asseman (☎ 29 096, fax 29 021), which has an office on Tāleqānī Blvd, flies to Kīsh Island at 9pm on Monday and Wednesday for IR92,000/184,000 one way/return. Kīsh Airlines also has flights between Bandar and Kīsh that leave the island at 8 am, returning from Bandar at 9.30 am on Sunday, Tuesday and Thursday, for the same price as Iran Asseman.

International Services One interesting way in or out of Iran is to hop across the Persian Gulf to the UAE. Iran Air flies twice a week each to Dubai and Sharjah for US$60 one way. Iran Asseman, (four flights a week) and Qeshm Air (☎ 570 361, fax 570 360) (once a week via Qeshm Island) also have services to Dubai for the same price as Iran Air.

Bus Bandar enjoys better road communications with central Iran than any other place along the southern shores. However, heavy truck traffic, poor facilities along the road, endless expanses of desert and punishing temperatures make it an arduous bus journey.

The bus station, which is full of locals who wish they could afford to fly, is not far from the airport, in the far east of town. You may need to take two shared taxis: one to the turn-off to the bus station and another to the bus station itself.

There are several buses each day, from Bandar to the following places:

destination	distance (km)	duration (hrs)	cost (IR)
Bam	449	8	13,500
Bandar-é Langeh	255	4	6000
Būshehr	903	16	22,000
Esfahān	1082	18	21,500
Kermān	498	8	11,500
Shīrāz	601	10	18,000
Tehrān	1313	20	31,500
Yazd	671	11	17,000
Zāhedān	1039	17	24,000

Although the occasional bus leaves from the bus station for Mīnāb, there are regular and more convenient shared taxis (IR6000, two hours, 100km) from 50m south of Abūzar Square throughout the day.

Train The train starts its 1483km journey to Tehrān daily at 12.15 pm, taking a minimum of 19 hours (IR56,550 in 1st class). It travels via Sīrjān and Yazd (IR27,000, 9½ hours) among other places.

The train station is 8km away in the far north of town: As it's not on the way to anywhere else, you'll probably have to charter a private taxi to get there. There is a handy ticket office in town, one door east of the Bala Parvaz Travel Agency on the second floor. Hava Gasht Air Travel Agency (See Travel Agencies earlier in the section) also sells tickets.

Boat Boats from Bandar to the nearby islands of Hormoz and Qeshm leave from the main jetty (*eskelé*), near the bazaar. You must pay an IR1000 port tax before you enter the jetty, although sometimes foreigners are waved through. For Qeshm, buy a ticket from the small ticket booth about 200m from the shore (IR7500 for an open fibreglass speedboat; or IR10,000 in a covered, slightly quicker, less frequent launch with padded seats). The journey takes between 30 and 45 minutes.

The only reason to take the much slower daily ferry for Qeshm is if you intend to stay a few nights and have lots of luggage. Boats leave from the chaotic Shahīd Bāhonar docks, 5km west of the town centre, at 7.30 am daily and cost IR15,000. Tickets can be bought at the Valfarje-8 shipping company office (☎ 55 559) on Eskleh Shahīd Bāhonnar Blvd, 1km east of the docks (look for the building with a sign that reads 'South Shipping Line Iran'), or at the offices of Qeshm Air.

The speedboats to Hormoz (IR5000, about 30 minutes) leave less often than those to Qeshm. They go from the docks a few metres away from those to Qeshm every 15 to 20 minutes in the early morning. As the day wears on, they take longer to fill. There are no tickets; simply pay the owner of the boat.

If taking one of the open fibreglass boats in summer, take some protection from the sun and something to sit on to prevent a seriously scalded bottom.

There are no longer ferry services between Bandar and Kīsh Island.

International Services Valfarje-8 (see contact details above) also has ferries between Bandar-é Abbās and Dubai (once a week; IR400,000/450,000 for 1st/2nd class) and Sharjah (twice weekly; IR320,000 for one class only). There are also well-advanced plans to launch a high-speed ferry linking Bandar with other Persian Gulf ports (see Būshehr earlier in this chapter). Neither prices nor schedules were available at the time of research.

Getting Around
To/From the Airport The airport is about 8km east of the bazaar. It is easy enough to charter a taxi to or from the airport for about IR10,000. A shared taxi (which is harder to find *to* the airport) will cost about IR2500.

Bus Local buses criss-cross the town; tickets cost IR100 to IR200 depending on the distance.

Taxi Shared taxis are easy to find and cost a reasonable IR500 around town. To places like the bus station, train station and airport, you'll probably need to change taxis, so consider your comfort and charter a vehicle, especially in summer. For a private taxi, don't pay more than IR8000 to the bus station or the Shahīd Bāhonar docks from the centre of town.

Ani Taxi Service (☎ 555 539) has air-con Peugeots for which they charge IR20,000 per hour (including a driver) within Bandar-é Abbās. For a half day beyond the city limits (eg, Mīnāb), expect to pay IR175,000. To charter a non-air-con Paykan, pay IR10,000 an hour within Bandar and IR100,000 for a half day.

MĪNĀB   میناب
☎ 0765 or 07623
Although Mīnāb was one of the earliest and largest settlements in the area, it's better known for the luxuriant date plantations which dominate the area and, more recently, the cultivation of mangoes. Mīnāb is a

PERSIAN GULF

charming and quiet alternative to Bandar-é Abbās and one of the more pleasant towns in southern Iran. It is transformed on Thursday by the weekly market.

The approach to Mīnāb from Bandar-é Abbās is quite dramatic. On the left, on a hilltop as you approach, there is a picturesque **historic tower** with houses perched all the way up to it, all set to the backdrop of jagged mountains. It's the custom that couples from the town must walk once around this fortress, in the company of their families, before taking their marriage vows.

Places to Stay & Eat

The *Sadaf Hotel* (☎ 29 99) is well signposted along the road from Bandar and is located about 800m before the main bridge. The rooms are outstanding value at IR60,000/70,000 for a spotless and spacious single/double with bath and air-con. It's a very friendly place, English is spoken and there's even a gift shop selling zaribafi (see the

The Thursday Market of Mīnāb

If possible, try and arrange your visit to Mīnāb so that you are there for the Thursday market (*panjshambé bāzār*). The market, one of the most colourful in the country, is held on a patch of open ground along the banks of the seasonal riverbank 500m west of the main bridge. Famous throughout the region, the market attracts buyers and sellers from outlying villages, even as far afield as Bandar-é Abbās. Many of the women wear the *burqa* (see boxed text The Masked Women of Mīnāb), as well as bright headscarves and long dresses over pants with shiny brocaded trimmings around the ankles.

On display at the motley array of makeshift stalls is everything from fresh fruit, vegetables and clothing to the distinctive *zaribafi* – a range of items made from local palm leaves including mats, fans, brooms and baskets – and the brocaded strips of cloth used by local women to adorn their clothing. Whether you're there to buy or not, arrive as early as possible to soak up the atmosphere which is a cross between the colour and vibrancy of an African market and the discreet smiles of an Iranian bazaar.

The Masked Women of Mīnāb

If you travel around southern Iran, particularly near Mīnāb, you may come across Bandarī women wearing a burqa. This inflexible mask, often in bright reds with multi-coloured stitching along the border, covers all of the face not hidden by the chador, with the exception of two tiny slits for the eyes. Ethnologists do not believe these masks have any religious links, but rather think they are a fashion accessory dating back to the period when the Portuguese ruled the region.

boxed text 'The Thursday Market at Mīnāb'). The *restaurant* is good and the hotel is within easy walking distance of the bazaar.

The *Mīnāb Inn* (☎ 53 22) is pleasantly located inside a park, 3km past the main bridge as you come from Bandar. It's also good value at IR105,000 a double, even better in quieter periods when they don't bother bargaining and offer you the Iranian price of IR70,000 straight up. The rooms come with balcony, air-con and bathroom and the pleasant *restaurant* is open to guests and the public.

Getting There & Away

About every hour, a shared taxi/pik-up (IR6000) arrives from Bandar-é Abbās at the small bus station not far from the Sadaf Hotel. Transport for Mīnāb leaves Bandar from 50m south of Abūzar Square throughout the day. If you've been staying in Mīnāb and want to avoid Bandar, ask to be let out at the roundabout with the replica sailing ship as its centrepiece about 10km east of the city; buses pass this way en route to Sirjān, Kermān and Yazd although your choice of seats will be limited.

Chartering a private air-con taxi in Bandar for a half day trip to Mīnāb will set you back around IR175,000; a Paykan costs around IR100,000.

HORMOZ ISLAND   جزیره هرمز

If you only visit one island in the Persian Gulf, make it Hormoz. This delightfully sleepy 42-sq-km island is worlds away from

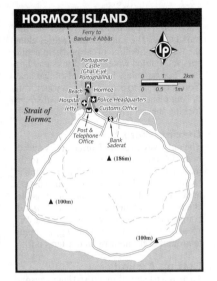

HORMOZ ISLAND

Ferry to
Bandar-é Abbás

Portuguese
Castle
(Ghal'é-yé
Portoghálíhá)

Beach   Hormoz
Hospital   Police Headquarters
Jetty   Customs Office
Strait of
Hormoz
Post &
Telephone
Office   Bank
Saderat

▲ (186m)

▲ (100m)

(100m) ▲

0   1   2km
0   0.5   1mi

---

the frantic bustle of Bandar-é Abbás, just across the water. The first thing you'll notice when the outboard motor is turned off is the silence and the fact that the locals greet you with a smile and a wave. For all its accessibility from the mainland, Hormoz feels like a remote outpost on the open seas, retaining the ramshackle charm that has all but disappeared from the islands of Qeshm and Kish. Its strategic location close to the Straits of Hormoz, where the Persian Gulf meets the Indian Ocean, and the oil tankers looming out of the haze make it easy to imagine a time when this was one of the most dangerous and hotly contested stretches of water in the world.

There's one small town called, naturally enough, Hormoz and a wonderful Portuguese castle on the northern tip. The rest of the island is virtually uninhabited, its interior hilly and infertile, the forbidding peaks seared by centuries of fierce Persian Gulf sun.

History

The island was, until the 14th century, known as Jarūn Island, while Hormoz was the name of a famous and long-established commercial town on the mainland, probably on the Mīnāb

River. Around 1300, the damage caused by repeated Mongol raids made the 15th Amīr of Hormoz shut up shop and move. He took many of his subjects with him and together they briefly stopped on Kīsh Island before finally settling on Jarūn Island.

This new Hormoz soon became the main emporium of the Persian Gulf, attracting immigrants from the mainland and traders from as far away as India. Visitors to Hormoz described it as heavily fortified, bustling and opulent. It naturally attracted some European traders, mainly Portuguese who built a castle there (see the boxed text 'The Portuguese on Hormoz' later in this chapter). After the Portuguese left Hormoz in the early 17th century, Shāh Abbās I selected the small mainland fishing town of Gāmerūn to be the new outlet for Persian trade, changing its name to Bandar-é Abbās. Hormoz quickly fell into a period of decline from which it has never recovered, with most of its former splendour reduced to ruins within a few years.

Today, the town of Hormoz is still an impoverished outpost where foraging goats and barefoot children are rarely disturbed by motorised traffic.

Portuguese Castle

Some 750m to the north of Hormoz beach is the famous Portuguese castle (ghal'é-yé Portoghālīhā) of Hormoz Island, without doubt the most impressive colonial fortress in Iran. Despite some signs of neglect, it is still hauntingly beautiful.

The castle is best reached from the boat jetty on foot – follow the waterfront around the arc of the bay all the way to the tip of the cape, past the fishing boats and via the occasional, easily negotiable rocky ledge and the west-facing cannon emplacements. Entrance to the castle is through a large open courtyard with the ancient armoury on the left. After the armoury, pass through the door that leads north, past the prison and more cannons facing north, to the sign in English that has some general historical information, including the surprising announcement that 'Hormoz is an island located in the south of Iran'.

Returning to the courtyard, cross to the partially underground church, which has some splendid, if simple, vaulted ceilings. Before following the path marked by stones up onto the ramparts, you can visit the ground-floor room of the watchtower if the door is open. Higher up is another door to the submerged 'Water Supply', a surprisingly deep cavern that is quite impressive and circled by an elevated, interior walkway amid the pillars.

From atop the ramparts the views back over the village and island are spectacular. The village, punctuated by palm trees and the pale stone minaret of the Sunni mosque, is surrounded by the deep blue waters of the Persian Gulf with the starkly beautiful backdrop of the mountains of Hormoz.

There is no gate or entrance fee and, if you're lucky, the old caretaker may be around to let you into the locked doors of the tower and water supply. There is no charge but a tip is appreciated.

Hormoz Village   هرمز

This pleasant little village is interesting, though there's nothing much to do except ramble through the small maze of kūchés. In the northern-most part of Hormoz village is the small Sunni Jāmeh-yé Emām Shāfe'ī mosque, with a fine single minaret of pale stone.

Places to Stay & Eat

There are no places to stay or eat on Hormoz Island. The small grocery stores along the western shoreline of the northern peninsula sell bottled water, soft drinks and limited food supplies. Bread is also available. You may want to bring food and water from the mainland, as a picnic at the castle overlooking the sea is wonderfully relaxing.

Getting There & Away

The only way to get to Hormoz is by speedboat (IR5000, about 30 minutes) from the main jetty in Bandar-é Abbās. In summer, Hormoz is witheringly hot with barely a breath of wind so start as early as possible. Boats leave whenever they have their full complement of about 18 passengers – every 15 or so minutes in the morning, dropping to around every hour by mid-afternoon.

Getting Around

There is a paucity of motorised land transport (and paved roads) around Hormoz. Exploring the village and castle is best done on foot. If you wish to explore the bone-dry interior, you could try and persuade one of the locals to carry you on their motorcycle or, more creatively, charter a boat from the jetty to circumnavigate the island (IR80,000 and

The Portuguese on Hormoz

In 1507, the talented Portuguese admiral and empire builder, Afonso de Albuquerque (also known as Afonso the Great), besieged and, after a battle, conquered Hormoz in an attempt to establish a network of Portuguese bases, including Goa, Aden and Malacca (in present-day Malaysia). The castle of Hormoz, which he started the same year, was completed in 1515; in the meantime he took Goa in 1510 and Malacca in 1511. In 1515 he left Hormoz to return to Goa, only to be informed by the ungrateful Portuguese authorities that he was out of a job – he died in Goa later the same year.

With Hormoz Island as their fortified base, the Portuguese quickly extended their gains and came to hold sway over all shipping in the Persian Gulf. Virtually all trade with India, the Far East, Muscat (Oman) and the Gulf ports was funnelled through Hormoz, to which the Portuguese, under an administration known for its justice and religious tolerance, brought great prosperity for over a century.

But Portugal's stranglehold over vital international trading routes could hardly fail to arouse the resentment of Persia and the other rising imperial powers of the day. In 1550, Ottoman forces besieged the fortress of Hormoz for a month but failed to take the island.

Early the next century, Shāh Abbās I granted the British East India Company trading rights with Persia through the port of Jāsk to the south-east, thus enraging the Portuguese. Abbās cajoled the English into sending a force to assist him and in 1622 the joint expedition, despite a brave defence by the Portuguese, succeeded in gaining control of Hormoz Island.

120,000) or drop you around the uninhabited southern shores. If you choose to do this, be wary of tides and leave a detailed explanation of your plans with the police. You should also be self-sufficient in food and water and understand that the only trails are those left by shepherds or intermittent watercourses.

QESHM ISLAND   جزیره قشم
☎ 076352 or 0763522

By far the largest island (1335 sq km) in the Persian Gulf, Qeshm is more than twice the size of Bahrain but with less than 15% of its population. The island is mountainous, with a largely rocky coastline, dotted with villages and small towns; there are few settlements of any size in the interior.

In 1990 it was decided that Qeshm Island should become a duty-free area along the lines of Kīsh, despite the lack of local enthusiasm. The island has managed to retain some charm away from the main centres, but large-scale development has irretrievably changed the character of the island.

History
Qeshm Island was referred to briefly in documents from the Achaemenid period, and has for many centuries been a trading centre between the continents and subcontinents. The island was mentioned by Marco Polo, and later marked out for potential colonisation by Vasco da Gama. However, Qeshm lacks the historical status of the smaller Hormoz Island, and very little is known of its early development. Qeshm Island came under the sway of the Dutch, French, Germans and British until it was brought back firmly under the control of Iran shortly after WWI.

Orientation & Information
Qeshm is the largest town on the island. Outside the entrance to the port and main jetty area is a taxi stand where shared taxis are available. Alternatively, follow the small lane directly opposite the gate to Emām Khomeinī Ave and the bazaar area. The main north-south road begins at Pāsdārān Square, 150m east; it then becomes Shahīd Montazeri Ave, then Valiasr Ave and finally Emām Golikhan Blvd as it passes through the main shopping district a few kilometres to the south.

There are plans to build a bridge at Lāft-é Kohneh, linking the island to the mainland at Bandar-é Pol, but this is many years away from completion.

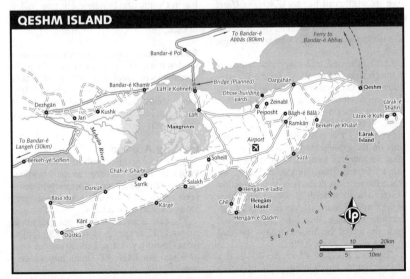

PERSIAN GULF

You can usually change money at the Bank Melli on Pāsdārān Square.

Things to See & Do

The village of Lāft, at the end of the road that continues west from Qeshm town, is the highlight of any trip to Qeshm. Only here is it possible to catch a glimpse of the fast-disappearing traditional cultures of the Persian Gulf fishing villages and communities. The roofscape of Lāft is a breathtaking forest of windtowers, and old dhows (sailing ships) sit anchored offshore in the channels of the mangrove swamps. Climb the hill above the town for marvellous views. You might also come across some activity in the dhow-building yards as you enter town, although there are larger yards on the barren coastline north of Zeinabi, accessible by dirt track off the main road.

Places to Stay & Eat

There are some OK cheapies scattered around Qeshm town. *Hotel Sahel* (☎ *47 23, fax 32 96*) on Emām Khomeinī Ave is handy for the jetty and has decent doubles with shared bath for IR50,000. Rooms at the *Mehmunsara Sittaré* (☎ *58 89*) on Valiasr Ave are a little cell-like for IR40,000. *Hotel Hamyaren* (☎ *58 31*) at the southern end of town off Felastīn Ave is rather overpriced at IR84,000 for a clean but uninspiring triple room.

One of the best mid-range places to stay is the *Qeshm Inn* (☎ *82 32, fax 55 57*), also known as 'Jahāngardī Inn' (or, to locals, as the Tourist Hotel). It's a friendly place and has great views overlooking both town and Gulf. Very pleasant doubles with a fridge, air-con and TV cost IR150,000. The *restaurant* on the ground floor is very good, and ideal for lunch or a cup of tea if you are taking a day trip from Bandar-é Abbās. To reach the hotel from the port, you can either charter a taxi for the short ride, or walk west along Emām Khomeinī Ave as far as Jahadsazandegy Square, then take Sayadan Blvd up to the top of the hill and follow the road to the right for about 200m.

The *Sara Hotel* (☎ *45 71, fax 45 72*) is a little isolated, but is quiet with attractive

doubles for IR115,000 including breakfast. It also has a good *restaurant*. The *Qeshm International Hotel* (☎/fax *49 05*) is Qeshm's finest with two restaurants and rooms starting at a surprisingly accessible US$20, before soaring to US$125 for a luxurious suite. Both places are at the southern end of Qeshm town.

There are very few exciting places to eat; stick to your hotel. The *Dallaho Restaurant* opposite the Sāhel Hotel is a good cheapie and there are plenty of **snack bars** and **kabābīs** along the main streets, particularly around the bazaar.

Getting There & Away

When arriving and departing, you may be subjected to a search for smuggled duty-free goods, though foreigners are often waved through.

Air Qeshm International Airport is around 43km south-west of Qeshm town. Qeshm Air (☎ 85 51) on the northern end of Emām Golikhan Blvd flies daily (except Saturday) to Tehran for IR215,000 one way and daily to Dubai for IR290,000/500,000 one way/return. There are also occasional flights between Qeshm and Bandar-é Langeh. Naderi Travel Agency (☎ 51 55) can help with air tickets.

Boat The main jetty is at the northern end of Qeshm town. There are two types of regular speedboats (open/closed for IR7500/10,000, 30 to 45 minutes) between Qeshm and Bandar-é Abbās (see Bandar-é Abbās earlier in the chapter for details). There is also a much slower daily ferry.

Getting Around

There's no organised public transport, but things are likely to change as the island becomes more developed. Currently, shared taxis, vans and pik-ups take passengers along the coastal road.

The fare between Qeshm and Dargahān is about IR2000 per person. For Lāft (58km from Qeshm), you may have to charter your own taxi for IR30,000, including waiting time.

Farsi (Persian)

Farsi (or Persian as it's also known) is an Indo-Iranian language and a member of the Indo-European language family. It's written in Arabic script, which runs from right to left, but the language itself isn't related to Arabic at all. There are a number of different mutually-intelligible dialects spoken in Iran. This language section is based on the Tehrani dialect, which is considered to be the standard dialect and is spoken by most Farsi speakers.

For a more comprehensive guide to Farsi, pick up a copy of Lonely Planet's new *Farsi (Persian) phrasebook*.

Transliteration

Transliterating from non-Roman script into the Roman alphabet is always a tricky affair. Formal transliterations of Farsi are overly complicated in the way they represent vowels and do not accurately represent the spoken language. In this language guide the system used is designed to be as simple as possible for spoken communication.

Elsewhere in this book, transliterations (especially of place names) use the more formal system, where vowels appear both with and without diacritical marks.

Pronunciation

This guide mostly uses colloquial expressions. Classical Farsi is not the language of everyday speech, but a literary form of the language, normally only used in books or speeches. Colloquial Farsi is the language of everyday speech, that spoken by most Iranians most of the time.

Hyphens have been used between compound words which are pronounced as one word but written as two, and where a combination of consonants would otherwise be mispronounced.

In general, the last syllable of a multisyllable word is stressed, unless the last vowel in the word is a short vowel, eg, *emām* but *bal-e* (bolded 'a' indicates stress).

Vowels & Diphthongs

A macron over a vowel (ā) indicates a longer vowel sound. This is very important, as the wrong vowel length can completely change the meaning of a word, or make it incomprehensible, eg, *māst* (rhyming with 'passed') means 'yogurt', while *mast* (rhyming with 'gassed') means 'drunk'.

a   as in 'father',
ā   as in 'far' (longer than a)
e   as in 'bed'
i   as in 'marine'
o   as in 'mole'
u   as in 'rule'

Consonants

The letters **b, d, f, j, m, n, p, sh, t** and **z** are pronounced as in English.

ch as in 'cheese'
g   as in 'goose'
gh a guttural sound like a heavy French 'r' pronounced at the back of the mouth
h   as in 'hot'
kh as the 'ch' in Scottish *loch*
l   always as in 'leg', never as in 'roll' (see note below)
r   trilled
s   as in 'sin'
y   as in 'yak'
zh as the 'g' in 'mirage'
'   a very weak glottal stop, like the sound made between the words 'uh-oh' or the 'tt' in Cockney 'bottle'

Note: doubled consonants are always pronounced distinctly, as in 'hat trick' not 'battle'; the sole exception is *Allāh* (God), in which the l's are swallowed as in English 'doll'.

Be Polite!

When addressing a stranger, especially one older than you, it's polite to include *āghā* (sir) or *khānom* (madam) at the beginning

Help! I Can't Speak Farsi

English is understood by well-educated people in the major cities, by some employees of middle and top-end restaurants and hotels, and by just about everyone working at a travel agency or airline office. Away from tourist areas, however, very few people speak English and when they do, because they are not used to listening to native speakers, they may not be able to understand your replies, making for some very frustrating 'conversations'. Since Iran does more business with France and Germany than with the English-speaking countries, you may have better success with French or German.

If you are travelling independently and using budget accommodation and restaurants, it would certainly help to learn a few basic Farsi phrases. At the very least, learn the Arabic numerals so you can identify prices, bus and train numbers, and addresses.

Whenever possible get your hotel receptionist to write down the Farsi for wherever you're going so you can show it to people. And don't forget to pick up your hotel's bilingual business card in case you get lost!

Thankfully, just about every village, town and city, and most streets and squares within the towns and cities, have signs in English.

of the first sentence, or after one of the standard greetings. *Āghā ye* and *Khānom e* are the equivalents of Mr, and Mrs/Miss/Ms. *Āghā* can be used before or after the first name as a title of respect, eg, *Mohammad Āghā* or, more likely, *Āghā Mohammad*.

The pronoun *shomā* is the polite form of 'you' singular, and should be used when addressing people you don't know well – *to* is only generally used when talking to close friends and relatives of the same generation or older, and to children and animals.

Greetings & Civilities

The all-purpose greeting in Iran is *salām aleykom*, which does duty for good morning, good afternoon and good evening. The same expression is used throughout the Muslim world, so if you learn only one phrase in Iran, this is it!

Welcome.	*khosh āmadin*
Hello.	*salām*
Good morning.	*sob bekheyr*
Good day. (noon)	*rux bekheyr*
Good evening.	*shab bekheyr*
Goodbye.	*khodā hāfez*
How are you?	*hāletun chetor e?*
Fine – and you?	*khubam – shomā chetoin?*
Yes.	*bale*
No.	*na*
Please.	*lotfan*
Thank you.	*motashakkeram*
Thank you very much.	*kheyli mamnum*
You're welcome.	*khāhesh mikonam*
Excuse me/ I'm sorry.	*bebakhshid*
What's your name?	*esmetun chi ye?*
My name is ...	*esmam ... e*
God has willed it	*māshallāh*
mother	*mādar*
father	*pedar*
sister	*khāhar*
brother	*bavadār*
daughter	*dokhtār*
son	*pesar*
aunt	*āmeh* (maternal)
	khāleh (paternal)
uncle	*āmu* (maternal)
	dāi (paternal)
wife	*zan*
husband	*shohar*

Language Difficulties

Do you speak English?	*shomā ingilisi baladin?*
Does anyone here speak English?	*injā kesi ingilisi balad e?*
I understand.	*mifahman*
I don't understand.	*na mifahman*
Please write it down.	*lotfan un o benevisin*

Getting Around

Where is the ...?	*... kojā st?*
airport	*furudgāh*
bus stop	*istgāh e utubus*
train station	*istgāh e ghatār*

Signs

Entrance	ورود
Exit	خروج
Open	باز
Closed	بسته
No Entry	ورود ممنوع
No Smoking	دخانیات ممنوع
Prohibited	ممنوع
Hot	گرم
Cold	سرد
Toilets	توالت
Men	مردانه
Women	زنانه

What time does … che sā'ati harekat
the … leave/arrive? mikone/mirese?
  aeroplane   havāpeymā
  boat   ghāyegh
  bus   utubus
  train   ghatār

What time is utubus e … key miyād?
the … bus?
  first   avval
  last   ākhar
  next   ba'di

I'd like a … . … mikhām
  one-way ticket belit e ye sare
  return ticket belit e do sare

1st class daraje yek
2nd class daraje do

Accommodation
Do you have any otāgh khāli dārin
  rooms available?

I'd like a … room ye otāgh e … mikhām
  single taki
  shared moshtarak

How much is it barāye … cheghadr
for …? mishe?
  one night ye shab
  a week ye hafte
  two people do nafar

We want a room mā ye otāgh bā ye …
with a … mikhāyim
  bathroom dastshuyi
  shower dush
  TV televiziyon
  window panjere

Around Town
Where is the …? … kojā st?
  bank bānk
  church kelisā
  city centre markaz e shahr
  consulate konsulgari
  embassy sefārat
  hotel hotel
  lodging house mosāferkhūneh
  mosque masjed
  market bāzār
  police polis
  post office edāre ye post
  public telephone telefon e umumi
  public toilet tuvālet e umumi
  tourist office edāre ye jahāngardi
  town square meydun a shahr

Is it far from here? un az injā dur e?
Go straight ahead. mostaghim berin
To the left. samt e chap
To the right. samt e rāst
here injā
there unjā

Health
Where is the …? … kojā st?
  chemist dārukhune
  dentist dandun pezeshk
  doctor doktor
  hospital bimārestān

I'm sick. mariz am

I have … … dāram
  anaemia kam khuni
  asthma āsm
  diabetes diyābet

antiseptic	*zedd e ufuni konande*
aspirin	*āsperin*
condom	*kāndom*
contraceptive	*zedd e hāmelegi*
diarrhoea	*es-hāl*
medicine	*dāru*
sunblock	*kerem e zedd e āftāb*
tampon	*tāmpon*

Time & Dates

What time is it?	*sā'at chand e?*
today	*emruz*
tomorrow	*fardā*
yesterday	*diruz*
tonight	*emshab*
morning, am	*sob*
afternoon, pm	*ba'd az zohr*
day	*ruz*
month	*māh*
year	*sāl*

Monday	*dos hanbe*
Tuesday	*se shanbe*
Wednesday	*chahār shanbe*
Thursday	*panj shanbe*
Friday	*jom'e*
Saturday	*shanbe*
Sunday	*yekshanbe*

Numbers

1	*yek*
2	*do*
3	*se*
4	*chāhār*
5	*panj*
6	*shish*
7	*haft*
8	*hasht*
9	*noh*
10	*dah*
11	*yāzdah*
12	*davāzdah*
13	*sizdah*
14	*chāhārdah*
15	*punzdah*
16	*shānzdah*
17	*hifdah*
18	*hijdah*
19	*nuzdah*
20	*bist*
21	*bist o yek*
22	*bist o do*

Emergencies

Help!	*komak!*
Stop!	*ist!*
Go away!	*gom sho!*
Call ...!	*... khabar konin!*
a doctor	*ye doktor*
an ambulance	*ye āmbulans*
the police	*polis o*
I wish to contact my embassy/consulate.	*mikham bā sefārat/ konsulgari khod am tamās begiram*
Where is the toilet?	*tuvālet kojā st?*
Shame on you!	*khejalāt bekesh!* (said by a woman to a man bothering her)

30	*si*
40	*chehel*
50	*panjāh*
60	*shast*
70	*haftād*
80	*hashtād*
90	*navad*
100	*sad*
167	*sad o shast o haft*
200	*divist*
1000	*hezār*

one million	*yek milyon*

Food

restaurant	*chelo kababi*
teahouse	*chāy khune*
breakfast	*sobhune*
lunch	*nāhār*
dinner	*shām*
supper	*asrune*

I'm a vegetarian.	*sabzikhār am*

I don't eat ...	*... nemikhoram*
meat	*gusht*
chicken	*morgh*
fish	*māhi*

bread	*nun*
butter	*kare*
cheese	*panir*
eggs	*tokhm e morgh*
fork	*changāl*

honey	asal
knife	chāghu
pepper	felfel
salt	namak
yogurt	māst

Vegetables

cucumber	khiyār
eggplant	bādemjun
garlic	sir
lettuce	kāhu
olive	zeytun
onion	piyāz
peas	nokhod
potato	sib zamini
tomato	goje farangi
vegetables	sabzijāt

Meat & Poultry

beef	gusht e gāv
chicken	morgh
goat meat	gusht e boz
lamb/mutton	gusht e gusfand
meat	gusht

Fruit & Nuts

apple	sib
apricot	zard ālu
fig	anjir

fruit	mive
grape	angur
lemon	limu
melon	kharboze
orange	porteghāl
pomegranate	anār

almond	bādum
hazelnut	fandogh
pistachio	peste

Drinks

boiled drinking water	āb e jush
coffee	ghahve
drink	nushābe
fruit juice	āb mive
mineral water	āb e ma'dani
soft drink	nushābe
tea	chāyi
water	āb
yogurt drink	dugh

with/without ...	bā/bedun e ...
ice	yakh
milk	shir
sugar	shekar

Glossary

Here, with definitions, are some unfamiliar words and abbreviations that you may encounter in this book. Where there are two forms of a word, the Farsi term is indicated by (F). Generally, the Persian words in this book are transliterations of colloquial usage. See the Language chapter for other useful words and phrases.

ābgūsht – a stew-soup combination, commonly served in teahouses and roadside cafes; also known as *dīzī*
āghā – sir; gentleman
Allāh – Muslim name for God
ārāmgāh – resting-place; burial-place; tomb
arg, ark – citadel
āsh – a type of soup often made from yogurt and barley
āstān-é – sanctuary; threshold
āteshkadeh – a Zoroastrian fire-temple where a flame was kept burning all the time
ayatollah, āyatollāh (F) – Shiite cleric of the highest rank, used as a title before the name; literally means a 'sign or miracle of God'
āzād – free; liberated
āzādī – freedom

bādgīr – windtower or ventilation shaft used to catch breezes and funnel them down into a building to cool it
bāgh – garden
bandar – port; harbour
Bandarī – indigenous inhabitant of the Persian Gulf coast and islands
bāstān – ancient; ancient history; antiquity
bāzār – bazaar; market place
bāzārī – shopkeeper in the bazaar
behesht – paradise
berenj – generic term for rice
bolvār – boulevard
boq'eh – mausoleum
borj – tower
borqa – a mask worn by some Bandarī women with tiny slits for the eyes
bozorg – big, large, great

caliphate – the dynasty of the successors of the Prophet Mohammed as rulers of the Islamic world
caravanserai – an inn or way-station for camel trains; usually consisting of rooms arranged around a courtyard
CFZ – Chābahār Free Zone; the duty-free port of Chābahār
chador – literally 'tent'; a cloak, usually black, covering all parts of a woman's body except the hands, feet and face
chāy – tea
chāykhūneh – teahouse ('chāykhāneh' in Kermān province)
chelō – boiled or steamed rice
chelō kabāb – a long thin strip of meat or mince served with a mound of rice or with bread and grilled tomatoes; a staple at Iranian restaurants
chelō kabābī – place serving *chelō kabāb* or restaurant in general
chelō morgh – chicken and rice

darvāzeh – gate or gateway, especially a city gate
daryā – sea
dasht – plain; plateau; desert, specifically one of sand or gravel
dīzī – another name for *ābgūsht*; also the name of the container the ābgūsht is traditionally served in
dūgh – a popular Iranian cold drink made from churned sour milk or yogurt, mixed with either sparkling or still water and sometimes flavoured with mint and other herbs

eivān – see *iwan*
emām – see *imam*
Emām Rezā – the 12th Shiite imam, also known as The Hidden One or the Mahdi; he is said to have disappeared in AD 878, and his return will, it is believed, signal an end to tyranny and injustice
emāmzādeh – descendant of an imam; shrine or mausoleum of an emāmzādeh
enqelāb – revolution

farsh – carpet
Farsi – Persian language or people
Ferdōsī – one of the great Persian poets, born about AD 940 in Tūs, near Mashhad; wrote the first epic poem, the *Shāh-namah*
fesenjān – a meat stew made with pomegranate juice, walnuts, aubergine and cardamom
fire temple – see *āteshkadeh*

givehs – lightweight shoes
golestān – rose garden; name of poem by Sa'dī
gonbad – dome, domed monument or tower tomb; also written 'gombad'

Hāfez – one of the great Persian poets, born in Shīrāz in about AD 1324
haj – pilgrimage to Mecca
halāl – permitted by Islamic law; lawful to eat or drink
hammam, hammūm (F) – bath, public bathhouse; bathroom
Hazrat-é – title used before the name of Mohammed, any other apostle of Islam or a Christian saint
hejab – veil; the 'modest dress' required of Muslim women and girls
Hossein – the eighth of the 12 imams recognised by Shiites as successors of the Prophet Mohammed; he was martyred at the battle of Karbala, an event that is commemorated in rituals acted out during the mourning month of Moharram
Hosseinieh – see *takieh*

imam – emām in Farsi; religious leader, also title of one of the 12 descendants of Mohammed who, according to Shiite belief, succeeded him as religious and temporal leader of the Muslims
IRISL – Islamic Republic of Iran Shipping Line
īstgāh – station (especially railway station)
ITTO – Iranian Touring & Tourism Organisation; a government-run travel agency
iwan – eivān in Farsi; rectangular hall opening onto a courtyard

Jāmeh Mosque – Masjed-é Jāmeh in Farsi; meaning Friday Mosque, this is the mosque Muslims go to on their holy day, Friday
jazīreh – island

kabāb – kebab
kabābī – anywhere that sells kebabs; general term for snack bar
kabīr – great
kalīsā – church (sometimes cathedral)
kavīr – salt desert
khalīj – gulf; bay
khan, khān (F) – feudal lord, title of respect
kheyābūn – street; avenue
khōresht – a blanket term for any kind of thick meaty stew made with vegetables and chopped nuts and served with rice
khūneh – house; home
KFZO – Kīsh Free Zone Organisation; the organisation which runs the duty-free island of Kīsh
Komīteh – local 'committee' of the Islamic Revolutionary Guards Corps, or religious police
kūché – lane; alley

lavāsh – least appetising of Iranian breads: it's flat, thin and cardboard-like, and keeps for months
lux – regular class of bus

madraseh – school; also Muslim theological college
maghbareh – tomb; burial ground
Majlis – Iranian Parliament
manār – minaret: tower of a mosque
markaz – centre; headquarters
markazī telefon – main telephone office
masjed – mosque: Muslim place of worship
Masjed-é Jāmeh – see *Jāmeh Mosque*
māst – yogurt
mehmūn – guest
mehmūnkhūneh – hotel
mehmūnpazīr – a simple hotel
mehmūnsarā – government-owned resthouse or hotel
MFA – Iranian Ministry of Foreign Affairs
mihrab – niche inside a mosque indicating the direction of Mecca, often ornately decorated with tiling and calligraphy; in Iran,

specifically the hole cut in the ground before the niche

minbar – pulpit of a mosque

Moharram – first month of the Muslim lunar calendar, the Shiite month of mourning

mosāferkhūneh – lodging-house or hotel of the cheapest, simplest kind; 'mosāfer' means traveller or passenger

muezzin – person at mosque who calls Muslims to prayer

mullah – Islamic cleric; title of respect

Nō Rūz – Iranian New Year's Day, celebrated on the vernal equinox (usually around 21 March)

Omar Khayyām – born in Neishābūr in about 1047 and famous as a poet, mathematician, historian and astronomer; his best known poem is the *Rubaïyat*

Pārs – Farsi for Persia or Iran

pāsāzh – passage; shopping arcade

Persia – old name for Iran

Persian – adjective and noun frequently used to describe the Iranian language, people and culture

pol – bridge

polō – rice cooked with other ingredients

qal'eh – fortress; fortified walled village

qalyan – water pipe, usually smoked in traditional teahouses

qanāt – underground water channel

qar – cave

Quran – Muslim holy book

Ramadan, Ramazān (F) – ninth month in the Muslim lunar calendar; the month of fasting

rial – currency of Iran; equal to one-tenth of a *tōmān*

rūd, rūdkhūneh – river; stream

rūz – day

Sā'dī – one of the great Persian poets (AD 1207-91); his most famous works are the *Golestān* (Rose Garden) and *Būstan* (Garden of Trees)

sahn – court; courtyard

savārī – private car; local word for a *shared taxi*

shah, shāh (F) – king; the usual title of the Persian monarch

shahīd – martyr; used as a title before the forename of a fighter killed during the Islamic Revolution or the Iran-Iraq War

shahr – town or city

Shāh-nama – *Ferdōsī's* famous epic poem

shared taxi – common form of public transport within and between cities; they usually run on set routes and generally don't leave until full

super – superior class of bus; see also *lux*

takht – throne

takieh – building used during the rituals to commemorate the death of Emām Hossein during Moharram; sometimes called a *Hosseinieh*

tappeh – hill; mound

termīnāl – terminal; bus station

tōmān – unit of currency equal to 10 *rials*

ziggurat – pyramidal temple with a series of tiers on a square or rectangular plan

Zoroastrianism – ancient religion, the state creed before the Islamic conquest; today, Zoroastrians are found mainly in Yazd, Shīrāz, Kermān, Tehrān and Esfahān

Thanks

Many thanks to the travellers who used the last edition and wrote to us with helpful hints, useful advice and interesting anecdotes:

Moha Abdulla, Ali Akbary, Alexander Akopian, Gonzalo Alaez, Paivi Alatalo, Josep Albeniz Fornells, Bruce Allen, Venise Alstergren, William Altaffer, Ali Amiris, Rob Anderson, Michel & Sandra Andeweg-Hannon, Cesar Andres, Fredrik Angsmark, Philippe Antzenberger, Joaquin Arcas, Antonio Arce, Jun Asakura, Zmrouthe Aubozian, Johan van Audekerke, Leonor de Bailliencourt, Renske Bakker, Alison Ball, Pawel Banczyk, Evan Barneveld-de Bock, D Barr, Guenther Bauer, John Bedford, Georges Bellet, Rob & Geisje van den Berg, Laura Bertolotto, Roland Beutler, David N Biacsi, Jonathan Bickley, Mike & Liz Bissett, Francisco Blaha, Tony Blair, Geoff Bolton, Richard Bone, Richard GA Bone, Myriam Born, Ernest-Jan van den Bosch, Dr Ken Bowes, Sophie Brancherau, Johanna de Bresser, Eric Bringuier, David Brown, Jamie Brown, Louis Burgers, A Capelle, Brian Christie, Mogens Christoffersen, Peter Clark, Lainey Cohen, Silvia Cosimini, Bill Crowley, Brian Daken, Adam Danek, Paul Daniels, Paul Davison, Koupal Davoudi, Arno van Deuzen, Emmmanuelle Devaux, Leendert Develing, Christoph Dreyer, Ruud & Irene Duijm, Laurens den Dulk, Isabel Durack, Hakon Dyrkoren, Saman Ebady, Mahyar Ebrahimi, Lindsay Eccles, Michael Eckert, Nicky Efron, B Eggermont, Jorn Eide, Homeyra Emami, Jan Ewens, Alireza Fatehi, Tibo Faures, Tamas Feher, Bernard Feilden, Gerard Ferlin, Dr Pierre Flener, Neil Flintham, Sebastian Florian, Paul Freatonby, Doug Friesen, Yacan & Leo Gaill, James Gallantry, A Ganjtoma, Ray George, Marcus Gerhardt, Farshid Ghafourpour, Massimo Giannini, Nicolas Gizardin, Luis Gonzalez, Maria Gonzalez, Martin Gonzalo, Gail Gorham, Francois Gossiaux, Pascal Graillot, Eugenie Greig, Evert Jan Groeskamp, Martin Gutjahr, Matthias Gutzeit, Claude Haberer, Maria Hager, Nancy Hall, Aisling Halleman, Slim Hamdani, Ziaul Haq, Nicholas Harding, Mat Hardy, T Harish, Mario S Harlow, Nigel Harris, Peggy Hasselgren, Brian Hasson, Michael Heim, Marianne Heredge, Manon van der Hilst, Thomas Hintze, Len Hobbs, Sebastian Hoffman, Fam Hoger, Milena Holcova, Annabel Holley, Rene Holtel, Rene Horfel, Mark Horobin, Mark Hunt, Kate Hunter, Andy Hurst, Doms Hussmann, Trygve Inda, Pixie & Ted James, Simon James, Gordon Janow, Ton Janusch, Ramtin Jazayeri, Petr Jebacek, Trygve Jensen, Kjerstin Johnsen, Tiffany Johnston, John Jones, Mary Carol Jones, Martin Jorgsen, Maric Josephe Felce, Peter & Fiona von Kaehne, Juray Kaman, Jean Kennedy-Roy, George Kechagioglou, Mary Kelley, Nick Khaira, Laleh Khalili, Heather Kidlay, Fritti de Kiel, Timothy King, Olivier Klein, Brian Knox, Denise Switzer Kofod, Klaas Koers, Lorna Konopka, Maike Kramer, Martine van de Kreeke, Blaz Krhin, Hank Kryger, Dr Rolf-Peter Lacher, Mario Lague, Chris Lane, George Lane, Luc Lauwers, Lars Lemoine, Ernst Lessan, R P Lidbetter, Cameron Lindsay Adrian Lloyd, Jasper Lloyd, Alison & Graham Loader, Karl Loring, Yolanda Louwinger, Jonathan Lynn, Stefan M, Zohreh Majidian, Mazen Makareem, Constantine Mandylas, Marue-Jose Manini, Eugenia Manolopoulou, Richard Mansfield, Alex Marcovitch, Yann Martel, Almudena Martinez, Eduardo Martino, Peter Matersdorff, NA Matthews, Frauce Mazoyer, Sarah McAlpine, Wendy McCarty, Nick McGhee, Reyhan Mehran, Holger Meinck, Eric Mendelsohn, Reza Mokarram, Katarina Moller, Joel Montague, Dave Mountain, Pawel Mroczkowski, D Mulder, Daniel Muller, Alan Murphy, Mehdi Nassehi, Dallas Newby, T Nhu, Stephane Nicolopoulos, Aernout Nieuwkerk, Rune Norheim, Julie Norton, Lyn Oettli, Erik Olafsen, Radek Ondrusak, Barunka O'Shaughnessy, Len Outram, Ted Papenfuss, JS Parkes, Federico Parodi, Domenico Paterna, Sharon Peake, Ms Sigrid Pearson, Emily Peckham, Martin Peterson, R & H Pfeiffer, Ben Pillonel, Reyco van der Pol, Gregor Preac, Lukas Pribyl, Dr Gisela Prochazka-Eisl, Ad Ragas, Jason Ray, Margaret Rey, Espen Rikter-Svendsen, Cheryl Rivers, Jody Robbins, Magnus Roeger, Pius Rohner, Guido Rooijackers, Jonathan Ruel, Samuel Samuelian, Yvonne & Thimo Scheffer, Nora Schep, Wilma Scholte E Schotman, Henk Schreuders, Anik See, Sandra Self, Mitra Sharafi,

R Sheikhi, Chris Shenfield, Hiro Shimai, Iraj Zoghi Shiraz, Philip Shulman, Hanne Siewartz, John Silver, Nathalie Silvestre, Dr J Simpson, Greg Skora, Kasom Skultab, Eirik Softeland, Lex Spek, Gary Spinks, R Spreeuw, Peter Stein, Dafydd Stephens, Feher Tamas, Garry Telford, Stéphane Tiberghien, Clark Toes, Romul Torrents, Marietta Vazquez, Tony Verschoor, Ioannis Vikelidis, Jerry Vinal, Daria Vyncke, Chrisian Wagner, Sean Wayman, AD Weaver, David Weaver, Volkmar Weiler, Josh Welbaum, Ian Whitby, Wolfgang Wiedmann, Marie-Jose Wijntjes, Catherine Willemart, Dr Neil Wilson, JP Wispelaere, James Woods, David Yaghoubian, Blaz Zabukovec, Aernout Zappey, Pablo de Zardain, Ziemowit Zaworski, Negar Zoka and Arian Zwegers

LONELY PLANET

You already know that Lonely Planet produces more than this one guidebook, but you might not be aware of the other products we have on this region. Here is a selection of titles that you may want to check out as well:

Black on Black
ISBN 0 86442 795 6
US$12.95 • UK£6.99

Farsi (Persian) phrasebook
ISBN 0 86442 581 3
US$7.99 • UK£4.50

Istanbul to Kathmandu
ISBN 1 86450 214 2
US$21.99 • UK£13.99

Middle East
ISBN 0 86442 701 8
US$24.95 • UK£14.99

Oman & the United Arab Emirates
ISBN 1 86450 130 8
US$15.99 • UK£9.99

Pakistan
ISBN 0 86442 535 X
US$17.95 • UK£11.99

Turkey
ISBN 1 86450 213 4
US$21.99 • UK£13.99

Bahrain, Kuwait & Qatar
ISBN 1 86450 132 4
US$15.99 • UK£9.99

Georgia, Armenia & Azerbaijan
ISBN 0 86442 680 1
US$19.99 • UK£12.99

Central Asia
ISBN 0 86442 673 9
US$24.95 • UK£14.99

Available wherever books are sold

Index

Text

Bold indicates maps.

Bold indicates maps.

Boxed Text & Special Sections

MAP LEGEND

CITY ROUTES

Freeway	Freeway	Unsealed Road	
Highway	Primary Road	One Way Street	
Road	Secondary Road	Pedestrian Street	
Street	Street	Stepped Street	
Lane	Lane	Tunnel	
	On/Off Ramp	Footbridge	

REGIONAL ROUTES

Tollway, Freeway
Primary Road
Secondary Road
Minor Road

BOUNDARIES

International
State
Disputed
Fortified Wall

HYDROGRAPHY

River, Creek
Canal
Lake
Dry Lake; Salt Lake
Spring; Rapids
Waterfalls

TRANSPORT ROUTES & STATIONS

Train
Metro
Cable Car, Chairlift
Ferry
Walking Trail
Walking Tour
Path
Pier or Jetty

AREA FEATURES

Building
Park, Gardens
Market
Sports Ground
Beach
Cemetery
Campus
Plaza

POPULATION SYMBOLS

✪ CAPITAL	National Capital	● CITY	City	● Village	Village
◉ CAPITAL	State Capital	● Town	Town		Urban Area

MAP SYMBOLS

■	Place to Stay	▼	Place to Eat	●	Point of Interest
✈	Airport	⚓	Fountain	▲)(	Mountain; Pass	◙	Synagogue
⊖	Bank	⊕	Hospital	🏛	Museum	◙	Taxi Rank
🚌 🚍	Bus Stop/Terminal	ⓘ	Information	⊙	Petrol	◙	Telephone
⌂	Cave	◙	Internet Cafe	✦	Police Station	�	Temple, Hindu
⊞ 🏠	Church	♠	Islamic Monument	◪	Post Office	▥	Temple, Zoroastrian
⊞ ⊡	Cinema; Theatre	☼	Lookout	⊠	Ruins	◼	Tomb
◙	Embassy	⚭	Monument	⚶	Ski Resort	❶	Tourist Information
▣	Fort	◙	Mosque	🏛	Stately Home	◙	Transport

Note: not all symbols displayed above appear in this book

LONELY PLANET OFFICES

Australia
Locked Bag 1, Footscray, Victoria 3011
☎ 03 8379 8000 fax 03 8379 8111
email: talk2us@lonelyplanet.com.au

USA
150 Linden St, Oakland, CA 94607
☎ 510 893 8555 TOLL FREE: 800 275 8555
fax 510 893 8572
email: info@lonelyplanet.com

UK
10a Spring Place, London NW5 3BH
☎ 020 7428 4800 fax 020 7428 4828
email: go@lonelyplanet.co.uk

France
1 rue du Dahomey, 75011 Paris
☎ 01 55 25 33 00 fax 01 55 25 33 01
email: bip@lonelyplanet.fr
www.lonelyplanet.fr

World Wide Web: www.lonelyplanet.com *or* AOL keyword: lp
Lonely Planet Images: www.lonelyplanetimages.com